ATRILL*McLANEY*HARVEY*JENNER

Accounting
an introduction

PEARSON
Prentice
Hall

3
edition

Pearson Education Australia
Unit 4, Level 3
14 Aquatic Drive
Frenchs Forest NSW 2086

www.pearsoned.com.au

Senior Acquisitions Editor: Karen Hutchings
Editorial Team Leader: Carolyn Robson
Associate Editor: Jill Gillies
Editorial Coordinator: Laura Chapman
Copy Editor: Janice Keynton
Senior Permissions Coordinator: Louise Burke
Cover and internal design by Wideopen
Typeset by Midland Typesetters, Australia

Printed in China (SWTC)

3 4 5 10 09 08 07 06

National Library of Australia
Cataloguing-in-Publication Data

Accounting: an introduction.

    3rd ed.
    Includes index.
    ISBN 0 7339 6918 6.

    1. Accounting – Textbooks. I. Atrill, Peter.

657

Extracts on pages 598 and 599 are reproduced with permission of the ASX on behalf of the ASX Corporate Governance Council.

Every effort has been made to trace and acknowledge copyright. However, should any infringement have occurred, the publishers tender their apologies and invite copyright owners to contact them.

An imprint of Pearson Education Australia
(a division of Pearson Australia Group Pty Ltd)

BRIEF CONTENTS

CONTENTS

MEASURING AND REPORTING FINANCIAL POSITION 70

MEASURING AND REPORTING FINANCIAL PERFORMANCE 119

MEASURING AND REPORTING CASH FLOWS — 186

ANALYSIS AND INTERPRETATION OF FINANCIAL STATEMENTS 238

COST–VOLUME–PROFIT ANALYSIS AND MARGINAL ANALYSIS 287

PROJECTED FINANCIAL STATEMENTS 403

CAPITAL INVESTMENT DECISIONS 443

ABOUT THE AUSTRALIAN AUTHORS

 **David Harvey** has recently retired after a long academic career. After qualifying as an accountant in the United Kingdom, David originally began lecturing in 1971 at Portsmouth Polytechnic (now Portsmouth University) and Plymouth Polytechnic (now the University of Plymouth). During this period he developed a keen interest in curriculum development and teaching methods and was involved with the writing of a number of books with an open learning style. Many of these were in collaboration with Peter Atrill and Eddie McLaney. In 1991 he moved to Australia to take up the position of Professor of Accounting and Head of the Centre for Accounting and Finance at UNE (Northern Rivers) which subsequently became Southern Cross University. In 1992 he became the Dean of the Faculty of Business and Computing, a position he held until 1996, before reverting to his Professorship. In 2000 he took up the position of the Dean of the Faculty of Commerce at the University of Southern Queensland. In 2001 the Faculty of Commerce was merged with the Faculty of Business and David became Dean of the enlarged Faculty of Business. His most recent position was as Pro Vice-Chancellor (International Quality), a position he held from 2004 until his retirement in 2005.

 **Maurice Jenner** is currently on secondment from the University of Southern Queensland Toowoomba to South China Normal University, Guangzhou, China. Maurice is head of Degree Studies in the Joint USQ-SCNU International Accounting Programme. He lectures in the BCom Accounting degree course for a wide range of subjects including Accounting for Decision Making, Accounting Information Systems, Financial Accounting, Accounting Theory and Management Accounting. Maurice is also a co-author of the Atrill *Workbook* and the companion website for the textbook. He is a supplements author for Deegan *Financial Accounting* and Peirson & Ramsay *Accounting*. Maurice also works as a financial consultant and as a CPA monitor for graduate students.

PREFACE

This text is the third Australian edition of a UK book. It provides a broad-based introduction to accounting and finance for those who wish, or need, to acquire an understanding of the main concepts and their practical application in decision making, but who do not require in-depth theoretical or technical detail. It is aimed primarily at students who are studying a single unit in accounting and finance as part of a university or MBA course, including courses in business studies, economics, engineering and a range of other non-specialist accounting courses. Given the content and style of the text it is suitable for students studying at a distance, and for those who are studying independently, perhaps with no formal qualification in mind.

In writing the text we have been particularly mindful that most of its readers will not have studied accounting and finance before. We have therefore tried to write in an accessible style, avoiding technical jargon. Throughout, we have tried to ensure that basic concepts are thoroughly explained. Underpinning the text's coverage is an 'open-learning' approach – that is to say, it involves the reader in a manner which is traditionally not found in textbooks, delivering topics much as a good lecturer would do and encouraging readers to interact with the text. This approach distinguishes itself through a variety of integrated and end-of-chapter assessment material, including the following.

✳ Interspersed throughout each chapter are numerous activities. These are short 'quick-fire' questions of a type a lecturer might pose to students during a lecture or tutorial, and are intended to serve two purposes: to give readers the opportunity to check that they have understood the preceding section; and to encourage them to think beyond the immediate topic and make linkages to topics either previously covered or covered in the next section. An answer to each activity is provided at the end of the chapter, to which readers should refer only after they have attempted the activity.

✳ Towards the end of the chapter, but also at an appropriate point within a chapter, there is a self-assessment question or questions. These are much more demanding and comprehensive than an activity, in terms both of the breadth and depth of the material they cover. A solution to each of these questions is given at the end of the text. As with the activities, it is important to make a thorough attempt at each question before referring to the solution.

✳ At the end of each chapter there are a number of discussion questions. These are relatively short, typically require a descriptive or analytical answer, and are intended to enable readers to assess their recollection and critical evaluation of the main principles in each chapter. They might be used as the basis for tutorial discussion.

✳ Also at the end of each chapter there are a number of application exercises, categorised as easy, intermediate or challenging. These are typically of a numerical type, and are designed to enable readers to further apply and consolidate their understanding of topics. Solutions to a limited number of these questions are given at the end of the text. Here, too, a thorough attempt should be made to complete each exercise before referring to the solution.

The third edition contains many more new and revised discussion questions and practical application exercises than the second edition.

COVERAGE AND STRUCTURE

Although the topics included are, to some extent, relatively conventional, the coverage and treatment of material is designed to meet the needs of non-specialists; therefore, the emphasis is on the application and interpretation of information for decision making, and the underlying concepts, rather than on the collection of data and the preparation of statements and reports.

Two additional chapters have been added to the third edition, covering share and business valuations, as a natural flow-on from the chapter on capital investment appraisal, and trends and issues in accounting. This latter chapter deals with issues such as governance, social and environmental accounting, now commonly referred to as sustainability reporting, and the link between management accounting and strategy development.

We have ordered the chapters and their component topics to reflect what we consider to be a logical sequence. For this reason, we advise readers to work through the text in the order presented, particularly since we have been careful to ensure that earlier chapters do not refer to concepts or terms that are not covered until a later chapter.

Chapter 1 provides a general introduction to the scope, purpose and interrelationships of the text's core coverage – financial accounting, management accounting and financial management – together with a brief overview of the three main financial statements. It also examines user groups and their needs, a topic which links with the key issues identified in Chapter 15. Chapter 2 deals with the main types of business structures, namely sole proprietorships, partnerships and limited companies. The latter are discussed in some detail. Chapters 3–5 consider the measurement and basic reporting aspects of the principal accounting statements prepared by businesses – the balance sheet, income statement (traditionally known as the profit and loss account), and the cash flow statement. The analysis and interpretation of these statements assessing the financial position and performance of a business is the subject of Chapter 6. Our coverage of management accounting begins in Chapter 7 with a discussion of the interrelationships between costs, volume and profit in decision making. The new edition provides more emphasis on the use of spreadsheets in this analysis and goes into this area in a little more detail than the second edition. Chapter 8 covers full costing and activity-based costing. Chapter 9 focuses on short-term planning and control and deals with various aspects of budgeting. Chapter 10 enables us to put the financial accounting framework firmly on a decision-making track by using it for projection and planning purposes. Projected financial statements are a key element in most companies' strategic planning. Chapter 11 deals with capital budgeting, the decision to invest in medium- and long-term assets, and considers how businesses appraise such projects. Coverage is slightly extended in the third edition. Chapter 12 extends the idea of investing in long-term assets to the area of appraisal and valuation of financial assets, bonds and shares, with some reference to valuation of businesses. The chapter discusses risk–return trade-offs and the idea of portfolios of shares and their impact on risk. Chapter 13 deals with the management of short-term assets and liabilities. Chapter 14 deals with the main sources of finance available to a business in making an investment. Finally, Chapter 15 provides a review of some of the main issues confronting accounting at this time. It deals with issues relating to corporate governance, in the light of a number of scandals in recent years, the area of social and environmental accounting (including triple bottom line reporting and sustainability reporting) and the links between management accounting and strategy (including the balanced scorecard approach).

The extensions of content in some chapters, together with the inclusion of two new chapters, reflect our interpretation of the main comments made by reviewers. Given the resulting length we have decided to take the appendix on Accounting in Practice from the main text and place it on the companion website so that students and lecturers may still refer to it.

The instructor's manual that accompanies this Australian edition includes outline answers to the discussion questions, solutions to the remaining application questions and cases. There is also a wide variety of other supplementary resources available for both lecturers and students. Please refer to the 'For students: How do I use this book?' and 'For instructors: How do I teach with this book?' sections for more detail on these resources.

We would like to thank the Chartered Association of Certified Accountants for their permission to use some questions from the Certified Diploma.

Peter Atrill

Eddie McLaney

David Harvey

Maurice Jenner

ACKNOWLEDGEMENTS

The dedicated contributions of many individuals helped make this book a reality and contributed to refinements and improvements in this edition. An impressive cast of reviewers provided many helpful suggestions, constructive criticism and enthusiasm for the organisation and content of the text. Both the authors and publisher are grateful to each one of them. These include:

Daryll Cahill, RMIT

Sally Chaplin, University of Tasmania

Peter Collett, University of Tasmania

Scott Copeland, University of South Australia

Lyndal Drennan, QUT

Mary Dunkley, Swinburne University

Chris Durden, University of Southern Queensland

Peter Hall, University of South Australia

David Hay, University of Auckland

Gary Heaton, University of Otago

Jim Larkin, University of Adelaide

Stephen Marks, Southern Cross University

Mark Silvester, University of Southern Queensland

Allan Tunstall, Charles Sturt University

Arabella Volkov, University of Southern Queensland

Brian West, University of Ballarat

Belinda Williams, University of Tasmania

Special thanks from the authors and publisher to Mark Silvester, University of Southern Queensland, technical editor and reviewer for *Accounting: An Introduction 3rd edition* and co-author of the *Workbook*, companion website and PowerPoint slides. We are extremely appreciative of the important contribution he has made to the Atrill teaching package.

FOR STUDENTS: HOW DO I USE THIS BOOK?

OBJECTIVES

These are listed at the beginning of each chapter and explain the key concepts that you should understand after studying the chapter. End-of-chapter questions are then keyed to the objectives.

OBJECTIVES

When you have completed your study of this chapter you should be able to:

1. state the purpose of the income statement (profit and loss)
2. explain the relationship between the income statement and the balance sheet
3. present the equation and identify alternative formats for the income statement
4. demonstrate an understanding of income in relation to definition, recognition, classification and measurement
5. demonstrate an understanding of expenses in relation to definition, recognition, classification and measurement
6. distinguish between accrual- and cash-based transaction recognition
7. analyse expense recognition for non-current tangible assets
8. analyse expense recognition for inventory
9. analyse expense recognition for accounts receivable
10. prepare an income statement from relevant financial information
11. review and interpret income statements.

KEY TERMS

To help you understand key accounting terminology and concepts, these are in bold with a 'key' icon in the margin. All these terms are in the glossary at the end of the book for easy reference.

Note that an asset does not have to be a physical item—it may also be a non-physical right to certain benefits. Assets that have a physical substance and that can be touched are referred to as **tangible assets** (inventory, plant and equipment). Assets that have no physical substance but, nevertheless, provide expected future benefits are referred to as **intangible assets** (copyright, trademark, patent, franchise, goodwill).

CLAIMS AGAINST THE ASSETS

The other side of the balance sheet includes **claims** against the assets of an entity, or simply the different interests in those assets. There are essentially two types of claims: external claims, known as liabilities; and internal, or ownership, claims, labelled **owners' equity**, equity or capital.

IN-CHAPTER ACTIVITIES

These are designed to test your comprehension of the material you have just read, as well as to make links to topics already covered or still to be covered. Answers to the activities are provided at the end of each chapter.

ACTIVITY 2.2

Why would the regulation related to financial records and reporting be simpler for sole proprietors than for more complex entity structures such as companies?

● *Limited access to funds.* Access to funds is potentially limited. With a sole proprietorship the ownership funding is restricted to the personal resources of a single owner. Additionally, certain forms of borrowing are not available to sole proprietors that may be available to companies, and lenders may be more reluctant to provide credit or funds to sole proprietorships.

ACTIVITY 2.3

What sort of business activities would normally be carried out using the sole proprietorship structure?

Two companies, X Ltd and Y Ltd, commence business with the following long-term capital structures:

	X Ltd $	Y Ltd $
Paid-up ordinary capital	100,000	200,000
10% loan	200,000	100,000
	300,000	300,000

In the first year of operations they both make a profit before interest and taxation of $50,000. In this case X Ltd would be considered highly geared as it has a high proportion of borrowed funds in its long-term capital structure. Y Ltd is lowly geared. The profit available to the shareholders of each company in the first year of operations will be:

	X Ltd $	Y Ltd $
Profit before interest and taxation	50,000	50,000
Interest expense	20,000	10,000
Profit before taxation	30,000	40,000
Taxation (say 30%)	9,000	12,000
Profit available to ordinary shareholders	21,000	28,000

The return on owners' equity for each company will be (using year-end figures for owners' equity):

X Ltd	Y Ltd
$\dfrac{21,000 \times 100}{100,000}$	$\dfrac{28,000 \times 100}{200,000}$
= 21%	= 14%

EXAMPLES

EXAMPLE 6.3

The worked examples take you step by step through accounting processes and calculations.

IN-CHAPTER SELF-ASSESSMENT QUESTIONS

More demanding and comprehensive than the activities, these challenge you to put your understanding of key concepts into practice. Solutions are provided at the end of the book.

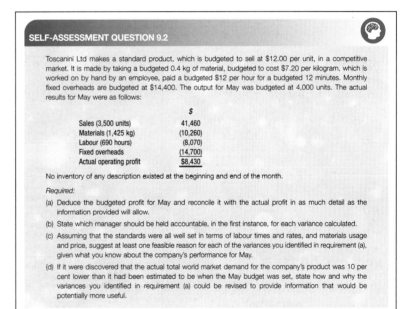

SELF-ASSESSMENT QUESTION 9.2

Toscanini Ltd makes a standard product, which is budgeted to sell at $12.00 per unit, in a competitive market. It is made by taking a budgeted 0.4 kg of material, budgeted to cost $7.20 per kilogram, which is worked on by hand by an employee, paid a budgeted $12 per hour for a budgeted 12 minutes. Monthly fixed overheads are budgeted at $14,400. The output for May was budgeted at 4,000 units. The actual results for May were as follows:

	$
Sales (3,500 units)	41,460
Materials (1,425 kg)	(10,260)
Labour (690 hours)	(8,070)
Fixed overheads	(14,700)
Actual operating profit	$8,430

No inventory of any description existed at the beginning and end of the month.

Required:

(a) Deduce the budgeted profit for May and reconcile it with the actual profit in as much detail as the information provided will allow.

(b) State which manager should be held accountable, in the first instance, for each variance calculated.

(c) Assuming that the standards were all well set in terms of labour times and rates, and materials usage and price, suggest at least one feasible reason for each of the variances you identified in requirement (a), given what you know about the company's performance for May.

(d) If it were discovered that the actual total world market demand for the company's product was 10 per cent lower than it had been estimated to be when the May budget was set, state how and why the variances you identified in requirement (a) could be revised to provide information that would be potentially more useful.

SUMMARY

In this chapter we have achieved the following objectives in the way shown.

OBJECTIVE	METHOD ACHIEVED
List the items making up working capital	Identified as current assets (cash + debtors + inventories) less current liabilities (creditors)
Discuss the nature and importance of working capital	Identified working capital as the pool of short-term assets necessary for the day-to-day operations of the entity
Illustrate the working capital cycle	Showed the net period that funding has to be provided for trading activities (inventory turnover period plus debtors turnover period less creditors turnover

SUMMARY

At the end of every chapter, the summary correlates learning objectives with the method used to achieve them. Use this as a great revision tool.

GLOSSARY

This quick reference guide at the end of the book helps jog your memory for all those important accounting terms and concepts.

END-OF-CHAPTER QUESTIONS AND PROBLEMS

These help reinforce your understanding of chapter content. All questions are keyed to the learning objectives to which they correspond so you can pick and choose the areas you want to work on. Each of the questions is also divided into level of difficulty – easy, intermediate and challenging.

✳ Discussion questions – help you assess your recall of the main principles covered in each chapter.

DISCUSSION QUESTIONS

EASY

<Obj 1>	8.1	Assuming a simple manufacturing operation in which only one product is produced, what problems arise in determining the unit output cost?
<Obj 1-3>	8.2	How is the term 'full cost' defined?
<Obj 2>	8.3	What is the point of distinguishing direct costs from indirect ones?
<Obj 2>	8.4	Provide a list of direct and indirect costs for a 'hot bread' shop.
<Obj 2>	8.5	Are direct costs and variable costs the same thing?
<Obj 2>	8.6	What other labels are used for 'indirect costs'?
<Obj 5>	8.7	What is a 'cost driver'?

INTERMEDIATE

<Obj 1, 3>	8.8	It is sometimes claimed that the full cost of pursuing some objective represents the long-run break-even selling price. Why is this said and what does it mean?
<Obj 3>	8.9	Under what circumstances does the allocation of overheads on the basis of labour hours lead to product costs distortions?

✳ Application exercises – help you apply and consolidate your understanding of accounting in practice.

APPLICATION EXERCISES

EASY

<Obj 5>   5.1   For each item listed identify the activity and whether it is an inflow, an outflow or of a non-cash nature.

	Activity	Cash flow
e.g. Cash received from customers	Operating	Inflow
(a) Dividends received		
(b) Taxation paid		
(c) Payments to suppliers and employees		
(d) Interest paid		
(e) Purchase of property, plant and equipment		
(f) Bonus issue of shares		
(g) Dividends paid		
(h) Proceeds on sale of investments		
(i) Interest received		
(j) Long-term borrowing		
(k) Goodwill write-down (impairment)		
(l) Profit on sale of equipment		

CASE STUDIES

These give you real-world examples of accounting in practice and encourage you to think critically about accounting issues and controversies.

Southcorp investors in two minds
Trevor Chappell and Mathew Charles

The Courier-Mail
Wednesday, 19 January 2005, p. 29

SHARES in winemaker Southcorp retreated yesterday and predator Foster's Group rose as analysts considered whether global beverage firms such as Diagea and Allied Domecq would make counterbids for Southcorp.

Allied Domecq, Diageo Pernod Ricard and Constellation Brands have been mentioned as possible rivals to the Foster's $3.1 billion takeover bid for Southcorp.

But reports in the UK have said Allied Domecq and Diageo might only be interested in wine brands that might be for sale should the Foster's takeover of Southcorp succeed—and they were unlikely to make full counterbids.

Foster's made the takeover bid for Southcorp on Monday at $4.17 per share, after securing an 18.8 per cent stake last week from Southcorp's largest shareholder, the Oatley family.

Southcorp shares were down 10¢ at $4.51 yesterday after jumping more than 8 per cent on Monday. Foster's shares were up 10¢ at $5.37.

Analysts said the bid heralded a new era of uncertainty for the Australian wine industry.

They predicted Foster's takeover attempt of Southcorp would take months to play out, with Macquarie Equities' Lucinda Chan comparing it with Xstrata's play for WMC Resources, which has dragged on since last October.

'Patience is a virtue for those of us who hold the stock,' she said.

CASE STUDY 6.2
→

SOLUTIONS TO ACTIVITIES

These allow you to check your answers to the in-chapter activities.

SOLUTIONS TO ACTIVITIES

Activity 4.1

Your answer should be along the following lines:

1. Accountancy practice—fees for services
2. Squash club—subscriptions, court fees
3. Bus company—ticket sales, advertising
4. Newspaper—newspaper sales, advertising
5. Finance company—interest received on loans
6. Songwriter—royalties, commission fees
7. Retailer—sale of goods
8. Magazine publisher—magazine subscriptions, sales and advertising.

Activity 4.2

The stock approach to determining the profit or loss may be used:

- to check on the accuracy of the transaction approach ('Revenue – Expenses')
- by regulatory bodies (e.g. taxation office) to determine the profit and loss where records are unavailable
- by insurance assessors or other parties where records have been destroyed.

WHAT ELSE CAN I USE WITH THIS BOOK?

WORKBOOK

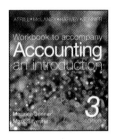

Use this as an excellent revision and study tool that is designed to match the structure and content of the textbook. This workbook gives you a wide variety of questions, e.g. multiple choice, true/false, matching, fill in the blanks, classification and practical questions, as well as a list of the textbook's chapter objectives and a chapter overview. Solutions to all of the question material are provided at the end of each chapter.

COMPANION WEBSITE

This interactive website gives you a wide range of multiple choice questions as well as true/false questions with instant feedback and hints as to where to find the information in the textbook. It also provides a reference list for each chapter of web links to visit for further information. The current events sections are regularly updated and give recent examples from the media of businesses facing accounting issues. A range of questions and relevant web links are also provided with each current event. Use Atrill's companion website as an excellent source of self-paced learning and revision.

ACTIVEBOOK

Activebook is an interactive on-line book that completely integrates media resources with your Atrill textbook to enhance your student learning experience. Carefully integrated self-testing checks your understanding of the concepts you have just read, while instant feedback provides an interactive study guide for a dynamic learning environment.

FOR INSTRUCTORS: HOW DO I TEACH WITH THIS BOOK?

ONEKEY: ALL YOU AND YOUR STUDENTS NEED TO SUCCEED

OneKey is Pearson's exclusive new resource for instructors and students, giving access to the best on-line teaching and learning tools – all available 24 hours a day, 7 days a week. Whether you prefer CourseCompass, BlackBoard, WebCT or a Companion Website, OneKey means all your resources are in one place for maximum convenience, simplicity and success.

INSTRUCTOR'S MANUAL INCLUDING POWERPOINT SLIDES

A comprehensive solutions manual prepared by the author team with a full set of PowerPoint® slides developed to tie in very closely with the text. These are fully customisable to meet individual teaching requirements. There are also some interactive Excel spreadsheets that you may choose to use in your teaching

COMPUTERISED TEST BANK

Allows you to customise the bank of questions to meet your individual teaching needs and add/revise questions as needed. The test bank consists of more than 2000 questions, exercises and problems complete with solutions and calculation support. The easy-to-use customisable format allows you the flexibility to create a range of exams, have the ability to conduct online testing and to track student results.

COURSE MANAGEMENT SYSTEMS

Including Course Compass and BlackBoard platforms (and WebCT on request), this allows you to deliver and manage your course online with specific material designed around the textbook.

AUDIENCE RESPONSE SYSTEM

Powered by TurningPoint™ software, Pearson Education offers an Audience Response System through a partnership with KEEpad™. TurningPoint allows you to create and deliver interactive questions in your lecture theatre or tutorial room and receive instant feedback from your students. Students respond to questions posed by you via an infra-red handheld device called a KEEPad. Their responses are automatically tallied and the results are graphed instantly on a PowerPoint slide. A bank of questions specifically created by an instructional designer matches the content of *Accounting: An introduction 3e* with the pedagogical functionality of the TurningPoint™ software.

ACTIVEBOOK

Activebook is an interactive on-line book that completely integrates media resources with your Atrill textbook to enhance the student learning experience. Carefully integrated self-testing checks student understanding of the concepts they have just read, while instant feedback provides an interactive study guide for a dynamic learning environment.

OBJECTIVES

When you have completed your study of this chapter you should be able to:

1 define accounting

2 discuss the role of accounting information

3 list the main user groups for a business entity

4 summarise the different uses that can be made of accounting information

5 explain the different procedures involved in the accounting information system

6 state the key characteristics of accounting information

7 relate the steps in the planning process

8 discuss the nature of control in the decision-making process

9 list alternative objectives of business

10 compare and contrast financial and management accounting

11 provide an overview of the main financial reports.

1

INTRODUCTION TO ACCOUNTING AND FINANCE

People need economic information to help them to make decisions and judgments about businesses. Whether we are talking about managers within a business making decisions on what is the most appropriate level of production, a bank manager responding to a request from the business for a bank loan, or trade unionists deciding on the level of pay increase to seek for their members, accounting information should help them with their decision. In this chapter we shall look at accounting as a tool in the decision-making, planning and control process.

NATURE AND ROLE OF ACCOUNTING

Accounting is concerned with the collection, analysis and communication of economic information. Such information can be used as a tool of decision making, planning and control. This is to say that accounting information is useful to those who need to make decisions and plans about businesses and for those who need to control those businesses. Though managers working within a particular business are likely to be significant users of accounting information, they are by no means the only people who are likely to use accounting information about that particular business.

It is generally recognised that accounting fulfils two distinct roles, a 'stewardship' role and a 'decision usefulness' role. Traditionally, accounting focused more on providing a stewardship, or accountability, report on the status of transactions for the period: that is, what was the position at the beginning of the period, what happened during the period, and what was the position at the end of the period. More recently, accounting has been seen as a mechanism to assist a wide range of users in making informed choices about the allocation of scarce resources. Sometimes, the impression is given that the purpose of accounting is simply to prepare financial reports on a regular basis. While it is true that accountants undertake this kind of work, it does not represent an end in itself. The ultimate purpose of accountants' work is to both discharge the accountability function of management and to influence the decisions of users of the information produced. This decision-making perspective of accounting fits in with the theme of this book and shapes the way in which we deal with each topic.

ACTIVITY 1.1

How would you define 'accountability'?

Accounting seeks to satisfy the needs of a wide range of users. In relation to a particular business, there may be various groups who are likely to have an interest in its financial health. (Although the points that will be made in this chapter and throughout this book may apply to a variety of organisations, such as public sector business enterprises, local authorities and charities, we concentrate on private sector businesses.)

The major user groups for a business organisation are shown in Figure 1.1.

ACTIVITY 1.2

Why do each of the user groups identified in Figure 1.1 need accounting information relating to a business?

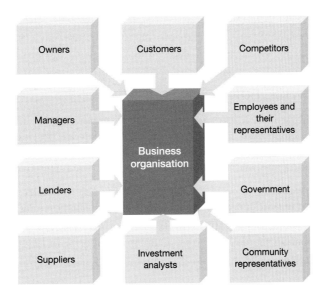

The figure shows that there are several user groups with an interest in the financial information relating to a business organisation. Most of them are outside the business but nevertheless have a stake in it. This is not meant to be an exhaustive list of potential users, but the user groups identified here are normally the most important.

FIGURE 1.1 Main users of financial information relating to a business organisation

ACCOUNTING AS AN INFORMATION SYSTEM

Accounting can be seen as an important part of the total information system within a business. Users, both inside and outside the business, have to make decisions concerning the allocation of scarce economic resources. To try to ensure that these resources are allocated in an efficient and effective manner, users require economic information and other information, on which to base decisions. It is the role of the accounting system to provide much of that information. Thus, we can view accounting as an information gathering, processing and communication system. The accounting system will involve the following procedures shown in Figure 1.2:

* identifying and capturing relevant economic information
* recording the information collected in a systematic manner
* analysing and interpreting the information collected
* reporting the information in a manner that suits the needs of users.

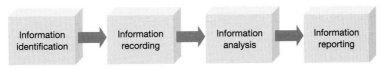

The figure shows the four sequential stages of an accounting information system. The first two stages are concerned with preparation, whereas the last two stages are concerned with using the information collected.

FIGURE 1.2 The accounting information system

Given the decision-making emphasis of the text, we shall be concerned primarily with the final two elements of the process—the analysis and reporting of financial information. We are concerned with the way in which information is used by, and is useful to, decision makers rather than with the way in which it is collected and recorded.

ACCOUNTING AS A SERVICE FUNCTION

Another way of viewing accounting is as a form of service. Accountants provide financial information to their 'clients', who are the various users identified earlier. The quality of the service provided will be determined by the extent to which the information needs of the various user groups have been met. It can be argued that, in order to meet the needs of users, accounting information should possess certain key qualitative characteristics. These are:

* *Relevance.* Accounting information must have the ability to influence decisions. Unless this characteristic is present, there really is no point in producing the information. The information may be relevant to the prediction of future events or relevant in helping to confirm past events.
* *Reliability.* Accounting information should be free from any material error or bias.
* *Comparability.* Items which are basically the same should be treated in the same manner for measurement and presentation purposes.
* *Understandability.* Accounting reports should be expressed as clearly as possible and should be understood by those at whom the information is aimed.

These qualitative characteristics apply to accounting information reported to any of the user groups identified. The key characteristics (listed above) are frequently in conflict.

ACTIVITY 1.3

Try to think of an example in which there is a conflict between relevance and reliability.

COSTS AND BENEFITS OF ACCOUNTING INFORMATION

In the previous section the four key characteristics of relevance, reliability, comparability and understandability were identified. In fact, there is also a fifth key characteristic which is at least as important as any of these four.

ACTIVITY 1.4

An item of information is capable of being produced or discovered. It is relevant to a particular decision, it is also reliable, comparable and can be understood by the decision maker concerned.

Can you think of a reason why, in practice, you might choose not to produce or discover it?

Suppose that you wish to buy a particular portable radio which you have seen in a local shop for sale at $50. You believe that other local shops may have the same model of radio on offer for as little as $45. The only way in which you can find out the prices at other shops is to telephone or visit them. Telephone calls cost money and involve some of your time. Visiting the shops may not involve the outlay of money, but more of your time will be involved. Is it worth the cost of finding out the price of the radio at various shops?

The answer is, of course, that if the cost of discovering the price is less than the potential benefit, it is worth having that information.

Supplying accounting information to users is similar. The provision of accounting information costs money. If no accounting information were produced, no accounting staff would need to be employed. Salaries of accounting staff are normally only a part of the cost of producing accounting information. In order to be worth having, the potential benefits from having the information need to outweigh the cost of producing it. A real problem with making decisions about the relative cost and benefits of having accounting information is that the costs and benefits are normally very difficult, if not impossible, to identify with accuracy.

Going back to the portable radio, identifying the cost of finding out the various selling prices in advance is problematical. It will probably involve considerations of the following factors:

❋ How many shops will you phone or visit?
❋ What will be the cost of each phone call?
❋ How long will it take you to make all of the phone calls or to visit all of the shops?
❋ What value do you put on your time?

The economic benefit of having the information on the price of radios is probably even harder to assess, the following probably being relevant:

❋ What is the cheapest price which you might be quoted for the radio?
❋ How likely is it that you will be quoted prices cheaper than $50?

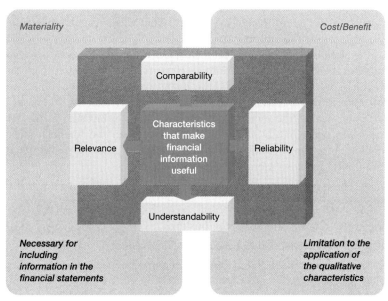

The figure shows that there are four main qualitative characteristics that influence the usefulness of accounting information. In addition, accounting information should be material and the benefits of providing the information should outweigh the costs.

FIGURE 1.3 The characteristics that influence the usefulness of accounting information

As you can see, a decision as to whether it is economically advantageous to discover other shops' prices for the radio is very difficult. It is possible to apply some 'science' to the decision, but a lot of subjective judgment is likely to be involved. It is normally exactly the same with decisions on producing accounting information in a business context.

No one would seriously advocate that the typical business should produce no accounting information. At the same time no one would advocate that every item of information that could be seen as possessing one or more of the key characteristics (relevance, reliability, comparability or understandability) should be produced, irrespective of the cost of producing it.

DECISION MAKING, PLANNING AND CONTROL

It is vitally important that businesses plan their future. Whatever a business is trying to achieve it is unlikely to be successful unless its managers have clear in their minds what the plans are. Planning is vital for businesses of all sizes, but where a business involves more than one manager it is vital also that the actions of all the managers coordinate. For example, it is crucially important to a manufacturing business that production levels and sales levels are related to one another. It is not feasible for sales and production to go their own separate ways. It is necessary, therefore, that plans exist that will lead to production and sales levels matching each other. This is not to say that plans, once made, are incapable of being revised. Unexpected changes in the market or unforeseen production problems may well demand revision of the plans, but they require revision of all of the plans that are likely to be affected by the new circumstances.

Closely linked to planning is decision making. Planning involves making decisions about the best course of action.

STEPS IN THE PLANNING PROCESS

Planning is usually broken down into three stages:

1. *Setting the objectives or mission of the business*—that is, what the particular business is basically trying to achieve. These are likely to reflect the attitudes of owners (shareholders) and of the managers. Objectives tend to be framed in broad, generalised, non-numerical terms. Once the objectives have been established they are likely to remain in force for the long term—for example, 10 years. It is probably true to say that, for most private sector businesses, wealth generation is likely to be the main financial/economic objective. This broadly means that businesses tend to take actions that will increase the wealth of the business. Increases in wealth may be paid to the government in taxes, paid to the owners, paid to employees, reinvested in the business or deployed in some other way. Businesses will typically have objectives other than the financial ones—for example, being environmentally friendly or providing employment for the family. In practice, therefore, any decision is likely to be the result of a compromise between more than one objective.

2. *Setting long-term plans.* These are plans setting out how the business will work towards the achievement of its objectives over a period of, say, five years. They are likely to deal with such matters as:

   * type of products or services to be offered by the business
   * amounts and sources of finance needed to be raised by the business
   * capital investments (e.g. in new plant and machinery) required
   * sources of raw materials
   * labour requirements.

   In the case of each of these the pursuit of the established objectives of the business over the planning horizon (perhaps five years) will lay the foundation for the plans. Long-term plans tend to be stated in financial terms.

3. *Setting detailed short-term plans or budgets.* **Budgets** are financial plans for the short term, typically one year. They are likely to be expressed mainly in financial terms. Their role is to convert the long-term plans into actionable blueprints for the immediate future. Budgets usually define precise targets in areas such as:

* cash receipts and payments
* sales, broken down into amounts and prices for each of the products or services provided by the business
* detailed inventory (i.e. stock of goods held for sale) requirements
* detailed labour requirements
* specific production requirements.

It must be emphasised that planning (and decision making) is not the role of accountants; it is the role of managers. However, much of the planning will be expressed in financial terms and most of the data for decision making are of an accounting nature. Therefore accountants, because of their background knowledge, expertise and skills, together with their understanding of the accounting system, are very well placed to give technical advice and assistance to managers in this context. It is the managers of the various departments of the business who must actually do the planning, however. Only in respect of the accounting department, of which the most senior accountant will be the manager, should an accountant be taking decisions and making plans.

CONTROL

However well planned the activities of the business may be they will come to nothing unless steps are taken to try to implement them in practice. The process of making planned events actually occur is known as control. **Control** can be defined as compelling events to conform to plan. This definition of control is valid in any context. For example, when we talk about controlling a motor car we mean making the car do what we plan that it should do. In the case of a car the plan may only be made split seconds before the plan is enacted, but if the car is under control it is doing what the driver intended.

In a business context, accounting is very useful in the control process. This is because it is possible to state plans in accounting terms and it is also possible to state actual outcomes in the same terms, thus making comparison between actual and planned outcomes relatively easy. Where actual outcomes are at variance with detailed plans (which are called budgets) this should be highlighted by the accounting information. Managers can then take steps to get the business back on track towards the achievement of the plans (budgets). Figure 1.4 shows the decision-making, planning and control process in diagrammatic form.

The accountant must be aware of the fact that people have a restricted ability to process information. Too much information can be as bad as too little information as it can overload individuals and create a sense of confusion. This, in turn, can lead to poor evaluations and poor decisions. The information provided to managers must be restricted to that which is relevant to the particular decision and which is capable of being absorbed. This may mean that, in practice, information is produced in summarised form and that only a restricted range of options will be considered.

ACTIVITY 1.5

The approach described above suggests that decision makers will examine all the various courses of action available and then systematically rank them in order of preference.

Do you think this is what decision makers really do? Is this how you approach decisions—for example, choosing a career?

The figure shows the key steps in the planning and control process as described in this chapter.

FIGURE 1.4 The planning and control process

BUSINESS OBJECTIVES

In the previous section, enhancement of wealth was identified as the principal financial objective that businesses tend to pursue. We shall now briefly consider other financial objectives that have been identified, by various commentators, as likely practical targets for businesses. We shall also try to justify the assertion that wealth enhancement is the most likely in practice.

The popular suggested objectives include:

1. *Maximisation of sales revenue.* Most businesses seek to sell as many of their wares as possible; as a business objective, however, this is far from adequate. Almost any business could sell enormous quantities of goods and/or services if it were to lower its prices to gain market share. This may well lead, however, to the business collapsing as a result of the sales revenues being insufficient to cover the costs of running the business.

2. *Maximisation of profit.* This is an improvement on sales maximisation as it takes account both of sales revenues and of expenses. It is probably also too limited as a business goal.

ACTIVITY 1.6

Can you think of any reasons why making the maximum possible profit this year may not be in the best interests of the business and those who are involved with it? (We could think of several reasons.)

3. *Maximisation of return on capital employed.* This suggestion overcomes the last of the objections of Activity 1.6 to the profit maximisation suggestion, since it takes account of both the level of profit and the investment made to achieve it. It still suffers, however, from the risk and short-termist weaknesses of profit maximisation.

4. *Survival.* Businesses obviously aim to survive, but this is not what most businesses seem to be seeking, except in exceptional short-term circumstances.

5. *Long-term stability.* Though businesses pursue this goal, to some extent, it is not a primary objective for most businesses in that stability, like survival, is too limited a goal.

6. *Growth.* This is probably fairly close to what most businesses seek to do. The growth objective does seek to strike a balance between long-term and short-term benefits. It also encompasses survival and, probably, long-term stability. Growth is probably not specific enough to act as a suitable target. Is any level of growth acceptable or is a specific level of growth necessary? Is it growth of profits, of assets, or perhaps of something else?

7. *Satisficing.* It has been argued that all of the other suggested objectives are too concerned with profits and the welfare of the owners of the business. The business can be seen as an alliance of various 'stakeholders', which includes owners but also includes employees, suppliers, customers and the community in which the business operates. Thus, it is suggested, the objective should not be to maximise the returns of any one of these stakeholders, but to give all of them a satisfactory return. It is difficult to argue against this general principle, but it is not clear how this can be stated as a practical touchstone for making business decisions.

8. *Achieving sustainable development.* This means that the entity will seek to maximise economic growth within the bounds of minimising or eliminating impacts on the environment, and while conforming with society's expectations of a good corporate citizen.

9. *Enhancement/maximisation of the wealth of the business.* This means that the business would take decisions that would result in it being worth more. When valuing businesses people logically tend to take account of future profitability, both long-term and short-term, and of the risk attaching to future profits. Thus all of the valuable features of suggestions 1 to 6 (above) are taken into account by a wealth-enhancement objective.

It can also be argued that a wealth-enhancing business is one that has the maximum potential to satisfy the stakeholders (suggestion 7). Not only that, but any decision that failed to consider the position of the various

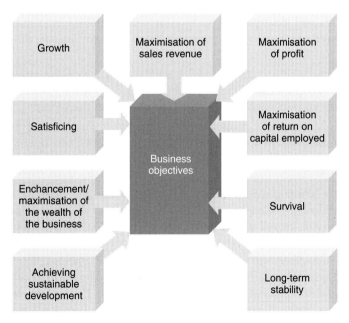

FIGURE 1.5 Business objectives

stakeholders could be a bad one from a wealth-enhancement point of view. For example, a decision which led to customers being exploited and not getting a satisfactory deal would pretty certainly not be one that had a wealth-enhancing effect. This is because disenchanted customers would avoid dealing with the business in future and, possibly, influence others to do the same.

Though wealth enhancement may not be a perfect description of what businesses seek to achieve, in the financial/economic context, wealth is certainly something which businesses cannot ignore. A particular business only has a certain amount of wealth, so it can only make a limited number of 'wrong' decisions before it collapses.

For the remainder of this book we shall treat enhancement/maximisation of business wealth as the key objective against which decisions will be assessed. There will usually be other non-financial/non-economic factors that also tend to bear on decisions. The final decision may well involve some compromise.

FINANCIAL AND MANAGEMENT ACCOUNTING

In providing information for the various user groups identified, accounting has divided into two main areas: management accounting and financial accounting. Management accounting, as the name suggests, is concerned with providing managers with the information they require for the day-to-day running of the organisation. Financial accounting is concerned with providing the other users identified with information they will find useful.

The differences between the two types of accounting reflect the different audiences they address. Briefly, the main differences are as follows:

✳ *Nature of the reports produced.* Financial accounting tends to produce general purpose financial reports. That is, they contain financial information that will be useful for a broad range of users and decisions. Management accounting reports, on the other hand, are often specific purpose reports. That is, they are designed either with a particular decision in mind or for a particular manager.

✳ *Level of detail.* Financial accounting reports provide users with a broad overview of the position, performance and cash flows of the business for a period. As a result, information is aggregated and detail is often lost. Management accounting reports, however, often provide managers with considerable detail to help them with a particular decision.

✳ *Restrictions.* Financial reporting for many businesses is subject to accounting regulations that seek to ensure specified content is presented in a fairly standardised form. Because management accounting reports are for internal use only, there are no restrictions on the form and content of the reports.

✳ *Reporting interval.* For most businesses, financial accounting reports are produced on an annual basis. However, large companies may produce semi-annual reports and a few produce quarterly reports. Management accounting reports may be produced as frequently as required by managers. In many businesses, managers are provided with certain reports on a weekly or monthly basis which allows them to check progress frequently.

✳ *Time horizon.* Financial accounting reports reflect the performance and position of the business to date. In essence, they are backward looking. Management accounting reports, on the other hand, often provide information concerning future performance as well as past performance. It is an oversimplification, however, to suggest that financial accounting reports never incorporate expectations concerning the future. Occasionally, businesses will release forecast information to other users in order to raise capital or to fight off unwanted takeover bids.

✳ *Range of information.* Financial accounting reports concentrate on information that can be quantified in monetary terms. Management accounting also produces such reports, but is also more likely to produce reports which contain information of a non-financial nature such as measures of physical quantities of inventory (stocks) and output. Financial accounting places greater emphasis on the use of objective, verifiable evidence when preparing reports. Management accounting reports may use information that is less objective and verifiable in order to provide managers with the information they require.

We can see from the above list that management accounting is less constrained than financial accounting. It may draw from a variety of sources and use information that has varying degrees of reliability. The only real test to be applied when assessing the value of the information produced for managers is whether or not it improves the quality of decisions made.

ACTIVITY 1.7

Do you think this distinction between management accounting and financial accounting may be misleading? Is there any overlap between the information needs of managers and the needs of other users?

The distinction between the two areas reflects, to some extent, the differences in access to financial information. Managers have much more control over the form and content of information they receive. Other users have to rely on what managers are prepared to provide or what the financial reporting regulations state must be provided. Although the scope of financial accounting reports has increased over time, fears surrounding loss of competitive advantage and of user ignorance concerning the reliability of forecast data have led businesses to resist providing information which is available for managers to other users.

Broadly, Chapters 2 to 6 (inclusive) of the book deal with areas that are usually considered to be in the area of financial accounting, the next five chapters (7–11) are concerned with management accounting, the next three chapters (12–14) are considered to be the domain of the finance director, while the last chapter (15) includes material relevant to all three areas.

THE MAIN FINANCIAL REPORTS—AN OVERVIEW

The main financial statements are designed to provide a picture of the overall financial position and performance of the business. In order to provide this overall picture, the accounting system will normally produce four main financial reports on a recurring basis. The financial statements are concerned with answering the following questions:

* What cash movements (i.e. cash in and cash out) took place over a particular period?
* How much did wealth increase over a particular period as a result of operating and other activities? In other words, how much profit was generated by the business from its overall activities and what other changes occurred in the ownership interests?
* What is the financial position of the business at the end of a particular period?

These questions are addressed by the four financial reports, with each one addressing one of the questions. The financial reports produced are:

* the **cash flow statement**
* the **income statement**, traditionally known as the statement of financial performance or profit and loss account
* the statement of changes in owners' equity for the period (sometimes included as part of the balance sheet)
* the **balance sheet**, traditionally known as the statement of financial position.

Taken together, they provide an overall picture of the financial health of the business.

Perhaps the best way to introduce the financial reports is to look at an example of a very simple business. From this we shall be able to see the sort of useful information which each of the statements can provide.

EXAMPLE

1.1

Paul was unemployed and was unable to find a job. He therefore decided to embark on a business venture in order to meet his living expenses. Christmas was approaching and so he decided to buy gift wrapping paper from a local supplier and sell it on the corner of his local main street. He felt that the price of wrapping paper in the shops was excessive and that this provided him with a useful business opportunity.

He began the venture with $100 in cash. On the first day of trading he purchased wrapping paper for $100. This is called stock (of goods) or inventory. Later in the day he sold three-quarters of his inventory for $110 *cash.*

What cash movements took place in the first day of trading?

On the first day of trading a cash flow statement, showing the cash movements for the day, can be prepared as follows:

Cash flow statement for day 1	
	$
Opening balance (cash introduced)	100
Sale of wrapping paper	110
	210
Purchase of wrapping paper	100
Closing balance	110

How much did wealth increase as a result of operations in the first day of trading? In other words, how much profit was generated by the business?

An income statement (profit and loss account) can be prepared to show the increase in wealth (profit) generated on the first day. The wealth generated will represent the difference between the sales made and the cost of the goods (i.e. wrapping paper) sold.

Income statement for day 1	
	$
Sales	110
Cost of goods sold (¾ of $100)	75
Profit	35

Note that it is only the cost of the wrapping sold which is matched against the sales in order to find the profit and not the whole of the cost of wrapping paper acquired. Any unsold wrapping paper (known as inventory or stock) will be charged against future sales.

What is the financial position at the end of the first day?

In order to establish this we can draw up a balance sheet which will list the resources held at the end of the day.

Balance sheet at the end of day 1	
	$
Cash (closing balance)	110
Inventory (stock of goods for resale: ¼ of $100)	25
Total business wealth	135

You should note that the profit has led to an increase in wealth ($35).

We can see from the above financial reports that each provides part of a picture which sets out the financial performance and position of the business. We begin by showing the cash movements. Cash is a vital resource which is necessary for any business to function effectively. Cash is required to meet obligations, to acquire other resources (such as stock/inventory), to satisfy operating expenses and to meet ownership distributions. Cash has been described as the 'life blood' of a business and movements in cash are usually given close scrutiny by users of financial statements.

However, it is clear that reporting cash movements alone would not be enough to portray the financial health of the business. The changes in cash over time do not give an insight into the profit generated. The income statement provides an insight into this aspect of performance. For day 1, for example, we saw that the cash balance increased by $10 but the profit generated, as shown in the income statement, was $35. The increase in wealth ($35) was represented by $10 cash and $25 in the form of stock (inventory).

In order to gain an insight into the total wealth of the business a balance sheet is drawn up at the end of the day. Cash is only one form in which wealth can be held. In the case of this business, wealth is also held in the form of inventory (stock of goods for resale). Hence when drawing up the balance sheet, both forms of wealth held will be listed. In the case of a large business, there may be many other forms in which wealth will be held, such as land and buildings, equipment and motor vehicles.

Let us now continue with our example.

EXAMPLE

1.1

continued

On the second day of trading, Paul purchased more wrapping paper for $50 cash. He managed to sell all of the new wrapping paper and half of the earlier stock for a total of $90.

The cash flow statement on day 2 will be as follows:

Cash flow statement for day 2	
	$
Opening balance (i.e. closing balance from day 1)	110
Sale of wrapping paper	90
	200
Purchase of wrapping paper	50
Closing balance	150

The income statement for day 2 will be as follows:

Income statement for day 2	
	$
Sales	90
Cost of goods sold ($50 + ½ of $25)	62.50
Profit	27.50

The balance sheet at the end of day 2 will be:

Balance sheet at the end of day 2	
	$
Cash	150
Inventory (stock of goods for resale: ½ of $25)	12.50
Total business wealth	162.50

The statement of changes in owner's equity for day 2 will be:

Statement of changes in owner's equity for day 2 (additional part of the balance sheet)	
	$
Owner's capital (wealth) at the beginning of day 2	135
Profit for day 2	27.50
Owner's capital (wealth) at the end of day 2	162.50

We can see that the total business wealth increased to $162.50 by the end of day 2. This represents an increase of $27.50 (i.e. $162.50–$135) over the previous day. You should note that this is the amount of profit made during day 2 as shown on the income statement.

ACTIVITY 1.8

On the third day of his business venture, Paul purchased more stock for $100 cash. However, it was raining hard for much of the day and sales were slow. After Paul had sold half of his total stock for $65, he decided to stop trading until the following day. Have a go at drawing up the four financial reports for day 3 of Paul's business venture.

The solution to Activity 1.8 shows that the total business wealth increased by $8.75 (i.e. the amount of the day's profit) even though the cash balance declined. This is due to the fact that the business is holding more of its wealth in the form of inventory rather than cash, compared with the end of day 2.

Note that the income statement and cash flow statement are both concerned with measuring flows (of wealth and cash respectively) over time. The period of time may be one day, one month, one year, etc. The balance sheet, however, is concerned with the financial position (or wealth) at a particular moment in time (the end of one day, one week, etc.). Figure 1.6 illustrates this point. The income statement, statement of changes in owner's equity, cash flow statement and balance sheet, when taken together, are often referred to as the 'final accounts' of the business.

For external users of the accounts these reports are normally backward looking and are based on information concerning past events and transactions. This can be useful for users in providing feedback on past performance and in identifying trends that provide clues to future performance. However, the reports can also be prepared using projected data in order to help assess likely future profits, cash flows, etc. The financial reports are normally prepared on a projected basis for internal decision-making purposes only. Managers are usually reluctant to publish these projected figures for external users.

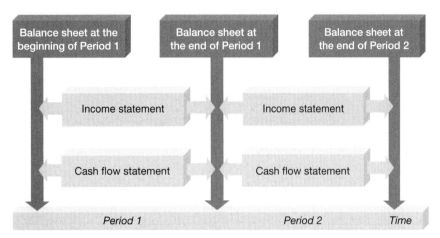

The figure shows how the income statement and cash flow statement are concerned with measuring flows of wealth over time. The balance sheet, however, is concerned with measuring the stock of wealth at a particular moment in time.

FIGURE 1.6 The relationship between the balance sheet, the income statement and the cash flow statement

Nevertheless, as external users have to make decisions about the future, projected financial reports prepared by managers are likely to be useful for this purpose. Managers are, after all, in a good position to assess future performance and so their assessments are likely to provide a valuable source of information. In certain circumstances, such as raising fresh capital or resisting a hostile takeover bid, managers are prepared to depart from normal practice and issue projected figures to external users. Where publication does occur, some independent verification of the assumptions underlying the forecasts is often provided by a firm of accountants to lend credibility to the figures produced.

SELF-ASSESSMENT QUESTION 1.1

While on holiday on the Gold Coast, Helen had her credit cards and purse stolen from a beach where she was swimming. She was left with only $40, which she had left in her hotel room. There were three days of her holiday remaining. She was determined to continue her holiday and decided to make some money in order to be able to complete her holiday. She decided to sell orange juice to holidaymakers using the local beach. On day 1 she purchased 80 cartons of orange juice at $0.50 each for cash and sold 70 of these at $0.80 each. On the following day she purchased 60 cartons for cash and sold 65 at $0.80 each. On the third and final day she purchased another 60 cartons for cash. However, it rained and, as a result, business was poor. She managed to sell 20 at $0.80 each but sold off the rest of her stock at $0.40 each.

Required:

Prepare an income statement and a cash flow statement for each day's trading and prepare a balance sheet at the end of each day's trading.

SUMMARY

In this chapter we have achieved the following objectives in the way shown.

OBJECTIVE	METHOD ACHIEVED
Define accounting	Illustrated that it is an information system concerned with the collection, analysis and communication of economic information.
Discuss the role of accounting information	Identified the role as the provision of economic information to assist in: • Decision making • Planning • Control
List the main user groups for a business entity	Identified the following groups: • Resource providers—owners, lenders, suppliers, employees • Recipients of goods and services—customers • Reviewers—auditors, government, unions, competitors, special interest groups • Managers
Summarise the different uses that can be made of accounting information	Identified the following uses: • Financial performance—efficient use of resources • Financial position—longer-term stability • Liquidity—short-term survival • Compliance—with plans, sales, expectations, regulations • Social responsibility—in relation to physical, environmental and human resources
Explain the different procedures involved in the accounting information system	Explained the nature of the accounting information system as including: • Information identification—relevant economic information • Information recording—systematic • Information analysis—including interpretation • Information reporting—matching user needs
State the key characteristics of accounting information	Identified the key characteristics as: • Relevance—decision usefulness in confirmation or prediction • Reliability—to faithfully represent • Comparability—in classification, measurement and presentation • Understandability—user friendly • Cost/benefit—benefits exceed the cost of processing
Relate the steps in the planning process	Explained the planning process and identified the following steps: • Setting the objectives or mission—explains what the business is trying to achieve • Setting long-term plans—explains how the objectives will be achieved over the medium term • Setting the budget—represents the short-term financial plan
Discuss the nature of control in the decision-making process	Identified control as compelling events to conform to the plan

OBJECTIVE	METHOD ACHIEVED
List alternative objectives of business	Reviewed the range of possibilities, including the following: • Maximise sales • Maximise profit • Maximise investors' return • Financial survival • Financial stability • Growth • Satisficing • Sustainable development • Wealth enhancement

Compare and contrast financial and management accounting — Identified differences as follows:

	Financial accounting	Management accounting
Report nature	General purpose	Special purpose
Level of detail	Aggregated	Dissected
Restrictions	Standardised or regulated	Minimum restrictions
Reporting interval	Less frequently	More frequently
Time horizon	Backward looking	Forward looking
Range of information	Primarily monetary and objective	Often non-monetary with less objective constraints

Provide an overview of the main financial reports — Illustrated the need for and development of cash flow statements, the balance sheet, the statement of changes in owner's equity and income statement (profit and loss account)

DISCUSSION QUESTIONS

EASY

<Obj 5> **1.1** Accounting is often defined as an 'information system'. Identify the:
- input
- process
- output.

<Obj 6> **1.2** 'Understandability' is identified in the text as a key characteristic of accounting information. By whom should the financial reports be readily understood?

<Obj 7> **1.3** What is the difference between an organisation's 'mission' and its 'long-term plans'?

<Obj 8> **1.4** Distinguish between planning and control.

<Obj 8> **1.5** Within the business, how can accounting facilitate control?

<Obj 11> **1.6** Identify the similarities and differences between the three major external financial reports (income statement, balance sheet, cash flow statement).

INTERMEDIATE

<Obj 1> **1.7** Is 'accounting' what 'accountants' do?

<Obj 2> **1.8** What is the purpose of producing accounting information?

<Obj 2> **1.9** What economic principle should be the determinant of what accounting information is produced? Should economics be the only issue here? (Consider who are the users of accounting information.)

<Obj 3,4> **1.10** There are three categories of external report users: 'resource providers', 'recipients of goods and/or services' and 'reviewers'. Who are the resource providers? What financial information do they seek from the financial reports?

<Obj 4> **1.11** Accounting is said to perform a 'decision-usefulness' role as well as an 'accountability (stewardship) role'. Distinguish between these two roles and provide an example of each.

<Obj 6> **1.12** Relevance and reliability represent two key qualitative characteristics of accounting information. What do these two terms mean in an accounting context? Are they in conflict?

<Obj 9> **1.13** Review the mission statements of several business entities and identify the stated objectives in terms of the list on pages 8 and 9.

<Obj 9> **1.14** Briefly explain the differences between the following alternative objectives for a business:
- to maximise sales
- to maximise the return on assets
- to maximise profits
- to maximise sustainable profits.

<Obj 10> **1.15** Reconcile financial accounting with management accounting. Your textbook clearly distinguishes between them; what are the similarities?

<Obj 10> **1.16** What restrictions impact on the financial accounting reports produced in Australia?

CHALLENGING

<Obj 1> **1.17** Accounting is normally defined in terms of 'recording, classifying, summarising and communicating economic information about a reporting entity'. Explain and provide an example of the following 'key' terms in such a definition:
- classifying
- summarising
- communicating
- economic information.

<Obj 2> **1.18** Many organisations provide financial information to external users in excess of what the regulators require. Can you suggest why they would incur the cost of producing such information?

<Obj 2> **1.19** Financial accounting statements tend to reflect past events. In view of this, how can they be of assistance to a user in making a decision when decisions, by their very nature, can only be made about future actions?

<Obj 3, 9> **1.20** It is claimed today that organisations must meet the needs or demands of various stakeholders.
- What is meant by the term 'stakeholder'?
- Who are the stakeholders?
- What are their needs or demands?
- Why must they be met?

<Obj 11> **1.21** The income statement reflects the financial performance for the period and explains the changes in the balance sheet.
Do you agree or disagree with this statement? Why?

Qantas Audit Report 2004

Independent Audit Report to the members of Qantas Airways Limited

CASE STUDY 1.1

SCOPE

THE FINANCIAL REPORT AND DIRECTORS' RESPONSIBILITY

The Financial Report comprises the Statements of Financial Position, Statements of Financial Performance, Statements of Cash Flows, accompanying notes to the Financial Statements notes 1 to 39, and the Directors' Declaration for both Qantas Airways Limited (the 'Company') and Qantas Airways Limited and its controlled entities (the 'Consolidated Entity'), for the year ended 30 June 2004. The Consolidated Entity comprises both the Company and the entities it controlled during that year.

The directors of the Company are responsible for the preparation and true and fair presentation of the Financial Report in accordance with the Corporations Act 2001. This includes responsibility for the maintenance of adequate accounting records and internal controls that are designed to prevent and detect fraud and error, and for the accounting policies and accounting estimates inherent in the Financial Report.

AUDIT APPROACH

We conducted an independent audit in order to express an opinion to the members of the Company. Our audit was conducted in accordance with Australian Auditing Standards in order to provide reasonable assurance as to whether the Financial Report is free of material misstatement. The nature of an audit is influenced by factors such as the use of professional judgement, selective testing, the inherent limitations of internal control, and the availability of persuasive rather than conclusive evidence. Therefore, an audit cannot guarantee that all misstatements have been detected.

We performed procedures to assess whether in all material respects the Financial Report presents fairly, in accordance with the Corporations Act 2001, Australian Accounting Standards and other mandatory financial reporting requirements in Australia, a view which is consistent with our understanding of the Company's and the Consolidated Entity's financial position, and of their performance as represented by the results of their operations and cash flows.

We formed our audit opinion on the basis of these procedures, which included:

- examining, on a test basis, information to provide evidence supporting the amounts and disclosures in the Financial Report; and
- assessing the appropriateness of the accounting policies and disclosures used and the reasonableness of significant accounting estimates made by the directors.

While we considered the effectiveness of management's internal controls over financial reporting when determining the nature and extent of our procedures, our audit was not designed to provide assurance on internal controls.

INDEPENDENCE

In conducting our audit, we followed applicable independence requirements of Australian professional ethical pronouncements and the Corporations Act 2001.

AUDIT OPINION

In our opinion, the Financial Report of Qantas Airways Limited is in accordance with:

(a) the Corporations Act 2001, including:
    i. giving a true and fair view of the Company's and the Consolidated Entity's financial position as at 30 June 2004 and of their performance for the year ended on that date; and

ii. complying with Accounting Standards in Australia and the Corporations Regulations 2001; and

(b) other mandatory financial reporting requirements in Australia.

KPMG   Mark Epper
                                         Partner

Sydney, 30 August 2004

1   Clearly distinguish between the functions of the three financial reports covered by the auditor's report:
    * statement of financial position (now balance sheet)
    * statement of financial performance (now income statement)
    * statement of cash flows (now cash flow statement)

2   What are some examples of good internal controls that organisations such as Qantas would have to minimise the risk of fraud or error in the records?

3   The audit is conducted in accordance with Australian Auditing Standards. Who is responsible for preparing these standards?

4   In relation to the procedures undertaken by the auditors the following were mentioned:
    * examining evidence to support amounts included in the financial reports
    * assessing the appropriateness of the accounting policy
    * assessing the reasonableness of significant accounting estimates.
    Provide an example for each of these aspects (what is being assessed? and how it may be assessed?).

5   What sorts of things would you expect to be covered by the accounting professional's ethical pronouncements?

6   The audit report provides reasonable assurance that as to whether the financial statements are free from material misstatement. How do accountants define 'material'?

7   The audit opinion is expressed in terms of a 'true and fair view of the entity's financial position and financial performance'. What does 'true and fair' mean? Is it different to 'complying with Accounting Standards'?

CASE STUDY 1.2

Go green and boost profits

Joanna Tovia

Business Owner (section), *The Courier-Mail*
Wednesday, 19 January 2005, p. 34

Experts say small businesses wanting to grow and compete against big business should follow their lead.

A shift in consumer values, demand for greater transparency and alarming environmental evidence is starting to force businesses into going green.

Businesses who do take environmental issues into account are discovering some unexpected benefits.

Research shows big businesses that toe the green line earn higher profits as a result and the same can be true for small businesses.

Australian Conservation Foundation legal adviser Chuck Berger says although it's often more difficult for a small business to understand and implement sustainability, in principle the issues are the same.

'There are competitive advantages and savings in terms of efficiency and resource usage that are just the same as for big businesses,' Mr Berger says.

Social and environmental factors, economics and shareholder value make up what is often referred to as the 'triple bottom line', a term coined by US sustainability expert John Elkington.

In his chapter of the book, *The Triple Bottom Line,* Mr Elkington says growing numbers of companies are already finding themselves challenged by consumers and the financial markets about aspects of their triple bottom line commitments and performance.

Mr Elkington says the power of people's values should not be underestimated.

He says values change every generation and have the power to cause companies to crash and burn.

'Companies that have felt themselves standing on solid ground for decades suddenly find that the world as they knew it is being turned upside down and inside out.'

This, combined with the demand for increased transparency, will have companies contemplating their triple bottom line more than ever before.

'Pressures will continuously build on both corporations and governments to make a transition to sustainable development,' he writes.

If sustainability is the way of the future, it makes sense to turn your business green sooner rather than later.

According to the Small Business Development Corporation, sustainability involves considering not only the economic impacts of your key business decisions, but also the social and environmental impacts as well.

The good news is that turning your business green needn't involve sacrifices. In fact, the opposite is true.

The SBDC says green businesses benefit in the following ways:

• Increased profits—sustainability can save you money and even make you money.
• Satisfying customer demand—customer values are shifting and customers want to support businesses that have adopted sustainable practices and want to buy products and services that are environmentally and socially friendly.
• Increased innovation—there is plenty of opportunity for new markets and products and services to be identified and developed in response to demand for sustainable solutions.
• Contributing to sustainability also offers good marketing opportunities that put your business in a positive light.

1 What does it mean for a business to 'go green'?
2 What is 'sustainable development'?
3 What sort of actions, or non-actions, can the management of a business undertake (or not undertake) to enhance its environmental performance?
4 The author of the article states that businesses that 'toe the green line earn higher profits as a result'. Why might this be so?

5 Triple bottom line reporting is a term coined by John Elkington, a US expert on sustainability. What three separate performance measures are to be assessed in such a report?

6 The article highlights that apart from meeting changing societal expectations about environmental and social performance, organisations today must satisfy 'the demand for increased transparency'. What is meant by 'increased transparency'?

CASE STUDY 1.3

Audit queries mystery $8.4 m

Brendan O'Keefe

The Australian, Higher Education
Wednesday, 12 January 2005, p. 25

Operations of a research centre at the University of NSW have been referred to the state's Independent Commission Against Corruption after an internal audit revealed alleged mismanagement, conflicts of interest and millions in unaccounted funds.

The Audit Office of NSW in its 2004 report to state parliament, says an internal audit of the Co-operative Research Centre for Eye Research and Technology uncovered 'poor governance with unmanaged conflicts of interest; allegations of mismanagement; duplicate payments of approximately $4 million that may not be recoverable; and unaccounted industry funds of approximately $6.5 million'.

The university was unable to give any details about the allegations.

The report says CRCs had poor systems, understanding of governance and standards of record-keeping.

'Nobody seems to take responsibility for managing corporate governance, making sure that there's adequate reporting,' a spokesman said.

'They focus on the research and the rest of it falls by the wayside.'

An ICAC spokesman said the anti-corruption body was working with the university's Internal Audit Office on the matter. UNSW referred the matter to ICAC.

'We have been liaising with the university, providing information and advice,' he said.

ICAC was keeping a watching brief on the IAO investigation.

The university also has an unaccounted-for $8.4 million on its books; no one is sure where it came from or how long it has been there.

After an intensive three-month search, even the Audit Office is at a loss. It reported to parliament that the university had, in its financial report to December 31, 2003, recognised the $8.4 million as 'revenue and cash to adjust a prior period error'.

'The university performed significant work investigating this error, but was unable to identify its cause or nature,' the 2004 report says.

'The work performed by the university indicates this error did not occur in 2003 but has been carried forward from a prior period.'

In a statement, the university said it believed the error may have occurred in 2000-01, when its financial systems were transferred to a new software program.

'The fact that the error was not detected earlier demonstrates that the university's reconciliation process was not operating satisfactorily,' it said.

1   What is the function of an audit?

2   What is the difference between an internal and an external audit?

3   The review highlighted 'poor governance with unmanaged conflicts of interest; allegations of mismanagement; duplicate payments of approximately $4 million that may not be recoverable; and unaccountable industry funds of approximately $6.5 million'.

  ✳ What does 'governance' involve?

  ✳ Identify possible conflicts of interest that may have applied here.

  ✳ How would you easily prevent duplicate payments?

  ✳ Why might duplicate payments not be recoverable?

  ✳ How could the problem of unaccountable industry funds have been resolved?

4   The University of NSW itself recognised an imbalance of $8.4 million carried forward as revenue and cash to resolve a possible error in earlier periods. Is this appropriate? How else could it have been treated?

5   In relation to the error the review stated that 'the fact that the error was not detected earlier demonstrates that the university's reconciliation process was not operating satisfactorily'. What is the 'reconciliation process'?

SOLUTIONS TO ACTIVITIES

Activity 1.1

Accountability is normally divided into two parts:

- agreeing to undertake certain actions, or not to undertake them as the case may be
- providing a retrospective report on those actions (or non-actions).

Activity 1.2

Your answer may be as follows:

User group	Use
Customers	To assess the ability of the business to continue in business and to supply the needs of the customers.
Suppliers	To assess the ability of the business to pay for the goods and services supplied.
Government	To assess how much tax the business should pay, whether it complies with agreed pricing policies, whether financial support is needed, etc.
Owners	To assess how effectively the managers are running the business and to make judgments about likely levels of risk and return in the future.
Lenders	To assess the ability of the business to meet its obligations and to pay interest and to repay the principal.
Employees (non-management)	To assess the ability of the business to continue to provide employment and to reward employees for their labour.
Investment analysts	To assess the likely risks and returns associated with the business in order to determine its investment potential and to advise clients accordingly.

| Community representatives | To assess the ability of the business to continue to provide employment for the community and use community resources, to help fund environmental improvements, etc. |
| Managers | To help make decisions and plans for the business and to help exercise control to try to ensure that plans come to fruition. |

This is not an exhaustive list. You may have thought of other reasons why each group would find accounting information useful.

Activity 1.3

The example we thought of relates to a decision as to whether or not to sell an asset, such as a unique cutting tool. The most reliable figure could well be the original historic cost. Is such a figure particularly relevant to the decision? It is far more likely that managers will require information concerning the likely current realisable (i.e. disposal) value of the asset. The current realisable value of the machine may be highly relevant to the final decision but may not be very reliable, particularly as the machine is unique and there is likely to be little information concerning market values.

There are other examples you may have thought of.

Activity 1.4

The reason that you may decide not to produce or discover the information is that you judge the cost of doing so to be greater than the potential benefit of having the information.

Activity 1.5

In practice, decision makers may not be as rational and capable as implied in the process described above. Individuals may find it difficult to handle large amounts of information relating to a wide range of options. As a result, they may restrict their range of possible options or discard some information in order to prevent themselves from being overloaded. They may also adopt rather simple approaches to evaluating the mass of information provided. One such simple approach is to ignore any information that may not fit very well with the outcome that the decision makers would like to achieve.

Activity 1.6

The reasons that we thought of are:

- *Risk*. Next year could be particularly profitable if large risks are taken, like not having expensive quality control mechanisms. This may make the business profitable, but it could lead to disaster sooner or later.

- *Short-termism*. Concentrating on the short term and ignoring the long term could lead to immediate profitability. For example, cutting out spending on things that are likely to pay off in the longer-term, such as research and development and training, will have immediate profitability benefits at the cost of longer-term ones.

- *Increased size*. Expanding the business, through increased investment, could lead to higher profit, but the effectiveness of the investment may diminish with expansion.

Activity 1.7

The distinction between management and financial accounting suggests that there are differences between the information needs of managers and those of other users. While differences undoubtedly exist, there is also a good deal of overlap between the needs of managers and the needs of other users. For example, managers will, at times, be interested in receiving an historic overview of business operations of the sort provided to other users. Equally, the other users would be interested in receiving information relating to the future such as the forecast level of profits and non-financial information such as the state of the order book and product innovations.

Activity 1.8

Cash flow statement for day 3	
	$
Opening balance (from day 2)	150
Sale of wrapping paper	65
	215
Purchase of wrapping paper	100
Closing balance	115

Income statement for day 3	
	$
Sales	65
Cost of goods sold (½ of $(100 + 12.50))	56.25
Profit	8.75

Balance sheet at the end of day 3	
	$
Cash	115
Inventory (½ of $(100 + 12.50))	56.25
Total business wealth	171.25

Statement of changes in owner's equity for day 3 (additional part of the balance sheet)	
	$
Owner's capital (wealth) at the beginning of day 3	162.50
Profit for day 3	8.75
Owner's capital (wealth) at the end of day 3	171.25

OBJECTIVES

When you have completed your study of this chapter you should be able to:

1 list the three most common entity structures used for business operations in Australia

2 discuss the main characteristics of the three entity structures

3 discuss the advantages and disadvantages of the three entities

4 assess the alternative bases for profit or loss distribution among partners

5 distinguish between different types of companies

6 discuss the role and responsibilities of company directors

7 compare and contrast ordinary and preference shares

8 identify and discuss the role of the alternative regulatory bodies in relation to company operations and financial reporting.

DIFFERENT ACCOUNTING ENTITIES

In Chapters 3 to 5 we will deal with the three main financial reports in detail. Before doing this, however, it is important to recognise that the reports relate to a particular business. Each business is known as a business entity. The financial reports relate to each particular business entity. In practice there are a number of different kinds of entity, including non-profit organisations such as clubs and societies, businesses run by a single owner, businesses run by a number of people collectively as a partnership, and businesses that are run in the form of a limited company. There are even entities which are effectively groups of companies run through a holding company. The form of the financial reports differs, depending on the nature of the particular entity concerned. In this chapter we will examine the nature of the most common forms of business structures used in Australia. The structures examined include the sole proprietorship, the partnership and the limited company.

In examining the nature of each entity, we are particularly interested in how that nature will affect the financial recording and reporting process and the relationship between key stakeholders of the enterprise. Included in these stakeholders will be the managers, resource providers, recipients of the products or services of the entity, and external reviewers. The external reviewers may include regulatory bodies, auditors, trade unions and special interest groups.

THE NATURE OF SOLE PROPRIETORSHIPS

A **sole proprietorship** represents that form of business where there is a single owner (called the proprietor). From a legal perspective there is no distinction between the owner (Bill Bloggs) and the business (Bill's Diner). However, from an accounting perspective we distinguish clearly between the owner (Bill Bloggs) and the business (Bill's Diner).

In Chapter 3 (on the balance sheet) we will highlight that the accounting entity (Bill's Diner) will recognise transactions between the owner (Bill Bloggs) and the business. These transactions will relate to capital (funds) contributed to the business by the owner, profit earned by the business and not distributed to the owner, and distributions to the owner.

ACTIVITY 2.1

What might distributions to the sole owner of the business represent?

The important characteristics of the sole proprietorship entity structure from the perspective of both the owner and other people or other entities dealing with this business include the following:

* *No separate legal entity.* While the business is a separate accounting (recording/reporting) entity, it is not a separate legal entity. It cannot enter into contractual arrangements (borrow, lend, purchase, sell, sue, be sued) in its own right; rather, it is the legal owner who must negotiate such contracts.
* *Limited life.* The sole proprietorship structure has a limited life. The life of the business is restricted to the period the owner continues in that position. This does not mean that the activity of the business necessarily stops

when the owner dies, retires or leaves the business, but that sole proprietorship business ceases and possibly another commences (e.g. new owner, new name).

✳ *Unlimited liability.* The owner of a sole proprietorship has unlimited liability with respect to the activities of the business. That is, he or she will be fully responsible for the obligations and debts of the business.

✳ *Minimum reporting regulations.* Regulations with respect to financial recording and reporting are minimal compared with other entity structures. However, the introduction of GST has increased the requirement to produce regular detailed reports.

 ACTIVITY 2.2

Why would the regulation related to financial records and reporting be simpler for sole proprietors than for more complex entity structures such as companies?

✳ *Limited access to funds.* Access to funds is potentially limited. With a sole proprietorship the ownership funding is restricted to the personal resources of a single owner. Additionally, certain forms of borrowing are not available to sole proprietors that may be available to companies, and lenders may be more reluctant to provide credit or funds to sole proprietorships.

 ACTIVITY 2.3

What sort of business activities would normally be carried out using the sole proprietorship structure?

✳ *The costs to establish a sole proprietorship structure are normally much lower than for other entity structures.* By costs we are referring to those involved in setting up the business entity, not the costs to make the business operational (e.g. the necessary resources, property, plant, equipment, inventories, staff and other expenditure).

 ACTIVITY 2.4

Can you think of any restrictions on a person establishing a sole proprietorship business?

Having highlighted a number of the key features of the sole proprietorship entity structure we can determine its advantages and disadvantages. The advantages include:

✳ simple and inexpensive to establish and operate
✳ minimal financial reporting regulation
✳ ownership and management are normally combined
✳ the financial rewards flow directly to the owner
✳ timely decision making.

ACTIVITY 2.5

Can you think of possible disadvantages to an owner selecting the sole proprietorship entity structure?

THE NATURE OF PARTNERSHIPS

The **partnership** business entity structure represents the relationship that exists between two or more individuals and which is focused on generating a financial profit. This relationship may have been established by a formal partnership agreement or an informal arrangement between the parties, or in fact it may be simply inferred by the actions of two or more individuals.

The partnership represents a separate accounting entity distinct from the owners (partners). However, as with the sole proprietorship, there is no separate legal entity. From the viewpoint of the law there are just the individual owners.

In terms of financial record keeping, individual records will be maintained by the partnership for each partner's transactions with the partnership. These records will relate to:

❊ resource contributions (capital)

❊ resource withdrawals (drawings)

❊ share of undistributed profits (either current or retained earnings—earnings made in earlier periods but not withdrawn by the owners).

The important characteristics of the partnership entity structure from the perspective of both the owners and external parties dealing with the business include the following:

❊ *No separate legal entity.* While the partnership is a separate accounting entity, there is no legal distinction between the business and the partners. As with a sole proprietorship, it is the partners, not the partnership, who enter into all contractual arrangements (e.g. borrow, lend, buy, sell, employ, dismiss, sue, be sued).

❊ *Limited life.* The partnership has a limited life, as each time there is a change in ownership (partners leave, new partners are introduced) the existing partnership concludes and a new partnership commences.

❊ *Unlimited liability.* The liability of partners jointly and separately is unlimited with respect to the debts of the business. This means that personal assets of each partner can be called upon to satisfy the claims of business creditors, well beyond the amount of the individual partner's share of the business.

❊ *Mutual agency.* Each partner is responsible for the business actions of all other partners as if they had undertaken the action themselves.

❊ *Co-ownership of assets.* The partnership assets are owned by the partners in aggregate rather than individually.

❊ *Co-ownership of profits.* The partnership profits belong to the partners equally or in otherwise agreed proportions.

❊ *Limited membership.* There are certain restrictions on the number of partners that can belong to a partnership entity structure. While this is normally limited to 20, there are some exceptions in relation to professions (e.g. accounting practices). Given the expanded number of owners, the access to ownership funds is normally much greater than for a sole proprietorship.

❊ *Increased regulation.* Most states have Partnership Acts which provide direction in relation to the activities of partnerships and the rights and responsibilities of partners.

ACTIVITY 2.6

Having reviewed the characteristics of partnerships, can you think of some of the advantages of this structure over the sole proprietorship structure?

When considering the potential disadvantages of partnerships it is important to identify the entity structure with which the partnership is being compared.

In comparison with a sole proprietorship the disadvantages could include:

* a higher level of regulation
* giving up profit share to other owners (co-ownership)
* giving up individual asset ownership (co-ownership)
* reduced decision-making authority (shared management)
* mutual agency imposes an added responsibility for the business actions of other partners.

In comparison with a company the disadvantages could include:

* a limited life may affect long-term planning
* unlimited liability creates greater risk for ownership investment
* absence of a specialist management team
* mutual agency imposes an added responsibility for the business actions of the partners
* limited access to both ownership funds and debt funds.

It is important for partners to have a formal and detailed partnership agreement so as to avoid the problems that invariably arise in relation to the operation of the partnership and the relations between partners. Where problems arise between partners that cannot be resolved without recourse to the law, the requirements of the Partnership Act will apply.

ACTIVITY 2.7

What matters should a partnership agreement cover?

In relation to the distribution of partnership profit, most Partnership Acts indicate:

* Partners are not entitled to a 'salary or wage equivalent' related to their input (physical or mental) into the business operations.
* Partners are not entitled to an 'interest equivalent' on the capital contributions they make to the business.
* The profit or loss is to be divided equally among the partners.

However, these rules only apply in the absence of an agreement. Partners can agree to share profits in any way they choose.

ACTIVITY 2.8

If you were setting up in partnership, suggest an equitable basis for sharing profits or losses.

THE NATURE OF COMPANIES

There are a wide variety of company types, but the most common in Australia is the company limited by share capital. In this chapter we will largely restrict our focus to this entity structure. Basically, a company is a business entity which is owned by many people who have invested in the business. This ownership interest is broken down into small shares; hence the use of the term 'shareholders' to describe the owners.

The most important characteristics of the **limited company** are as follows:

* *Separate legal entity.* A limited company has the legal capacity of a person and has a separate legal status from those who own the entity (shareholders). Thus, a company in its own right is able to enter into contracts with external parties (buy, sell, borrow, lend, employ, sue, be sued). An Australian company comes into existence as a 'body corporate' when it is registered under the Corporations Act and is issued a certificate of registration.
* *Unlimited (perpetual) life.* The life of the company is indefinite and is not related to the life of the individuals who own it. The ownership interest may change over time as shares are transferred or sold from one shareholder to another.
* *Limited liability.* Since the company is a legal person in its own right, it must take responsibility for its own debts and losses. This means that once the shareholders have paid what they have agreed to pay for the shares, their obligation to the company, and to the company's creditors, is satisfied.

ACTIVITY 2.9

Can you think of any other economic benefits that limited liability might bring?

ACTIVITY 2.10

Can you list three different suppliers of goods or services to a company entity?

ACTIVITY 2.11

Consider how suppliers of goods and services might be protected, given that the liability of company owners is limited to their agreed contributions.

While limited liability is an advantage to the owners, it can be seen as a problem to the external parties providing goods and services to the company.

✳ *Company ownership of assets.* The company assets are owned by the company in its own right as a legal person.

✳ *Company profits belong to the shareholders.* The company profits are either distributed or retained for the benefit of shareholders. Other things being equal, the fact that profits are retained in the business, and reinvested in more assets, or to reduce debt, would tend to increase the value of the shares.

✳ *Extensive membership.* While for some forms of companies the membership may be restricted, for public companies the number of shareholders can be very large. In the case of several significant Australian privatisations (Commonwealth Bank, Telstra) the initial number of owners exceeded 250,000.

With such a large number of owners corporate entity structures have the potential to raise significant amounts of ownership funds. Also, public companies have access to certain types of debt funding that is not available to other entity structures. This will be discussed further in Chapter 14.

✳ *Separation of ownership and management.* With sole proprietorships and partnerships the owner(s) and manager(s) are by and large the same. However, with companies there will generally be a separate specialist management team outside of the ownership interest.

Increasingly today, the key personnel in this management team may well be allocated shares (ownership interests) on the basis of the company's performance, and therefore may be managers and owners at the same time.

✳ *Extensive regulation.* The corporate entity will be subject to much stricter regulation than the partnership and sole proprietorship entity structure. This additional regulation is required given the 'limited liability' benefit granted to owners (shareholders) and the fact that most shareholders are widely removed from the day-to-day activities of the business and its management.

ACTIVITY 2.12

What are some of the regulations you might expect to apply to the corporate entity?

Having highlighted a number of the key features of the company entity structure, we can identify its potential advantages and disadvantages compared with the other commonly used entity structures. The advantages would normally include:

✳ the separation of ownership and management and the existence of a specialist management team

✳ perpetual existence of the entity provides for the stability of operations and long-term planning

✳ the existence of a separate legal entity facilitates the operational and financial freedom of the entity

✳ the limited liability for the owners (shareholders) removes significant barriers to investment

✳ greater access to ownership funding enhances the business's ability to operate and expand

✳ potentially greater access to debt funding

✳ potential taxation advantages given the company tax rate (currently 30 per cent) is less than the maximum personal taxation rate (currently 47 per cent)

✳ potential increases in share values where shares are listed on the stock exchange.

We have looked at the general features of companies. However, it is important with this more complex entity structure to consider in greater detail its component parts before looking in subsequent chapters at financial reports and the use of those reports in management decision making.

ACTIVITY 2.13

What are some of the potential disadvantages of the corporate entity structure compared with the other entity structures?

MANAGEMENT OF COMPANIES—THE ROLE OF DIRECTORS

A limited company may have a legal personality but it is not a human being capable of making decisions and plans about the business and exercising control over it. These management tasks must be undertaken by human beings. The most senior level of management of a company is the board of **directors**.

The shareholders elect directors to manage the company on a day-to-day basis on behalf of those shareholders. By law there must be at least one director for a proprietary company and three for a public company. In a small company the board may be the only level of management and consist of all the shareholders. In larger companies the board may consist of ten or so directors, out of many thousands of shareholders. The directors need not even be shareholders. Below the board of directors could be several layers of management comprising thousands of people.

Whatever the size of the company the directors are responsible to the shareholders, and to some extent to the world at large, for the conduct of the company. The directors' term of office is limited and they must stand for election at the end of that term if they wish to continue in office.

PUBLIC AND PROPRIETARY (PRIVATE) COMPANIES

Several different types of companies operate under the Corporations Act. A limited company uses the word 'Limited' (Ltd) in its name. The two main categories are public and proprietary (private) companies.

Public companies can offer their shares for sale to the general public. Proprietary companies cannot. There is no maximum number of shareholders for public companies, so ownership can be very widely spread. Many public companies, provided that they meet the requirements of the stock exchange, have their shares listed on the exchange, which means that they can be freely traded. This means that shareholders can sell their shares at the going market price, or existing shares can be purchased. Public companies are more rigorously regulated than proprietary companies.

Proprietary companies tend to be smaller businesses where the ownership is divided between relatively few shareholders who are usually fairly close to one another—for example, a family company. Numerically, there are more private limited companies in Australia and New Zealand than there are public ones. Since the public ones tend to be individually larger, they represent a much more important group economically. Many proprietary companies are no more than the vehicle through which businesses that are effectively little more than sole proprietorships or small partnerships operate.

Proprietary companies have the words 'Proprietary Limited' (Pty Ltd) in their name. They are restricted to no more than 50 (non-employee) shareholders and are restricted in their ability to raise money from the public. Proprietary companies generally are less regulated than public companies. Small proprietary companies are relieved from many of the reporting requirements of large proprietary companies or public companies. A company is deemed to be small if it satisfies at least two of the following three requirements:

* it has consolidated gross operating revenue of less than $10 million
* its consolidated gross assets at the end of the financial year are less than $5 million
* it employs fewer than 50 employees at the end of the financial year.

CAPITAL (OWNERS' CLAIM) OF LIMITED COMPANIES

Our simple balance sheet of Chapter 1 was effectively a statement of wealth. In practice the **balance sheet** sets out the things that are owned, and deducts from this figure the amounts owed to outsiders. The difference represents the wealth of the business. Given that the business is run for the benefit of the owners, this wealth can be seen as a measure of the owners' claim. As a business makes more profit and increases its wealth, so the owners' claim increases. If the business pays out some of its profits the wealth will decrease, as will the owners' claim.

The owners' claim of a sole proprietorship is normally encompassed in one figure on the balance sheet, usually labelled 'capital'. This figure can be increased by further injections of funds or by making of profits, or reduced by incurring losses or by drawings made by the owner. With companies, this is usually a little more complicated, though in essence the same broad principles apply. With a company the owners' claim is divided between shares (i.e. the original investment) on the one hand, and reserves (i.e. profits and gains subsequently made) on the other. Capital and reserves are generally referred to as shareholders' equity. There is also the possibility that there will be shares of more than one type and reserves of more than one type, so within the basic divisions of share capital and reserves there may well be further subdivisions. This probably seems quite complicated. Shortly we shall consider the reasons for these subdivisions and all should become clearer.

THE BASIC DIVISION

When a company is first formed, those who take steps to form it, usually known as the 'promoters' of the company, will decide how much needs to be raised by the potential shareholders to set up the company with the necessary assets to operate.

EXAMPLE

2.1

Let us imagine that several people get together and decide to form a company to operate a particular business. They estimate that the company will need $50,000 to obtain the necessary assets to operate the business. Between them they raise the cash which they use to buy shares in the company. The company issues 50,000 shares at $1 each.

At this point the balance sheet of the company would be:

Balance sheet as at 31 March 2005	
Net assets (all in cash)	$50,000
Shareholders' equity	
Share capital—50,000 shares	$50,000

For simplicity, in this and succeeding balance sheets which are being used to illustrate points relating to shareholders' equity, we have simply added together current and non-current assets and deducted external liabilities, giving net assets. This figure must equal shareholders' equity.

The company now buys the necessary non-current assets and inventory and starts to trade. During the first year the company makes a profit of $10,000. This, by definition, means that both the net assets and the owners' claim expand by $10,000. During the year the shareholders (owners) make no drawings of their capital (such drawings are known as dividends when applied to companies), so at the end of the year the summarised balance sheet looks like this:

Balance sheet as at 31 March 2006

Net assets (various assets less liabilities)	$60,000
Shareholders' equity	
Share capital—50,000 shares	50,000
Reserves (retained profits)	10,000
	$60,000

The profit is shown in a 'reserve', known as retained profits. Note that we do not simply add the profit to the share capital. We must keep the two amounts separate (to satisfy the Corporations Act). The reason for this is that there is a legal restriction on the maximum drawings of capital (or 'dividends') that the owners can make. This is defined by the amount of distributable reserves, so it is helpful to show these separately. We shall look at why there is this restriction, and how it works, later in the chapter.

SHARE CAPITAL

Shares represent the basic units of ownership of the business. All companies issue **ordinary shares**. Ordinary shares are the main risk-bearing shares issued by companies. All other claims on the business have a higher priority in terms of repayment. The returns obtained by ordinary shareholders will be through distributions of profit (known as **dividends**) or in the form of increases in the value of the shares. Under normal circumstances retaining profits is likely to lead to such increases. Until recently each share had a value, known as par value, attached to it. The *Company Law Review Act 1998* eliminated this and shares are now deemed to have no par value.

Suppose a company wishes to raise $250,000 in cash and issues 250,000 ordinary shares at a price of $1 a share.

The resulting balance sheet will be:

Net assets	
Cash	$250,000
Shareholders' equity	
Paid-up share capital (250,000 ordinary	
shares issued at $1)	$250,000

EXAMPLE
2.2

A company can issue **partly paid shares**. Suppose that instead of issuing 250,000 shares at $1, the company decided to raise the $250,000 it needs by issuing 500,000 partly paid shares, but asks for (calls) only 50 cents per share now, with the remaining 50 cents per share to be called and collected at some future date.

The result will be:

Net assets
Cash $250,000
Shareholders' equity
Share capital (500,000 ordinary shares
 issued at $1—called to 50 cents) $250,000

The shareholders, in agreeing to buy shares issued at $1, have agreed to commit $1 when required. At this stage the company has only asked for half of this, so the further liability of the shareholders is restricted to 50 cents per share. Once this has been paid the shares become **fully paid shares** and the shareholders have no further liability to the company.

Where calls are unpaid this will be reflected on the balance sheet. If, for example, the call was unpaid on 5,000 shares, the balance sheet would appear as follows:

Net assets
Cash $247,500
Shareholders' equity
Share capital (500,000 ordinary shares issued
 at $1—called to 50 cents)   250,000
Less calls in arrears (5,000 shares at 50 cents)   2,500
                                                                        $247,500

ACTIVITY 2.14

Show the balance sheet of a company after each of the following transactions:
1. The issue of 100,000 shares at an issue price of $2, of which $1 is payable immediately.
2. A further call of 50 cents per share.

Some companies also issue other classes of shares, preference shares being the most common. **Preference shares** usually guarantee that if a dividend is paid, the preference shareholders will be entitled to the first part of it up to a maximum value. This maximum is normally defined as a fixed percentage of the preference shares. If, for example, a company issues 10,000 preference shares issued at $1 each with a dividend rate of 6 per cent, this means that the preference shareholders are entitled to receive the first $600 of any dividend which is paid by the company for a year. The profit in excess of the preference dividend is the entitlement of the ordinary shareholders, though this amount is not necessarily (or even normally) paid out as a cash dividend. Normally, any undistributed profits and gains accrue to the ordinary shareholders. Thus the ordinary shareholders are the primary risk takers. Their potential rewards reflect this risk. Power normally resides in the hands of the ordinary shareholders. Normally, only the ordinary shareholders are able to vote on issues that affect the company, such as who the directors should be. One ordinary share usually carries with it one vote.

It is open to the company to issue shares of various classes, perhaps with some having unusual and exotic conditions, but it is rare to find other than straightforward ordinary and preference shares. Though a company may have different classes of shares whose holders have different rights, within each class all shares must be treated equally. The rights of the various classes of shareholders, as well as other matters relating to a particular company, are contained in that company's constitution, or in the special resolution approving the issue.

A company can issue more share capital at a later date. Given that the value of the company (and therefore of the shares) is likely to increase over time as profits are retained, the asking price for the new shares is likely to be higher than the original asking price. Generally it would be expected that new shareholders would buy new shares at a price that would be very close to the current market value of the shares. The proceeds will be added to cash and capital.

ACTIVITY 2.15

A company issues 100,000 shares on formation at $1 per share. Five years later its balance sheet is as shown below:

Net assets	$170,000
Shareholders' equity	
Capital	100,000
Retained profits	70,000
	$170,000

The current market price of the shares is $2. A further 100,000 shares are issued at market price. Show the balance sheet assuming the issue is successful.

You need to be clear as to why it is important that any new issues are at a price close to market price. Given that the new shareholders have the same rights as the old, it is necessary for the new shareholders to 'buy in' their share of any increases in value since the initial share purchase. If this does not occur, then new shareholders will benefit at the expense of the old shareholders.

The balance sheet of a company is as follows:

Net assets	$1,500,000
Shareholders' equity	
Capital (1 million shares)	1,000,000
Retained profits	500,000
	$1,500,000

EXAMPLE

2.3

Assuming that the market value of the shares is the same as the book value, the share price would be $1.50. The company wishes to raise an additional $600,000 of cash for expansion and has decided to raise it by issuing new shares. If the shares are issued for $1.50 each, 400,000 shares will need to be issued. This will lead to the following balance sheet:

Net assets	$2,100,000
Shareholders' equity	
Capital (1.4 million shares)	1,600,000
Retained profits	500,000
	$2,100,000

This should lead to maintenance of the share price at $1.50.

If the new issue of 400,000 shares was at a price less than $1.50, say $1, the end result would be as follows:

Net assets	$1,900,000
Shareholders' equity	
Capital (1.4 million shares)	1,400,000
Retained profits	500,000
	$1,900,000

If we continue our assumption that book value and market value are the same, the market value per share will change to 1.9 million dollars/1.4 million shares = $1.36 per share. The old shareholders are disadvantaged whereas the new ones are better off.

In practice the situation is more complicated than this, with book value and market value almost never being the same, but the principles remain the same.

RESERVES

Reserves are profits and gains that have been made by the company and that still form part of the shareholders' (owners') claim. Profits and gains tend to lead to cash flowing into the company. It might be worth mentioning here that retained profits represent the largest source of new finance for Australian companies, more than share issues and borrowings combined for most companies. These ploughed-back profits create most of the typical company's reserves. Retained profits can be held in an account with the same name, 'retained profits' or in an account labelled 'general reserve'.

ACTIVITY 2.16

Are reserves amounts of cash?

Can you think of a reason why this is an odd question?

Not all reserves result from profits earned and therefore reserves may not be distributable as a cash dividend. An example might be one in which a company revalues (upwards) non-current assets. For example, a company might have property which was bought several years ago for $250,000 revalued to reflect its current value of, say, $400,000. The property would be increased by $150,000 and a revaluation reserve will be increased by the same amount. It is probably important to note that such capital gains can be distributed if they are the result of a bona fide revaluation of all assets, but such distributions are relatively rare.

BONUS SHARES

It is always open to the company to take reserves of any kind and turn them into share capital. The new shares are known as **bonus shares** as they involve no cost to the shareholders. Issues of bonus shares are quite frequently encountered in practice.

EXAMPLE 2.4

The summary balance sheet of a company is as follows:

Balance sheet as at 31 March 2006	
Net assets (various assets less liabilities)	$128,000
Shareholders' equity	
Share capital 50,000 shares issued at $1 each	50,000
Reserves	78,000
	$128,000

The company decides that it will issue, to existing shareholders, one new $1 share for every share owned by each shareholder. The balance sheet immediately following this will appear as follows:

Balance sheet as at 31 March 2006	
Net assets (various assets less liabilities)	$128,000
Shareholders' equity	
Share capital 100,000 shares issued at $1 each	100,000
Reserves (78,000 – 50,000)	28,000
	$128,000

ACTIVITY 2.17

A shareholder of the company in Example 2.4 owned 100 shares in the company before the bonus issue. How will things change for this shareholder, as a result of the bonus issue, in regard to the number of shares owned and to the value of the shareholding?

In practice, events are not likely to take place with quite the precision implied above. One of the arguments used to support a bonus issue is that a reduction in share price might lead to higher levels of activity in the market for shares, with the result that the price might not fall as much as logic would expect, with the end result being an increase in the market value of the company. Using the above example, such a result might leave the shares trading at a value slightly higher than 50 per cent of the pre-bonus share price. Such a reaction may be short term if the fundamental value of the business, based on future earnings, has not changed. However, the fact that a firm undertakes a bonus issue may indicate that management has reason to believe that future earnings will improve, and if the market supports this position then the bonus issue may be associated with increased overall share value.

However, if the share value increases overall after the bonus issue, it is not possible to determine whether the share value may have increased anyhow, had the bonus not taken place.

A bonus issue simply takes one part of the owners' claim (part of a reserve) and puts it into another part of the owners' claim (share capital).

ACTIVITY 2.18

Can you think of any reasons why a company might want to make a bonus issue if it has no economic consequence?

RIGHTS ISSUES

It is quite common for companies that have been established for some time to seek to raise additional share capital for expansion, or even to solve a liquidity problem (cash shortage), by issuing additional shares for cash. In general, companies usually give existing shareholders the first right of refusal on these new shares. So they would be offered to existing shareholders, in proportion to their existing holding. Thus existing shareholders are each given the 'right' to buy some new shares. Where the existing shareholders agree to waive their right the shares would be offered to others.

The company (i.e. the existing shareholders) would typically prefer that the shares are bought by existing shareholders in any case. This is because:

* the ownership (and therefore control) of the company remains in the same hands
* the costs of making the issue (advertising, complying with various Corporations Act requirements) tend to be less if the shares are to be offered to existing shareholders.

To encourage existing shareholders to take up their 'rights' to buy some new shares, those shares are virtually always offered at a price below the current market price of the existing ones. Rights to buy shares can be sold, so shareholders who do not wish to take up their rights can sell them and benefit accordingly. You should note, however, that in the case of proprietary companies the directors may have the discretion to refuse to register transfers.

ACTIVITY 2.19

In Example 2.3 the point was illustrated that issuing new shares at below their current worth was to the advantage of the new shareholders at the expense of the old ones.

In view of this, does it matter that rights issues are almost always made at below the current value of the shares?

You should be clear that a **rights issue** is a totally different thing from a bonus issue. Rights issues result in an asset (cash) being transferred from shareholders to the company. Bonus issues involve no transfer of assets in either direction.

TRANSFERRING SHARE OWNERSHIP—THE ROLE OF THE STOCK EXCHANGE

The point has already been made that shares in companies may be transferred from one owner to another without this change of share ownership having any direct impact on the company's business, or on the shareholders not involved with the particular transfer. With major companies, the desire of some existing shareholders to sell their shares, coupled with the desire of others to buy those shares, has led to the existence of a formal market, or **stock exchange**, in which the shares can be bought and sold. The Australian Stock Exchange, and similar organisations around the world, are simply market places in which shares in major companies are bought and sold. Prices are determined by the law of supply and demand. Supply and demand are themselves determined by investors' perceptions of the future economic prospects of the companies concerned.

ACTIVITY 2.20

If, as has been pointed out above, the change in ownership of the shares of a particular company does not directly affect that company, why would a particular company welcome the fact that the shares are traded in a recognised market?

RESTRICTIONS ON THE RIGHTS OF SHAREHOLDERS TO MAKE DRAWINGS OR REDUCTIONS OF CAPITAL

Limited companies are required by law to distinguish between that part of their capital (shareholders' claim) which may be withdrawn by the shareholders and that part which may not be.

The distributable (withdrawable) part, that which has arisen from trading profits and from realised profits on the disposal of fixed assets (both on an after-tax basis), is called **retained profit**. As mentioned earlier, unrealised capital profits as a result of a bona fide revaluation of all assets are also distributable.

The non-distributable part (which cannot be withdrawn) normally consists of that which arose from funds injected by shareholders buying shares in the company. In fact, many companies treat unrealised capital gains as a result of a revaluation as effectively a non-distributable revaluation reserve.

ACTIVITY 2.21

Can you think why limited companies are required to distinguish different parts of their equity, whereas sole trading businesses are not?

The law does not specify how large the non-distributable part of a particular company's capital should be, simply that anyone dealing with the company should be able to tell from looking at the company's balance sheet how large it is. In the light of this, a particular prospective lender, or supplier of goods or services on credit, can make a commercial judgment as to whether or not to deal with the company.

The law is quite specific that it is illegal, under normal circumstances, for shareholders to withdraw that part of their claim which is represented by capital. This means that potential creditors of the company know the maximum amount of the shareholders' claim that can be drawn or withdrawn by the shareholders.

EXAMPLE

2.5

The summary balance sheet of a company is as follows:

Balance sheet as at 30 June 2006	
Net assets	
Current and non-current assets less	
short-term liabilities	$43,000
Shareholders' equity	
Share capital 20,000 shares issued at $1 each	20,000
Retained profits	23,000
	$43,000

A bank has been asked to make a $25,000 long-term loan to the company. If the loan were to be made, immediately following, the balance sheet would appear as follows:

Balance sheet as at 30 June 2006	
Net assets	
Current and non-current assets less	
short-term liabilities (43,000 + 25,000)	68,000
Less non-current (long-term) liabilities	25,000
	$43,000
Shareholders' equity	
Share capital 20,000 shares issued at $1 each	20,000
Retained profits	23,000
	$43,000

As things stand, there are net assets to a total balance sheet value of $68,000 to meet the bank's claim of $25,000. It would be possible, however, for the company to pay a dividend of $23,000, perfectly legally. If this happened then the balance sheet would appear as follows:

Net assets	
Current and non-current assets less	
short-term liabilities (68,000 – 23,000)	45,000
Less Non-current liabilities	25,000
	$20,000
Shareholders' equity	
Share capital 20,000 shares issued at $1 each	20,000
Retained profits (23,000 – 23,000)	–
	$20,000

This leaves the bank in a very much weaker position in that there are now net assets which are shown as having a value of $45,000 to meet a claim of $25,000. Note that the difference between the amount of the bank loan and the net assets always equals the capital and reserves total. The capital represents a 'margin of safety' for creditors. The larger the amount of the owners' claim which is withdrawable by the shareholders, the smaller is the potential margin of safety for creditors.

It is important to remember that company law says nothing about how large this margin of safety must be. What is desirable is left as a matter of commercial judgment of the company concerned. The larger it is, the easier the company will find it to persuade potential lenders to lend and suppliers to supply goods and services on credit.

ACTIVITY 2.22

Would you expect a company to pay out all of its retained profits as a dividend?

What factors might be involved with a dividend decision?

Sometimes a potential creditor may insist that some of the retained profits are converted to bonus shares (or 'capitalised') to increase the margin of safety, as a condition of granting the loan.

Most potential long-term lenders would seek to have their loan secured against a particular asset of the company, particularly an asset such as freehold property. This would give them the right to seize the specific asset concerned, sell it and satisfy their claim should the company default. Lenders often place restrictions or covenants on the borrowing company's freedom of action as a condition of granting the loan. These covenants typically restrict the level of risk to which the company, and the lender's asset, is exposed.

It is possible for certain preference shares (called redeemable preference shares) to be redeemed (repurchased by the company). Where any such preference shares redeemed are replaced by new shares there is no real problem, as the creditor's position relative to shareholders is unchanged. However, where preference shares are redeemed without any new capital issue there would appear to be a direct contradiction of what has been said so far in this section, as the shareholders' equity would be reduced. It is therefore necessary for an amount equivalent to the amount of preference capital redeemed to be transferred from retained profits directly to capital, thus maintaining the total capital of the business. Without this proviso, it would be possible for unscrupulous directors to redeem capital and pay out retained profits, with the result that creditors and lenders would be disadvantaged.

A company is not allowed to acquire shares in itself. It can, however, buy back shares and cancel them, as long as the buyback does not materially prejudice the creditors.

Figure 2.1 shows the important division between that part of the shareholders' claim that can be withdrawn and that part which cannot.

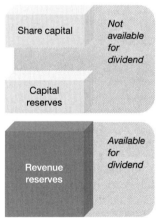

Total equity finance of limited companies consists of share capital, capital reserves and revenue reserves. Only the revenue reserves (which arise from realised profits and gains) can be used to fund a dividend. In other words, the maximum legal dividend is the amount of the revenue reserves.

FIGURE 2.1 Availability for dividends of various parts of the shareholders' claim

SELF-ASSESSMENT QUESTION 2.1

The summarised balance sheet of Bonanza Ltd is as follows:

Balance sheet as at 31 December 2005	
Net assets (various assets less liabilities)	$235,000
Shareholders' equity	
Share capital—100,000 shares issued at	
$1.30 each	130,000
Revaluation reserve	37,000
Retained profits	68,000
	$235,000

1. Without any other transactions occurring at the same time, the company made a one-for-five rights share issue at $2 per share payable in cash (all shareholders took up their rights) and, immediately after, made a one-for-four bonus issue, at an issue price of $2.

    Show the balance sheet immediately following the bonus issue, assuming that the directors wanted to retain the maximum dividend payment potential for the future.

2. Explain what external influence might cause the directors to choose not to retain the maximum dividend payment possibilities.

3. Show the balance sheet immediately following the bonus issue, assuming that the directors wanted to retain the minimum dividend payment potential for the future.

    (For purposes of Questions 3 and 4 assume that the revaluation reserve is not considered by the company to be distributable as a cash dividend.)

4. What is the maximum dividend that could be paid before and after the events described in Question 1 above if the minimum dividend payment potential is achieved?

5. Lee owns 100 shares in Bonanza Ltd before the events described in Question 1 above. Assuming that the net assets of the company have a value equal to that shown in the accounts, show how these events will affect Lee's wealth.

THE DIRECTORS' DUTY TO ACCOUNT—THE ROLE OF COMPANY LAW (CORPORATIONS ACT)

As we have already seen, it is not usually possible for all of the shareholders to be involved in the general management of the company, nor do most of them wish to be involved, so they elect directors to act on their behalf. It is both logical and required by company law that directors are accountable for their actions in respect of their stewardship of the company's assets.

In this context directors of all disclosing entities, all public companies and all large proprietary companies are required by law to prepare true and fair financial statements. Disclosing entities include companies listed on the stock exchange and companies raising funds through a prospectus (i.e. public) issue. Small proprietary companies are required to do the same if directed to by at least 5 per cent of their shareholders or by the Australian Securities and Investments Commission (ASIC). They are not required to prepare formal financial statements or to have them audited. They must, however, maintain sufficient accounting records to be able to allow annual accounts to be prepared and audited.

The financial statements are to include the balance sheet, income statement and the cash flow statement and related notes.

'True and fair' has not been specifically defined, nor tested in court. However, it is normally considered in terms of the provision of all necessary financial information of a material nature related to the directors' stewardship (discharge of accountability) and financial information (general purpose users' decisions related to the allocation of scarce resources) roles.

The Australian accounting standard on 'Materiality' (AASB 1031) explains 'material' as:

Information is material if its omission, misstatement or non-disclosure has the potential, individually or collectively, to:

(a) influence the economic decisions of the users taken on the basis of the financial report; or

(b) affect the discharge of accountability by the management or governing body of the entity.

The Corporations Act also requires directors of disclosing entities to provide with the financial statements both a 'directors' declaration' and a 'directors' report'.

In the 'directors' declaration' the directors must state whether, in their opinion, the financial statements comply with the applicable accounting standards and represent a 'true and fair' view of both the financial performance and financial position of the company. They must also state that at the date of the declaration they believe that there are reasonable grounds to believe that the company can meet its debts as and when they fall due.

The 'directors' report' is generally much longer and contains certain required information together with an increasing level of voluntary disclosures. Included in the required disclosures are the names of directors, the emoluments of directors, the principal activities of the company, a review of the operations for the year, details of significant changes in the state of affairs of the company, the financial significance of probable future events, details of significant events that have occurred after the balance date that affect the company, and details of compliance with environmental regulations. Obviously, the voluntary disclosures extend beyond the required disclosures, and may include financial forecasts, details of human resources management strategies, significant contributions to community life, and additional environmental initiatives. When one company owns a controlling interest in another so that management of the controlled company is effectively carried out by the controlling company, 'consolidated accounts' (group accounts) are prepared in addition to the individual company accounts. The consolidated accounts represent the accounts as if both controlling and controlled companies were a single company. More commonly the controlling company is referred to as the holding company (parent company), and the controlled company as the subsidiary. Holding company–subsidiary company relationships can become quite complex as effective control can be obtained by owning less than 100 per cent of the shares of a company.

The financial reports must comply with **accounting standards**. Companies' financial reports need to be checked by an **auditor** and reported on (unless the company is a small proprietary company—and even then shareholders or ASIC may require an audit). The auditor's report provides a check on the credibility and reliability of the financial reports, and an indication as to whether or not the report complies with the Corporations Act. The auditor's report tends to be fairly short and normally includes:

✳ the identification of the financial reports covered by the audit report, together with responsibilities

✳ a statement that the audit (the check) was carried out in accordance with Australian Auditing Standards

✳ a statement that the financial statements comply with Australian Accounting Standards

✳ an opinion section, in which the auditor gives an opinion as to whether or not the financial reports present fairly the financial performance, financial position and cash flows of the company. If the auditor does not think that this is the case the report will be 'qualified' with a section explaining why, and the extent to which, the statements do not comply with the statements and tests reviewed above.

You should note that an audit report gives an opinion but no guarantees. In general, however, given the number of legal cases which have been made against auditors, it is true to say that given the care and attention to detail that is associated with audit work, an unqualified audit report provides reassurance for the investing public. Even qualified reports rarely pose problems when the rationale for the qualification is understood.

Overall, the requirements on the directors of limited companies to report on the activities are quite extensive. Originally, the prime motivation was the provision of a 'stewardship' report, in which the directors reported to the shareholders on their stewardship of the resources entrusted to them. Over the last 30 years the stewardship report has developed into a general purpose report of use to a variety of users and potential users such as shareholders, potential shareholders, lenders, creditors, employees, social activists and environmentalists.

It must be emphasised that there is no difference in principle between the accounts of a company and those of a sole proprietor. Company accounts look a bit different in detail, especially in the area of ownership claims, because the relationships are rather more complex than those of a sole proprietor. You should note that the use of the term 'profit and loss account' is still commonly found in the accounts of sole proprietors.

THE ROLE OF ACCOUNTING STANDARDS IN COMPANY ACCOUNTING

In considering the role of accounting standards in company accounting, it is important to briefly review accounting standard setting in Australia.

For much of the 20th century accounting practice and financial reporting in Australia was guided by a body of loosely connnected ideas labelled 'generally accepted accounting principles' (GAAP). Some of these ideas are discussed in more detail in Chapter 3. Included among these ideas (variously labelled as principles, doctrines or conventions) were:

Principle	Brief explanation
Entity	The reporting entity (e.g. company) is separate from the owners.
Monetary basis	The common denominator for recording transactions and events is money.
Historical cost	Transactions are to be initially recorded on the basis of an external transaction price or its equivalent.
Stable monetary unit	The assumption that the value of the monetary measuring unit does not change over time.
Accounting period	The life of the business is divided up into unique periods of time (usually one year) for reporting purposes.
Objectivity	The recognition of transactions is to be based on reliable and verifiable measures.
Prudence (conservatism)	The tendency to caution or pessimism rather than optimism. This will be reflected in lower profits and asset amounts and higher liabilities amounts.
Going concern (continuity)	The assumption that a business will continue to operate in the future as it has in the past.

Consistency	Applying comparable methods from one period to the next.
Realisation	That stringent conditions should be met before revenue could be recognised (the entity must have completed its contractual commitments and must have an unavoidable claim against the customer).
Matching	That expenses should be aligned with the revenue to which they relate, and in the same period in which the revenue is recognised.

Up until the 1970s a limited number of specific and formal accounting directives related to external financial reporting were imposed on management by the accounting profession and corporate regulators. However, around this time there were significant numbers of corporate crashes and the accuracy and reliability of accounting reports came under question. How was it that seemingly profitable organisations with substantial assets on their balance sheet had apparently overnight become worthless?

ACTIVITY 2.23

Can you think of any reasons why the application of the above GAAP could lead to financial reports that do not fairly represent the financial performance or financial position of the company?

When voters lose money, pressure is brought on governments to act. In a real sense pressure was placed on the accounting profession in Australia to codify accounting rules and restrict the variety of unacceptable accounting practices. So from the 1970s through to the early 1980s the two major Australian accounting bodies (the Institute of Chartered Accountants and the Australian Society of Accountants [now CPA Australia]) through their joint research body (the Australian Accounting Research Foundation) produced a significant number of accounting standards. However, professional regulation in accounting in Australia had failed by the early 1980s.

ACTIVITY 2.24

Why do you think professional regulation of accounting failed?

In the mid-1980s a statutory body was set up to issue accounting standards that would be mandatory for all companies and certain other disclosing entities. This body was initially known as the 'Accounting Standards Review Board' but later, its name was changed to the 'Australian Accounting Standards Board'(AASB). For a time there were two sets of accounting standards being issued from two separate boards, and they applied either to companies (AASB standards) or to other entities (AAS standards).

Another criticism of the professional regulation period in Australia was the fact that inconsistent standards and rules were being produced because of the lack of a logical theoretical structure on which to base accounting practice. As a result, during the late 1980s and 1990s the two standard-setting bodies in Australia (the Public Sector Accounting Standards Board of the AARF and the AASB) were working towards the development of a conceptual framework for accounting, a conceptual framework being a logical theoretical structure to aid in the development of consistent accounting practices. We will return to discussion of the conceptual framework later.

ACTIVITY 2.25

How would having a 'conceptual framework' for financial accounting assist the stakeholders (regulators, practitioners, report users)?

During the first few years of the 21st century there have been further changes within the Australian accounting standard-setting environment. Only the AASB now sets standards, and we are working towards just the one set of standards (AASBs). Following concern over differences between Australian Accounting Standards and the accounting standards in other trading partner countries, Australia actively moved towards harmonising (making similar but not the same) Australian Accounting Standards with the International Accounting Standards.

ACTIVITY 2.26

What would be possible benefits of harmonising Australian Accounting Standards with the International Accounting Standards?

In a further development in 2002, it was announced by the Financial Reporting Council (FRC), which is the supervisory body that oversees the AASB, that by 2005 Australia would 'adopt' the International Accounting Standards. Therefore, in the space of a decade we have moved from national accounting standards that highlighted differences between them and the international equivalent standard (reconciled), to accounting standards compatible with international standards (adapted), to accounting standards that are the same as the international standards (adopted).

ACTIVITY 2.27

Can you think of disadvantages of Australia adopting the International Accounting Standards?

Accounting standards narrow the choice available to management in recording and reporting given transactions and therefore lead to greater consistency and comparability in application and assessment. Companies are required by law to comply with the accounting standards. If management is of the view that complying with a particular accounting standard will not lead to a true and fair view of the financial position or financial performance, they still must adhere to the standard. They can then, if they so choose, provide additional information in the notes related to their concerns in applying that standard.

ACTIVITY 2.28

When the law in Australia for the first time made compliance with accounting standards mandatory, there was a 'true and fair' override clause. That was, where the directors were of the view that adherence to the standard would not lead to a true and fair view, then they did not have to adhere to the standard. Do you think this was a better rule as there have been calls in Australia for its re-introduction?

THE ROLE OF THE AUSTRALIAN STOCK EXCHANGE IN COMPANY ACCOUNTING

The Australian Stock Exchange extends the accounting rules for those companies that are listed as being eligible to have their shares traded on the exchange. These extensions include summarised interim (half-year) accounts in addition to the statutorily required annual accounts, together with a number of specific requirements including things such as takeovers, capital, options and sundry administrative matters.

Figure 2.2 illustrates the sources of accounting rules with which listed Australian companies must comply.

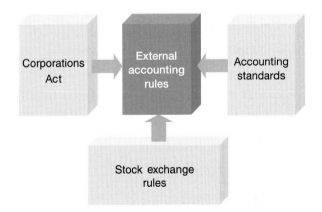

The Corporations Act provides the basic framework of company accounting regulation. This is augmented by accounting standards, which have virtually the force of law. The ASX imposes additional rules for companies listed on the Australian Stock Exchange.

FIGURE 2.2 Sources of accounting regulations for an Australian company listed on the Australian Stock Exchange

AUDITORS

Shareholders are required to appoint a qualified and independent person or, more usually, a firm to act as auditor (though there is an exception for small proprietary companies). The main duty of auditors is to make a report as to whether, in their opinion, the statements do what they are supposed to do—namely, fairly reflect the financial performance, financial position and liquidity of the reporting entity and that they comply with statutory and accounting standards requirements. In order to be able to make such a statement, the auditors must scrutinise the annual accounting statements prepared by the directors and the evidence on which they are based. The auditors' opinion must be included with the accounting statements which are sent to the shareholders and to ASIC.

The relationship between the shareholders, the directors and the auditors is illustrated in Figure 2.3. The figure shows that the shareholders appoint the directors to act on their behalf in the day-to-day running of the company. The directors are required to 'account' to the shareholders on the performance, position and cash flows of the company on an annual basis (and on a half-yearly basis for disclosing entities). The shareholders also appoint auditors whose role is to give the shareholders an impression of the extent to which they can regard the accounting statements prepared by the directors as reliable.

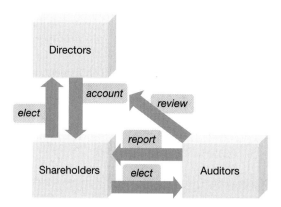

The directors are appointed by the shareholders to manage the company on the shareholders' behalf. The directors are required to report each year to the shareholders, principally by means of financial statements, on the company's performance and position. To lend greater credibility to the financial statements, the shareholders also appoint auditors to investigate the statements and to express an opinion on their reliability.

FIGURE 2.3 The relationship between the shareholders, the directors and the auditors

SUMMARY

In this chapter we have achieved the following objectives in the way shown.

OBJECTIVE	METHOD ACHIEVED		
List the three most common entity structures used for business operations in Australia	Identified as follows: • Sole proprietorship • Partnership • Company		
Discuss the main characteristics of the three entity structures	Identified as:		
		Sole proprietorship	*Partnership*	*Company*

	Sole proprietorship	*Partnership*	*Company*
• Entity	Accounting	Accounting	Legal
• Life	Limited	Limited	Perpetual
• Liability of owner(s)	Unlimited	Unlimited	Limited
• Access to capital	One owner	Normally limited to 20 owners	50 owners—private; unlimited owners—public
• Asset ownership	Proprietor	Partners co-ownership	Company ownership
• Set-up costs	Minimal	Moderate	Significant
• Regulation (financial reporting)	Minimal	Moderate	Maximum
• Separation of ownership and management	No	Not normally	Normally
• Transfer of ownership	Business sold	Partner retires or new partner introduced	Simple market sale for listed companies

Discuss the advantages and disadvantages of sole proprietorships

Identified as follows:

Advantages
• Simple to establish
• Minimum regulatory costs
• Flexible decision making
• All profits to the owner

Disadvantages
• Limited life
• Limited access to ownership funds
• Unlimited ownership liability

Discuss the advantages and disadvantages of partnerships compared to companies

Identified as follows:

Advantages
• Lower set-up costs
• Limited financial regulations

Disadvantages
• Limited life
• Unlimited liability
• Limited access to ownership funds
• Mutual agency

OBJECTIVE	METHOD ACHIEVED
Discuss the advantages and disadvantages of companies compared to other entity structures	Identified as follows: *Advantages* • Perpetual life • Specialist management • Greatest access to ownership funds • Unlimited liability • Possible taxation advantages • Ease of ownership transfer *Disadvantages* • Significant set-up costs • Less flexible decision making • Stringent financial regulation • Loss of control by owners
Assess the alternative bases for profit/loss distribution among partners	Identified the contributions of each partner in terms of capital contributed, physical effort and entrepreneurship

Distinguish between private and public companies — Distinguishing features identified as follows:

	Private	Public
Can they offer shares to the general public?	No	Yes
The number of shareholders	50 maximum	No maximum
Can the shares be listed?	No	Yes
The criteria for a proprietary company to be classified as small and thereby avoid significant corporate regulation?	It must satisfy at least two of the following requirements: • gross revenue less than $10m • gross year-end assets less than $5m • less than 50 employees at year-end	

OBJECTIVE	METHOD ACHIEVED
Discuss the role and responsibilities of company directors	Identified as follows: • The board of directors • Directors' report • Directors' declaration • Audit report
Compare and contrast ordinary and preference shares	Main differences discussed as follows: • A preference share has some specified preference or priority over ordinary shares (e.g. specified dividend) • An ordinary share has no preference or priority but has voting rights and residual ownership of profits and assets
Identify and discuss the role of the alternative regulatory bodies in relation to company operations and financial reporting	Main bodies identified as follows: • The Australian Stock Exchange (ASX) • The Australian Securities and Investments Commission (ASIC) • The Australian Accounting Standards Board (AASB) • Auditors

DISCUSSION QUESTIONS

EASY

<Obj 2> **2.1** Distinguish between 'accounting entities' and 'legal entities' in relation to business structures.

<Obj 2> **2.2** Explain 'mutual agency' in relation to partnerships.

<Obj 2> **2.3** Is a partnership taxed?

<Obj 2> **2.4** When does a partnership cease?

<Obj 2> **2.5** How can a company be said to have a 'perpetual life'?

<Obj 3> **2.6** What are the potential advantages of the partnership structure over the sole proprietorship structure?

<Obj 4> **2.7** How should partnership profit or losses be divided between the partners?

<Obj 5> **2.8** How do you determine whether a company can be classified as 'small' under the Australian Corporations Act?

<Obj 7> **2.9** In what sense do preference shares have an 'advantage' or 'priority' over ordinary shares?

<Obj 7> **2.10** A share is described as being a 'non-redeemable, participating, cumulative, non-voting, 8% preference share'. You are required to explain each of the descriptive terms:
   (a) 'non-redeemable'
   (b) 'participating'
   (c) 'cumulative'
   (d) 'non-voting'
   (e) '8%'.

INTERMEDIATE

<Obj 1> **2.11** In relation to business entity structures:
   (a) What are the most common forms in Australia?
   (b) Indicate the major reasons for the use of each form?

<Obj 2> **2.12** Why is a limit placed on the maximum number of partners that can be included in the one business entity?

<Obj 2> **2.13** Why is it important for partners to have a formal partnership agreement?

<Obj 3> **2.14** In relation to companies, in what sense is 'limited liability' an *advantage* at the same time as it is a *disadvantage*?

<Obj 3> **2.15** How can a supplier to a company minimise the risk related to the limited liability of shareholders?

<Obj 3> **2.16** A sole proprietorship converts to a limited liability company.
   (a) What are the potential advantages of the change from the viewpoint of the owner?
   (b) What are the potential disadvantages from the viewpoint of suppliers of goods and services to that company?

<Obj 3> **2.17** Why would a business choose to undertake the following entity structure changes:
   (a) from a sole proprietorship to a partnership
   (b) from a partnership to a private company
   (c) from a public company to a private company?

<Obj 4> **2.18** Why is it important to have a partnership agreement specifying the arrangement for allocating (dividing) profits between the partners?

<Obj 8> **2.19** Why is the Corporations Act particularly interested in distinguishing between 'a return *on* capital' and 'a return *of* capital'?

<Obj 8> **2.20** In terms of financial reporting how does the focus of the Australian Stock Exchange differ from the Australian Accounting Standards Board?

<Obj 8> **2.21** What are the duties of company directors in relation to the financial records of companies?

CHALLENGING

<Obj 5> **2.22** In this chapter we focused on limited liability companies. There are two other categories classified as 'no liability' and 'unlimited liability'.
(a) What do you think these terms represent?
(b) Why do you think certain businesses may wish to have such a classification?

<Obj 6> **2.23** In the 'directors' declaration', the directors must state that in their opinion:
- the financial statements are 'true and fair'
- the financial statements comply with the accounting standards
- the company will be able to pay its debts when they fall due.
(a) What does 'true and fair' mean?
(b) Which financial statements does the declaration refer to?
(c) Which accounting standards does the declaration refer to?
(d) Does compliance with accounting standards lead to financial statements that present a 'true and fair' view of the reporting entity?

<Obj 8> **2.24** Over the past five years Australia has moved through the following stages:
- producing its own standards with reference to differences between the national standards and the international equivalent accounting standard
- changing our standards to be compatible with the equivalent international accounting standard. The process was labelled 'harmonisation' and involved adapting international accounting standards for use in Australia.
- changing our standards to be consistent with the equivalent international accounting standards. The process was labelled 'convergence' and involved adopting the international accounting standards for use in Australia.
(a) Why would Australia give up its standards in favour of international accounting standards?
(b) What are the potential limitations of Australia giving up setting its own individual accounting standards?

Qantas Financial Report 2004, pp. 59–60

Notes to the Financial Statements continued
for the year ended 30 June 2004

CASE STUDY
2.1
→

39. International Financial Reporting Standards

For the reporting period beginning on or after 1 January 2005, the Qantas Group must comply with International Financial Reporting Standards (IFRS) as issued by the Australian Accounting Standards Board (AASB).

The areas of significant difference between Australian Generally Accepted Accounting Principles (GAAP) and IFRS, as applied to the Qantas Group, have been identified and work has commenced to quantify the impact of adoption. To date, quantification has not been completed or presented to the Board for approval.

MANAGING THE TRANSITION TO IFRS

The Board has established a Project Group, reporting through to the Chief Financial Officer, to achieve the transition to IFRS reporting.

The Qantas implementation project consists of three phases.

Assessment Phase

The IFRS Project Group has completed the Assessment Phase. In completing the Assessment Phase, a high level overview of the impacts of IFRS reporting on existing accounting and reporting policies, procedures, systems, processes, business structures and staff has been undertaken.

Design Phase

The Design Phase is well progressed. This phase aims to formulate the changes required to existing accounting policies, procedures, systems and processes in order to transition to IFRS.

The Design Phase will incorporate:
- formulating revised accounting policies and procedures for compliance with IFRS and quantifying their impact;
- developing revised IFRS disclosures; and
- designing accounting and business processes to support IFRS reporting obligations.

At the conclusion of the Design Phase, Board approval will be sought for each proposed change in accounting policy and disclosure. The Design Phase will be completed during the 2004/05 financial year.

Implementation Phase

The Implementation Phase will include the implementation of identified changes to accounting and business procedures, processes, systems and training. It is expected that the Implementation Phase will be completed during the 2004/05 financial year.

KEY DIFFERENCES BETWEEN AUSTRALIAN GAAP AND IFRS

The potential implications of the conversion to IFRS on the Qantas Group are outlined below. The summary should not be taken as an exhaustive list of all the differences between Australian GAAP and IFRS. The impact on future years will depend on the particular circumstances prevailing in those years. Accordingly, there can be no assurances that the consolidated Statements of Financial Performance and financial position would not be significantly different if determined in accordance with IFRS.

Frequent Flyer

Qantas is considering the application of AASB 118 'Revenue' to the accounting for the frequent flyer program. Australian GAAP and IFRS do not specifically address accounting for frequent flyer/loyalty schemes. Under both GAAPs there are two acceptable accounting treatments including the Deferral and Incremental Cost approaches.

The Deferral approach results in the deferral of frequent flyer revenue until earned points are redeemed. The Incremental Cost approach recognises revenue when points are allocated to individuals participating in the scheme, with the recognition of a corresponding provision for the incremental cost of providing the service at a later date.

Both approaches are used by airlines globally and the most appropriate accounting policy is dependent upon factors such as the size of the program, the mechanism for managing redemptions and the potential for frequent flyers to displace fare-paying passengers. Under Australian GAAP, Qantas has adopted the Incremental Cost approach, as historically it has best reflected the commercial operation of the program.

AASB 1 'First Time Adoption of Australian Equivalents to International Financial Reporting Standards', requires that all accounting policies be reconsidered having regard to both their current and future suitability.

As part of the Qantas IFRS transition project, the Company is considering changing to the Deferral approach. Future growth in the scheme and a desire to make redemptions easier, may require changes to the current marginal management of the scheme. Should a decision to change to the Deferral method be approved, revenue previously recognised would be deferred and retained earnings reduced. In future periods, deferred revenue would be released to the Statement of Financial Performance as points are redeemed. This treatment would no longer necessitate the raising of a provision for future incremental costs.

The quantification of the financial impact of the possible change in treatment is complex and requires the calculation of the fair value of unredeemed frequent flyer points, breakage rates and a detailed analysis of revenues previously brought to account. To date, the financial effect of the change being considered has not been determined. It is anticipated that should it be adopted, a reduction in retained earnings will be made. The impact on future profits is largely dependent on the extent to which the program grows and as such cannot be quantified at this time.

Defined Benefit Superannuation Plans

Qantas is considering the application of AAS8 119 'Employee Benefits' to the recognition of the funding surplus or deficit of the Qantas sponsored defined benefit superannuation plans. Under the requirements of IFRS, any surpluses and deficits in the defined benefit superannuation plans within the consolidated entity will be recognised in the Statement of Financial Position and movements in the surplus or deficit recognised in the Statement of Financial Performance.

Actuarial valuations of the Plans will be conducted as at 30 June 2004. The expected impact is likely to be a one-off reduction in retained earnings and the corresponding recognition of a retirement liability.

Leases

Qantas is considering the application of AASB 117 'Leases' to the classification of lease transactions. Under IFRS some leases currently classified as operating may require recognition in the Statement of Financial Position. To date the financial effect of the change has not been determined, however, it is not expected to have a significant impact on the Statement of Financial Performance in future years.

Financial Instruments Recognition and Measurement

1. Fuel Hedging

Qantas is considering the application of AASB 139 'Financial Instruments: Recognition and Measurement' to aviation fuel hedging transactions. Extensive hedge effectiveness testing and documentation is required under IFRS in order to apply hedge accounting to these transactions. The potential application and impact of this accounting standard on aviation fuel hedging has not been determined.

2. Revenue Hedging

Qantas is considering the application of AASB 139 'Financial Instruments: Recognition and Measurement' to revenue hedging transactions. The potential application and impact of this accounting standard on revenue hedging has not been completed. It is anticipated that, after initial adoption adjustments are made, the existing accounting treatment will continue under IFRS, although it will be subject to increased effectiveness testing and documentation requirements.

Impairment of Assets

Qantas is considering the application of AASB 136 'Impairment of Assets' to the valuation of assets. Under IFRS, assets are tested for impairment on the basis of their ability to generate independent cash inflows from continuing use. If assets do not generate cash flows they may be aggregated into groups for the purposes of determining the smallest identifiable group of assets that generate cash inflows which are largely independent. Aircraft do not directly generate cash flows as passenger revenue is derived from the sale of seats on flights rather than seats on particular aircraft. The aggregation of aircraft cash flows is therefore performed on the basis of route groupings.

Impairment testing upon transition to IFRS is required. The financial effect of the change is not expected to result in significant impairment losses upon transition. The impact on future financial years is dependent on the cash flows generated by each grouping of assets and is therefore unable to be determined.

1   Why must the Qantas Group comply with International Financial Reporting Standards (IFRS) from 1 January 2005?

2   What is the process called whereby Australia is adopting international accounting standards from 2005?

3   What benefits are supposed to arise from the adoption of international accounting standards (IFRS) by the Australian accounting standard setters (AASB)?

4   In relation to accounting for frequent flyer/loyalty schemes:
     (a) Briefly explain what such schemes represent.
     (b) Distinguish between the two methods for accounting for such schemes by airlines.
     (c) Critically evaluate the grounds provided by Qantas for making the choice between the two methods, bearing in mind:
          • the size of the programme
          • the mechanism for managing redemptions
          • the potential for frequent flyers to displace fare-paying passengers.
     (d) Accounting for such schemes requires the calculation of the 'fair value of unredeemed frequent flyer points'. How would you approach such a calculation?

5   In relation to defined benefit superannuation plans:
     (a) What is a defined benefit superannuation scheme?
     (b) What is meant by a deficit in a defined benefit superannuation plan?

(c) Why would the application of the IFRS on 'employee benefits' be likely to lead to Qantas reducing retained profits and increasing a retirement liability?

(d) What factors would the actuary take into account in determining the adequacy of the retirement provision made by Qantas?

6 In relation to accounting for leases:

(a) What is the difference between a finance lease and an operating lease?

(b) Why would companies such as Qantas prefer to have leases classified as 'operating' rather than 'financial'?

(c) On what basis are leases to be classified as 'operating' or 'financial' (finance leases)?

7 In relation to the impairment of assets:

(a) The impairment of assets is a new concept introduced with the adoption of international accounting standards. What is an 'asset impairment'?

(b) How would you determine the amount of an individual asset's impairment for the period under review?

(c) How does the impairment of an asset differ from depreciation of that asset?

CASE STUDY 2.2

ERG holds hand out again

Neale Prior

Australian Financial Review
8 July 2004, p. 22

Smartcard and ticketing company ERG finalised last night the details of a $67 million rights issue that it hopes will mark the end of its recent status as a market mendicant.

Melbourne billionaire Dick Pratt is believed to have come to the company's aid by taking part in the issue.

ERG, which has lost more than $400 million over the past four years and raised about $600 million in equity over the past two decades, has reached agreement with underwriter Patersons Securities and sub-underwriters for a renounceable issue.

The company had hoped to have the terms of the issue finalised by Monday night but had to seek a full trading suspension while it continued to pitch its equity offering to potential institutional backers in Melbourne.

The 5-for-4 rights issue will be at 20¢—a third of the market price before ERG called a trading halt last Thursday and 99 per cent lower than the peaks when it was a sharemarket darling in 2000 and 2001.

A prospectus will be lodged on July 16 and trading of the rights will commence on July 21.

Sources said sub-underwriters for the issue include the funds management group Acorn and Thorney, an investment company ultimately owned by Pratt Group Holdings, Mr Pratt's private company.

Major ERG stakeholder Duncan Saville is taking a sizeable role by sub-underwriting $30 million of the issue.

Company supporters have sought to paint it as the final stage of a restructuring process embarked upon in 2002 that involved interests linked to Mr Saville taking an estimated 29 per cent stake in the company through a swap of convertible notes into equity.

ERG lost more than $400 million between the 2001 and 2003 financial years amid massive write-downs of the value of its transit ticketing and smartcard technologies, made worse by its 2001 buy-out of its partners in Belgian smartcard technology group Proton World and then a retreat from that business.

In the past, analysts queried whether ERG was charging enough to cover the significant cost of developing its technology.

Its woes continued in the first half of 2003–04, with a $43 million loss—including $36 million in write-downs.

ERG struck a $25 million financing deal with a Saville-linked company in February for extra working capital, which is likely to be repaid from the proceeds of the rights issue.

ERG will use $15.8 million of the proceeds to pay a settlement to its former Proton World partners Banksys, Visa and Interpay, who were given ERG scrip and cash in return for their stakes. The ERG scrip was subject to share price guarantees.

---

1   What is an 'underwriter'?
2   What is a 'renounceable rights issue'?
3   Why was a trading halt called while details of the rights issue was finalised?
4   What would have been the theoretical price for the shares after the rights issue was finalised (assume the shares were selling for 60c prior to the announcement of the rights issue)?
5   What price do you think each right would have traded at?
6   How did the swap of 'convertible notes' into 'equity' assist in the restructure of ERG back in 2002?
7   Which factors highlighted in the article impacted on the company's past losses?
8   In February 2004, a Saville-linked company provided $25 million in working capital to ERG. What is 'working capital'?
9   Why is $15.8 million still owed to the former Proton World partners who were previously given cash and scrip (shares) to fully meet their claims?

Creditors creamed in Parmalat restructure

A correspondent in Milan

The Australian
16 July 2004, p. 21

CASE STUDY

2.3

→

Parmalat plans to sweep aside most of its debt by paying creditors much less than expected as it struggles to survive after a massive accounting scandal.

The investments of Parmalat's creditors all but disappeared when the Italian milk and juices group unveiled a multi-billion-euro hole in its accounts in December.

They had hoped its new managers would pay back about 15 per cent of their money in a restructuring.

But Parmalat yesterday said it would convert €1.9 billion ($3.2 billion) of debt into shares in a new, slimmed-down company. Most creditors would recover less than 12 per cent of their money.

Parmalat's debts totalled €14.3 billion in 2003, including €9.5 billion in bonds and €4.2 billion in bank loans.

Its restructuring plan must be approved by Industry Ministry Antonio Marzano and creditors. A source close to the company said government approval was expected by July 21. The company said creditors to Parmalat Finance Corporation, which had issued millions of euros worth of bonds backed by the operating company Parmalat SpA, would be given shares worth 4.6 per cent of debt plus 7.3 per cent from Parmalat SpA.

Creditors to holding company Parmalat Finanziaria SpA were offered a recovery ratio of 11.3 per cent, while people owed money by smaller units would recover between zero and 100 per cent.

Creditors would also be given one warrant per share, up to a maximum of 500, giving them the right to buy more Parmalat shares at a nominal price between 2005 and 2015.

'The ratios are low,' DebtTraders analyst Ceki Medina said.

'In this scenario, creditors of Parmalat Finance Corp . . . will get around 12c return on the dollar, far below the 15 per cent of face value where they have been trading,' he said.

Reuters

1   What were the key aspects of the accounting scandal at Parmalat?
2   Basically, in an Australian context, what is the priority in repayments of obligations to creditors?
3   The predominant debt of Parmalat being 'bonds':
    (a)   What are bonds?
    (b)   What is another name for bonds?
    (c)   How do bonds differ from shares?
4   Debt is being satisfied by the issue of shares.
    (a)   What are the merits and limitations of this approach to the existing owners of the company?
    (b)   What are the merits and limitations of this approach to the existing debt holders?
5   Debt holders are also being given one warrant per share up to a maximum of 500.
    (a)   What is a 'warrant'?
    (b)   Why would those attempting to restructure Parmalat include this instrument in the settlement?
6   Distinguish between the probable function of the following companies within the Parmalat Group:
    • Parmalat Finanziaria Spa
    • Parmalat Finance Corporation
    • Parmalat SpA.

CASE STUDY
2.4

Village buyback moves fuel speculation about privatisation

Bryan Frith

The Australian
8 July 2004, p. 29

The board faces tough decisions on how it treats its preference shareholders during any on-market buyback.

The additional information required by the Takeovers Panel in relation to Village Roadshow's latest on-market share buyback arguably fuels the long-standing speculation that the ultimate aim of the founding Kirby family is to privatise the company.

Village has been offside with much of the investment community since it suspended ordinary dividends two years ago, followed last year by suspension of dividends on the company's A class preference shares.

Village's ability to pay ordinary dividends is hamstrung because prefs are entitled to a dividend of 10.175c a share, or 3c more than the ordinary dividend, whichever is the greater.

The Village board believes that adversely affects the price of the company's shares and last year proposed a $312.5 million buyback of all of the prefs, via a scheme of arrangement. But it was rejected by shareholders, who considered the $1.25 a share consideration too low.

Village responded with two on-market pref buybacks (which didn't require shareholder approval) resulting in the acquisition of 56 per cent, or 140 million, of the prefs, for $170 million, or $1.20 a share.

Village is now seeking to acquire up to 10 per cent, or 23.4 million, of the ordinary shares, at a cost of $42 million.

However, the panel considered that the market didn't have enough information to assess the merits of the buyback and required further explanation by Village of its capital management objectives, the effects of the buybacks and the dividend policy.

Logic suggests the priority should be to remove all the remaining 110 million prefs before buying back any ords.

But Village explains that it is taking this route because further buybacks are appropriate, its capital management objective can be met by buying either ords or prefs, and the directors consider it unlikely that many more prefs can be obtained through another buyback.

The ordinary buyback would reduce the total number of shares on issue to 321 million (211 million ords and 110 million prefs). Village directors suggest that 'over time and as business circumstances permit' a total capital in the range of 235 million to 285 million shares can sustain future dividends on a reasonably consistent basis.

Village will consider further buybacks to reduce the capital.

Village's largest shareholder is Village Roadshow Corp, which is controlled by three Village directors — John Kirby (chairman), Graham Burke (managing director) and Robert Kirby. VRC owns 118.6 million, or 50.5 per cent, of the ords.

VRC has told Village that it has not decided if it will participate in the current buyback. As Village directors, the VRC trio consider the buyback to be in Village shareholders' interests, but apparently are undecided if it is in VRC's interest.

In any case, VRC won't decide until the 'closed window' period has ended. This stops Village directors from trading in Village shares until after the full-year results are released, which must be by August 27.

The buyback may be over by then, especially if speculation that Granada-ITV wants to sell its 18 per cent shareholding is accurate, and that it may be prepared to tip 10 per cent into the buyback and seek to place the remainder.

If the directors are right that Village has exhausted the prefs as an avenue for buybacks, they would have to come via the ords. A total of 235 million to 285 million shares on issue would mean that the ords on issue would fall to 125 million to 175 million.

Assuming that VRC didn't participate, that would increase its shareholding from 68 per cent at the higher end, to 95 per cent at the lower, sufficient to enforce the general compulsory power.

And it would have reached that point with the company, rather than VRC, buying the shares, and without paying any control premium. Village pref holders may also have cause to feel aggrieved at the directors' preference for a policy of maintaining a 'roughly proportionate' dividend payout to ords and prefs holders.

If any dividends are paid on the ords, Village also must pay a dividend of at least 10.175c on the prefs. Before the pref buybacks, that would have required $25.45 million.

The proportionate payment on the ords would have been 7.175c or $16.85 million.

The pref buyback would have reduced any pref dividend to $11.2 million which, together with an ordinary dividend, would require $28 million.

The directors maintain that level of dividend continues to be 'difficult to support', despite forecasting a profit of $52 million for the year to June.

Village directors appear to approach the question of pref and ordinary dividends in tandem—you can't have one without the other.

But while Village cannot pay an ordinary dividend without paying a pref dividend, it can pay a pref dividend without an ordinary dividend. Village directors know that's so because they did it in 2002 when they suspended ordinary dividend payments but paid the pref dividend.

And it's arguably how the board should go about it. Instead of treating the dividends in tandem, they should consider them separately, first deciding whether a pref dividend can be paid and, if so, whether an ordinary dividend can also be paid.

A pref dividend would now cost only $11 million, when the company expects to earn $52 million. Do the Village directors consider that amount difficult to support?

It's true the prefs have some attributes of ordinary equity—they are perpetual and dividends are non-cumulative. But if the Village board continues to tie the payment of a pref dividend to whether it also can afford an ordinary dividend, the pref dividend right counts for little. If Village wants to treat the prefs as ordinaries, give them voting rights.

1   Why would a company in general choose a 'buyback' of its shares?
2   The Village preference shares are said to be 'non-cumulative' and 'perpetual':
    (a)   What do these two terms mean?
    (b)   How does this make them similar to 'ordinary shares'?
    (c)   How are they different to 'ordinary shares'?
3   Why are the regulators particularly interested in reviewing proposed 'share buybacks'?
4   Assuming the proposed ordinary share 'buyback' takes place, what is the mimimum dividend amount required for an annual payment to ordinary and preference shareholders?
5   'Logic suggests the priority should be to remove all the remaining 110 million preference shares before buying back any ordinary shares'.
    (a)   On what grounds did Bryan Frith make this statement?
    (b)   Why is Village then focusing on buying back 'ordinary shares'?
6   Bryan Frith suggests that the proposed restructure would give VRC the power to acquire all shares without having to pay a control premium.
    (a)   What does he mean by 'a control premium'?
    (b)   How do they achieve that power under this proposed buyback arrangement?
    (c)   Why might they want Village Roadshow to become a private company?

SOLUTIONS TO ACTIVITIES

Activity 2.1

Distributions to the owner, which are often labelled drawings, may be any of the following:

*   cash taken out of the business on a regular (weekly) or irregular basis
*   other assets taken out of the business for personal consumption or use (e.g. merchandise or equipment)

- personal accounts paid by the business (e.g. insurance, rent, electricity)
- personal benefits derived from business assets (e.g. accommodation, use of motor vehicle)

Activity 2.2

Much of the regulation related to financial record keeping and reporting is concerned with protecting the interests of those parties providing funding for the business. In the case of companies, many of the owners (shareholders) are far removed from the day-to-day activities of the business and the actions of management and require timely, detailed and accurate reports.

In addition, with companies the liability of owners (shareholders) is limited and therefore there is a greater need to regulate the activities of management to protect both shareholders and external providers of finance, goods and services.

With sole proprietors the management is by the owner, so one source of conflict disappears. Also the size of a sole proprietorship is likely to be much smaller than that of a limited company so any damage done is likely to be limited. Finally, creditors can sue the sole proprietor for any loss caused by his or her actions (although this does not help in the event of bankruptcy).

Activity 2.3

Sole proprietorship will normally be related to a wide range of small-business activities in retailing, manufacturing service and rural pursuits. For example:

- professional services—doctors, dentists, accounting, legal, real estate, architecture, engineering
- trade activities—mechanics, carpentry, painting, television repair, plumbing
- retail outlets—corner store, hot bread shops, service station, florist
- rural pursuits—animal husbandry, horticulture, fishing.

Activity 2.4

You may have identified one or more of the following and possibly others:

- legal restrictions—a sole proprietor cannot operate a bank, a building society or an insurance firm
- licence requirements—it is necessary to have a licence to operate certain types of business (e.g. liquor licence, taxi licence, food services licence)
- professional qualifications may be required to operate a business (e.g. doctors, lawyers, surveyors, accountants, chemists, engineers).

Activity 2.5

Potential disadvantages of the sole proprietorship structure when compared to other structures include:

- the liability of the owner is unlimited and personal assets may have to be used to satisfy business debts
- access to ownership funds is restricted to the personal resources of the proprietor
- inflexibility in management to the extent that the sole owner is frequently the sole manager
- access to non-ownership funding (credit supplier of goods and services, external loans) is often limited.

Activity 2.6

The potential advantages of partnerships might include the following:

- there would normally be greater access to capital given there are two or more owners
- the partners would normally bring different skills to the partnership (professional, administrative, technical)

- there will be greater management flexibility arising from having more than one owner
- taxation advantages often arise through being able to spread the partnership income among the partners. This is particularly applicable in 'husband and wife' activities.

Activity 2.7

You may have included in your list some of the following:

- the name of the partnership
- the activities of the partnership
- the contributions of partners
- the basis of valuing partners' contributions
- details in relation to partners' responsibilities in the partnership
- profit and loss sharing arrangements
- provision for resolution of disputes
- provision for the retirement of partners
- provision for the introduction of new partners
- provision for partnership dissolution
- details related to financial record keeping.

Activity 2.8

The profit and loss sharing arrangements should take into account the following three input factors:

- actual physical input into the partnership for which the respective partners should be entitled to a profit share equivalent to what they would have had to pay an external party for that input
- capital (funds) contributed to the partnership for which the respective partners should be entitled to a profit share equivalent to the interest that would have to be paid on loan funds
- a return for entrepreneurship or the ideas and risks taken. This may be split evenly or on some other equitable basis.

    In practical terms this may be represented as follows:

	Partners				Total
	A	B	C		
	$	$	$	$	$
Profit available					150,000
• Salary equivalent	Nil	20,000	30,000	50,000	
• Interest equivalent	15,000	10,000	5,000	30,000	
• Residual profit share	21,000	35,000	14,000	70,000	
	30%	50%	20%		
Total	36,000	65,000	49,000	150,000	150,000

Activity 2.9

With a sole proprietorship and a partnership the owners are closely involved with the day-to-day activities of the business. With companies, the structure was established to allow a large number of investors to have an ownership but generally not a daily management interest in the business activities. To encourage this sort of non-management investment the limited liability aspect was important to reduce the level of risk for investors.

Activity 2.10

You may have included:

- employees provide labour
- wholesalers provide goods (e.g. merchandise, supplies)
- professionals provide services (e.g. auditing, legal, marketing)
- financial institutions provide funds (e.g. bank overdraft, fully drawn advances, commercial bills, lease finance).

Activity 2.11

Obviously not all suppliers of goods and services are protected as we read regularly that they lose all or part of what is owed to them when companies are liquidated (e.g. Harris Scarfe, Ansett, HIH). However, a number of factors, requirements or actions are designed to provide protection, including:

- the legal requirement for companies to prepare financial reports in conformity with statutory accounting standards
- suppliers require payment to be made in advance
- creditors require personal guarantees by the owners or management
- lenders take out a specific claim against tangible assets of the company (mortgage, bill of sale)
- lending agreements restrict the financial practices:
  —maximum level of debt to assets
  —minimum required return on assets
  —limitations on profit distributions
  —restrictions on asset sales
  —specification of accounting methods that can be used
- the creditors will rank before the shareholders in the distribution of assets in the event of a liquidation of the company.

Activity 2.12

The additional regulations that apply to the limited liability company will depend on the classification of that company. However, these regulations may relate to:

- company registration requirements before a company is granted a certificate of incorporation
- the requirement to submit annual accounts to the Australian Securities and Investments Commission (ASIC)
- the requirement to have accounts audited by registered auditors
- the requirement to prepare reports in conformity with statutory Australian Accounting Standards
- reporting and other obligations imposed on the company management (directors).

Activity 2.13

You may have included:

- more expensive to establish
- more extensive regulatory requirements
- less management flexibility
- control may be lost by the original owners
- greater scrutiny by analysts and other special interest groups
- greater pressure to perform over the short term by external (non-management) investors
- potential taxation disadvantages as tax is paid at 30% on all profit (from the first $1).

ACCOUNTING an introduction

Activity 2.14

The answers are as shown below:

1. *Net assets*
   Cash $100,000
   Shareholders' equity
   Share capital (100,000 ordinary shares issued at $2—called to $1) $100,000

2. *Net assets*
   Cash $150,000
   Shareholders' equity
   Share capital (100,000 ordinary shares issued at $2—called to $1.50) $150,000

Activity 2.15

The balance sheet would appear as follows:

Net assets	$370,000	
Capital (200,000 shares)	300,000	(i.e. 100,000 issued at $1 plus 100,000 issued at $2)
Retained profits	70,000	
	$370,000	

Activity 2.16

To deal with the second point first, it is an odd question because reserves are a claim, or part of one, whereas cash is an asset. So reserves cannot be cash.

Activity 2.17

The answer should be that the number of shares will double from 100 to 200. Now the shareholder owns one five-hundredth of the company (200/100,000). Before the bonus issue the shareholder also owned one five-hundredth of the company (100/50,000). The company's assets and liabilities have not changed one bit as a result of the bonus issue, so logically one five-hundredth of the value of the company should be identical to what it was before. Thus each share is worth half as much, but the shareholder now owns twice as many shares.

Activity 2.18

Three possible reasons are:

1. To lower the value of each share, without reducing the shareholders' collective or individual wealth. This is the same effect as 'splitting' and may be seen as an alternative to splitting.

2. To provide the shareholders with a 'feel good factor'. It seems to be believed that shareholders like bonus issues, because it seems to make them better off, though in practice it should not affect their wealth.

3. Where reserves arising from operating profits and/or realised gains on the sale of non-current assets are used to make the bonus issue, it has the effect of taking part of that portion of the owners' claim which could be drawn by the shareholders, as drawings (or dividends), and locking it up. We shall see, a little later in this chapter, that there are severe restrictions on the extent to which shareholders may make drawings from their capital. An individual or organisation contemplating lending money to the company may insist that the dividend payment possibilities are restricted as a condition of making the loan. This point will be explained in a little more detail later.

Activity 2.19

The answer is that it does not matter *in these particular circumstances*. This is because, in a rights issue, the existing shareholders and the new shareholders are exactly the same people. Not only this, but the new shares will be held by the shareholders in the same proportion as they held the existing shares. Thus a particular shareholder will be gaining on the new shares exactly as much as he or she is losing on the existing ones.

Shareholders who do not wish to take up their rights can sell their rights, at a price which is likely to be very close to the reduction in the value of their holding (though you should note that in the case of proprietary companies the directors may have the discretion to refuse to register transfers). Thus, in the end, no one is better or worse off as a result of the rights issue being made at a discount.

Activity 2.20

The main reason is that investors are generally very reluctant to pledge their money unless they can see some way in which they can turn their investment back into cash. In theory, the shares of a particular company may be very valuable, as a result of the company having a very bright economic future, but unless this value is capable of being realised in cash the benefit to the shareholders is dubious. After all, you cannot spend shares; you generally need cash. This means that potential shareholders are much more likely to be prepared to buy new shares from the company (thus providing the company with new finance) where they can see a way of liquidating their investment (turning it into cash).

The stock exchanges provide the means of liquidation.

Though the buying and selling of 'second-hand' shares does not provide the company with cash, the fact that the buying and selling facility exists will make it easier for the company to raise new share capital as and when it wishes to do so.

Activity 2.21

The reason for this is the limited liability, which company shareholders enjoy, but which owners of unincorporated businesses do not. If a sole trader withdraws all of the owner's claim or even an amount in excess of this, the position of the creditors of the business is not weakened since they can legally enforce their claims against the sole trader as an individual. With a limited company, in which the business and the owners are legally separated, such legal right does not exist. However, to protect the company's creditors the law insists that a specific part of the capital of a company cannot legally be withdrawn by the shareholders.

Activity 2.22

It would be very rare for a company to pay all of its revenue reserves as a dividend: a legal right to do so does not necessarily make it a good idea. Most companies see ploughed-back profits as a major, usually *the* major, source of new finance.

The factors which influence the dividend decision are likely to include:

- the availability of cash to pay a dividend: it would not be illegal to borrow to pay a dividend, but it would be unusual and, possibly, imprudent
- the needs of the business for finance for investment
- possibly a need for the directors to create good relations with investors, who may regard a dividend as a positive feature.

You may have thought of others.

Activity 2.23

A number of the underlying ideas within GAAP potentially conflict with other ideas within GAAP and also with the economic reality. Examples of underlying ideas that could create conflict would be:

(a) *historic cost*: while at the time of acquisition the price paid represents a useful measure of value, over time, that measure will become out of date with changes in such things as exchange rates, inflation, technology and general market conditions. This is of particular concern for non-current (long-term) assets and liabilities.

(b) *the stable monetary unit*: money is both a 'measure of value' and a 'good' in its own right, subject to supply and demand conditions. As a result the significance (purchasing power) of money changes over time and it is not logical to compare, add or subtract dollars of different time periods, and this is unfortunately what accountants do. It has been suggested that to overcome this problem we need to adjust exchange prices to either current values or purchasing power equivalents.

(c) *the accounting period*: the idea of dividing the business up into equal periods of time for reporting purposes (e.g. years) creates significant problems where at the end of the period there are incomplete transactions (e.g. a building under construction, inventory unsold, amount owing on credit sales, research incomplete, crops not harvested etc.). At the end of the period management has to estimate the amount of revenue earned, expenses incurred, obligation outstanding and assets remaining.

(d) *prudence*: the idea of caution in recognising transactions (e.g. overstating expenses and liabilities and understating revenues and assets) conflicts with full disclosure and leads to future reverses (e.g. overstating revenues and assets and understating expenses and liabilities in subsequent periods).

(e) *going concern*: this assumption is especially relevant to property, plant and equipment where the particular item is depreciated over its useful life on the basis of the economic benefits consumed. As a result such assets are often recorded at a value well in excess of their market or liquidation value.

You may have thought of others.

Activity 2.24

There are many reasons why professional regulation of accounting failed in Australia, but of major significance was the fact that the profession was unable to enforce compliance with the professional standards.

For managers responsible for preparing accounts who were not members of the profession, there was little that the profession could do to ensure compliance.

Even where the profession was able to act in response to non-compliance, the penalties that it could impose were limited.

Activity 2.25

The rationale for preparing a conceptual framework included the ideas that:

(a) accounting standards developed from using the framework would be more consistent and logical

(b) the accounting standards developed would be more comparable with those in other countries using similar frameworks

(c) the accounting standard setting body would be more accountable for its decisions, as they would be based on a specific set of ideas

(d) accountants would be better able to communicate the underlying basis of the reported figures, and the framework would also provide a basis to support their position in the event of conflict

(e) framework should lead to fewer standards and a more efficient standard-setting process.

Activity 2.26

The stated benefits of harmonising Australian accounting standards with the international equivalent standards are:

(a) improved comparability of financial reports between countries

(b)   enhanced international capital flows resulting from the use of consistent standards across countries

(c)   reduced accounting and reporting costs from multinational enterprises as fewer separate reports will have to be produced

(d)   greater understanding of financial reports by the stakeholders given uniform recording and reporting regulations.

Activity 2.27

You may have identified some of the following as potential disadvantages of adopting international standards in favour of the existing nationally developed standards.

(a)   International standards by their very nature must be general and involve compromise to gain broad acceptance. As a result they may be inferior to the national standards in terms of providing report users with optimal financial information. It is interesting to note that the Australian standard setting body has, in adopting the international standards, made changes to further restrict the choices available to Australian companies and also to require additional disclosures.

(b)   In general it will be more expensive for purely domestic (not multinational) Australian companies to comply with the new international accounting standards. This results from there being more standards, and from the need to make changes from existing practices.

(c)   A single set of accounting standards for worldwide use cannot take into account the wide divergence in economic, political, legal and cultural attributes of different countries.

Activity 2.28

This is a widely debated issue, and because there is no clear guidance as to what constitutes a 'true and fair view' it is difficult to resolve the debate.

The standards setters have concluded that the 'true and fair' override is inappropriate because users can potentially avoid complying with accounting standards that are unfavourable to their financial performance and/or financial position.

On the other side, requiring firms to always adhere to the accounting standards may deprive them of the ability to efficiently communicate their financial performance and financial position.

OBJECTIVES

When you have completed your study of this chapter you should be able to:

1 explain the nature and purpose of the balance sheet

2 demonstrate an understanding of assets in terms of definition, recognition, measurement and classification

3 demonstrate an understanding of liabilities in terms of definition, recognition, measurement and classification

4 discuss the nature and classification of owners' equity

5 explain the basic accounting equation

6 contrast the alternative balance sheets

7 discuss the main factors that influence the content and values in a balance sheet

8 prepare a simple balance sheet

9 analyse balance sheets of reporting entities

10 state the potential limitations of the balance sheet in portraying the financial position of an entity.

3

MEASURING AND REPORTING FINANCIAL POSITION

In this chapter we examine the first of the three financial reports—that which is concerned with establishing financial position. The balance sheet represents the assets and claims against those assets of an entity at a given point in time. The interests in, or claims against, the assets are divided into external (liability) and internal (owners') interests. We will see how the statement is made up and how the report is prepared. We will also consider the basis on which accounts are included, measured and reported. Finally, its usefulness in decision making will be considered and possible deficiencies highlighted.

NATURE AND PURPOSE OF THE BALANCE SHEET

The purpose of this first statement is to set out the financial position of a business at a particular moment in time. This has generally been known as the balance sheet. It represents a summary of the information provided in the accounts, and is effectively a listing of the balances in all of the detailed accounts—this is where the term balance sheet comes from. The balance sheet sets out the assets of the business on the one hand, and the claims against the business on the other. Before looking at the statement in more detail, we need to be clear what these terms mean.

ASSETS

An **asset**, for accounting purposes, is essentially a resource which has certain characteristics and which is held by the business. The main characteristics of an asset are:

✳ *An expected future economic benefit.* This simply means that the item is expected to have some future monetary value. This value can arise through its use within the business or through its hire or sale. Thus, an obsolete piece of equipment that can be sold for scrap would still be considered an asset, whereas an obsolete piece of equipment that could not be sold for scrap would not be regarded as an asset.

✳ *The business has an exclusive right to control the benefit.* Unless the business has exclusive rights over the resource it cannot be regarded as an asset of the business. Thus, for a business offering holidays on houseboats, the canal and river system may be a very valuable resource. However, as the business will not be able to control the access of others to the system it cannot be regarded as an asset of the business (but the houseboats owned by the business would be regarded as assets).

✳ *The benefit must arise from some past transaction or event.* This means the transaction (or other event) giving rise to the business's right to the benefit must have already occurred and will not arise at some future date. Thus, an agreement by a business to purchase a piece of machinery at some future date would not mean the item is currently an asset of the business.

✳ *The asset must be capable of reliable measurement in monetary terms.* Unless the item can be measured in monetary terms with a reasonable degree of reliability the item will not be regarded as an asset for inclusion on the balance sheet. For example, the loyalty of customers may be extremely valuable to the business but may be impossible to quantify.

The AASB Framework defines an asset as 'a resource controlled by the entity as a result of past events and from which economic benefits are expected to flow to the entity'.

We can see that these conditions will strictly limit the kind of items that may be referred to as 'assets' in financial reports. Certainly not all resources exploited by a business will be assets of the business. Once an asset has been acquired by a business, it will continue to be considered an asset until the benefits are exhausted or the business disposes of it in some way.

ACTIVITY 3.1

State which of the following items could appear on the balance sheet of business A as an asset. Explain your reasoning in each case.

1. $1,000 owing to business A by a customer who will never be able to pay.

2. The purchase of a licence from business B giving business A the right to produce a product designed by that business. Production of the new product under licence is expected to increase profits over the period in which the licence is held.

3. The hiring by business A of a new marketing director who is confidently expected to increase profits by at least 30 per cent over the next three years.

4. Purchase of a machine which will save business A $10,000 per annum. It is currently being used by the business but has been acquired on credit and is not yet paid for.

The sorts of items that often appear as assets in the balance sheet of a business include:

❋ freehold premises
❋ machinery and equipment
❋ fixtures and fittings
❋ patents and trademarks
❋ debtors
❋ investments.

ACTIVITY 3.2

Suggest three additional items that might appear as assets in the balance sheet of a business.

Note that an asset does not have to be a physical item—it may also be a non-physical right to certain benefits. Assets that have a physical substance and that can be touched are referred to as **tangible assets** (inventory, plant and equipment). Assets that have no physical substance but, nevertheless, provide expected future benefits are referred to as **intangible assets** (copyright, trademark, patent, franchise, goodwill).

CLAIMS AGAINST THE ASSETS

The other side of the balance sheet includes **claims** against the assets of an entity, or simply the different interests in those assets. There are essentially two types of claims: external claims, known as liabilities; and internal, or ownership, claims, labelled **owners' equity**, equity or capital.

Liabilities

Liabilities represent the claims of individuals and organisations, apart from the owner(s), which have arisen from past transactions or events such as supplying goods and services or lending money to the business.

ACTIVITY 3.3

Can you list four liabilities that might appear in the balance sheet of a business?

In recent years concern has been raised at the inclusion as liabilities of what appear to be non-obligations in the balance sheet of reporting entities. Examples of such items are:

✳ provision for major maintenance
✳ provision for future losses
✳ deferred gains on foreign transactions.

In an effort to restrict the classification of such items as liabilities, the definition of liabilities has been extended. According to the AASB Framework, liabilities are: 'a present obligation of the entity arising from past events, the settlement of which is expected to result in an outflow from the entity of resources embodying economic benefits'.

In addition to the extended definition, a new recognition criterion was introduced. That is, even where an item may satisfy the definition it also needs to meet the recognition criterion to be included in the balance sheet liability account. The recognition criterion for all account types, including liabilities, is twofold:

✳ probability of occurrence (i.e. in the case of liabilities it is more likely rather than less likely that a future sacrifice of economic benefits will occur)
✳ reliability of measurement (i.e. in the case of liabilities the amount of the claim can be determined with acceptable precision or accuracy).

ACTIVITY 3.4

State which of the following items could appear on the balance sheet of business A as a liability. Explain your reasoning in each case.

1. $2,000 owing to business B for the satisfactory supply of goods during the past month.
2. A provision (estimate) is made each year of $50,000 for future relining of the blast furnace that takes place every three years. The current estimate is $100,000.
3. Magazine subscriptions have been received in advance by a publisher amounting to $27,400.
4. The business has guaranteed a manager's personal loan of $100,000. The manager has maintained the account in good order and $79,000 is currently owing.
5. There is a legal claim against the business for negligence in relation to faulty workmanship. It is likely they will settle out of court for $50,000.

Most liabilities will represent legal claims by external parties against the entity for satisfaction in cash (e.g. bills or accounts payable) or for the provision of goods and services (e.g. subscriptions received in advance). However, it is possible for non-legal claims to be recognised on the basis of past industry or business behaviour, such as the provision (estimate) for employee bonuses or owners' distribution (constructive obligation), or on the basis of social or moral behaviour related to such things as extended warranties (equitable obligations).

ACTIVITY 3.5

Can you list additional liability accounts based on satisfaction in both cash and kind (goods or services)?

Owners' equity (or simply 'equity')

This represents the claim of the owner(s) against the business. This claim is sometimes referred to as the owners' capital. The AASB Framework defines equity as the 'residual interest in the assets of the entity after deducting all its liabilities'.

Some find it hard to understand how the owner can have a claim against the business, particularly when we consider the example of a sole proprietor-type business where the owner is, in effect, the business. However, for accounting purposes, a clear distinction is made between the business (whatever its size) and the owner(s). The business is viewed as being quite separate from the owner, irrespective of whether the business has a separate legal identity or not. This means that when financial reports are prepared, they are prepared for the business rather than the owner(s). Viewed from this perspective, therefore, any funds contributed by the owner to help finance the business will be regarded as a claim against the business in its balance sheet.

In addition to the owners' equity contributed we will find two other owners' equity accounts:

✳ *Owners' equity retained.* This represents the profits left in the business by the owners.

ACTIVITY 3.6

Can you think of reasons why owners would leave profits in the business rather than withdrawing them for personal use?

✳ *Reserves.* These represent special purpose owners' equity accounts and in many cases are related to retained profits being transferred to a separate account to identify the nature of those profits (e.g. profits made on the sale of long-term assets—*capital profits reserve*) or to a future intended action (e.g. a decision to ensure owners' distributions (dividends) are relatively constant over time—*dividend equalisation reserve*; a decision to redeem preference dividends—*capital redemption reserve*; a decision to replace assets—*capital replacement reserve*). The most commonly found reserve of major significance that does not relate to retained profit transfers is the *revaluation reserve*. It represents the increases recognised in assets related to inflation and other price changes.

ACTIVITY 3.7

If you have access to any published financial reports, either hard copy or via the Internet, identify the names of other reserve accounts.

It is important to note that reserves represent ownership interests in the assets, not the assets themselves. Reserves are not separate deposits of cash available for a specified purpose.

While we have discussed three distinct categories of owners' equity accounts, it is common today for *retained profits* and *other reserves* to simply be classified separately under the general heading of 'reserves'.

Now that the meaning of the terms 'assets', 'liabilities and 'owners' equity' has been established we can go on to discuss the relationship between them. This relationship is quite simple and straightforward. If a business wishes to acquire assets it will have to raise the necessary funds from somewhere. It may raise the funds from the owner(s) or from other outside parties or from both. To illustrate the relationship let us take the example of a new business as set out in Example 3.1 below.

EXAMPLE

3.1

Jerry and Co. deposits $20,000 in a bank account on 1 March in order to commence business. Let us assume that the cash is supplied by the owner ($6,000) and an outside party ($14,000). The raising of the funds in this way will give rise to a claim on the business by both the owner (capital) and the outside party (liability). If a balance sheet of Jerry and Co. is prepared following the above transactions, the assets and claims of the business would appear as follows:

JERRY AND CO.
Balance sheet as at 1 March

Assets	$	Claims	$
Cash at bank	20,000	Owner's equity	6,000
		Liability—loan	14,000
Total assets	20,000	Total liabilities and owner's equity	20,000

We have chosen to use a two-sided, traditional-style statement for illustration purposes. Later in the chapter we will discuss other formats.

We can see from the statement that has been prepared that the total claims are the same as the total assets. Thus:

$$Assets = Owner's\ equity + Liabilities$$

The equation shown above—which is often referred to as the accounting equation—will always hold true. Whatever changes may occur to the assets of the business or the claims against the business, there will be compensating changes elsewhere which will ensure that the balance sheet always 'balances' (i.e. both sides agree). By way of illustration consider some further possible transactions for Jerry and Co. Assume that, after the $20,000 had been deposited in the bank, the following transactions took place:

March 2 Purchased a motor vehicle for $5,000 paying by cheque.

March 3 Purchased inventory (stock-in-trade) on one month's credit for $3,000.

March 4 Repaid $2,000 of the loan from outside party.

March 6 Owner introduced $4,000 into the business bank account.

A balance sheet may be drawn up after each day in which transactions have taken place. In this way, the effect can be seen of each transaction on the assets and claims against the assets of the business. The balance sheet as at 2 March will be as follows:

JERRY AND CO.

Balance sheet as at 2 March

Assets	$	Claims	$
Cash at bank	15,000	Owner's equity	6,000
Motor vehicle	5,000	Liabilities—loan	14,000
Total assets	20,000	Total liabilities and owner's equity	20,000

As can be seen, the effect of purchasing a motor vehicle is to decrease the balance at the bank by $5,000 and to introduce a new asset—a motor vehicle—onto the statement. The total assets remain unchanged. It is only the 'mix' of assets which has changed. The claims against the business remain the same as there has been no change in the funding arrangements for the business.

The balance sheet as at 3 March, following the purchase of inventory, will be as follows:

JERRY AND CO.

Balance sheet as at 3 March

Assets	$	Claims	$
Cash at bank	15,000	Owner's equity	6,000
Motor vehicle	5,000	Liabilities—loan	14,000
Inventory	3,000	Liabilities—trade creditor	3,000
Total assets	23,000	Total liabilities and owner's equity	23,000

The effect of purchasing inventory has been to introduce another new asset (inventory) onto the balance sheet. In addition, the fact that the goods have not yet been paid for means that the claims against the business have been increased by the $3,000 owed to the supplier, who is referred to as a 'trade creditor' on the balance sheet. Creditors are also known as 'accounts payable' or simply 'payables'.

 ACTIVITY 3.8

Try drawing up a balance sheet for Jerry and Co. as at 4 March.

 ACTIVITY 3.9

Try drawing up a balance sheet for Jerry and Co. as at 6 March.

This example illustrates the point made earlier that the accounting equation (owner's equity plus liabilities equals assets) will always hold true. This is because the equation is based on the fact that, if a business wishes to acquire assets, it must raise funds equal to the cost of those assets. These funds must be provided by the owners (owner's equity), or other outside parties (liabilities), or both. Hence, the total cost of assets acquired should always equal the total owner's equity (capital) plus liabilities.

It is worth pointing out that a business would not draw up a balance sheet after each day of transactions as shown in the example above. Such an approach is likely to be impractical given even a relatively small number of transactions each day. A balance sheet for the business is usually prepared at the end of a defined reporting period. Determining the length of the reporting interval will involve weighing up the costs of producing the information against the perceived benefits of the information for decision-making purposes. In practice, the reporting interval will vary between businesses and could be monthly, quarterly, half-yearly or annually. For external reporting purposes an annual reporting cycle is the norm (although certain large companies report more frequently than this). However, for internal reporting purposes, many businesses produce monthly financial reports.

EFFECT OF TRADING OPERATIONS ON THE BALANCE SHEET

In the example we considered earlier (Jerry and Co.), we dealt with the effect on the balance sheet of a number of different types of transactions that a business might undertake. These transactions covered the purchase of assets for cash and on credit, the repayment of a loan and the injection of owner's equity. However, one form of transaction, namely trading (an asset is sold for a price different from the cost to acquire or manufacture that asset), has not yet been considered. In order to deal with the effect of trading transactions on the balance sheet let us return to our earlier example.

Let us use the balance sheet drawn up for Jerry and Co. as at 6 March in the solution to Activity 3.9. The balance sheet at that date was as follows:

JERRY AND CO.

Balance sheet as at 6 March

EXAMPLE 3.1 *continued*

Assets	$	Claims	$
Cash at bank	17,000	Owner's equity	10,000
Motor vehicle	5,000	Liabilities—loan	12,000
Inventory	3,000	Liabilities—trade creditor	3,000
Total assets	25,000	Total liabilities and owner's equity	25,000

Let us assume that, on 7 March, the business managed to sell all of the inventory for $5,000 and received a cheque immediately from the customer for this amount. The balance sheet on 7 March, after this transaction has taken place, will be as follows:

JERRY AND CO.
Balance sheet as at 7 March

Assets	$	Claims	$
Cash at bank	22,000	Owner's equity	
Motor vehicle	5,000	[10,000 + (5,000 – 3,000)]	12,000
		Liabilities—loan	12,000
		Liabilities—trade creditor	3,000
Total assets	27,000	Total liabilities and owner's equity	27,000

We can see that the inventory ($3,000) has now disappeared from the balance sheet but the cash at bank has increased by the selling price of the inventory ($5,000). The net effect has therefore been to increase assets by $2,000 (i.e. $5,000 – $3,000). This increase represents the net increase in wealth (profit) which has arisen from trading. Also note that the owner's equity of the business has increased by $2,000 in line with the increase in assets. This increase in owner's equity reflects the fact that increases in wealth as a result of trading or other operations will be to the benefit of the owner and will increase his or her stake in the business.

ACTIVITY 3.10

What would have been the effect on the balance sheet if the inventory had been sold on 7 March for $1,000 rather than $5,000?

Thus, we can see that any decrease in wealth (loss) arising from trading or other transactions will lead to a reduction in the owner's stake in the business. If the business wished to maintain the level of assets as at 6 March it would be necessary to obtain further funds from the owner or outside parties, or both.

What we have just seen means that the balance sheet equation can be extended as follows:

Assets = Owner's equity beginning + Profit (or – Loss) +/– Other owner's equity changes + Liabilities

The profit for the period is usually shown separately in the balance sheet as an addition to owner's equity. Any funds introduced by the owner, or withdrawn by the owner for living expenses or other reasons, are also shown separately. Thus, if we assume that the above business sold the inventory for $5,000, as in the earlier example, and further assume that the owner withdrew $1,500 of the profit, the owner's equity would appear as follows on the balance sheet:

	$
Owner's equity	
Opening balance	10,000
Add profit	2,000
	12,000
Less drawings	1,500
Closing balance	10,500

If the drawings were in cash, then the balance of cash would decrease by $1,500 in the balance sheet.

In Example 3.1 we have been looking at the basic accounting equation and the effects of various transactions on that equation. Table 3.1 below illustrates the above transactions.

TABLE 3.1 Accounting equation and effects of transactions

| | Assets | | = | Liabilities | + | Owner's equity | | |
| | | | | | | Owner's | Retained | |
	Cash	Inventory	Motor vehicle	Trade creditor	Loan	contribution	profit	Drawings
1 March	20,000				14,000	6,000		
2 March	−5,000		+5,000					
	15,000		5,000		14,000	6,000		
3 March		+3,000		+3,000				
	15,000	3,000	5,000	3,000	14,000	6,000		
4 March	−2,000				−2,000			
	13,000	3,000	5,000	3,000	12,000	6,000		
6 March	+6,000					+6,000		
	19,000	3,000	5,000	3,000	12,000	12,000		
7 March	+5,000	−3,000					+2,000	
	24,000	Nil	5,000	3,000	12,000	12,000	2,000	
or								
Drawings	−1,500							+1,500
	22,500	Nil	5,000	3,000	12,000	12,000*	2,000*	1,500*

*single account $12,500
It should be noted that the drawings figure is effectively a negative figure in the owner's equity section of the balance sheet.

THE CLASSIFICATION OF ASSETS

To help users of financial information easily locate items of interest on the balance sheet, it is customary to group assets and equities into categories. Assets are normally categorised as being either current or non-current. The distinction between these two categories is as follows:

✳ **Current assets** are assets which are not held on a continuing basis. They include cash and other assets which are expected to be consumed or converted to cash within the next 12 months or within the **operating cycle**. The operating cycle would normally represent the time between the acquisition of the assets (e.g. raw materials or finished goods) and their ultimate realisation in cash or cash equivalents. Current assets are normally held as part of the day-to-day trading activities of the business. The most common current assets are inventory (stock), accounts receivable (trade debtors), pre-payments and cash itself. The current assets mentioned are interrelated and circulate within a business as shown in Figure 3.1. We can see that cash can be used to purchase stock which is then sold on credit. When the trade debtors pay, the business receives an injection of cash.

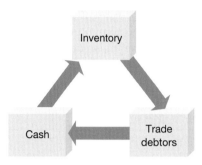

The figure shows how inventory may be sold on credit to customers. When the customers pay, the trade debtors will be converted into cash, which can then be used to purchase more inventory, and so the cycle begins again.

FIGURE 3.1 The circulating nature of current assets

The Australian Accounting Standard AASB 101 'Presentation of Financial Statements' requires an asset to be classified as current when it satisfies any of the following criteria:

(a) *the asset is expected to be realised in, or is intended for sale or consumption in, the entity's normal operating cycle;*

(b) *the asset is held primarily for the purpose of being traded;*

(c) *the asset is expected to be realised within twelve months after the reporting date; or*

(d) *the asset is cash or a cash equivalent unless it is restricted from being exchanged or used to settle a liability for at least twelve months after the reporting date.*

✳ **Non-current assets** are defined primarily according to the purpose for which they are held. They are held with the intention of being used to generate wealth rather than being held for resale (although they may be sold by the business when there is no further use for the asset). They can be seen as the tools of the business. Non-current assets are normally held by the business on a continuing basis. The minimum period a non-current asset is expected to be held is one year.

ACTIVITY 3.11

Can you think of two examples of assets which may be classified as non-current assets within a particular business?

It is important to appreciate that the classification of an asset may vary (i.e. between current and non-current) according to the nature of the business being carried out. This is because the purpose for which a particular type of business holds a certain asset may vary. For example, a motor vehicle manufacturer will normally hold the motor vehicles produced for resale and would therefore classify them as inventory. On the other hand, a business which uses motor vehicles for transportation purposes would classify them as non-current assets.

ACTIVITY 3.12

The assets of Kunalun and Co., a large metalworking business, are shown below:
- cash at bank
- fixtures and fittings
- office equipment
- motor vehicles
- freehold factory premises
- goodwill purchased from business taken over
- plant and machinery
- computer equipment
- stock of work-in-progress (i.e. partly completed goods)
- short-term investments.

Which of the above do you think should be defined as current assets and which should be defined as non-current assets?

AASB 101 'Presentation of Financial Statements' requires assets to be classified as non-current when they do not satisfy any of the criteria for being classified as current.

The item 'goodwill purchased' in the list of non-current assets above requires some explanation. When a business takes over another business, the amount paid for the business taken over will often exceed the fair value (market value) of identifiable net assets acquired. This additional amount represents a payment for 'goodwill' which arises from such factors as the quality and reputation of products produced, the location of the business, the skill and competence of the workforce, and the relationship with customers and suppliers. 'Qualitative' items such as these are normally excluded from the balance sheet as they are difficult to measure. However, when they have been acquired by a business at an agreed price, the amount paid provides an objective basis for measurement. Hence, 'goodwill purchased' can be regarded as an asset and included on the balance sheet. Goodwill is regarded as a non-current asset as it is not held primarily for resale and will be held on a continuing basis. It is also a good example of an intangible asset, since it has no physical substance.

In the Australian context an accounting standard, AASB 101 'Presentation of Financial Statements', was issued in July 2004 and applies to companies from 1 January 2005. This standard requires that assets be classified according to their nature or function. It then indicates that this classification could be either on:

✳ a current/non-current basis,
✳ the basis of the order of liquidity (receipt).

While it is expected that the current/non-current classification will predominate, there is provision for companies to use the liquidity classification categories for their assets where the presentation on a liquidity basis will provide more relevant and reliable information.

THE CLASSIFICATION OF LIABILITIES

Liabilities are normally classified into two groups:

1. **Current liabilities** represent amounts due and payable to outside parties within 12 months or one operating cycle of the balance sheet date.

AASB 101 'Presentation of Financial Statements' requires liabilities to be classified as current when they satisfy any of the following criteria:

(a) the liability is expected to be settled in the entity's normal operating cycle;

(b) the liability is held primarily for the purpose of being traded;

(c) the liability is due to be settled within twelve months after the reporting date; or

(d) the entity does not have an unconditional right to defer settlement of the liability for at least twelve months after the reporting date.

2. Non-current liabilities represent those amounts due to other parties which are not liable for repayment within the next 12 months or the next operating cycle after the balance sheet date.

AASB 101 'Presentation of Financial Statements' requires liabilities to be classified as non-current when they do not satisfy any of the criteria to be classified as current.

Unlike assets, the purpose for which the liabilities are held is not an issue. It is only the period for which the liability is outstanding that is important. Thus, a long-term liability will turn into a current liability when the settlement date comes within 12 months or one operating cycle of the balance sheet date.

ACTIVITY 3.13

Can you think of examples of non-current liabilities and current liabilities?

The Australian Accounting Standard AASB 101 'Presentation of Financial Statements' also requires that liabilities be classified according to their nature. As for the assets, this classification can be on:

✳ a current/non-current basis, or

✳ the basis of the order of liquidity (payment).

While it is expected that the current/non-current classification will predominate, there is provision for companies to use the alternative liquidity classification category for their liabilities where it provides information that is more relevant and reliable.

THE CLASSIFICATION OF OWNERS' EQUITY

Owners' equity can represent a single account in sole proprietorships (owner's capital); however, for most businesses it is either useful, or required (companies), to provide three separate categories:

1. owners' equity contributed (paid-up capital, partners' capital, accumulated funds)

2. reserves

3. retained profit (retained earnings).

As we noted earlier it is now common for categories 2 and 3 to be combined:

1. owners' equity

2. reserves:
   (a) retained profits
   (b) other reserves.

The statement of changes in owners' equity discussed in Chapter 1 essentially represents the owners' equity section of the balance sheet.

FORMATS FOR BALANCE SHEETS

Now that the classification of assets, liabilities and owners' equity has been completed, it is possible to consider the format of the balance sheet. Although there is an almost infinite number of ways in which the same information could be presented, there are in practice two basic choices; the overall format of the report, and the nature of the balance sheet equation.

In terms of the overall format of the report you can either use the T format (horizontal—across the page) or the narrative format (vertical—down the page).

In terms of the balance sheet equation you can either use the entity (from the viewpoint of the entity) approach (A = L + OE) or the proprietary (from the view point of the owner) approach (OE = A − L).

Figures 3.2 and 3.3 provide an overview of these two perspectives.

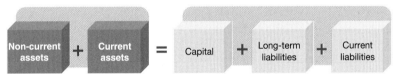

The figure sets out the equation for the entity perspective of balance sheet layout.

FIGURE 3.2 The equation for the entity perspective

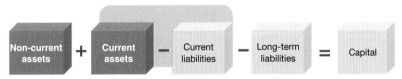

The figure sets out the equation for the proprietary perspective of balance sheet layout.

FIGURE 3.3 The equation for the proprietary perspective

The style we adopted with Jerry and Co. earlier represents a T format using the entity equation. A more comprehensive example of this style is shown below:

BRIE MANUFACTURING
Balance sheet as at 31 December 2005

	$	$		$	$
Current assets			*Current liabilities*		
Cash at bank	12,000		Trade creditors	37,000	
Trade debtors	18,000				
Inventory	23,000		*Non-current liabilities*		
		53,000	Loan	50,000	
			Total liabilities		87,000

Non-current assets			Owners' equity		
Motor vehicles	19,000		Opening balance	50,000	
Plant and machinery	30,000		Add profit	14,000	
Freehold premises	45,000			64,000	
		94,000	Less drawings	4,000	
			Ending balance		60,000
Total assets		147,000	Total liabilities and owners' equity		147,000

Note that within each category of asset (current and non-current) the items are listed with the most liquid (starting with cash) first, going down to the least liquid. This is a standard practice which is followed irrespective of the format used. Liquidity generally relates to cash or closeness to cash.

You should note that this approach is not used in all countries. For example, in the United Kingdom the order is typically reversed, with the listing going from the least liquid to the most liquid. Overall content is basically the same; only the order changes.

An obvious change to this format is to show claims on the left and assets on the right. Some people prefer this approach because the claims can be seen as the source of finance for the business and the assets show how that finance has been deployed. It could be seen as more logical to show sources first and uses second.

The format shown above is sometimes referred to as the 'horizontal layout' or T account. However, in recent years, a more common form of layout for the balance sheet is the 'narrative' or 'vertical' form of layout. This format is really based on a rearrangement of the accounting equation. With the horizontal format above, the accounting equation is set out as:

$$\text{Current assets }(CA) + \text{Non-current assets }(NCA) = \text{Owners' equity }(OE)$$
$$+ \text{ Non-current liabilities }(NCL) + \text{Current liabilities }(CL)$$

The vertical format merely rearranges this to:

$$CA$$
$$+ NCA$$
$$=$$
$$CL$$
$$+ NCL$$
$$+ OE$$

We can therefore rearrange the layout of Brie Manufacturing as follows:

BRIE MANUFACTURING
Balance sheet as at 31 December 2005

	$	$
Current assets		
Cash at bank	12,000	
Trade debtors	18,000	
Inventory	23,000	
		53,000

Non-current assets		
Motor vehicles	19,000	
Plant and machinery	30,000	
Freehold premises	45,000	
		94,000
Total assets		147,000
Current liabilities		
Trade creditors		37,000
Non-current liabilities		
Loan		50,000
Total liabilities		87,000
Owners' equity		
Opening balance	50,000	
Add profit	14,000	
	64,000	
Less drawings	4,000	
Ending balance		60,000
Total liabilities and owners' equity		147,000

In terms of published balance sheets in Australia the most commonly presented is the vertical format based on the entity equation. Irrespective of the format, or the equation, all balance sheets contain the same information.

Figure 3.4 illustrates the relationship between the balance sheet accounts together with the respective classifications within those accounts.

FIGURE 3.4 Classification of balance sheet accounts

FINANCIAL POSITION AT A POINT IN TIME

As we have already seen, the balance sheet is a statement of the financial position of the business at a specified point in time. The balance sheet has been compared to a photograph. A photograph 'freezes' a particular moment in time and will only represent the situation at that moment in time. Hence, events may be quite different immediately before and immediately after the photograph was taken. Similarly, the balance sheet represents a 'snapshot' of the business at a particular moment in time. When examining a balance sheet, therefore, it is important to establish the date at which it has been drawn up. This information should be prominently displayed in the heading as shown above. The more current the date the better when you are trying to assess current financial position.

SELF-ASSESSMENT QUESTION 3.1

The following information relates to the Simonson Engineering Company as at 30 September 2005:

	$
Plant and machinery	25,000
Trade creditors	18,000
Bank overdraft	26,000
Inventory	45,000
Freehold premises	72,000
Long-term loans	51,000
Trade debtors	48,000
Capital at 1 October 2004	117,500
Cash in hand	1,500
Motor vehicles	15,000
Fixtures and fittings	9,000
Profit for the year to 30 September 2005	18,000
Drawings for the year to 30 September 2005	15,000

Required:

Prepare a balance sheet in narrative form.

A business will normally prepare a balance sheet as at the close of business on the last day of its accounting year. In Australia and New Zealand, businesses are free to choose their accounting year. When making a decision on which year-end date to choose, commercial convenience can often be a deciding factor. Thus a business operating in the retail trade may choose to have a year-end date early in the calendar year (e.g. 31 January) because trade tends to be slack during that period and more staff time is available to help with the tasks involved with the preparation of the annual accounting statements (e.g. checking the amount of inventory held). Since trade is slack, it is also a time when the amount of inventory held by the business is likely to be atypically low as compared with other times of the year. Thus the balance sheet, though showing a fair view of what it purports to show, may not show a picture of what is more typically the position of the business over the year.

FACTORS INFLUENCING THE FORM AND CONTENT OF THE BALANCE SHEET

We will briefly consider three significant factors that have influenced the accounts included in the balance sheet and the financial measures assigned to those accounts. These influences are:

1. traditional accounting conventions and doctrines that have underpinned accounting practice for decades
2. more recent theoretical developments in relation to conceptual framework projects
3. professional and statutory accounting standards.

CONVENTIONAL ACCOUNTING PRACTICE

Accounting is based on a number of **conventions** or doctrines which have evolved over time. By conventions or doctrines is meant the principles, assumptions or accepted ideas on which accounting rules, records and reports were or are based. These concepts have been collectively known in the past as GAAP (generally accepted accounting principles/practices). They have evolved in order to deal with practical problems experienced by preparers and users rather than to reflect some theoretical ideal. In preparing the balance sheet earlier, we have adhered to various conventions although they have not been explicitly mentioned. Below we identify and discuss the main conventions (principles or assumptions or doctrines) that have been employed.

Business entity convention

For accounting purposes, the business and its owner(s) are treated as quite separate and distinct. This is why owners are treated as claimants against their own business in respect of their investment in the business. The **business entity convention** must be distinguished from the legal position that may exist between businesses and their owners. For sole proprietorships and partnerships, the law does not make any distinction between the business and its owner(s). For limited companies, on the other hand, there is a clear legal distinction between the business and its owners. (As we saw in Chapter 2, the limited company is regarded as having a separate legal existence.) For accounting purposes, these legal distinctions are irrelevant and the business entity convention applies to all forms of business entity.

Money measurement convention

Accounting normally deals with only those items that are capable of being expressed in monetary terms, hence the convention **money measurement**. Money has the advantage that it is a useful common denominator with which to express the wide variety of resources held by a business. However, not all resources held by a business may be capable of being measured in monetary terms and so some may be excluded from the balance sheet.

ACTIVITY 3.14

Can you think of resources held by a business that are not normally included on the balance sheet because they cannot be quantified in monetary terms?

Accounting is a developing subject and the boundaries of financial measurement can change. In recent years, attempts have been made to measure particular resources of a business previously excluded from the balance sheet. For example, we have seen the development of human resource accounting which attempts to measure the 'human assets' of the business. It is often claimed that employees are the most valuable 'assets' of a business. By measuring these assets and putting the amount on the balance sheet, it is sometimes argued that we would have a more complete picture of financial position. For similar reasons, we have also seen attempts by certain large businesses to measure the value of brand names they hold. However, some of the measurement methods proposed have been controversial and often conflict with other accounting conventions. There are mixed views as to whether extending the boundaries of financial measurement will succeed in making the balance sheet a more useful representation of the financial position of a business.

Another approach to overcoming some of the limitations of money measurement is to publish a narrative financial report. Rather than trying to 'quantify the unquantifiable', a narrative financial report could be published to help users assess financial health. Thus, in order to give a more complete picture of financial position, a narrative statement might incorporate a discussion of such matters as investment policy, financial structure, liquidity and valuable resources that have not been quantified.

The size of published annual reports continue to grow, and much of the information provided is outside of the financial reports themselves, and includes extensive disclosures related to human resources, contributions to the community, and other positive social and environmental policies and actions.

Historic cost convention

Assets are generally shown on the balance sheet at a value that is based on their historic (acquisition) cost or its equivalent. This method of measuring asset value has been adopted by accountants in preference to methods based on some form of current value. Many commentators find this particular convention difficult to support, as outdated historical costs are unlikely to help in the assessment of current financial position. It is often argued that recording assets at their current value would provide a more realistic view of financial position and would be more relevant for a wide range of decisions. However, a system of measurement based on current values can present a number of problems.

ACTIVITY 3.15

Can you think of reasons why current value accounting may pose problems for both preparers and users of financial reports?

By reporting assets at their historic cost, it is argued that more reliable information is produced. Reporting in this way reduces the need for subjective opinion as the amount paid for a particular asset is usually a matter of demonstrable fact. However, information based on past costs may not always be relevant to the needs of users in terms of decisions about the allocation of scarce resources.

Later in the chapter we will consider the valuation of assets in the balance sheet in more detail. We will see that the **historic cost convention** is not always rigidly adhered to and that departures from this convention often occur.

Going concern or continuity convention

The **going concern (or continuity) convention** holds that the business will continue operations for the foreseeable future. In other words, there is no intention or need to liquidate the business. This convention is important because the value of non-current assets on a liquidation basis (which is the alternative to the going concern basis) is often low in relation to the recorded values and an expectation of winding up would mean that anticipated losses on sale should be fully recorded. However, where there is no expectation of liquidation, the value of non-current assets can continue to be shown at their recorded values (i.e. based on historic cost). This convention therefore provides support for the historic cost convention under normal circumstances.

Dual aspect convention

The **dual aspect convention** states that each transaction has two aspects, both of which will affect the balance sheet. Thus, the purchase of a car for cash results in an increase in one asset (car) and a decrease in another (cash). The repayment of a loan results in the decrease in a liability (loan) and the decrease in an asset (cash/bank).

ACTIVITY 3.16

What are the two aspects of each of the following transactions?

- Purchase $1,000 inventory on credit.
- Owner withdraws $2,000 in cash.
- Sale of inventory (purchased for $1,000) for $2,000 cash.

Recording the dual aspect of each transaction ensures that the balance sheet will continue to balance. Another name for the 'dual aspect' is double entry accounting.

Conservatism/prudence convention

The terms 'conservatism' and 'prudence' are frequently used interchangeably. The **conservatism/prudence convention** holds that financial reports should err on the side of caution. The convention represents a pessimistic view of financial position and evolved to counteract the excessive optimism of some managers and owners which resulted in an overstatement of financial position. Operation of this convention results in the recording of both actual and anticipated losses in full, whereas profits are not recognised until they are realised (i.e. there is reasonable certainty the profit will be received). In essence, conservatism means that revenues are deferred or understated, and that expenses are brought forward or overstated. The direct implication of these two practices is that assets will be understated and liabilities overstated. When the conservatism convention conflicts with another convention, it is conservatism that will normally prevail. We will see an example of this when we consider the valuation of current assets later in the chapter.

ACTIVITY 3.17

Can you think of a situation where certain users might find that a pessimistic view of the financial position of a business will work to their disadvantage?

The extent of this bias towards understatement may be difficult to judge. It is likely to vary according to the views of the individual carrying out the valuation.

An interesting aspect of prudent or conservative accounting practices is that they reverse, so if profits or losses in this period are understated (revenues deferred, expenses brought forward), in a future period the profits will be overstated as the deferred revenues are then recognised, but the related expenses had been recognised in an earlier period. This will be covered in chapter 4.

Stable monetary unit convention

The **stable monetary unit convention** holds that money, which is the unit of measurement in accounting, will not change in value over time. However, throughout much of the world, inflation has been a persistent problem over the years. This has meant the value of money has declined in relation to other assets. In past years, high rates of inflation resulted in statements that were drawn up on an historic cost basis, reflecting figures for assets that were much lower than if current values were employed. The value of freehold land and buildings, in particular, increased rapidly during much of the 1970s and 1980s. Where this asset was held for some time by a business, there was often a significant difference between its original cost and the current market value. This led to the criticism that asset values were seriously understated and, as a result, some businesses broke away from the use of historic cost as the basis for valuing this particular asset. Instead, land and buildings are periodically revalued in order to provide a more realistic balance sheet. Although this represents a departure from accounting convention, it is a practice which has become increasingly common.

ACTIVITY 3.18

Refer to the vertical format balance sheet of Brie Manufacturing shown earlier. What would be the effect of revaluing the freehold land to a figure of $110,000 on the balance sheet?

In practice, the revaluation of land and buildings often has a significant effect on the size of the figures for tangible non-current assets. In past years, the effect on the balance sheet has usually been beneficial as property has risen in value throughout much of the past three decades. However, in years when we have witnessed a fall in property values we have seen some reluctance among those businesses who revalued their land and buildings upwards in earlier years to make downward revaluations in recessionary years. A common reason cited is that the fall in value is only considered to be temporary.

Inflation creates problems other than those discussed above relating to land and buildings. These problems generally relate to the identification of profit and will be dealt with in more detail in later chapters.

The essential issue is that the measuring unit in accounting, money, is a 'good' in its own right and therefore is subject to supply and demand conditions. As a result the measuring unit used by accountants changes in value over time (general or specific purchasing power changes). Over the years critics of the 'stable monetary unit assumption' have proposed alternative accounting models, and some of these will be considered later in this chapter and in Chapter 4.

Objectivity/reliability convention

The **objectivity convention** seeks to reduce personal bias and error in financial reports. As far as possible, financial reports should be based on objective, verifiable evidence rather than on matters of opinion.

ACTIVITY 3.19

Which of the above conventions does the objectivity convention support and which does it conflict with?

The application of the objectivity convention provides reliable measures of assets, liabilities and owners' equity. This satisfies the stewardship (or accountability) role of accounting, but may not be all that relevant to users assessing the decision usefulness role of accounting in terms of the allocation of scarce resources (e.g. suppliers, investors, lenders, employees, government, customers).

Accounting period convention

Reporting entities operate over long periods of time, and as a result periodic reports on financial performance and position need to be prepared. The time period selected is normally one year, and different entities have their financial years ending at different times (e.g. 31 December, 30 June, 31 January).

The implications of this convention are that estimates and allocations will have to be made, as transactions will not be complete as at the end of each period. In relation to revenues we may need to compute the percentage of completion (e.g. building contracts), the amount of returns, the amount of early settlement discounts, the amount of doubtful debts, the warranty claims and so on. In relation to assets we may need to compute the service potential or economic benefits used up during the period (e.g. cost of goods sold, depreciation, net realisable value, other write-downs).

The other aspect concerns whether the period end date gives rise to asset and liability measures that are representative of balances during the year. In a cyclical business (production or sales) there will be times in the year where assets and liabilities are higher or lower than at other times.

Realisation convention

This principle is normally associated with income and the issue is essentially when should income (revenue or gains) be recognised.

The traditional guidance related to the entity having a contractual arrangement with an external party, having completed its part of the contract (provision of goods or services), having received cash from the client in satisfaction for the goods or services provided (or having an unavoidable claim against the client), and being able to reliably estimate any outstanding costs (e.g. returns, bad debts, warranty).

Matching convention

While the matching principle relates directly to the income statement that is covered in Chapter 4, it has indirect implications for the balance sheet.

Matching relates to bringing together in a given period the income earned in that period with the costs (expenses) which were incurred in generating that income. In many cases there is a direct association (e.g. cost of goods sold, sales commission, delivery expenses, direct labour), however in other cases the association is less obvious (e.g. advertising, insurance, rent, administration), or does not exist (e.g. exploration or research that is abandoned and does not result in any future income). In the cases where there is no direct association between income and expenses, a decision has to be made about recognising those costs as expenses (e.g. charging the costs against revenues on a subjective basis or simply recognising them as expenses in the period when they were incurred).

THE CONCEPTUAL FRAMEWORK

During the last decade or so the accounting statutory and professional bodies have been working on the development of a conceptual framework for financial recording and reporting. A conceptual framework represents a logical theoretical structure to support and direct accounting practice.

Up until 2004, four statements of accounting concepts had been issued under the Australian Conceptual Framework Project:

* SAC 1 'Definition of the Reporting Entity'
* SAC 2 'Objective of General Purpose Financial Reporting'

✳ SAC 3 'Qualitative Characteristics of Financial Information'

✳ SAC 4 'Definition and Recognition of the Elements of Financial Statements'.

During 2004 the Australian Accounting Standards Board, in moving to adopt the International Accounting Standards, replaced the Australian Conceptual Framework with the International Framework. As a result SAC3 and SAC4 have been replaced by the Australian adoption of that framework which is now called the AASB Framework. As SAC1 and SAC2 were not covered by the International Accounting Framework, they have continued in their previous form.

While the framework and statements of accounting concepts are not mandatory, they are having a significant influence on new and revised accounting standards being issued.

In relation to the balance sheet the main significance lies in the new definitions and recognition rules that apply to assets, liabilities and owners' equity. The definitions used in this chapter are largely taken from the AASB Framework.

ACCOUNTING STANDARDS

The history and significance of accounting standard setting in Australia was covered in some detail in Chapter 2. In relation to the balance sheet there are a large number of standards that directly impact on recording and reporting assets, liabilities and owners' equity. In reviewing specific balance sheet accounts we will continue to consider the implications of the applicable Australian Accounting Standards.

 ACTIVITY 3.20

Can you identify Australian Accounting Standards that relate to the balance sheet accounts or presentation?

THE BASIS OF VALUATION OF ASSETS ON THE BALANCE SHEET

 ACTIVITY 3.21

Can you think of different financial measurements that could be used for assets?

While the historical cost convention underlies the conventional accounting system, other conventions and doctrines have led to departures from using the initial price (historical cost) measure. Additionally, there may not be an initial transacted price where assets are donated, internally developed or acquired in an aggregate transaction. In particular, the following underlying ideas have led to these departures.

Prudence convention

The notion of caution or pessimism has emphasised that losses or declines in value should be recognised as early as possible, but gains should not be recognised until they are realised and certain. The implication here is that assets will be written down in advance of being realised (i.e. exchanged for cash).

Evidence of the application of this principle can be seen in how the following assets are valued:

Current assets

✳ Debtors—the 'net realisable value' (what you expect to collect)

✳ Inventory—the lower of 'cost' and 'net realisable amount' (expected sales proceeds less expected selling costs).

Non-current assets

✳ Property, plant and equipment—the lower of 'cost' and 'recoverable amount' (the amount expected to be recovered in future cash flows through use and/or sale)

✳ Goodwill—only externally acquired goodwill is to be recorded; internally generated goodwill may not be included as an asset.

ACTIVITY 3.22

Can you identify another example of assets being recorded at less than cost, or being immediately expensed in response to the prudence assumption?

Accounting period/going concern conventions

The issue here is that the life of an enterprise is divided up into equal time intervals (normally one year). As a result of this arbitrary subdivision there is a need for subjective allocation of the consumption of the future economic benefits embodied in long-term assets during each period.

Evidence of the application of these assumptions can be seen in the treatment of non-current tangible and intangible assets:

✳ Tangibles (property, plant and equipment)—these assets are depreciated and their valuation is therefore based on unexpired or **unimpaired** (unallocated) cost (or other valuation)

✳ Intangibles which are identifiable (patent, copyright, franchise, masthead, trademark, development)—these assets are amortised and their valuation is therefore based on unexpired or unimpaired cost (or other valuation).

Depreciation and amortisation reflect the fact that assets have a limited life. The life of an asset may be limited by law (e.g. copyright) or it may be limited by physical capacity (e.g. equipment) or by technological factors (e.g. computer obsolescence). The depreciation or amortisation charge or impairment write-down for the period and consequent reduction in the financial measure of the asset normally reflects the cost of the asset used up during the period. This aspect will be discussed further in Chapter 4.

Full disclosure/relevant financial information

There has been an increasing tendency for many non-current assets to be valued on the basis of market values. Examples of such valuations are:

✳ Property, plant and equipment can be revalued to 'fair valuation', fair value being based on an equivalent current exchange price between independent, knowledgeable and willing parties.

✳ Assets of a life insurer must be measured at net market value, net market value being the amount that could be expected to be received from disposal after deducting the expected costs of disposal.

✳ Leased assets and other assets subject to deferred settlement should be valued on the basis of the present value of expected future settlement payments, using an appropriate discount rate.

✳ Biological assets are to be recorded at fair value.

THE BASIS OF VALUATION OF LIABILITIES IN THE BALANCE SHEET

While liabilities in general do not have the same range of alternative measures as assets, there are still a number of alternative bases for measurement, both in practice and within the accounting standards. These include:

✳ the contracted amount (initial price or historical cost). Many of the liability measures are based on this concept (accounts payable, bank overdraft, loans).

✳ an estimate of the expected future sacrifice. A number of liability magnitudes are based on expected future sacrifices in cash or in goods and services provided (provision for taxation, provision for warranty, provision for sick leave).

✳ in relation to liabilities with deferred settlement, there is an increasing tendency for those liabilities to be determined on the basis of the present value of the future known or expected cash outflows (financial lease liability, long-service leave, insurance claims, superannuation payments).

INTERPRETING THE BALANCE SHEET

We have seen that the conventional balance sheet has a number of limitations. This has led some users of financial information to conclude that the statement has little to offer in the way of useful information. However, this is not necessarily the case. The balance sheet can provide useful insights into the financing and investing activities of a business. In particular, the following aspects of financial position can be examined:

✳ *the liquidity of the business.* This is the ability of the business to meet its short-term obligations (current liabilities) from its liquid (cash and near cash) assets. Liquidity is particularly important because business failures occur when the business cannot meet its maturing obligations, whatever the root cause of that inability may be.

✳ *the 'mix' of assets held by the business.* The relationship between current assets and non-current assets is important. Businesses with too much of their funds tied up in non-current assets could be vulnerable to financial failure. This is because non-current assets are typically not easy to turn into cash in order to meet short-term obligations. Converting many non-current assets into cash may well lead to substantial losses for the business because such assets are not always worth, on the open market, what the business paid to acquire the asset or what the asset is worth to the business. For example, a specialised piece of equipment may have little value to any other business, yet it could be worth a great deal to the business.

✳ *the financial structure of the business.* The relative proportion of total finance contributed by the owners and outsiders can be calculated to see whether the business is heavily dependent on outside financing. Heavy borrowing can bring with it a commitment to pay large interest charges and make large capital repayments at regular intervals. These are legally enforceable obligations which can be a real burden as they have to be paid irrespective of the financial position of the business. Funds raised from the owners of the business, on the other hand, do not impose such obligations on the business.

The interpretation of the balance sheet will be considered in more detail in Chapter 6.

SELF-ASSESSMENT QUESTION 3.2

Consider the following balance sheet of a manufacturing business:

RUSSELL MANUFACTURING COMPANY
Balance sheet as at 30 April 2006

	$	$
Current assets		
Cash at bank	12,000	
Trade debtors	44,000	
Inventory	48,000	
		104,000
Non-current assets		
Fixtures and fittings	14,000	
Motor vehicles	13,000	
Plant and machinery	46,000	
Freehold premises	88,000	
		161,000
Total assets		265,000
Current liabilities		
Trade creditors	24,000	
Bank overdraft	18,000	
		42,000
Non-current liabilities		
Loan		160,000
Total liabilities		202,000
Owner's equity		
Opening balance	42,000	
Add profit	32,000	
	74,000	
Less drawings	11,000	
		63,000
Total liabilities and owner's equity		265,000

What can you deduce about the financial position of the business from the information contained in the balance sheet shown above?

SUMMARY

In this chapter we have achieved the following objectives in the way shown.

OBJECTIVE	METHOD ACHIEVED
Explain the nature and purpose of the balance sheet	Explained the nature and purpose as follows: • Statement of financial position • List of balances in the assets, liabilities and owners' equity accounts • At a point in time
Demonstrate an understanding of assets in terms of definition, recognition, measurement and classification	Identified and analysed the nature of assets in the following terms: • Definition—based on future economic benefits, control and past transactions or events • Recognition—based on probability of occurrence and reliability of measurement • Accounts—based on property or rights (e.g. cash, accounts receivable, inventory, prepayments, land, buildings, equipment, patents, investments, goodwill) • Classification—the most common being based on liquidity (current, non-current) • Measurement—traditionally based on historical cost but with considerable variety as a result of accounting conventions and standards (e.g. realisable value, fair value, current cost, recoverable amount, present value)
Demonstrate an understanding of liabilities in terms of definition, recognition, measurement and classification	Identified and analysed the nature of liabilities in the following terms: • Definition—based on the sacrifice of future economic benefits, a present obligation and past transactions or events • Recognition—based on probability of occurrence and reliability of measurement • Accounts—based on legal, equitable or constructive obligations (e.g. accounts payable, bank overdraft, unearned revenue, accrued expenses, loans, money provisions) • Classification—the most common being based on the timing of satisfaction (e.g. current, non-current) • Measurement—traditionally contract based but with some variation as a result of accounting conventions and standards (e.g. present value of expected cash outflows)
Discuss the nature and classification of owners' equity	Identified and analysed the nature of owners' equity in the following terms: • Definition—based on the residual interest in the assets • Classification—based on contributions, retained profits and reserves
Explain the basic accounting equation	Identified the basic equation as: • Proprietary $\quad OE = A - L$ • Entity $\quad\quad A = L + OE$
Contrast the alternative balance sheet formats	Examined the following formats: • Horizontal (T account) • Vertical (narrative)

OBJECTIVE	METHOD ACHIEVED	
Discuss the main factors that influence the balance sheet accounts and magnitudes	Identified and analysed the following factors:	
	• Conventional accounting practice (assumptions/ conventions/ principles	– business entity – accounting period – continuity (going concern) – monetary measurement – historical cost – stable monetary unit – prudence (conservatism) – dual aspect – objectivity (reliability)
	• Conceptual framework	– AASB Framework – SAC 3 (qualitative characteristics) – SAC 4 (definition and recognition of the elements)
	• Accounting standards	– professional (AAS) – statutory (AASB)
Analyse balance sheet of reporting entities	Identified the ways in which the balance sheet can provide useful insights into the entity's:	
	• Liquidity (ability to meet short-term obligation)	
	• Asset mix (productive or unproductive)	
	• Financial structure (optimal mix of owners and external funds; appropriate levels of short-term and long-term funds)	
State the potential limitations of the balance sheet in portraying the financial position of an entity	Explained that the limitations of the balance sheet in portraying financial position largely relate to:	
	• Limitations related to the element definitions	
	• Limitations related to transaction recognition	
	• The range of alternative asset and liability financial measures	

DISCUSSION QUESTIONS

EASY

<Obj 2>   **3.1**   What are the main characteristics of assets from an accounting perspective?

<Obj 2>   **3.2**   What sort of items would be included in the intangible asset category?

<Obj 4>   **3.3**   Your textbook examples use the term 'owners' equity' in the accounting equation and in the balance sheet. What other titles could be used for this accounting term?

<Obj 5>   **3.4**   Do all accounting transactions affect the balance sheet?

INTERMEDIATE

<Obj 2>   **3.5**   Valuable resources of a business are sometimes not included in its balance sheet assets.

    (a) Why does this occur?

    (b) Can you provide examples?

<Obj 2>   **3.6**   Assets are classified as current or non-current.

    (a) What does the term 'current' refer to in accounting?

    (b) Refer to a published report and list the categories of non-current assets.

    (c) How do these two terms relate to the liquidity of the organisation?

<Obj 2>   **3.7**   Goodwill can be 'internally generated' or 'externally acquired'.

    (a) What is goodwill?

    (b) Distinguish between the two categories of goodwill.

    (c) Why do the accounting regulations only permit 'externally acquired' goodwill to appear in the statement of financial position?

<Obj 2>   **3.8**   Why is the statement of financial position called a 'balance sheet'?

<Obj 2>   **3.9**   Identify as many different ways of measuring an asset in financial terms as you can think of.

<Obj 2>   **3.10** Non-current assets such as plant and equipment are shown at cost (or fair value) less accumulated depreciation.

    (a) What is the net figure called?

    (b) What does depreciation represent?

    (c) What sort of account is 'accumulated depreciation'?

<Obj 2, 7>   **3.11** Inventories are required to be recorded at 'the lower of cost or net realisable value'.

    (a) What is net realisable value?

    (b) How does this practice relate to the following conventions (i.e. is it consistent with or in conflict with them)?

       • historical cost

       • prudence.

<Obj 3>   **3.12** Claims against the business assets are of two types.

    (a) What are the two types?

    (b) Provide examples of each.

    (c) Discuss the key differences between these two categories of claims.

<Obj 3>   **3.13** You observe in a balance sheet:

Current liability:	Provision for long-service leave	73,000
Non-current liability:	Provision for long-service leave	122,000

    (a) Define the accounting term 'non-current'.

    (b) Explain the difference between these two figures.

<Obj 3>   **3.14** Liabilities can be described as what the business 'owes' external parties. Is this an adequate definition of liabilities for accounting purposes?

<Obj 5>   **3.15** Why is the accounting equation always in balance?

<Obj 7>   **3.16** What is an accounting convention?

<Obj 7>   **3.17** Distinguish between a 'legal entity' and an 'accounting entity' in relation to different business types.

<Obj 7>   **3.18** The prudence convention has significantly influenced financial transaction recording and reporting.

    (a) What is the prudence convention?

    (b) Provide examples of how it has influenced transaction recording and reporting.

<Obj 7>   **3.19** The stable monetary unit convention does not hold up over time.

(a) What is the stable monetary unit convention?

(b) How have companies addressed this deficiency during periods of inflation?

CHALLENGING

<Obj 2>   **3.20** In recent years there have been attempts to place a value on the 'human assets' of a business in order to derive a figure which can be included on the balance sheet. Do you think people should be treated as assets? Would 'human assets' meet the conventional definition of an asset for inclusion on the balance sheet?

<Obj 4>   **3.21** In what ways is 'owners' equity' different from 'liabilities'? Can you think of an owners' equity account that could or should be classified as a liability?

<Obj 6>   **3.22** An accountant prepared a balance sheet for a business using the horizontal layout. In this statement, the capital of the owner was shown next to the liabilities. This confused the owner who argued: 'My capital is my major asset and so should be shown as an asset on the balance sheet'. How would you explain this misunderstanding to the owner?

<Obj 9>   **3.23** The balance sheet can be used to assess the following aspects of the reporting entity:

- liquidity
- asset mix
- financial structure (solvency).

(a) What do these terms mean?

(b) How could they be assessed from the balance sheet figures?

(c) Which external stakeholders would have a particular interest in each aspect?

<Obj 10>   **3.24** A balance sheet reveals:

	$
Total assets	310,000
Total liabilities	170,000
Capital	140,000

What reservations would you have about all three figures as a measure of financial position at that point in time?

<Obj 10>   **3.25** 'The balance sheet shows how much a business is worth.' Do you agree with this statement? Discuss.

APPLICATION EXERCISES

EASY

<Obj 2>   **3.1** Would the following accounts would be classified as liabilities? If not, how would they be classified?

	Account	Yes	No—reason
1	Accounts payable		
2	Provision for depreciation		
3	Debentures issued		
4	Loan guarantee		

5	Unused bank overdraft
6	Provision for major maintenance
7	Provision for warranty
8	Rent revenue received in advance

<Obj 2>   **3.2**   Match the following asset measurements with the most appropriate (one or more) accounting principles listed.

	Asset measurement		Accounting principle
1	Inventories at the lower of cost or market	A	Historical cost
2	Equipment at residual cost	B	Prudence or conservatism
3	Debtors at estimated amount collectible	C	Accounting period
4	Land at fair value	D	Going concern
5	Prepayments at unexpired cost	E	Full disclosure
6	Patent at unamortised cost	F	Matching
7	Goodwill at recoverable amount		
8	Leased assets at net present value		

<Obj 5>   **3.3**   Business transactions have a dual, or double, effect. (They affect two or more accounts but leave the accounting equation in balance.)

Identify a transaction for each of the following accounting equation changes.

Accounting equation: Assets (A) = Liabilities (L) + Owners' equity (OE)

Equation's effect   Examples
(a) $A{\uparrow} = L{\uparrow}$
(b) $A{\uparrow} = OE{\uparrow}$
(c) $A{\uparrow} = A{\downarrow}$
(d) $A{\downarrow} = L{\downarrow}$
(e) $A{\downarrow} = OE{\downarrow}$
(f) $L{\uparrow} = OE{\downarrow}$
(g) $L{\downarrow} = OE{\uparrow}$

<Obj 5, 8>   **3.4**   Complete the table by inserting the missing figures.

	(a)	(b)	(c)	(d)
Current assets	13,900	18,300	13,200	?
Non-current assets	51,600	71,600	110,700	69,600
Current liabilities	14,200	11,900	9,600	17,500
Non-current liabilities	17,900	?	41,500	51,200
Opening capital	20,700	29,200	?	26,700
Profit or loss	19,600	17,900	37,400	(9,500)
Drawings	?	8,700	11,700	7,200

<Obj 6, 8>   **3.5**   The following is a list of assets and claims of a manufacturing business at a particular point in time:

	$
Bank overdraft	22,000
Freehold land and buildings	245,000
Inventory of raw materials	18,000
Trade creditors	23,000
Plant and machinery	127,000
Loan from National Australia Bank	100,000
Inventory of finished goods	28,000
Delivery vehicles	54,000
Trade debtors	34,000

Prepare a balance sheet in the standard vertical format incorporating these figures.
Hint: There is a missing figure which needs to be deduced and inserted.

<Obj 6, 8>   **3.6**   The following is a list of the assets and claims of Crafty Engineering Ltd as at 30 June 2006:

	$
Creditors	86,000
Motor vehicles	38,000
Loan from St George Bank	260,000
Machinery and tools	207,000
Bank overdraft	116,000
Inventory	153,000
Freehold premises	320,000
Debtors	185,000

Required:
(a) Using the vertical format prepare the balance sheet of the business as at 30 June 2006 from the above information.
(b) Discuss the significant features revealed by this financial report.

INTERMEDIATE

<Obj 2, 3>   **3.7**   Complete the table of assets below by classifying each account in terms of being:
- current
- non-current: investments
- non-current: property, plant and equipment
- non-current: intangibles.

Account	*Classification*
Cash at bank	
Patent	
Equipment	
Prepayment	
Land	
Goodwill	

Accounts receivable
Shares in Telstra
Accumulated depreciation—equipment
Inventories
Leasehold improvements
Preliminary expense
Interest prepaid
Government bonds

<Obj 2, 3>   **3.8** The following is a list of assets and claims against the assets of a manufacturing business at a particular point in time.

Account	Amount $
Cash at bank	2,000
Bank loan—mortgage	25,000
Initial capital	89,000
Freehold land and buildings	80,000
Owner's drawings	15,000
Accounts receivable	11,000
Plant and equipment	27,000
Prepayments	1,000
Accrued expenses	3,000
Profit for the period	27,000
Bank overdraft	15,000
Finished goods inventory	23,000

Use the above information to prepare a balance sheet in vertical format.

<Obj 5>   **3.9** You are provided with the following balance sheet at the start of the week and the seven transactions for the week.

Complete the table to show how each transaction affected the accounts together with the balances at the end of the period.

	Beginning	Transactions				Ending		
Assets	$	1	2	3	4	5	6	7
Cash	3,000							
Accounts receivable	5,000							
Inventory	7,000							
Freehold premises	60,000							
Furniture and fittings	18,000							
	93,000							
Liabilities								
Trade creditors	3,000							
Bank loan	30,000							
	33,000							
Capital	60,000							
	93,000							

Transactions for the week:

1. Purchased inventory on credit for $5,000
2. Collected $4,000 from customers
3.   Sales: Cash $2,000   (Cost $1,500)
                        Credit $6,000   (Cost $4,500)
4. Paid creditors $7,000
5. Owner's additional cash contribution $10,000
6. Purchased furniture for cash $6,000
7. Loan repayment of $2,000.

<Obj 5>   **3.10** Following the example shown below, complete the table for the effects of the transactions listed in relation to the balance sheet accounts of A. Dunn, solicitor (sole proprietor).

Transaction	Asset	Liability	Owner's capital
e.g. Cash purchase of computer	↑ Equipment ↓ Cash at bank		
(a) Billed client for services			
(b) Paid building rental for the month			
(c) Paid quarterly electricity account			
(d) Purchased stationery supplies on credit			
(e) Paid staff monthly salary and wages			
(f) Received payment from client			
(g) Paid stationery supplier			
(h) Withdrew cash for personal use			
(i) Paid personal tax			
(j) Repairs to computer on account			
(k) Rendered services to customer for cash			
(l) Purchased furniture on account			
(m) Paid for computer repairs			
(n) Returned some of the furniture (faulty)			

<Obj 5, 8>   **3.11** The balance sheet of a business at the start of a week is as follows:

Assets	$	Claims	$
Trade debtors	33,000	Trade creditors	23,000
Inventory	28,000	Bank overdraft	43,000
Furniture and fittings	63,000	Owner's equity	203,000
Freehold premises	145,000		
Total assets	269,000	Total liabilities and owner's equity	269,000

During the week the following transactions take place:

*   Sold inventory for $11,000 cash. This inventory had cost $8,000.
*   Sold inventory for $23,000 on credit. This inventory had cost $17,000.
*   Received cash from trade debtors totalling $18,000.
*   The owners of the business introduced $100,000 of their own money which was placed in a business bank account.
*   The owners bought a motor vehicle, valued at $10,000, to be used in the business.

- Bought inventory on credit for $14,000.
- Paid trade creditors $13,000.

Prepare the balance sheet after all these transactions have been reflected.

<Obj 6, 8> **3.12** On 1 March 2006 Joe Conday started a new business. During March he carried out the following transactions:

March 1 Deposited $20,000 in a bank account.
     2 Purchased fixtures and fittings for $6,000 cash, and inventory valued at $8,000 on credit.
     3 Borrowed $5,000 from a relative and deposited it in the bank.
     4 Purchased a car for $7,000 cash and withdrew $200 for own use.
     5 Purchased another car costing $9,000. The car purchased on 4 March was given in part exchange at a value of $6,500. The balance of purchase price for the new car was paid in cash.
     6 Conday won $2,000 in a lottery and paid the amount into the business bank account. He also repaid $1,000 of the loan.

Required:
(a) Prepare a balance sheet for the business at the end of each day using the horizontal format.
(b) Show how the balance sheet you have prepared as at 6 March 2006 would be presented in the vertical format.

CHALLENGING

<Obj 2> **3.13** For each of the following transactions determine:
(a) Should an asset be recognised?
(b) If yes, what would it be called?
(c) If no, why is no asset recognised?

	Transaction	Yes—asset name	No—reason
1	Signed a contract for a $300,000 building		
2	Undertook basic research of $40,000 on a new product		
3	Delivered goods to a customer related to credit sales contract		
4	Special staff training programme related to new regulations cost $10,000		
5	Cash purchase of a new computer for $23,000		
6	Paid initial payment of $5,000 related to the financial lease of a bus		

<Obj 4> **3.14** The 'owners' equity' is made up of two components:

- owners' contributions
- reserves.

The major reserve account is normally 'retained profits'. However, on reviewing a number of balance sheets you identified other reserve accounts listed in the table below. In relation to each of the reserves listed answer the following:

(a) What does it represent?
(b) How was it created?
(c) Is it distributable?

	(a)	(b)	(c)
Asset revaluation			
Dividend equalisation			
Capital profits			
Asset replacement			
Capital reduction			
Foreign translation			

<Obj 8>

3.15 You are presented with the following balance sheet which is an incorrect draft. Assuming the accounts and amounts are correct, re-present the balance sheet making the necessary corrections.

	$	$
Current assets		
Cash at bank	9,000	
Trade creditors	11,000	
Plant and machinery	26,000	46,000
Non-current assets		
Inventory	15,000	
Asset revaluation increment	20,000	
Motor vehicles	18,000	53,000
Total assets		99,000
Current liabilities		
Trade debtors	6,000	
Prepayments	1,000	7,000
Non-current liabilities		
Bank overdraft	14,000	
Land and buildings	50,000	
Loan	10,000	74,000
Owner's equity		
Opening balance	40,000	
Minus profit	32,000	
Add drawings	10,000	18,000
Total liabilities and owner's equity		99,000

<Obj 9>

3.16 Provide a report based on your evaluation of the following three balance sheets in terms of:

(a) liquidity

(b) solvency

(c) asset mix.

	A $'000	B $'000	C $'000
Current assets	500	300	700
Non-current assets	500	700	300
Total assets	1000	1000	1000
Current liabilities	300	100	100
Non-current liabilities	200	200	600
Total liabilities	500	300	700
Owners' contributions	400	100	200
Reserves	100	600	100
Total owners' equity	500	700	300

Qantas Financial Report 2004, p. 3

*Statements of Financial Position
as at 30 June 2004*

	Notes	Qantas Group 2004 $M	Qantas Group 2003 $M	Qantas 2004 $M	Qantas 2003 $M
CURRENT ASSETS					
Cash	7	335.9	121.9	254.7	99.6
Receivables	8	2,116.3	2,867.0	2,203.4	2,875.2
Net receivables under hedge/swap contracts		302.1	330.9	301.8	331.2
Inventories	9	375.5	430.3	348.4	400.9
Other	11	192.2	204.3	210.5	143.7
Total current assets		3,322.0	3,954.4	3,318.8	3,850.6
NON-CURRENT ASSETS					
Receivables	8	304.6	176.5	1,977.9	1,879.9
Net receivables under hedge/swap contracts		997.0	1,014.9	952.3	958.2
Investments accounted for using the equity method	30	339.7	68.3	–	–
Other investments	10	110.1	101.9	777.2	374.8
Property, plant and equipment	12	12,256.6	11,432.5	10,673.0	9,548.5
Intangible assets	13	152.4	119.6	47.2	–
Deferred tax assets		0.9	44.7	–	14.6
Other	11	90.9	61.0	64.9	24.9
Total non-current assets		14,252.2	13,019.4	14,492.5	12,800.9
Total assets		17,574.2	16,973.8	17,811.3	16,651.5
CURRENT LIABILITIES					
Payables	14	2,167.5	2,109.1	2,078.9	1,984.2
Interest-bearing liabilities	15	821.9	971.1	826.4	980 2
Net payables under hedge/swap contracts		250.8	46.6	262.9	44.2
Provisions	16	381.6	435.9	328.8	372.5
Current tax liabilities/(receivables)	17	30.1	(4.7)	27.2	(32.2)
Revenue received in advance		1,493.3	1,158.4	1,348.1	1,056.3
Deferred lease benefits/income		45.0	50.6	40.2	45.9
Total current liabilities		5,190.2	4,767.0	4,912.5	4,451.1
NON-CURRENT LIABILITIES					
Interest-bearing liabilities	15	5,081.8	5,391.9	6,134.3	6,055.6
Net payables under hedge/swap contracts		131.6	340.9	131.6	340.9
Provisions	16	331.7	354.1	302.3	324.4
Deferred tax liabilities		806.9	603.0	788.3	489.4
Deferred lease benefits/income		191.7	254.8	166.2	221.5
Total non-current liabilities		6,543.7	6,944 7	7,522.7	7,431.8
Total liabilities		11,733.9	11,711.7	12,435.2	11,882.9
Net assets		5,840.3	5,262.1	5,376.1	4,768.6

EQUITY					
Contributed equity	18	3,994.9	3,757.9	3.994.9	3.757.9
Reserves	19	54.4	54.0	82.9	82.9
Retained profits	20	1,776.3	1,435.9	1,298.3	927.8
Equity attributable to members of the Company		5,825.6	5,247.8	5,376.1	4,768 6
Outside equity interests in controlled entities	22	14.7	14.3	–	–
Total equity	21	5,840.3	5,262.1	5,376.1	4,768.6

The Statements of Financial Position are to be read in conjunction with the Notes to the Financial Statements on pages 5 to 60.

1 While these statements are labelled 'Statements of Financial Position', in future what will they be called?
2 Figures are provided for both 'Qantas' and the 'Qantas Group'.
   (a) What is the difference between these two entities?
   (b) Why are the two sets of figures provided?
3 The assets are classified as 'current and non-current'.
   (a) What is the difference between these two categories?
   (b) How else could the assets be categorised?
4 What sort of items would be included in the inventory of the 'Qantas Group'?
5 Both the current and non-current liability categories include an account category labelled 'Provisions'.
   (a) What does the term 'provision' mean?
   (b) Provide possible examples of liability provision accounts.
   (c) How can a provision be both a 'current liability' and a 'non-current liability'?
6 What would the liability account 'Deferred lease benefits/income' represent?
7 Why would an airline have such a high balance in the current liability labelled 'Revenue received in advance'?
8 Does this report represent an 'entity' or 'proprietary' approach to the accounting equation?
9 List names of possible 'Reserve' accounts.
10 Why would the receivables of 'Qantas' be greater than the receivables of the 'Qantas Group'?
11 Why would property, plant and equipment of the 'Qantas Group' be greater than property, plant and equipment of 'Qantas'?

Insuring for the loss of key people

Business Owner (section), *The Courier-Mail*
Wednesday, 19 January 2005, p. 34

No one is indispensable, runs the age-old adage—but the loss of key people can have a serious impact on company revenue.

ING's Andrew Lowe says it is good sense for business owners to protect themselves against the loss of key people as part of their overall financial planning. 'Loss of expected profit, diminished customer base and reduced confidence by shareholders and employees are just a few of the potential outcomes that could result from the loss of a key person in the business,' Mr Lowe says.

CASE STUDY 3.2

Key-person insurance is one way to minimise the impact if it is caused by the death, total and permanent disablement or if the person suffers a trauma condition.

Insurance can be an effective way to protect revenue and profit or any other measure of economic performance that may be affected.

This can also cover internal and external indebtedness and liquidity as well as the recruitment and training costs of a replacement person.

The tricky part is deciding the value of key people. This can be difficult, Mr Lowe says. This valuation method can be useful: add up what the key person contributes to the net profit of the business, or calculate their average gross remuneration.

Key-person insurance is usually owned by the business, but if a policy is taken to protect personal guarantees it may be more appropriate for the guarantor or spouse to own the policy. Policies may also be taken in the name of sole proprietor, the partners, a trustee, or the corporate entity. Who owns the policy depends on the way the business is set up and the purpose of the cover.

The proceeds of an insurance claim, whether for capital or revenue cover, will have taxation treatment implications as well.

1   ING's Andrew Lowe 'says it is good sense for business owners to protect themselves against the loss of key people as part of their overall financial planning'.
    (a)   How should they protect themselves?
    (b)   Why do they need to protect themselves?
    (c)   How do they determine what level of protection is needed?
2   The article suggests that with the loss of key personnel there may well be a loss of profit, a reduction in the customer base, and reduced confidence by shareholders and employees. If key staff therefore generate such significant future economic benefits should they not be classified as assets in the balance sheet?
3   The insurance coverage for key personnel is said to cover among other things the costs of recruiting and training replacement staff. Should staff recruitment and training costs in general be capitalised (deferred) and treated as assets in the short-term?
4   Should the insurance premium paid related to key staff be classified as a 'deferred asset' or an 'expense'?
5   Who should own the insurance policy related to 'key' personnel?
6   On what basis would you determine the amount of insurance to be taken out for a given key staff member?

CASE STUDY 3.3

Enron boss to turn himself in

Rodney Dalton
New York correspondent

The Australian
9 July 2004, p. 17

ENRON: THE KEY PLAYERS
To be indicted
Kenneth Lay
To be indicted overnight on charges relating to accounting fraud that drove Enron into bankruptcy.

Guilty pleas

Andrew Fastow

Pleaded guilty in January to two counts of wire fraud and conspiracy to commit wire and securities fraud. His wife Lea, a one-time director and assistant treasurer of corporate finance at Enron, faces one year in jail after pleading guilty to a single count of filing a false income tax return.

Awaiting trial

Jeffrey Skilling

Former CEO was indicted on 35 counts of securities fraud, insider trading, wire fraud and conspiracy in February. He pleaded not guilty and is free on bond.

Richard Causey

Former chief accountant was indicted in January. He faces 31 counts of fraud, conspiracy and insider trading.

The company

Enron could emerge from Chapter 11 bankruptcy protection by July 15, the deadline for when a bankruptcy judge may issue his approval of the company's reorganisation plan. Under the plan, creditors stand to receive 20c for every dollar owed—92 per cent in cash and the rest in equity in Prisma Energy International, which owns Enron's foreign assets. Enron's other assets have been sold, or are in the process of being sold.

Thirty months after the collapse of Enron shook US market capitalism to its core, former boss Ken Lay will turn himself in to the FBI today and appear in court to face criminal charges that he conspired to defraud investors.

A friend of President George W. Bush and a member of Houston society, Mr Lay, 62, is expected to suffer the indignity of wearing handcuffs as he is paraded like the catch of the day for the media on his way into the courtroom.

He will plead not guilty to the long-awaited charges, which are yet to be specified but were said to include fraud and insider trading.

'I have been advised that I have been indicted,' Mr Lay said last night. 'I will surrender in the morning. I have done nothing wrong and the indictment is not justified.'

Mr Lay became the public face of corporate greed after Enron—the energy trader he built into the seventh-largest US company by sales—filed for bankruptcy in December 2001.

Thousands lost their jobs and billions of dollars of shareholder wealth evaporated in what was then the largest bankruptcy filing in US history.

The collapse of telecommunications giant WorldCom almost two years ago dwarfed Enron in terms of assets destroyed but the Enron disaster dented America's faith in the capital markets by revealing that some companies' balance sheets were garbage wrapped in glossy paper.

As rumours that the indictment was imminent drew stronger in past weeks, Mr Lay broke his silence to profess his innocence, blaming underlings such as former chief financial officer Andrew Fastow for cooking up the off-balance-sheet schemes that hid Enron's ballooning debt.

The Enron collapse brought down accounting giant Arthur Andersen and prompted Washington to enact corporate governance reforms.

Mr Lay, whose wealth was largely tied up in Enron stock, suffered along with investors.

Worth more than $US400 million at the start of 2001, Mr Lay told *The New York Times* recently that of his remaining $US20 million, about $US19 million would be used for legal fees and to pay off debt.

The indictment is a huge step in a two-year investigation by the Justice Department which has so far yielded criminal charges against 30 individuals, including Fastow and Jeffrey Skilling, who resigned as Enron chief executive in August 2001 after only six months in charge.

Skilling's departure ended Mr Lay's thoughts of moving on from Enron, ensuring the Texas titan, who was once rumoured to be in line for a cabinet post in the Bush administration, was at the helm when the ship went down.

Enron investigators are believed to have focused on this period, when Mr Lay made numerous public announcements expressing confidence in Enron while he was selling the stock and while whistleblowers such as Sherron Watkins — later named one of *Time* magazine's Persons of the Year in 2002 — were sending him warning emails.

Federal prosecutors scored a coup in January when Fastow pleaded guilty to two counts of conspiracy and agreed to assist the investigation.

A similar strategy was used in the WorldCom investigation, with prosecutors waiting for CFO Scott Sullivan to agree to co-operate before they charged CEO Bernie Ebbers.

---

1   Briefly highlight key aspects of the Enron financial disaster.
2   Mr Lay, the CEO of Enron, is to be charged with fraud and insider trading:
    (a)   What is 'insider trading'?
    (b)   Why does the corporations law view 'insider trading' so severely?
3   It was stated in the article 'that some companies' balance sheets were garbage wrapped in glossy paper'.
    (a)   What is a balance sheet supposed to reveal about a reporting entity?
    (b)   What is the balance sheet equation?
    (c)   Why might the assets and asset balances be incorrect?
    (d)   Why might the liability and liability balances be incorrect?
    (e)   Why might the owners' equity and owners' equity balances be incorrect?
4   What is 'off-balance-sheet' debt?
5   How did the collapse of Enron bring down the giant auditing firm of Arthur Andersen?
6   Is it wrong for the CEO to sell shares in the company while at the same time be making 'numerous announcements expressing confidence in Enron'?

CASE STUDY
3.4

Let the market fix a price

Alan Moran

The Australian Financial Review
Tuesday, 3 July 2004, p. 62

The saga of the price determination for the Moomba-to-Sydney pipeline is compelling evidence of the reasons for avoiding government price regulation.

The pipeline has been in negotiation with the regulatory authorities since May 1999. Last week the Australian Competition Tribunal rejected the Australian Competition and Consumer

Commission's valuation of the pipeline (and, therefore, its price determination), with a decision that can only bring further price paralysis.

The basic pipeline, commissioned in 1976, was a Whitlam government project built at a cost of $240 million. It was privatised by the Keating government for $534 million in 1994. The ACCC now says its value is $559 million while the pipeline's owners, the Australian Pipeline Trust, say it is worth between $784 million and $998 million.

The owners appealed to the tribunal against the ACCC's decision. The tribunal ordered the ACCC to reassess its calculations applying an accountancy approach, depreciated optimised replacement cost, plus other adjustments that might result in a value approaching $800 million.

Clearly, the different means of calculating the capital base on which prices should be set is proving both tortuous and controversial. We have witnessed five years of arguing, establishing positions, and shoring these up with reports from expensive consultancies. Nor is the Moomba-to-Sydney pipeline unique.

This experience is duplicated in the case of Australia's five other major gas pipeline systems, a sad commentary on the bureaucratic system of price determination that we have put in place.

Also the regulation is unnecessary. The peregrinations around the capital base are misplaced. There are, in fact, sufficient market disciplines on this and most other gas pipelines for the regulatory authorities to exit the game. Since it first had to seek the ACCC's agreement to its prices, the Moomba-to-Sydney pipeline has seen its competitive situation revolutionised thanks to the August 2000 commissioning of the rival Eastern Gas Pipeline transporting gas from Bass Strait to Sydney. Within the next decade, there is likely to be another pipeline to Sydney from Queensland, unless the regulatory authorities stifle competition by establishing an artificially low price for gas sent along existing pipelines.

The increased competition from the East Coast Pipeline has already resulted in the haulage price from Moomba to Sydney being marked down from 72¢ to 65¢ per gigajoule. The ACCC capital costs were developed to establish a price similar to that which their consultants had estimated to be the competitive price equivalent (53¢). But this is simply an artificial construct, one that nobody regards as superior to a price that is the outcome of a competitive market.

Clearly, the market for the haulage of gas can never approach a 'perfect market' comprising many sellers and many buyers, but very few markets do. However, the past five years' experience clearly demonstrates the superiority even of the imperfect competition that stems from lumpy capital to the rituals of price determination by the ACCC.

The government, recognising the existing regulatory deficiencies, has commissioned several reviews of the industry. The latest, from the Productivity Commission, is awaiting release. The PC is unlikely to have changed its draft advice that seeks a relaxation of controls on gas transport in line with the emerging competition evident in the industry.

Both the ACCC and the tribunal will claim that the regulatory rules confine them to making decisions within the confines set by the regulation itself. This, they say, requires them to set a synthetic price and not to allow the price to emerge from market interaction.

There is some merit in such claims by the tribunal. The ACCC had, however, a suite of criteria it could have used either to establish price or to allow the market to do so. The fact is that, stemming from its own interests and its personnel's flimsy experience outside of government, it is predisposed towards regulation.

Indeed, the ACCC makes liberal use of its taxpayer funding to promote, in a wide number of forums, additional regulation (and of course more funding). This licence means the confused ACCC is both a policy body and an arbitrator. The government has successfully removed the advocacy role in taxation policy from the Australian Taxation Office, and if it is to restore confidence in its competition commission it should adopt a similar approach with the ACCC.

In the meantime the government needs to release the latest report of the Productivity Commission and restore price determination in the gas industry to the marketplace.

Alan Moran is the director, deregulation unit at the Institute of Public Affairs.

_____

1 Distinguish between the roles of the following bodies:
   (a) Australian Competition and Consumer Commission (ACCC)
   (b) Australian Competition Tribunal
   (c) Productivity Commission (PC)
   (d) Australian Pipeline Trust (APT).

2 Why is the valuation of the pipeline an important issue?

3 The value of the pipeline varies between $559m (ACCC's valuation) and $998m (APT's valuation).
   (a) Identify different ways the pipeline could be valued.
   (b) Discuss how different values could be of importance to different stakeholders.
   (c) For the purpose of the current valuation, which method of valuation is appropriate?

4 What is 'depreciated replacement cost'?

5 What are the arguments in favour of a regulated approach to price fixing?

6 What are the arguments in favour of a free market approach to price fixing?

SOLUTIONS TO ACTIVITIES

Activity 3.1

Your answer should be along the following lines:

1. Under normal circumstances a business would expect a customer to pay the amount owed. Such an amount is therefore typically shown as an asset under the heading 'debtors', also referred to as 'accounts receivable' or simply 'receivables'. However, in this particular case the debtor is unable to pay. Hence, the item is incapable of providing future benefits and the $1,000 owing would not be regarded as an asset. Debts that are not paid are referred to as 'bad debts'.

2. The purchase of the licence would meet all of the conditions set out on page 71 and would therefore be regarded as an asset.

3. The hiring of a new marketing director would not be considered as the acquisition of an asset. One argument against its classification as an asset is that the organisation does not have exclusive rights of control over the director. Nevertheless, it may have an exclusive right to the services that the director provides. Perhaps a stronger argument is that the value of the director cannot be measured in monetary terms with any degree of reliability.

4. The machine would be considered an asset even though it is not yet paid for. Once the organisation has agreed to purchase the machine and has accepted it, the machine is legally owned by the organisation even though payment is still outstanding. (The amount outstanding would be shown as a claim.)

Activity 3.2

You may be able to think of a number of other items which could appear as an asset on the balance sheet of a business. Some items you may have identified are:

- motor vehicles
- inventory/stock of goods
- computer equipment
- cash at bank
- cash on hand
- prepayments
- goodwill
- leasehold improvements
- copyright.

Activity 3.3

Some of the items you may have identified are:

- accounts payable (creditors)
- bank overdraft
- loans
- debentures
- provisions for (warranty, long-service leave, holiday pay, taxation).

Activity 3.4

Your answer should be along the lines of testing each item against the definition and recognition criterion. If it fails the definition criterion, then the recognition criterion is irrelevant. Your assessment should have been as follows:

	Definition			Recognition	
	Sacrifice FEB	Past event	Present obligation	Probability 50%	Measurement reliability
(1) Accounts payable	✓	✓	✓	✓	✓
(2) Future maintenance	✓	X	X	NA	NA
(3) Subscriptions	✓	✓	✓	✓	✓
(4) Guarantee	?	?	?	X	X
(5) Legal suit	✓	✓	✓	✓	✓

Item 2 related to future maintenance fails the definition test as it does not represent a current obligation to any external party and the relevant transaction will arise in the future.

Item 4 related to the guarantee would certainly fail the recognition test of probability of occurrence and measurement reliability.

Activity 3.5

Some of the accounts you may have identified are:

Satisfaction in cash

- Bank overdraft
- Debentures
- Loans
- Wages payable
- Provision for taxation

Satisfaction in kind

- Provision for warranty
- Deposit received in advance
- Rent received in advance

Activity 3.6

Some of the reasons you may have identified are:

- The business is growing and requires additional funding to support that growth (more inventories, more debtors, more equipment) and retaining profits is an important source of funds.
- From the owners' perspective the business may be able to generate a greater return on the profits retained for the owners than they could have obtained by withdrawing the profit share and investing it elsewhere.
- Retaining profits may facilitate debt repayment by the business and therefore lead to increased future profits (and distributions) as the interest costs are reduced.
- There may be personal taxation advantages to the owners if profits are retained in the business.

Activity 3.7

Some of the reserves you may have identified are:

- capital profits reserve
- capital reduction reserve
- foreign currency translation reserve
- asset replacement reserve
- forfeited shares reserve
- general reserve.

Activity 3.8

The balance sheet as at 4 March, following the repayment of part of the loan, will be as follows:

JERRY AND CO.

Balance sheet as at 4 March			
Assets	*$*	*Claims*	*$*
Cash at bank	13,000	Owner's equity	6,000
Motor vehicle	5,000	Liabilities—loan	12,000
Inventory	3,000	Liabilities—trade creditor	3,000
Total assets	21,000	*Total liabilities and owner's equity*	21,000

The repayment of $2,000 of the loan will result in a decrease in the balance at the bank of $2,000 and a decrease in the loan claim against the business by the same amount.

Activity 3.9

The balance sheet as at 6 March will be as follows:

JERRY AND CO.

Balance sheet as at 6 March

Assets	$	Claims	$
Cash at bank	17,000	Owner's equity	10,000
Motor vehicle	5,000	Liabilities—loan	12,000
Inventory	3,000	Liabilities—trade creditor	3,000
Total assets	25,000	Total liabilities and owner's equity	25,000

The introduction of more funds by the owner will result in an increase in the capital of $4,000 and an increase in the cash at bank by the same amount.

Activity 3.10

The balance sheet on 7 March would be as follows:

JERRY AND CO.

Balance sheet as at 7 March

Assets	$	Claims	$
Cash at bank	18,000	Owner's equity [10,000 + (1,000 – 3000)]	8,000
Motor vehicle	5,000	Liabilities—loan	12,000
		Liabilities—trade creditor	3,000
Total assets	23,000	Total liabilities and owner's equity	23,000

As we can see, the inventory ($3,000) will disappear from the balance sheet but the cash at bank will only rise by $1,000. This will mean a net reduction in assets of $2,000. This reduction will be reflected in a reduction in the capital of the owner.

Activity 3.11

Examples of assets which are often defined as being non-current are:

- Freehold premises
- Plant and machinery
- Motor vehicles
- Patents
- Goodwill
- Investments
- Copyright
- Franchise

This is not an exhaustive list. You may have thought of others.

Activity 3.12

Your answer should be as follows:

Non-current assets	*Current assets*
Fixtures and fittings	Cash at bank
Office equipment	Stock of work-in-progress
Motor vehicles	Short-term investments
Freehold factory premises	
Goodwill purchased	
Plant and machinery	
Computer equipment	

Activity 3.13

Examples of current and non-current liabilities are:

Current
- Accounts payable
- Bank overdraft
- Bank loan (repayable within 12 months)
- Revenue received in advance (e.g. subscriptions)
- Provisions (payable within 12 months—holiday pay, warranty, long-service leave, taxation)

Non-current
- Mortgage loan (payable after 12 months)
- Debentures (payable after 12 months)
- Provisions (payable after 12 months' warranty, long-service leave)

Activity 3.14

In answering this activity you may have thought of the following:
- the quality of the workforce
- the reputation of the business's products
- the location of the business
- the relationship with customers
- the quality of management.

Activity 3.15

The term 'current value' can be defined in a number of ways. For example, it can be defined broadly as either the current replacement cost or the current realisable value (selling price) of an item. These two types of valuation may result in quite different figures being produced to represent the current value of an item. (Think, for example, of second-hand car values: there is often quite a difference between buying and selling prices.) In addition, the broad terms 'replacement cost' and 'realisable value' can be defined in different ways. We must therefore be clear about what kind of current value accounting we wish to use. There are also practical problems associated with attempts to implement any system of current value accounting. For example, current values, however defined, are often difficult to establish with any real degree of objectivity. This may mean that the figures produced are heavily dependent on the opinion of managers. Unless the current value figures are capable of some form of independent verification, there is a danger that the financial reports will lose their credibility among users.

Activity 3.16

Your answer should be as follows:

- Inventory increases by $1,000, creditors increase by $1,000.
- Capital reduces by $2,000, cash reduces by $2,000.
- Assets show a net increase of $1,000 (cash + $2,000, inventory – $1,000), profit (and therefore capital) increases by $1,000.

Activity 3.17

Applying the conservatism convention will result in an understatement of financial position. This bias towards understatement may result in owners selling their stake in the business at a price which is lower than they would have received if a more realistic approach to valuation was employed.

Activity 3.18

The effect on the balance sheet would be to increase the freehold land to $110,000 and the gain on revaluation (i.e. $110,000 – $45,000 = $65,000) would be added to the capital of the owner as it is the owner who will benefit from the gain. The revised balance sheet would therefore be as follows:

BRIE MANUFACTURING

Balance sheet as at 31 December 2005

	$	$
Current assets		
Cash at bank	12,000	
Trade debtors	18,000	
Inventory	23,000	
		53,000
Non-current assets		
Motor vehicles	19,000	
Plant and machinery	30,000	
Freehold premises	110,000	
		159,000
Total assets		212,000
Current liabilities		
Trade creditors		37,000
Non-current liabilities		
Loan		50,000
Total liabilities		87,000
Owners' equity		
Opening balance	50,000	
Add revaluation gain	65,000	
Add profit	14,000	
	129,000	
Less drawings	4,000	
Closing balance		125,000
Total liabilities and owners' equity		212,000

Activity 3.19

The objectivity convention provides further support (along with the going concern convention) for the use of historic cost as a basis of valuation. It can conflict, however, with the prudence convention which requires the use of judgment in determining values.

Activity 3.20

Included in your list may have been some of the following:

AASB 101: Presentation of Financial Statements

AASB 102: Inventories

AASB 111: Construction Contracts

AASB 114: Segment Reporting

AASB 116: Property, Plant and Equipment

AASB 117: Leases

AASB 123: Borrowing Costs

AASB 128: Investments in Associates

AASB 131: Interests in Joint Ventures

AASB 132: Financial Instruments: Disclosure and Presentation

AASB 136: Impairment of Assets

AASB 137: Provisions, Contingent Liabilities and Contingent Assets

AASB 138: Intangible Assets

AASB 140: Investment Property

AASB 141: Agriculture

Activity 3.21

We will find that many of the following alternative financial measures for assets are used within financial reports and allowed within the accounting standards:

- historical cost (initial exchange price)
- replacement price (alternatively labelled current cost)
- net realisable value (selling price less costs to sell)
- fair value (the value in exchange between knowledgeable and willing independent parties)
- recoverable amount (what you expect to recover in the future through either use or sale)
- net present value (the present value of expected future net cash inflows).

Activity 3.22

There are many examples of where the prudence assumption has led to a reduction in the valuation of assets. You may have included one of the following:

- Development expenditure can only be capitalised and treated as an asset where it is 'probable' that future economic benefits will be generated to cover the research and development expenditure.
- In the extractive industries a similar principle applies to the recognition of valuable resources discovered.
- With the revaluation of non-current assets, upward revaluations are allocated to a reserve account while downward revaluations are treated as expenses.

OBJECTIVES

When you have completed your study of this chapter you should be able to:

1 state the purpose of the income statement (profit and loss)

2 explain the relationship between the income statement and the balance sheet

3 present the equation and identify alternative formats for the income statement

4 demonstrate an understanding of income in relation to definition, recognition, classification and measurement

5 demonstrate an understanding of expenses in relation to definition, recognition, classification and measurement

6 distinguish between accrual- and cash-based transaction recognition

7 analyse expense recognition for non-current tangible assets

8 analyse expense recognition for inventory

9 analyse expense recognition for accounts receivable

10 prepare an income statement from relevant financial information

11 review and interpret income statements.

4

MEASURING AND REPORTING FINANCIAL PERFORMANCE

In this chapter the income statement will be examined. The statement has traditionally been called the profit and loss account, and this terminology may continue in many areas other than companies. The term profit and loss account is likely to continue to be used by accountants as there will always be a need for such an account in the detailed records. The published income statement is simply a summary of the content of the detailed account called profit and loss.

THE INCOME STATEMENT

In the previous chapter we examined the nature and purpose of the balance sheet. We saw that this statement was concerned with setting out the financial position of a business at a particular moment in time. However, it is not usually enough for users to have information relating only to the amount of wealth held by a business at one moment in time. Businesses exist for the primary purpose of generating wealth, or profit, and it is the profit generated during a period that is the primary concern of many users. Although the amount of profit generated is of particular interest to the owners of a business, other groups, such as managers, employees and suppliers, will also have an interest in the profit-making ability of the business. The purpose of the income statement is to measure and report how much profit (wealth) the business has generated over a period. Profit (or loss) is the difference between the increases in capital attributable to operations or trading (known as income) and the decreases in owner's equity attributable to operations or trading (known as expenses).

The measurement of profit requires that the total income of the business, generated during a particular period, be calculated. **Income** is simply a measure of the inflow of assets (e.g. cash or amounts owed to a business by debtors) or the reduction in liabilities that arise as a result of operating or trading operations. Income is comprised of both 'revenues' and 'gains'. **Revenues** represents the gross inflows of future economic benefits related to the different categories of operating activities. Gains represent the net inflows from the non-operating activities, for example the gain on sale of investments, or the gain on foreign transactions. Different forms of business enterprise will generate different forms of revenue. Some examples of the different forms that revenue can take are as follows:

* sales of goods (e.g. of a manufacturer)
* fees for services (e.g. of a solicitor)
* subscriptions (e.g. of a club)
* interest received (e.g. of an investment fund).

It is quite possible for a business to have more than one source of income.

ACTIVITY 4.1

The following represent different forms of business enterprise:

1. Accountancy practice
2. Squash club
3. Bus company
4. Newspaper
5. Finance company
6. Songwriter
7. Retailer
8. Magazine publisher

Can you identify the main source(s) of revenue for each type of business enterprise?

The total expenses relating to the period must also be calculated. An **expense** represents the outflow of assets (or increase in liabilities) which is incurred as a result of generating income. The nature of the business will again determine the type of expenses that will be incurred. Examples of some of the more common types of expense are:

❋ the cost of buying goods which are subsequently sold—known as cost of sales or cost of goods sold

❋ salaries and wages

❋ rent and rates

❋ motor vehicle running expenses

❋ insurances

❋ printing and stationery

❋ heat and light

❋ telephone and postage

The income statement (profit and loss account) for a period simply shows the total income generated during a particular period and deducts from this the total expenses incurred in generating that income. The difference between the total income and total expenses will represent either profit (if income exceeds expenses) or loss (if expenses exceed income). Thus, we have:

Profit (loss) for the period = Total income – Total expenses incurred in generating the income

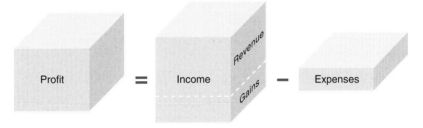

FIGURE 4.1 The transaction approach to computing profit

RELATIONSHIP BETWEEN THE INCOME STATEMENT AND THE BALANCE SHEET

The two statements should not be viewed in any way as substitutes for each other. Rather, they should be seen as performing different functions. The balance sheet of a business occurs at a single point in time, and is effectively a 'snapshot' of the stock of wealth held by the business. The income statement, on the other hand, is concerned with the generation of wealth over a period of time. The two statements are closely related. The income statement can be viewed as linking the balance sheet at the beginning of the period with that at the end of the period. Thus, at the commencement of the business a position statement (balance sheet) will be produced to reveal the opening financial position:

$$A_{beg} = OE_{beg} + L_{beg}$$

After an appropriate period, a profit and loss account will be prepared (which will be summarised as an income statement) to show the wealth generated over the period:

$$\text{Profit (loss)} = I_{\text{period}} - E_{\text{period}}$$

At the end of the period a revised balance sheet will be prepared which incorporates the changes in wealth that have occurred since the opening financial position statement was drawn up. This will include an adjustment to capital reflecting the amount of profit or loss for the period.

We saw in the previous chapter that the effect of making a profit (or loss) on the balance sheet means that the accounting equation can be extended as follows:

$$\text{Assets} = OE_{\text{beg}} + \text{Profit (or} - \text{Loss)} +/- \text{Other } OE \text{ adj} + \text{Liabilities}$$

This equation can be further extended to:

$$\text{Assets} = OE_{\text{beg}} + \text{(Income} - \text{Expenses)} +/- \text{Other } OE \text{ adj} + \text{Liabilities}$$

In theory, it would be possible to calculate profit and loss for the period by making all adjustments for income and expenses through the capital account. However, this would be rather cumbersome. A better solution is to have an 'appendix' to the owners' equity (capital) account in the form of a profit and loss account which is then presented as an income statement. By deducting expenses from the income for the period, the profit (loss) can be derived for adjustment in the capital account. This figure represents the net effect of operating and other activities for the period. Providing this 'appendix' means that a detailed and more informative view of financial performance is presented to users.

As a result of the relationship between the income statement and two consecutive balance sheets, it is possible to compute the profit or loss for a period based on the stock approach.

The stock approach computes the profit or loss by adjusting the change in net assets for the period by other changes in owners' equity during the period:

* new contributions by the owners
* withdrawals by the owners
* other owners' equity changes not related to income or expense (e.g. revaluation of property).

The accounting equation for the stock approach is:

$$\text{Profit (or loss)} = (A_{\text{end}} - A_{\text{beg}}) - (L_{\text{end}} - L_{\text{beg}}) - \text{New contributions}$$
$$+ \text{Owners' distributions} +/- \text{Other changes in owners' equity}$$

Figure 4.2 illustrates the stock approach which is alternatively called the 'increment in wealth' method.

ACTIVITY 4.2

Why might the stock approach to determining profit or loss be used?

THE FORMAT OF THE INCOME STATEMENT

The format of the income statement will vary according to both the entity structure (e.g. non-profit entity, sole proprietorship, partnership, company) and the nature of its operations (e.g. manufacturing, retail, service).

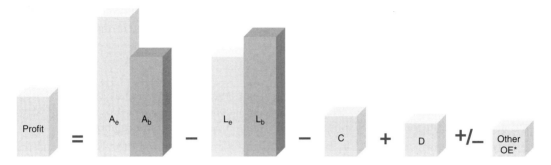

e = end of the period
b = beginning of the period
D = Distributions (Dividends or Drawings)
C = Contributions
* = Other owners' equity changes

FIGURE 4.2 The stock approach to computing profit

In practice you will observe at least three forms of income statements:

1. simple listings of accounts for small organisations
2. classified reports for larger organisations
3. regulatory presentations for companies.

SIMPLE REPORTS

For smaller organisations the financial performance report may well consist of a listing of income and expenses in alphabetic or financial magnitude order. The following example sets out a typical structure:

NEWLANDS SOCCER CLUB

Income statement for the year ended 31 October 2005		
Income	$	$
Ticket sales	9,200	
Fundraising	5,700	
Members' fees	3,500	
Government grant	2,700	
Interest	600	21,700
Expenses		
Players' payments	8,300	
Ground fees	2,900	
Insurance	2,100	
Travel costs	1,900	
Uniforms	1,500	
Repairs and maintenance	900	
Telephone and postage	600	
Sundries	400	18,600
Period profit (surplus)		3,100

The income statement simply lists and summarises the income and expenses. The difference is the net profit or the net loss. In the case of a not-for-profit organisation such as the one shown above, the terms 'surplus' or 'deficit' are often used. For other than companies the report may be labelled the 'profit and loss account'.

LARGER ORGANISATIONS

The second broad category of income statement relates to larger organisations with more detailed transactions and is called the classified financial report. This simply means that income and expenses are not simply listed but are grouped into meaningful categories for the purpose of providing more relevant information.

Income (revenues in particular) would be broken down to reflect the nature of the business and the relative significance of each item. For organisations selling goods, sales will normally be the major revenue items, with other revenues (e.g. interest, commission, rent, dividends) frequently being categorised as 'other revenues'.

In relation to expenses there are often four categories for retailers and three for other activities. However, the categories tend not to be regulated and are decided upon by the individual entity's management. The four categories are:

1. Cost of sales
2. Selling and distribution
3. Administration and general
4. Financial.

ACTIVITY 4.3

How would you classify the following expenses?

	Cost of sales	Selling and distribution	Administration and general	Financial
Freight inward				
Freight outward				
Sales staff salaries				
Interest				
Rates				
Depreciation—showcase				
Depreciation—building				
Repairs and maintenance—cash register				
Cleaning				
Bad debts				
Discounts given				
Telephone and postage				
Insurance—inventory				
Audit fee				
Administration staff salaries				
Advertising				

The following example sets out a typical format for a classified income statement of a retail business.

HI-PRICE STORES

Income statement for the year ended 31 October 2005

	$	$
Sales		432,000
Less cost of sales		254,000
Gross profit		178,000
Other revenue		
Interest from investments	2,000	
Rent from properties	5,000	7,000
		185,000
Less expenses		
Selling and distribution		
Advertising	5,000	
Commissions	4,000	
Delivery	3,000	
Display	2,000	
Salary and wages	37,000	51,000
Administration and general		
Salary and wages	41,000	
Rates	2,000	
Heat and light	3,000	
Telephone and postage	2,000	
Insurance	1,000	
Repairs and maintenance	5,000	
Motor vehicle running expenses	4,000	
Depreciation plant and equipment	1,000	
Depreciation motor vehicles	2,000	
Depreciation buildings	3,000	64,000
Financial		
Interest	3,000	
Bad debts	7,000	10,000
Total expenses		125,000
Net profit		60,000

This statement is sometimes called the 'trading and profit and loss account', the trading section being up to the 'gross profit' stage and the profit and loss representing the rest. The trading section is concerned with calculating the gross profit for the period. The trading revenues (sales), which arise from selling the goods, produce the first item that appears. Deducted from this is the trading expense (cost of sales), which is the cost of acquiring the goods sold during the period. The difference between the trading revenues and trading expenses is referred to as **gross profit**. This represents the profit from simply buying and selling goods without taking into account any other expenses or income associated with the business. We will look in greater detail at the 'cost of sales' expense account later in this chapter when we examine inventories.

Having calculated the gross profit, any additional revenues or gains of the business are then added to this figure. In the above example, interest and rent represent additional revenues. From this subtotal of gross profit and other revenues or gains, the other expenses (overheads) that have to be incurred in order to operate the business (salaries and wages, rates, etc.) are deducted. The final figure derived is the net profit for the period. This net profit figure represents the wealth generated during the period which is attributable to the owner(s) of the business and which will be added to their capital figure in the balance sheet and statement of changes in owners' equity. As can be seen, net profit is a residual—that is, the amount left over after deducting all expenses incurred in generating the income for the period.

ACTIVITY 4.4

The following information relates to the activities of H & S Retailers for the year ended 30 April 2006:

	$
Motor vehicle running expenses	1,200
Rent received from subletting	2,000
Closing inventory	3,000
Rent and rates	5,000
Motor vans	6,300
Annual depreciation—motor vans	1,500
Heat and light	900
Telephone and postage	450
Sales	97,400
Goods purchased	68,350
Insurance	750
Loan interest payable	620
Balance at bank	4,780
Salaries and wages	10,400
Opening inventory	4,000

Prepare an income statement in the form of a trading and profit and loss account for the year ended 30 April 2006. (*Hint*: Not all items shown above should appear on this statement.)

COMPANIES

The third format for the income statement is that which is required to be produced by companies and other entities in accordance with the statutory standards. Such companies are often reluctant to provide detailed classified reports and generally only disclose what is required under the applicable standard.

ACTIVITY 4.5

Why might companies be reluctant to provide a fully classified income statement?

AASB 101 'Presentation of Financial Statements' requires that with respect to the 'income statement' the 'expenses' are to be classified on the basis of either their nature or by function.

 ACTIVITY 4.6

What is the difference between the two terms 'nature' and 'function'? Can you think of examples for each?

AASB 101 specifies a number of required disclosures to be included in the income statement:

(a) revenue

(b) finance costs

(c) certain investment income (associates and joint ventures)

(d) tax expense

(e) the after-tax gain or loss related to discontinued operations or business disposals

(f) the overall profit or loss.

Additionally, either within the income statement itself, or in the notes attached to the income statement, details of any items of income or expense related to the following should be disclosed:

(g) write-downs, or reversals of previous write-downs, to significant tangible assets (inventory, property, plant and equipment)

(h) restructuring activities

(i) disposal of property, plant and equipment

(j) disposals of investments

(k) discontinuing operations

(l) litigation settlements

(m) other provision reversals.

You obviously do not need to be familiar with the details of all of these accounting disclosures, but it is interesting to consider why these particular disclosures were specifically selected as required disclosures by the standard setters.

 ACTIVITY 4.7

Select several of the above required disclosures in the income statement and explain why the regulators (AASB) may have required that information to be presented for all companies?

The following example represents a typical format for an income statement prepared to comply with the accounting standard.

Statements of Financial Performance (since 2005 it would be labelled 'Income Statement')
for the year ended 30 June 2004

	Notes	Qantas Group 2004 $M	2003 $M	Qantas 2004 $M	2003 $M
SALES AND OPERATING REVENUE					
Net passenger revenue[1,2]		8,978.3	8,992.8	8,182.7	8,242.5
Net freight revenue[1]		469.7	511.3	467.3	508.9
Tours and travel revenue		711.1	696.3	–	–
Contract work revenue		502.6	530.9	276.5	281.0
Other sources[3,4]		692.0	643.6	943.3	930.9
Sales and operating revenue	2	11,353.7	11,374.9	9,869.8	9,963.3
EXPENDITURE					
Manpower and staff related		2,938.5	3,017.7	2,501.9	2,587.7
Selling and marketing		466.1	546.6	434.7	517.0
Aircraft operating – variable		2,226.8	2,405.0	2,150.9	2,352.1
Fuel and oil		1,355.6	1,540.4	1,232.8	1,423.8
Property		309.8	286.5	284.8	262.6
Computer and communication		439.1	412.3	411.6	387.7
Depreciation and amortisation		1,005.6	891.4	871.0	774.2
Non-cancellable operating lease rentals		263.5	283.9	237.3	233.2
Tours and travel		570.9	564.0	–	–
Capacity hire		287.4	381.6	255.5	350.4
Other[5]		411.9	488.1	424.0	551.0
Share of net profit of associates and joint ventures	30	(19.7)	(9.6)	–	–
Expenditure	3	10,255.5	10,807.9	8,804.5	9,439.7
Earnings before interest and tax	34	1,098.2	567.0	1,065.3	523.6
Borrowing costs	3	(259.5)	(172.4)	(263.5)	(173.6)
Interest revenue	2	125.9	107.7	112.3	93.5
Net borrowing costs		(133.6)	(64.7)	(151.2)	(80.1)
Profit from ordinary activities before related income tax expense		964.6	502.3	914.1	443.5
Income tax expense relating to ordinary activities	4	(315.8)	(155.7)	(238.1)	(71.0)
Net profit		648.8	346.6	676.0	372.5
Outside equity interests in net profit		(0.4)	(3.1)	–	–
Net profit attributable to members of the Company	20	648.4	343.5	676.0	372.5
Non-owner transaction changes in equity:					
Net decrease in retained profits on the initial adoption of AASB 1028 "Employee Benefits"		–	(3.7)	–	(3.7)
Net exchange differences relating to self-sustaining foreign operations		0.4	(2.3)	–	–
Total changes in equity from non-owner related transactions attributable to members of the Company	21	648.8	337.5	676.0	368.8
Basic earnings per share	35	35.7 cents	20.0 cents		
Diluted earnings per share	35	35.5 cents	19.8 cents		

1 Passenger and freight revenue is disclosed net of both sales discount and interline/IATA commission.

2 Passenger recoveries are disclosed as part of net passenger revenue.

3 Revenue from 'Other sources' includes revenue from aircraft charters and leases, property income, Qantas Club and Frequent Flyer membership fees, freight terminal and service fees, commission revenue, and other miscellaneous income.

4 Excludes interest revenue of $125.9 million (2003: $107.7 million) which is included in net borrowing costs. Also excluded are proceeds on sale and operating leaseback of non-current assets of $221.8 million (2003: $36.7 million), which are offset against the relevant asset's written down value before recognition of the profit or loss on sale. Net loss on sale of non-current assets was $0.5 million (2003: $12.4 million).

5 'Other expenditure' includes contract work materials, printing, stationery, insurance and other miscellaneous expenses.

The Statements of Financial Performance are to be read in conjunction with the Notes to the Financial Statements on pages 5 to 60.

In the case of the balance sheet, we saw that the information could be presented in either a horizontal format or a vertical format. This is also true of the income statement (trading and profit and loss account). Where a horizontal format is used, expenses are listed on the left-hand side and revenues on the right-hand side, the difference being either net profit or net loss. The vertical format has been used above as it is easier to understand and is now almost always used.

THE REPORTING PERIOD

We have seen already that for reporting to those outside the business a financial reporting cycle of one year is the norm, although some large businesses will prepare quarterly or half-yearly financial statements to provide more frequent feedback on progress (often called interim reporting). However, for those who manage a business it is important to have much more frequent feedback on performance. Thus, it is quite common for profit figures to be prepared on a monthly basis in order to show the progress made during that period.

PROFIT MEASUREMENT AND THE RECOGNITION OF INCOME

A key issue in the measurement of profit concerns the point at which income (revenue) is recognised. It is possible to recognise income at different points in the production/selling cycle and the particular point chosen could have a significant effect on the total income reported for the period. Many business failures and corporate crashes relate to situations where profit has been inflated from recognising income before it was realised, and in most of these cases it was never realised.

ACTIVITY 4.8

Can you think of four points in the production/selling cycle at which income might be recognised for a manufacturing business that sells goods on credit (i.e. where cash is received some time after the goods have been passed to the customer)?

A number of different points in the production/selling cycle of a manufacturer are identified in Figure 4.3.

Traditionally, the **realisation convention** in accounting was used to solve the revenue recognition problem (or at least to provide some consistency). This convention stated that revenue should only be recognised when it has been realised. Normally, realisation is considered to have occurred when:

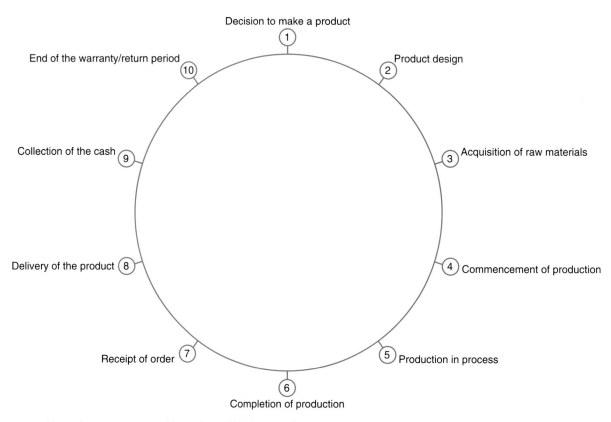

FIGURE 4.3 Alternative revenue recognition points within the manufacturing cycle

* the activities necessary to generate the revenue (e.g. delivery of goods, carrying out of repairs) are substantially complete
* the amount of revenue generated can be objectively determined
* there is reasonable certainty that the amounts owing from the activities will be received
* any other outstanding items (e.g. returns, warranty) can be determined with reasonable certainty.

 **ACTIVITY 4.9**

Look at the various points in the production/selling cycle set out in the answer to the previous activity. At which of these points do you think the criteria for realisation will be fulfilled for the manufacturing business?

In recent times the realisation convention has been replaced by consistent recognition criterion for all accounts, including income and expenses. This rule is similar to the old 'realisation' concept and is based on the dual notion of 'probability that the change has occurred' and being able to 'reliably measure that change'.

Within the old Australian accounting conceptual framework (replaced in 2004 by the international framework) was useful guidance concerning when revenue should be recognised.

SAC 4 para 130:

(a)   *an agreement for the provision of goods or services exists between the entity and one or more of the parties external to the entity;*

(b)   *cash has been received, or the entity has a claim against an external party or parties that:*

   (i)   *is for a specified consideration, in the form of cash, other assets, or a reduction in a liability of the entity; and*

   (ii) *cannot be avoided by the external party or parties without the incurrence of a penalty set sufficiently large as, in normal circumstances, to deter avoidance;*

(c)   *all acts of performance necessary to establish a valid claim against the external party or parties have been completed; and*

(d)   *it is possible to estimate reliably the collectability of debts or the return of the goods sold.*

The application of both the earlier realisation convention and the new transaction recognition criteria in accounting means that a sale on credit is usually recognised before the cash is ultimately received. Thus, the total sales figure shown in the income statement may include sales transactions for which the cash has yet to be received. The total sales figure in the income statement will therefore be different from the total cash received from sales.

Not all businesses will wait to recognise income until all of the work necessary to generate the income is complete. A construction business, for example, which is engaged in a long-term project such as building a dam, will not usually wait until the contract is complete. To do this would mean that no income would be recognised by the business until several years after the work first commenced. Instead, the business will normally recognise a proportion of the total expected income on the contract when an agreed stage of the contract has been completed. This approach to income recognition is consistent with the recognition criterion.

ACTIVITY 4.10

Apart from long-term construction projects, can you think of other activities where it may be appropriate to recognise income earlier in the production/selling cycle—that is, to recognise the income before the goods or services are completed or before there is a firm sales contract in place?

Alternatively, situations may also arise where benefits (normally cash) have been received in advance of the receiving entity providing all of the related goods and services. For example, it is common for customers to pay a deposit in advance or in fact to pay for goods or services for a specified future time period (e.g. subscriptions, insurance premiums and service fees are regularly paid in advance). For such transactions the income recognition criteria are not fully satisfied and the reporting entity receiving these benefits in advance should classify the advance receipts as liabilities in the balance sheet. They represent an obligation to provide the customer, member or client goods or services (or a refund where goods or services are not provided) at some time in the future. The notion that we have introduced in this section is that of cash and accrual-based accounting. Cash accounting recognises income when it is received. Accrual accounting recognises income on the basis that it has been earned irrespective of whether the cash receipt is in arrears or advance.

For accounting purposes we have deemed that income is earned when it is realised, realisation being closely linked to probability of occurrence and reliability of measurement.

PROFIT MEASUREMENT AND THE RECOGNITION OF EXPENSES

Traditionally, the recognition of expenses was closely linked to the recognition of income. The notion of 'matching' dictated that expenses should be matched (linked with, assigned to, recognised against) to the income they helped to generate. In other words, expenses must be taken into account in the same period and in the income statement in which the associated sale or other income is recognised.

While many of the current accounting practices are derived from this accounting principle, there have been moves in recent years to shift from this notion to a common basis for recognising both income and expenses. This common basis is that, provided an item satisfies the respective definition of income or expense, it will be recognised where its occurrence is probable (more likely than less likely) and it can be reliably measured.

The traditional **matching convention** posed problems where it was difficult to link expenditure with income, or where expenditure was carried forward to be matched against future projected income.

ACTIVITY 4.11

What is the difference between 'expenditure' and 'expense'? What is meant by the concept of 'carrying-forward expenditure'?

In recognising expenses in a specific period, three possibilities arise:

1. The cash payments match the expenses incurred (benefits used up or consumed).
2. The cash payments are less than the expenses incurred.
3. The cash payments exceed the expenses incurred.

The first poses no problems as the expense that is recognised on both a cash basis and an accrual basis is the same. However, with the others there is a difference between the expense recognised on a cash basis and an accrual basis. We will review these two in more detail.

The cash basis of recognising expenses being to recognise the expense at the time that the cash payment is made. The accrual method of recognising expenses being to recognise the expense when it is incurred (economic benefits used up).

When the expense for the period is more than the cash paid during the period

Suppose that sales staff are paid a commission of 2 per cent of sales generated and that total sales during the period amounted to $300,000. This will mean that the commission to be paid in respect of the sales for the period will be $6,000. Let us say, however, that, by the end of the period, the sales commission paid to staff was $5,000. If the business took no action on this and only reported the amount paid, it would mean that the profit calculation would not reflect the full expense for the year. This would contravene both the matching convention and the expense recognition criterion because not all of the expenses associated with the revenues of the period would have been matched or recognised in calculating profit. This will be remedied as follows:

✳ Sales commission expense in the profit and loss account/income statement will include the amount paid plus the amount outstanding (i.e. $5,000 + $1,000 = $6,000).

✳ The amount outstanding ($1,000) represents a liability and will be included under the heading 'accruals' or '**accrued expenses**' in the balance sheet. As this item will have to be paid within 12 months of the balance sheet date, it will be treated as a current liability.

Ideally, all expenses should be matched to the income (e.g. sales) to which they relate, in the period in which they are reported. However, it is often difficult to match closely certain expenses to income in the same way that we have matched sales commission to sales. It is unlikely, for example, that electricity charges incurred can be linked directly to particular sales in this way. As a result, the electricity charges incurred will normally be recognised in (assigned or allocated to) the period to which they relate.

  Suppose a business has reached the end of its accounting year and it has only been charged electricity for the first three-quarters of the year (amounting to $1,900), simply because the electricity company has yet to send out bills for the quarter that ends on the same date as the business's year-end. In this situation, an estimate should be made of the electricity expense outstanding (i.e. the bill for the last three months of the year is estimated). This figure (let us say the estimate is $500) is dealt with as follows:

✳ Electricity expense in the profit and loss account/income statement will include the amount paid, plus the amount of the estimate (i.e. $1,900 + $500 = $2,400) in order to cover the whole year.

✳ The amount of the estimate ($500) represents a liability (outstanding obligation) and will be included under the heading 'accruals' or 'accrued expenses' in the balance sheet. As this item will have to be paid within 12 months of the balance sheet date, it will be treated as a current liability.

The above treatment will have the desired effect of increasing the electricity expense to the 'correct' figure for the year in terms of the profit calculation, presuming that the estimate is reasonably accurate. It will also have the effect of showing that at the end of the accounting year the business owed the amount of the last quarter's electricity bill. Dealing with the outstanding amount in this way reflects the dual aspect of the item and will ensure the accounting equation is maintained.

ACTIVITY 4.12

Let us say the estimate for outstanding electricity was correct. How will the payment of the electricity bill be dealt with?

If there is a slight error in the estimate, a small adjustment (either negative or positive, depending on the direction of the error) can be made to the following year's expense. Dealing with the estimation error in this way is not strictly correct, but the amount is likely to be insignificant. The current accounting standard would require that corrections of estimates be made directly against the owners' equity account at the beginning of the period and shown in the 'statement of changes in owners' equity'.

ACTIVITY 4.13

Can you think of other expenses that cannot be linked directly to income and where matching will therefore be done on a time basis?

Where the amount paid during the year is more than the full expense for the period

Suppose a business pays rent for its premises quarterly in advance (on 1 January, 1 March, 1 June and 1 September) and that, on the last day of the accounting year (say, 31 December), it pays the next quarter's rent to the following 31 March ($400), which is a day earlier than required. This would mean that a total of five quarters' rent was paid during the year. If the business reports the cash paid in the income statement, this would be more than the full expense for the year. This treatment would also contravene the matching convention and transaction recognition criterion because a higher figure than the expenses associated with the income of the year appears in the income statement.

The problem is overcome by dealing with the rental payment as follows:

✳ Reduce cash to reflect the full amount of the rent paid during the year (i.e. 5 × $400 = $2,000).

✳ Show the rent for four quarters as the appropriate expense in the income statement (i.e. 4 × $400 = $1,600).

✳ Show the quarter's rent paid in advance ($400) as a prepayment on the asset side of the balance sheet. It is an asset because it represents future economic benefits in terms of the right to use rented premises for 3 months next year.

The prepaid expense will appear as a current asset in the balance sheet, under the heading 'prepayments'. In the next period, this prepayment will cease to be an asset and become an expense in the income statement of that period when the three months' usage expires. This is because the rent prepaid relates to that period.

Figure 4.4 illustrates the cash and accrual components of a typical expense account and the relationship of this expense account to the three financial reports.

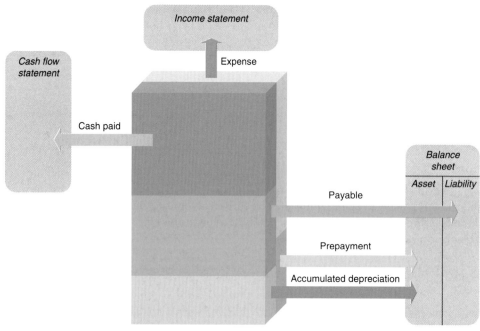

FIGURE 4.4 Accounting for expenses

In practice, the treatment of accruals and prepayments will be subject to the **materiality convention** in accounting. This convention states that, where the amounts involved are immaterial (insignificant), we should consider only what is expedient. This may mean that an item will be treated as an expense in the period in which it is paid, rather than being strictly matched to the income to which it relates. For example, a business may find that, at the end of an accounting period, there is a bill owing for stationery used during the year, of $5. The time and effort involved in recording this as an accrual would have little effect on the measurement of profit or financial position for a business of any size and so it would be ignored when preparing the income statement for the period. The bill would, presumably, be paid in the following period and therefore be treated as an expense of that period.

Profit and cash

The foregoing sections on income and expenses reveal that income does not usually represent cash received and expenses are not the same as cash paid. As a result, the net profit figure (i.e. total income minus total expenses) will not normally represent the net cash generated from operations during a period. It is therefore important to distinguish between profit and liquidity. Profit is a measure of achievement, or productive effort, rather than a measure of cash generated. Although making a profit will increase wealth, we have already seen in the previous chapter that cash is only one form in which that wealth may be held.

Figure 4.5 illustrates the cash and accrual components of a typical income account and the relationship of this income account to the three financial reports.

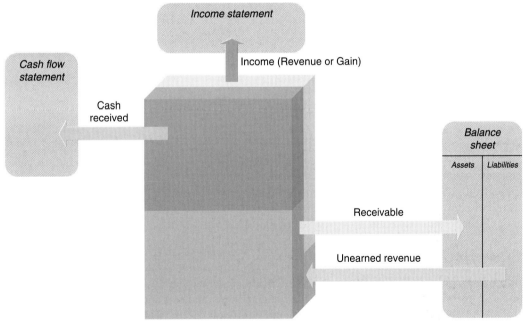

FIGURE 4.5 Accounting for income

Up until now we have been looking at simple differences between income and expense recognition under 'cash' and 'accrual' based accounting systems. We label these differences 'deferrals' and 'accruals'. Deferred revenue relates to the situation where the cash has been received in advance of it being earned (e.g. subscriptions). Deferred expense relates to the situation where the expense has been paid in advance of being incurred (e.g. rental). Accrued revenue relates to the situation where the revenue has been earned but not received (e.g. credit sales, interest on investments). Accrued expense relates to the situation where the expense has been incurred (economic benefits have been used up) but the payment has not been paid (e.g. wages owing at year end).

We now need to consider several more complex examples of significant deferral and accrual transactions where the cash outlay (cash-based recognition) will not be an appropriate measure of the expense (accrual based).

PROFIT MEASUREMENT AND THE CALCULATION OF DEPRECIATION

The expense of **depreciation**, which appeared in the income statement earlier, is an example of a deferred expense, where the cash is paid in advance of the expense being recognised. Property, plant and equipment (normally with the exception of freehold land) do not have a perpetual existence. They are eventually used up in the process of generating income for the business. Depreciation is an attempt to measure the cost of the future economic benefits (service potential) of an item of property, plant and equipment which has been used up in generating the income recognised during a particular period. As it is nearly impossible to measure the consumption of the economic benefits of such assets during a period, we normally refer to this measurement process as 'cost allocation'. That is, management estimate how much of the economic benefits of the related asset has been used up during the period. The depreciation charge (the measure of the economic benefits used up) is considered to be an expense of the period to which it relates.

To calculate a depreciation expense for a period, four factors have to be considered:

1. the cost (or other value) of the asset
2. the useful life of the asset
3. the estimated residual value of the asset
4. the depreciation method.

The cost of the asset

This will include all costs incurred by the business to bring the asset to its required location and to make it ready for use. Thus, in addition to the costs of acquiring the asset, any delivery costs, installation costs (e.g. plant) and legal costs incurred in the transfer of legal title (e.g. freehold property) will be included as part of the total cost of the asset. Similarly, any costs incurred in improving or altering an asset in order to make it suitable for its intended use within the business will also be included as part of the total cost.

The useful life of the asset

An item of property, plant and equipment has a physical life, an economic life and a useful life to the entity. The physical life of an asset will be exhausted through the effects of wear and tear and the passage of time. It is possible, however, for the physical life to be extended considerably through careful maintenance and improvements. The economic life of an asset is determined by the effects of technological progress and commercial realities (changes in demand). After a while, the benefits of using the asset may be less than the costs involved. This may be because the asset is unable to compete with newer assets or because it is no longer relevant to the needs of the business. The economic life of an asset to the business may be much shorter than its physical life. For example, a computer may have a physical life of eight years and an economic life of three years. It is the economic life of an asset to the business which will determine the expected useful life for the purpose of calculating depreciation. Forecasting the economic life of an asset to the business, however, may be extremely difficult in practice. Both the rate at which technology progresses and shifts in consumer tastes can be swift and unpredictable.

Figure 4.6 provides an overview of the depreciation process related to property, plant and equipment.

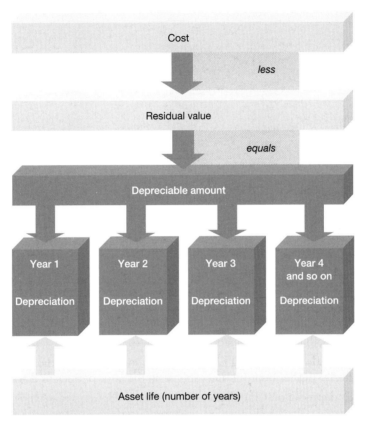

The figure shows how an annual depreciation charge is derived. The cost of an asset less the estimated residual value will represent the amount to be depreciated. This amount is depreciated over the useful life (four years in this particular case) of the asset using an appropriate depreciation method.

FIGURE 4.6 Calculating an annual depreciation charge

Estimated residual value (disposal value)

When a business disposes of an item of property, plant and equipment it may still be of value to others, and some payment may be received. This payment will represent the residual value, or disposal value, of the asset. To calculate the total amount to be depreciated with regard to an asset, the estimated residual value must be deducted from the cost of the asset. The likely amount to be received on disposal is, once again, often difficult to predict.

Depreciation method

Once the amount to be depreciated (called depreciable amount) has been estimated, the business must select a method of allocating this depreciable amount over the useful life of the item of property, plant or equipment. There

ACTIVITY 4.14

Dalton Engineering Ltd purchased a new car for its marketing director. The invoice received from the car supplier revealed the following:

	$	$
New Holden Vectra		24,000
Delivery charge	500	
Alloy wheels	660	
Sun roof	200	
Petrol	30	
Registration	500	
Plates	200	
		2,090
		26,090
Trade-in: Commodore		14,000
Amount outstanding		12,090

What is the total cost of the new car?

are various ways in which the total depreciation may be allocated and a depreciation expense for a period derived. These methods would normally be of three types:

* straight-line depreciation—with equal depreciation expense in each period
* accelerated depreciation—with systematically higher depreciation expense in the earlier periods of the asset's useful life, and systematically smaller depreciation expense in the later periods of the asset's useful life
* units of production based depreciation—the depreciation expense allocated to each period reflects an objective measure of the asset's life (e.g. kilometres travelled, units produced, hours of operation).

The first of these is known as the **straight-line method**. This method simply allocates the amount to be depreciated equally over each year of the useful life of the asset.

EXAMPLE
4.1

To illustrate this method, consider the following information:

Cost of machine	$40,000
Estimated residual value at the end of its useful life	$1,024
Estimated useful life	4 years

To calculate the depreciation expense for each year, the total amount to be depreciated must be calculated. This will be the total cost less the estimated residual value, i.e. $40,000 – $1,024 = $38,976. Having done this, the annual depreciation charge can be derived by dividing the amount to be depreciated by the estimated useful life of the asset of four years. The calculation is therefore:

$$\$38,976 \div 4 = \$9,744$$

Thus, the annual depreciation expense which appears in the income statement in relation to this asset will be $9,744 for each of the four years of the asset's life.

When property, plant and equipment is depreciated we are effectively recognising in each period a reduction in the asset (e.g. equipment) and an increase in expense (e.g. depreciation expense—equipment). It is exactly the same as the earlier treatment of prepaid rental expense, except that the time period is much longer. As a result of this extended time period between the acquisition of property, plant and equipment and its disposal, we account for the asset reduction differently. Instead of reducing directly the asset account (e.g. equipment), we use a **contra** (alternatively called 'negative') **asset** account (called 'accumulated depreciation equipment') for all reductions. The balance in the contra asset account progressively gets bigger, and represents the cost of the economic benefits of the asset used up to date. Having two accounts to explain each item of property, plant and equipment provides relevant information to users compared with having a single account. The amount of depreciation relating to the asset will be accumulated for as long as it is held. This accumulated amount will be deducted from the cost of the asset on the balance sheet. Thus, for example, at the end of the second year the accumulated depreciation will be $9,744 × 2 = $19,488 and the asset details will appear on the balance sheet as follows:

	$	$
Machine at cost	40,000	
Less accumulated depreciation	19,488	
		20,512

The balance of $20,512 shown above is referred to as the written-down value or net book value or carrying amount of the asset. It represents that portion of the cost of the asset which has still to be written off (or allocated against future income generated from using the asset). This figure does not represent the current market value, which may be quite different.

ACTIVITY 4.15

How can the use of a contra asset account provide more relevant information to report users?

The straight-line method derives its name from the fact that the written-down value of the asset at the end of each year, when graphed against time, will result in a straight line, as shown in Figure 4.7.

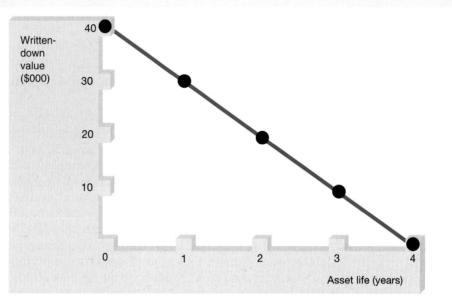

The figure shows that the written-down value of the asset declines by a constant amount each year. This is because the straight-line method provides a constant depreciation charge each year. The result, when plotted on a graph, is a straight line.

FIGURE 4.7 Graph of written-down value against time using the straight-line method

The second approach to calculating depreciation for a period is referred to as **accelerated depreciation**. The most common accelerated depreciation method is known as the **reducing-balance** (or declining-balance) **method**. This method applies a fixed percentage rate of depreciation to the written-down value of an asset each year. The effect of this will be higher annual depreciation charges in the early years and lower charges in the later years.

Deriving the fixed percentage to be applied requires the use of the following formula:

$$P = (1 - \sqrt[n]{\tfrac{R}{C}}) \times 100\%$$

where P = the depreciation percentage
n = the useful life of the assets (in years)
R = the residual value of the asset
C = the cost of the asset.

The fixed percentage rate will be given in all examples used in this text.

To illustrate this method let us take the same information used in our earlier example. Let us, however, use a fixed percentage (60 per cent) of the written-down value to determine the annual depreciation charge. The calculations will be as follows:

	$
Cost of machine	40,000
Year 1 depreciation charge (60% of cost)	24,000

Written-down value (WDV)	16,000
Year 2 depreciation charge (60% WDV)	9,600
Written-down value	6,400
Year 3 depreciation charge (60% WDV)	3,840
Written-down value	2,560
Year 4 depreciation charge (60% WDV)	1,536
Residual value	1,024

If we plot the written-down value of the asset which has been derived using the reducing-balance method against time, the result will be as shown in Figure 4.8.

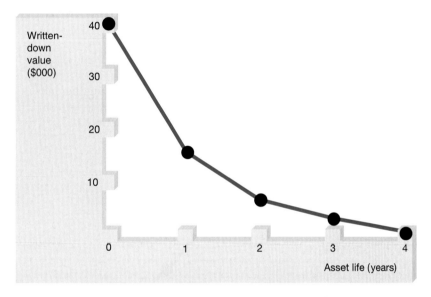

The figure shows that, under the reducing-balance method, the written-down value of an asset falls by a larger amount in the earlier years than in the later years. This is because the depreciation charge is based on a fixed-rate percentage of the written-down value.

FIGURE 4.8 Graph of written-down value against time using the reducing-balance method

The third approach to calculating depreciation is based on the units of output. Under this method the useful life of the asset changes from 'time' to 'output'. This method multiplies the depreciable amount by the relative output for each period. Referring to Example 4.1, we now need to know the expected total output, and the output for each year.

Year	Units of output
1	2000
2	4000
3	3000
4	1000

The formula is:

$$\frac{\text{cost} - \text{residual value}}{\text{total estimated units}} \times \text{output units in the period}$$

($40,000 – $1,024) ÷ 10,000 units = $3.8976 per unit

Applying this method gives us the following schedule of depreciation over the four years.

Cost of machine	40,000
Year 1 depreciation charge 1000 × $3.8976	3,898
Written-down value (WDV)	36,102
Year 2 depreciation charge 4000 × $3.8976	15,590
Written-down value	20,512
Year 3 depreciation charge 3000 × $3.8976	11,693
Written-down value	8,819
Year 4 depreciation charge 2000 × $3.8976	7,795
Residual value	1,024

If we plot the written-down value of the asset which has been derived using the units of production method, the result is shown in Figure 4.9.

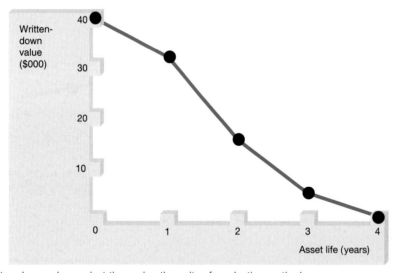

FIGURE 4.9 Graph of written-down value against time using the units of production method

ACTIVITY 4.16

Assume that the machine used in the example above was owned by a business that made a profit before depreciation of $20,000 for each of the four years in which the asset was held. Calculate the net profit for the business for each year under each depreciation method and comment on your findings.

We can see that the pattern of depreciation is quite different for the three methods. In practice, the use of different depreciation methods may not have such a dramatic effect on profits as suggested in the solution to the activity above. Where a business replaces some of its assets each year, the total depreciation charge calculated under the reducing-balance method or units of output approach will reflect a range of charges (from high through to low), as assets will be at different points in the replacement cycle. This could mean that the total depreciation charge under these methods may not be significantly different from the total depreciation charge that would be derived under the straight-line method.

Selecting a depreciation method

How does a business choose which depreciation method to use for a particular asset? The most appropriate method is the one that best matches the depreciation expense to the income it helped generate. The business may therefore decide to undertake an examination of the pattern of benefits flowing from the asset. Where the benefits are likely to remain fairly constant over time (e.g. buildings), the straight-line method may be considered appropriate. Where assets lose their efficiency over time and the benefits decline as a result (e.g. certain types of machinery), the reducing-balance method may be considered more appropriate. The units of output method is particularly relevant where depreciation relates more to use than to time, or technological or commercial factors.

There is an accounting standard to deal with the problem of depreciation—AASB 116 'Property, Plant and Equipment'. As we saw in Chapter 1, the purpose of accounting standards is to narrow the areas of difference in accounting between businesses by producing financial reports based on best accounting practice. However, the standard provides no clear statement on the suitability of the various methods of depreciation available. It simply states that management should select a depreciation method that is most appropriate to a particular asset and its use in the business. The standard does, however, require that limited companies disclose, in their financial reports, the methods of depreciation employed and either the depreciation rates applied or the useful lives of the assets.

Depreciation and the replacement of fixed assets

A view often heard is that the purpose of depreciation is to provide for the replacement of an asset when it reaches the end of its useful life. However, this is not the purpose of depreciation as conventionally defined. It was mentioned earlier that depreciation represents an attempt to allocate the cost (less any residual value) of an asset over its expected useful life to the business. The resulting depreciation expense in each period is then used in the calculation of net profit for the period. Calculating the depreciation expense for a period is therefore necessary for the proper measurement of both financial position (the carrying amount of assets) and financial performance, and must be calculated whether or not the business intends to replace the asset in the future.

ACTIVITY 4.17

Suppose that a business sets aside liquid funds, equivalent to the depreciation charge each year, with the intention of using them to replace the asset at the end of its useful life.

Will this ensure that there will be sufficient funds available for this purpose?

If there is an intention to replace the asset, the depreciation expense in the income statement will not ensure that liquid funds are set aside by the business specifically for this purpose. Although the effect of a depreciation charge is to reduce net profit and, therefore, to reduce the amount available for distribution to owners, the amounts retained within the business as a result may be invested in ways that are unrelated to the replacement of the specific assets.

Depreciation and judgment

When reading the above sections on depreciation it may have struck you that accounting is not as precise and objective as is sometimes suggested. There are areas where judgment is required, and depreciation provides a good illustration of this.

ACTIVITY 4.18

What kind of judgments must be made to calculate a depreciation charge for a period?

Making different judgments on these matters would result in a different pattern of depreciation expense over the life of the asset and therefore a different pattern of reported profits. However, under- or over-estimations that are made in relation to the above will be adjusted for in the final year of an asset's life (as a gain or loss on disposal), so the total depreciation charge (and total profit) over the asset's life will not be affected by estimation errors.

PROFIT MEASUREMENT AND THE VALUATION OF INVENTORY

As with property, plant and equipment, so inventory represents another example of a deferred expense, where the payment for the inventory precedes the recognition of the expense. In relation to the valuation of inventory and its impact on profit measurement a number of issues need to be considered.

* What is inventory?
* What is the cost of inventory?
* What is the basis for transferring the inventory cost to cost of sales?
* What is the net realisable value of inventory?

In considering these questions we will refer to the Australian Accounting Standard AASB 102 'Inventories'.

WHAT IS INVENTORY?

Inventory for accounting purposes consists of finished goods (e.g. merchandise for a retailer), raw materials (e.g. inputs to the manufacturing process—metal, paint, timber), stores or supplies (e.g. consumables—paper, cleaning liquid), and work-in-progress (e.g. partly finished goods of a manufacturer).

WHAT IS THE COST OF INVENTORY?

All costs directly related to bringing the inventory into a saleable state (ready to sell) should be included as part of the cost of inventory. This is covered in the accounting standard paragraph 10:

(a) cost of purchase;

(b) costs of conversion; and

(c) other costs incurred in bringing the inventories to their present location and condition.

ACTIVITY 4.19

Can you think of costs that could be included within each category of the definition?

The implication of the 'cost of inventory' for profit measurement is that any costs included in inventory will be deferred as an asset (inventory), and only be recognised as an expense when the inventory is sold (cost of goods sold) or written down (inventory write-down). Costs that are not included in inventory will be recognised immediately as expenses.

WHAT IS THE BASIS FOR TRANSFERRING THE INVENTORY COST TO COST OF SALES?

In the last chapter, we saw that historic cost is the traditional basis for valuing assets and so you may think that inventory valuation should not be a difficult issue. However, in a period of changing prices, the determination of which inventory costs should be allocated to the 'cost of goods sold' (expense) during the period, and which should be allocated to 'closing inventory' (asset) can have a significant impact on both the financial performance and the financial position of an entity in a given period.

Consider the example of a business that supplies coal to factories and which has the following transactions during a period:

		Tonnes	Cost per tonne
May 1	Opening stock/inventory	1,000	$10
2	Purchased	5,000	$11
3	Purchased	8,000	$12
		14,000	
6	Sold	9,000	
	Closing stock/inventory	5,000	

The business must determine the cost of the inventory sold during the period and the cost of the inventory remaining at the end of the period. However, it may be difficult to match precisely particular purchases with sales. When inventory is acquired, it may enter a common pool and become indistinguishable from earlier inventory purchased, in which case, how do we know which inventory was sold and which remains? Additionally, is it logical that the profit on the sale of a particular selection (item or batch) of inventory (where all inventory is the same) is dependent on which item of inventory is selected by the customer, or, more importantly, provided to the customer by the reporting entity? Where it is difficult to trace particular inventory movements, or where the costs in doing so outweigh the benefits, the solution is often to make an assumption concerning the physical flow of inventory through the business. This will enable the business to identify which inventory has been sold and which is still being held. The two most common assumptions used are:

✳ first in, first out (FIFO)—that is, the earlier inventory held is the first to be sold

✳ last in, first out (LIFO)—that is, the latest inventory held is the first to be sold.

These assumptions need not correspond to the actual flow of inventory through the business. They simply provide a useful and convenient way of deriving cost figures.

A further approach to deriving the cost of inventory sold is to assume that inventory entering the business loses its separate identity and any issues of inventory reflect the average cost of the inventory which is held. Weighted average cost (AVCO) is based on this idea. The weights used in deriving the average cost figure are the quantities of each batch of inventory purchased.

Let us now use the information contained in the example above to calculate the cost of goods sold and closing inventory figures for the business.

First in, first out

The example shows that purchases of 14,000 tonnes were made, that 9,000 tonnes were used up and sold, and 5,000 tonnes remained as closing inventory. The question is, what value do we put on the 9,000 tonnes which is sold, and what value on the closing inventory? Using FIFO, the first 9,000 tonnes of the purchases are assumed to be those which are sold and the remainder will comprise the closing inventory. Thus we have:

		Cost of sales				Closing inventory		
	No. of tonnes	Cost per tonne $	Total $		No. of tonnes	Cost per tonne $	Total $
May 1	1,000	10	10,000				
2	5,000	11	55,000				
3	3,000	12	36,000		5,000	12	60,000
	9,000						
	Cost of sales		101,000		Closing inventory		60,000

Last in, first out

Using this approach, the later purchases are assumed to be the first to be sold and the earlier purchases will comprise the closing inventory. Thus we have:

		Cost of sales				Closing inventory		
	No. of tonnes	Cost per tonne $	Total $		No. of tonnes	Cost per tonne $	Total $
May 3	8,000	12	96,000				
2	1,000	11	11,000		4,000	11	44,000
1	–		–		1,000	10	10,000
	9,000				5,000		
	Cost of sales		107,000		Closing inventory		54,000

Average cost

Using this approach, a weighted average cost will be determined which will be used to derive both the cost of sales and the cost of the remaining inventory held. Thus we have:

| | Purchases | | |
	No. of tonnes	Cost per tonne $	Total $
May 1	1,000	10	10,000
2	5,000	11	55,000
3	8,000	12	96,000
	14,000		161,000

Average cost = $161,000 / 14,000
= $11.5

Cost of sales				Closing inventory		
No. of tonnes	Cost per tonne $	Total $		No. of tonnes	Cost per tonne $	Total $
9,000	11.5	103,500		5,000	11.5	57,500

ACTIVITY 4.20

Suppose the 9,000 tonnes of inventory (coal) was sold for $15 per tonne.

(a) Calculate the gross profit for the period under each of the three methods.

(b) What observations concerning the portrayal of financial position can you make about each method when prices are rising?

ACTIVITY 4.21

Assume that prices are falling rather than rising. How would your observations concerning the portrayal of financial performance and position be different for the various inventory valuation methods?

It is important to recognise that the different inventory cost allocation methods will only have an effect on the reported profit between years. The figure derived for closing inventory will be carried forward and matched with sales in a later period. Thus, if the cheaper purchases of inventory are matched to sales in the current period, it will mean that the dearer purchases will be matched to sales in a later period. Over the life of the business, therefore, the total profit will be the same whichever cost allocation method has been used.

In reviewing the different cost allocation methods we have used a very simple method under which all inventory purchases occur before any sales arise. In reality, the sales and purchases will be interspersed over the period. This leads us to consider briefly the two main inventory recording systems:

1. the perpetual inventory system
2. the physical or periodic inventory system.

Perpetual inventory system

The perpetual inventory system maintains continuous records of all inventory movements at both cost and selling price. The following table summarises these records in relation to the inventory and cost of sales.

	Accounts	
Transaction	Inventory	Cost of sales
Purchase	Increase (+)	
Purchase returns	Decrease (–)	
Sales (at cost price)	Decrease (–)	Increase (+)
Sales returns (at cost price)	Increase (+)	Decrease (–)
Owner's drawings of inventory	Decrease (–)	
Stock count losses	Decrease (–)	

The advantage of the perpetual system is that at any point in time the business knows what inventory should be on hand and what the cost of sales for the period to date has been. Physical inventory counts are still undertaken to confirm the inventory balances and to assess inventory losses.

ACTIVITY 4.22

Why might the accounting inventory balance under the perpetual inventory system reveal a higher balance than the physical inventory count?

The implication of the perpetual inventory system for cost allocation is that for the LIFO and average approaches the appropriate costing is determined progressively over time and not at the end of the period.

Modifying our earlier example as follows, let us recalculate the inventory and cost of sales figures:

		Tonnes	Cost per tonne
May 1	Opening stock/inventory	1,000	$10
2	Purchased	5,000	$11
3	Sold	4,000	
4	Purchased	8,000	$12
6	Sold	5,000	
	Closing stock/inventory	5,000	

In relation to the three methods let us recalculate the figures.

First in, first out

This will be the same irrespective of when the sales are made, and is shown below.

Detailed records can be kept as described below. The opening balance provides a starting point. To this can be added any new purchases of stock. A record could be kept as follows:

May 1	Opening balance	1,000 tonnes at $10 = $10,000
May 2	Purchased	5,000 tonnes at $11 = $55,000

So total inventory at this stage equals:

> 1,000 tonnes at $10 = $10,000 plus
> 5,000 tonnes at $11 = $55,000

May 3 Sold 4,000 tonnes

A reduction would be made reflecting the cost of sales (using FIFO) on this date:

> 1,000 tonnes at $10 = $10,000 plus
> 3,000 tonnes at $11 = $33,000

The cost of this particular set of sales would be $43,000, while the remaining inventory on this date would be:

> 2,000 tonnes at $11 = $22,000

May 4 Purchased 8,000 tonnes at $12 = $96,000.

So total inventory on this date equals:

> 2,000 tonnes at $11 = $22,000 plus
> 8,000 tonnes at $12 = $96,000

May 6 Sold 5,000 tonnes

A reduction would be made reflecting the cost of sales (using FIFO) on this date:

> 2,000 tonnes at $11 = $22,000 plus
> 3,000 tonnes at $12 = $36,000

The cost of this particular set of sales would be $58,000, while the remaining inventory on this date would be:

> 5,000 tonnes at $12 = $60,000

The perpetual inventory method would give us a cost of sales figure in total of $43,000 + $58,000 = $101,000, which is the same as using the FIFO method (see page 146). The closing inventory is $60,000.

Last in, first out

Use of the perpetual inventory method and LIFO will often result in different figures to those calculated under the earlier system. Using the same example we find the following.

> May 1 Opening balance   1,000 tonnes at $10 = $10,000
> May 2 Purchased   5,000 tonnes at $11 = $55,000

So total inventory at this stage equals:

> 1,000 tonnes at $10 = $10,000 plus
> 5,000 tonnes at $11 = $65,000

May 3 Sold 4,000 tonnes

A reduction would be made reflecting the cost of sales (using LIFO) on this date:

> 4,000 tonnes at $11 = $44,000

The cost of this particular set of sales would be $44,000, while the remaining inventory on this date would be:

1,000 tonnes at $10 = $10,000 plus
1,000 tonnes at $11 = $11,000

May 4 Purchased 8,000 tonnes at $12 = $96,000.

So total inventory on this date equals:

1,000 tonnes at $10 = $10,000 plus
1,000 tonnes at $11 = $11,000 plus
8,000 tonnes at $12 = $96,000

May 6 Sold 5,000 tonnes

A reduction would be made reflecting the cost of sales (using LIFO) on this date:

5,000 tonnes at $12 = $60,000

The cost of this particular set of sales would be $60,000, while the remaining inventory on this date would be:

1,000 tonnes at $10 = $10,000 plus
1,000 tonnes at $11 = $11,000 plus
3,000 tonnes at $12 = $36,000

The net effect of this method is to show cost of sales as $44,000 + $60,000 = $104,000, and closing stock as $57,000.

Average cost

Using this approach you will adjust the average price each time there is a purchase. Using the same example we find the following:

May 1 Opening balance	1,000 tonnes at $10	=	$10,000
May 2 Purchased	5,000 tonnes at $11	=	$55,000
Balance equals	6,000 tonnes at $10.8333	=	$65,000
May 3 Cost of sales	4,000 tonnes at $10.8333	=	$43,333
Inventory balance	2,000 tonnes at $10.8333	=	$21,667
May 4 Purchase	8,000 tonnes at $12	=	$96,000
Inventory balance	10,000 tonnes at $11.7667	=	$117,667
May 6 Cost of sales	5,000 tonnes at $11.7667	=	$58,833
Inventory balance	5,000 tonnes at $11.7667	=	$58,833

The net effect of this method is to show cost of sales as $43,333 + $58,833 = $102,166 and closing stock as $58,833.

Figure 4.10 visually illustrates the alternative inventory cost allocation methods related to the example used.

Physical or periodic inventory system

The physical or periodic inventory system is much simpler and does not maintain detailed records of the cost of inventory sold. Returning to our earlier illustration of transactions and the records maintained under the periodic system we see that:

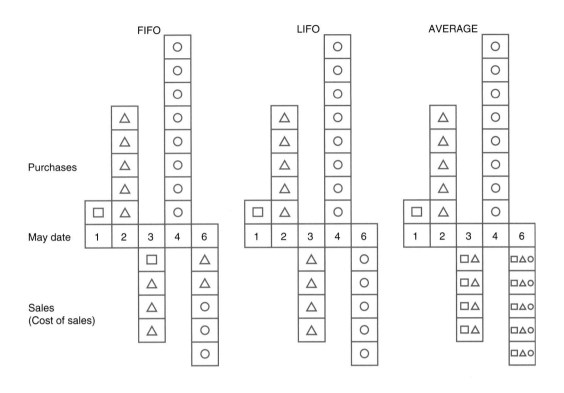

FIGURE 4.10 Inventory cost allocation methods

Transaction	Inventory	Accounts Purchases (expense)	Cost of sales
Opening balance	✓	Nil	
Purchases		Increase (+)	
Purchase returns		Decrease (−)	
Sales (at cost price)			
Sales returns (at cost price)			
Owner's drawings of inventory		Decrease (−)	
Stock count	Adjust	Close	Calculate

As can be observed in the table:

✳ The inventory (asset) account remains unchanged during the year and is updated at the end of the period following the stock count.

✳ Net purchases are recorded in the purchases account, which is an expense account. It is assumed that what is purchased will be sold during the period.

151

* At year end a stock count is undertaken to update the inventory balance and calculate the cost of sales.
* Under this system it is not directly possible to determine stock losses as the assumption is that stock not on hand must have been sold (i.e. is in cost of sales).

Another way of determining cost of sales is to prepare a summary report as follows:

	Inventory at the beginning		x
(+)	Purchases	x	
(+)	Freight inward	x	
(−)	Purchase returns	(x)	x
(=)	Inventory available		x
(−)	Inventory at the end		(x)
=	Cost of sales		x

The implication of the periodic inventory system for cost allocation is that all purchases and sales are assumed to be at the end of the period and therefore the results of applying the three methods will be the same as in the original example where all sales occurred after the purchases for the period were complete.

The Australian accounting standard permits the use of a number of inventory cost allocation methods, being:

* specific identification
* first in, first out
* average
* standard cost.

However, it does not allow the use of the 'last in, first out' method.

ACTIVITY 4.23

Why do you think that LIFO is not an allowed inventory cost allocation method within Australia?

WHAT IS THE NET REALISABLE VALUE OF INVENTORY?

We saw in the previous chapter that the closing inventory figure will appear as part of the current assets of the business and that the prudence (conservatism) assumption requires that current assets be valued at the lower of cost and **net realisable value**. (The net realisable value of inventory is the estimated selling price less any further costs that may be necessary to complete the goods and any costs involved in selling and distributing those goods.) The application of this rule would lead to lower profits and lower assets in the period when it is applied. In practice, however, the cost of the inventory held is usually below the current net realisable value—particularly during a period of rising prices. It is therefore the cost figure that will normally appear in the balance sheet.

ACTIVITY 4.24

Can you think of any circumstances where the net realisable value will be lower than the cost of inventory held, even during a period of generally rising prices?

AASB 102 'Inventories' requires that inventory be valued on the basis of the lower of cost and net realisable value on an item-by-item basis.

Inventory valuation and depreciation provide two examples of where the **consistency convention** should be applied. This convention holds that when a particular method of accounting is selected to deal with a transaction, this method should be applied consistently over time. Thus, it would not be usual to switch from, say, FIFO to AVCO between periods. The purpose of this convention is to try to ensure that users are able to make valid comparisons between periods. Where changes of this type do occur, appropriate disclosures regarding reasons and effects are required.

ACTIVITY 4.25

Inventory valuation provides a further example of the judgment required to derive the figures for inclusion in the financial statements. Can you identify the main areas where judgment is required in inventory valuation?

PROFIT MEASUREMENT AND THE PROBLEM OF BAD AND DOUBTFUL DEBTS

THE TRADITIONAL APPROACH

The recognition of bad and doubtful debts is associated with accrued income. Most businesses sell goods on credit. When credit sales are made the revenue is usually recognised as soon as the goods are passed to, and accepted by, the customer. Recording the dual aspect of a credit sale will involve:

✴ increasing the sales and

✴ increasing debtors/receivables

by the amount of the credit sale.

However, with this type of sale there is always the risk that the customer will not pay the amount due. Where it is reasonably certain that the customer will not eventually pay, the debt is considered to be 'bad' and this must be taken into account when preparing the financial statements.

ACTIVITY 4.26

When preparing the financial statements, what would be the effect of not taking into account the fact that a debt is bad on the portrayal of financial performance and position?

To provide a more realistic picture of financial performance and financial position, the bad debt must be 'written off'. This will involve:

✴ reducing accounts receivable (debtors) and

✴ increasing expenses (by creating an expense known as 'bad debts written off') by the amount of the bad debt.

The matching convention requires that the bad debt is written off in the same period as the sale that gave rise to the debt is recognised.

Note that when a debt is bad the accounting response is not simply to cancel the original sale. If we did this, the income statement would not be so informative. Reporting the bad debts as an expense can be extremely useful in the evaluation of management performance, particularly credit-granting policies.

At the end of the accounting period it may not be possible to identify, with reasonable certainty, all the bad debts that have been incurred during the period. It may be that some debts are unlikely to be collected, but only at some later point in time will the true position become clear. The uncertainty that exists does not mean that, when preparing the financial reports, we should ignore the possibility that some of the debtors outstanding will eventually prove to be bad. It would not be prudent to do so, nor would it comply with the need to match expenses to the period in which the associated sale is recognised. As a result, the business will normally try to identify all those debts that, at the end of the period, can be classified as 'doubtful' (i.e. there is a possibility that they may eventually prove to be bad). The determination of doubtful debts would normally be achieved either on the basis of the credit sales or by analysing the debtors' balances outstanding.

With a credit sales approach a given percentage based on past experience and current expectations is often applied to the credit sales figure to determine the doubtful debts expense. The analysis of the debtors' balances outstanding could involve an account-by-account analysis of individual debtors, or alternatively categorising the total 'debtors outstanding' balance into categories in terms of how long the amounts have been outstanding. For the total of each aged category (e.g. current, 31–60 days, 61–90 days) a different percentage is applied to determine the amount that is not expected to be collected. The percentages applied to each aged category are determined from past experience and future expectations. This analysis might appear as follows:

Aged category	Amount $	Percentage %	Doubtful debts $
Current	32,000	1	320
31–60 days	21,000	3	620
61–90 days	12,000	8	960
91–120 days	8,000	15	1,200
120+ days	5,000	30	1,500
Total	78,000		4,600

Analysis using either the percentage of credit sales or the aged listing of debtors will facilitate the determination of the amount of the debtors balance that is not expected to be received. This will be recorded as:

❋ an expense labelled 'doubtful debts expense' to be included in the income statement

❋ a deduction from the debtors account labelled 'allowance for doubtful debts' to be included in the balance sheet. This is another example of a contra asset account.

By recognising doubtful debts we take full account, in the appropriate accounting period, of those debtors for which there is a risk of non-payment. This accounting treatment of doubtful debts will be in addition to the treatment of bad debts described earlier. The following example illustrates the reporting of bad and doubtful debts.

Boston Enterprises has debtors of $350,000 at the end of the accounting year to 30 June 2006. Investigation of these debtors reveals that $10,000 is likely to prove irrecoverable and that recovery of a further $30,000 is doubtful.

Extracts from the financial statements would be as shown below.

EXAMPLE

4.2

Income statement (extracts) for the year ended 30 June 2006	
	$
Bad debts written off	10,000
Doubtful debts expense	30,000

Balance sheet (extracts) as at 30 June 2006	
	$
Debtors	340,000*
Less allowance for doubtful debts	30,000
	310,000

*(i.e. $350,000 − $10,000)

The allowance for doubtful debts is, of course, an estimate and it is quite likely that the actual amount of debts that ultimately prove to be bad will be different from the estimate. Let us say that during the next accounting period it was discovered that $26,000 of the debts that were considered to be doubtful proved to be irrecoverable. These debts must now be written off as follows:

• reduce debtors by $26,000
• reduce allowance for doubtful debts by $26,000.

However, an allowance for doubtful debts of $4,000 will still remain. This amount represents an overestimate made when creating the allowance for the year to 30 June 2006. As the allowance is no longer needed it should be eliminated. Remember that the allowance was created by raising an expense in the income statement for the year to 30 June 2006. As the expense was too high, the amount of the overestimate should be 'written back' in the next accounting period. In other words, it will be treated as income for the year to 30 June 2007. This will mean:

• reducing the allowance for doubtful debts by $4,000
• increasing income by $4,000.

Ideally, of course, the amount should be written back to the 2006 income statement, however, it is too late to do this, and the accounting standards applying in Australia from 2005 would indicate that errors in a prior period should be adjusted directly against the owners' equity account.

It is more likely that the income shown above would be seen as an off-set to the doubtful debts expense of the next year (2007).

In practice, you will observe at least three alternative approaches by firms to recording bad and doubtful debts.

✳ Those firms that only recognise 'bad debts expense' on the basis of a realised uncollectible amount (customer is bankrupt, customer deceased, customer cannot be located etc.).

✳ Those firms that recognise 'bad debts expense' and 'doubtful debts expense' separately. The 'bad debts expense' is always written off directly against the accounts receivable (debtors) account as for the conditions discussed above. The 'doubtful debts expense/income' represents the adjustment required each year to the allowance for doubtful debts account on the basis of the aged listing analysis.

✴ Those firms that recognise a single 'bad and doubtful debts expense'. The expense figure is based on either the percentage of credit sales or aged listing approach. When bad debts are realised the amount is deducted from both accounts receivable and the allowance for doubtful debts account.

ACTIVITY 4.27

Clayton Conglomerates had debts outstanding at the end of the accounting year to 31 March 2005 of $870,000. The chief accountant believed that $40,000 of those debts were irrecoverable and that a further $60,000 were doubtful. In the subsequent period, it was found that an overestimate had been made and that only a further $45,000 of debts actually proved to be bad.

Show the relevant extracts in the income statement for both 2005 and 2006 to report the bad debts written off and allowance for doubtful debts. Also show the relevant balance sheet extract as at 30 June 2006.

ACTIVITY 4.28

Bad and doubtful debts represent further areas where judgment is required in deriving expenses figures for a particular period. What will be the effect of different judgments concerning the amount of bad and doubtful debts on the profit for a particular period and on the total profit reported over the life of the business?

THE IMPAIRMENT OF ASSETS APPROACH

With the harmonisation of Australian accounting standards with international accounting standards an overall **impairment** test is now being applied to many of the assets held by business entities.

The impairment test being that assets should not be carried at amounts that exceed the future cash flows expected to be recovered from the use and/or disposal of that asset. Where the recoverable amount is less than the carrying amount, the assets are to be written down to the recoverable amount and the write-down will be labelled 'impairment loss'.

Accounting for accounts receivable (debtors) is covered under the accounting standard on financial instruments (AASB 132).

The implications of this standard for accounting for bad and doubtful debts are:

✴ In calculating the bad and doubtful debts expense consideration will be given to the amount expected to be recovered. This is essentially the same as what has already been discussed under the traditional approach.

✴ The name of the bad and doubtful debts expense may be changed to 'impairment loss' on debtors.

✴ The name of the contra-debtors' account may be changed from the 'allowance for doubtful debts' to the 'allowance for impairment loss'.

✴ The asset (accounts receivable) will be said to be recorded on the basis of unimpaired cost. That is, it will be recorded on the basis of the residual transaction amount (cost) that has not been written down for impairment.

SELF-ASSESSMENT QUESTION 4.1

TT Ltd is a new business which started trading on 1 January 2005. The following is a summary of transactions which occurred during the first year of trading:

1. The owners introduced $50,000 of capital which was paid into a bank account opened in the name of the business.

2. Premises were rented from 1 January 2006 at an annual rental of $20,000. During the year, rent of $25,000 was paid to the owner of the premises.

3. Rates on the premises were paid during the year as follows:
   - For the period 1 January 2005 to 31 March 2005, $500.
   - For the period 1 April 2005 to 31 March 2006, $1,200.

4. A delivery vehicle was bought on 1 January for $12,000. This is expected to be used in the business for four years and then to be sold for $2,000.

5. Wages totalling $33,500 were paid during the year. At the end of the year, the business owed $630 of wages for the last week of the year.

6. Electricity bills for the first three-quarters of the year were paid totalling $1,650. After 31 December 2005, but before the accounts had been finalised for the year, the bill for the last quarter arrived showing a charge of $620.

7. Inventory totalling $143,000 was bought on credit.

8. Inventory totalling $12,000 was bought for cash.

9. Sales on credit totalled $152,000 (cost $74,000).

10. Cash sales totalled $35,000 (cost $16,000).

11. Receipts from trade debtors totalled $132,000.

12. Payments to trade creditors totalled $121,000.

13. Vehicle running expenses paid totalled $9,400.

At the end of the year it was clear that a trade debtor who owed $400 would not be able to pay any part of the debt.

Required:

Prepare a balance sheet as at 31 December 2005 and an income statement for the year to that date.

INTERPRETING THE INCOME STATEMENT

When an income statement is presented to users it is sometimes the case that the only item with which they will be concerned will be the final net profit figure, or 'bottom line', as it is sometimes called. Although the net profit figure is a primary measure of performance, and its importance is difficult to overstate, the income statement contains other information that should also be of interest. In order to evaluate business performance effectively, it is important to find out how the final net profit figure was derived. Thus, the level of sales, the nature and amount of expenses incurred and the profit in relation to sales are important factors in understanding the financial performance of the business over a period. The analysis and interpretation of financial statements is considered in detail in Chapter 6. However, it may be useful at this point to consider some of the ways in which users will use the information contained within the income statement.

EXAMPLE
4.3

Consider the income statement set out below:

PATEL WHOLESALERS
Income statement for the year ended 31 March 2006

	$	$
Sales		460,500
Less cost of sales		345,800
Gross profit		114,700
Less		
Salaries and wages	45,900	
Rent and rates	15,300	
Telephone and postage	1,400	
Motor vehicle expenses	3,900	
Loan interest	4,800	
Depreciation—motor vehicle	2,300	
Depreciation—fixtures and fittings	2,200	
		75,800
Net profit		38,900

To evaluate financial performance the following points might be considered:

- The sales figure represents an important measure of output and can be compared with the sales figure of earlier periods and the planned sales figure for the current period in order to assess the achievement of the business.
- The gross profit figure can be related to the sales figure in order to find out the profitability of the goods that are sold. In the statement shown above we can see that the gross profit is about 25 per cent of the sales figure or, to put it another way, for every $1 of sales generated the gross profit is 25c. This level of profitability may be compared with past periods, with planned levels of profitability or with comparable figures of similar businesses.
- The expenses of the business may be examined and compared with past periods in order to evaluate operating efficiency. Individual expenses can be related to sales to assess whether the level of expenses is appropriate. Thus, for example, in the above statement the salaries and wages represent almost 10 per cent of sales, or for every $1 of sales generated 10c is absorbed by employee costs.
- Net profit can also be related to sales. In the statement shown above, net profit is about 8 per cent of sales. Thus, for every $1 of sales the owners of the business benefit by 8c. Whether or not this is acceptable will again depend on making the kind of comparisons

referred to earlier. Net profit as a percentage of sales can vary substantially between different types of business. There is usually a trade-off to be made between profitability and sales volume. Some businesses are prepared to accept a low net profit percentage in return for generating a high volume of sales. At the other extreme, some businesses may prefer to have a high net profit percentage but accept a relatively low volume of sales. For example, a supermarket may fall into the former category while a trader in luxury cars may fall into the latter category.

SELF-ASSESSMENT QUESTION 4.2

Chan Exporters provides the following income statement:

Income statement for the year ending 31 May 2006		
	$	$
Sales		840,000
Less cost of sales		620,000
Gross profit		220,000
Less		
Salaries and wages	92,000	
Selling and distribution expenses	44,000	
Rent and rates	30,000	
Bad debts written off	86,000	
Telephone and postage	4,000	
Insurance	2,000	
Motor vehicle expenses	8,000	
Loan interest	5,000	
Depreciation—motor vehicle	3,000	
Depreciation—fixtures and fittings	4,000	
		278,000
Net loss		(58,000)

In the previous year sales were $640,000. The gross profit was $200,000 and the net profit was $37,000.

Required:

Analyse the performance of the business for the year to 31 May 2006 insofar as the information allows.

SELF-ASSESSMENT QUESTION 4.3

Presented below is a draft set of simplified accounts for Pear Ltd for the year ended 30 September 2006.

PEAR LTD

Income statement for the year ended 30 September 2006

	$'000	$'000
Sales		1,456
Cost of sales		768
Gross profit		688
Less expenses		
Salaries	220	
Depreciation	249	
Other operating expenses	131	
		600
Operating profit		88
Interest expense		15
Profit before taxation		73
Taxation—30%		22
Profit after taxation		51

Balance sheet as at 30 September 2006

	$'000	$'000
Current assets		
Cash at bank	21	
Trade debtors	182	
Inventory	207	
		410
Non-current assets		
Cost	1,570	
Accumulated depreciation	(690)	
		880
Total assets		1,290
Current liabilities		
Bank overdraft	105	
Tax payable	22	
Trade creditors	88	
Other creditors	20	
		235
Non-current liabilities		
10% Debentures—repayable 2009		300
Total liabilities		535

Shareholders' equity		
Share capital	600	
Retained profit	155	
		755
Total liabilities and shareholders' equity		1,290

The following additional information is available:

1. Depreciation has not yet been charged on office equipment with a written-down value of $100,000. This class of asset is depreciated at 12 per cent per annum using the reducing-balance method.

2. A new machine was purchased on credit for $30,000 and delivered on 29 September but has not been included in the financial statements.

3. A sales invoice to the value of $18,000 for September has been omitted from the accounts. (The cost of sales is stated correctly.)

4. A dividend has been proposed of $25,000.

5. The interest expense on the debenture for the second half of the year has not been included in the accounts.

6. A general allowance for doubtful debts is to be made at the rate of 2 per cent of debtors.

7. An invoice for electricity to the value of $2,000 for the quarter ended 30 September 2006 arrived on 4 October and has not been included in the accounts.

8. The charge for taxation will have to be amended to take into account the above information.

Required:

Prepare a revised set of financial statements for the year ended 30 September 2006 incorporating the additional information in points 1–8 above.

SUMMARY

In this chapter we have achieved the following objectives in the way shown.

OBJECTIVE	METHOD ACHIEVED
State the purpose of the income statement	Identified the purpose as being the measurement of the increment in wealth during the period
Explain the relationship between the income statement and the balance sheet	Explained the increment in owners' equity from operating or trading activities
Present the profit and loss equation and identify alternative formats for the income statement	Explained the profit and loss equation: • Profit or loss = Income – Expenses or • Profit or loss = Change in net assets for the period – Owners' contributions for the period + Owners' distributions for the period and illustrated alternative formats

Demonstrate an understanding of income in relation to definition, recognition, classification and measurement	Defined and explained income:
	• Inflows of future economic benefits in the form of asset increases or liability reductions that result in an increase in owners' equity of a non-contribution nature
	• Recognition:
	  —Probable that the inflow has occurred
	  —The inflow can be reliably measured

Demonstrate an understanding of expenses in relation to definition, recognition, classification and measurement	Defined and explained expenses:
	• Outflows of future economic benefits in the form of assets down or liabilities up that result in a decrease in owners' equity of a non-distribution nature
	• Classification:
	  —Cost of sales
	  —Selling and distribution
	  —Administration and general
	  —Financial
	• Recognition:
	  —Probable that the outflow has occurred
	  —The outflow can be reliably measured

Distinguish between accrual- and cash-based transaction recognition	Illustrated difference between cash-based and accrual-based, with emphasis on:
	• Income:
	  —Cash-based relates to benefits being received during the period
	  —Accrual-based relates to revenues being earned during the period
	• Expenses:
	  —Cash-based relates to expenses being paid during the period
	  —Accrual-based relates to expenses being incurred during the period

Analyse expense recognition for non-current tangible assets	Explained the allocation of the cost of a tangible asset to reflect the consumption of that asset's economic benefits during the period (physical deterioration, technical obsolescence, commercial obsolescence, depreciation)

OBJECTIVE	METHOD ACHIEVED
	The most common allocation methods are: • Straight-line • Reducing-balance (accelerated)
Analyse expense recognition for inventory	Explained inventory recording methods: • Perpetual (continuous) • Periodic (physical stock count) Inventory cost allocation methods: • First in, first out (FIFO) • Last in, first out (LIFO) • Average (weighted or moving) To conform with the matching and prudence assumptions, inventory is valued on the basis of the lower of cost and net realisable value (the amount expected to be obtained from orderly sale less the costs to sell)
Analyse expense recognition for accounts receivable	Explained the problems associated with debtors and bad debts, and examined alternative recognition methods: • Bad debts are realised in the sense that both the debtor and the amount can be established • Doubtful debts relate to amounts not expected to be collected from debtors but are not currently uncollectible Alternative doubtful debt calculation methods: • Applying a given percentage to sales • Analysing the balances in debtors' accounts
Review and interpret income statements	Explained and analysed such statements by comparison with: • Past performance • Expectations or budget • Other firms in the same industry

DISCUSSION QUESTIONS

EASY

<Obj 1>   **4.1** What other labels are given to the income statement?

<Obj 2>   **4.2** How does the income statement articulate (link) with the balance sheet?

<Obj 7>   **4.3** Under what circumstances should you choose the following alternative depreciation methods?
(a) Straight-line
(b) Reducing-balance

<Obj 9>   **4.4** Distinguish between bad and doubtful debts.

INTERMEDIATE

<Obj 1>   **4.5** Company Xcel Ltd announces an increase of 10% in net profit for the year to $1,700,000. As an potential investor in the company:

(a) what does this announcement tell you?

(b) what other information do you require in relation to deciding whether to invest or not in the company?

<Obj 2>   **4.6** Distinguish between the 'transaction approach' and the 'stock approach' to calculating profit.

<Obj 3, 4>   **4.7** Income is essential to all profit-oriented businesses.

(a) Define income.

(b) Discuss the basis of income recognition by accountants.

<Obj 4>   **4.8** When should income be recognised in the following situations?

(a) a long-term construction project

(b) investment in a new-growth forest

(c) wine held in storage for the purposes of selective ageing

(d) mining exploration.

<Obj 4>   **4.9** Within the income statement, the following terms are frequently used:

- Income
- Revenue
- Gains
- Profit
- Surplus.

Are these labels alternative titles for the same thing, or do they represent different transactions or computations?

<Obj 5>   **4.10** 'An asset is similar to an expense.' Do you agree?

<Obj 5>   **4.11** Within the income statement, the following terms are used:

- Expenditure
- Cost
- Expense
- Loss
- Deficit.

Are these labels alternative titles for the same thing, or do they represent different transactions or computations?

<Obj 5>   **4.12** Income is normally associated with expenses.

(a) Define expenses.

(b) Discuss the basis of expense recognition by accountants.

<Obj 5>   **4.13** It has been said that 'all costs become expenses'.

(a) Distinguish between 'costs' and 'expenses'.

(b) Do you agree with this statement? Why or why not?

<Obj 5>   **4.14** A retailer will normally calculate 'gross profit'.

(a) What is gross profit?

(b) How is it related to 'mark-up'?

(c) Why is it such an important measure?

<Obj 6>   **4.15** Accounting transactions can be recognised on a 'cash' or an 'accrual' basis.

(a) Explain these two terms.

(b) Why have government bodies and councils moved in recent years from a 'cash basis' to an 'accrual basis' of transaction recognition?

<Obj 6>   **4.16** Some 'provision' accounts are classified as 'contra assets' and others as 'liabilities'.

(a) What is the difference?

(b) Provide examples of each.

<Obj 6>   **4.17** 'Although the income statement is a record of past achievement, the calculations required for certain expenses involve estimates of the future.' What is meant by this statement? Can you think of examples where estimates of the future are used?

<Obj 7>   **4.18** 'Depreciation is a process of allocation and not valuation.' What do you think is meant by this statement?

<Obj 8>   **4.19** The Australian Accounting Standard on inventories precludes the use of the LIFO inventory cost allocation methods. What is LIFO?

<Obj 8>   **4.20** It is claimed that in periods of rising inventory purchase prices, the use of FIFO inventory cost allocation leads to a profit overstatement.
(a) How does this inventory method lead to an overstatement of profits?
(b) How could this problem be resolved?

<Obj 9>   **4.21** How would you suggest a business determine the 'bad and doubtful debts expense' for a given period?

<Obj 11>   **4.22** In terms of expenses, in this chapter you have specifically reviewed:
(a) depreciation of property, plant and equipment
(b) cost of goods sold and inventory valuation
(c) bad and doubtful debts and debtors.
For each of these expenses discuss the significance or influence of the accounting conventions.

CHALLENGING

<Obj 2>   **4.23** The profit after tax for the period was $70,000, but the net assets increased by $180,000. What are the possible explanations for the discrepancy between the two figures?

<Obj 4>   **4.24** Revenue could be recognised at different points in the discovery/extraction/production/sales cycle.
(a) How does the decision on which point is selected affect performance?
(b) How does the 'realisation convention' of accounting assist in the decision process?
(c) Identify situations where income could be recognised earlier in the cycle and also where it should not be recognised until later in the cycle.

<Obj 7>   **4.25** Critically evaluate the following statements about depreciation.
(a) Depreciation is a valuation adjustment.
(b) Depreciation equals physical wear and tear.
(c) Depreciation provides funds for replacement.
(d) There is no point depreciating buildings because their value is increasing.

<Obj 7>   **4.26** In relation to 'property, plant and equipment', the following expenses can be observed in the income statements or attached notes:
• depreciation of equipment
• write-down of equipment to fair value
• write-down of equipment to recoverable amount (impairment)
• carrying amount of equipment sold
• immediate expensing of equipment purchased.
(a) Explain the difference between these 'expenses'.
(b) Identify an accounting principle that is closely linked with each of these expenses.

APPLICATION EXERCISES

EASY

<Obj 10>

4.1 The following information on the income statement relates to a trading enterprise and covers four independent situations.

Calculate the missing figures.

	(a) $	(b) $	(c) $	(d) $
Net sales	200,000	600,000	800,000	?
Opening inventory	54,000	120,000	?	230,000
Net purchases	130,000	?	500,000	?
Available inventory	184,000	?	?	?
Closing inventory	44,000	85,000	150,000	255,000
Cost of sales	?	390,000	?	660,000
Gross profit	60,000	210,000	260,000	240,000
Operating expenses	70,000	165,000	205,000	?
Net profit (loss)	?	?	?	(25,000)

INTERMEDIATE

<Obj 3>

4.2 Joe's profit and loss records for the year ended 30 June 2006 have been lost. However, you are able to extract the following balance sheet information together with the owner's contributions and drawings for the year.

	Beginning	Ending
Current assets		
Cash	5,300	3,700
Accounts receivable	7,900	8,700
Inventory	6,400	7,500
Prepayments	800	600
Non-current assets		
Land	20,000	20,000
Building	60,000	68,000
Plant and equipment	18,000	16,500
Motor vehicles	23,000	31,000
Current liabilities		
Trade creditors	9,000	6,900
Bank overdraft	Nil	7,400
Accruals	1,300	1,500
Non-current liabilities		
Bank loan	40,000	36,000

Additional information: The owner did not make any further contributions during the year but did withdraw cash of $12,000.

Calculate the profit made by Joe's sole proprietorship during the year ended 30 June 2006.

<Obj 7>   **4.3**   Calculate the fixed percentage rate of depreciation (P) to be used with the reducing-balance method given the following alternative circumstances:

	(a)	(b)	(c)
The cost of the asset (C)	$10,000	$20,000	$40,000
The estimated useful asset life (n)	5 years	8 years	10 years
The estimated residual value of the asset (R)	$2,000	$5,000	$4,000

$$\text{Formula: } P = \left(1 - \sqrt[n]{\frac{R}{C}}\right) \times 100\%$$

<Obj 8>   **4.4**   Spratley Ltd is a builders' merchant. On 1 September the business had 20 tonnes of sand in stock at a cost of $18 per tonne and at a total cost of $360. During the first week in September the business purchased the following amounts of sand:

September	Tonnes	Cost per tonne
2	48	$20
4	15	$24
6	10	$25

On 7 September the business sold 60 tonnes of sand to a local builder.

Calculate:
(a) The cost of goods sold based on perpetual inventory and FIFO cost allocation.
(b) The closing inventory based on periodic inventory and weighted average cost allocation.

<Obj 10>   **4.5**   Prepare an income statement for the year ended 30 June 2006 given the following account balances. (*Note*: Some accounts may not be relevant.)

Cash	3,000
Sales	280,000
Salary and wages	37,000
Accounts receivable	15,000
Loan interest	4,000
Insurance	2,000
Loan	40,000
Telephone and postage	1,500
Rent and rates	12,400
Cost of sales	160,000
Inventory	11,000
Accounts payable	9,100
Heat and light	3,700
Motor vehicles	32,000
Equipment repairs	1,600
Depreciation—motor vehicles	4,500
Motor vehicle running costs	1,700
Depreciation—equipment	3,200
Royalties received	1,700
Accounting and audit	3,400
Bad and doubtful debts	800

CHALLENGING

<Obj 3>

4.6 The following table highlights the impacts on the balance sheet and income statement of using three alternative approaches to recognising bad and doubtful debts:

Account	Method A	Method B	Method C
Income statement	$	$	$
* Bad debts expense	10,000	10,000	
* Doubtful debts expense		7,000	
* Bad and doubtful debts expense			17,000
Balance sheet			
* Accounts receivable	189,000	189,000	189,000
* Allowance for doubtful debts		(15,000)	(15,000)

(a) What is the approach used in Method A called?
(b) What is the approach used in both Method B and Method C called?
(c) What is the rationale for the approach used in Method A?
(d) What accounting principles support the approach used in Method B and Method C?
(e) What is the basic difference between Method B and Method C?
(f) How is the $17,000 expense determined under Method C?
(g) How is the balance in the 'Allowance for doubtful debts' determined under Method B?

<Obj 3>

4.7 Using the 'stock approach' calculate the profit for the period given:
- assets for the period went up by $33,400
- liabilities for the period went down by $15,700
- the owners contributed $5,000 in new capital
- the owners' drawings were $7,500
- land was revalued upwards to the asset revaluation reserve by $20,000
- a negative adjustment was made against the opening retained earnings account for $3,100 related to the introduction of a new accounting standard
- debt of $12,000 was extinguished by issuing an equivalent amount in ownership capital.

<Obj 5, 6>

4.8 On what basis would the following expenses be measured or calculated (i.e. what does the amount for each represent)?

Expense account	Amount $	Basis of measurement
A Insurance	2,400	
B Depreciation—Buildings	5,700	
C Cost of goods sold	89,500	
D Bad and doubtful debts	4,700	
E Long-service leave	5,800	
F Warranty	6,300	
G Write-down of land	15,000	
H Impairment of goodwill	23,000	

<Obj 6, 10>   **4.9**   Ambrose prepares his income statement on a cash basis.

Sales		100,000
Less inventory purchases		30,000
Equals gross profit		70,000
Less expenses		
Salary and wages	20,000	
Rent	15,000	
Insurance	2,000	
Advertising	3,000	
Other	4,000	44,000
Equals net profit		26,000

On further investigation you find the following accrual balances:

	Beginning	Ending
Debtors	6,000	1,500
Creditors (for inventory)	700	4,100
Inventory	8,400	6,500
Prepaid rent	3,000	1,200
Prepaid insurance	800	1,000
Accrued advertising	Nil	600

Also there should be depreciation of plant and equipment of $2,400, and bad and doubtful debts of $300.

Prepare an accrual-based income statement.

<Obj 7>   **4.10**   Equipment was acquired on 1 July 2004 for $50,000 by HiLite Ltd. Its life was determined as being:

- useful—5years
- economic—8 years
- physical—10 years.

The estimated residual values at the end of these respective periods are:

- after 5 years, $20,000
- after 8 years, $4,000
- after 10 years, nil.

(a) Over what period should HiLite depreciate the equipment?

(b) What would be the difference in the depreciation expense for the year ending 30 June 2006 based on using either the 'straight-line method' or the 'reducing-balance method'?

(c) On what basis should management select one or other of these two methods to depreciate the equipment?

<Obj 8>

4.11 The following table summarises the inventory movements of a particular product for the year under the perpetual inventory recording system.

Opening balance   100 @ $1

	1st qtr	2nd qtr	3rd qtr	4th qtr
Purchases	60 @ 1.10	40 @ 1.20	80 @ 1.40	100 @ 1.70
Sales	80 @ 2.10	70 @ 2.20	60 @ 2.30	120 @ 2.40
Closing stock count	47 units			

(a) Calculate inventory shortage.
(b) Determine cost of goods sold using FIFO cost allocation.
(c) Determine the value of closing inventory using LIFO cost allocation.
(d) Determine the value of inventory loss (shortage) using average cost allocation.

<Obj 9>

4.12 The following represents a review of credit sales and bad debts realised over a five-year period together with details of the origin of the bad debts (what year's credit sales they relate to).

Year	Credit sales $	Bad debts $	1	2	3	4	5
				Origin of bad debts Year ($)			
1	160,000	1,920	1,920				
2	190,000	4,130	1,280	2,850			
3	240,000	6,120		2,280	3,840		
4	310,000	9,360		570	3,840	4,960	
5	390,000	13,200			1,920	5,580	4,680
6	na					4,960	9,360
7	na						9,360

na = not applicable

Prepare a report to the business owners in respect of credit management based on the above analysis.

In this report you should discuss:
(a) The changing significance of bad debts expense.
(b) The trends in recognising bad debts realised.
(c) Alternative methods for determining the uncollectables (bad and/or doubtful debts).

<Obj 9>

4.13 The following is the balance sheet of TT Ltd at the end of its first year of trading (from Self-assessment question 4.1):

TT LTD

Balance sheet as at 31 December 2005

	$	$
Current assets		
Cash at bank	750	
Prepaid expenses	5,300	
Trade debtors	19,600	
Inventory	65,000	
		90,650
Non-current assets		
Motor vehicles—cost	12,000	
Accumulated depreciation	2,500	
		9,500
Total assets		100,150
Current liabilities		
Accrued expenses	1,250	
Trade creditors	22,000	
		23,250
Owner's equity		
Original	50,000	
Retained profit	26,900	
		76,900
Total liabilities and owner's equity		100,150

During 2006, the following transactions took place:

1. The owners withdrew capital in the form of cash of $20,000.
2. Premises continued to be rented at an annual rental of $20,000. During the year, rent of $15,000 was paid to the owner of the premises.
3. Rates on the premises were paid during the year for the period 1 April 2006 to 31 March 2007, $1,300.
4. A second delivery vehicle was bought on 1 January for $13,000. This is expected to be used in the business for four years and then to be sold for $3,000.
5. Wages totalling $36,700 were paid during the year. At the end of the year, the business owed $860 of wages for the last week of the year.
6. Electricity bills for the first three quarters of the year were paid totalling $1,820. After 31 December 2006, but before the accounts had been finalised for the year, the bill for the last quarter arrived showing a charge of $690.
7. Inventory totalling $67,000 was bought on credit.
8. Inventory totalling $8,000 was bought for cash.
9. Sales on credit totalled $179,000 (cost $89,000).
10. Cash sales totalled $54,000 (cost $25,000).
11. Receipts from trade debtors totalled $178,000.
12. Payments to trade creditors totalled $71,000.
13. Vehicle running expenses paid totalled $16,200.

Prepare a balance sheet as at 31 December 2006 and an income statement for the year to date.

<Obj 10>

4.14 Rose Ltd operates a small chain of retail shops which sell high-quality teas and coffees. Approximately half of the sales are on credit. Abbreviated and unaudited accounts are given below.

ROSE LTD

Income statement for the year ended 31 March 2006

	$'000	$'000
Sales		12,080
Cost of sales		6,282
Gross profit		5,798
Labour costs	2,658	
Depreciation	625	
Other operating costs	1,003	
		4,286
Net profit before interest		1,512
Interest expense		66
Net profit before tax		1,446
Tax expense		434
Net profit after tax		1012
Dividend declared		300
Retained profit for the year		712
Retained profit brought forward		756
Retained profit carried forward		1,468

Balance sheet as at 31 March 2006

	$'000	$'000
Current assets		
Cash at bank	26	
Trade debtors	996	
Inventory	1,583	
		2,605
Non-current assets		2,728
Total assets		5,333
Current liabilities		
Bank overdraft	296	
Tax payable	434	
Dividend payable	300	
Trade creditors	1,118	
Other creditors	417	
		2,565
Non-current liabilities		
Secured loan—repayable 2009		300
Total liabilities		2,865
Shareholders' equity		
Share capital	1,000	
Retained profits	1,468	
		2,468
Total liabilities and shareholders' equity		5,333

Since the unaudited accounts for Rose Ltd were prepared, the following information has become available:

1. An additional $74,000 of depreciation should have been charged on fixtures and fittings.
2. Invoices for credit sales on 31 March 2006 amounting to $34,000 have not yet been included; cost of sales is not affected.
3. Bad debts should be provided at a level of 2 per cent of debtors at the year end.
4. Inventory which had been purchased for $2,000 was damaged and is now unsaleable.
5. Fixtures and fittings to the value of $16,000 have been delivered just before 31 March 2006, but these assets were not included in the accounts and the purchase invoice has not been processed.
6. Wages for Saturday-only staff, amounting to $1,000, have not been paid for the final Saturday of the year.
7. Tax is payable at 30 per cent of net profit.

Prepare a balance sheet as at 31 March 2006 and an income statement for the year ended 31 March 2006 for Rose Ltd, incorporating the information in points 1–7 above.

Statements of Financial Performance
for the year ended 30 June 2004

CASE STUDY 4.1

	Notes	Qantas Group		Qantas	
		2004 $M	2003 $M	2004 $M	2003 $M
SALES AND OPERATING REVENUE					
Net passenger revenue[1,2]		8,978.3	8,992.8	8,182.7	8,242.5
Net freight revenue[1]		469.7	511.3	467.3	508.9
Tours and travel revenue		711.1	696.3	–	–
Contract work revenue		502.6	530.9	276.5	281.0
Other sources[3,4]		692.0	643.6	943.3	930.9
Sales and operating revenue	2	11,353.7	11,374.9	9,869.8	9,963.3
EXPENDITURE					
Manpower and staff related		2,938.5	3,017.7	2,501.9	2,587.7
Selling and marketing		466.1	546.6	434.7	517.0
Aircraft operating – variable		2,226.8	2,405.0	2,150.9	2,352.1
Fuel and oil		1,355.6	1,540.4	1,232.8	1,423.8
Property		309.8	286.5	284.8	262.6
Computer and communication		439.1	412.3	411.6	387.7
Depreciation and amortisation		1,005.6	891.4	871.0	774.2
Non-cancellable operating lease rentals		263.5	283.9	237.3	233.2
Tours and travel		570.9	564.0	–	–
Capacity hire		287.4	381.6	255.5	350.4
Other[5]		411.9	488.1	424.0	551.0

continued

	Notes	Qantas Group 2004 $M	Qantas Group 2003 $M	Qantas 2004 $M	Qantas 2003 $M
Share of net profit of associates and joint ventures	30	(19.7)	(9.6)	–	–
Expenditure	3	10,255.5	10,807.9	8,804.5	9,439.7
Earnings before interest and tax	34	1,098.2	567.0	1,065.3	523.6
Borrowing costs	3	(259.5)	(172.4)	(263.5)	(173.6)
Interest revenue	2	125.9	107.7	112.3	93.5
Net borrowing costs		(133.6)	(64.7)	(151.2)	(80.1)
Profit from ordinary activities before related income tax expense		964.6	502.3	914.1	443.5
Income tax expense relating to ordinary activities	4	(315.8)	(155.7)	(238.1)	(71.0)
Net profit		648.8	346.6	676.0	372.5
Outside equity interests in net profit		(0.4)	(3.1)	–	–
Net profit attributable to members of the Company	20	648.4	343.5	676.0	372.5
Non-owner transaction changes in equity:					
Net decrease in retained profits on the initial adoption of AASB 1028 "Employee Benefits"		–	(3.7)	–	(3.7)
Net exchange differences relating to self-sustaining foreign operations		0.4	(2.3)	–	–
Total changes in equity from non-owner related transactions attributable to members of the Company	21	648.8	337.5	676.0	368.8
Basic earnings per share	35	35.7 cents	20.0 cents		
Diluted earnings per share	35	35.5 cents	19.8 cents		

1 Passenger and freight revenue is disclosed net of both sales discount and interline/IATA commission.
2 Passenger recoveries are disclosed as part of net passenger revenue.
3 Revenue from "Other sources" includes revenue from aircraft charters and leases, property income, Qantas Club and Frequent Flyer membership fees, freight terminal and service fees, commission revenue, and other miscellaneous income.
4 Excludes interest revenue of $125.9 million (2003: $107.7 million) which is included in net borrowing costs. Also excluded are proceeds on sale and operating leaseback of non-current assets of $221.8 million (2003: $36.7 million), which are offset against the relevant asset's written down value before recognition of the profit or loss on sale. Net loss on sale of non-current assets was $0.5 million (2003: $12.4 million).
5 "Other expenditure" includes contract work materials, printing, stationery, insurance and other miscellaneous expenses.

The Statements of Financial Performance are to be read in conjunction with the Notes to the Financial Statements on pages 5 to 60.

1 What will the statement of financial performance be called from 2005 in Australia?
2 Have the expenses been classified according the their 'nature' or their 'function'? Explain?
3 Earnings before interest and taxes increased significantly for the year while overall revenues fell. How was this made possible?
4 What is the difference between 'depreciation' and 'amortisation'?

5   Borrowing costs are shown separately from the other expenses. Why do you think this separation is made?

6   The report has a major sub-heading labelled 'Expenditure'. Do you think this is the appropriate term for the items listed under this sub-heading?

7   Non-cancellable operating lease rentals are disclosed separately.
    (a)   What is a non-cancellable operating lease?
    (b)   How does its treatment differ from a financial lease?

8   What are 'non-owner related transactions'?

Lump sum turns Envestra loss into sizeable profit

Ian Howarth

The *Australian Financial Review*
9 July 2004, p. 64

CASE STUDY 4.2

Envestra has clarified how it will account for a $54.6 million payment from the South Australian government: the gas distribution company now expects a full-year profit of $24.6 million rather than an after-tax loss of $10 million.

The cash payment is to cover the cost of introducing systems that will allow SA gas consumers to choose their gas supplier. Envestra has spent more than two years developing such systems. At first it expected to recoup up to $30 million that was spent on the project, plus annual operating costs of about $6 million, through a special tariff to be levied on gas retailers for five years.

That would have meant that gas retailers would have been charged an extra $26 a year for every retail customer to cover the increased cost of distributing gas. Instead, the SA government opted to pay Envestra $54.6 million in a lump sum, which will be included as revenue in the year to June 30. The lump sum allows the cost of gas distribution in the state to be held steady for the next five years.

Envestra said the payment included $28 million to cover the actual amount spent on developing the systems for retail contestability, plus five years' worth of annual operating costs.

Envestra managing director Ian Little said the company has been advised by its auditor, PricewaterhouseCoopers, that accounting standards require the entire payment of $54.6 million to be treated as revenue for the year ended June 30. However, the capital expenditure is depreciated over the next five years, starting in 2004–05.

1   How is revenue defined under the AASB Framework?

2   Reconcile the figures provided in terms of the original proposal for the project cost recoupment and that resulting from the single payment by the SA government.

3   While this article does not provide full details of the transactions it seems that:
    Cash received from the government for past outlays is being treated as revenue, while some of those past outlays are currently being treated as deferred assets to be expensed over the next five years.
    (a)   What are the potential limitations of treating the full $54.6 million payout as revenue in this period?
    (b)   How would you have recommended the cash receipt from the SA government be classified?

4   What is the role of auditors in relation to this issue?

Timber shares notch up strong growth

Greg Tubby

The Courier-Mail
Friday, 2 July 2004, p. 31

Shares in Great Southern Plantations surged yesterday after the plantation forestry group announced that its sales had more than doubled for the second consecutive year.

Investors also got behind agricultural investment company Timbercorp after it forecast a surge in net profit of 50 per cent for fiscal 2004.

Sales from Great Southern Plantation's eucalypt plantation projects grew by 120 per cent to about $224 million for the year to June 30 2004, after having doubled in the previous year.

Coupled with the group's first viticulture project, which closed oversubscribed in March after raising about $16 million, total sales from Great Southern's managed investment scheme projects for the year climbed to about $240 million.

However, at least 20 per cent of total sales will not be recognised in the results for the 2003–04 financial year—instead being deferred until completion of the relevant services.

This is in line with the group's revenue recognition policies, which will also result in revenue of $17.6 million, deferred at June 30, 2003, being recognised in the current year's results.

Shares in Great Southern leapt almost 10 per cent to $3.15 within minutes of opening, before dropping back to end the day up 17¢ at $3.05.

Timbercorp shares rose as high as $1.66 before settling at $1.57, up 2¢ and at a two-and-a-half-year closing high.

The company forecast net profit of more than $40 million for the year to September 30, 2004, which represents earnings per share of about 17¢, up from 11.1¢ in 2002–03.

Timbercorp is expecting revenue of $162 million for the year, up from $112 million in the previous corresponding period.

The revenue boost comes from recurring contractual revenues of $85 million and new sales revenue of $77 million for the nine months to June 30, 2004.

Consequently, Timbercorp has reintroduced an interim dividend, declaring a 2¢ fully franked dividend with a record date of August 16 and payment on August 31.

Executive director Sol Rabinovich said there had been structural improvements in perception and acceptance of agribusiness investment.

1   Why did the shares price of Great Southern Plantations surge after the announcement of the doubling of sales?

2   The article states that 'at least 20 per cent of total sales will not be recognised in the results for the 2003–04 financial year—instead being deferred until the completion of the relevant services':
    (a)   What is the definition of revenue (or income) under the AASB Framework?
    (b)   Is 'sales' a revenue account?
    (c)   What does the author mean by 'not recognised in the results'?
    (d)   When should revenue be recognised?
    (e)   To what account would it be 'deferred'?

3   In relation to growing timber for sale:
    When should the revenue be recognised?
    How should it be measured?
    How should costs incurred during the pre-production stage be classified?

4   In relation to dividends:
   (a) Distinguish between 'interim' and 'final' dividends.
   (b) Distinguish between the dividend 'record' and 'payment' dates.
   (c) Why would they re-introduce an interim dividend?
   (d) What does it mean that dividends are 'fully franked'?

SOLUTIONS TO ACTIVITIES

Activity 4.1

Your answer should be along the following lines:

1. Accountancy practice—fees for services
2. Squash club—subscriptions, court fees
3. Bus company—ticket sales, advertising
4. Newspaper—newspaper sales, advertising
5. Finance company—interest received on loans
6. Songwriter—royalties, commission fees
7. Retailer—sale of goods
8. Magazine publisher—magazine subscriptions, sales and advertising.

Activity 4.2

The stock approach to determining the profit or loss may be used:

* to check on the accuracy of the transaction approach ('Revenue – Expenses')
* by regulatory bodies (e.g. taxation office) to determine the profit and loss where records are unavailable
* by insurance assessors or other parties where records have been destroyed.

Activity 4.3

	Cost of sales	Selling and distributions	Administration	Financial
Freight inward	✓			
Freight outward		✓		
Sales staff salaries		✓		
Interest				✓
Rates			✓	
Depreciation—showcase		✓		
Depreciation—building		✓	✓	
Repairs and maintenance—cash register		✓		
Cleaning		✓	✓	
Bad debts				✓
Discounts given				✓

• Telephone and postage	✓	✓
• Insurance—inventory	✓	
• Audit fee		✓
• Administration staff salaries		✓
• Advertising	✓	

Activity 4.4

Your answer should be as follows:

H & S RETAILERS

Income statement for the year ended 30 April 2006

	$	$
Sales		97,400
Less cost of sales		
Opening inventory	4,000	
Purchases	68,350	
	72,350	
Closing inventory	3,000	
		69,350
Gross profit		28,050
Rent received		2,000
		30,050
Less		
Salaries and wages	10,400	
Rent and rates	5,000	
Heat and light	900	
Telephone and postage	450	
Insurance	750	
Motor vehicle running expenses	1,200	
Loan interest	620	
Depreciation—motor van	1,500	
		20,820
Net profit		9,230

The two items not included in the income statement are in fact assets (motor vans and cash) and would appear in the balance sheet.

Activity 4.5

Probably the major reason is that they do not wish to provide that level of detail to competitors (e.g. gross profit margin, selling expenses).

Additionally, many companies are involved in a diverse range of activities and the presentation of a classified aggregate report may be complex, costly and potentially confusing.

Activity 4.6

The 'nature' of an item refers to its essential characteristic or unique attribute. In the case of an expense the classification based on nature could for example be related to any of the following:

- immediate consumption of the economic benefits (services or goods). Examples would include fuel, repairs and advertising.
- allocated consumption of the economic benefits over time. Examples would include insurance expense, and depreciation of property, plant and equipment.
- the consumption of the economic benefits is directly related to a revenue account. Examples would include cost of goods sold and sales commission.
- the economic benefits relate to employees. Examples would include salaries, bonuses, annual leave, sick leave, long-service leave, superannuation, other non-cash benefits (housing, vehicle, travel, medical, educational).

The 'function' of an item refers to its role, or purpose, or rationale. In relation to expenses this could relate to such things as:

- procurement of resources
- research and development
- manufacture
- selling and distribution
- assets management
- customer collection
- long-term financing
- administration and general.

Activity 4.7

There are two primary purposes of regulation in accounting and financial reporting. Firstly, the provision of reliable information that satisfies the stewardship or accountability function of accounting, which is sometimes referred to in terms of assessing the compliance of the management with acceptable practices.

Secondly, the provision of relevant information that satisfies the decision usefulness function of accounting, and is related to decisions about the allocation of scarce resources. The information related to decision usefulness will assist in both confirmation and prediction.

Of the listed regulator disclosures you could select possible examples to fulfil each of these roles.

(a) Examples of stewardship or accountability disclosures might include total 'revenue', 'taxation expense'; 'the overall profit or loss'; 'disposals of property or equipment' and 'litigation settlements'.

(b) Examples of decision usefulness disclosures might include 'certain investment income', 'the after tax gain or loss related to discontinued operations or business disposals', 'reversals of previous write-downs', restructuring activities', 'disposals', 'discontinuing operations' and 'other provision reversals'.

Activity 4.8

In answering this activity you may have thought of the following:

- when the goods are produced
- when an order is received from a customer
- when the goods are delivered to the customer, and accepted by them
- when the cash is received from the customer.

A significant amount of time may elapse between these different points.

Activity 4.9

The criteria will probably be fulfilled when the goods are passed to the customers and are accepted by them. This is the normal point of recognition when goods are sold on credit. It is also the point at which there is a legally enforceable contract between the parties.

Activity 4.10

In answering this question you may have identified one or more of the following or other similar situations:

- where there is a ready market at a given price for all production output (e.g. precious minerals, oil, grains, wool)
- where there is an extended period related to the growth, maturity or extraction of the produce (e.g. the growth of timber, the maturity of wine, the discovery of a major oilfield).

Activity 4.11

'Expenditure' would conventionally refer to the outlay of cash. This would include payments for goods and services that have already been consumed (e.g. past wages owing or goods bought on credit), are immediately consumed (e.g. rent or supplies) or will be consumed in the future (e.g. inventory or depreciation of equipment).

'Expense' is used to describe the situation where the future economic benefits have been used up in that period. Where the cash payment coincides with the using up of the economic benefits, the expenditure and the expense are the same. However, where an expense is accrued (benefits used up before the cash payment), the expense is recognised earlier than the expenditure. Where an expense is deferred (payment occurs before the benefits are used up or consumed), the expense is recognised after the expenditure.

'Carry-forward expenditure' represents a description of the deferred expense discussed above. The cash outlay occurs before the entity uses up the economic benefits generated from the outlay. The cash outlay may relate to such things as the acquisition of inventory, the purchase of plant and equipment, the prepayment of expenses, or other cash outlays that are likely generate future benefits to the entity. It is often in relation to this last category that the term 'carry-forward expenditure' is specifically used. Examples could include 'development expenditure' on a new product or process; or 'set-up costs' related to a new business venture.

Activity 4.12

When the electricity bill is eventually paid it will be dealt with as follows:

- reduce cash by the amount of the bill
- reduce the amount of the accrued expense (liability) as shown on the statement of financial position.

Activity 4.13

You may have thought of the following examples:

- rent and rates
- insurance
- interest payments
- licences.

This is not an exhaustive list. You may have thought of others.

Activity 4.14

The cost of the new car will be as follows:

	$	$
New Vectra		24,000
Delivery charge	500	
Alloy wheels	660	
Sun roof	200	
Plates	200	
	1,560	
	25,560	

These costs include delivery costs and plates as they are a necessary and integral part of the asset. Improvements (alloy wheels and sunroof) are also regarded as part of the total cost of the car. The petrol costs and registration, however, represent a cost of operating the asset rather than a part of the total cost of acquiring the asset and making it ready for use, hence these amounts will be charged as an expense in the period incurred (although part of the cost of the registration may be regarded as a prepaid expense if the period of the registration goes beyond the end of the current financial year). The trade-in figure shown is part payment of the total amount outstanding and is not relevant to a consideration of the total cost.

Activity 4.15

A contra asset account reveals how much of the associated asset account has been used up, or is not expected to be realised. It is deducted from the associated asset account to determine the book value (or carrying amount) of that asset. Without having a contra account there would simply be a single account showing the book value of the asset and potentially valuable information would be lost.

Common examples of the use of contra accounts are:

Asset	Buildings	$250,000
Contra asset	Accumulated depreciation—buildings	$160,000
Book value		$90,000
Asset	Accounts receivable	$80,000
Contra asset	Allowance for doubtful debts	$13,000
Book value		$67,000
Asset	Development expenditure	$60,000
Contra asset	Accumulated amortisation	$50,000
Book value		$10,000

Activity 4.16

Your answer should be as follows:

Straight-line method

	Profit before depreciation $	Depreciation $	Net profit $
Year 1	20,000	9,744	10,256
Year 2	20,000	9,744	10,256
Year 3	20,000	9,744	10,256
Year 4	20,000	9,744	10,256
		38,976	41,024

Reducing-balance method

	Profit before depreciation $	Depreciation $	Net profit/ (loss) $
Year 1	20,000	24,000	(4,000)
Year 2	20,000	9,600	10,400
Year 3	20,000	3,840	16,160
Year 4	20,000	1,536	18,464
		38,976	41,024

Unit of production method

	Profit before depreciation $	Depreciation $	Net profit $
Year 1	20,000	3,898	16,102
Year 2	20,000	15,590	4,410
Year 3	20,000	11,693	8,307
Year 4	20,000	7,795	12,205
		38,976	41,024

The above calculations reveal that the straight-line method of depreciation results in a constant net profit figure over the four-year period. This is because both the profit before depreciation and the depreciation charge are constant over the period. The reducing-balance method, however, results in a changing profit figure over time. In the first year a net loss is reported and thereafter a rising net profit is reported. The unit of production method reflects the usage of the machine and profit is quite variable, as the production is quite variable.

Although the pattern of net profit over the period will be quite different, depending on the depreciation method used, the total net profit for the period will remain the same. This is because both methods of depreciating will allocate the same amount of total depreciation over the four-year period. It is only the amount allocated between years that will differ.

Activity 4.17

No. Even if funds are set aside each year that are equal to the depreciation expense for the year, the total amount accumulated at the end of the asset's useful life may be insufficient for replacement purposes. This may be because inflation or technological advances have resulted in an increase in the replacement cost.

Activity 4.18

In answering this activity, you may have thought of the following:

- the cost of the asset (e.g. deciding whether to include interest charges or not)
- the expected residual or disposal value of the asset
- the expected useful life of the asset
- the choice of depreciation method.

Activity 4.19

The 'cost of inventory purchase' would include the purchase price, government taxes and duties and freight-inwards costs.

The 'cost of conversion' would largely relate to goods being manufactured and would include both direct costs (those that can be readily or physically traced to the product, e.g. direct labour and direct materials) and indirect costs of manufacture (those that cannot be readily or physically traced to the product, e.g. indirect materials, indirect labour, and manufacturing overheads).

The 'other costs' would include such outlays as receival, storage, security and display.

Activity 4.20

Your answer should be along the following lines.

Gross profit calculation	FIFO $'000	LIFO $'000	AVCO $'000
Sales (9,000 @ $15)	135.0	135.0	135.0
Cost of sales	101.0	107.0	103.5
Gross profit	34.0	28.0	31.5
Closing inventory figure	$60.0	$54.0	$57.5

The above figures reveal that FIFO will give the highest gross profit during a period of rising prices. This is because sales are matched with the earlier (and cheaper) purchases. LIFO will give the lowest gross profit as sales are matched against the more recent (and dearer) purchases. The AVCO method will normally give a figure that is between these two extremes.

The closing inventory figure in the statement of financial position will be highest with the FIFO method. This is because the cost of goods still held will be based on the more recent (and dearer) purchases. LIFO will give the lowest closing inventory figure as the goods held in stock will be based on the earlier (and cheaper) inventory purchased. Once again, the AVCO method will normally give a figure that is between these two extremes.

Activity 4.21

When prices are falling, the position of FIFO and LIFO is reversed. FIFO will give the lowest gross profit as sales are matched against the earlier (and dearer) goods purchased. LIFO will give the highest gross profit as sales are matched against the more recent (and cheaper) goods purchased. AVCO will give a cost of sales figure between these two extremes. The closing inventory figure in the statement of financial position will be lowest under FIFO as the cost of inventory will be based on the more recent (and cheaper) stocks purchased. LIFO will provide the highest closing inventory figure and AVCO will provide a figure between the two extremes.

Activity 4.22

Your answer could focus on errors in the inventory accounting records or errors within the stock count.

Errors within the accounting records could include:

- missed cost of sales transactions
- cost of sales transactions at incorrect prices (too low)
- physical loss of stock (i.e. theft)
- summation and processing errors with stock records.

Errors with the stock count could include:

- missed stock items
- incorrect costing of stock (too low)
- incorrect stock sheet extractions or summations.

Activity 4.23

There are at least three reasons why the Australian accounting profession has consistently excluded LIFO as an approved inventory cost allocation method.

Firstly, it is contrary to the actual physical flow of inventory where the earliest inventory purchased will normally be sold first.

Secondly, where inventory levels are increasing over time, the inventory on hand valuation can become very much out of date. That is, if the quantity of inventory was to increase each month over five years the inventory on hand at the end of two years would be based on inventory prices two years earlier.

Thirdly, the use of LIFO can lead to manipulation of the financial position, and financial performance by management. A large purchase of inventory at the end of the period at a high price will reduce profits (higher cost of sales) or at a low price will inflate profits (lower cost of sales).

Activity 4.24

The net realisable value may be lower where:

- goods have deteriorated or become obsolete
- there has been a fall in the market price of the goods
- the goods are being used as a 'loss leader'
- bad purchasing decisions have been made.

Activity 4.25

The main areas are:

- the choice of cost method (FIFO, LIFO, AVCO)
- deciding which items should be included in the cost of inventory (particularly for work-in-progress and the finished goods of a manufacturing business)
- deriving the net realisable value figures for inventory held.

Activity 4.26

The effect would be to overstate the assets (debtors) on the balance sheet and profit in the income statement, as the sale (which has been recognised) will not result in any future benefits arising.

Activity 4.27

Your answer should be as follows:

Income statement (extracts) for the year ended 31 March 2005	
	$
Bad debts written off	40,000
Doubtful debts expense	60,000

Income statement (extracts) for the year ended 31 March 2006	
	$
Doubtful debts expense written back	15,000*
(a revenue or a reduction in the expense)	

Balance sheet (extract) as at 31 March 2006	
	$
Debtors	830,000**
Less allowance for doubtful debts	60,000
	770,000

* This figure will usually be netted off against any allowance created for doubtful debts in respect of 2007.
** $870,000 – $40,000

Activity 4.28

Judgment is often required in order to derive a figure for bad debts incurred during a period. There may be situations where views will differ concerning whether or not a debt is irrecoverable. The decision concerning whether or not to write off a bad debt will have an effect on the expenses for the period and, hence, the reported profit. However, over the life of the business the total reported profit will not be affected as incorrect judgments in one period will be adjusted for in a later period. Suppose, for example, that a debt of $100 was written off in a period and that, in a later period, the amount owing was actually received. The increase in expenses of $100 in the period in which the bad debt was written off would be compensated for by an increase in revenues of $100 when the amount outstanding was finally received (bad debt recoverable). If, on the other hand, the amount owing of $100 was never written off in the first place, the profit for the two periods would not be affected by the bad debt adjustment and would therefore be different, but the total profit for the two periods would be the same.

The same situation would apply where there are differences in judgments concerning doubtful debts.

OBJECTIVES

5

When you have completed your study of this chapter you should be able to:

1 explain the importance of cash to the reporting entity

2 define cash and cash equivalents

3 distinguish between accrual- and cash-based transaction recognition

4 compare and contrast the roles of the three external financial reports (income statement, balance sheet, cash flow statement)

5 discuss the three components of the cash flow statement (operating activities, investing activities, financing activities)

6 identify non-cash transactions

7 recognise the alternative approaches to preparing a cash flow statement

8 prepare a simple cash flow statement

9 prepare a reconciliation of net profit to cash flow from operations

10 explain how the cash flow statement can be useful in identifying cash flow management strengths, weaknesses and opportunities.

MEASURING AND REPORTING CASH FLOWS

Despite the undoubted value of the income statement (profit and loss account) as a means of assessing the effect on a company's wealth of its trading activities, it has increasingly been recognised that the accrual-based approach can mask problems, or potential problems, with cash flow, leading to shortages of cash. This is principally because large expenditures on such things as non-current assets and inventories do not necessarily have an immediate effect on the income statement. Cash is important because in practice without it no business can operate. Companies are required to produce a cash flow statement as well as the more traditional income statement (profit and loss account) and balance sheet. In this chapter we are going to consider the deficiencies of these traditional statements, in the context of assessing cash flow issues. We shall then go on to consider how the cash flow statement is prepared and how it may be interpreted.

THE IMPORTANCE OF CASH AND CASH FLOW

Simpler organisations, such as small clubs and other not-for-profit associations, limit their accounting activities to a record of cash receipts and cash payments. Periodically (normally annually), a summary of all cash transactions for the period is produced for the members. The summary will show one single figure for each category of payment or receipt—for example, membership subscriptions. This summary is usually the basis of decision making for the club and the main means of the committee fulfilling its moral duty to account to the club members. This is normally found to be sufficient for such organisations.

The following illustrates such a report:

XYZ SOCIAL CLUB

Statement of receipts and payments for the year ended 30 June 2006

Cash at bank 1/7/05		10,320
Receipts		
Members' subscriptions	4,370	
Fundraising	3,190	
Government grants	2,500	
Interest	470	
Other	380	10,910
		21,230
Payments		
Administration and accounting	1,360	
Functions	3,410	
Insurance	920	
Repairs and maintenance	2,670	
Telephone and postage	1,290	
Utilities	1,430	
Other	670	11,750
Cash at bank 30/6/06		9,480

Clearly, organisations that are more complicated than simple clubs need to produce statements which reflect movements in wealth and the net increase (profit) or decrease (loss) for the period concerned. However, prior to 1983 in Australia, there was no need for companies to produce any statements to show how funds had been raised or used. It seemed to be believed that all that shareholders and other interested parties needed to know, in accounting terms, about a company could be taken more or less directly from the two main financial statements. This view was based partly on the implicit belief that if a company were profitable, then automatically it would have plenty of cash. Though in the very long run this is likely to be true, it certainly is not necessarily true in the short to medium term.

In 1991 an accounting standard was introduced that required entities to produce and publish, in addition to the income statement and balance sheet, a cash flow statement which would reflect movements in cash. The reason for this requirement was the increasing belief that, despite their usefulness, the income statement and the balance sheet do not concentrate sufficiently on liquidity. It was believed that the 'accrual-based' nature of the income statement tended to obscure the question of how and where a company is generating the cash it needs to continue its operations.

Why is cash so important to businesses that are pursuing a goal which is concerned with profit/wealth? The solution to Activity 5.2 illustrates the fact that cash and profit do not go hand in hand, so why the current preoccupation with cash? After all, cash is just an asset that a business needs to help it to function. The same could be said of inventory or non-current assets.

The reason for the importance of cash is that people and organisations will not normally accept other than cash in settlement of their claims against the business. If a business wants to employ people, it must pay them in cash. If it wants to buy a new asset to exploit a business opportunity, the seller of the asset will normally insist on being paid in cash, probably after a short period of credit, usually a month or two. When businesses fail, it is their inability to find the cash to pay claimants that really drives them under. These factors lead to cash being the pre-eminent business asset and, therefore, the one that analysts and others watch carefully in trying to assess the ability of the business to survive and to take advantage of commercial opportunities as they arise.

CASH AND CASH EQUIVALENTS

The Australian accounting standard on the 'cash flow statement' incorporates a broad concept of cash in terms of both 'cash' and 'cash equivalents'. Cash represents 'cash on hand' and 'demand deposits', while cash equivalents represent short-term, highly liquid investments that can readily be converted to a fixed amount of cash.

Details of the balance sheet accounts making up the 'cash and cash equivalent' balance in the cash flow statement must be separately disclosed. Examples of such accounts would include 'cash on hand', 'cash deposits at the bank', 'bank overdrafts', 'short-term money market deposits' and 'bank bills'.

DIFFERENCES BETWEEN THE THREE EXTERNAL FINANCIAL REPORTS

The three external financial reports required to be produced by regulated reporting entities are:

1. the balance sheet
2. the income statement (profit and loss)
3. the cash flow statement.

The balance sheet is a static financial report at a given point in time based on the balances in assets, liabilities and owners' equity (capital). It would normally be based on accrual transactions (recognising accounts and changes in account balances on the basis of economic reality rather than changes in cash).

The income statement is a financial report measuring the financial performance over a period of time (usually one year). It would normally be based on accrual transactions related to revenues earned less expenses incurred.

The cash flow statement is a financial report identifying all cash receipts and cash payments for the period. It is therefore based on cash, not accrual, transactions and would incorporate all account types (assets, liabilities, owners' equity, revenues, expenses and distributions).

The relationship between the three statements is shown in Figure 5.1.

THE CASH FLOW STATEMENT

The cash flow statement is, in essence, a summary of the cash receipts and payments over the period concerned. All payments of a particular type (e.g. cash payments to acquire additional non-current assets) are added together to give just one figure which appears in the statement. The net total of the statement is the net increase or decrease of the cash of the business over the period. The statement is basically an analysis of the business's cash movements for the period.

The balance sheet shows the position, at a particular point in time, of the business's assets and claims. The income statement explains how, over a period between two balance sheets, the owners' claim figure in the first balance sheet has altered as a result of trading operations to become the figure in the second balance sheet. The cash flow statement also looks at changes over the accounting period, but this statement explains the alteration in the cash balances shown in the two consecutive balance sheets.

FIGURE 5.1 The relationship between the balance sheet, the income statement and the cash flow statement

THE LAYOUT OF THE CASH FLOW STATEMENT

The standard layout for the statement in Australia is as follows:

XYZ LTD

Cash flow statement for the financial year ended 30 June 2006	
Cash flows from operating activities	
Cash receipts from customers	x
Cash paid to suppliers and employees	(x)
Interest paid	(x)
Income taxes paid	(x)
Net cash provided by (used in) operating activities	x(x)
Cash flows from investing activities	
Purchase of property, plant and equipment	(x)
Acquisition of subsidiary, net of cash acquired	(x)
Proceeds from sale of property, plant and equipment	x
Interest received	x
Dividends received	x
Net cash provided by (used in) investing activities	x(x)
Cash flows from financing activities	
Proceeds from issue of share capital	x
Proceeds from long-term borrowings	x
Repayment of long-term borrowings	(x)
Payment of finance lease liabilities	(x)
Dividends paid	(x)
Net cash provided by (used in) financing activities	x(x)
Net increase (decrease) in cash and cash equivalents held	x(x)
Cash and cash equivalents at the beginning of the financial year	x(x)
Cash and cash equivalents at the end of the financial year	x(x)

The headings in italics are the primary categories into which cash payments and receipts for the period must be analysed.

✳ *Cash flows from operating activities.* This is the net inflow from operations. It is equal to the sum of cash receipts from trade debtors (and cash sales where relevant) less the sums paid to buy inventory, to pay rent, to pay wages etc. Note that it is the amounts of cash received and paid, not the revenues and expenses, which feature in the cash flow statement. It is, of course, the income statement that deals with the expenses and revenues.

✳ *Cash flows from investing activities.* This part of the statement is concerned with cash payments made to acquire additional non-current assets and cash receipts from the disposal of such assets. These non-current assets could be tangible assets such as plant and machinery, or such things as loans made by the business, shares in another company bought by the business, or other investments.

✳ *Cash flows from financing activities.* This part of the statement is concerned with financing the business, except to the extent of trade credit and other very short-term credit. So we are considering borrowings (other than very short-term) and finance from share issues. This category is concerned with procuring long-term finance from debt and equity sources together with debt repayment/redemption and the returns to equity holders.

✳ *Net increase in cash and cash equivalents held.* Naturally, the total of the statement must be the net increase or decrease in cash over the period covered by the statement.

The standard layout for the cash flow statement is summarised in Figure 5.2.

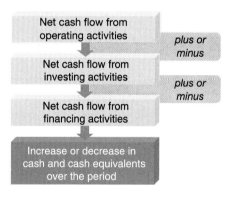

FIGURE 5.2 Standard layout of the cash flow statement

Under normal circumstances we would expect (or at least hope) that the cash flows from operations would be positive. Given that the cash flows will not include non-cash expenses such as depreciation the cash flow from operations would normally be higher than the profit recorded. Interest and tax payments are separately identified. Companies pay tax on profits, so where the company is profitable the cash flow would be from the company to the tax authority. There would not normally be a cash outflow where the company is not profitable. The cash flow from operating activities enables users to get a reasonable understanding of the trends over the years and hence likely sustainability in the future. Given that a high proportion of the funding for expansion comes from retained profits—which is approximately the cash flow from operating activities less dividends—a full understanding of the cash flow from operating activities is important.

The section on investing activities needs to be linked with the other two sections, in that we would normally expect long-term assets to be paid for (funded) by either operations or other financing. Of course, sometimes asset sales can fund further asset purchases. Because most types of fixed asset wear out and because companies tend to seek to expand their asset base, the normal direction of cash in this area is out of the company—that is, negative.

The section on financing enables us to understand what cash has been raised and repaid in financing transactions. Normally a company would pay out more to service its finance than it receives from financial investments (loans made and shares owned) which it has itself made. Financing can go in either direction, depending on the financing strategy at the time. Since companies seek to expand, there is a general tendency for this area to be associated with cash coming into the business rather than leaving it.

Comparison of cash flow statements over time enables us to identify trends and facilitates comparison with other companies.

ACTIVITY 5.3

Assume that last year's statement of cash flows for Angus Ltd showed a 'negative' cash flow from operating activities.

What could be the reason for this and should the company's management be alarmed by it?

PREPARATION OF THE CASH FLOW STATEMENT—AN OVERVIEW

The cash flow statement is based on an analysis and classification of cash receipts and cash payments for the period into three activity sets (operations, investing, financing) and then several categories within each activity.

Essentially the cash flow statement can be produced in one of two ways:

1. Independently viewing the cash receipts and cash payments for the period and allocating transactions to the different activities and categories.

2. Reconstructing the income statement by tracking the changes in the balance sheet for the period and eliminating accrual transactions. Once the accrual transactions are eliminated (or reversed) only the cash changes will remain and form the basis for preparing the cash flow statement.

In practice, it is frequently the second approach that is used—that is, constructing the cash flow statement by making adjustments to the income statement by tracking the changes in the balance sheet for accrual (non-cash) transactions for the period. In undertaking this reconstruction, three alternative approaches can be used. These approaches are:

1. schedules using additions and subtractions

2. ledger reconstructions

3. worksheets.

The last two approaches require a knowledge of the double entry system as discussed in the appendix to this text (located on the Companion Website). As some students using this text may not cover that material, these two approaches will not be discussed in this chapter. The **schedule approach** using additions and subtractions will be discussed and illustrated as it does not require an understanding of the formal double entry framework.

PREPARATION OF THE CASH FLOW STATEMENT — A SIMPLE EXAMPLE

Given that the emphasis of this book is on users rather than preparers, a section on preparation of a cash flow statement might seem redundant. However, a broad understanding of the issues faced by accountants in preparation of such a statement will provide you with a better understanding of the statement itself. With this in mind we shall use Example 5.1 to illustrate the preparation of a cash flow statement.

EXAMPLE 5.1

Income statement for the year ended 31 December 2006

	$m	$m
Sales		100
Cost of sales		60
Gross profit		40
Depreciation	5	
Interest expense	3	
Other expenses	17	
		25
Net profit before tax		15
Tax		5
Profit after taxation		10
Retained profit brought forward from last year		30
		40
Proposed dividend on ordinary shares		20
Retained profit carried forward		20

Balance sheet as at 31 December 2005 and 2006

	2005 $m	2006 $m
Current assets		
Cash at bank and in hand	12	5
Accounts receivable	15	20
Inventory	22	30
	49	55
Non-current assets		
Land and buildings	50	60
Plant and machinery—cost	40	50
—accumulated depreciation	(10)	(15)
	80	95
Total assets	129	150

Current liabilities		
Accounts payable	10	15
Income tax payable	4	5
Dividend proposed	<u>15</u>	<u>20</u>
	<u>29</u>	<u>40</u>
Non-current liabilities		
Debenture loans	<u>20</u>	<u>25</u>
Shareholders' equity		
Paid-up ordinary capital	50	65
Retained profits	<u>30</u>	<u>20</u>
	<u>80</u>	<u>85</u>
Total liabilities and shareholders' equity	<u><u>129</u></u>	<u><u>150</u></u>

During 2006 the company spent $10 million on additional land and buildings and $10 million on additional plant and machinery. There were no other non-current asset acquisitions or disposals. A new issue of shares occurred.

DEDUCING 'CASH FLOWS FROM OPERATING ACTIVITIES'

The first category of cash flow that appears in the statement, and the one which is typically the most important for most companies, is the cash flow from operations. Basically, this requires an analysis of the cash records of the business for the period, picking out all payments and receipts relating to operating activities. These are summarised to give the net figure for inclusion in the cash flow statement. You should remember that the layout for the 'operating' section is as shown below.

Cash flows from operating activities	
Cash receipts from customers	x
Cash paid to suppliers and employees	(x)
Interest paid	(x)
Income taxes paid	<u>(x)</u>
Net cash provided by operating activities	<u>x</u>

The first stage is to calculate the *cash receipts from customers*. Basically, we would expect the following relationship to be true:

Opening balance of accounts receivable	x
plus sales for the period	<u>x</u>
gives the amount we might expect to receive for the period	x

This amount either has been received or has not been received (in which case it will be reflected in a figure for accounts receivable at the end of the period). Hence cash received from customers can be calculated as follows:

Opening balance of accounts receivable	x
plus sales for the period	<u>x</u>
gives the amount we might expect to receive for the period	x
less closing balance of accounts receivable (the amount not received)	<u>(x)</u>
equals the cash received from customers	<u>x</u>

Using the figures from Example 5.1 we have:

Opening balance of accounts receivable	15
plus sales for the period	100
gives the amount we might expect to receive for the period	115
less closing balance of accounts receivable	(20)
equals the cash received from customers	95

The same kind of approach can be used to calculate *cash paid to suppliers and employees*, although the process is generally a little more complicated.

The calculation of *payments relating to creditors* for inventory purchases can be derived as follows:

Opening balance of accounts payable	X
plus purchases of inventory for the period	X
gives the amount we might expect to pay for the period	X
less closing balance of accounts payable (the amount unpaid)	(x)
equals the cash paid to accounts payable	X

However, this requires knowledge of the purchases figure. The purchases figure can be derived as follows:

Opening inventory	X
plus purchases	X
equals the amount available for sale	X
less closing inventory (the amount unsold)	(x)
equals the cost of sales (the cost of the amount sold)	X

Using Example 5.1, inserting the known figures, we get:

Opening inventory	22
plus purchases	X
equals the amount available for sale	22 + X
less closing inventory (the amount unsold)	(30)
equals the cost of sales (the cost of the amount sold)	60

We can calculate the figure for purchases (x) by solving the equation $22 + x - 30 = 60$, so $x = 60 + 30 - 22 = 68$. This figure can then be inserted in the earlier table relating to creditors.

Opening balance of accounts payable	10
plus purchases of inventory for the period	68
gives the amount we might expect to pay for the period	78
less closing balance of accounts payable	(15)
equals the cash paid to accounts payable	63

Payments relating to other expenses may be presumed to have been paid in cash, as they reflect expenses of the year and there are no prepayments or accruals at either the beginning or end of the year. Depreciation will not involve a cash outflow.

Interest paid is usually fairly straightforward, but where there is an associated interest payable or interest prepaid, a calculation process similar to the one above for accounts payable will be required.

The calculation of *interest paid relating to interest payable* can be derived as follows:

Opening balance of interest payable	X
plus interest expense for the period	X
gives the amount we might expect to pay for the period	X
less closing balance of interest payable (the amount unpaid)	(X)
equals the interest paid	X

The calculation of *interest paid relating to prepaid interest* can be derived as follows:

Closing balance of prepaid interest	X
plus interest expense for the period	X
gives the amount we might expect to pay for the period	X
less opening balance of prepaid interest	(X)
equals the interest paid	X

With regard to payments of tax, we have already flagged that the actual payment of tax tends to lag behind profits, so we would expect payments in the current year to reflect last year's (possibly adjusted) tax liability. In the case of Example 5.1 it should be clear that the figure for tax due at the end of 2005 will be paid in 2006, and the amount included against profit for 2006 remains outstanding at the end of 2006, presumably to be paid in 2007. Alternatively, it can be calculated in the same way that we calculated *interest paid* where there was a payable at the beginning and end of the period.

The 'operating' section can now be completed for Example 5.1 as follows:

Cash flows from operating activities	
Cash receipts from customers	95
Cash paid to suppliers and employees	
(63 + other expenses of 17)	(80)
Interest paid	(3)
Income taxes paid (2005 liability)	(4)
Net cash provided by operating activities	8

DEDUCING 'CASH FLOWS FROM INVESTING ACTIVITIES'

The basis of this section is as set out below:

Cash flows from investing activities		
Purchase of property, plant and equipment	(x)	
Proceeds from sale of property, plant and equipment	x	
Net cash used in investing activities		(x)

We clearly need to know how much has been spent on non-current assets, and any sale proceeds relating to non-current asset sales. In Example 5.1 we are told that the company spent $10 million on additional land and buildings and $10 million on additional plant and machinery. We were also told that there were no other non-current asset acquisitions or disposals. There was no investment income and therefore no cash received from dividends or interest. If there was income from either of these investments, then the cash received would be calculated the same way that cash from customers was calculated.

Opening balance of _____ receivable	x
plus _____ revenue for the period	x
gives the amount we might expect to receive for the period	x
less closing balance of _____ receivable	(x)
equals the cash received from _____	x

The 'investing' section for Example 5.1 would appear as follows:

Cash flows from investing activities

Purchase of property, plant and equipment (10 + 10)	(20)	
Net cash used in investing activities		(20)

DEDUCING 'CASH FLOWS FROM FINANCING ACTIVITIES'

The basis of this section is as set out below:

Cash flows from financing activities

Proceeds from issue of share capital	x	
Proceeds from long-term borrowings	x	
Repayment of long-term borrowings	(x)	
Dividends paid	(x)	
Net cash provided by (used in) financing activities		x/(x)

A comparison of the opening and closing capital figures should enable us to calculate the amount of new share capital issued. In the case of Example 5.1 we find that ordinary share capital increased by $15 million (50 to 65) over the year.

A comparison of the long-term liabilities at the beginning and end of the year should provide an indication of the net cash flows from borrowings. In the case of Example 5.1 it is assumed that there was new borrowing of $5 million as the loans figure increased by that amount over the year.

With regard to dividends, we would usually expect final dividends for the year to be shown as a current liability in the year-end balance sheet and to be paid early in the following year. In Example 5.1 this means that the $15 million dividends proposed at the end of 2005 will be paid in 2006. The proposed dividends shown in the income statement for the year ended 30 June 2006 are also shown as outstanding in the year-end balance sheet, so clearly they cannot have been paid.

The 'financing' section can now be completed for Example 5.1 as follows:

Cash flows from financing activities

Proceeds from issuance of share capital	15	
Proceeds from long-term borrowings	5	
Dividends paid	(15)	
Net cash provided by financing activities		5

Putting the above sections together enables us to complete the cash flow statement for Example 5.1 as follows:

Cash flow statement for the year ended 30 June 2006		
	$m	$m
Cash flows from operating activities		
Cash receipts from customers	95	
Cash payments to suppliers and employees		
(63 + other expenses of 17)	(80)	
Interest paid	(3)	
Income taxes paid (2005 liability)	(4)	
Net cash provided by operating activities		8
Cash flows from investing activities		
Purchase of property, plant and equipment (10 + 10)	(20)	
Net cash used in investing activities		(20)
Cash flows from financing activities		
Proceeds from issue of share capital	15	
Proceeds from long-term borrowings	5	
Dividends paid	(15)	
Net cash provided by financing activities		5
Net decrease in cash and cash equivalents held		(7)
Cash and cash equivalents at the beginning of the financial year		12
Cash and cash equivalents at the end of the financial year		5

A legitimate question to ask is 'what does this statement add?'

Chapter 6 deals specifically with financial analysis. However the cash flow statement should be linked with this analysis, with the following points being relevant. The statement clearly shows that cash decreased by $7 million over the course of the year, and it clearly identifies the factors that contributed to this decrease. This enables users of the financial reports to assess efficiency relative to liquidity management. The following points might be considered and questions asked:

* Is a decline in cash resources to $5 million acceptable?

* Does it pose any problems regarding liquidity in the future?

* Will it signal any problem with creditworthiness/credit ratings?

* The cash flow from operating activities is positive, but is it enough? Could it be increased?

* $20 million has been spent on new property, plant and equipment.

* $15 million has been raised by a new share issue.

* $5 million has been borrowed.

* Rather strangely, $15 million of dividends has been paid out, a figure that is higher than the after-tax profit for the year. The logic of this should be questioned given that a new share issue has been made. Normally new asset purchases (investing activities) are associated with similar-sized inputs in the financing section. The dividends payment appears to be something of an aberration.

* The impact of the new shares on control of the company needs consideration.

Consideration of the balance sheets also raises further questions, which should be reinforced after study of Chapter 6:

✳ Accounts receivable have increased by one-third, or $5 million—is this increase justified relative to sales, or is it the result of tighter trading conditions or inefficient debt collection and credit policy?

✳ Inventory has increased by just over one-third, or $8 million—is this justified, or does it reflect poor inventory control?

✳ Accounts payable have increased by 50 per cent, or $5 million. To some extent this may offset the increase in inventory. It could also reflect a lengthening of the time that it takes the business to pay its debts. Whether the new time is appropriate is a question that needs to be addressed in the context of the industry.

The cash flow statement enables the main liquidity issues to be identified.

RECONCILING CASH FROM OPERATIONS WITH OPERATING PROFIT

The accounting standard also requires a note that reconciles the net operating profit or loss after tax with the cash flows from operating activities. The reconciliation is broadly as follows:

Operating profit (loss) after tax	x/(x)
add non-cash expenses related to non-current assets	
e.g. depreciation/amortisation/loss on sale (or carrying amount of asset sold)	x
adjust for changes over the period in non-cash current assets/current liabilities	
inventory	x/(x)
accounts receivable (debtors)	x/(x)
deferred tax asset	x/(x)
prepayments and accruals	x/(x)
deferred tax payable	x/(x)
accounts payable (creditors)	x/(x)
income tax payable	x/(x)
subtract non-cash revenues related to non-current assets, e.g. profit on	
sale (or proceeds on sale of asset)	(x)
equals the cash flow from operating activities	x/(x)

Figure 5.3 summarises this indirect method of deducing the net cash flow from operating activities.

This reconciliation is based on the following logic.

The starting point is the operating profit after income tax. Broadly, we would expect sales to give rise to cash inflows and expenses to give rise to outflows, so our starting point is with operating profit.

We have already seen that this relationship does not follow precisely within a particular accounting period. It is not strictly true that net profit equals the net cash inflow from operating activities. Referring back to Example 5.1 we saw that there was a difference between the sales figure in the income statement and the cash received from customers calculated as follows:

Opening balance of accounts receivable	15
plus sales for the period	100
gives the amount we might expect to receive for the year	115
less closing balance of accounts receivable	(20)
equals the cash received from customers	95

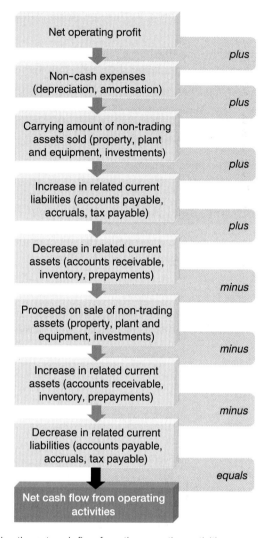

FIGURE 5.3 The indirect method of deducing the net cash flow from the operating activities

Put another way, the cash from customers can be arrived at as follows:

Sales for the period	100
less the increase or plus the decrease in accounts receivable over the year	(5)
Cash received from customers	95

An increase in accounts receivable over the year means that the cash received will be less than the amount included as revenue over the year, by the amount of the increase. A reduction in accounts receivable over the year means that the cash received will be greater than the amount included as revenue over the year, by the amount of the decrease.

Basically the accounts receivable figure is affected by sales and cash receipts. It is increased when a sale is made and decreased when cash is received from a debtor. If, over the year, the sales and the cash receipts had been equal, the accounts receivable figures *would have remained the same*. Since the accounts receivable figure increased it must mean that less cash was received than the figure for sales included in the income statement. Thus the cash receipts from sales must be $95 million (i.e. 100 – (20 – 15)). Put slightly differently, we can say that as a result of sales, assets of $100 million flowed into the business during the year. If $5 million of this went to increasing the asset of trade debtors, this leaves $95 million which went to increase cash.

The same general point is true in respect of nearly all of the other items that are taken into account in deducing the operating profit figure. The exception is depreciation. This is not associated with any movement in cash during the accounting period, but rather represents an estimate of *service potential* or *economic benefits* of property, plant and equipment used up during the period.

Using Example 5.1 we see that this would result in a reconciliation as shown below:

	$m
Operating profit after tax	10
Depreciation	5
Increase in inventory	(8)
Increase in accounts receivable	(5)
Increase in accounts payable	5
Increase in tax payable	1
Net cash flow provided by operating activities	8

The net cash inflow of $8 million from operating activities is the same as was shown on the cash flow statement.

Basically this reconciliation starts with the assumption that the net profit equals the cash generated. We know that this is not true. It is not true because certain things happen that prevent it being true. These things are:

✳ Depreciation does not involve a cash outflow, so the cash flow from operations will be higher than the net profit by the amount of the depreciation.

✳ Any increase in current assets (accounts receivable, prepayments or inventory) over the course of the year can be seen as representing a drain of cash (accounts receivable—cash not collected from sales during the period; inventory and prepayments—cash paid related to inventory and other expenses exceeds the cost of goods sold and expense amounts). So increases can be seen as an effective decrease in cash flow. Any decrease in current assets means that these assets over the course of the year can be seen as releasing cash (accounts receivable—cash collected exceeds the sales; inventory and prepayments—cash paid related to inventory and other expenses is less than the cost of goods sold and expense amounts). So reductions represent an effective increase in cash flow.

✳ Any increase in current liabilities (accounts payable, income tax payable, deferred tax payable and accruals) must mean that less has been paid out over the course of the year than might have been expected on the basis of the expenses included in the income statement. This means that an increase in such liabilities over the year can be seen as representing an effective increase in cash flow, over and above those included from profit. Any decrease in these current liabilities must mean that more has been paid out over the course of the year than might have been expected on the basis of the expenses included in the income statement. This means that a decrease in such liabilities over the year (they have been paid off) can be seen as representing an effective decrease in cash flow compared with profit.

✳ Any gain or loss on the disposal of non-trading assets (e.g. property, plant and equipment; investments; intangibles) needs to be adjusted for. Both the gain and the loss are non-cash in nature and simply represent the difference between the *proceeds on disposal* and the *carrying amount* of the asset sold. The cash proceeds are included as a cash inflow within the investing activities section of the cash flow statement. Therefore, the *loss* is added back in the reconciliation and the *gain* is deducted.

All of this means that, if we take the operating profit for the year, add back the depreciation charged in arriving at that profit and adjust this total by movements in non-cash current asset and current liability accounts (e.g. inventory, accounts receivable, accounts payable, prepayments and accruals), we have the effect of operations on cash.

In many ways the reconciliation provides more useful information than the cash flow statement. Cash can be positively or negatively affected by changes in working capital. These are not well highlighted in the cash flow statement. The reconciliation focuses on them. Certainly inefficient working capital management can more easily be identified by the reconciliation.

ACTIVITY 5.4

The relevant information from the accounts of Dido Ltd for last year is as follows:

	$m
Sales	500
Cost of sales	300
Depreciation	34
Other expenses	44
Net operating profit	122
At the beginning of the year	
Inventory	15
Debtors	24
Creditors	18
At the end of the year	
Inventory	17
Debtors	21
Creditors	19

Required:

1. Prepare a statement of cash flows from operating activities.

2. Prepare a statement reconciling the net operating profit with the cash flows from operating activities.

PREPARATION OF THE CASH FLOW STATEMENT—A MORE COMPLICATED EXAMPLE AND FURTHER PROBLEMS

In preparing the cash flow statement we need to adjust for non-cash transactions together with accrual transactions. In the simple example covered in Example 5.1 there were only a limited number of adjustments required:

✳ Depreciation

✳ Changes in year-end balances

   —Accounts receivable

   —Inventory

—Accounts payable

—Income tax payable

—Dividend payable.

All other changes were of a cash nature.

ACTIVITY 5.5

Can you think of other non-cash transactions that arise in business that must be adjusted for in preparing the cash flow statement?

With more complicated and realistic situations, additional non-cash transactions occur and must be adjusted for (eliminated) in preparing the cash flow statement.

Further problems are discussed in the next section, some of which are based around the following example. A number of the additional non-cash transactions identified in Activity 5.5 will be illustrated using Example 5.2.

Torbryan Ltd's income statement for the year ended 31 December 2006 and the balance sheet as at 31 December 2005 and 2006 are as follows:

TORBRYAN LTD

Income statement for the year ended 31 December 2006

EXAMPLE

5.2

	$m	$m
Sales		591
Cost of sales		307
Gross profit		284
Other expenses (including amortisation and depreciation of $79m)		91
		193
Other operating income		21
		214
Interest revenue (and similar income)		2
		216
Interest expense (and similar charges)		23
		193
Tax on profit		46
Profit after taxation		147
Retained profit brought forward from last year		16
		163
Transfer to reserves	60	
Proposed dividend on ordinary shares	50	110
Retained profit carried forward		53

TORBRYAN LTD

Balance sheet as at 31 December 2005 and 2006

	2006 $m	2007 $m
Current assets		
Cash at bank and in hand	2	17
Trade debtors	115	123
Prepaid expenses	6	16
Inventory	44	41
	167	197
Non-current assets		
Intangible assets: patents and trademarks	44	37
Land and buildings	241	310
Plant and machinery	110	125
Fixtures, fittings, tools and equipment	155	163
	550	635
Total assets	717	832
Current liabilities		
Bank overdraft	14	–
Trade creditors	44	39
Income tax payable	32	46
Dividend payable	40	50
Accrued expenses	11	15
	141	150
Non-current liabilities		
Debenture loans	400	250
Shareholders' equity		
Paid-up ordinary capital	150	240
Asset revaluation reserve	–	69
Other reserves	10	70
Retained profits	16	53
	176	432
Total liabilities and shareholders' equity	717	832

During 2006 the company spent $40 million on additional plant and $55 million on additional fixtures. There were no other non-current asset acquisitions or disposals. A new issue of shares occurred. The land and buildings were revalued. At the end of 2005 there were 150,000 shares on issue.

ACTIVITY 5.6

Before preparing the cash flow statement for this more complicated example, what is a simple rule for converting:
- revenues to cash received?
- expenses to cash paid?

Returning to Example 5.2 we will initially calculate the cash flow magnitudes related to operating activities.

DEDUCING 'CASH FLOWS FROM OPERATING ACTIVITIES'

There should be no real problems calculating cash received from customers. Using the figures from Example 5.2 we have:

Opening balance of accounts receivable	115
plus sales for the period	591
gives the amount we might expect to receive for the year	706
less closing balance of accounts receivable	(123)
equals the cash received from customers	583

To this must be added any other operating income (adjusted for any related opening and closing balance amounts). In Example 5.2 this amounted to $21 million, making cash from customers 583 + 21 = $604 million.

With regard to *payments to suppliers and employees*, there are likely to be both prepaid and accrued expenses at both the beginning and end of the year. Where this happens the payment of operating expenses can be derived as follows:

Opening balance of accrued expenses	x
less any opening prepaid expenses	(x)
plus relevant expenses for the period	x
gives the amount we might expect to pay for the year	x
plus any closing prepaid expenses	x
less closing balance of accruals (amounts not paid)	(x)
equals the cash paid for operating expenses	x

Using Example 5.2 we get:

Opening balance of accruals	11
less opening balance of prepaid expenses	(6)
plus relevant expenses for the period	12*
gives the amount we might expect to pay for the year	17
plus closing balance of prepaid expenses	16
less closing balance of accruals	(15)
equals the cash paid for operating expenses for the year	18

*$91m expenses less $79m amortisation and depreciation

With payment to suppliers, using Example 5.2, inserting the known figures, we get:

Opening inventory	44
plus purchases	x
equals the amount available for sale	44 + x
less closing inventory—the amount unsold	(41)
equals the cost of sales—the amount sold	307

We can calculate the figure for purchases (x) by solving

$$44 + x - 41 = 307, \text{ so } x = 307 + 41 - 44 = 304.$$

This figure can then be inserted in the earlier table relating to creditors.

Opening balance of accounts payable	44
plus purchases of inventory for the period	304
gives the amount we might expect to pay for the year	348
less closing balance of accounts payable	(39)
equals the cash paid to accounts payable	309

Interest paid is usually fairly straightforward. With regard to payments of tax, we have already flagged that tax tends to lag behind profits so we would expect payments in the current year to reflect last year's (possibly adjusted) tax liability. In the case of Example 5.2 it should be clear that the figure for tax due at the end of 2005 will be paid in 2006, and the amount included against profit for 2006 remains outstanding at the end of 2006, presumably to be paid in 2007.

The 'operating' section can now be completed for Example 5.2 as follows:

Cash flows from operating activities

Cash receipts from customers (583 + 21)	604
Cash paid to suppliers and employees (18 + 309)	(327)
Interest paid	(23)
Income taxes paid (2005 liability)	(32)
Net cash provided by operating activities	222

ACTIVITY 5.7

How would each of the following transactions affect the balance in the associated property, plant or equipment account?

Transaction	Cost	Accumulated depreciation	Net
Depreciation expense equipment for the period	———	———	———
Revaluation of land to a higher value	———	———	———
Acquisition cost of a new plant	———	———	———
Cost of the vehicle sold during the period	———	———	———
Accumulated depreciation on asset sold	———	———	———
Trade-in allowance on the new plant	———	———	———
Direct exchange of shares for property	———	———	———
Write-down of buildings to recoverable amount	———	———	———

Returning to Example 5.2 we will now calculate the cash flow magnitudes for investing activities.

DEDUCING 'CASH FLOWS FROM INVESTING ACTIVITIES'

We clearly need to know how much has been spent on non-current assets, and any sale proceeds relating to non-current asset sales. In addition we want to know the cash receipts from investments in terms of interest and dividends received.

In Example 5.2 we are told that the company spent $40 million on additional plant and $55 million on additional fixtures. We were also told that there were no other non-current asset acquisitions or disposals but that interest income of $2 million was earned during the year. The 'investing' section for Example 5.2 would appear as follows:

Interest received	2
Purchase of plant and fixtures (40 + 55)	(95)
Net cash used in investing activities	(93)

In passing it is worth noting the movements in non-current assets over the year. These can generally be summarised in the following table.

Asset	Cost	Accumulated depreciation	Net
Balance at the start of the year	X	(X)	X
less any disposals	(X)	X	(X)
	X	(X)	X
plus new acquisitions	X	–	X
plus any revaluations	X	–	X
less depreciation for the year	–	(X)	(X)
equals closing balance	X	(X)	X

The following points need to be recognised:

* Proceeds of asset sales will be reflected in the investing section.
* Only when an asset is sold can we calculate the actual depreciation incurred with complete accuracy. Depreciation charged previously is only an estimate. Profits or losses on disposal reflect an underprovision (too little) or overprovision (too much) of depreciation. A loss on disposal would represent additional depreciation and would be a non-cash expense. A profit on disposal would offset the depreciation.
* Any revaluations of assets will be reflected in an increase in the asset and an increase in shareholders' equity—shown in asset revaluation reserve.
* By setting out a table of this sort it is possible to follow through movements in assets relatively easily.

In the case of Example 5.2 the property, plant and equipment can be summarised as shown below. You should note that in this example there is insufficient information given to separate cost and accumulated depreciation (also known as provision for depreciation) so we can only use the net column. In practice, disclosure requirements will usually mean that the full information relating to property, plant and equipment will be available from the notes to the accounts.

In the case of intangible assets in this question there are no disposals, acquisitions or revaluations. The amortisation for the year can be calculated by solving for y in the following table.

Asset	Cost	Accumulated amortisation	Net
Balance at the start of the year	X	(X)	44
less any disposals	(X)	X	–
	X	(X)	44
plus new acquisitions	X	–	–
plus any revaluations	X	–	–
less amortisation for the year	–	(X)	$y = (7)$
equals closing balance	X	(X)	37

In the case of land and buildings we are told that no assets were bought or sold, but land and buildings were revalued. The figure of $69 million is matched with an entry in the asset revaluation reserve, thus completing the table.

Land and buildings	Cost	Accumulated depreciation	Net
Balance at the start of the year	X	(x)	241
less any disposals	(x)	X	–
	X	(x)	241
plus new acquisitions	X	–	–
plus any revaluations	X	–	69
less depreciation for the year	–	(x)	–
equals closing balance	X	(x)	310

In the case of plant and machinery we are told that $40 million was spent on new assets; there are no disposals or revaluations, so completion of the table enables us to solve for y to arrive at the depreciation for the year.

Plant and machinery	Cost	Accumulated depreciation	Net
Balance at the start of the year	X	(x)	110
less any disposals	(x)	X	–
	X	(x)	110
plus new acquisitions	X	–	40
plus any revaluations	X	–	–
less depreciation for the year	–	(x)	$y = (25)$
equals closing balance	X	(x)	125

Using similar logic the figure for depreciation for fixtures can be derived as follows.

Fixtures, etc.	Cost	Accumulated depreciation	Net
Balance at the start of the year	X	(x)	155
less any disposals	(x)	X	–
	X	(x)	155
plus new acquisitions	X	–	55
plus any revaluations	X	–	–
less depreciation for the year	–	(x)	(47)
equals closing balance	X	X	163

Total amortisation and depreciation of $79 million can be seen to be made up of $7 million amortisation for intangibles, $25 million depreciation for plant and $47 million depreciation for fixtures.

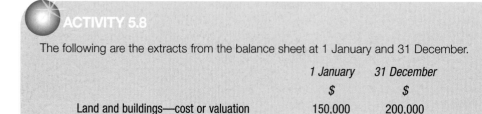

ACTIVITY 5.8

The following are the extracts from the balance sheet at 1 January and 31 December.

	1 January	31 December
	$	$
Land and buildings—cost or valuation	150,000	200,000

208

Plant and machinery		
Cost	80,000	100,000
Accumulated depreciation	(20,000)	(30,000)
Net	60,000	70,000
Fixtures and fittings		
Cost	20,000	25,000
Accumulated depreciation	(10,000)	(12,000)
Net	10,000	13,000

You are told that:

- land and buildings were revalued upwards by $20,000
- fixtures and fittings which had cost $5,000, and which had been depreciated by $3,000, were sold for $1,000.

1. Calculate the depreciation for the year.

2. Show the relevant extracts from the cash flow statement.

Continuing with Example 5.2 we will now calculate the cash flow magnitudes for financing activities.

DEDUCING 'CASH FLOWS FROM FINANCING ACTIVITIES'

Problems can arise in establishing the cash flow from owners' contribution. Generally, a comparison of the opening and closing capital figures ('paid-up capital' for companies) should enable us to calculate the amount of owners' contributions received (new share capital issued for companies). However, possible problems can arise with:

✳ bonus issues (which result in an increase in share capital without any cash inflow)

✳ issue of shares directly for non-cash assets or to extinguish debt

✳ re-purchase or redemption of shares.

In the case of Example 5.2 we find that called-up share capital increased by $90 million ($150 million to $240 million) over the year. This suggests that there was a cash inflow of $90 million from shares. Of course, if we were told that some of this was in the form of a bonus issue the cash proceeds from shares would need to be adjusted. Suppose that you had been told that in the course of the year, and prior to the new issue of shares, a bonus issue on a one-for-five basis, at an issue price of $1 per share, had occurred. This would have led to a bonus issue of $30 million which would have meant that the cash issue could only have been $60 million ($90 million – $30 million).

A comparison of the long-term liabilities at the beginning and end of the year should provide an indication of the net cash flows from borrowings. However, as with the issue of shares the calculation of cash received from long-term liabilities, or cash repaid on long-term loans, may be more complicated than just computing the change for the year in the liability balance.

These problems include:

✳ The issue of debt directly for non-monetary assets (e.g. debentures issued in exchange for a building). In this case the increase in the liability does not represent a cash inflow.

* The conversion of debt directly into shares (e.g. convertible notes). In this case the reduction of the liability does not represent a cash outflow.
* The accounting standard requires that the gross borrowing and gross repayments be shown. The change in the long-term liability for the period only shows the net change.

In the case of Example 5.2 it is assumed that there were no new borrowings but $150 million was repaid, as the figure for long-term loans went down from $400 million to $250 million over the course of the year.

With regard to dividends, we would usually expect final dividends for the year to be shown as a current liability in the year-end balance sheet, and to be paid early in the following year. Care needs to be taken when there are interim dividends paid part way through the year as these will also be paid in the year. Generally, we would expect the cash outflow for dividend payments to include any proposed dividends outstanding from the preceding year, plus any interim dividends (if any) declared in the current year.

The 'financing' section can now be completed for Example 5.2 as follows:

Cash flows from financing activities

Proceeds from issuance of share capital	90	
Repayment of long-term borrowings	(150)	
Dividends paid	(40)	
Net cash used in financing activities		(100)

Putting the above sections together enables us to complete the cash flow statement for Example 5.2 as follows:

TORBRYAN LTD

Cash flow statement for the year ended 30 June 2006

	$m	$m
Cash flows from operating activities		
Cash receipts from customers (583 + 21)	604	
Cash paid to suppliers and employees (18 + 309)	(327)	
Interest paid	(23)	
Income taxes (2005 liability)	(32)	
Net cash provided by operating activities		222
Cash flows from investing activities		
Interest received	2	
Purchase of plant and fixtures (40 + 55)	(95)	
Net cash used in investing activities		(93)
Cash flows from financing activities		
Proceeds from issuance of share capital	90	
Repayment of long-term borrowings	(150)	
Dividends paid	(40)	
Net cash used in financing activities		(100)
Net increase in cash and cash equivalents held		29
Cash and cash equivalents at the beginning of the financial year		(12)
Cash and cash equivalents at the end of the financial year		17

The reconciliation between operating profit and operating cash flows is as follows:

Operating profit		147
Adjusted for:		
Add: Depreciation	72	
Amortisation	7	
Increase in accrued expenses	4	
Increase in tax liability	14	
Decrease in inventory	3	100
Subtract:		
Increase in debtors	(8)	
Increase in prepaid expenses	(10)	
Interest received (not operating)	(2)	
Reduction in creditors	(5)	(25)
		222

The reconciliation focuses fairly clearly on key issues. For example, why were prepaid expenses allowed to increase? Why would a reduction in creditors occur? Why is there an increase in debtors and a reduction in inventory? As we will see in a later chapter on working capital management, the management of current assets and liabilities is a critical feature of management which can easily be overlooked.

WHAT DOES THE CASH FLOW STATEMENT TELL US?

The statement tells us how the business has generated cash during the period and where that cash has gone. Since cash is properly regarded as the life blood of just about any business, this is potentially very useful information.

Tracking the sources and uses of cash over several years could very well show financing trends that a reader of the statements could use to help make predictions about likely future behaviour of the company.

Looking specifically at the cash flow statement for Torbryan Ltd, we can see the following:

* Net cash flow from operations was strong, much larger than the profit figure. This would be expected because depreciation is deducted in arriving at profit.
* There was a general tendency for working capital to absorb some cash. This would not be surprising had there been an expansion of activity (sales output) over the year. From the information supplied, we do not know whether there was an expansion or not. If there had not been an increase, questions would arise regarding working capital management.
* There were net outflows of cash in servicing of finance, payment of tax and purchasing non-current assets.
* There seems to be a healthy figure of net cash inflows before financing.
* There was a fairly major outflow of cash to redeem some debt finance, partly offset by the proceeds of a share issue.
* The net effect was a rather healthier looking cash position in 2006 than was the case in 2005.

SELF-ASSESSMENT QUESTION 5.1

Touchstones Ltd's income statements for the years ended 31 December 2005 and 2006 and the balance sheet as at 31 December 2005 and 2006 are as follows:

Income statements for the years ended 31 December 2005 and 2006

	2005 $m	2006 $m
Sales	173	207
Cost of sales	(96)	101
Gross profit	77	106
Other expenses (including depreciation)	(43)	(48)
	34	58
Other operating income	3	4
	37	62
Interest revenue and similar income	1	2
	38	64
Interest expense and similar charges	(2)	(4)
	36	60
Tax on profit or loss	(8)	(16)
Profit after taxation	28	44
Retained profit brought forward from last year	16	30
	44	74
Proposed dividend on ordinary shares	(14)	(18)
Retained profit carried forward	30	56

Balance sheet as at 31 December 2005 and 2006

	2005 $m	2006 $m
Current assets		
Inventory	25	24
Debtors	16	26
Cash at bank and in hand	8	27
	49	77
Non-current assets		
Land and buildings	94	110
Plant and machinery	53	62
	147	172
Total assets	196	249

Current liabilities		
Trade creditors	26	23
Income tax payable	8	16
Dividend payable	12	14
	46	53
Non-current liabilities		
Debenture loans (10%)	20	40
Shareholders' equity		
Paid-up share capital	100	100
Retained profits	30	56
	130	156
Total liabilities and shareholders' equity	196	249

In 'other expenses', depreciation was included as follows:

	2005	2006
	$m	*$m*
Land and buildings	5	6
Plant and machinery	6	10

There were no non-current asset disposals in either year. In both years an interim dividend was paid within the financial year and a final dividend was paid just after the end of the year concerned.

Required:

Prepare a cash flow statement for the company for 2006 together with the reconciliation of operating profit and cash flow from operations.

SUMMARY

In this chapter we have achieved the following objectives in the way shown.

OBJECTIVE	METHOD ACHIEVED
Explain the importance of cash to the reporting entity	Explained that cash is the life blood of business and the medium by which assets are acquired, expenses are met, debts are paid and owners receive returns
Distinguish between accrual- and cash-based transaction recognition	Explained that transactions can either be recognised on a cash basis (cash in–out) or an accrual basis (economic reality)
Compare and contrast the roles of the three external financial reports (income statement, balance sheet, cash flow statement)	Examined the three external reports and found the following: • Income statement—flow statement; based on accruals; covers *R and E* • Balance sheet—static statement; based on accruals; covers *A, L and OE* • Cash flow—flow statement; based on cash; covers *A, L, OE, R, E and D*
Discuss the three components of the cash flow statement (operating activities, investing activities, financing activities)	Identified the main components of the cash flow statement as: • Operating activities—commercial or trading objectives • Investing activities—non-current or non-trading assets • Financing activities—non-current finance
Identify non-cash transactions	Identified the following as non-cash transactions: • Management allocations (depreciation, revaluations, write-downs, discounts, doubtful debts, bonus issues of shares) • Accruals/deferrals (receivables, inventories, prepayments, payables, accruals, provisions) • Direct exchanges (shares for assets)
Recognise the alternative approaches to preparing a cash flow statement	Examined the alternative approaches, identified as follows: • Review cash receipts and payments • Reconstruct by adjusting for non-cash transactions using one of the following: (a) Schedule—used in this textbook (b) Ledger reconstruction—based on double entry accounting (c) Worksheet—based on double entry accounting
Prepare a simple cash flow statement	Identified the main components listed below and worked through examples

Operating activities

Inflows	Outflows
• Cash received from customers	• Cash paid to suppliers and employees

Sales	Cost of goods sold	Expenses
+ Debtors (b)	+ Inventory (e)	+ Prepayments (e)
− Debtors (e)	+ Creditors (b)	+ Accruals (b)
	− Inventory (b)	− Prepayments (b)
	− Creditors (e)	− Accruals (e)

• Interest received	• Interest paid
• Dividends received	• Taxation paid

OBJECTIVE	METHOD ACHIEVED

Investing activities

Inflows

- Cash proceeds on sale

Outflows

- Cash purchase of assets

> Asset (e)
> – Asset (b)
> – Upward revaluation*
> – Direct issue of shares/debt for assets*
> + Depreciation*
> + Carrying amount of assets sold*
> + Write-downs*

* for that period (year)

Financing activities

Inflows

- Owners' equity contributed

> Owners' equity (e)
> – Owner's equity (b)
> – Bonus issues

Outflows

- Dividends paid

> Dividends declared
> + Dividends payable (b)
> – Dividends payable (e)

- Borrowing (if positive)

> Debt (e)
> – Debt (b)
> – Direct issue of debt for assets
> – Forgiveness of debt

- Debt repayment (if negative)

> Debt (e)
> – Debt (b)
> – Direct issue of debt for assets
> – Forgiveness of debt

(e) = end of period   (b) = beginning of period

Prepare a reconciliation of net profit to cash flow from operations	Identified and worked through the necessary steps:

> Net profit after tax
> + Non-cash expenses (e.g. depreciation, carrying amount of assets sold, write-downs)
> + Changes in non-cash current assets (increase in liabilities, decrease in assets)
> – Non-cash/operating revenues (proceeds on sale of non-trading assets)
> – Changes in non-cash current assets (increase in assets, decrease in liabilities)
> = Cash flow from operating activities

Explain how the cash flow statement can be useful in identifying cash flow management strengths, weaknesses and opportunities	Analysed the main uses of the cash flow statement:

- Identify operating cash flows, which should be positive (provided)
- Identify main investing activities, which are normally negative (used)
- Assess financing activities, which should be balanced over time (provided/used)
- Identify and observe changing patterns of cash flows
- Review reconciliation for efficient use of working capital
- Identify future sources of cash

DISCUSSION QUESTIONS

EASY

<Obj 2> **5.1** The cash flow statement provides an explanation of the change in cash for a reporting entity. What is included in 'cash'?

<Obj 4> **5.2** In what ways is the cash flow:
(a) similar to the income statement?
(b) different from the income statement?

<Obj 5> **5.3** Identify the three categories of sources/uses of cash summarised in the cash flow statement.

<Obj 6> **5.4** What are 'non-cash' transactions?

<Obj 6, 9> **5.5** What factors could give rise to the accounting 'accrual profit' exceeding the 'cash flow from operating activities'?

<Obj 10> **5.6** If you were to review the cash flow statements for a particular entity over several years, what would you expect to observe in relation to the net flow from each of the three different activities?

INTERMEDIATE

<Obj 1> **5.7** The typical business has about 50 per cent more of its resources tied up in inventory than in cash, yet there is no call for an 'inventory flow statement' to be prepared. Why is cash regarded as more important than inventory?

<Obj 2> **5.8** For each of the following following items explain why they would, or would not be, included in 'cash and cash equivalents' within the cash flow statement?
(a) Bank overdraft
(b) Accounts receivable
(c) Debentures payable with a 3-month maturity date
(d) Deposits at call with a bank
(e) Shares in listed companies acquired with short-term surplus cash
(f) Bills receivable that are secured
(g) The unused but approved bank overdraft facility
(h) Cash advances made to staff

<Obj 3> **5.9** Distinguish between an 'accrual' and a 'deferral'.

<Obj 3, 5> **5.10** Does the cash flow statement incorporate 'bad and doubtful debts expense'?

<Obj 5> **5.11** How would you classify cash advances to employees within the cash flow statement?

<Obj 5> **5.12** Several income items have been classified differently in the cash flow statement over time and between countries. For example, 'dividends received' and 'interest received' previously were classified as 'operating cash inflows', but are now classified as 'investing cash inflows' within the Australian accounting standards. Some countries would even allow them to be classified within the 'financing cash inflows', or allow reporting entities discretion in choosing how they are to be classified.
(a) How would you classify these two items within the cash flow statement?
(b) Is it important to have a standard classification?

<Obj 6> **5.13** Explain how the following accounts could change as indicated without there being a cash flow consequence:
(a) an increase in the land account

    (b) an increase in share capital (issued)

    (c) a decrease in the long-term liabilities

    (d) a decrease in inventory

    (e) a decrease in accounts receivable.

<Obj 6, 9>   **5.14** Where does 'depreciation' appear in the statement of cash flows?

<Obj 7>   **5.15** There are two methods of calculating 'cash flow from operating activities': the direct method (gross flows) and the indirect method (reconciliation).

    (a) Explain the difference between the two methods.

    (b) Which method is required by the Australian accounting standards?

    (c) Which do you prefer? Why?

<Obj 9>   **5.16** Under the indirect (reconciliation method) what is added back to 'net profit after tax' to calculate the 'cash flow from operating activities'?

<Obj 9>   **5.17** Explain the reconciliation of operating cash flows with operating profit.

<Obj 10>   **5.18** What sort of questions does the cash flow statement provide answers to?

CHALLENGING

<Obj 4>   **5.19** Compare and contrast 'cash from operating activities' with the accrual 'profit' as a relevant and reliable measure of financial performance for a given period for an entity.

<Obj 9>   **5.20** Explain how you could use the 'reconciliation of net profit after tax' to 'cash flow from operating activities' over a period of years for a reporting entity to identify potential financial problems?

<Obj 10>   **5.21** The cash flow statement represents a reconstruction from the other financial reports, and therefore does not provide new information to report users.

    (a) What other financial reports are being referred to?

    (b) Do you think the cash flow statement provides useful information to report users? If so, what is this useful information?

APPLICATION EXERCISES

EASY

<Obj 5>   **5.1** For each item listed identify the activity and whether it is an inflow, an outflow or of a non-cash nature.

	Activity	Cash flow
e.g. Cash received from customers	Operating	Inflow
(a) Dividends received		
(b) Taxation paid		
(c) Payments to suppliers and employees		
(d) Interest paid		
(e) Purchase of property, plant and equipment		
(f) Bonus issue of shares		
(g) Dividends paid		
(h) Proceeds on sale of investments		
(i) Interest received		
(j) Long-term borrowing		
(k) Goodwill write-down (impairment)		
(l) Profit on sale of equipment		

ACCOUNTING an introduction

INTERMEDIATE

<Obj 5>   **5.2**   Determine how each of the following affects the cash flow from operating activities.

			Effect	
Item	Cash flow category	No effect	Increase	Decrease
e.g. Increase in debtors	Cash received from customers			✓

(a) Increase in prepayments
(b) Decrease in provision for tax
(c) Increase in interest receivable
(d) Bad debts expense
(e) Decrease in inventory
(f) Decrease in accrued expenses
(g) Increase in accounts payable
(h) Discounts given
(i) Discounts received
(j) Increase in provision for doubtful debts

<Obj 6>   **5.3**   Identify the impacts of the following non-cash transactions on the accounts listed in the following table:

Transaction	Assets	Liabilities	Owners' equity
(a) Revaluation upwards of land			
(b) Bonus issue of shares			
(c) Write-down of inventory			
(d) Depreciation of equipment			
(e) Issue of debentures in exchange for buildings			
(f) Conversion of notes (debt) into shares			
(g) Write-down of goodwill			
(h) Recognising doubtful debts			
(i) Receiving early settlement discount from supplier			

<Obj 8>   **5.4**   *Investing activities*
You extract the following information relating to plant and equipment:

		Year 1 $	Year 2 $
Balance sheet:	Assets: Non-current plant and equipment	67,293	76,937
	Accumulated depreciation	(27,961)	(32,411)
Income statement:	Loss on sale of plant and equipment		3,764
	Depreciation expense—plant and equipment		8,216
Other:	The book value of the plant and equipment sold was $6,179.		

Calculate for the period:

(a) cash purchase of plant and equipment
(b) proceeds on sale of plant and equipment.

<Obj 8>   **5.5** *Financing activities*

You extract the following information:

Balance sheet:

		Year 1 $	Year 2 $
Owners' equity:	Paid-up capital	100,000	150,000
	Retained profits	50,000	60,000
	Reserves	30,000	45,000
Liabilities:	Provision for dividends	5,000	8,000
	Debentures	70,000	110,000
Income statement:	Net profit after tax	32,000	
	Dividends appropriated*	12,000	

* Allocated

Other:
- There was a 1 for 4 bonus issue of shares during the year.
- Assets were revalued upwards by $30,000.
- There was a transfer of $10,000 from retained profit to reserves.
- $20,000 in debentures was directly exchanged for land acquisition.

Complete the financing section of the cash flow statement:

Cash inflows—issues of shares	_____
—borrowing	_____
Cash outflows—dividends paid	(_____)
Net cash provided (used) by financing activities	_____

<Obj 8>   **5.6** The following information relates to the non-current assets of TAO Ltd for the years ended 30 June 2006 and 2005.

Non-current assets	2006 $m	2005 $m
Land	231	93
Buildings	237	212
Plant and equipment	69	63

You also extract the following information relating to the non-current assets for the year ended 30 June 2006.

Land	• Revalued upwards by $15 million
	• Direct issue of debentures for land $80 million
Buildings	• Depreciation of $8 million
Plant and equipment	• Depreciation $13 million
	• Sale of plant and equipment at a gain of $3 million (carrying amount $9 million)

Prepare the cash flow statement extract for investing activities for TAO Ltd for the year ending 30 June 2006.

<Obj 8> **5.7** Heins Ltd had a $11,000 net loss from operations for 2006. Depreciation expense for 2006 was $5,700 and a dividend of $5,000 was declared and paid. The balances in the working capital accounts at the start and end of the year are shown below.

	Start $	End $
Cash	3,700	5,100
Debtors	7,400	6,300
Inventory	21,300	17,200
Prepayments	1,900	700
Creditors	8,300	11,500
Accrued expenses	700	1,500

Did Heins Ltd generate 'cash from operating activities' in 2006? (Show workings.)

<Obj 8, 9> **5.8** Nu Bold Ltd's income statement for the years ended 31 December 2005 and 2006 and the balance sheet as at 31 December 2005 and 2006 are as follows:

NU BOLD LTD
Income statement for the years ended 31 December 2005 and 2006

	2005 $m	2006 $m
Sales	170	190
Cost of sales	(90)	(100)
Gross profit	80	90
Other expenses	(31)	(37)
Other operating income	–	–
	49	53
Interest revenue	–	–
	49	53
Interest expense	(5)	(7)
	44	46
Tax on profit or loss	(9)	(10)
Profit after taxation	35	36
Retained profit brought forward from last year	25	44
	60	80
Proposed dividend on ordinary shares	(16)	(18)
Retained profit carried forward	44	62

NU BOLD LTD

Balance sheet as at 31 December 2005 and 2006

	2005 $m	2006 $m
Current assets		
Inventory	17	21
Debtors	24	18
Cash at bank and in hand	12	17
	53	56
Non-current assets		
Land and buildings	130	157
Plant and machinery	61	55
	191	212
Total assets	244	268
Current liabilities		
Trade creditors	15	16
Income tax payable	9	10
Dividend payable	10	12
	34	38
Non-current liabilities		
Long-term loans	66	68
Shareholders' equity		
Paid-up share capital	100	100
Retained profits	44	62
	144	162
Total liabilities and shareholders' equity	244	268

In 'other expenses', depreciation was included as follows:

	2006 $m	2007 $m
Buildings	11	10
Plant and machinery	12	11

There were no non-current asset disposals in either year.

In both years an interim dividend was paid within the financial year and a final dividend was paid just after the end of the year concerned.

Prepare a cash flow statement for the company for 2006 together with a reconciliation of operating profit and cash from operations.

ACCOUNTING an introduction

<Obj 8, 9>

5.9 The following information has been taken from the accounts of Tuna Ltd for the last two years (year ending 30 June).

	2005 $m	2006 $m
Income statement		
Sales	627	591
Cost of sales	411	382
Gross profit	216	209
Interest expense	19	13
Other expenses (excluding depreciation)	126	109
Depreciation	27	32
Net operating profit	44	55
Balance sheet extract (ending balance)		
Accounts receivable	95	72
Inventories	103	81
Prepayments	5	7
Accounts payable	84	57
Accruals	9	5
Interest payable	7	3

Using the information provided prepare for Tuna Ltd for the year ending 30 June 2006:
(a) the cash flow statement extract for operating activities (direct method)
(b) a statement which reconciles the 'net operating profit' with the 'cash flow from operations'.

<Obj 8, 9>

5.10 The following information has been taken from the accounts of Juno Ltd for last year and the year before last:

	Last year $m	Year before last $m
Summary of the income statement		
Sales	572	505
Cost of sales	300	270
Gross profit	272	235
Interest payable	(5)	(4)
Other expenses (including depreciation)	(80)	(75)
Net operating profit	187	156
Depreciation charged in arriving at net operating profit	55	47
Inventory held at the end of period	31	27
Debtors at the end of	23	24
Creditors at the end of period	17	15

Using the above information, prepare for Juno Ltd:
(a) a statement of cash flow from operations
(b) a statement which reconciles the net operating profit with the cash flow from operations.

<Obj 8, 9>

5.11 Hi View Ltd's income statement for the years ended 31 December 2005 and 2006 and the balance sheet as at 31 December 2005 and 2006 are as follows:

HI VIEW LTD

Income statements for years ended 2005 and 2006		
	2005	2006
	$m	$m
Sales	207	153
Cost of sales	(101)	(76)
Gross profit	106	77
Other expenses	(48)	(48)
Other operating income	4	–
	62	29
Interest revenue and similar income	2	–
	64	29
Interest expense and similar charges	(4)	(4)
	60	25
Tax on profit or loss on ordinary activities	(16)	(6)
Profit on ordinary activities after taxation	44	19
Retained profit brought forward from last year	30	56
	74	75
Proposed dividend on ordinary shares	(18)	(18)
Retained profit carried forward	56	57

HI VIEW LTD

Balance sheet as at 31 December 2005 and 2006		
	2005	2006
	$m	$m
Current assets		
Inventory	24	25
Debtors	26	25
Cash at bank and in hand	27	1
	77	51
Non-current assets		
Land and buildings	110	130
Plant and machinery	62	56
	172	186
Total assets	249	237
Current liabilities		
Trade creditors	23	20
Income tax payable	16	6
Dividend payable	14	14
	53	40

Non-current liabilities		
Debenture loans (10%)	40	40
Shareholders' equity		
Paid-up share capital	100	100
Retained profits	56	57
	156	157
Total liabilities and shareholders' equity	249	237

In 'other expenses', depreciation was included as follows:

	2006	2007
	$m	*$m*
Land and buildings	6	10
Plant and machinery	10	12

There were no non-current asset disposals in either year.

In both years an interim dividend was paid within the financial year and a final dividend was paid just after the end of the year concerned.

Prepare a cash flow statement for the company for 2006 together with a reconciliation of operating profit and cash from operations.

<Obj 8, 9>   **5.12** Torbryan Ltd's income statement for the year ended 31 December 2006 and the balance sheet as at 31 December 2005 and 2006 are as follows:

TORBRYAN LTD
Income statement

	$m	$m
Sales		623
Cost of sales		(353)
Gross profit		270
Other expenses		(101)
		169
Other operating income		13
		182
Interest revenue and similar income		4
		186
Interest expense and similar charges		(16)
		170
Tax on profit		(35)
Profit after taxation		135
Retained profit brought forward from last year		53
		188
Transfer to general reserve	(40)	
Proposed dividend on ordinary shares	(60)	(100)
Retained profit carried forward		88

TORBRYAN LTD

Balance sheet as at 31 December 2005 and 2006		
	2005	2006
	$m	$m
Current assets		
Inventory	41	35
Debtors		
Trade debtors	123	132
Prepayments and accrued income	16	13
Cash at bank and in hand	17	5
	197	185
Non-current assets		
Intangible assets		
Patents and trademarks	37	32
Tangible assets		
Land and buildings	310	310
Plant and machinery	125	102
Fixtures, fittings, tools and equipment	163	180
	635	624
Total assets	832	809
Current liabilities		
Bank overdraft	–	16
Trade creditors	39	30
Income tax payable	46	35
Dividends payable	50	60
Accrued expenses	15	11
	150	152
Non-current liabilities		
Debenture loans	250	150
Shareholders' equity		
Paid-up share capital	240	300
Asset revaluation reserve	69	9
Reserves	70	110
Retained profits	53	88
	432	507
Total liabilities and shareholders' equity	832	809

During 2006 the company spent $67 million on additional fixtures, etc. There were no other non-current asset acquisitions or disposals.

There was no share issue for cash during the year.

Prepare the cash flow statement for Torbryan Ltd for the year ended 31 December 2006, together with a reconciliation of operating profit and cash flow from operations.

Briefly comment on what the cash flow statement that you have prepared tells us about Torbryan Ltd during the year.

<Obj 9>   **5.13** Using the reconciliation approach calculate the 'cash flow from operating activities' given the following financial information extracted from the reports.

Note: It may not all be relevant.

Income statement items	$
• Net profit after tax	26,310
• Bad and doubtful debts	1,400
• Depreciation expense—equipment	6,100
• Amortisation of goodwill	3,400
• Loss on sale of equipment	2,500

Balance sheet changes for the period	$	Change
• Accounts receivable	3,700	Increase
• Cash at bank	4,100	Increase
• Inventory	1,500	Decrease
• Equipment	7,800	Increase
• Goodwill	3,400	Decrease
• Accounts payable	3,200	Increase
• Accrued expenses	400	Decrease
• Provision for taxation	3,700	Increase

<Obj 10>   **5.14** The following represents the reconciliation of 'net profit after tax' with 'cash flow from operating activities' for Sealands Ltd over a three-year period.

	2005 $m	2006 $m	2007 $m
Net profit after tax	19	22	27
Depreciation	8	7	9
Impairment of goodwill	5	5	5
Carrying amount of assets sold	7	4	11
Accounts payable	5	(3)	(7)
Accrued expenses	(1)	1	(1)
Tax payable	7	4	2
Prepayments	1	(1)	(2)
Accounts receivable	(9)	(5)	(3)
Inventories	(7)	(2)	1
Proceeds on sale of assets	(2)	(3)	(17)
Cash flow from operations	33	29	25

Management is concerned with the downward trend in operating cash flows compared to profits over the three-year period. Provide a report.

<Obj 10>

5.15 The following schedule identifies the reconciliation provided in the notes for XYZ Ltd related to the cash flow statement for the period 2005 to 2007.

	2005 $m	2006 $m	2007 $m
Net profit after tax	19	22	27
Depreciation	8	9	11
Impairment of goodwill	8	0	4
Carrying amount of assets sold	7	4	11
Accounts payable	(2)	(5)	(9)
Accrued expenses	(1)	1	(1)
Tax payable	4	5	7
Prepayments	(2)	(1)	1
Accounts receivable	(3)	(5)	(7)
Inventories	1	(4)	(6)
Proceeds on sale of assets	(11)	(3)	(2)
Cash flow from operations	28	23	36

What can you conclude about the financial management of this company over the three-year period covered by the reconciliation?

CHALLENGING

<Obj 8, 9>

5.16 The management of your company is perplexed as to why the company's bank balance has gone down in the last year, even though profits have been satisfactory. Relevant information is given below.

Balance sheet as at 2006

	1 January $'000	31 December $'000
Current assets		
Cash	50	10
Debtors	60	80
Inventory	70	100
	180	190
Non-current assets		
Premises	110	120
Plant —cost	50	70
—accumulated depreciation	(30)	(35)
Vehicles—cost	25	30
—accumulated depreciation	(12)	(10)
	143	175
Total assets	323	365
Current liabilities		
Creditors	100	80
Dividends proposed	10	15

Income tax payable	20	25
	130	120
Non-current liabilities		
Loans	80	50
Shareholders' equity		
Paid-up ordinary capital	80	100
Retained profits	33	95
	113	195
Total liabilities and shareholders' equity	323	365

Income statement for the year ending 31 December 2006

	$'000	$'000
Sales		379
Opening inventory	70	
Purchases	250	
	320	
Less closing inventory	(100)	
Cost of sales		(220)
Gross profit		159
Depreciation		
Plant	5	
Vehicles	4	
Profit on disposal of vehicles	(3)	
Loan interest	7	
Other expenses	44	
		(57)
Net profit		102
Income tax	25	
Dividends	15	
		40
Added to retained profits		62

During the year vehicles that had cost $10,000, which had been depreciated by $6,000, were sold for $7,000.

Sales in the previous year had been $350,000.

(a) Prepare the cash flow statement for the year, together with the reconciliation of operating cash flows and operating profit.

(b) Comment on the cash flows and suggest ways of resolving the problem.

<Obj 9>

5.17 Using the reconciliation approach calculate the 'net profit after tax' given the following financial information extracted from the reports.

Note: It may not all be relevant.

Income statement items	$
Net profit after tax	
Bad and doubtful debts	(1,300)
Depreciation expense—equipment	(5,300)
Impairment of goodwill	(2,500)
Gain on sale of equipment	2,500

Balance sheet changes for the period	$	Change
Accounts receivable	4,300	Increase
Bank overdraft	4,500	Increase
Inventory	1,500	Increase
Equipment	9,900	Increase
Goodwill	2,500	Decrease
Accounts payable	1,200	Decrease
Prepaid expenses	700	Increase
Provision for taxation	4,700	Increase

Qantas Financial Report 2004

Statements of Cash Flows
for the year ended 30 June 2004

CASE STUDY 5.1 →

	Notes	Qantas Group		Qantas	
		2004 **$M**	2003 $M	**2004** **$M**	2003 $M
CASH FLOWS FROM OPERATING ACTIVITIES					
Cash receipts in the course of operations		**12,328.5**	12,567.3	**10,111.3**	10,995.0
Cash payments in the course of operations		**(10,128.6)**	(10,960.6)	**(8,396.0)**	(9,891.7)
Interest received		**126.0**	114.4	**112.3**	98.9
Borrowing costs paid		**(305.6)**	(268.1)	**(312.1)**	(277.2)
Dividends received		**12.4**	7.0	**222.6**	220.7
Income taxes paid		**(33.3)**	(169.2)	**134.8**	(61.0)
Net cash provided by operating activities	37	**1,999.4**	1,290.8	**1,872.9**	1,084.7
CASH FLOWS INVESTING ACTIVITIES					
Payments for property, plant and equipment		**(2,007.0)**	(3,137.2)	**(1,210.8)**	(1,625.3)
Receipts for aircraft security deposits		**63.1**	197.7	**59.3**	162.0

Net payments for puchase of property, plant, equipment and aircraft security deposits	**(1,943.9)**	(2,939.5)	**(1,151.5)**	(1,463.3)
Proceeds from sale of property, plant and equipment	**50.1**	36.7	**46.6**	6.0
Proceeds from sale and leaseback of non-current assets	**171.7**	–	**171.7**	–
Payments for investments, net of cash acquired	**(271.9)**	(92.9)	**(271.7)**	(3.2)
Advances of investment loans	**(128.2)**	–	**(128.2)**	–
Payments for other intangibles	**(47.3)**	–	**(47.3)**	–
Net cash used in investing activities	**(2,169.5)**	(2,995.7)	**(1,380.4)**	(1,460.5)
CASH FLOWS FROM FINANCING ACTIVITIES				
Repayments of borrowings/swaps	**(1,822.9)**	(798.3)	**(2,834.9)**	(678.1)
Proceeds from borrowings/swaps	**1,413.2**	3,205.2	**1,701.4**	2,167.5
Net proceeds from the issue of shares	**90.6**	701.0	**90.6**	701.0
Dividends paid	**(161.4)**	(172.3)	**(159.1)**	(170.9)
Net cash provided by/(used in) financing activities	**(480.5)**	2,935.6	**(1,202.0)**	2,019.5
RECONCILIATION OF CASH PROVIDED BY/(USED IN):				
Operating activities	**1,999.4**	1,290.8	**1,872.9**	1,084.7
Investing activities	**(2,169.5)**	(2,995.7)	**(1,380.4)**	(1,460.5)
Financing activities	**(480.5)**	2,935.6	**(1,202.0)**	2,019.5
Net increase/(decrease) in cash held	**(650.6)**	1,230.7	**(709.5)**	1,643.7
Cash at the beginning of the financial year	**2,015.9**	785.2	**1,993.6**	349.9
Cash at the end of the financial year	37	**1,365.3**	2,015.9	**1,284.1**	1,993.6

The statements of Cash Flows are to be read in conjunction with the Notes to the Financial Statements on pages 5 to 60.

_____

1 Interest received and interest paid (part of borrowing costs) are both classified as 'operating activities'.
   (a) Is this different to the classification of dividends received and dividends paid?
   (b) Will the classification of these four cash flows change from 2005?
   (c) How do you think 'interest received' should be classified in the cash flow statement?
2 What will the 'Statement of Cash Flows' be labelled from 2005?
3 Which cash flow activity section is most likely to vary from year to year in terms of either providing or using cash?
4 Which three cash flow line items have changed by the greatest dollar amount over the year?
5 Which three cash flow line items have changed by the greatest relative amount over the year?
6 The 'cash at the end of the financial year' ($1,365.3m) is not the same as the 'cash' in the statement of financial position ($335.9m). Why is there a difference between these two figures?
7 The 'proceeds on sale and lease back' are reported as investing cash inflows in this statement. How will this sale and leaseback transaction be recorded:
   (a) In the statement of financial performance (income statement)?
   (b) In the statement of financial position (balance sheet)?

Qantas Financial Report 2004

Notes to the Financial Statements continued
for the year ended 30 June 2004

37. Notes to the Statements of Cash Flows

CASE
STUDY
5.2
→

	Qantas Group		Qantas	
	2004	2003	**2004**	2003
	$M	$M	**$M**	$M
RECONCILIATION OF CASH				
Cash as at the end of the financial year as shown in the Statements of Cash Flows is reconciled to the related items in the Statements of Financial Position as follows:				
Cash on hand and at bank	**110.8**	88.6	**30.0**	66.7
Cash as call	**225.1**	33.3	**224.7**	32.9
Short-term money market securities and term deposits	**1,029.4**	1,894.0	**1,029.4**	1,894.0
	1,365.3	2,015.9	**1,284.1**	1,993.6
RECONCILIATION OF PROFIT FROM ORDINARY ACTIVITIES AFTER INCOME TAX EXPENSE TO NET CASH PROVED BY OPERATING ACTIVITIES				
Net profit after tax attributable to members of the Company	**648.4**	343.5	**676.0**	372.5
Add: depreciation and amortisation	**1,005.6**	891.4	**871.1**	774.2
Add: loss on sale of aircraft, engines and spares	**4.0**	12.4	**3.0**	12.6
Less: profit on sale of land and buildings	**(3.4)**	(0.4)	**(3.3)**	–
Add: loss/(profit) on sale/disposal of property, plant and equipment	**(0.1)**	0.4	**0.8**	0.1
Add: loss on scrappage of aircraft spares	–	47.8	–	46.6
Less: capitalised interest	**(49.2)**	(82.7)	**(49.2)**	(82.7)
Less: share of associates' and joint ventures' net profit	**(19.7)**	(9.6)	–	–
Add: dividends received from associates and joint ventures	**11.9**	6.7	–	–
Reversal of provision against intercompany investment	–	–	**(130.7)**	–
Write-off of intercompany loan	–	–	**5.2**	–
Add: other items	**(35.6)**	66.7	**(12.3)**	(36.8)
Movements in operating assets and liabilities:				
(Increase)/decrease in receivables	**(173.9)**	590.4	**(181.3)**	625.9
(Increase)/decrease in inventories	**98.9**	(44.9)	**96.6**	(58.4)
(Increase) in other assets	**(17.8)**	(63.5)	**(106.8)**	(27.7)
Increase/(decrease) in provisions	**(76.8)**	54.1	**(65.8)**	54.3
Increase/(decrease) in current tax liabilites	**34.8**	(82.6)	**59.4**	(64.1)
(Increase)/decrease in deferred tax assets	**43.8**	(10.0)	**14.6**	(14.6)
Increase in deferred tax liabilities	**203.9**	78.3	**298.9**	88.1
Increase/(decrease) in trade/other payables	**58.4**	(306.9)	**2.1**	(265.7)
Increase/(decrease) in net intercompany payables	–	–	**163.8**	(152.4)
Increase/(decrease) in revenue received in advance	**334.9**	(126.8)	**291.8**	(121.9)
Decrease in deferred lease benefits	**(68.7)**	(66.0)	**(61.0)**	(57.8)
(Decrease) in other liabilities	–	(7.5)	–	(7.5)
Net cash provided by operating activities	**1,999.4**	1,290.8	**1,872.9**	1,084.7

1   Why is depreciation added to net profit in computing the net cash flow from operating activities?

2   Why is an increase in receivables deducted from net profit in computing the net cash flow from operating activities?

3   Why is the loss on sale added to net profit in computing the net cash flow from operating activities?

4   Why is capitalised interest added to net profit in computing the net cash flow from operating activities?

5   Net income increased by $304.9m in 2004 over 2003 while cash flow from operating activity increased by $708.6m. What three items made the greatest contribution to the surplus of operating cash inflow over the net profit?

6   The change in which two current assets had the biggest positive impact on the cash flows from operating activities?

7   The change in which two current liabilities had the biggest negative impact on the cash flows from operating activities?

CASE STUDY 5.3

The following article provides insights into Telstra's financial performance in 2000–2001. After reading this brief report, answer the questions that follow.

Cash flow is shareholders' silver lining

Comment reproduced with permission of the author, Alan Kohler
The Australian Financial Review
Thursday, 30 August 2001, p. 13

When Telstra shareholders get their copy of the company's profit report in the next few days, they should turn straight to the cash flow summary.

Their wealth is now entirely dependent on Ziggy Switkowski and the board wisely spending the company's free cash flow on cash acquisitions: privatisation is off the agenda, and if the Labor Party is elected it will be off it for a very long time.

That means scrip cannot be issued to make big growth-oriented mergers and acquisitions, and as for the business itself, the best that can be hoped for is no further decline for a while.

As it happens, that is actually what Switkowski and his team have achieved in the past 12 months: Telstra's overall market share has apparently levelled out at just above 70 per cent.

Whether it can hang on to between two-thirds and three-quarters of the telecommunications market in Australia indefinitely is another matter, although any pause in market share decline is definitely worth having.

Every day that Telstra gets through to nightfall without losing more market share is a great day for shareholders.

So let's tick off the prospects for shareholders over the next few years: there will be no dramatic growth in sales volumes in the phone business, no increase in Telstra's market share of it, no big scrip-based acquisitions, no further big cost reductions, and probably no surprise boost to the share price because of management changes.

With the share price wallowing at about $5 this is a grim checklist. The only alleviation of the gloom for shareholders can come from an examination of the cash flow statement. It is a pretty document.

In financial year 2000, the company coughed up its free cash flow—and then some—to the Government in a special dividend; in 2001 the money was spent, and largely wasted, on investments near the top of the market.

Telstra has been an investment-free zone for more than 12 months and Switkowski says there are no immediate plans to buy anything. Cash is pouring into the Telstra bank account, which stood at a billion dollars at balance date, at the rate of $70 million a week: meanwhile the market prices of telcos around the world are continuing to fall, with few buyers.

This is the silver lining in the Telstra shareholders' cloud. Market conditions look difficult, and although market share has stopped falling for the time being, in the long term it is only heading south.

But this is a rich company getting richer: the important thing for shareholders is that the board buys better than it did in the past.

1   What does the author mean by 'free cash flow'?
2   In general, what are the main options a company has in utilising surplus operating cash flows?
3   What business factors does the author suggest potentially lead to an increase in share price?
4   Why is Telstra's cash position so strong?
5   Why might profits be stable or declining but operating cash flows increasing?

SOLUTIONS TO ACTIVITIES

Activity 5.1

The difference between the two is that while a receipts and payments summary confines itself to cash movements, an accrual-based (i.e. profit and loss type) statement is concerned with movements in wealth. Increases and decreases in wealth do not necessarily involve cash. A business making a sale (a revenue) increases its wealth, but if the sale is made on credit no cash changes hands, at least not at the time of the sale. Here the increase in wealth is reflected in another asset—that is, an increase in trade debtors. If an item of inventory is the subject of the sale, the business incurs an expense in order to make the sale—that is, wealth is lost to the business through the reduction in inventory. Here an expense has been incurred, but no cash has changed hands. There is also the important distinction for profit-seeking organisations that the participants are going to be very concerned with wealth generation, not just with cash generation.

For an organisation with any real level of complexity a cash receipts and payments summary would not tell the participants all that they would want to know. A so-called accrual-based statement is necessary.

A simple club organisation may simply collect subscriptions from its members, perhaps raise further cash from activities and spend cash on pursuing the purposes of the club—for example, making payments to charity. Here everything that accounting is capable of reflecting is reflected in a simple cash receipts and payments statement. The club has no inventory. There are no non-current assets. All transactions are for cash, rather than on credit.

Where clubs and societies are involved with more complicated transactions the accrual-based 'profit and loss account' is generally referred to as an 'income and expenditure account'.

Activity 5.2

You should have come up with the following:

	Effect	
Event	On profit	On cash
Repayment of a loan	none	decrease
Making a sale on credit	increase	none
Buying a non-current asset for cash	none	decrease
Depreciating a non-current asset	decrease	none
Receiving cash from a trade debtor	none	increase
Buying some inventory for cash	none	decrease
Making a share issue for cash	none	increase

Activity 5.3

There are two broad possible reasons for a negative cash flow.

1. The company is unprofitable. This leads to more cash being paid out to employees, suppliers of goods and services, etc. than is being received from operating revenues. This would be particularly alarming because a major expense for most companies is depreciation of fixed assets. Since depreciation does not lead to a cash flow it is not considered in cash flow from operating activities. Thus a negative operating cash flow might well indicate a very much larger negative trading profit—that is, a significant loss of the company's wealth.

2. The other reason might be less alarming. A business that is expanding its activities (level of sales) would tend to spend quite a lot of cash relative to the amount of cash coming in from sales. This is because it will probably be expanding its inventory holdings to accommodate the increased demand. In the first instance, it would not necessarily benefit, in cash flow terms, from all of the additional sales. Normally, a business may well have to have the inventory in place first before additional sales could be made. Even when the additional sales are made, the sales would normally be made on credit, with the cash inflow lagging behind the sale. This is particularly likely to be true of a new company which would be expanding inventories, debtors, etc. from zero. Expansion typically causes cash flow strains for the reasons just explained. This can be a particular problem because the company's increased profitability might encourage a feeling of optimism which could lead to necessary concern not being shown for the cash flow problem.

Activity 5.4

Workings for the cash flow statement	
Cash received from customers	
Opening balance of debtors	24
plus sales for the period	500
gives the amount we might expect to receive for the year	524
less closing balance of debtors	(21)
equals the cash received from customers	503
Cash paid to suppliers, etc.	
Opening balance of creditors	18
plus purchases of inventory for the period (see below)	302
gives the amount we might expect to pay for the year	320
less closing balance of creditors	(19)
equals the cash paid to creditors	301

Calculation of purchases figure

Opening inventory	15
plus purchases	x
equals the amount available for sale	$x+15$
less closing inventory—the amount unsold	(17)
equals the cost of sales—the cost of the amount sold	300

Therefore $15 + x - 17 = 300$ or $x = 300 + 17 - 15 = 302$.

Cash flows from operating activities

Cash received from customers	503	
Cash paid to suppliers and employees		
(301 + other expenses of 44)	(345)	
Net cash provided by operating activities		158

The *reconciliation* is as follows:

		$m	
		$m	
Net operating profit		122	
Add depreciation		34	
Net inflow of working capital from operations		156	
Less increase in inventory		(2)	
		154	
Add decrease in debtors	3		
Increase in creditors	1	4	
Net cash inflow from operating activities		158	

Thus, the net increase in working capital was $156 million. Of this, $2 million went into increased inventory. More cash was received from debtors than sales were made and less cash was paid to creditors than purchases were made of goods and services on credit. Both of these had a favourable effect on cash.

Activity 5.5

Possible additional non-cash transactions:

Management allocation expenses

- Amortisation or impairment of intangibles
- Loss on sale of property, plant and equipment
- Write-down of inventory
- Revaluation downwards or impairment of property, plant and equipment
- Doubtful debts recognition
- Discounts given (early settlement)

Management allocation revenues

- Gain on sale of property, plant and equipment
- Discounts received (early settlement)

Asset increases

- Donations
- Revaluation upwards
- Direct issue of shares or debt for assets
- Self-constructed assets

Liability changes

- Direct issue of debt for assets
- Forgiveness of debt
- Conversion of debt for owners' equity

Owners' equity changes

- Revaluations
- Transfers
- Bonus issues
- Direct issues for assets
- Conversion of debt

Activity 5.6

Revenues	*Expenses*
+ Asset (beg)	+ Liability (beg)
− Asset (end)	+ Asset (end)
= Cash received	− Liability (end)
	− Asset (beg)
	= Cash paid

Activity 5.7

Transaction	*Cost*	*Accumulated depreciation*	*Net*
Depreciation expense equipment for the period	−	+	−
Revaluation of land to a higher value	+	−	+
Acquisition cost of a new plant	+	−	+
Cost of the vehicle sold during the period	−	−	−
Accumulated depreciation on asset sold	−	−	+
Trade-in allowance on the new plant	+	−	+
Direct exchange of shares for property	+	−	+
Write-down of buildings to recoverable amount	−	−	−

Activity 5.8

Using the format on page 208 we get the following:

Land and buildings	*Cost*	*Accumulated depreciation*	*Net*
Balance at the start of the year	150,000	−	150,000
less any disposals	−	−	−
	150,000	−	150,000
plus new acquisitions	*x* = 30,000	−	30,000
plus any revaluations	20,000	−	20,000
less depreciation for the year	−	−	−
equals closing balance	200,000	−	200,000

The new acquisitions were calculated by essentially filling in the gap.

Plant and machinery	Cost	Accumulated depreciation	Net
Balance at the start of the year	80,000	(20,000)	60,000
less any disposals	–	–	–
	80,000	(20,000)	60,000
plus new acquisitions	$x = 20,000$	–	20,000
plus any revaluations	–	–	–
less depreciation for the year	–	$x = (10,000)$	(10,000)
equals closing balance	100,000	30,000	70,000

The new acquisitions and the depreciation for the year are obtained by solving for x as shown.

Fixtures and fittings	Cost	Accumulated depreciation	Net
Balance at the start of the year	20,000	(10,000)	10,000
less any disposals	(5,000)	3,000	(2,000)
	15,000	(7,000)	8,000
plus new acquisitions	$x = 10,000$	–	10,000
plus any revaluations	–	–	–
less depreciation for the year		$x = (5,000)$	(5,000)
equals closing balance	25,000	(12,000)	13,000

Note that it is the cost and accumulated depreciation of the asset being disposed of that gets taken off. The fact that assets which had cost $5,000, and which had been depreciated by $3,000 (giving a book value of $2,000), are sold for $1,000 means that there will be a loss on disposal of $1,000, which would be a non-cash expense in the income statement. The sale proceeds will be reflected in the statement of cash flows.

The relevant extracts from the statement of cash flows will be:

Cash flow from investing activities

Purchase of land and buildings	(30,000)
Purchase of plant and machinery	(20,000)
Purchase of fixtures and fittings	(10,000)
Proceeds from sale of fixtures and fittings	1,000
Net cash used in investing activities	(59,000)

In passing it is worth noting that the reconciliation would include depreciation totalling $15,000 plus $1,000 loss on disposal.

OBJECTIVES

When you have completed your study of this chapter you should be able to:

1   define what a ratio is

2   identify the key aspects of financial performance and financial position that are evaluated by the use of ratios

3   explain the terms *profitability*, *efficiency*, *liquidity*, *gearing* and *investment*

4   summarise the alternative bases of comparison for ratio analysis

5   present the ratio formulae for the basic ratios

6   calculate ratios to analyse the profitability, efficiency, liquidity, gearing and investment of a given entity's financial statements over several periods

7   interpret basic ratios relating to profitability, efficiency, liquidity, gearing and investment

8   discuss the limitations of ratios as a tool of financial analysis

9   understand index or percentage analysis as an alternative to ratios.

ANALYSIS AND INTERPRETATION OF FINANCIAL STATEMENTS

In this chapter we will consider the analysis, interpretation and evaluation of financial statements. We will see how financial ratios can help in developing a financial profile of a business. We will also consider problems that are encountered when applying this technique.

FINANCIAL RATIOS

Financial ratios provide a quick and relatively simple means of examining the financial health of a business. A ratio simply expresses the relationship between one figure appearing in the financial statements and some other figure appearing in the financial statements (e.g. net profit in relation to capital employed) or perhaps some resource of the business (e.g. net profit per employee, sales per square metre of counter space).

By calculating a relatively small number of ratios, it is often possible to build up a reasonably good picture of the financial position and performance of a business. Thus, it is not surprising that ratios are widely used by those who have an interest in businesses and business performance. Although ratios are not difficult to calculate they can be difficult to interpret. For example, a change in the net profit per employee of a business may be due to a number of possible reasons, such as:

✳ a change in the number of employees without a corresponding change in the level of output

✳ a change in the level of output without a corresponding change in the number of employees

✳ a change in the mix of goods or services being offered, which in turn changes the level of profit.

It is important to appreciate that ratios are really only the starting point for further analysis. They help to highlight the financial strengths and weaknesses of a business but they cannot, by themselves, explain why certain strengths or weaknesses exist or why certain changes have occurred. Only a detailed investigation will reveal these underlying reasons.

A major problem when comparing the financial health of different businesses is the differences that exist in the scale of operations. Thus, a direct comparison of (say) the profits of each business may be misleading due to differences in size. By expressing profit in relation to some other measure (e.g. sales) the ratio derived can be used as a basis for comparison with similarly derived ratios for other similar businesses.

Ratios can be expressed in various forms—for example, as a percentage, as a fraction, as a proportion. The way a particular ratio is presented will depend on the needs of those who will use the information. Although it is possible to calculate a large number of ratios, only a relatively few, based on key relationships, may be required by the user. Many ratios that could be calculated from the financial statements (e.g. rent payable relative to taxation) may not be considered because there is no clear or meaningful relationship between the items.

There is no generally accepted list of ratios that can be applied to the financial statements, nor is there a standard method of calculating many ratios. Variations in both the choice of ratios and their calculation will be found in the literature and in practice. However, it is important to be consistent in the way in which ratios are calculated for comparison purposes. The ratios discussed below are those which many consider to be among the more important for decision-making purposes.

FINANCIAL RATIO CLASSIFICATION

Ratios can be grouped into certain categories, each of which reflects a particular aspect of financial performance or position. The following broad categories provide a useful basis for explaining the nature of the financial ratios to be dealt with.

* *Profitability.* Businesses come into being with the primary purpose of creating wealth for the owners. Profitability ratios provide an insight into the degree of success in achieving this purpose. They express the profits made (or figures bearing on profit such as overheads) in relation to other key figures in the financial statements or to some business resource.

* *Efficiency.* Ratios may be used to measure the efficiency with which certain resources have been utilised within the business. These ratios are also referred to as activity or turnover ratios.

* *Liquidity.* It is vital to the survival of a business for there to be sufficient liquid resources available to meet maturing obligations. Certain ratios may be calculated which examine the relationship between liquid resources held and accounts due for payment in the near future.

* *Gearing.* Gearing is an important issue which managers must consider when making financing decisions. The relationship between the amount financed by the owners of the business and the amount contributed by outsiders reflects the degree of risk associated with a business, as we will see. Gearing is also referred to as leverage.

* *Investment.* Certain ratios are concerned with assessing the returns and performance of shares held in a particular business.

THE NEED FOR COMPARISON

Calculating a ratio by itself will not tell you very much about the position or performance of a business. For example, if a ratio revealed that the business was generating $100 in sales per square metre of counter space, it would not be possible to deduce from this information alone whether this level of performance was good, bad or indifferent. It is only when you compare this ratio with some 'benchmark' that the information can be interpreted and evaluated.

ACTIVITY 6.1

Can you think of any bases (benchmarks) that could be used to compare a ratio you have calculated from the financial statements of a particular period?

THE KEY STEPS IN FINANCIAL RATIO ANALYSIS

When employing financial ratios, a sequence of steps is carried out by the analyst. The first step involves identifying the key indicators and relationships that require examination. In order to carry out this step the analyst must be clear *who* the target users are and *why* they need the information. Different types of users of financial information are likely to have different information needs which will, in turn, determine the ratios they find useful. For example, shareholders are likely to be interested in their returns in relation to the level of risk associated with their investment. Thus, profitability, investment and gearing ratios will be of particular interest. Long-term lenders are concerned with the long-term viability of the business. In order to help them to assess this, the profitability ratios and gearing ratios of the business are also likely to be of particular interest. Short-term lenders, such as suppliers, may be interested in the ability of the business to repay the amounts owing in the short term. As a result, the liquidity ratios should be of interest.

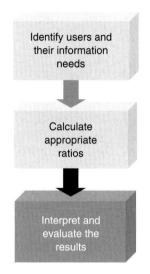

The next step in the process is to calculate ratios that are considered appropriate for the particular users and the purpose for which they require the information. The final step is interpretation and evaluation of the ratios. Interpretation involves examining the ratios in conjunction with an appropriate basis for comparison and any other information that may be relevant. The significance of the ratios calculated can then be established. Evaluation involves forming a judgment concerning the value of the information uncovered in the calculation and interpretation stage. While calculation is usually straightforward, the interpretation and evaluation are more difficult and often require high levels of skill. This skill can only really be acquired through much practice.

The three steps described are shown in Figure 6.1.

FIGURE 6.1 Financial ratio analysis: the key steps

THE RATIOS CALCULATED

Probably the best way to explain financial ratios is to work through an example. The following example provides a set of financial statements from which we can calculate important ratios.

The following financial statements relate to Alexis Ltd, which owns a small chain of wholesale/retail carpet stores.

EXAMPLE

6.1

ALEXIS LTD

Balance sheet as at 31 March						
	2005		2006		2007	
	$'000	$'000	$'000	$'000	$'000	$'000
Current assets						
Bank	6.1		33.5		41.0	
Trade debtors	281.0		240.8		210.2	
Inventory at cost	241.0		300.0		370.8	
		528.1		574.3		622.0
Non-current assets						
Fixtures and fittings at cost	107.8		129.0		160.4	
Less accumulated depreciation	37.4	70.4	64.4	64.6	97.2	63.2
Freehold land and buildings at cost	351.2		451.2		451.2	
Less accumulated depreciation	65.0	286.2	70.0	381.2	75.0	376.2
		356.6		445.8		439.4
Total assets		884.7		1,020.1		1,061.4
Current liabilities						
Trade creditors	247.0		221.4		228.8	
Dividends payable	32.0		40.2		60.0	
Income tax	46.4		60.2		76.0	
		325.4		321.8		364.8

Non-current liabilities					
12% Debentures (secured)		200.0		200.0	60.0
Capital and reserves					
Paid-up ordinary capital	280.0		300.0		334.1
(shares all issued at 50 cents each)					
Reserves	26.5		26.5		40.0
Retained profit	52.8		171.8		262.5
		359.3		498.3	636.6
Total liabilities and shareholders' equity		884.7		1,020.1	1,061.4

ALEXIS LTD

Income statement for the year ended 31 March

	2006		2007	
	$'000	$'000	$'000	$'000
Sales		2,240.8		2,681.2
Less cost of sales				
Opening stock	241.0		300.0	
Purchases	1,804.4		2,142.8	
	2,045.4		2,442.8	
Less closing stock	300.0	1,745.4	370.8	2,072.0
Gross profit		495.4		609.2
Wages and salaries	137.8		195.0	
Directors' salaries	48.0		80.6	
Rates	12.2		12.4	
Heat and light	8.4		13.6	
Insurance	4.6		7.0	
Interest expense	24.0		6.2	
Postage and telephone	3.4		7.4	
Audit fees	5.6		9.0	
Depreciation				
Freehold buildings	5.0		5.0	
Fixtures and fittings	27.0	276.0	32.8	369.0
Net profit before tax		219.4		240.2
Less income tax		60.2		76.0
Net profit after tax		159.2		164.2
Add retained profit brought forward		52.8		171.8
		212.0		336.0
Transfer to reserves		–		(13.5)
Dividends proposed		(40.2)		(60.0)
Retained profit carried forward		171.8		262.5

ALEXIS LTD

Cash flow statement for the year ended 31 March				
	2006		2007	
	$'000	$'000	$'000	$'000
Cash flows from operations				
Cash receipts from customers	2,281		2,711.8	
Cash paid to suppliers and employees	(2,050)		(2,460.4)	
Interest paid	(24)		(6.2)	
Tax paid	(46.4)		(60.2)	
Net cash provided by operating activities		160.6		185
Investing activities				
Purchase of non-current assets	(121.2)		(31.4)	
Net cash used in investing activities		(121.2)		(31.4)
Financing activities				
Dividends paid	(32.0)		(40.2)	
Proceeds from issuance of share capital	20.0		34.1	
Repayment of long-term loan	–		(140.0)	
Net cash used in financing activities		(12)		(146.1)
Increase in cash and cash equivalents		27.4		7.5

The company employed 14 staff in 2006 and 18 in 2007.

All sales and purchases are made on credit.

The market value of the shares of the company at the end of each year was $2.50 and $3.50 respectively. The issue of equity shares during the year ended 31 March 2007 occurred at the beginning of the year.

As a general rule, where a ratio involves a comparison between two balance sheets, we use year-end figures. However, where the ratio involves both balance sheet and income statements we would use the average of the two balance sheets figures rather than the year-end figure, because it is more directly comparable with the figures from the income statement.

PROFITABILITY

The following ratios may be used to evaluate the profitability of the business:

* return on owners' equity
* return on total assets
* net profit margin
* gross profit margin.

Return on owners' equity (ROE)

This ratio compares the amount of profit for the period available to the owners with the owners' stake in the business. For a limited company, the ratio (which is normally expressed in percentage terms) is as follows:

$$ROE = \frac{\textit{Net profit after taxation and preference dividend (if any)}}{\textit{Average ordinary share capital plus reserves}} \times 100$$

The net profit after taxation and any preference dividend is used in calculating the ratio as this figure represents the amount of profit available to the owners. In the above equation, 'reserves' means all reserves including general reserves, revaluation reserves and retained profits.

In the case of Alexis Ltd the ratio for the year ended 31 March 2006 is:

$$\frac{159.2}{(359.3 + 498.3)\,/\,2} \times 100 = 37.1\%$$

ACTIVITY 6.2

Calculate the return on owners' equity (ROE) for Alexis Ltd for the year to 31 March 2007.

Note that in calculating the ratios above it can be argued that it is preferable to use an average figure for the year as this would be more representative of the amount invested by owners during the period. The easiest approach to calculating the average equity investment would be to take a simple average based on the opening and closing figures for the year. However, where these figures are not available it is acceptable to use the year-end figures.

Return on total assets (ROA)

Return on total assets is a fundamental measure of business performance. This ratio expresses the relationship between the net profit generated by the business and the assets owned by the business. The ratio is expressed in percentage terms and is as follows:

$$ROA = \frac{\textit{Net profit before interest and taxation}}{\textit{Average total assets}} \times 100$$

Note in this case that the profit figure used in the ratio is the net profit *before* interest and taxation. This figure is used because the ratio attempts to measure both the efficiency and effectiveness with which assets are used. Interest is a financing expense, not an operating expense. Taxation is subject to fluctuation over time as the rules change and, for comparison purposes, a before-tax figure is more useful.

In the case of Alexis Ltd the ratio for the year to 31 March 2006 is:

$$ROA = \frac{243.4}{(884.7 + 1,020.1)\,/\,2} \times 100 = 25.6\%$$

ACTIVITY 6.3

Calculate the return on total assets for Alexis Ltd for the year to 31 March 2007.

Return on total assets is considered by many to be a primary measure of profitability. It compares inputs (assets invested) with outputs (profit). This comparison is of vital importance in assessing the effectiveness with which assets have been utilised. Once again, an average figure for total assets is used where the information is available.

Net profit margin

This ratio relates the net profit for the period to the sales during that period. The ratio is expressed as follows:

$$Net\ profit\ margin = \frac{Net\ profit\ before\ interest\ and\ taxation}{Sales} \times 100$$

The net profit before interest and taxation is used in this ratio as it represents the profit from trading operations before any costs of servicing long-term finance are taken into account. This is often regarded as the most appropriate measure of operational performance for comparison purposes, as differences arising from the way in which a particular business is financed will not influence this measure. However, this is not the only way in which this ratio may be calculated in practice. The net profit after taxation is also used on occasions as the numerator.

For Alexis Ltd for the year ended 31 March 2006 the net profit margin ratio (based on the net profit before interest and taxation) is:

$$\frac{243.4}{2,240.8} \times 100 = 10.9\%$$

This ratio compares one output of the business (profit) to another output (sales). The ratio can vary considerably between types of business. For example, a supermarket will often operate on low net profit margins in order to stimulate sales and thereby increase the total amount of profit generated. A jeweller, on the other hand, may have a high net profit margin but have a much lower level of sales volume. Factors such as the degree of competition, the type of customer, the economic climate and industry characteristics (such as the level of risk) will influence the net profit margins of a business.

ACTIVITY 6.4

Calculate the net profit margin for Alexis Ltd for the year to 31 March 2007.

Gross profit margin

This ratio relates the gross profit of the business to the sales generated for the same period. Gross profit represents the difference between sales and the cost of sales. The ratio is therefore a measure of profitability in buying (or producing) and selling goods before any other expenses are taken into account. As cost of sales represents a major expense for retailing and manufacturing businesses, a change in this ratio can have a significant effect on the 'bottom line' (i.e. the net profit for the year). The gross profit ratio is calculated as follows:

$$Gross\ profit\ margin = \frac{Gross\ profit}{Sales} \times 100$$

For Alexis Ltd for the year to 31 March 2006 the ratio is as follows:

$$Gross\ profit\ margin = \frac{495.4}{2,240.8} \times 100 = 22.1\%$$

Calculate the gross profit margin for Alexis Ltd for the year to 31 March 2007.

An adequate gross profit margin for manufacturing and retail operations is essential to the success of that operation. An inadequate gross profit margin will mean that the business has little likelihood of success. The gross profit needs to be sufficient to cover the other expenses, and provide a satisfactory return to the owners. The adequacy of this margin is dependent on both the buying price (or manufactured cost) and the selling price.

The profitability ratios for Alexis Ltd over the two years can be set out as follows:

	2006	*2007*
Return on owners' equity	37.1%	28.9%
Return on total assets	25.6%	23.7%
Net profit margin	10.9%	9.2%
Gross profit margin	22.1%	22.7%

What do you deduce from a comparison of the profitability ratios for Alexis Ltd over the two years?

EFFICIENCY

Efficiency ratios examine the productive or timely ways in which various resources of the business are managed. The following ratios consider some of the more important aspects of resource management:

✳ average inventory turnover period
✳ **average settlement period** for debtors
✳ average settlement period for creditors
✳ asset turnover period.

Average inventory turnover period

Inventory often represents a significant investment for a business. For some types of business (e.g. manufacturers), inventory may account for a substantial proportion of the total assets held. The average inventory turnover period measures the average period for which inventory is being held. The ratio is calculated thus:

$$\textit{Inventory turnover periods} = \frac{\textit{Average inventory held}}{\textit{Cost of sales}} \times 365$$

The average inventory for the period can be calculated as a simple average of the opening and closing inventory levels for the year. However, in the case of a highly seasonal business, where inventory levels may vary considerably over the year, a monthly average may be more appropriate.

For Alexis Ltd the inventory turnover period for the year ended 31 March 2006 is:

$$\frac{(241 + 300) / 2}{1,745.4} \times 365 = 57 \text{ days (to nearest day)}$$

This means that, on average, the inventory held is being 'turned over' every 57 days. A business will normally prefer a low inventory turnover period to a high period, as funds tied up in inventory cannot be used for other profitable purposes. In judging the amount of inventory to carry, the business must consider such things as the likely future demand, the possibility of future shortages, the likelihood of future price rises, the cost advantages of buying in larger quantities, the amount of storage space available and the perishability of the product. The management of inventory will be considered in more detail in Chapter 13.

This ratio is sometimes expressed in terms of months rather than days. Multiplying by 12 rather than 365 will achieve this.

ACTIVITY 6.7

Calculate the average inventory turnover period for Alexis Ltd for the year ended 31 March 2007.

Average settlement period for accounts receivable (debtors)

A business will usually be concerned with how long it takes for customers to pay the amounts owing. The speed of payment can have a significant effect on the cash flows of the business. The average settlement period calculates how long, on average, credit customers take to pay the amounts they owe to the business. The ratio is as follows:

$$\text{Average settlement period} = \frac{\text{Average trade debtors}}{\text{Credit sales}} \times 365$$

We are told that all sales made by Alexis Ltd are on credit and so the average settlement period for debtors for the year ended 31 March 2006 is:

$$\frac{(281.0 + 240.8) / 2}{2,240.8} \times 365 = 43 \text{ days (to nearest day)}$$

ACTIVITY 6.8

Calculate the average settlement period for debtors for Alexis Ltd for the year ended 31 March 2007.

A business will normally prefer a shorter average settlement period than a longer one as, once again, funds are being tied up which may be used for more profitable purposes. Although this ratio can be useful, it is important to remember that it produces an *average* figure for the number of days debts are outstanding. This average may be badly distorted by, for example, a few large customers who are very slow payers.

Average settlement period for accounts payable (creditors)

This ratio measures how long, on average, the business takes to pay its trade creditors. The ratio is calculated as follows:

$$Average\ settlement\ period = \frac{Average\ trade\ creditors}{Credit\ purchases} \times 365$$

In the case of Alexis Ltd, for the year ended 31 March 2006 the average settlement period is:

$$\frac{(247.0 + 221.4)\ /\ 2}{1,804.4} \times 365 = 47\ days\ (to\ nearest\ day)$$

ACTIVITY 6.9

Calculate the average settlement period for creditors for Alexis Ltd for the year ended 31 March 2007.

This ratio provides an average figure which, like the average settlement period for debtors ratio, can be distorted by the payment period for one or two large suppliers.

As trade creditors provide a free source of finance for the business, it is perhaps not surprising that some businesses attempt to increase their average settlement period for trade creditors. However, such a policy can be taken too far and can result in a loss of suppliers' goodwill. We will return to the issues concerning the management of trade debtors and trade creditors in Chapter 13.

Asset turnover period

This ratio examines how effectively the assets of the business are being employed in generating sales revenue. The ratio is calculated as follows:

$$Average\ asset\ turnover\ period = \frac{Average\ total\ assets\ employed \times 365}{Sales}$$

For the year ended 31 March 2006 this ratio for Alexis Ltd is as follows:

$$\frac{(884.7 + 1,020.1)\ /\ 2}{2,240.8} \times 365 = 155\ days$$

ACTIVITY 6.10

Calculate the average asset turnover period for Alexis Ltd for the year ended 31 March 2007.

Generally speaking, a lower asset turnover period is preferred to a higher period. A lower turnover period will normally suggest that assets are being used more productively in the generation of revenue. However, a very low turnover period may suggest that the business is 'overtrading on its assets'—that is, it has insufficient assets to match the level of sales achieved. When comparing this ratio between businesses, such factors as the age and condition of assets held, the valuation bases for assets, and whether assets are rented or purchased outright can complicate interpretation.

A variation of this formula is to use the total assets less current liabilities (which is equivalent to long-term capital employed) in the numerator.

The efficiency ratios for Alexis Ltd may be summarised as follows:

	2006	2007
Inventory turnover period	57 days	59 days
Average settlement period for debtors	43 days	31 days
Average settlement period for creditors	47 days	38 days
Asset turnover period	155 days	142 days

The efficiency ratios have been expressed in terms of a turnover period (number of days). An alternative is to express them simply as the number of times that asset (or liability) turns over on average during the year (repeats itself). The formula for such ratios is simple: income statement figure (sales, credit sales, cost of goods sold, credit purchases) divided by the average balance sheet figure (total assets, debtors, inventory, creditors).

If you know the 'turnover' figure (e.g. 3.2 times) you can get the 'turnover period' by dividing 365 days by the 'turnover' (e.g. 365 days / 3.2 equals 114 days). Similarly, if you know the 'turnover period' (e.g. 49 days) you can get the 'turnover' by dividing 365 days by the turnover period (e.g. 365 days / 49 days = 7.45 times).

For the worked examples the 'turnovers' would be:

	2006	2007
Inventory turnover	6.4 times	6.2 times
Average debtors turnover	8.5 times	11.8 times
Average creditors turnover	7.8 times	9.6 times
Asset turnover	2.4 times	2.6 times

ACTIVITY 6.11

What do you deduce from a comparison of the efficiency ratios for Alexis Ltd over the two years?

THE RELATIONSHIP BETWEEN PROFITABILITY AND EFFICIENCY

In our earlier discussions concerning profitability ratios you will recall that return on total assets (ROA) is regarded as a key ratio by many businesses. The ratio is:

$$ROA = \frac{Net\ profit\ before\ interest\ and\ taxation}{Average\ total\ assets} \times 100$$

This ratio can be broken down into two elements as shown in Figure 6.2. The first ratio is, of course, the net profit margin ratio and the second ratio is the asset turnover ratio, which we discussed earlier.

By breaking down the ROA ratio in this manner, we highlight the fact that the overall return on funds employed within the business will be determined both by the profitability of sales and by efficiency in the use of assets.

Consider the following information concerning two different businesses, A and B, operating in the same industry:

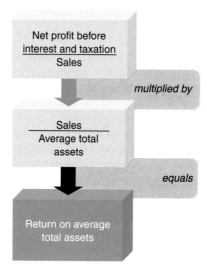

FIGURE 6.2 The main elements comprising the ROA ratio

EXAMPLE

6.2

	Business	
	A	*B*
Profit before interest and tax	$20m	$15m
Average total assets	$100m	$75m
Sales	$200m	$300m

The ROA for each business is identical (i.e. 20 per cent). However, the manner in which the return was achieved by each business was quite different. In the case of business A, the net profit margin is 10 per cent and the asset turnover is two times (hence ROA = 10% × 2 = 20%). In the case of business B, the net profit margin is 5 per cent and the asset turnover ratio is four times (hence ROA = 5% × 4 = 20%).

This demonstrates that a relatively low net profit margin can be compensated for by a relatively high asset turnover ratio and a relatively low asset turnover ratio can be compensated for by a relatively high net profit margin. In many areas of retailing and distribution (e.g. supermarkets and delivery services) the net profit margins are quite low but the ROA can be high, providing the assets are used productively.

LIQUIDITY

Liquidity ratios assess the ability of the business to meet short-term commitments or claims against the assets when they fall due. It is sometimes expressed in terms of the ability or speed with which assets can be converted to cash.

Current ratio

This ratio compares the 'liquid' assets (i.e. cash and those assets held that will soon be turned into cash) of the business with the short-term liabilities (current liabilities). The ratio is calculated as follows:

$$Current\ ratio = \frac{Current\ assets}{Current\ liabilities}$$

For the year ended 31 March 2006 the current ratio of Alexis Ltd is:

$$\frac{574.3}{321.8} = 1.8\ times$$

The ratio reveals that the current assets cover the current liabilities by 1.8 times. In some texts the notion of an 'ideal' current ratio (usually two times or 2:1) is suggested for businesses. However, this fails to take into account the fact that different types of business require different current ratios. For example, a manufacturing business will often have a relatively high current ratio because it is necessary to hold stocks of finished goods, raw materials and work-in-progress. It will also normally sell goods on credit, thereby incurring debtors. A supermarket chain, on the other hand, will have a relatively low ratio as it will hold only fast-moving stocks of finished goods and will generate mostly cash sales.

The higher the ratio the more liquid the business is considered to be. As liquidity is of vital importance to the survival of a business, a higher current ratio is normally preferred to a lower ratio. However, if a business has a very high current ratio this may suggest that funds are being tied up in cash or other liquid assets and are not being used as productively as they might otherwise be.

ACTIVITY 6.12

Calculate the current ratio for Alexis Ltd for the year ended 31 March 2007.

Acid test ratio

This ratio (also known as the liquid or quick ratio) represents a more stringent test of liquidity. It can be argued that, for many businesses, the inventory on hand cannot be converted into cash quickly. (Note that in the case of Alexis Ltd the inventory turnover period was more than 50 days in both years.) As a result, it may be better to exclude this particular asset from any measure of liquidity. The acid test ratio is based on this idea and is calculated as follows:

$$Acid\ test\ ratio = \frac{Current\ assets\ (excluding\ inventory\ and\ prepayments)}{Current\ liabilities}$$

The acid test ratio for Alexis Ltd for the year ended 31 March 2006 is:

$$\frac{(574.3 - 300)}{321.8} = 0.9\ times$$

We can see that the 'liquid' current assets do not quite cover the current liabilities and so the business may be experiencing some liquidity problems. In some types of business, however, where cash flows are strong, it is not unusual for the acid test ratio to be below 1.0 without causing liquidity problems for the particular businesses.

The current and acid test ratios for 2006 can be expressed as 1.8:1 and 0.9:1 respectively, rather than as a number of times. This form can be found in some texts. The interpretation of the ratios, however, will not be affected by this difference in form.

ACTIVITY 6.13

Calculate the acid test ratio for Alexis Ltd for the year ended 31 March 2007.

Both the current ratio and acid test ratio derive the relevant figures from the balance sheet. As this statement is simply a 'snapshot' of the financial position of the business at a single moment in time, care must be taken when interpreting the ratios. It is possible that the figures from the balance sheet are not representative of the liquidity position during the year. This may be due to exceptional factors or simply due to the fact that the business is seasonal in nature and these figures represent the cash position at one particular point in the seasonal cycle only.

Cash flows from operations ratio

This ratio compares the operating cash flows with the current liabilities of the business. It provides a further indication of the ability of the business to meet its maturing obligations. The ratio is calculated as follows:

$$\text{Cash flows from operations ratio} = \frac{\text{Operating cash flows}}{\text{Current liabilities}}$$

The higher this ratio, the better the liquidity of the business. This ratio has the advantage that the operating cash flows for a period usually provide a more reliable guide to the liquidity of a business than the current assets held at the reporting date. Alexis Ltd's ratio for the year ended 31 March 2006 is:

$$\frac{160.6}{321.8} = 0.5 \text{ times}$$

This ratio indicates that the operating cash flows for the period are not sufficient to cover the current liabilities at the end of the period.

ACTIVITY 6.14

Calculate the operating cash flows to maturing obligations ratio for Alexis Ltd for the year ended 31 March 2007.

The liquidity ratios for the two-year period for Alexis Ltd may be summarised as follows:

	2006	2007
Current ratio	1.8 times	1.7 times
Acid test ratio	0.9 times	0.7 times
Cash flow from operations ratio	0.5 times	0.5 times

ACTIVITY 6.15

What do you deduce from a comparison of the liquidity ratios for Alexis Ltd over the two years?

GEARING (LEVERAGE)

Gearing occurs when a business is financed, at least in part, by contributions from outside parties. The level of gearing (i.e. the extent to which a business is financed by outside parties) associated with a business is often an important factor in assessing risk. Where a business borrows heavily it takes on a commitment to pay interest charges and make capital repayments. This can be a financial burden and can increase the risk of a business becoming insolvent. Nevertheless, it is the case that most businesses are geared to some extent.

Given the risks involved, you may wonder why a business would want to take on gearing. One reason may be that the owners have insufficient funds and therefore the only way to finance the business adequately is to borrow from others. Another reason is that gearing can be used to increase the returns to owners. This is possible providing the returns generated from borrowed funds exceed the cost of paying interest. An example can be used to illustrate this point.

EXAMPLE

6.3

Two companies, X Ltd and Y Ltd, commence business with the following long-term capital structures:

	X Ltd	Y Ltd
	$	$
Paid-up ordinary capital	100,000	200,000
10% loan	200,000	100,000
	300,000	300,000

In the first year of operations they both make a profit before interest and taxation of $50,000. In this case X Ltd would be considered highly geared as it has a high proportion of borrowed funds in its long-term capital structure. Y Ltd is lowly geared. The profit available to the shareholders of each company in the first year of operations will be:

	X Ltd	Y Ltd
	$	$
Profit before interest and taxation	50,000	50,000
Interest expense	20,000	10,000
Profit before taxation	30,000	40,000
Taxation (say 30%)	9,000	12,000
Profit available to ordinary shareholders	21,000	28,000

The return on owners' equity for each company will be (using year-end figures for owners' equity):

X Ltd	Y Ltd
$\dfrac{21,000 \times 100}{100,000}$	$\dfrac{28,000 \times 100}{200,000}$
= 21%	= 14%

We can see that X Ltd, the more highly geared company, has generated a better return on equity than Y Ltd.

An effect of gearing is that returns to equity become more sensitive to changes in profits. For a highly geared company a change in profits can lead to a proportionately greater change in the returns to equity.

We can see from the solution to Activity 6.16 that for X Ltd, the higher geared company, the returns to equity have increased by 33 per cent whereas for the lower geared company the benefits of gearing are less pronounced. The increase in the returns to equity for Y Ltd is less than 25 per cent. The effect of gearing, of course, can work in both directions. Thus, for a highly geared company a small decline in profits may bring about a much greater decline in the returns to equity.

Figure 6.3 illustrates the effects of gearing with the movement of the larger cog (profit before interest and taxes) causing a more than proportionate movement in the smaller cog (returns to ordinary shareholders).

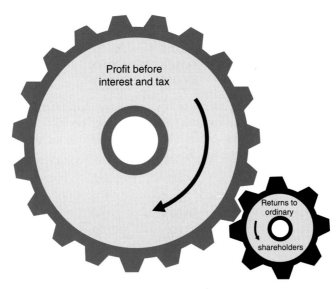

The two wheels are linked by the cogs, so that a relatively small circular movement in the large wheel (profit before interest and tax) leads to a relatively large circular movement in the small wheel (returns to ordinary shareholders).

FIGURE 6.3 The effect of financial gearing

Gearing ratio

The following ratio measures the contribution of long-term lenders to the long-term capital structure of a business:

$$Gearing\ ratio = \frac{Long\text{-}term\ liabilities}{Share\ capital + Reserves + Long\text{-}term\ liabilities} \times 100$$

The gearing ratio for Alexis Ltd for the year ended 31 March 2006 is:

$$\frac{200}{(498.3 + 200)} \times 100 = 28.6\%$$

This ratio reveals a level of gearing that would not normally be considered to be very high.

ACTIVITY 6.17

Calculate the gearing ratio of Alexis Ltd for the year ended 31 March 2007.

There are other variations of the gearing ratio which essentially focus on the proportion of outside debt to owners' equity. These are:

✳ total liabilities to total assets
✳ total liabilities to total owners' equity
✳ long-term liabilities to total owners' equity.

Interest cover ratio (times interest earned)

This ratio measures the amount of profit available to cover interest expense. The ratio may be calculated as follows:

$$Interest\ cover\ ratio = \frac{Profit\ before\ interest\ and\ taxation}{Interest\ expense}$$

The ratio for Alexis Ltd for the year ended 31 March 2006 is:

$$\frac{(219.4 + 24)}{24} = 10.1\ times$$

This ratio shows that the level of profit is considerably higher than the level of interest expense. Thus, a significant fall in profits could occur before profit levels failed to cover interest expense. The lower the level of profit coverage the greater the risk to lenders that interest payments will not be met.

ACTIVITY 6.18

Calculate the interest cover ratio of Alexis Ltd for the year ended 31 March 2007.

ACTIVITY 6.19

What do you deduce from a comparison of the gearing ratios of Alexis Ltd over the two years?

The gearing ratio at the end of 2007 would normally be considered to be very low and may indicate that the business has some debt capacity (i.e. it is capable of borrowing more if required). However, the availability of adequate security and profitability must also be taken into account before the debt capacity of a business can be properly established.

INVESTMENT RATIOS

There are a number of ratios available that are designed to help investors assess the returns on their investment. Below we consider some of these ratios.

Dividends per share

The dividends per share ratio relates the dividends announced during a period to the number of shares on issue during that period. The ratio is calculated as follows:

$$\text{Dividends per share} = \frac{\text{Dividends announced during the period}}{\text{Number of shares on issue}}$$

In essence, the ratio provides an indication of the cash return that an investor receives from holding shares in a company.

Although it is a useful measure, it must always be remembered that the dividends received will usually only represent a partial measure of return to investors. Dividends are usually only a proportion of the total earnings generated by the company and available to shareholders. A company may decide to plough back some of its earnings into the business in order to achieve future growth. These ploughed-back profits also belong to the shareholders and should, in principle, increase the value of the shares held.

When assessing the total returns to investors we must take account of both the cash returns received and any change in the market value of the shares held.

In Example 6.1, Alexis Ltd, you should note that the capital was issued at a price of 50 cents per share, so the number of shares is twice the amount recorded in the accounts. The figure for dividends per share for Alexis Ltd for the year ended 31 March 2006 is therefore:

$$\frac{40.2}{600} = 6.7c$$

This ratio can be calculated for each class of share issued by a company. Alexis Ltd has only ordinary shares on issue and therefore only one dividend per share ratio can be calculated.

In practice, the calculation of 'the average number of shares on issue for the period' can be quite complex. The calculation will need to take into account the timing of the issues, the type of issue (e.g. fresh public issue at market price, a rights issue to existing shareholders at a price below the market price at the time of the issue, and a bonus issue to existing shareholders at no cost to the shareholder), and possible future issues related to contracts currently in place (e.g. convertible notes or management options).

Dividends per share can vary considerably between companies. A number of factors will influence the amount a company is prepared to distribute in the form of dividends to shareholders. These include cash availability, future commitments and investor expectations.

ACTIVITY 6.20

Calculate the dividends per share of Alexis Ltd for the year ended 31 March 2007.

Dividend payout ratio

The dividend payout ratio measures the proportion of earnings that a company pays out to shareholders in the form of dividends. The ratio is calculated as follows:

$$\text{Dividend payout ratio} = \frac{\text{Dividends announced for the year} \times 100}{\text{Earnings for the year available for dividends}}$$

In the case of ordinary shares, the earnings available for dividends will normally be the net profit after taxation and after any preference dividends announced during the period. This ratio is normally expressed as a percentage.

The dividend payout ratio for Alexis Ltd for the year ended 31 March 2006 is:

$$\text{Dividend payout ratio} = \frac{40.2}{159.2} \times 100 = 25.3\%$$

ACTIVITY 6.21

Calculate the dividend payout ratio of Alexis Ltd for the year ended 31 March 2007.

Dividend yield ratio

The **dividend yield** ratio relates the cash return from a share to its current market value. This can help investors to assess the cash return on their investment in the company. The ratio is:

$$\text{Dividend yield} = \frac{\text{Dividends per share} / (1-t)}{\text{Market value per share}} \times 100$$

The symbol t represents the company tax rate and is explained below. This ratio is also expressed as a percentage.

The numerator of this ratio requires some explanation. In Australia, investors are subject to income tax, with rates being dependent on income. Companies are also subject to income tax at the company tax rate. It is clearly not fair that investors should pay tax on income (i.e. dividends) that has already been taxed (company profits). In order to avoid double taxation a system known as the 'imputation credit' system has been adopted. Under this system an investor who receives a dividend from a company generally also receives a tax credit. This tax credit is effectively the amount of income tax that would be payable by the company. In other words, any dividend is deemed to have been paid out of profits taxed at the company tax rate. To avoid double taxation a tax credit is 'imputed'. This means that, assuming a company tax rate of, say, 30 per cent, a dividend of $70 will be given a tax credit of $30. The investor will be deemed to have received gross income of $100 ($70 + $30) and to have paid tax of $30. The dividend is assumed to have been paid net of tax at 30 per cent with a recognition that the 30 per cent has been paid by the taxpayer. The 'gross' dividend will be calculated by multiplying the cash dividend by $(1 / (1-t))$ where t is the company tax rate. Hence if dividends received are $70 the gross dividends will be $70 \times (1 / (1 - 0.30))$, assuming the tax rate is 30 per cent, which gives $100. As far as the individual shareholder is concerned the tax authorities will treat the $100 as income on which 30 per cent tax has been paid. It will then be up to the individual shareholder to make a return.

Investors may wish to compare the returns from shares with the returns from other forms of investment. As these other forms of investment are often quoted on a 'gross' (i.e. pre-tax) basis it is useful to 'gross up' the dividend in order to facilitate comparisons. This can be done by dividing the dividend per share by $(1-t)$ where t is the company tax rate.

Assuming an income tax of 30 per cent, the dividend yield for Alexis Ltd for the year ended 31 March 2006 is:

$$Dividend\ yield = \frac{0.067 / (1 - 0.30)}{2.50} \times 100 = 3.8\%$$

ACTIVITY 6.22

Calculate the dividend yield for Alexis Ltd for the year ended 31 March 2007 assuming a company tax rate of 30 per cent.

Earnings per share

The earnings per share (EPS) of a company relates the earnings generated by the company during a period and available to shareholders to the number of shares on issue. For ordinary shareholders the amount available will be represented by the net profit after tax (less any preference dividend where applicable). The ratio for ordinary shareholders is calculated as follows:

$$Earnings\ per\ share = \frac{Earnings\ available\ to\ ordinary\ shareholders}{Number\ of\ ordinary\ shares\ on\ issue}$$

In the case of Alexis Ltd, the earnings per share for the year ended 31 March 2006 will be as follows:

$$Earnings\ per\ share = \frac{159.2}{600} = 26.5c$$

This ratio is regarded by many investment analysts as a fundamental measure of share performance. The trend in earnings per share over time is used to help assess the investment potential of a company's shares.

Although it is possible to make total profits rise through ordinary shareholders investing more in the company this will not necessarily mean that the profitability *per share* will rise as a result.

ACTIVITY 6.23

Calculate the earnings per share of Alexis Ltd for the year ended 31 March 2007.

The number of shares on issue during the period may change and therefore the number used in the calculation should be a weighted average, the weighting being related to how long the shares have been issued.

In this case, the new issue of shares occurred at the beginning of the financial year. Where an issue is made part the way through the year, a weighted average of the shares on issue will be taken based on the date at which the new share issue took place.

It is not usually very helpful to compare the earnings per share of one company with another. Differences in capital structures can render any such comparison meaningless. However, like dividends per share, it can be very useful to monitor the changes that occur in this ratio for a particular company over time.

Operating cash flow per share

It can be argued that, in the short run at least, operating cash flows provide a better guide to the ability of a company to pay dividends and to undertake planned expenditures than the earnings figure. The operating cash flow per share is calculated as follows:

$$\text{Operating cash flow per share} = \frac{\text{Operating cash flows} - \text{Preference dividends}}{\text{Number of ordinary (equity) shares on issue}}$$

The ratio for Alexis Ltd for the year ended 31 March 2006 is as follows:

$$\frac{160.6}{600.0} = 26.8c$$

ACTIVITY 6.24

Calculate the operating cash flow per share for Alexis Ltd for the year ended 31 March 2007.

Note that, for both years, the operating cash flow per share is higher than the earnings per share. This is not unusual. The effect of adding back depreciation in order to derive operating cash flows will usually ensure that a higher figure results.

Price earnings ratio

The **price earnings (P/E) ratio** relates the market value of a share to the earnings per share. This ratio can be calculated as follows:

$$\text{Price earnings ratio} = \frac{\text{Market value per share}}{\text{Earnings per share}}$$

The P/E ratio for Alexis Ltd for the year ended 31 March 2006 will be:

$$\frac{\$2.50}{26.5c} = 9.4 \text{ times}$$

This ratio reveals that the capital value of the share is 9.4 times higher than its current level of earnings. The ratio is, in essence, a measure of market confidence concerning the future of a company. The higher the P/E ratio the greater the confidence in the future earning power of the company and, consequently, the more investors are prepared to pay in relation to the earnings stream of the company.

P/E ratios provide a useful guide to market confidence concerning the future and therefore can be helpful when comparing different companies. However, differences in accounting policy choice (methods) between businesses can lead to different profit and earnings per share figures and this can distort comparisons.

The reciprocal of the P/E ratio, expressed as a percentage (i.e. (earnings × 100) / market price per share) provides a measure of earning yield. Hence a share with a P/E ratio of 10 would have an earnings yield of 10 per cent, while one with a P/E ratio of 20 would have an earnings yield of only 5 per cent.

ACTIVITY 6.25

Calculate the P/E ratio of Alexis Ltd for the year ended 31 March 2007.

The investment ratios for Alexis Ltd over the two-year period are as follows:

	2006	2007
Dividends per share	6.7c	9.0c
Dividend payout ratio	25.3%	36.5%
Dividend yield ratio	3.8%	3.7%
Earnings per share	26.5c	24.6c
Operating cash flow per share	26.8c	27.7c
P/E ratio	9.4 times	14.2 times

ACTIVITY 6.26

What do you deduce from the investment ratios for Alexis Ltd set out above?

SELF-ASSESSMENT QUESTION 6.1

A Ltd and B Ltd operate electrical wholesale stores in Sydney. The accounts of each company for the year ended 30 June 2006 are as follows:

Balance sheet as at 30 June 2006

	A Ltd		B Ltd	
	$'000	$'000	$'000	$'000
Current assets				
Cash at bank	100.6		109.0	
Debtors	176.4		321.9	
Inventory at cost	592.0		403.0	
		869.0		833.9
Non-current assets				
Freehold land and buildings at cost	436.0		615.0	
Less accumulated depreciation	76.0	360.0	105.0	510
Fixtures and fittings at cost	173.4		194.6	
Less accumulated depreciation	86.4	87.0	103.4	91.2
		447.0		601.2
Total assets		1,316.0		1,435.1

Current liabilities			
Trade creditors	271.4		180.7
Dividends payable	135.0		95.0
Income tax payable	32.0		34.8
		438.4	310.5
Non-current liabilities			
Debentures		190.0	250.0
Capital and reserves			
Paid-up ordinary capital (issued at $1)	320.0		250.0
Reserves	355.9		289.4
Retained profit	11.7		335.2
		687.6	874.6
Total liabilities and shareholders' equity		1,316.0	1,435.1

Income statement for the year ended 30 June 2006

	A Ltd		B Ltd	
	$'000	$'000	$'000	$'000
Sales		1,478.1		1,790.4
Less cost of sales				
Opening inventory	480.8		372.6	
Purchases	1,129.5		1,245.3	
	1,610.3		1,617.9	
Less closing inventory	592.0	1,018.3	403.0	1,214.9
Gross profit		459.8		575.5
Less				
Wages and salaries	150.4		189.2	
Directors' salaries	45.4		96.2	
Rates	28.5		15.3	
Heat and light	15.8		17.2	
Insurance	18.5		26.8	
Interest expense	19.4		27.5	
Postage and telephone	12.4		15.9	
Audit fees	11.0		12.3	
Depreciation				
—Freehold buildings	8.8		12.9	
—Fixtures and fittings	17.7	327.9	22.8	436.1
Net profit before tax		131.9		139.4
Income tax		32.0		34.8
Net profit after taxation		99.9		104.6
Add retained profit brought forward		46.8		325.6
		146.7		430.2
Dividends proposed		135.0		95.0
Retained profit carried forward		11.7		335.2

All purchases and sales are on credit.

The market value of the shares in each company at the end of the year were $6.50 and $8.20 respectively.

Required:

Calculate six different ratios which are concerned with liquidity, gearing and investment. What can you conclude from the ratios you have calculated?

TREND ANALYSIS

It is important to see whether there are trends occurring that can be detected from the use of ratios. Thus, key ratios can be plotted on a graph to provide users with a simple visual display of changes occurring over time. The trends occurring within a company may be plotted against trends occurring within the industry as a whole for comparison purposes. An example of trend analysis is shown in Figure 6.4.

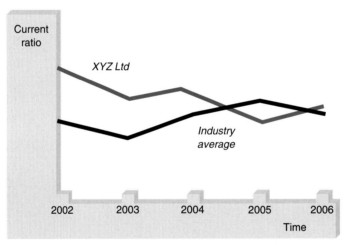

The current ratio for a particular business (XYZ Ltd) is plotted over time. On the same graph the same ratio for the average of businesses in the same industry is also plotted, enabling comparison to be made between the ratio for the particular business and the industry average

FIGURE 6.4 Graph plotting current ratio against time

Some companies publish certain key financial ratios as part of their annual report in order to help users identify important trends. These ratios may cover several years.

RATIOS AND PREDICTION MODELS

Financial ratios, based on current or past performance, are often used to help predict the future. However, both the choice of ratios and the interpretation of results are normally dependent on the judgment of the analyst. In recent years attempts have been made to develop a more rigorous and systematic approach to the use of ratios for prediction purposes. In particular, researchers have shown an interest in the ability of ratios to predict financial distress in a business. A number of methods and models employing ratios have now been developed which claim to predict future financial distress. Researchers have also developed ratio-based models which claim to assess the vulnerability of a business to takeover by another business. These areas, of course, are of interest to all those connected with the business. In the future, it is likely that further ratio-based models will be developed which predict other aspects of future performance.

LIMITATIONS OF RATIO ANALYSIS

Although ratios offer a quick and useful method of analysing the financial position and financial performance of a business, they are not without their problems and limitations. Some of the more important limitations are considered below.

✳ *Quality of financial statements.* It must always be remembered that ratios are based on financial statements and that the results of ratio analysis are dependent on the quality of these underlying statements. Ratios will inherit the limitations of the financial statements on which they are based. These limitations may relate to the accounting policy choice (methods used) and the resultant effect on the financial magnitude for that account.

ACTIVITY 6.27

Identify how different accounting methods can affect the ratio calculated.

Account type	Methods	Ratio (examples)
_____	_____	_____
_____	_____	_____
_____	_____	_____

✳ *The restricted vision of ratios.* It is important not to rely exclusively on ratios, thereby losing sight of information contained in the underlying financial statements. Some items reported in these statements can be of vital importance in assessing financial position and financial performance. For example, the total sales, capital employed and profit figures may be useful in assessing changes in absolute size that occur over time, or differences in scale between businesses. Ratios do not provide such information. In comparing one figure with another, ratios measure relative performance and position and therefore provide only part of the picture. Thus, when comparing two businesses it will often be useful to assess the absolute size of profits as well as the relative profitability of each business. For example, company A may generate $1 million profit and have an ROA of 15 per cent and company B may generate $100,000 profit and have an ROA of 20 per cent. Although company B has a higher level of profitability, as measured by ROA, it generates lower total profits.

✳ *The basis for comparison.* We saw earlier that ratios require a basis for comparison in order to be useful. Moreover, it is important that the analyst compares like with like. When comparing businesses, however, no two businesses will be identical and the greater the differences between the businesses, the greater the limitations of ratio analysis. Furthermore, when comparing businesses, differences in such matters as accounting policies, financing policies and financial year ends will add to the problems of evaluation.

※ *Financial position ratios.* Because the balance sheet is only a 'snapshot' of the business at a particular moment in time, any ratios based on balance sheet figures, such as the liquidity ratios above, may not be representative of the financial position of the business for the year as a whole. For example, it is common for a seasonal business to have a financial year end that coincides with a low point in business activity. Thus, inventories and debtors may be low at the reporting date and, as a result, the liquidity ratios may also be low. A more representative picture of liquidity can only really be gained by taking additional measurements at other points in the year.

Index or percentage analysis

Ratios represent the most important and powerful tool for analysing financial statements. However, a simple technique that can be used to highlight potential strengths and weaknesses in financial performance, financial position and liquidity over time or between entities, is index or percentage analysis. With index or percentage analysis the monetary figures are simply replaced with an index or percentage. As a result it is very easy to see trends that emerge over time, or differences between different entities.

There are basically three alternative index or percentage methods.

(1) *The common size reports, also known as vertical analysis.* Under this method the key magnitude in the report becomes 100 and all other subsidiary figures are expressed as a percentage of that figure. In the income statement the key figure would normally be 'sales'. In the balance sheet the key figure would normally be 'total assets', or 'total liabilities plus equity'. However, you can modify the key figure to match the analysis you wish to undertake.

(2) *Trend percentage.* Under this method all figures in an allocated base year are indexed as 100 and all subsequent years' figures are expressed as a percentage of the base year figure.

(3) *Percentage change, also known as horizontal analysis.* Under this method the percentage change for the year is shown for each line item.

Index analysis is easy to implement and can readily highlight pleasing and disturbing trends in the financial reports over time.

The best way to explain these techniques is by way of an example based on a very basic income statement.

	2005	2006	2007
Income statement	$	$	$
Sales	270,000	310,000	360,000
Cost of sales	130,000	160,000	200,000
Gross profit	140,000	150,000	160,000
Selling expenses	28,000	31,000	34,000
Administration expenses	52,000	62,000	77,000
Financial expenses	22,000	22,000	22,000
Total expenses	102,000	115,000	133,000
Net profit	38,000	35,000	27,000
	2005	2006	2007
Common size			
Sales	100	100	100
Cost of sales	48.1	51.6	55.6
Gross profit	51.9	48.4	44.4
Selling expenses	10.4	10.0	9.4

Administration expenses	19.3	20.0	21.4
Financial expenses	8.1	7.1	6.1
Total expenses	37.8	37.1	36.9
Net profit	14.1	11.3	7.5
	2005	*2006*	*2007*
Trend percentage			
Sales	100	114.8	133.3
Cost of sales	100	123.1	153.8
Gross profit	100	107.1	114.3
Selling expenses	100	110.7	121.4
Administration expenses	100	119.2	148.1
Financial expenses	100	100	100
Total expenses	100	112.7	130.4
Net profit	100	92.1	71.1

	2005–6	*2006–7*
	%	*%*
Percentage change		
Sales	+ 14.8	+ 16.1
Cost of sales	+ 23.1	+ 24.9
Gross profit	+ 7.1	+ 6.7
Selling expenses	+ 10.7	+ 9.7
Administration expenses	+ 19.2	+ 24.2
Financial expenses	0	0
Total expenses	+ 12.7	+ 15.7
Net profit	− 7.9	− 22.8

A review of any of the above should reveal a number of favourable and unfavourable financial trends that may warrant further investigation.

ACTIVITY 6.28

What favourable and unfavourable trends did you observe?

SUMMARY

In this chapter we have achieved the following objectives in the way shown.

OBJECTIVE	METHOD ACHIEVED		
Define what a ratio is	Defined as a comparison between two financial magnitudes within the financial statements that gives an important insight into financial performance or financial position.		
Identify the key aspects of financial performance and financial position that are evaluated by the use of ratios	Identified as: • Profitability • Efficiency • Liquidity • Gearing • Investment		
Explain the terms *profitability*, *efficiency*, *liquidity*, *gearing* and *investment*	Explained as follows: • Profitability—success in wealth creation • Efficiency—effective utilisation of resources • Liquidity—ability to meet short-term obligations • Gearing—financial stability • Investment—market investment performance		
Summarise the alternative bases of comparison for ratio analysis	Summarised as: • Intertemporal—past performance • Budget—planned performance • Intra-industry—interfirm		
Present the ratio formula for the basic ratios	Profitability	Return on owners' equity	Net profit after tax + Preference dividends / Av. OE
		Return on assets	Net profit before interest and tax / Av. assets
		Net profit margin	Net profit before interest and tax / Sales
		Gross profit margin	Gross profit/Sales
	Efficiency	Average inventory turnover period	(Av. inventory × 365) / Cost of sales
		Average debtors settlement	(Av. debtors × 365) / Credit sales
		Average creditors settlement	(Av. creditors × 365) / Credit purchases
		Asset turnover period	(Av. total assets × 365) / Sales
	Liquidity	Current	Current assets / Current liabilities
		Acid test	Liquid current assets / Current liabilities
		Cash flows from operations	Operating cash flow / Current liabilities

OBJECTIVE	METHOD ACHIEVED		
	Gearing	Gearing	Long-term liabilities / (OE + Long-term liabilities)
		Interest cover	Net profit before interest and tax / Interest
	Investment	Dividends per share	Dividends / No. of shares
		Dividend payout	Dividends / Earnings
		Dividend yield	Dividends per share / (l – t) / Mkt. price share
		Earnings per share	Earnings available / No. of shares
		Operating cash flow per share	(Operating cash flow – Pref. dividends) / No. of shares
		Price earnings ratio	Mkt. price per share / Earnings per share
Discuss the limitations of ratios as a tool of financial analysis	Identified limitations as: • Alternative ratio formulae for a given ratio • Variety in accounting policy choice • Emphasis on financial rather than non-financial measures • Emphasis on past financial measures rather than future expectations • Focus on relative rather than absolute measures • Year-end determination leads to averaging distortions • Potentially invalid comparisons between firms or over time		
Understand index or percentage analysis as an alternative to ratios	Discussed and assessed • Common size reports • Trend percentage • Percentage change		

DISCUSSION QUESTIONS

EASY

<Obj 1>   **6.1**   What is a financial ratio?

<Obj 4>   **6.2**   Ratios in isolation provide little insight into the financial performance and the financial position of any entity. Discuss.

<Obj 5>   **6.3**   Some businesses operate on a low net profit margin (e.g. a supermarket chain). Does this mean that the return on assets used by the business will also be low?

<Obj 9>   **6.4**   An alternative to ratio analysis is index or percentage analysis.
   (a)   What is a common size report?
   (b)   What are the benefits of preparing common size reports?
   (c)   How else could we utilise 'indexes' or 'percentages' in financial report analysis?

<Obj 9>   **6.5**   Distinguish between the index (percentage) tools labelled 'horizontal' and 'vertical' analysis.

INTERMEDIATE

<Obj 2>   **6.6** What are the potential advantages of 'debt finance' (borrowing) over 'owners' equity finance' (contributions)?

<Obj 3>   **6.7** Distinguish between liquidity and solvency (gearing).

<Obj 3>   **6.8** Contrast the benefits and risks of financial leverage.

<Obj 3>   **6.9** The reciprocal of the P/E ratio is the 'earnings yield'. Explain the relationship between 'earnings yield' and 'return on owners' equity'.

<Obj 3>   **6.10** The determination of the cash cycle is a useful aid in assessing liquidity rather than solvency.
   (a) What is the 'cash cycle'?
   (b) What is the difference between 'liquidity' and 'solvency'?
   (c) Do you agree with the statement?

<Obj 3, 5> **6.11** In relation to efficiency the textbook discusses four ratios:
   - inventory turnover period
   - debtors settlement period
   - creditors settlement period
   - asset turnover.

   Identify another five ratios for a retailer that would be useful in assessing resource efficiency.

<Obj 3, 5> **6.12** Profitability versus efficiency:
   (a) Distinguish between these two aspects of business performance.
   (b) Identify ratios to assess each of these measures.
   (c) Discuss whether these ratios complement each other or are in conflict.

<Obj 4>   **6.13** Identify and discuss three benchmarks that could be used for assessing the financial structure (solvency) of a reporting entity?

<Obj 5>   **6.14** In the 'return on total assets' ratio, why is interest excluded from the profit determination?

<Obj 5>   **6.15** Identify and discuss three reasons why the P/E ratio of two companies operating within the same industry may differ.

<Obj 5, 7> **6.16** The gross profit margin for Inca Ltd falls for the year from 31 per cent to 29 per cent.
   (a) What is the gross profit margin?
   (b) Why is it an important financial measure?
   (c) What may have given rise to the fall identified?
   (d) Under what circumstances would such a fall be of limited concern?

<Obj 7>   **6.17** Different stakeholders with an interest in financial reports require different ratio analysis. List key stakeholders and their particular interests.

<Obj 7>   **6.18** The debtors turnover reduced for the year from 8 times to 7.2 times. Explain the possible implications of this to management.

<Obj 7>   **6.19** Two businesses operate in the same industry. One has an inventory turnover period that is higher than the industry average and one has an inventory turnover period that is lower than the industry average. Give three possible explanations for each ratio.

<Obj 7>   **6.20** Compared with the industry averages the business being reviewed has a favourable current ratio, but an unfavourable quick (acid test) ratio.
   (a) What aspect of the business is being reviewed?
   (b) What might give rise to this conflicting result of the analysis?
   (c) What other ratios would you refer to in resolving this conflict?

<Obj 8>   **6.21** The current ratio focuses on liquidity. A rough rule of thumb is that this ratio should be 2:1. What are the probable limitations of using such a guide?

<Obj 8>   **6.22** While ratios are an important tool in analysis and interpretation of financial reports, a number of limitations have been identified. Briefly discuss each of the following identified limitations.
  (a) The use of averages for figures from the balance sheet.
  (b) The range of choice available to management in recording financial transactions.
  (c) The historical focus of financial reports.
  (d) The age of the business and stage in business cycle (growth, maturity, decline).
  (e) The preoccupation with financial information.
  (f) Invalid comparison with previous periods of other firms within the same industry.

<Obj 8>   **6.23** What potential problems arise for the external analyst from the use of figures from the balance sheet in the calculation of financial ratios?

CHALLENGING

<Obj 8>   **6.24** Critically evaluate the statement that 'financial reports are largely based on historical financial information and are therefore useful in assessing the stewardship (accountability) of management, but of little use to external decision makers in decisions about the allocation of scarce resources'.

APPLICATION EXERCISES

EASY

<Obj 6>   **6.1**

Balance sheet extracts as at 30 June			
	2005	*2006*	*2007*
Current assets	$	$	$
Cash	3,000	16,000	20,000
Receivables	100,000	45,000	35,000
Inventories	120,000	68,000	65,000
Total current assets	223,000	129,000	120,000
Non-current assets	240,000	210,000	198,000

Income statements for the years ended 30 June		
	2006	*2007*
	$	$
Net sales (all credit)	600,000	500,000
Less cost of sales	360,000	380,000
Gross profit	240,000	220,000
Less operating expenses		
General	170,000	140,000
Interest	25,000	15,000
Net profit	45,000	65,000
Less tax	13,500	19,500
Net profit after tax	31,500	45,500

Calculate the following ratios for 2006 and 2007:

(a) return on assets

(b) net profit margin

(c) gross profit margin

(d) asset turnover

(e) average inventory turnover period

(f) average settlement period for debtors

(g) interest cover ratio (times interest earned).

INTERMEDIATE

<Obj 5>

6.2 Complete the following table in relation to:

- ratio name
- ratio focus
- ratio formula.

Name		Focus	Formula
(a)	Return on owners' equity	Profitability	
(b)			(Average inventory/Cost of sales) × 100
(c)	Gearing		
(d)	Asset turnover ratio	Efficiency	
(e)			Current assets/Current liabilities
(f)			Net profit before interest and tax/Interest expense
(g)		Profitability	(Net profit before interest and tax/Total assets) × 100
(h)	Average settlement period for debtors		
(i)	Acid test ratio		
(j)	Dividends per share	Investment	
(k)	Gross profit margin		
(l)			Operating cash flows/Current liabilities
(m)			Market value per share/Earnings per share
(n)	Dividend yield ratio		

<Obj 5>

6.3 Complete the following table with respect to the transaction effect on the stated ratios.

Transaction		Ratio	Effect Increase	Decrease	None
(a)	Sold merchandise on credit	Current ratio			
(b)	Sold merchandise on credit	Inventory turnover period			
(c)	Collected a receivable account	Acid test ratio			
(d)	Wrote off an uncollectable account	Settlement period for debtors			
(e)	Paid a payable account	Current ratio			
(f)	Declared cash dividend	Return on owners' equity			
(g)	Incurred advertising expense	Net profit margin			
(h)	Issued bonus share dividend	Gearing			
(i)	Issued debentures payable	Asset turnover ratio			
(j)	Accrued interest expense	Current ratio			

(k)	Paid previously declared cash dividend	Dividend yield ratio
(l)	Repurchased shares	Return on total assets
(m)	Recorded depreciation expense	Cash flow from operations ratio

<Obj 5, 7>

6.4 C. George (Western) Ltd has recently produced its accounts for the current year. The board of directors met to consider the accounts and, at this meeting, concern was expressed that the return on assets had decreased from 14 per cent last year to 12 per cent for the current year.

The following reasons were suggested as to why this reduction in ROA had occurred:
(a) increase in the gross profit margin
(b) reduction in sales
(c) increase in overhead expenses
(d) increase in amount of inventory held
(e) repayment of a loan at the year end
(f) increase in the time taken for debtors to pay.

State, with reasons, which of the above might lead to a reduction in ROA.

<Obj 5, 7>

6.5 Business A and business B are both engaged in retailing, but seem to take a different approach to this trade according to the information available. This information consists of a table of ratios, shown below.

Ratio	Business A	Business B
Return on total assets (ROA)	20%	17%
Return on owners' equity	30%	18%
Average settlement period for debtors	63 days	21 days
Average settlement period for creditors	50 days	45 days
Gross profit percentage	40%	15%
Net profit percentage	10%	10%
Inventory turnover period	52 days	25 days

(a) Explain how each ratio is calculated.
(b) Describe what this information indicates about the differences in approach between the two businesses. If one of them prides itself on personal service and the other on competitive prices, which do you think is which and why?

<Obj 6, 7>

6.6 The working capital cycle represents that period from when inventory is paid for until cash is received on inventory sales. The following discloses the key turnover ratios related to working capital accounts for Duval Ltd.

	2005	2006	2007	Industry
Inventory turnover	6.2 times	5.7 times	5.5 times	6.4 times
Debtors turnover	7.7 times	7.2 times	6.8 times	8.0 times
Creditors turnover	8.4 times	8.7 times	9.2 times	7.5 times

(a) Convert the turnover times to days.
(b) Calculate the working capital cycle for each year (days).
(c) Comment on the possible significance of your findings for management.

<Obj 6, 7> **6.7** The following information relates to the business of N. Shakey, who is concerned about the profitability and financial structure of his business at 30 June 2007, especially since the bank is requiring repayment of the business's overdraft.

	30 June 2006	30 June 2007
Sales (credit)	$60,000	$90,000
Cost of goods sold	39,000	63,000
All other expenses	12,000	21,000
Cash at bank	12,000	(18,000)
Inventory	18,000	33,000
Trade debtors (net)	12,000	30,000
Non-current assets (net)	24,000	48,000
Creditors	6,000	9,000
N. Shakey, Capital	60,000	72,000
Non-current liabilities	–	12,000

Inventory at 1 July 2005 was $15,000.
Trade debtors at 1 July 2005 were $10,000.

(a) Calculate the following ratios for 2006 and 2007:
   (i) net profit margin
   (ii) rate of return on owners' equity
   (iii) current ratio
   (iv) acid test ratio
   (v) gearing
   (vi) inventory turnover period.
(b) Write a short report to the owner in relation to:
   (i) profitability
   (ii) short-term liquidity
   (iii) long-term solvency

<Obj 6, 7> **6.8** Threads Ltd manufactures nuts and bolts which are sold to industrial users. The abbreviated accounts for 2006 and 2007 are given below.

THREADS LTD

Income statement for the year ended 30 September

	2007 $'000	2007 $'000	2006 $'000	2006 $'000
Sales		1,200		1,180
Less cost of sales		(750)		(680)
Gross profit		450		500
Less				
Operating expenses	(208)		(200)	
Depreciation	(75)		(66)	
Interest	(8)		(–)	
		(291)		(266)

Net profit before tax	159		234
Tax	(48)		(80)
Profit after tax	111		154
Dividends	(72)		(70)
Retained profit for the year	39		84

THREADS LTD

Balance sheet as at 30 September

	2007		2006	
	$'000	$'000	$'000	$'000
Current assets				
Bank	4		32	
Debtors	156		102	
Inventory	236		148	
		396		282
Non-current assets (see note 1)		687		702
Total assets		1,083		984
Current liabilities				
Bank overdraft	26			
Creditors	76		60	
Accruals	16		18	
Dividends payable	72		70	
Income taxation	48		80	
		238		228
Non-current liabilities				
Bank loan (see note 2)		50		–
Shareholders' equity				
Paid-up capital (issued at $1 per share)	500		500	
Retained profits	295		256	
		795		756
Total liabilities and shareholders' equity		1,083		984

Notes

1. Non-current assets:

	Buildings $'000	Fixtures and fittings $'000	Vehicles $'000	Total $'000
Cost 1.10.2006	900	100	80	1,080
Purchases	–	40	20	60
Cost 30.9.2007	900	140	100	1,140
Accumulated depreciation 1.10.2006	288	50	40	378
Charge for year	36	14	25	75
Accumulated depreciation 30.9.2007	324	64	65	453
Net book value 30.9.2007	576	76	35	687

2. The bank loan was taken up on 1 July 2006 and is repayable in six years from that date. It carries a fixed rate of interest of 12 per cent per annum and is secured by a fixed and floating charge on the assets of the company.

   (a) Calculate the following financial statistics for both 2007 and 2006, using end-of-year figures where appropriate:
   (i)   return on total assets
   (ii)   net profit margin
   (iii)   gross profit margin
   (iv)   current ratio
   (v)   liquid or acid test ratio
   (vi)   average settlement period for debtors
   (vii) average settlement period for creditors
   (viii) average inventory turnover period.

   (b) Comment on the performance of Threads Ltd from the viewpoint of a company considering supplying a substantial amount of goods to Threads Ltd on usual credit terms.

   (c) What action could a supplier take to lessen the risk of not being paid should Threads Ltd be in financial difficulty?

<Obj 6, 7>   **6.9**   The following financial information is provided for Metal Recyclers Ltd.

	2005 $'000	2006 $'000	2007 $'000
Net assets	1,000	1,053	1,095
Total liabilities	1,200	1,600	1,600
Paid-up capital ($1)*	800	800	800
Retained profit and reserves	80	100	120
Profit before interest and tax	270	294	325
Interest	120	160	160
Taxation	45	40	51
Dividends per share (cents)	5	6	7
Average market price per share	$1.08	$1.12	$1.23

*All shares initially issued at $1.

(a) Calculate for each year:
   (i)   gearing or leverage level
   (ii)   price earnings (P/E) ratio
   (iii) dividend yield
   (iv) dividend payout ratio.

(b) Calculate the historical return on owners' equity for 2006 and 2007 and compare with the market earnings yield.

(c) Discuss any significant trends or anomalies.

<Obj 7>

6.10 The following ratios have been extracted from the financial reports of Wayward Ltd in relation to liquidity and efficiency for the years 2005–2007.

Ratio	2005	2006	2007	Industry average (2007)
Current ratio	1.6:1	1.8:1	1.9:1	2.1:1
Acid test ratio	1.2:1	1.1:1	0.9:1	1.1:1
Inventory turnover period	31.3 days	33.4 days	37.9 days	27.4 days
Average settlement period for debtors	47.3 days	45.2 days	41.3 days	45.1 days
Average settlement period for creditors	74.5 days	70.2 days	66.5 days	62.1 days

Provide a report to management based on this analysis.

<Obj 9>

6.11 A common size analysis of the income statements of Justine Ltd is presented below:

	2005	2006	2007
Sales	100	100	100
COGS	65	63	61
Expenses	28	31	34
Net profit	7	6	5

Answer the following questions in relation to the above index analysis:
(a) What is a common size report?
(b) From the above analysis what are the two obvious trends that explain the change in net profit margin over the three periods?
(c) Identify possible factors giving rise to these trends.

CHALLENGING

<Obj 5, 7>

6.12 Utilising the reported figures and ratios provided, complete the missing figures in the following table.

		Alpha	Delta	Gamma
Sales (all credit)	($)	427,000		
Cost of goods sold	($)	291,000		
Gross profit	($)		79,600	137,611
Average inventory	($)	32,000		11,310
Average receivables	($)	48,000	36,400	
Inventory turnover	(times)		7.4	17.4
Average collection period for debtors (days)			46	52

<Obj 6, 7> **6.13** Conday and Co. Ltd has been in operation for three years and produces antique reproduction furniture for the export market. The most recent set of accounts for the company is set out below.

CONDAY AND CO.

Balance sheet as at 30 November 2007

	$'000	$'000
Current assets		
Debtors	820	
Inventory	600	
		1,420
Non-current assets		
Freehold land and buildings at cost		228
Plant and machinery at cost	942	
Less accumulated depreciation	180	762
		990
Total assets		2,410
Current liabilities		
Bank overdraft	385	
Creditors	665	
Taxation	95	1,145
Non-current liabilities		
12% debentures		200
Shareholders' equity		
Paid-up capital (issued at $1 each)		700
Retained profits		365
		1,065
Total liabilities and shareholders' equity		2,410

CONDAY AND CO.

Income statement for the year ended 30 November 2007

	$'000
Sales	2,600
Less cost of sales	1,620
Gross profit	980
Less other expenses	660
Net profit	320
Income tax	95
Net profit after tax	225
Proposed dividends	160
Retained profit for the year	65

Notes

The debentures are secured on the freehold land and buildings.

An investor has been approached by the company to invest $200,000 by purchasing ordinary shares in the company at $6.40 each. The company wishes to use the funds to finance a program of further expansion.

(a) Assess the financial position and performance of the company and comment on any features you consider to be significant.

(b) State, with reasons, whether or not the investor should invest in the company on the terms outlined.

<Obj 6, 7>   **6.14** The directors of Helena Beauty Products Ltd have been presented with the following abridged accounts for the current year and the preceding year:

HELENA BEAUTY PRODUCTS LTD

Income statement for the year ended 30 September				
	2006		2007	
	$'000	$'000	$'000	$'000
Sales		3,600		3,840
Less cost of sales				
Opening inventory	320		400	
Purchases	2,240		2,350	
	2,560		2,750	
Less closing inventory	400	2,160	500	2,250
Gross profit		1,440		1,590
Less expenses		1,360		1,500
Net profit		80		90

HELENA BEAUTY PRODUCTS LTD

Balance sheet as at 30 September				
	2006		2007	
	$'000	$'000	$'000	$'000
Current assets				
Bank	8		4	
Debtors	750		960	
Inventory	400		500	
		1,158		1,464
Non-current assets		1,900		1,860
Total assets		3,058		3,324
Current liabilities		390		450
Shareholders' equity				
Paid-up capital (issued at $1)	1,650		1,766	
Retained profits	1,018		1,108	
		2,668		2,874
Total liabilities and shareholders' equity		3,058		3,324

Using six ratios, comment on the profitability and efficiency of the business as revealed by the accounts shown above.

<Obj 9>   **6.15** A trend percentage analysis of Damien Ltd is presented below:

		2005	2006	2007	2008
Assets:	Current				
	Cash	100	86	73	45
	Accounts receivable	100	105	111	123
	Inventory	100	101	96	85
	Other	100	99	102	101
Assets:	Non-current				
	PP&E	100	110	123	145
	Investments	100	95	89	79
	Intangibles	100	95	90	85
	Other	100	98	97	101
Total assets		100			

(a) What is trend percentage analysis?

(b) From the above identify potential strengths and weaknesses in the financial management of Damien Ltd over the four year period.

(c) Identify possible factors giving rise to these trends.

(d) What are the potential deficiencies of this index (percentage) tool?

Convert the above analysis into a 'percentage change' (horizontal analysis) table.

CASE STUDY 6.1

Qantas Financial Report 2004

On the basis of the three financial reports presented for the years 2003 and 2004 for the Qantas Group:

- Statements of Financial Performance (Income statements) (page 173)
- Statements of Financial Position (Balance sheets) (page 106)
- Statements of Cash Flows (Cash flow statements) (page 229)

provide an assessment of Qantas in relation to:

(a) profitability

(b) liquidity

(c) efficiency

(d) solvency (financial stability)

(e) investment.

CASE STUDY 6.2

Southcorp investors in two minds

Trevor Chappell and Mathew Charles

The Courier-Mail
Wednesday, 19 January 2005, p. 29

Shares in winemaker Southcorp retreated yesterday and predator Foster's Group rose as analysts considered whether global beverage firms such as Diagea and Allied Domecq would make counterbids for Southcorp.

Allied Domecq, Diageo Pernod Ricard and Constellation Brands have been mentioned as possible rivals to the Foster's $3.1 billion takeover bid for Southcorp.

But reports in the UK have said Allied Domecq and Diageo might only be interested in wine brands that might be for sale should the Foster's takeover of Southcorp succeed—and they were unlikely to make full counterbids.

Foster's made the takeover bid for Southcorp on Monday at $4.17 per share, after securing an 18.8 per cent stake last week from Southcorp's largest shareholder, the Oatley family.

Southcorp shares were down 10¢ at $4.51 yesterday after jumping more than 8 per cent on Monday. Foster's shares were up 10¢ at $5.37.

Analysts said the bid heralded a new era of uncertainty for the Australian wine industry.

They predicted Foster's takeover attempt of Southcorp would take months to play out, with Macquarie Equities' Lucinda Chan comparing it with Xstrata's play for WMC Resources, which has dragged on since last October.

'Patience is a virtue for those of us who hold the stock,' she said.

Foster's will release its formal takeover documents within the week, outlining its exact game plan.

'It's all pure speculation right now,' Ms Chan said.

FW Holst and Co analyst David Spry said the movement in Foster's and Southcorp shares yesterday might be linked to a view among some investors that a counterbid for Southcorp was less likely.

'You can't rule them (counterbids) out. But Foster's can derive more synergies (from acquiring Southcorp) than the others,' Mr Spry said.

'If they (the other beverages companies) are going to pay a premium price, it will certainly test their nerve a bit in making the arithmetic work, in the short term anyway.'

It was hard to say if Foster's would have to bid more for Southcorp.

But analysts believe the potential synergies could prove too tempting for overseas rivals to sit aside and allow Foster's an easy victory over Australia's increasingly scarce and valuable wine assets.

One possibility is for them to join forces or seek a smaller Australian partner such as McGuigan Simeon to carve up Southcorp's top-shelf brands that include Australia's most expensive wine, Penfold's Grange.

This may also allow a takeover to pass the competition regulator's scrutiny, which may yet force Foster's to agree to sell some key brands such as Lindemans.

'Together they could be quite powerful if they merged together in one whole and attacked it all at once,' Ms Chan said.

Southcorp on Monday rejected the Foster's offer as opportunistic and inadequate.

---

1   Why do you think Southcorp's (potential acquiree) share price dropped the previous day, while Foster's (potential acquiror) share price increased?

2   David Spry (analyst) claimed that 'Foster's can derive more synergies (from acquiring Southcorp) than the others' (potential bidders). What does he mean by 'synergies'?

3　David Spry (analyst) stated that if the other beverages companies 'are going to pay a premium price, it will certainly test their nerve a bit in making the arithmetic work, in the short term anyway'. What is meant by:

(a)　a 'premium price'?

(b)　'making the arithmetic work'?

(c)　the 'short term'?

4　Why do we need a 'competition regulator' to scrutinise takeover arrangements?

5　Is it logical for Southcorp's directors to claim the offer of Foster's is inadequate when it was above the existing market price at the time of the takeover offer?

6　What actions could Southcorp's directors undertake to minimise the takeover threat, or boost the offer price of potential bidders?

CASE STUDY

6.3

Brokers pummel NAB shares

Tim Boreham

Business (section), *The Australian*
Friday, 16 July 2004, p. 17

National Australia Bank shares plunged to their lowest level yesterday since September 2001 as analysts took the knife to results forecasts and recommendations in the wake of Wednesday's profit downgrade, which delayed profit recovery until late next year.

Brokers have reduced their earnings expectations for 2004 and 2005, with at least one—UBS — rescinding its 'buy' recommendation on the stock.

Investors made it clear they were not willing to believe that new chief executive John Stewart had taken an overly cautious approach in warning of a 10 per cent to 15 per cent fall in the bank's current half-cash earnings.

'We do not view (the profit downgrade) as underpromising and see clear potential for further share price weakness in the next 12 months, especially as the bank still trades at a premium to its peers,' Burdett Buckeridge & Young analyst John Buonaccorsi said.

Marcus Padley of the *Marcus Today* newsletter said: 'We thought Stewart was just keeping expectations under wraps in his first set of results.

'Now it just looks like he was telling the truth.'

Following the previous day's $2.12 sell-off, NAB shares plunged another 59c before bargain hunters moved in and closed 40c lower at $28.45. Volume was heavy at more than 20 million shares.

'It looks like everybody was selling. You would be fairly bold to try to swim against the tide,' said HTM Wilson client adviser Henry Edgar.

In his profit warning, Mr Stewart warned of the heavy cost of protecting the bank's Australian business from brand damage stemming from this year's $360 million foreign exchange disaster.

Mr Stewart also offered little hope for the near future, warning "no real improvement" was expected until the second half of 2005.

Citigroup Smith Barney, which maintained its 'sell' recommendation, also scotched the theory that Mr Stewart was 'clearing the decks' as new CEO.

'Instead it largely reflects the outworking of a damaged franchise, the cost of defending the business and the long painful road to recovery,' the firm said.

Research house Fat Prophets warned of 'ominous things to come'.

'NAB is a cornerstone stock held in many institutional and retail investment portfolios and, with perceptions towards future earnings becoming more sedate, we believe further downside is inevitable.'

Further large share price falls seem unlikely, given NAB's commitment to maintaining its second-half dividend at 83c.

NAB was 'close to the bottom of the downgrade cycle', broker ABN Amro said. The firm also believes NAB's brand damage is 'not irreparable', more akin to last year's horror period for AMP than Westpac's and ANZ's 'near death' experiences with problem loans in the early 1990s.

'The one major difference versus AMP is that NAB has four strong competitors that are aggressively courting its customers,' ABN said.

As if to illustrate this point. ANZ yesterday launched an online account-switching service to enable other bank customers to transfer their accounts to ANZ.

_____

1   How is share price determined?
2   The article mentions 'cash earning' and 'profit':
    (a)   What is the difference?
    (b)   Which of the two will be of most interest to investors and analysts?
3   NAB is said to trade at a premium to its peers:
    (a)   Who are the peers?
    (b)   What is meant by 'trading at a premium'?
    (c)   Why would NAB shares trade at a premium to its peers?
4   'Mr Stewart warned of the heavy cost of protecting the bank's Australian business from brand damage stemming from this year's $360 million foreign exchange disaster.'
    (a)   What was the $360 million foreign exchange disaster referred to?
    (b)   What is meant by the term 'brand' in this context?
    (c)   What would be included in the 'costs' of protecting the brand damage?
5   Mention is made of the new CEO 'clearing the decks':
    (a)   What is meant by this expression?
    (b)   What actions might be representative of 'clearing the decks'?
    (c)   Why might a new CEO undertake such activities?
    (d)   Why is it concluded that the actions taken by NAB's new CEO (John Stewart) did not represent 'clearing the decks'?
6   Why would 'further large share price falls seem unlikely, given NAB's commitment to maintaining its second-half dividend at 83 cents'?

SOLUTIONS TO ACTIVITIES

Activity 6.1

In answering this activity you may have thought of the following bases:

- *Past periods*. By comparing the ratio you have calculated with the ratio of a previous period, it is possible to detect whether there has been an improvement or deterioration in performance. Indeed, it is often useful to track particular ratios over time (say, five or 10 years) in order to see whether it is possible to detect trends. However, the comparison of ratios from different time periods brings certain problems. In particular, there is always the possibility that trading conditions may have been quite different in the periods being compared. There is the further problem that when comparing the performance of a single business over time, operating inefficiencies may not be clearly exposed. For example, the fact that net profit per employee has risen by 10 per cent over the previous period may at first sight appear to be satisfactory; however, this may not be the case if similar businesses have shown an improvement of 50 per cent for the same period. Finally, there is the problem that inflation may have distorted the figures on which the ratios are based. Inflation can lead to an overstatement of profit and an understatement of asset values.

- *Planned performance.* Ratios may be compared with the targets that management developed before the commencement of the period under review. The comparison of planned performance with actual performance may therefore be a useful way of revealing the level of achievement attained. However, the planned levels of performance must be based on realistic assumptions if they are to be useful for comparison purposes.

- *Similar businesses.* In a competitive environment, a business must consider its performance in relation to that of other businesses operating in the same industry. Survival may depend on the ability to achieve comparable levels of performance. Thus, a very useful basis for comparing a particular ratio is the ratio achieved by similar businesses during the same period. This basis is not, however, without its problems. Competitors may have different year ends and therefore trading conditions may not be identical. They may also have different accounting policies which have a significant effect on reported profits and asset values (e.g. different methods of calculating depreciation, different methods of valuing inventory). Finally, it may be difficult to get hold of the accounts of competitor businesses. Sole proprietorships and partnerships, for example, are not obliged to publish their financial statements. In the case of limited companies, there is a legal obligation to publish accounts. However, a diversified company may not provide a breakdown of activities detailed enough for analysts to compare with the activities of other businesses.

Activity 6.2

The return on owners' equity for the following year will be as follows:

$$\text{ROE} = \frac{164.2}{(498.3 + 636.6)\,/\,2} \times 100 = 28.9\%$$

Activity 6.3

For the year ended 31 March 2007 the ratio is:

$$\text{ROA} = \frac{246.4}{(1{,}020.1 + 1{,}061.4)\,/\,2} \times 100 = 23.7\%$$

Activity 6.4

The net profit margin for the year to 31 March 2007 will be:

$$\text{Net profit margin} = \frac{246.4}{2{,}681.2} \times 100 = 9.2\%$$

Activity 6.5

The gross profit margin for the year to 31 March 2007 is as follows:

$$\text{Gross profit margin} = \frac{609.2}{2{,}681.2} \times 100 = 22.7\%$$

Activity 6.6

The gross profit margin shows a slight increase in 2007 over the previous year. This may be due to a number of reasons, such as an increase in selling prices and a decrease in the cost of sales. However, the net profit margin has shown a slight decline over the period. This means that operating expenses (wages, rates, insurance, etc.) are absorbing a greater proportion of sales income in 2007 than in the previous year.

The net profit available to equity shareholders has risen only slightly over the period, whereas the share capital and reserves of the company have increased considerably (see the financial statements). The effect of this has been to reduce the return to owners' equity. The ROA has decreased slightly in 2007. This is primarily due to the fact that the net profit has not increased in line with the increase in total assets.

Activity 6.7

The stock turnover period for the year to 31 March 2007 will be:

$$\frac{(300 + 370.8) / 2}{2,072} \times 365$$
$$= 59 \text{ days}$$

Activity 6.8

The average debtors settlement period for the year to 31 March 2007 is:

$$\frac{(240.8 + 210.2) / 2}{2,681.2} \times 365$$
$$= 31 \text{ days}$$

Activity 6.9

The average creditor settlement period is:

$$\frac{(221.4 + 228.8) / 2}{2,142.8} \times 365$$
$$= 38 \text{ days}$$

Activity 6.10

The asset turnover period for the year ended 31 March 2007 will be:

$$\frac{(1,020.1 + 1,061.4) / 2}{2,681.2} \times 365$$
$$= 142 \text{ days}$$

Activity 6.11

A comparison of the efficiency ratios between years provides a mixed picture. The average settlement period for both debtors and creditors has reduced. The reduction may have been the result of deliberate policy decisions—for example, tighter credit control for debtors, paying creditors promptly in order to maintain goodwill or to take advantage of discounts. However, it must always be remembered that these ratios are average figures and therefore may be distorted by a few exceptional amounts owed to, or owed by, the company.

ACCOUNTING an introduction

The inventory turnover period has shown a slight increase over the period but this may not be significant. Overall there has been an increase in the asset turnover ratio, which means that the sales have increased by a greater proportion than the assets of the company.

Activity 6.12

The current ratio for the year ended 31 March 2007 is:

$$\frac{622.0}{364.8}$$
$$= 1.7 \text{ times}$$

Activity 6.13

The acid test ratio for the year ended 31 March 2007 is:

$$\frac{(622.0 - 370.8)}{364.8}$$
$$= 0.7 \text{ times}$$

Activity 6.14

The cash flow from operations ratio is:

$$\frac{185}{364.8}$$
$$= 0.5 \text{ times}$$

Activity 6.15

The liquidity ratio summary reveals a decrease in both the current ratio and the acid test ratio. These changes suggest a worsening liquidity position for the business. The company must monitor its liquidity carefully and be alert to any further deterioration in these ratios. The operating cash flows to maturing obligations ratio has not changed over the period. This ratio is quite low and reveals that the cash flows for the period do not cover the maturing obligations. This ratio should give some cause for concern.

Activity 6.16

The revised profit available to the shareholders of each company in the first year of operations will be:

	X Ltd $	Y Ltd $
Profit before interest and taxation	60,000	60,000
Interest payable	20,000	10,000
Profit before taxation	40,000	50,000
Taxation (say 30%)	12,000	15,000
Profit available to ordinary shareholders	28,000	35,000

The return on owners' equity for each company will now be:

$$\frac{28,000 \times 100}{100,000} \qquad \frac{35,000 \times 100}{200,000}$$
$$= 28\% \qquad\qquad = 17.5\%$$

Activity 6.17

The gearing ratio for the following year will be:

$$\frac{60}{(636.6 + 60)} \times 100$$
$$= 8.6\%$$

This ratio reveals a substantial fall in the level of gearing over the year.

Activity 6.18

The interest cover ratio for the year ended 31 March 2007 is:

$$\frac{(240.2 + 6.2)}{6.2}$$
$$= 39.7 \text{ times}$$

Activity 6.19

The gearing ratios are:

	2006	2007
Gearing ratio	28.6%	8.6%
Interest cover ratio	10.1 times	39.7 times

Both the gearing ratio and interest cover ratio have improved significantly in 2007. This is mainly due to the fact that a substantial part of the long-term loan (debentures) was repaid during 2007. This repayment has had the effect of reducing the relative contribution of long-term lenders to the financing of the company and reducing the amount of interest expense.

Activity 6.20

Your answer to this activity should be as follows:

$$\frac{60.0}{668.2}$$
$$= 9.0c$$

Activity 6.21

Your answer to this activity should be as follows:

$$\frac{60.0}{164.2} \times 100$$
$$= 36.5\%$$

Activity 6.22

Your answer to this activity should be as follows:

$$\frac{9.0 / (1 - 0.30)}{3.50} \times 100$$
$$= 3.67\%$$

Activity 6.23

The earnings per share for the year ended 31 March 2007 will be:

$$\frac{164.2}{668.2}$$

$$= 24.6c$$

Activity 6.24

Your answer should be as follows:

$$\text{OCF per share} = \frac{185}{668.2}$$

$$= 27.7c$$

Activity 6.25

Your answer to this activity should be as follows:

$$\frac{3.50}{0.246}$$

$$= 14.2c$$

Activity 6.26

There has been a significant increase in the dividends per share in 2007 when compared to the previous year. The dividend payout ratio reveals that this can be attributed, at least in part, to an increase in the proportion of earnings distributed to equity shareholders. However, the payout ratio for the year ended 31 March 2007 is still fairly low. Only about a third of earnings available for dividends is being distributed. The dividend yield has changed very little over the period and remains fairly low at approximately 4.0 per cent.

Earnings per share shows a slight fall in 2007 when compared with the previous year. A slight increase occurs in the operating cash flows per share. However, the P/E ratio shows a significant improvement. The market is clearly much more confident about the future prospects of the business at the end of the year to 31 March 2007.

Activity 6.27

Account type	Methods	Ratio (examples)
Inventories	Specific identification, FIFO, average	Current, ROA, net profit margin
Property, plant and equipment	Depreciation—straight line, sum of years digits, reducing balance	ROA, net profit margin, gearing
Accounts receivable	Bad and doubtful debts—direct; provision	Current, acid test, net profit margin

Activity 6.28

In terms of the favourable trends revealed you may have considered:

(a) the growth in sales

(b) the relative decline in selling expenses

(c) the stable financial expenses.

In terms of the unfavourable trends you may have noted:

(a) the relative increase in cost of sales (declining gross profit margin)

(b) the relative increase in administration costs.

OBJECTIVES

When you have completed your study of this chapter you should be able to:

1 explain the importance of a detailed understanding of cost behaviour

2 distinguish between fixed costs and variable costs

3 use knowledge of this distinction to deduce the break-even point for some activity

4 explain why knowledge of the break-even point is useful

5 explain and apply the concept of contribution

6 explain the concept of a margin of safety

7 identify the weaknesses of break-even analysis

8 use a spreadsheet to develop profit profiles and associated charts, using historic or forecast costs, for simple and more complex relationships

9 explain and apply the idea of relevant costing

10 make decisions on the use of spare capacity, using knowledge of the relationship between fixed and variable costs

11 make decisions about the acceptance (or continuance) or rejection of a particular contract or activity, based on knowledge of the relationship between fixed and variable costs

12 choose between products when certain inputs are in scarce supply

13 identify whether it is better to buy a component or to make it, under specified circumstances.

7

COST–VOLUME–PROFIT ANALYSIS AND MARGINAL ANALYSIS

This chapter is concerned with the relationship between volume of activity, costs and profit. Broadly, costs can be divided between costs that are fixed, relative to the volume of activity, and those that vary with the volume of activity. We shall consider how we can use knowledge of this relationship to make decisions and assess risk, particularly in the context of short-term decisions.

THE BEHAVIOUR OF COSTS

It is an observable fact that for many commercial/business activities **costs** may be broadly classified as:

* those that stay fixed (the same) when changes occur to the volume of activity
* those that vary according to the volume of activity.

These are known as **fixed costs** and **variable costs** respectively.

We shall see in this chapter that knowledge of how much of each type of cost is involved with some particular activity can be of great value to the decision maker.

FIXED COSTS

The way in which fixed costs behave is depicted in Figure 7.1. 0F is the amount of fixed costs and this stays the same irrespective of the level of activity.

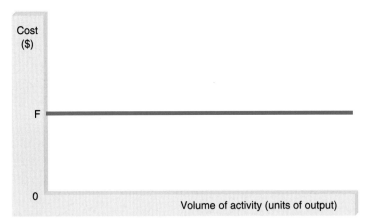

FIGURE 7.1 Graph of fixed cost(s) against the level of activity

ACTIVITY 7.1

A business operates a small chain of hairdressing salons. Can you give some examples of costs that are likely to be fixed for this business?

It is important to be clear that 'fixed', in this context, only means that the cost is not altered by changes in the level of activity.

Fixed costs are likely to be affected by inflation. If rent (a typical fixed cost) goes up due to inflation, a fixed cost will have increased, but not because of a change in the level of activity.

Fixed costs are not the same amount irrespective of the time period involved. Fixed costs are almost always 'time based'—that is, they vary with the length of time concerned. The rent charge for two months is normally twice that for one month. Thus fixed costs normally vary with time, but (of course) not with the level of output. You should note that when we talk of fixed costs being, say, $1,000, we must add the period concerned, say, $1,000 per month.

Fixed costs do not stay the same irrespective of the level of output. They are usually fixed for a particular range of output levels. Beyond a particular point, fixed costs often have to increase in order to facilitate the higher levels of output. They are often said to step up as activity levels increase.

ACTIVITY 7.2

What do you think will happen to the fixed costs associated with the cost of rent for the hairdressing business referred to in Activity 7.1 if there is dramatic growth in that business? Explain your thinking.

Figure 7.2 illustrates the idea of step functions as output increases.

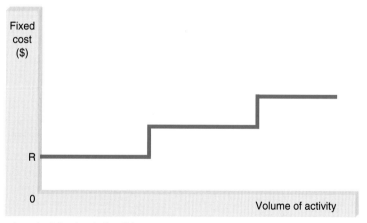

FIGURE 7.2 Graph of fixed cost against the level of activity

This might be applied to Activity 7.2 as follows. At lower levels of activity the rent cost would be 0R. As the level of activity expands, the accommodation becomes inadequate and further expansion requires an increase in premises and, therefore, cost. This higher level of accommodation provision will enable further expansion to take place. Eventually, further costs will need to be incurred if further expansion is to occur.

VARIABLE COSTS

These are costs which vary with the level of activity. In a manufacturing business, for example, this would include raw materials used.

ACTIVITY 7.3

Can you think of some examples of variable costs in the hairdressing business used in earlier activities?

Variable costs for the hairdressing business can be represented graphically as in Figure 7.3. At zero level of activity the cost is zero. This cost increases in a straight line as activity increases.

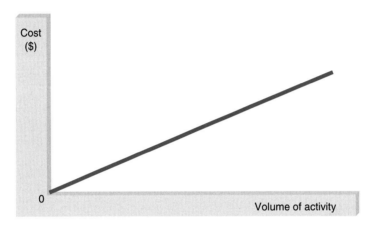

FIGURE 7.3 Graph of the variable cost of lotions and other materials against the level of activity

The straight line for variable cost on this graph implies that the cost of materials will normally be the same per unit of activity irrespective of the level of activity concerned. In some cases, however, the line is not straight because at high levels of output economies of scale may be available. For example, labour may be able to be employed more efficiently with higher volumes of activity. Similarly, the relatively large quantities of material and services bought may enable the business to benefit from bulk discounts and general power in the marketplace.

On the other hand, there are circumstances where a high level of demand may cause a shortage of a commodity, thus pushing prices up at the higher end of activity. To obtain more labour hours it may be necessary to pay higher salaries or wages to attract suitable additional employees or to pay overtime premiums to encourage existing employees to work longer hours.

The fact that the line may not, in practice, be perfectly straight is probably not worth taking into account in most cases. This is because all of the information used in the analysis is based on estimates of the future. Since this will inevitably be flawed to some extent, it seems pointless to be pedantic about minor approximations, such as assuming that the variable costs can be represented by a straight line when strictly this is invalid. Only where significant economies or diseconomies of scale are involved is it necessary to take into account the non-linearity of the variable costs.

SEMI-FIXED (SEMI-VARIABLE) COSTS

In some cases costs have both fixed and variable elements to them. These are usually called **semi-fixed** or **semi-variable costs**. An example might be the electricity cost for the hairdressing business. Some of this will be for heating and lighting and this part is probably fixed, at least until the volume of activity expands to a point where longer opening hours or larger premises are necessary. The other part of the cost will vary with the level of activity. Here we are talking about such things as power for hair dryers.

Usually it is not very obvious how much of each element a particular cost contains. It is usually necessary to look at past experience here. If we have data on what the electricity cost has been for various levels of activity—say, the relevant data over several three-month periods—we can estimate the fixed and variable portions. This is often done graphically, as shown in Figure 7.4. We tend to use past data here purely because it provides us with an estimate of future costs; past costs are not, of course, relevant for their own sake.

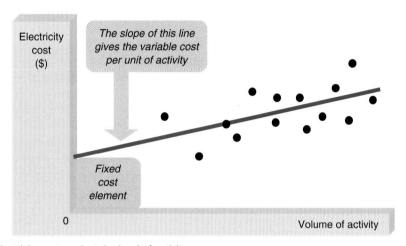

FIGURE 7.4 Graph of electricity cost against the level of activity

Each of the dots in the graph is a reading of the electricity charge for a particular level of activity (probably measured in term of sales revenue). The heavy line on the graph is an estimate of 'the line of best fit'. This means that, to us, it is the line that best seemed to represent the data. A better estimate can usually be made using a statistical technique ('least squares regression'), which does not involve drawing graphs and making estimates. In practice it probably does not make much difference which approach is taken.

From the graph we can say that the fixed element of the electricity cost is the amount represented by the vertical distance from the zero point (bottom left-hand corner) of the graph to the point where the heavy line crosses the vertical axis of the graph. The variable cost per unit is the amount that the graph rises for each increase in the volume of activity.

Now that we have considered the nature of fixed and variable costs we can go on to do something useful with that knowledge.

BREAK-EVEN ANALYSIS

If, in respect of a particular activity, we know the total fixed costs for a period and the total variable cost per unit, we can produce a graph like that in Figure 7.5.

Figure 7.5 shows a fixed cost area. Added to this is the variable cost, the wedge-shaped portion at the top of the graph. The uppermost line represents the total cost at any particular level of activity. This total is the vertical distance between the graph's horizontal axis and the uppermost line for the particular level of activity concerned.

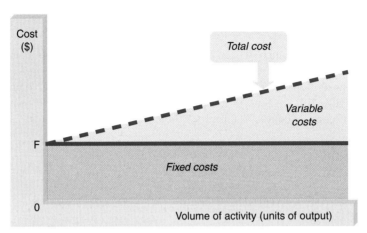

FIGURE 7.5 Graph of total cost against the level of activity

Logically enough, the total cost at zero activity is the amount of the fixed costs. This is because, even where there is nothing going on, the business will still be paying rent, salaries, etc., at least in the short term. The fixed cost is augmented by the amount of the relevant variable costs as the volume of activity increases.

If we superimpose on this total cost graph a line representing total revenue for each level of activity we obtain the graph shown in Figure 7.6.

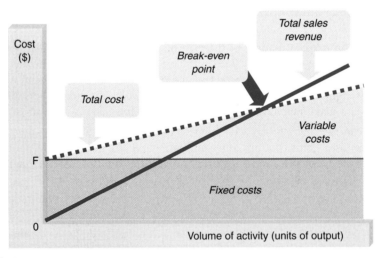

FIGURE 7.6 Break-even chart

Note that at zero level of activity (zero sales) there is zero sales revenue. The profit (total sales revenue less total cost) at various levels of activity is the vertical distance between the total sales line and the total cost line, at that particular level of activity. At the **break-even point** there is no vertical distance between these two lines and thus there is no profit—that is, the activity breaks even. Below the break-even point a loss will be incurred; above the break-even point there will be a profit. The further below the break-even point, the higher the loss; the further above, the higher the profit.

As you may imagine, deducing break-even points by graphical means is a laborious business. It may have struck you that since the relationships in the graph are all straight-line ones, it would be easy to calculate the break-even point.

We know that at break-even point (but not at any other point):

$$\textit{Total revenues = Total costs}$$
$$\textit{i.e. Total revenues = Fixed costs + Total variable costs}$$

If we call the number of units of output at break-even point b, then:

$$b \times \textit{Sales revenue per unit = Fixed costs + (b × Variable costs per unit)}$$

thus

$$(b \times \textit{Sales revenue per unit) – (b × Variable costs per unit) = Fixed costs}$$

and

$$b \times \textit{(Sales revenue per unit – Variable costs per unit) = Fixed costs}$$

giving

$$b = \textit{Fixed costs / (Sales revenue per unit – Variable costs per unit)}$$

If you look back at the break-even chart this looks logical. At an output of zero the total cost line is higher than revenue by an amount equal to the amount of the fixed costs. Because the sales revenue per unit is greater than the variable cost per unit, the sales revenue line will gradually catch up with the total cost line. The rate at which it will catch up is dependent on the relative steepness of the two lines and the amount that it has to catch up is the amount of the fixed costs. Bearing in mind that the slopes of the two lines are the variable cost per unit and the selling price per unit, the above equation for calculating b looks perfectly logical. We will return to calculation of the break-even point later in the chapter.

Cottage Industries Ltd makes baskets. The fixed costs of operating the workshop for a month total $1,500. Each basket requires materials which cost $6. Each basket takes two hours to make and the business pays the basket makers $9 an hour. The basket makers are all on contracts such that if they do not work for any reason, they are not paid. The baskets are sold to a wholesaler for $30 each.

What is the break-even point for basket making for the business?

The break-even point (in number of baskets)

$$= \textit{Fixed costs / (Sales revenue per unit – Variable costs per unit)}$$
$$= \$1,500 / [\$30 – (6 + 18)] = 250 \text{ baskets per month}$$

Note that the break-even point must be expressed with respect to a period of time.

EXAMPLE

7.1

ACTIVITY 7.4

Can you think of reasons why the managers of a business might find it useful to know the break-even point of some activity which they are planning to undertake?

ACTIVITY 7.5

Cottage Industries Ltd (see Example 7.1 above) expects to sell 500 baskets a month. The business has the opportunity to rent a basket-making machine. Doing so would increase the total fixed costs of operating the workshop for a month to $6,000. Using the machine would reduce the labour time to one hour per basket. The basket makers would still be paid $9 an hour.

How much profit would the business make each month from selling baskets:

(a) assuming that the business does not rent the basket-making machine?

(b) assuming that it is rented?

What is the break-even point if the machine is rented?

What do you notice about the figures you calculated?

The difference between the output and the break-even volume is known as the **margin of safety**, and provides an indication of the risks involved. We will consider this factor in more detail later in this chapter. We shall take a closer look at the relationship between fixed costs, variable costs, break-even and the advice we might give the management of Cottage Industries Ltd after we have considered the notion of 'contribution'.

CONTRIBUTION

The bottom part of the break-even formula (Sales revenue per unit – Variable costs per unit) is known as the **contribution per unit**. Thus for the basket-making activity, without the machine the contribution per unit is $6 and with the machine it is $15. This can be quite a useful figure to know in a decision-making context. It is known as contribution because it contributes to meeting the fixed costs and, if there is any excess, it also contributes to profit. The variable cost per unit is also known as the **marginal cost**—that is, the additional cost of making one more basket.

The idea of contribution can be seen more clearly in figure 7.7.

Figure 7.7 clearly shows how contribution grows as volume grows. The vertical distance between the sales revenue line and the variable cost line measure the amount of contribution at that level of output. It is important to note that there will be no profit made until the contribution covers the amount of the fixed costs.

The use of break-even and profit-volume charts (see next section) provides a useful picture of the relationship between costs, volume and profit. However, unless the charts are drawn with great care the results will not be as accurate as they might be. Mathematical techniques can be used to arrive at the break-even point or levels of output needed to achieve a prescribed amount of profit. The broad principles are outlined below.

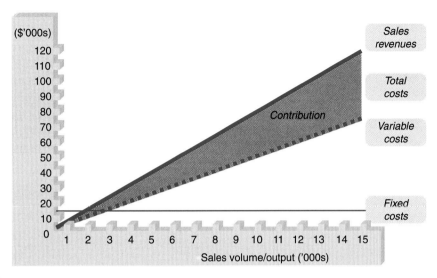

FIGURE 7.7 Contribution

Contribution per unit is calculated by deducting variable costs per unit from selling price per unit. Each unit of contribution goes towards fixed costs initially, then to profits. This means that the break-even point can be calculated by solving the following equation.

$$Break\text{-}even\ point = \frac{Fixed\ costs}{Contribution\ per\ unit}$$

Another way of looking at this is to ask the question how many lots of contribution per unit need to be obtained to cover the fixed costs.

The following are details of planned sales and costs of a business for a period. You are asked to construct a break-even chart and:

a) find the break-even point

b) find the margin of safety

c) estimate the sales necessary for a profit of $5,000.

EXAMPLE

7.2

Sales	10,000 units @ $6 each	$60,000
Variable costs	10,000 units @ $3.50 each	$35,000
Fixed costs		$15,000

You are also asked to convert this information into a profit–volume chart.

Using the information contained above, the break-even point could be calculated as follows:

Sales price per unit	$6
Variable costs per unit	$3.50
Contribution per unit	$2.50

Since the fixed costs were $15,000 the break-even point can be calculated as follows:

$$\frac{15{,}000}{2.50} = 6{,}000 \text{ units}$$

Given that the business plans to sell 10,000 units, the margin of safety is 4,000 units.

In order to calculate the level of sales necessary to make a prescribed level of profits it is necessary to recover the amount of the fixed costs plus the amount of profit desired. Hence, using the above example, the level of sales needed to obtain a profit of $5,000 can be obtained as follows:

$$\frac{\text{Fixed costs} + \text{Profit}}{\text{Contribution per unit}} = \text{Level of sales needed to achieve the desired profit}$$

that is,

$$\frac{\$15{,}000 + \$5{,}000}{\$2.50} = 8{,}000 \text{ units}$$

If a profit of $15,000 were desired it would be necessary to sell 12,000 units ([15,000 + $15,000] / 2.50).

PROFIT–VOLUME CHARTS

A slight variant of the break-even chart is the profit–volume (PV) chart. A typical PV chart is shown in Figure 7.8.

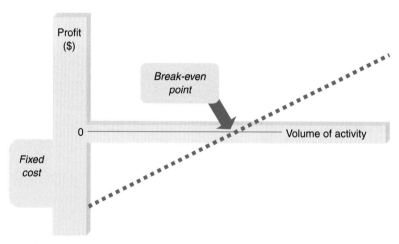

FIGURE 7.8 Profit–volume chart

The PV chart is obtained by plotting loss or profit against volume of activity. The slope of the graph is equal to the contribution per unit, since each additional unit sold decreases the loss, or increases the profit, by the sales revenue per unit less the variable cost per unit. At zero level of activity, there are no contributions so there is a loss equal to the amount of the fixed costs. As the level of activity increases, the amount of the loss gradually decreases until the break-even point is reached. Beyond the break-even point profits increase as activity increases.

It may have occurred to you that the PV chart does not tell us anything not shown by the break-even chart. Although it is true that nothing new is provided by the PV chart, information is perhaps more easily absorbed from this chart. This is particularly true of the profit at any level of volume. This information is provided by the break-even chart as the vertical distance between the total cost and total sales revenue lines. The PV chart, in effect, combines the total sales revenue and total variable cost lines, which means that profit (or loss) is actually plotted.

MARGIN OF SAFETY AND OPERATING GEARING

From the solution to Activity 7.5, we obtain the following situation:

	Without the machine	*With the machine*
Expected level of sales	500	500
Break-even point	250	400
Difference (margin of safety)		
Number of baskets	250	100
Percentage of estimated level of sales	50%	20%

ACTIVITY 7.6

What advice would you give Cottage Industries Ltd about renting the machine on the basis of the margin of safety figures?

The relative margins of safety are directly linked to the relationship between the selling price per basket, the variable costs per basket and the fixed costs per month. Without the machine the contribution (selling price less variable costs) per basket is $6. With the machine it is $15. Without the machine the fixed costs are $1,500 a month; with the machine they are $6,000. This means that with the machine the contributions have more fixed costs to 'overcome' or recover before the activity becomes profitable. On the other hand, the rate at which the contributions can overcome or recover fixed costs is higher with the machine, because variable costs are lower. This means that one more, or one less, basket sold has a greater impact on profit than it does if the machine is not rented.

The relationship between contribution and fixed costs is known as 'operating gearing'. An activity with relatively high fixed costs compared with its variable costs is said to have high operating gearing.

Thus Cottage Industries Ltd is more highly operationally geared with the machine than it would be without the machine. Renting the machine quite dramatically increases the level of operating gearing because it causes an increase in fixed costs, but at the same time it leads to a reduction in variable costs per basket.

The reason why the word 'gearing' is used in this context is that, as with intermeshing gear wheels of different circumferences, a movement in one of the factors (volume of output) causes a more than proportionate movement in the other (profit). The word 'leverage' is also used.

We can illustrate this with Cottage Industries Ltd's basket-making activities:

	Without the machine				With the machine			
Volume	300	500	1,000	1,500	300	500	1,000	1,500
	$	$	$	$	$	$	$	$
Contributions*	1,800	3,000	6,000	9,000	4,500	7,500	15,000	22,500
Less fixed costs	1,500	1,500	1,500	1,500	6,000	6,000	6,000	6,000
Profit	300	1,500	4,500	7,500	(1,500)	1,500	9,000	16,500

* $6 per basket without the machine and $15 per basket with it.

Note that without the machine (low operating gearing), a doubling of the output from 500 to 1,000 brings a trebling of the profit. With the machine (high operating gearing), doubling output causes profit to rise by six times. At a lower volume (300), high operating gearing is associated with a loss whereas, in this example, lower operating gearing is still associated with a profit, albeit small.

The effect of operating gearing is represented by Figure 6.3 (page 254). An amount of rotation by the larger gear wheel (representing volume of output) causes a larger amount of rotation by the smaller wheel (representing profit).

ACTIVITY 7.7

In general terms, what types of business activity tend to be most highly operationally geared? (*Hint*: Cottage Industries Ltd might give you some idea.)

WEAKNESSES OF BREAK-EVEN ANALYSIS

As we have seen, break-even analysis can provide some useful insights into the important relationship between fixed costs, variable costs and the volume of activity. It does, however, have its weaknesses. There are three general points:

1. *Non-linear relationships.* The normal approach to break-even analysis assumes that the relationships between sales revenues, variable costs and volume are strictly straight-line ones. In real life this is unlikely to be true.

    This is probably not a major problem, since break-even analysis is normally conducted in advance of the activity actually taking place. Our ability to predict future costs, revenues, etc., is somewhat limited, so minor variations from strict linearity are unlikely to be significant.

2. *Stepped fixed costs.* Most fixed costs are not fixed over all volumes of activity. They tend to be 'stepped' in the way depicted in Figure 7.2. This means that, in practical circumstances, great care must be taken in making assumptions about fixed costs. The problem is heightened because most activities will probably involve fixed costs of various types (rent, supervisory salaries, administration costs) all of which are likely to have steps at different points.

3. *Multi-product businesses.* Most businesses do not do just one thing. This is a problem for break-even analysis since it raises problems of the effect of additional sales of one product or service on sales of another of the business's products or services. There is also the problem of identifying the fixed costs of one particular activity. Fixed costs, such as rent, tend to relate to more than one activity—for example, two activities may be carried out in the same rented premises. There are ways of dividing fixed costs between activities, but these tend to be arbitrary, which calls the value of the break-even analysis into question.

USE OF SPREADSHEETS

It is frequently advisable or useful to prepare a break-even chart or some sort of profit profile under various assumptions. A spreadsheet provides a useful starting point. Given below is a very simple spreadsheet, and its accompanying charts, providing a picture of the profit/volume relationship under the status quo. This spreadsheet relates to the following example.

The following information relates to a business for the last three months.

	$
Sales 15,000 units @ $20	300,000
Variable costs 15,000 units @ $12	180,000
Contribution	120,000
Fixed costs	150,000
Loss	30,000

EXAMPLE 7.3

The managers of the business are now considering what to do about this loss. They hope to make a profit of $30,000 in the next three months and the following proposals have been made.

1. Launch an advertising campaign costing $50,000.
2. Reduce selling price to $19.
3. Reduce variable costs by $1.50 per unit by installing more efficient equipment which will increase fixed costs by $40,000.

You have been asked to advise on:

(a) the level of sales needed to make a profit of $30,000 assuming that none of the three proposals is adopted
(b) the break-even point under this assumption
(c) the level of sales needed for each of these proposals in order to generate the required profit
(d) the impact each proposal will have on the break-even point?

You may assume that revenues and costs will remain the same in the next three months, other than those relating to the three proposals.

The spreadsheet shown in Table 7.1 shows the profit profiles for a range of output levels. This spreadsheet is set up so that inputs are needed for those output levels for which a profit calculation is required, and for sales revenue (SR) per unit, variable costs (VC) per unit, fixed costs (FC) and any changes in these costs. These items are shown in italics. The rest of the spreadsheet uses formulae to provide profit figures at the various levels of output and to calculate the break-even point. The workings section of the spreadsheet is set out in this way so as to provide the necessary inputs for the charts which can be associated with an exercise of this type. Linked spreadsheets may be used so that the workings can be manipulated to obtain charts and graphs without cluttering up the main spreadsheet. In practice different spreadsheets may require slightly different layouts for purposes of preparing charts.

TABLE 7.1 A spreadsheet for calculating profit profiles and break-even charts

	A	B	C	D	E	F	G
1	**Profit profiles at various levels of output**			**Key**			
2			Profit	SR = Sales revenue			
3	Output levels for which figures required	12,000	−54,000	VC = Variable costs			
4		15,000	−30,000	FC = Fixed costs			
5		18,000	−6,000	TC = Total costs = Variable costs + Fixed costs			
6		20,000	10,000				
7		24,000	42,000				
8		27,000	66,000				
9		30,000	90,000				
10							
11	Sales revenue per unit	20					
12	Variable costs per unit	12					
13	Fixed costs—original	150,000					
14	Fixed costs—changes relating to proposal	0					
15	Target profit	30,000					
16							
17	Break-even point—units	18,750					
18	Break-even point—value	375,000					
19	Volume needed to achieve target profit	22,500					
20							
21	**Workings**						
22		SR	VC	FC	TC		Profit
23	0	0	0	150,000	150,000	0	−150,000
24	12,000	240,000	144,000	150,000	294,000	12,000	−54,000
25	15,000	300,000	180,000	150,000	330,000	15,000	−30,000
26	18,000	360,000	216,000	150,000	366,000	18,000	−6,000
27	20,000	400,000	240,000	150,000	390,000	20,000	10,000
28	24,000	480,000	288,000	150,000	438,000	24,000	42,000
29	27,000	540,000	324,000	150,000	474,000	27,000	66,000
30	30,000	600,000	360,000	150,000	510,000	30,000	90,000

The second spreadsheet shown in Table 7.2 shows the formulae used to build up the spreadsheet.

The bottom part of the spreadsheet is set up in a way that facilitates development of charts and graphs. Selection of the area covering A22 to E30 using the chart facility of the spreadsheet enables the break-even chart to be displayed. Selection of F22 to G30 enables the profit–volume graph to be developed.

TABLE 7.2 A spreadsheet for calculating profit profiles and break-even charts—formulae

	A	B	C	D	E	F	G
1	Profit profiles at various levels of output			Key			
2			Profit	SR = Sales revenue			
3	Output levels for which figures required	12,000	=G24	VC = Variable costs			
4		15,000	=G25	FC = Fixed costs			
5		18,000	=G26	TC = Total costs = Variable costs + Fixed costs			
6		20,000	=G27				
7		24,000	=G28				
8		27,000	=G29				
9		30,000	=G30				
10							
11	Sales revenue per unit	20					
12	Variable costs per unit	12					
13	Fixed costs—original	150,000					
14	Fixed costs—changes relating to proposal	0					
15	Target profit	30,000					
16							
17	Break-even point—units	=((B13+B14)/(B11–B12))					
18	Break-even point—value	=B17*B11					
19	Volume needed to achieve target profit	=(B13+B14+B15)/(B11–B12)					
20							
21	Workings						
22		SR	VC	FC	TC		Profit
23	0	0	0	=B13+B14	=C23+D23	0	=B23–E23
24	12,000	=A24*B11	=A24*B12	=B13+B14	=C24+D24	12,000	=B24–E24
25	15,000	=A25*B11	=A25*B12	=B13+B14	=C25+D25	15,000	=B25–E25
26	18,000	=A26*B11	=A26*B12	=B13+B14	=C26+D26	18,000	=B26–E26
27	20,000	=A27*B11	=A27*B12	=B13+B14	=C27+D27	20,000	=B27–E27
28	24,000	=A28*B11	=A28*B12	=B13+B14	=C28+D28	24,000	=B28–E28
29	27,000	=A29*B11	=A29*B12	=B13+B14	=C29+D29	27,000	=B29–E29
30	30,000	=A30*B11	=A30*B12	=B13+B14	=C30+D30	30,000	=B30–E30

Figures 7.9 and 7.10 show the charts provided by the spreadsheet set out in Table 7.1.

The next stage is to consider the impact of the various proposals on profit and the break-even point.

The results under the three proposals can be derived from this spreadsheet simply by changing the following:

1. grid B14   increase this by $50,000

2. grid B11   reduce this to $19

3. grid B12   reduce this by $1.50

   grid B14   increase to $40,000

The results should then be read off the spreadsheet and associated charts. Take care that you modify each of these three proposals independently.

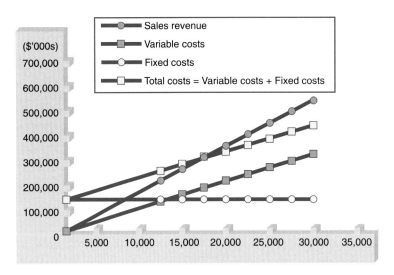

FIGURE 7.9 Break-even chart using the spreadsheet

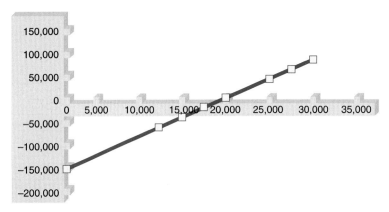

FIGURE 7.10 Profit–volume graph

Of course the above exercise can be solved manually as shown below. You should work through this using your own spreadsheet to verify these results.

(a) With the existing revenue/cost structure the sales needed to make a profit of $30,000 can be calculated as follows:

Amount of contribution needed = fixed costs $150,000 + profit of $30,000 = $180,000
Contribution per unit $8
Therefore sales needed $180,000 / 8 = 22,500 units or $450,000

(b) The current contribution per unit is $8.

Current fixed costs are $150,000.

Therefore current break-even point is 150,000 / 8 = 18,750 units.

(c) (1) The proposal to launch an advertising campaign will increase fixed costs by $50,000. The break-even point associated with this proposal will thus be ($150,000 + $50,000) / 8 = 25,000 units.

The sales level needed to make a profit of $30,000 will be ($150,000 + $50,000 + $30,000) / 8 = 28,750 units.

(2) A reduction in selling price to $19 will reduce the contribution per unit to $7. The break-even point can thus be calculated as $150,000 / 7 = 21,429 units.

The sales level needed to make a profit of $30,000 will be $180,000 / 7 = 25,715 units.

(3) If variable costs can be reduced by $1.50 the contribution will increase to $9.50 per unit.

Fixed costs will increase to $190,000.

The break-even point can thus be calculated as $190,000 / 9.50 = 20,000 units.

The sales level needed to make a profit of $30,000 will be $220,000 / 9.50 = 23,158 units.

These results can be summarised as follows:

	Break-even	Profit of $30,000
No change	18,750	22,500
Advertising campaign	25,000	28,750
Reduction in selling price	21,429	25,715
New equipment/reduced variable costs	20,000	23,158

This summary suggests that the third proposal is the best of the three, since it has the lowest break-even point and the lowest level of sales needed to make the desired profit. However, these results suggest that it would be better to maintain the existing revenue/cost structure, since this has lower figures than any of the proposals. Whether it will prove possible to actually achieve the desired profit level is another matter.

Further questions need to be asked about the likely impact of the various proposals on sales figures. If there is no particular reason to suppose that sales will increase above 15,000 units if the existing revenue/cost structure is maintained, the relevant profit figures will be:

Current position	loss	$30,000
Proposal 3	loss	$47,500
(contribution of 15,000 × $9.50)		
less $190,000 fixed costs		

The difference is caused by an increase in contribution of $22,500 (15,000 × $1.50) less the increase in fixed costs of $40,000.

So far, as indicated in the question, we have assumed that the existing revenue/cost structure will apply for the next three months. In practice it may well be the case that the existing revenue/cost structure will be associated with increases or decreases in sales in the future. Further market analysis is called for.

The contribution is $7 per unit.
A contribution of $120,000 is needed if a loss of $30,000 is to be made.
Therefore sales needed to be no worse off = 120,000 / 7 = 17,143 units.

EXPECTED COSTS RATHER THAN HISTORIC COSTS

Often the calculations need to be based on expected costs rather than historic costs. This is not a problem. It is simply necessary to ensure that the figures used are expected figures for the period for which decisions are being made, rather than simply those of the previous accounting period.

ACTIVITY 7.8

A business sold 10,000 units in 2005 at $100 each. Variable costs were $60 each while fixed costs totalled $250,000.

The business expects variable costs to increase by 5% in 2006 and fixed costs to increase by 10%. Because of current market conditions the selling price will not be increased in line with inflation, but will increase to $102 per unit. The business expects to sell 10,000 units in 2006.

What are the break-even points and the profits for each of the two years?

Clearly in this case the impact of inflationary increases in costs, when there is no equivalent increase in selling price (a situation frequently found in times of recession), is considerable, both in terms of profits and the break-even point.

In this kind of analysis it may be useful to consider building a spreadsheet model into which price rises can be put. This would enable results to be found under a variety of different assumptions about cost/revenue behaviour.

MORE COMPLEX COST AND REVENUE BEHAVIOUR PATTERNS

The analysis carried out so far assumes that selling price and variable costs change directly in proportion to changes in output. However, in practice costs may not change with this degree of precision. Higher levels of sales may only be achieved by reductions in selling price. Variable costs may reduce as output increases, due to discounts on bulk purchases. Alternatively they may increase as output increases, where the commodity is in short supply. Fixed costs may increase at certain levels of output.

The implication of these kinds of cost behaviour is that break-even charts and the analysis of relationships between costs, volume and profits, of the type discussed so far in the chapter, become far more complex. An example of a break-even chart modified to include some of the above cost behaviour patterns is shown in Figure 7.11.

Profit profiles using spreadsheets probably represent a more effective way of dealing with these patterns, although the spreadsheets are inevitably more complex than those used so far.

SEMI-VARIABLE COSTS

It was mentioned earlier that not all costs can be categorised as fixed or variable. Many costs are semi-variable, and some attempt must be made to split these into their fixed and variable elements, if the framework introduced earlier in this chapter is to be used. Typical examples of semi-variable costs are such things as wages for supervision and maintenance, administration costs, salaries and commission of sales staff.

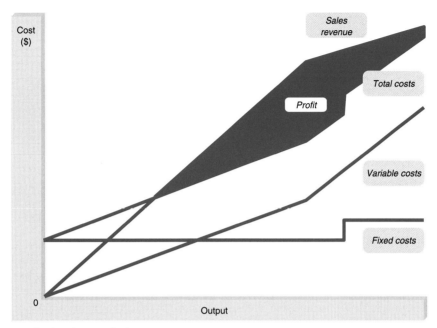

FIGURE 7.11 A more complex break-even chart

In making decisions about the likely behaviour of semi-variable costs it is highly likely that past behaviour patterns will be used as the base. If a number of cost figures are available for a range of production levels it is possible to plot these on a graph and put in a line of best fit. The aim is to calculate the equation of the line

$$y = mx + c$$

where y is cost, m is the variable cost element, x is the output level and c is a constant, the fixed costs.

The split into fixed and variable costs can be achieved in a number of ways. In its simplest form the cost line may be derived simply by drawing a line between the highest and lowest figures given, and extending this line to the y axis. This is known as the high–low or range method. A better method is to use all the observations. The line of best fit can be derived from these observations. This may be done 'by eye' or by statistical methods.

A business has the following figures for production overheads over the last five weeks.

Output	Production overheads ($)
20,000	30,500
22,000	31,000
18,000	28,500
19,000	29,000
20,000	29,800

These figures can be plotted on a graph and a line of best fit put in by eye, as shown in Figure 7.12.

EXAMPLE

7.4

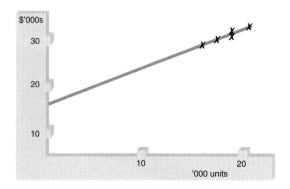

FIGURE 7.12 Line of best fit

When putting in a line of best fit in this way the line is inevitably approximate, and there is scope for error. Your graph may be slightly different to the graph shown in figure 7.12.

From this graph estimates of fixed and variable costs can be made. The fixed costs are the costs associated with an output level of zero. In the graph these are approximately $16,000. The variable cost, which is effectively the slope of the line, can be calculated by deducting the fixed costs of $16,000 from total costs at any level of output, and dividing it by that output. If we assume that the right-hand cross reflects a point of the graph at which 22,000 units of output causes $31,000 of costs, of which $16,000 is fixed, variable costs associated with an output of 22,000 must be $15,000 = $0.68 per unit of output. (The slope of the line is 15/22 = 0.68). Hence if we were to produce 24,000 units we would expect the total costs to be around $16,000 + (24,000 × $0.68) = $32,320.

If the high–low method were to be adopted the process would be as follows:

	Output	$
Lowest figure	18,000	$28,500
Highest figure	22,000	$31,000
Difference	4,000	$2,500 all of which is presumed to relate to the variable element of cost.

Hence the variable cost per unit could be calculated by dividing 2,500 by 4,000 units = 62.5 cents.

Since at an output level of 18,000 units variable costs would be 18,000 × 62.5c = $11,250, and total costs are $28,500, fixed costs can be estimated as $17,250. Clearly, these results are slightly different to those obtained when all five observations were used.

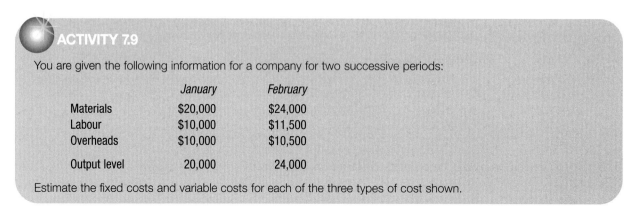

ACTIVITY 7.9

You are given the following information for a company for two successive periods:

	January	February
Materials	$20,000	$24,000
Labour	$10,000	$11,500
Overheads	$10,000	$10,500
Output level	20,000	24,000

Estimate the fixed costs and variable costs for each of the three types of cost shown.

If required, statistical techniques (e.g. linear regression) can be used to derive a more accurate line of best fit. Most spreadsheet packages have a function which enables this to be carried out fairly easily. More complex relationships can typically be handled using multiple regression techniques, while lines of best fit may be derived using exponential curves. Clearly, the use of spreadsheets is particularly advantageous in this area.

Considerable care is necessary when using figures based upon past information to help forecast future figures. The particular problem of changing prices has already been discussed. Two problems which arise, which can be related specifically to cost estimation, need to be considered. The first of these is that while a line of best fit can be calculated for two sets of figures, it may still not be a good fit, in the sense that the relationship is not close. This is illustrated in figure 7.13, which plots two different sets of observations.

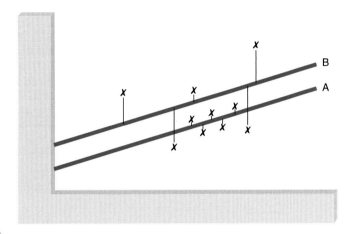

FIGURE 7.13 Lines of best fit

Clearly, the relationship between the observations which go to make up line A is far closer than that between those relating to B. The use of a supplementary statistical measure such as a correlation coefficient would enable users to assess the degree of confidence that could be associated with the regression line.

The second problem relates to the spread of observations used to estimate the fixed and variable elements of cost. This is probably something which occurred to you in a previous activity, when you were trying to put a line of best fit in by eye. The range of observations for that activity was for five output levels of between 18,000 and 22,000 units. Extrapolating a line beyond this range may be dangerous, since output levels outside this range may not be normal, and cost behaviour patterns may change quite dramatically, both above and below what may be regarded as 'normal' levels of activity. Some thought needs to be given to this if decisions are being made about output levels outside this normal or relevant range.

MARGINAL ANALYSIS/RELEVANT COSTING

When we are trying to decide between two or more possible courses of action and where economic costs and benefits are the decision-making criteria, only costs that vary with the decision should be included in the decision analysis. For example, a householder wants a house decorated. Two decorators have been asked to price the job. One of them will do the work for $2,000, the other one wants $2,400, in both cases on the basis that the householder will supply the materials. It is believed that either of the decorators will do an equally good job. The materials will cost $700 irrespective of which decorator does the work. Assuming that the householder wants the house decorated at the lower cost, the two contractors' prices will be compared and a decision made on that basis. The cost of the materials is irrelevant because it will be the same in each case. It is only possible to distinguish rationally between courses of action on the basis of differences between them.

For many decisions which involve relatively small variations from existing practice or are for relatively limited periods of time, fixed costs are not relevant to the decision because they will be the same irrespective of the decision made. This is because either:

✳ fixed costs tend to be impossible to alter in the short term, or

✳ managers are reluctant to alter them in the short term.

Suppose that a business occupies premises which it owns in order to carry out its activities. There is a downturn in demand for the service that the business provides and it would be possible to carry on the business from smaller, cheaper premises. Does this mean that the business will sell its old premises and move to new ones overnight? Clearly, it cannot mean this. This is partly because it is not usually possible to find a buyer for premises at very short notice and it may be difficult to move premises quickly where there is, say, delicate equipment to be moved. Apart from external constraints on the speed of the move, management may feel that the downturn might not be permanent and may thus be reluctant to take such a dramatic step as to deny itself the opportunity to benefit from a possible revival of trade.

The business's premises may provide an example of an area of one of the more inflexible types of cost, but most fixed costs tend to be broadly similar in this context.

We shall now consider some decision-making areas where fixed costs can be regarded as irrelevant and analyse decisions in those areas. Areas covered are:

✳ accepting/rejecting special contracts

✳ the most efficient use of scarce resources

✳ make or buy decisions

✳ closing or continuance of a section.

The fact that the decisions we are considering here are short term means that the objective of wealth enhancement will be promoted by pursuing a policy of seeking to generate as many net cash inflows as possible.

ACCEPTING/REJECTING SPECIAL CONTRACTS

 ACTIVITY 7.10

Cottage Industries Ltd (our old friend) has spare capacity, in that it has spare basket makers. An overseas retail chain has offered the business an order for 300 baskets at a price of $27 each.

Without considering any wider issues, should the business accept the order? Assume that the business does not rent the machine.

In considering any potential wider issues, there is a range of factors that are either difficult or impossible to quantify but which should be considered before reaching a final decision. In the present case these could include:

✳ The possibility that spare capacity will be 'sold off' cheaply when there is another potential customer who will offer a higher price, but by which time the capacity will be fully committed. It is a matter of commercial judgment as to how likely this will be.

✳ The problem that selling the same product, but at different prices, could lead to a loss of customer goodwill. The fact that each price will be to customers in different countries may be sufficient to avoid this potential problem.

✳ If the business is going to suffer continually from being unable to sell its full production potential at the 'regular' price, it might be better, in the long run, to reduce capacity and make fixed cost savings. Using the spare capacity to produce marginal benefits may lead to the business failing to address this issue.

✳ On a more positive note, the business may see this as a way of breaking into the overseas market. This is something that might be impossible to achieve if the business charges its regular price.

THE MOST EFFICIENT USE OF SCARCE RESOURCES

We tend to think in terms of the size of the market being the brake on output. That is to say that the ability of a business to sell is likely to limit production, rather than sales being limited by the ability to produce. In some cases, however, it is a limit on what can be produced which limits sales. Limited production might stem from a shortage of any factor of production—labour, raw materials, space, machinery, etc.

The most profitable combination of products will occur where the contribution per unit of the **limiting factor** is maximised.

A business provides three different services, the details of which are as follows:

Service (code name)	AX107	AX109	AX220
Selling price per unit	$50	$40	$65
Variable cost per unit	$25	$20	$35
Contribution per unit	$25	$20	$30
Labour time per unit	5 hours	3 hours	6 hours

EXAMPLE 7.5

Within reason the market will take as many units of each service as can be provided, but the ability to provide the service is limited by the availability of labour, all of which needs to be skilled. Fixed costs are not affected by the choice of service provided because provision of all three services uses the same production facilities. What is the most profitable service, given the limited number of labour hours available?

The most profitable service is AX109 because it generates a contribution of $6.67 (i.e. $20 / 3) per hour. The other two generate only $5.00 each per hour ($25 / 5 and $30 / 6).

Your first reaction may have been that the business should provide service AX220 only, because this is the one that yields the highest contribution per unit sold. If so, you are making the mistake of thinking of the ability to sell as being the limiting factor. If you are not convinced by the above analysis, take an imaginary number of available labour hours and ask yourself what is the maximum contribution (and therefore profit) that could be made by providing each service exclusively. Bear in mind that there is no shortage of anything else, including market demand, just a shortage of labour.

ACTIVITY 7.11

A business makes three different products, the details of which are as follows:

Product (code name)	B14	B17	B22
Selling price per unit	$25	$20	$23
Variable cost per unit	$10	$8	$12
Weekly demand (units)	25	20	30
Machine time per unit	4 hours	3 hours	4 hours

Fixed costs are not affected by the choice of product because all three products use the same machine. Machine time is limited to 148 hours a week.

Which combination of products should be manufactured if the business is to produce the highest profit?

ACTIVITY 7.12

What steps could be contemplated that could lead to a higher level of contribution for the business in Activity 7.11?

ACTIVITY 7.13

Going back to Activity 7.11, what is the maximum price that the business concerned would logically be prepared to pay to have the remaining B14s machined by a subcontractor, assuming that no fixed or variable costs would be saved as a result of not doing the machining 'in house'?

Would there be a different maximum if we were considering the B22s?

MAKE OR BUY DECISIONS

Businesses are frequently confronted by the need to decide whether to produce the product or service which they sell themselves or buy it in from some other business. Thus a producer of electrical appliances might decide to subcontract the manufacture of one of its products to another business, perhaps because there is a shortage of production capacity in the producer's own factory or because it believes it to be cheaper to subcontract than to make the appliance itself.

It might just be part of a product that is subcontracted. For example, the producer may have a component for the appliance made by another manufacturer. In principle, there is hardly any limit to the scope of make or buy decisions. Virtually any part, component or service required in production of the main product or service or the main product or service itself could be the subject of a make or buy decision. So, for example, the personnel function of a business, which is normally performed 'in house', could be subcontracted. At the same time, electrical power, which is typically provided by an outside electrical utility business, could be generated 'in house'.

Jones Ltd needs a component for one of its products. It can subcontract production of the component to a subcontractor who will provide the components for $20 each. The business can produce the components internally for total variable costs of $15 per component.

Jones Ltd has spare capacity. Should the component be subcontracted or produced internally?

The answer is that Jones Ltd should produce the component internally since the variable cost of subcontracting is greater by $5 than the variable cost of internal manufacture.

EXAMPLE 7.6

ACTIVITY 7.14

Shah Ltd needs a component for one of its products. It can subcontract production of the component to a subcontractor who will provide the components for $20 each. The business can produce the components internally for total variable costs of $15 per component.

Shah Ltd has no spare capacity, so it can only produce the component internally by reducing its output of another of its products. While it is making each component it will lose contributions of $12 from the other product.

Should the component be subcontracted or produced internally?

ACTIVITY 7.15

What factors, other than the immediately financially quantifiable, would you consider when making a make or buy decision?

CLOSING OR CONTINUANCE OF A SECTION OR DEPARTMENT

It is quite common for businesses to account separately for each department or section to try to assess the relative effectiveness of each one.

Goodsports Ltd is a retail shop that operates through three departments all in the same premises. The three departments occupy roughly equal areas of the premises.

The trading results for the year just finished showed the following:

EXAMPLE 7.7

	Total $'000	Sports equipment $'000	Sports clothes $'000	General clothes $'000
Sales	534	254	183	97
Costs	482	213	163	106
Profit/(loss)	52	41	20	(9)

It would appear that if the general clothes department were to close, the business would be more profitable, by $9,000 a year, assuming last year's performance to be a reasonable indication of future performance.

When the costs are analysed between those that are variable and those that are fixed, however, the following results were obtained:

	Total $'000	Sports equipment $'000	Sports clothes $'000	General clothes $'000
Sales	534	254	183	97
Variable costs	344	167	117	60
Contribution	190	87	66	37
Fixed costs (rent, etc.)	138	46	46	46
Profit/(loss)	52	41	20	(9)

Now it is obvious that closing the general clothes department, without any other developments, would make the business worse off by $37,000 (the department's contribution). The department should not be closed, because it makes a positive contribution. The fixed costs would continue whether the department closed or not. As can be seen from the above analysis, distinguishing between variable and fixed costs can make the picture a great deal clearer.

ACTIVITY 7.16

In our consideration of the Goodsports Ltd example, it was stated that the general clothes department should not be closed 'without any other developments'.

What 'other developments' could affect this decision, either making continuation more attractive or less attractive?

SELF-ASSESSMENT QUESTION 7.1

Khan Ltd can make three products (A, B and C) using the same machines. Various estimates for next year have been made as follows:

Product	A $	B $	C $
Selling price	30	39	20
Variable material cost	15	18	10
Other variable production costs	6	10	5
Share of fixed overheads	8	12	4
Time per unit required on machines (hours)	2	3	1

Fixed overhead costs for next year are expected to total $40,000.

Required:

(a) If the business were to make only product A next year, how many units would it need to make in order to break even? (Assume for this part of the question that there is no effective limit to market size and production capacity.)

(b) If the business has maximum machine capacity for next year of 10,000 hours, in which order of preference would the three products come?

(c) The maximum market for next year for the three products is as follows:

- Product A   3,000 units
- Product B   2,000 units
- Product C   5,000 units

What quantities of which product should the business make next year and how much profit would this be expected to yield?

SUMMARY

In this chapter we have achieved the following objectives in the way shown:

OBJECTIVE	METHOD ACHIEVED
Explain the importance of a detailed understanding of cost behaviour	• Illustrated relationships between volume and costs
Distinguish between fixed costs and variable costs	• Explained the nature of fixed and variable costs • Analysed costs and separation of the components of semi-variable costs into fixed and variable
Use knowledge of this distinction to deduce the break-even point for some activity	• Illustrated and prepared a break-even chart • Calculated break-even point
Explain why knowledge of the break-even point is useful	• Illustrated the uses to which break-even analysis can be put
Explain and apply the concept of contribution	• Illustrated the concept of contribution • Applied it to specific situations
Explain the concept of a margin of safety	• Illustrated the concept of margin of safety • Explained the concept of operating gearing
Identify the weaknesses of break-even analysis	• Identified problems such as non-linearity, stepped costs and multi-product businesses
Use a spreadsheet to develop a profit profile and associated charts, using historic or forecast costs, for simple and more complex relationships	• illustrated use of spreadsheets and related chart development • used both historic and forecast figures • illustrated more complex relationships

313

ACCOUNTING an introduction

OBJECTIVE	METHOD ACHIEVED
Explain and apply the idea of relevant costing	• Explained the concept • Applied it to a number of situations
Make decisions on the use of spare capacity, using knowledge of the relationship between fixed and variable costs	• Illustrated and applied the concepts to this area
Make decisions about the acceptance (or continuance) or rejection of a particular contract or activity, based on knowledge of the relationship between fixed and variable costs	• Illustrated and applied the concepts to this area
Choose between products when certain inputs are in scarce supply	• Illustrated and applied the concepts to this area
Identify whether it is better to buy a component or to make it, under specified circumstances	• Illustrated and applied the concepts to this area

DISCUSSION QUESTIONS

EASY

<Obj 1, 2> 7.1 Define the terms 'fixed cost' and 'variable cost'.

<Obj 1, 2> 7.2 In relation to classifying costs as 'fixed' or 'variable', the relevant range of activity is important. What is meant by the term 'relevant range'? How does it relate to the classification of costs into fixed and variable costs?

<Obj 2> 7.3 For a restaurant, list probable fixed costs.

<Obj 2> 7.4 For a service station, list possible variable costs.

<Obj 6> 7.5 What is the 'margin of safety'? Why is it important?

INTERMEDIATE

<Obj 1, 2> 7.6 Some costs are classified as semi-variable. What is a semi-variable cost? Provide examples in relation to a transport company. How does regression analysis assist in analysing semi-variable costs?

<Obj 3, 4, 5> 7.7 What is meant by the 'break-even point' for an activity? How is the break-even point calculated? Distinguish between a 'break-even chart' and a 'profit–volume chart'.

<Obj 4, 7> 7.8 What are the assumptions that underlie cost–volume–profit analysis? To what extent do these assumptions limit the usefulness of this analysis?

<Obj 5> 7.9 When we say that some business activity has 'high operating gearing', what do we mean?

<Obj 5>   **7.10** Contribution represents the unit selling price less the unit variable cost. How can this measure be used in break-even analysis? How does it relate to the concept of 'operating gearing'?

<Obj 9>   **7.11** What are 'relevant' costs in a decision-making context?

<Obj 10>   **7.12** Where there is a scarce resource, management should strive to maximise the contribution per unit of the limiting factor. What is meant by a scarce resource? How do we maximise the contribution per unit of the limiting factor? Should other factors be taken into consideration?

<Obj 10, 11> **7.13** If there is a scarce resource which is restricting sales, how will the business maximise its profit?

<Obj 11, 12> **7.14** If there is spare capacity should all contracts that contribute to fixed costs be accepted?

CHALLENGING

<Obj 13>   **7.15** Why might a business logically continue to make a product when it could be acquired externally at a cheaper total unit price?

APPLICATION EXERCISES

EASY

<Obj 1, 2, 3, 6> **7.1** From the following planned income statement construct a break-even chart and:
(a) find the break-even point
(b) find the margin of safety
(c) estimate the sales necessary for a profit of $5,000.

Sales	10,000 units @ $6 each	$60,000
Variable costs	10,000 units @ $3.50 each	$35,000
Fixed costs		$15,000

Convert this information into a profit–volume chart.

<Obj 3>   **7.2** A company breaks even with sales of $600,000. What profit will it make if it sells $800,000 worth of goods, the variable costs of which are $600,000? You may assume that variable costs change directly in proportion to sales.

<Obj 3>   **7.3** Given the situation where sales are $600,000 (at $10 per unit), fixed costs are $100,000 and profits are $100,000, what is the break-even point?

<Obj 3, 4>   **7.4** A company can sell its products for $15 each. The variable costs of each product are $10. Fixed costs are $20,000. Find:
(a) the break-even sales volume
(b) the sales volume needed to make a profit of $25,000
(c) the profit if sales revenues total $90,000.

<Obj 3, 4>   **7.5**   Lannion and Co. is engaged in providing and marketing a standard cleaning service. Summarised results for the past two months reveal the following:

	October	November
Sales (units of the service)	200	300
Sales ($)	5,000	7,500
Operating profit ($)	1,000	2,200

There were no price changes of any description during these two months.
(a) Deduce the break-even point (in units of the service) for Lannion.
(b) State why the company might find it useful to know its break-even point.

INTERMEDIATE

<Obj 2>   **7.6**   The following diagrams represent total cost patterns related to the activity level (volume) for different cost types.

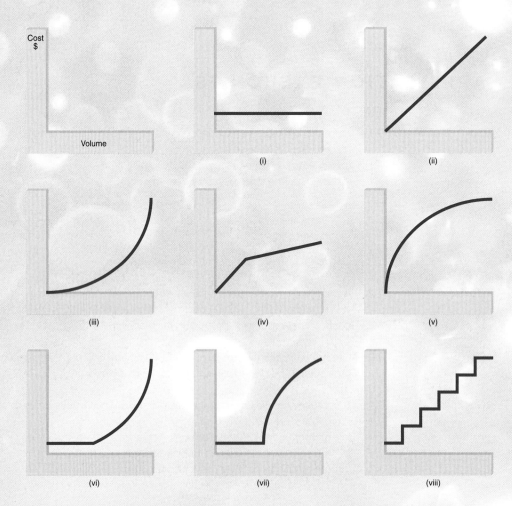

(i)   (ii)   (iii)   (iv)   (v)   (vi)   (vii)   (viii)

Required:

For the following costs select the diagram that you think most closely reflects that cost type and explain your selection.

1. Depreciation of a motor vehicle
2. Building insurance
3. Timber used in the manufacture of a table
4. A service contract for computer maintenance
5. Electricity
6. Telephone
7. Photocopying
8. Supervision.

<Obj 3>   **7.7**   Brown and Co. makes and sells a single product line. Summarised results for the past two months reveal the following:

	May	June
Sales (units of the product)	500	650
	$	$
Sales	7,500	9,750
Materials	2,000	2,600
Labour	3,000	3,900
Overheads	1,500	1,800
	6,500	8,300
Operating profit	1,000	1,450

There were no price changes of any description during these two months.

Deduce the break-even point (in units of the service) for Brown and Co.

(*Hint*: If there were no price changes over the two months, what is the only possible reason for the sales revenue and expenses figures being different from one month to the next?)

<Obj 3, 4, 5>   **7.8**   You are given the following information for a company for two successive periods.

	Period 6	Period 7
Materials	$300,000	$360,000
Labour	$212,000	$247,000
Overheads	$418,000	$453,000
Production level	10,000 units	12,000 units

All production is sold for $100 per unit.

Estimate the fixed costs and break-even point.

It is now proposed to introduce a machine whereby fixed costs will rise by $116,000 and variable costs will fall by $10 per unit. Estimate:

(a) the new break-even point
(b) the sales necessary to maintain profits at $140,000, using the new machine.

ACCOUNTING an introduction

<Obj 5>   **7.9**   Selected operating data for four (4) independent situations are shown below:

		A	B	C	D
Sales	$	120,000			100,000
Variable expense	$		30,000		
Fixed expense	$		15,000	18,000	52,000
Net income (loss)	$	10,000	10,000	12,000	(12,000)
Units sold	#	20,000	500		2,500
Contribution margin	$	4		3	
Contribution margin ratio*				0.40	

* (selling price per unit – variable cost per unit) ÷ selling price per unit.

Required:
Fill in the blanks for each independent situation together with supporting calculations.

CHALLENGING

<Obj 3, 4, 5, 8>   **7.10**   During the last three-month period B Ltd showed a net loss of $20,000 and the directors are holding a meeting to discuss what action to take. Each director has a proposal for consideration and you have been invited to attend and submit figures showing the result of each proposal. The one matter on which all the directors agree is a profit target of $40,000 for the next period.

You have the following information in respect of the last period and also for the period immediately preceding it:

	Last period	Preceding period
Production and sales	9,000 units	11,000 units
Revenues	$630,000	$770,000
Total costs	$650,000	$750,000
Result	$20,000 loss	$20,000 profit

Both of the above outputs were within the normal range of activity. It is estimated, however, that if the output exceeds 12,000 units the variable costs will increase by $10 for each unit in excess of 12,000.

The following proposals are put forward:
1. Improve packaging of the product at a cost of $2.50 per unit in an effort to increase sales.
2. Launch an advertising campaign costing $20,000 in an effort to increase sales.
3. Reduce selling price by $2.50 per unit.
4. Buy more efficient machinery which will reduce the variable costs per unit by $10. Fixed costs at present include $40,000 per annum depreciation in respect of the machinery to be replaced.

Required:
(a) Show how the figures for fixed and variable costs could be calculated.
(b) Assuming that the variable costs were $50 per unit and the fixed costs were $200,000, show the increases in sales necessary under each of the first three proposals to achieve the profit target.

318

<Obj 5>

(c) Show the amount which could be invested in new machinery under proposal 4, assuming that depreciation of 20 per cent per annum will be provided and that output will remain at 9,000 units.

Ignore inflation.

7.11 Contribution Margin Exercises

Information for four independent companies is presented below:

(a) W Ltd wishes to attain a before-tax net profit equal to 20% of sales revenue. Variable costs are 60% of sales and fixed costs are $360 000. Calculate the dollar amount of sales necessary for achieving the profit goal.

(b) X Ltd incurs variable costs of $24 per unit for a product that has a selling price of $36. If the break-even point is $84 000 of annual sales, what are the company's annual fixed costs?

(c) Y Ltd has annual fixed costs of $76 000. The variable costs are $5 per unit and the break-even point is 8,000 units. What is the selling price per unit?

(d) Z Ltd has a product that sells for $73 and is produced at a variable cost of $59 per unit. The variable costs can be reduced by 25% by installing a new piece of equipment. Installation of the new equipment will increase fixed costs from the present level of $120,000 to $170,000. Calculate the present break-even point and the new break-even point if the equipment is installed.

<Obj 8, 9, 10>

7.12 A hotel group prepares accounts on a quarterly basis. The senior management is reviewing the performance of one hotel and making plans for 2007.

They have in front of them the results for 2006 (based on some actual results and some forecasts to the end of 2006).

Quarter	Sales	Profit/(loss)
	$	$
1	400,000	(280,000)
2	1,200,000	360,000
3	1,600,000	680,000
4	800,000	40,000

The total estimated number of visitors (guest nights) for 2006 is 50,000. The results follow a regular pattern; there are no unexpected cost fluctuations beyond the seasonal trading pattern exhibited. The management intends to incorporate into their plans for 2007 an anticipated increase in unit variable costs of 10 per cent and a profit target for the hotel of $1 million.

(a) Determine the total variable and total fixed costs of the hotel for 2006, by the use of a PV chart or by calculation.

(b) (i) If there is no increase in visitors for 2007, what will be the required revenue rate per hotel visitor to meet the profit target?

(ii) If the required revenue rate per visitor is not raised above the 2006 level, how many visitors are required to meet the profit target?

(c) Outline and briefly discuss the assumptions that are contained within the accountants' typical PV or break-even analysis and assess whether they limit its usefulness.

<Obj 9, 10>

7.13 A company makes three products, A, B and C. All three products require the use of two types of machine, cutting machines and assembling machines. Estimates for next year include the following:

	Product A	Product B	Product C
Selling price (per unit)	$25.00	$30.00	$18.00
Sales demand (units)	2,500	3,400	5,100
Direct material cost (per unit)	$12.00	$13.00	$10.00
Variable production cost (per unit)	$7.00	$4.00	$3.00
Time required per unit on cutting machines	1.0 hours	1.0 hours	0.5 hours
Time required per unit on assembling machines	0.5 hours	1.0 hours	0.5 hours

Fixed overhead costs for next year are expected to total $42,000. It is the company's policy for each unit of production to absorb these in proportion to its total variable costs.

The company has cutting machine capacity of 5,000 hours per annum and assembling machine capacity of 8,000 hours per annum.

Required:

(a) State, with supporting workings, which products in which quantities the company should plan to make next year on the basis of the above information.

(b) State the maximum price per product that it would be worth the company paying a subcontractor to carry out that part of the work that could not be done internally.

<Obj 9, 10>

7.14 Darmor Ltd has three products that require the same production facilities. Information about their per unit production costs is as follows:

Product	A	B	C
	$	$	$
Labour—skilled	18	27	9
—unskilled	6	12	30
Materials	36	75	42
Variable overheads	9	21	21
Share of fixed overheads	15	30	30

All labour and materials are variable costs. Skilled labour is paid a basic rate of $18 an hour and unskilled labour is paid a basic rate of $12 an hour. The labour costs per unit, shown above, are based on basic rates of pay. Skilled labour is scarce, which means that the company could not sell more than the maximum it is able to make of any of the three products.

Product A is sold in a regulated market and the regulators have set a price of $90 per unit for it.

(a) State, with supporting workings, the price which must be charged for products B and C such that the company would be indifferent between making and selling any of the three products.

(b) State, with supporting workings, the maximum rate of overtime premium that the company would logically be prepared to pay its skilled workers to work beyond the basic time.

<Obj 9, 11>   **7.15**   Walker Ltd has furnished the following information for the year to 31 May 2006:

	$'000
Sales for the year—20,000 units (80% capacity)	1,600
Direct materials	500
Direct labour	200
Variable overheads	100

Break-even point is at 65% capacity.

Plans for the year to 31 May 2007 include the following:

- Selling price is to remain the same.
- Costs are expected to increase as follows:

Direct materials	2%
Direct wages	15%
Variable overheads	10%
Fixed overheads	No increase up to 100% capacity

- An order has been received from abroad, at a price which is 20 per cent lower than the domestic price, for 12,500 units to be supplied during the year. The order must be accepted in its entirety or be rejected.
- Home demand is unlikely to change.

Three options are being considered:
1. Reject the order.
2. Accept the order, work to 100 per cent capacity and turn away excess home demand.
3. Increase factory capacity so that the overseas order can be accepted and home demand met. This would involve purchasing new machinery at a cost of $500,000, increasing overheads by $125,000 (depreciation of $75,000 and $50,000 interest on borrowed capital), and renting additional factory space at a cost of $25,000 per annum.

    Advise management as to the most profitable option and calculate the net profit to be expected.

<Obj 10>   **7.16**   The management of your company is concerned about its inability to obtain enough fully trained labour to enable it to meet its present budget projection.

Product	Alpha	Beta	Gamma	Total
	$	$	$	$
Direct costs				
Materials	6,000	4,000	5,000	15,000
Labour	9,000	6,000	12,000	27,000
Expenses	3,000	2,000	2,000	7,000
Allocated fixed costs	13,000	8,000	12,000	33,000
Total cost	31,000	20,000	31,000	82,000
Profit	8,000	9,000	2,000	19,000
Sales	39,000	29,000	33,000	101,000

The amount of labour likely to be available amounts to $20,000. You have been asked to prepare a statement ensuring that at least 50 per cent of the budgeted sales are achieved for each product and the balance of labour used to produce the greatest profit.

(a) Prepare a statement showing the greatest profit available from the limited amount of skilled labour available, within the constraint stated.

(b) Provide an explanation of the method you have used.

(c) Provide an indication of any other factors that need to be considered.

<Obj 12>   **7.17** Noel Ltd makes three carton lots of products using the same machines. Various estimates for next year have been made as follows. Fixed overhead costs for next year are expected to total $30,000.

Product	A	B	C
	$	$	$
Selling Price	30	39	20
Variable material costs	15	18	10
Other variable production costs	6	10	5
Time per unit required on machines (hours)	0.5	0.7	0.3

Required:

(a) If the business were to make only B next year, how many cartons would it need to make in order to break-even assuming that there is no effective limit to market size or production capacity?

(b) If the business has maximum machine capacity for the next year of 10,000 hours, what will be the production priority for the three products if the demand for each product is 10,000 cartons per year.

(c) There is no restriction on machine hours, but the amount of variable material available is limited to $300,000.
   (1) What will be the production priorities?
   (2) How much profit would this be expected to yield?

CASE STUDY 7.1

The directors of a company are considering the following proposed budget for the year:

Summary of budget estimates			
Capacity 500,000 units			
Budgeted output 320,000 units			
	$	$	$
Sales			640,000
Cost of sales			
Factory			
Material	280,000		
Labour	96,000		
Variable overheads	64,000		
Fixed overheads	52,000		
		492,000	

Selling		
Commission	64,000	
Variable expenses	40,000	
Fixed expenses	10,000	
		114,000
Administration		
Variable expenses	16,000	
Fixed expenses	14,000	
	30,000	
		636,000
Budgeted profit		4,000

Note: Sales commission is equal to 10 per cent of sales.

The budgeted profit is not satisfactory and various proposals are put forward as to how the position could be improved.

1. The managing director would like to know the position if selling prices were increased by 7.5 per cent and an additional $40,000 spent on advertising to maintain the present budgeted output.
2. The production director feels the answer is an increased output. The sales director states that he could have the factory working at 100 per cent capacity if he were allowed to reduce selling prices by 5 per cent. He wishes to know what profit would be under these conditions and at what level of output the company would 'break even'.
3. The marketing director is opposed to proposal 2. He considers that more should be spent on sales promotion. He estimates that a sales promotion costing $15,000 would result in sales of 400,000 units per annum. He wishes to know what profit this would result in, and the maximum amount he could spend to achieve the desired sales level and not reduce profit below the $4,000 budgeted.
4. The sales director also reports that a European distributor is quite willing to take 100,000 units per annum, provided a reasonable selling price can be agreed. The quality required, however, would involve increased factory variable costs of 12.5 cents per unit and the company would pay half the distribution costs (estimated to total $30,000 per annum). No sales commission would, however, be payable. What is the minimum price at which the proposal could be accepted? What considerations would need to be taken into account in determining the finally agreed price?

---

1   Calculate the break-even point on the basis of the budgeted figures.
2   Prepare statements answering all the points raised, and comment on each one.
3   Identify the behavioural factors that are likely to be driving each of the proposals and consider how you might deal with these.

CASE STUDY 7.2

A business has the following revenue/cost patterns for the last three months:

Sales	10,000 units at $10 each
Variable costs	10,000 units at $5 each
Fixed costs	$40,000

Price indices for the period stood on average at 150 for variable costs and 200 for fixed costs. The equivalent figures are expected to be 155 and 210 for the next three months. Selling price is expected to increase by 3 per cent over the next three months.

If production and sales exceed 12,000 units, some old plant and equipment will need to be used. The variable cost per unit (for production in excess of 12,000 units) will then increase by a further 10 per cent, while fixed costs are expected to increase by $5,000.

It is expected that sales will only exceed 14,000 units if the selling price of the excess is reduced to $8 each. You may assume that these sales will be to a separate overseas market and will have no impact on domestic sales. Maximum production capacity is 15,000 units.

1 Using the information relating to the next three months, calculate (preferably using a spreadsheet):
   (a) the break-even point
   (b) the level of profits for output levels of 10,000 units, 11,000 units, 12,000 units, 13,000 units, 14,000 units and 15,000 units.
2 Prepare a break-even chart.

SOLUTIONS TO ACTIVITIES

Activity 7.1

We came up with the following:

- Rent
- Insurance
- Cleaning costs
- Staff salaries.

Staff salaries and wages are sometimes discussed in books as being variable costs. In fact, they tend to be fixed. People are generally not paid according to the level of output and it is not normal to sack staff when there is a short-term downturn in activity. If there is a long-term downturn in activity, or at least it looks that way to management, redundancies may occur, with fixed cost savings. This, however, is true of all costs. If there is seen to be a likely reduction in demand the business may decide to close some branches and make rent cost savings. Thus 'fixed' does not mean set in stone for all times; it usually means 'fixed' over the short to medium term.

Activity 7.2

In fact, the rent is only fixed over a particular range (known as the 'relevant' range). If the number of people wanting to have their hair cut, etc., by the business increased it would have to expand its physical size eventually. It might do this by opening additional branches, or perhaps by moving existing branches to larger premises in the same vicinity. It may be possible to cope with relatively minor increases in activity by using existing space more efficiently or having longer opening hours. If activity continued to expand, increased rent charges would seem inevitable. In practice the situation would look something like that in Figure 7.2, with the cost being rent.

Activity 7.3

We can think of a couple:

- Lotions and other materials used.
- Laundry costs to wash towels used to dry the hair of customers.

As with many types of business activity, variable costs of hairdressers tend to be relatively light in comparison to fixed costs—that is, fixed costs tend to make up the bulk of total costs.

Activity 7.4

The usefulness of being able to deduce the break-even point is to compare the planned or expected level of activity with the break-even point and so make a judgment concerning the riskiness of the activity. Operating only just above the level of activity necessary in order to break even may indicate that it is a risky venture, since only a small fall from the planned level of activity could lead to a loss.

Activity 7.5

Estimated profit, per month, from basket making:

	Without the machine		With the machine	
	$	$	$	$
Sales (500 × $30)		15,000		15,000
Less				
Materials (500 × $6)	3,000		3,000	
Labour (500 × 2 × $9)	9,000			
(500 × 1 × $9)			4,500	
Fixed costs	1,500		6,000	
		13,500		13,500
Profit		1,500		1,500

The break-even point (in number of baskets) with the machine

= Fixed costs / Sales revenue per unit – Variable costs per unit)

= $6,000 / [$30 – (6 + 9)] = 400 baskets per month

The break-even point without the machine is 250 baskets per month (see Example 7.1).

There seems to be nothing to choose between the two manufacturing strategies regarding profit at the estimated sales volume. There is, however, a distinct difference between the two strategies regarding the break-even point. Without the machine, the actual level of sales could fall by half of that which is expected (from 500 to 250) before the business would fail to make a profit. With the machine a 20 per cent fall (from 500 to 400) would be enough to cause the business to fail to make a profit. On the other hand, for each additional basket sold above the estimated 500 an additional profit of only $6 (i.e. $30 – 6 – 18) would be made without the machine, whereas $15 (i.e. $30 – 6 – 9) would be made with the machine.

Activity 7.6

It is a matter of personal judgment, which in turn is related to individual attitudes to risk, as to which strategy to adopt. Most people, however, would prefer the strategy of not renting the machine since the 'margin of safety' between the expected level of activity and the break-even point is much greater. The margin of safety gives the extent to which the planned level of output or sales lies above the break-even point.

Activity 7.7

In general, activities that are capital intensive tend to be more highly geared since renting or owning capital equipment gives rise to fixed costs and can also give rise to lower variable costs.

Activity 7.8

	2005	2006
Selling price per unit	100	102
Variable cost per unit	60	63
Contribution per unit	40	39
Total contribution	400,000	390,000
Fixed costs	250,000	275,000
Profit	150,000	115,000

Break-even point (fixed costs/contribution)

	6,250	7,051

Activity 7.9

Using the high/low method the figures can be calculated as follows:

Difference in costs / difference in output = variable cost per unit

Materials	$4,000 / 4,000 = $1
Labour	$1,500 / 4,000 = 37.5c
Overheads	$500 / 4,000 = 12.5c

At an output level of 20,000 units this implies total variable costs of:

Materials (20,000 × $1)	$20,000
Labour (20,000 × 37.5c)	$7,500
Overheads (20,000 × 12.5c)	$2,500

The difference between these figures and the total figures for each type of cost will give an estimate of fixed costs, as follows:

Materials	nil
Labour	$2,500
Overheads	$7,500

These figures could then be used to carry out CVP analysis and to prepare associated charts, with the figure for variable costs per unit being based on an estimated $1.50, while that for fixed costs would be based on an estimated $10,000.

Activity 7.10

Since the fixed costs will be incurred in any case, they are not relevant to this decision. All we need to do is to see whether the price offered will yield a contribution. If it will, the business will be better off by accepting the contract than by refusing it. We know that the variable costs per basket total $24; thus each basket will yield a contribution of $3 (i.e. $27 – 24)—$900 in all. Whatever else may be happening to the business, it will be $900 better off by taking this contract than by refusing it.

Activity 7.11

Product	B14	B17	B22
Selling price per unit	$25	$20	$23
Variable cost per unit	$10	$8	$12
Contribution per unit	$15	$12	$11
Machine time per unit	4 hours	3 hours	4 hours
Contribution per machine hour	$3.75	$4.00	$2.75
Order of priority	2nd	1st	3rd

Therefore:

Produce	20 units of product B17 using	60 hours
	22 units of product B14 using	88 hours
		148 hours

This leaves unsatisfied the market demand for a further three units of product B14 and 30 units of product B22.

Activity 7.12

The possibilities for improving matters which occurred to us are as follows:

- Contemplate obtaining additional machine time. This could mean obtaining a new machine, subcontracting the machining to another business or, perhaps, squeezing a few more hours per week out of the business's own machine. Perhaps a combination of two or more of these is a possibility.
- Redesign the products in a way that requires less time per unit on the machine.
- Increase the price per unit of the three products. This may well have the effect of dampening demand, but the existing demand cannot be met at present and it may be more profitable, in the long run, to make a greater contribution on each unit sold than to take one of the other courses of action to overcome the problem.

Activity 7.13

If the remaining three B14s were subcontracted at no cost, the business would be able to earn a contribution of $15 which it would not otherwise be able to gain. For any price up to $15 per unit, therefore, it would be worth paying a subcontractor to undertake the machining. Naturally the business would prefer to pay as little as possible, but anything up to $15 would still make it worthwhile to subcontract the machining.

This would not be true of the B22s because they have a different contribution per unit; $11 would be the relevant figure in their case.

Activity 7.14

The answer is to subcontract.

The relevant cost of internal production of each component is:

	$
Variable cost of production of the component	15
Opportunity cost of lost production of the other product	12
	$27

This is obviously more costly than the $20 per component which will have to be paid to the subcontractor. Therefore production of the component should be subcontracted.

Activity 7.15

We feel that there are two main factors:

1. The general problems of subcontracting:

   - loss of control of quality
   - potential unreliability of supply.

2. Expertise and specialisation. It is possible for most businesses, with sufficient determination, to do virtually everything 'in house'. This may, however, require a level of skill and facilities which most businesses do not have nor feel inclined to acquire. For example, although it is true that most businesses could generate their own electricity, their managements tend to take the view that this is better done by a specialist generating business.

Activity 7.16

The things we could think of are as follows:

- Expansion of the other departments or replacing the general clothes department with a completely new activity. This would only make sense if the space currently occupied by the general clothes department could generate contributions totalling at least $37,000 a year.
- Subletting the space occupied by the general clothes department. Once again, this would need to generate a net figure of $37,000 a year to make it more financially beneficial than keeping the department open.
- There may be advantages in keeping the department open even if it generated no contribution (assuming no other use for the space). This is because customers may be attracted into the shop because it has general clothing and they may then buy something from one of the other departments. By the same token the activity of a subtenant might attract customers into the shop. On the other hand, it might drive them away.

OBJECTIVES

When you have completed your study of this chapter you should be able to:

1 deduce the full cost of a unit of output in a single-product (single-service) environment

2 distinguish between direct and indirect costs

3 use this distinction to deduce the full cost of a job in a multi-product (multi-service) environment

4 discuss the problem of charging overheads to jobs in a multi-product (multi-service) environment, including the role of activity-based costing

5 explain cost drivers

6 explain the nature and role of activity-based costing

7 identify and explain the main uses of full cost information

8 identify the main criticisms of full costing

9 apply the concepts of relevant costing and full costing in an appropriate manner in a number of decision-making situations.

8

FULL COSTING

In this chapter we are going to look at an approach to deducing the cost of a unit of output which takes account of all of the costs. This approach is one that is very widely used in practice. The precise approach taken tends to depend on whether each unit output is identical to the next or whether each job has its own individual characteristics. It also tends to depend on whether the business accounts for overheads on a departmental basis or not. We shall look at how full costing is done, including the use of 'activity-based costing'. We shall then consider the usefulness of full costing for management purposes. Finally, we shall provide some illustrations as to how the concepts of relevant costing and full costing are applied in decision-making situations.

THE NATURE OF FULL COSTING

With full costing we are not concerned with variable costs, but with all costs involved with achieving some objective—for example, making a particular product. The logic of full costing is that all of the costs of running a particular facility—say, a factory—are part of the cost of the output of that factory. For example, the rent may be a cost that will not alter merely because we make one more unit of production, but if the factory were not rented there would be nowhere for production to take place, so rent is an important element of the cost of each unit of output.

 Full cost is the total amount of resources, usually measured in monetary terms, sacrificed to achieve a particular objective. It takes account of all resources sacrificed to achieve the objective. Thus if the objective was to supply a customer with a service or product, delivery of the service or product to the customer's premises would normally be included as part of the full cost.

If a business is trying to set prices for its output that will lead to the business making a profit, the prices charged must cover all costs. As we shall see later, pricing is one of the uses to which full cost information is put in practice.

DERIVING FULL COSTS IN A SINGLE-PRODUCT/SINGLE-SERVICE OPERATION

The simplest case for which to deduce the full cost per unit is where the business only has one product line or service—that is, each unit of its product or service is identical. Here it is simply a question of adding up all the costs of production incurred in the period (materials, labour, rent, fuel and power, etc.) and dividing this total by the total number of units of output for the period.

ACTIVITY 8.1

Rustic Breweries Ltd has just one product, a bitter beer which is marketed as 'Old Rustic'. During last month the company produced 4,300 litres of the product. The costs incurred were as follows:

	$
Ingredients	800
Fuel	250
Rent of brewery premises	900
Wear and tear of brewery equipment	200

What is the full cost per litre of producing 'Old Rustic'?

While the full cost can be found in this case quite simply by adding all of the costs and dividing by the number of litres produced, in practice there can be minor problems of deciding exactly how much cost was incurred. In the case of Rustic Breweries Ltd, for example, how is the cost of wear and tear deduced? It is almost certainly an estimate and so its reliability is open to question. Should we use the 'relevant' cost of the raw materials (almost certainly the replacement cost) or the actual price paid for the materials used? If it is worth calculating the cost per litre it must be because this information will be used for some decision-making purpose, so the replacement cost is probably more logical. In practice, however, it seems that historic costs are more often used to deduce full costs.

There can also be problems in deciding precisely how many units of output there were. Brewing beer is not a very fast process. This means that there is likely to be some beer that is in the process of being brewed at any given moment. This means that part of the costs incurred last month was in respect of some beer that was 'work-in-progress' at the end of the month and is not, therefore, included in the output quantity of 4,300 litres. Similarly, part of the 4,300 litres was started and incurred costs in the previous month, yet all of those litres were included in the 4,300 litres that we used in our calculation of the cost per litre. Work-in-progress is not a serious problem, but account does need to be taken of it if reliable full cost information is to be obtained.

This approach to full costing is often referred to as **process costing**.

MULTI-PRODUCT OPERATIONS

In many situations in which full costing is used, the units of output of the product or service are not identical. In such situations it will therefore not normally be acceptable to adopt the approach that we used with litres of 'Old Rustic' in Activity 8.1. For example, whereas customers would expect to pay the same price for each litre of a particular type of beer they buy, most people would not expect to pay the same price for each car repair carried out by a particular garage, without regard to the complexity and size of the repair. So, while it is reasonable to price litres of beer equally because the litres are identical, it is not acceptable to price widely different car repairs equally.

DIRECT AND INDIRECT COSTS

Where the units of output are not identical, we normally separate costs into two categories:

1. ***Direct costs***. These are costs that can be identified (or traced to) specific cost units. That is to say, the effect of the cost can be measured in respect of each particular unit of output. The normal examples of these are direct materials and direct labour. Collecting direct costs is a simple matter of having a cost recording system that is capable of capturing the cost of direct materials used on each job and the cost, based on the hours worked and the rate of pay, of direct workers.

2. ***Indirect costs (or overheads)***. These are all other product/service costs—that is, those that cannot be directly measured in respect of each particular unit of output.

   With both of these types of cost we include both production and non-production costs (such as marketing costs) as appropriate.

   We shall use the terms 'indirect costs' and 'overheads' interchangeably for the remainder of this book. Overheads are sometimes known as 'common costs' because they are common to all production of the production unit (for example, factory or department) for the period.

JOB COSTING

To deduce the full cost (usually referred to as costing) of a particular unit of output (or job) we usually ascribe all possible direct costs to the job which are allowed, by the definition of direct costs. We then seek to 'charge'

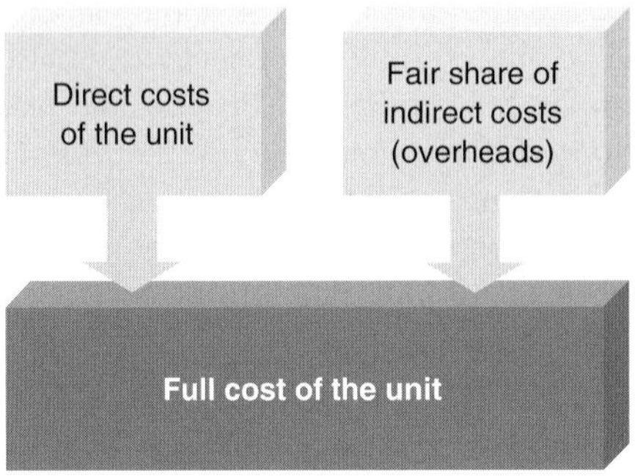

Direct costs of the unit

Fair share of indirect costs (overheads)

Full cost of the unit

FIGURE 8.1 The relationship between direct costs and indirect costs

each unit of output with a fair share of indirect costs. This is known as **job costing** and is shown graphically in Figure 8.1.

ACTIVITY 8.2

Sparky Ltd is a business that employs a number of electricians. The business undertakes a range of work for its customers, from minor repairs at one end of the range, to installing complete wiring systems in new houses at the other.

Into which category, direct or indirect, would each of the following costs fall in respect of a particular job done by Sparky Ltd?

- The wages of the electrician who did the job.
- Depreciation (wear and tear) of the tools used by the electrician.
- The salary of Sparky Ltd's accountant.
- The cost of cable and other materials used on the job.
- Rent of the premises where Sparky Ltd stores its stock of cable and other materials.

It is important to note that whether a cost is a direct one or an indirect one depends on the item being costed. People tend to refer to overheads without stating what the cost unit or object is; this is incorrect.

ACTIVITY 8.3

Into which category, direct or indirect, would each of the costs listed in Activity 8.2 fall if we were seeking to find the cost of operating the entire business of Sparky Ltd for a month?

Naturally, a cost unit that is defined broadly (e.g. operating Sparky Ltd for a month) tends to have a higher proportion of its costs identified as direct than do units that are more narrowly defined (such as a particular job—for example, a specific rewiring job for a particular customer). As we shall see shortly, this makes costing broader cost units rather more straightforward than costing narrower ones, since direct costs are easier to deal with.

THE COLLECTION OF COSTS AND THE BEHAVIOUR OF COSTS

We saw in Chapter 7 that the relationship between fixed and variable costs is that, between them, they make up the full cost (or **total cost**, as it is usually known in the context of marginal analysis). This is illustrated in Figure 8.2.

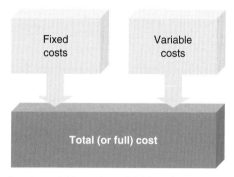

FIGURE 8.2 The relationship between fixed costs, variable costs and total costs

The similarity between what is shown in Figures 8.2 and 8.1 might lead us to believe that there might be some relationship between fixed, variable, direct and indirect costs. More specifically, some people seem to believe, mistakenly, that variable costs and direct costs are the same, as are fixed costs and overheads. This is incorrect.

The notion of fixed and variable costs is concerned entirely with the behaviour of costs in the face of changes to the volume of output. Directness of costs is entirely concerned with collecting together the elements that make up full cost—that is, with the extent to which costs can be measured directly in respect of particular units of output or jobs. These are entirely different concepts. Although it may be true that there is a tendency for fixed costs to be overheads and for variable costs to be direct costs, there is no automatic link and there are many exceptions to this tendency. For example, most operations have variable overheads. Also labour, a major element of direct cost in most production contexts, is usually a fixed cost, certainly over the short term.

To summarise this point, total cost is the sum of direct and indirect costs. It is also the sum of fixed and variable costs. These two facts are independent of one another. Thus a particular cost may, for example, be fixed relative to the level of output, on the one hand, and be either direct or indirect on the other.

The notion of distinguishing between direct and indirect costs is only related to deducing full cost in a job costing environment. You may recall that when we were considering costing a litre of 'Old Rustic' beer earlier in this chapter, whether particular elements of cost were direct or indirect was of absolutely no consequence. This was because *all* costs were shared equally between the litres of beer. Where we have units of output that are not identical we have to look more closely at the make-up of the costs to achieve a fair measure of the total cost of a particular job.

If the indirect costs of any activity form part of the cost of each unit of output, yet, by definition, they cannot be directly related to individual cost units, a major question is: how are they to be apportioned to individual cost units?

It is reasonable to view the overheads as rendering a service to the cost units. A manufactured product can be seen as having been rendered a service by the factory in which the product is made. In this sense, it is reasonable

333

to charge each cost unit with a share of the costs of running the factory (rent, lighting, heating, cleaning, building maintenance, etc.). It also seems reasonable to relate the charge for the 'use' of the factory to the level of service that the product received from the factory.

The next step is the difficult one. How might the cost of running the factory, which is a cost of all production, be apportioned (shared) between individual products that are not similar in size and/or complexity of manufacture?

One possibility is to share this overhead cost equally between each cost unit produced in the period. Most of us would not propose this method unless the cost units were close to being identical, in terms of the extent to which they had 'benefited' from the overheads.

If we are not to propose equal shares, we must identify something observable and measurable about the cost units that we feel provides a reasonable basis for distinguishing between one cost unit and the next.

In practice, time, measured by direct labour hours, is usually the basis that is most popular. It must be stressed that this is not the 'correct' way and it certainly is not the only way. We could, for example, use relative size of products as measured by weight or by relative material cost. Possibly we could use the relative lengths of time that each unit of output was worked on by machines.

EXAMPLE

8.1

Johnson Ltd has overheads of $30,000 each month. Each month 2,500 direct labour hours are worked and charged to units of output (the business's products). A particular job undertaken by the business used direct materials costing $138. Direct labour worked on the job was 15 hours and the wage rate is $15 an hour. Overheads are charged to jobs on a direct labour hour basis. What is the full cost of the job?

First, let us establish the 'overhead recovery rate' — that is, the rate at which jobs will be charged with overheads. This is $12 (i.e. $30,000 / 2,500) per direct labour hour. Thus the full cost of the job is:

	$
Direct materials	138
Direct labour (15 × $15)	225
	363
Overheads (15 × $12)	180
	543

You should note that if all of the jobs undertaken during the month are apportioned with overheads in a similar manner, all $30,000 of overheads will be charged to the jobs between them. Jobs with a lot of direct labour worked on them will be apportioned a lot of overheads and those with little direct labour will have few overheads charged to them.

ACTIVITY 8.4

Can you think of reasons why direct labour hours are regarded as the most logical basis for sharing overheads between cost units?

It cannot be emphasised often enough that there is no 'correct' way to apportion overheads to jobs. Overheads (indirect costs), by definition, do not naturally relate to individual jobs. If, nevertheless, we wish to take account of the fact that overheads are part of the cost of all jobs, we must find some acceptable way of including a share of the total overheads in each job. If a particular means of doing this is accepted by those who are affected by the full cost deduced as a result, then the method is as good as any other method. Accounting is only concerned with providing useful information to decision makers. In practice, the method that gains the most acceptability as being useful is the direct labour hour method.

ACTIVITY 8.5

Marine Supplier Ltd undertakes a range of work, including making sails for small sailing boats on a made-to-measure basis.

The following costs are expected to be incurred by the company during next month:

Indirect labour cost	$27,000
Direct labour time	6,000 hours
Depreciation (wear and tear) of machinery, etc.	$9,000
Rent and rates	$15,000
Direct labour costs	$90,000
Heating, lighting and power	$6,000
Machine time	2,000 hours
Indirect materials	$1,500
Other miscellaneous indirect costs	$600
Direct materials cost	$9,000

The company has received an inquiry about a sail and it is estimated that the sail will take 12 direct labour hours to make, and will require 20 square metres of sailcloth, which costs $6 per square metre.

The company normally uses a direct labour hour basis of charging overheads to individual jobs.

What is the full cost of making the sail detailed above?

ACTIVITY 8.6

Suppose that Marine Suppliers Ltd (Activity 8.5) used a machine hour basis of charging overheads to jobs. What would be the cost of the job detailed if it is expected to take five machine hours (as well as 12 direct labour hours)?

A question that now presents itself is: which of the two costs for this sail is the correct one or simply the better one? The answer is that neither is the correct one, as was pointed out earlier in the chapter. Which is the better one is a matter of judgment. This judgment is entirely concerned with the usefulness of the information, which in this context is probably concerned with the attitudes of those who will be affected by the figure used. Thus fairness, as it is perceived by those people, is likely to be the important issue.

Most people would probably feel that the nature of the overheads should influence the choice of the basis of charging the overhead to jobs. Where, because the operation is a capital-intensive one, the overheads are dominated by those relating to machinery (depreciation, machine maintenance, power, etc.), machine hours might be favoured. Otherwise direct labour hours might be preferred.

It could appear that one of these bases might be preferred to the other one because it apportions either a higher or a lower amount of overheads to a particular job. This would be irrational, however. Since the total overheads are the same irrespective of the method of charging the total to individual jobs, a method that gives a higher share of overheads to one particular job must give a lower share to the remaining jobs. There is one cake of fixed size. If one person is to be given a relatively large slice, the other people between them must receive relatively smaller slices.

EXAMPLE 8.2

A business expects to incur overheads totalling $20,000 next month. The total direct labour time worked is expected to be 1,600 hours and machines are expected to operate for a total of 1,000 hours.

During the month the business expects to do just two large jobs, the outlines of which are as follows:

	Job 1	Job 2
Direct labour hours	800	800
Machine hours	700	300

How much overheads will be charged to each job if overheads are to be charged on:

(a) a direct labour hour basis?

(b) a machine hour basis?

What do you notice about the two sets of figures you calculate?

Direct labour hour basis
Overhead recovery rate = $20,000 / 1,600 = $12.50 per direct labour hour.
Job 1 $12.50 × 800 = $10,000
Job 2 $12.50 × 800 = $10,000
Machine hour basis
Overhead recovery rate = $20,000 / 1,000 = $20.00 per machine hour.
Job 1 $20.00 × 700 = $14,000
Job 2 $20.00 × 300 = $6,000

It is clear from this that the total overheads charged to jobs is the same whichever method is used. So, whereas the machine hour basis gives job 1 a higher share than does the direct labour hour method, the opposite is true for job 2.

It is not possible to charge overheads on one basis to one job and on the other basis to the other job. This is because either total overheads will not be fully charged to the jobs, or the jobs will be overcharged with overheads. For example, the direct labour hour method for job 1 ($10,000) and the machine hour basis for job 2 ($6,000) will mean that only $16,000 of a total $20,000 of overheads will be charged to jobs. As a result, the objective of full costing, which is to charge all overheads to jobs done, will not be achieved. In this particular case, if selling prices are based on full costs the business may not charge prices high enough to cover all of its costs.

SEGMENTING THE OVERHEADS

As we have just seen, charging the same overheads to different jobs on different bases is not possible. It is possible, however, to charge one part of the overheads on one basis and another part, or other parts, on another basis.

ACTIVITY 8.7

Taking the same business as in Example 8.2, on closer analysis we find that of the expected overheads totalling $20,000 next month, $8,000 relates to machines (depreciation, maintenance, rent of the space occupied by the machines, etc.) and the remainder to more general overheads. The other information about the business is exactly as it was before.

How much overheads will be charged to each job if the machine-related overheads are to be charged on a machine hour basis and the remaining overheads are charged on a direct labour hour basis?

Segmenting the overheads in this way may well be seen as providing a better basis of charging overheads to jobs. This is quite often found in practice, usually by dividing a business into separate 'areas' for costing purposes, charging overheads differently from one area to the next.

Remember that there is no correct basis of charging overheads to jobs, so our frequent reference to the direct labour and machine hour bases should not be taken to imply that these are the correct methods. However, it should be said that these two methods do have something to commend them and are popular in practice. As we have already discussed, a sensible method needs to identify something about each job that can be measured and that distinguishes it from other jobs. There is also a lot to be said for methods that are concerned with time, because most overheads are time-related.

DEALING WITH OVERHEADS ON A DEPARTMENTAL BASIS

In general, all but the smallest businesses are divided into departments. Normally each department deals with a separate activity. The reasons for dividing a business into departments include the following:

* Many businesses are too large and complex to run as a single unit and it is more practical to run them as a series of relatively independent units with each one having its own manager.
* Each department normally has its own area of specialisation and is managed by a specialist.
* Each department can have its own accounting records which enable its performance to be assessed. This can lead to greater motivation among the staff.

Very many businesses deal with charging overheads to cost units on a department by department basis. They do this in the expectation that it will give rise to a more fair means of charging overheads. It is probably often the case that it does not lead to any great improvement in the fairness of the resulting full costs. Though it may not be of enormous benefit in many cases, it is probably not an expensive exercise to apply overheads on a departmental basis. Since costs are collected department by department for other purposes (particularly control), to apply overheads department by department is a relatively simple matter.

The departmental approach to deriving full costs works in the way depicted in Figure 8.3. Assume that the job starts life in the Preparation Department when some direct materials are taken from the stores and worked on by a Preparation Department direct worker. Thus the job will be charged with direct materials, direct labour and with

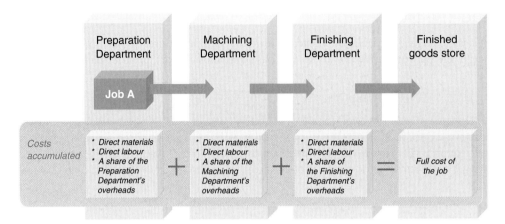

FIGURE 8.3 A cost unit passing through the production process

a share of the Preparation Department's overheads. The job then passes into the Machining Department, already valued at the costs which it picked up in the Preparation Department. Further direct labour and, possibly, materials are added in the Machining Department, plus a share of that department's overheads. The job now passes into the Finishing Department, valued at the cost of the materials, labour and overheads it accumulated in the first two departments. In the Finishing Department, further direct labour and, perhaps, materials are added and the job picks up a share of that department's overheads. The job, now complete, passes into the finished goods store or is despatched to the customer. The basis of charging overheads to jobs (for example, direct labour hours) might be the same for all three departments or it may be different from one department to another. In the present example, it is quite likely that machine-related costs dominate the Machining Department, so overheads might well be charged to jobs on a machine hour basis. The other two departments may well be labour intensive and direct labour hours may be seen as being appropriate there.

The passage of the job through the departments can be compared with a snowball being rolled across snow. As it passes, it picks up more and more snow.

Where costs are dealt with departmentally, each department is known as a **cost centre**. A cost centre can be defined as some physical area or some activity or function for which costs are separately identified. Charging direct costs to jobs, in a departmental system, is exactly the same as where the whole business is one single cost centre. It is simply a matter of keeping a record of:

* the number of hours of direct labour worked on the particular job and the grade of labour, assuming that there are different grades with different rates of pay
* the cost of the direct materials taken from stores and applied to the job
* any other direct costs—for example, subcontracted work—associated with the job.

This record keeping will normally be done departmentally in a departmental system.

It is obviously necessary to identify the production overheads of the entire organisation on a departmental basis. This means that the total overheads of the business must be divided between the departments, such that the sum of the departmental overheads equals the overheads for the entire business. By charging all of their overheads to jobs, between them the departments will charge all of the overheads of the business to jobs.

For our present purposes, it is necessary to distinguish between **product cost centres** (or departments) and **service cost centres**. Product cost centres are departments through which the jobs pass and which can be charged with a share of their overheads. The Preparation, Machining and Finishing Departments, in the example discussed above, are examples of product cost centres.

ACTIVITY 8.8

Can you guess what the definition of a service cost centre is? Can you think of an example of a service cost centre?

Service cost centre costs must be charged to product cost centres, and become part of the product cost centres' overheads so that they can be recharged to jobs. This must be done so that all of the overheads of the business find their way into the cost of the jobs done. If this is not done, the resulting 'full' cost of the jobs will not really be the full cost.

Logically, the costs of a service cost centre should be charged to product cost centres on the basis of the level of service provided to the product cost centre concerned. For example, a production department which has a lot of machine maintenance carried out, relative to other production departments, should be charged with a larger share of the Maintenance Department's costs than should those other product cost centres.

BATCH COSTING

The production of many types of goods and services, particularly goods, involves production of a batch of identical or nearly identical units of output, but where each batch is distinctly different from other batches. For example, a theatre may put on a production whose nature and therefore costs are very different from those of other productions. However, ignoring differences in the desirability of the various types of seating, all of the individual units of output (i.e. tickets to see the production) are identical.

In these circumstances, a system known as **batch costing** is used, in which we would normally deduce the cost per ticket by using a job costing approach (taking account of direct and indirect costs, etc.) to find the cost of mounting the production and then simply divide this by the number of tickets expected to be sold, to find the cost per ticket.

FULL COST AS THE BREAK-EVEN PRICE

It may have occurred to you by now that if all goes according to plan (direct costs, overheads and the basis of charging overheads—for example, direct labour hours—prove to be as expected), then selling the output for its full cost should cause the business exactly to break even. Therefore, whatever profit (in total) is loaded onto full cost to set actual selling prices will result in that level of profit being earned for the period.

THE FORWARD-LOOKING NATURE OF FULL COSTING

Though deducing full costs can be done after the work has been completed, it is often done in advance. In other words, costs are frequently predicted. This is because for one of the main uses to which cost information is put, namely the pricing of output, it is necessary to know the costs in advance. Where, for example, full costs are used as a basis on which to set selling prices, it is usually the case that prices need to be set before the customer will agree to the job being done. Even where no particular customer has been identified, some idea of the ultimate price will need to be known before the manufacturer will be able to make a judgment as to whether potential customers will buy the product and in what quantities. Obviously there is the risk that the actual outcome will differ from what was predicted.

SELF-ASSESSMENT QUESTION 8.1

Promptprint Ltd, a printing business, has received an inquiry from a potential customer for a quotation for a job. The business pricing policy will be based on the plans for the next financial year shown below.

	$
Sales (billings expected to be sent to customers)	196,000
Direct materials	(38,000)
Direct labour	(32,000)
Variable overheads	(2,400)
Advertising for business	(3,000)
Depreciation	(27,600)
Administration	(36,000)
Interest	(8,000)
Profit before tax	49,000

A first estimate for the direct costs of the job is shown below:

	$
Direct materials	4,000
Direct labour	3,600

Based on the estimated direct costs:

(a) Prepare a recommended quote for the job based on the plans, commenting on your method.

(b) Comment on the validity of using financial plans in pricing and recommend any improvements you would consider desirable for the business pricing policy used in (a).

ACTIVITY-BASED COSTING (ABC)

What we have considered so far for most of this chapter is the traditional, and still very widely used, approach to job costing, namely deriving the full cost of output where one unit of output differs from another. This approach is to collect for each job those costs which can be unequivocally linked to and measured in respect of the particular job (direct costs). All other costs (overheads) are thrown into a pool of costs and charged to individual jobs according to some formula. Traditionally this formula has been on the basis of the number of direct labour hours worked on each individual job.

This traditional approach to job costing developed when the notion of trying to cost industrial production first emerged, probably around the time of the Industrial Revolution in Britain. At that time, manufacturing industry was characterised by the following features:

✳ *Direct labour-intensive and direct labour-paced production.* Labour was at the heart of production. To the extent that machinery was used, it was to support the efforts of direct labour and the speed of production was dictated by direct labour.

✳ *A low level of overheads relative to direct costs.* Little was spent on power, personnel services, machinery (therefore, low depreciation charges) and other areas typical of the overheads of modern businesses.

✳ *A relatively uncompetitive market.* Transport difficulties limited industrial production worldwide, and lack of knowledge by customers of competitors' prices meant that businesses could prosper without being too scientific in pricing their output.

Since overheads represented a pretty small element of total costs, it was acceptable and practical to deal with overheads in a fairly arbitrary manner. Not too much effort was devoted to trying to control the cost of overheads because the rewards of better control were relatively small, certainly compared with the rewards from controlling direct labour and material costs. It was also reasonable to charge overheads to individual jobs on a direct labour hour basis. Most of the overheads were incurred directly in the support of direct labour: providing direct workers with a place to work, heating and lighting that workplace, employing people to supervise the direct workers, etc. At the same time all production was done by direct workers, perhaps aided by machinery.

The world is now a very different place and industrial production has fundamentally altered. Much of it is now characterised by:

✳ *Capital-intensive and machine-paced production.* Machines are at the heart of production. Most labour supports the efforts of machines, for example, technically maintaining them—and the speed of production is dictated by machines.

✳ *A high level of overheads relative to direct costs.* Modern industry is characterised by very high depreciation, servicing and power costs. There are also high costs of a nature scarcely envisaged in the early days of industrial production, such as personnel and staff welfare costs. At the same time there are very low, perhaps no, direct labour costs. The proportion of total cost accounted for by direct materials has typically not altered too much, but more efficient production tends to lead to less waste and therefore less material cost, again tending to make overheads more dominant.

✳ *A highly competitive international market.* Industrial production, much of it highly sophisticated, is carried out worldwide. Transport, including fast airfreight, is relatively cheap. Fax, telephone and email ensure that potential customers can quickly and cheaply know the prices of a range of suppliers. The market is therefore likely to be highly competitive. This means that businesses need to know their costs with a greater degree of accuracy than has historically been the case.

Whereas the traditional overhead recovery rate had been much less per direct labour hour than the actual rate paid to direct workers, recently there have been examples of overhead recovery rates five and 10 times the hourly rate of pay. When production is dominated by direct labour paid $10 an hour it might be reasonable to have a recovery rate of $2 an hour. When, however, direct labour plays a relatively small part in production, to have overhead recovery rates of $50 per direct labour hour is likely to lead to very arbitrary costing. Just a small change in the amount of direct labour worked on a job could massively affect the cost deduced, not because the direct worker is massively well paid, but for no better reason than this is the way in which it has always been done—overheads not particularly related to labour are charged on a direct labour hour basis.

The whole question of overheads, what causes them and how they are charged to jobs has, as a result of changes in the environment in which manufacturers operate, been receiving closer attention recently. Historically, businesses have been content to accept that overheads exist and to deal with them, for costing purposes, in as practical a way as possible. There has been a growing realisation that overheads do not just happen, they must be caused by something. The result is the development of **activity-based costing (ABC)**.

EXAMPLE

8.3

Modern Producers Ltd has, like virtually all manufacturers, an inventory storage area (stores). The costs of running the stores include a share of the factory rent and other establishment costs, such as heating and lighting. They also include salaries of staff employed to look after the inventory and the cost of financing the inventory held in the stores.

The company has two product lines, product A and product B. Production of both of these uses raw materials which are held in the stores. Product A is only made specifically to customers' orders, the finished product being transferred direct from the production area to be despatched to the customer. Product B is manufactured for inventory. The company prides itself on its ability to supply this product in relatively large quantities instantly. As a consequence, much of the stores is filled with finished stocks of product B ready to be despatched as an order is received.

Traditionally, the whole cost of operating the stores has been treated as a general overhead and included in the total of overheads that is charged to jobs, probably on a direct labour hour basis. This means that when assessing the cost of products A and B, the cost of operating the stores has fallen on them according to the number of direct labour hours worked on each one. In fact, most of the stores' cost should be charged to product B, since this product causes (and benefits) from the stores' cost much more than is true of product A. Failure to account more precisely for the costs of running the stores is masking the fact that product B is not as profitable as it seems to be; it may even be leading to losses as a result of the relatively high costs of operating the stores which it causes, but which so far have been charged partly to product A.

COST DRIVERS

The realisation that overheads do not just occur but are caused by activities, such as holding products in stores, which 'drive' the costs is at the heart of ABC, hence the term **'cost drivers'**. The traditional approach is that direct labour hours drive costs, which probably used to be true. It is now recognised to be no longer the case.

There is a basic philosophical difference between the traditional and ABC approaches. Traditionally we tend to think of overheads as rendering a service to cost units, the cost of which must be charged to those units. ABC sees overheads as being caused by cost units and that those cost units must be charged with the costs that they cause.

ACTIVITY 8.9

Can you think of any other purpose that identification of the cost drivers serves, apart from deriving more accurate costs?

The opaque nature of overheads has traditionally rendered them difficult to control relative to the much more obvious direct labour and material costs. If analysis of overheads can identify the cost drivers, questions can be asked about whether the activity that is driving costs is necessary at all and whether the cost justifies the benefit. In our example, it may be a good marketing ploy that product B can be supplied immediately from stock, but there is a cost and that cost should be recognised and assessed against the benefit.

Advocates of ABC argue that most overheads can be analysed and cost drivers identified. If this is true it means that it is possible to gain much clearer insights into the costs that are caused activity by activity. As a result, fairer and more accurate product costs can be identified and costs can be controlled more effectively.

ABC AND SERVICE INDUSTRIES

Much of the discussion of ABC so far in this chapter has concentrated on the manufacturing industry, perhaps because early users of ABC were manufacturing businesses. In fact, ABC is possibly even more relevant to service industries because, in the absence of a direct materials element, its total costs are likely to be particularly heavily affected by overheads. There certainly is evidence that ABC has been adopted by some businesses that sell services rather than goods.

ACTIVITY 8.10

What is the difference in the way in which direct costs are accounted for when using ABC relative to their treatment when taking a traditional approach to full costing?

CRITICISMS OF ABC

Critics of ABC argue that, in the analysis of overheads, trying to identify cost drivers is very time consuming and costly and that the benefit of doing so, in terms of more accurate costing and the potential for cost control, does not justify the cost.

ABC is also criticised for the same reason that full costing generally is criticised. This is that it does not provide very relevant information for decision making. This point will be addressed shortly.

USES OF FULL COST INFORMATION

Why do we need to deduce full cost information? There are probably two main reasons:

1. *For pricing purposes.* In some industries and circumstances, full costs are used as the basis of pricing. Here the full cost is deduced and a percentage is added on for profit. This is known as **'cost plus' pricing**. Garages carrying out vehicle repairs provide an example of this.

   In many circumstances suppliers are not in a position to set prices on a cost plus basis, however. Where there is a competitive market, a supplier will probably need to accept the price which the market offers—that is, most suppliers are 'price takers' not 'price makers'.

2. *For income measurement purposes.* To provide a valid means of measuring a business's income it is necessary to match expenses with the revenues realised in the same accounting period. Where manufactured inventory is made or partially made in one period but sold in the next, or where a service is partially rendered in one accounting period but the revenue is realised in the next, the full cost (including an appropriate share of overheads) must be carried from one accounting period to the next. Unless we are able to identify the full cost of work done in one period which is the subject of a sale in the next, the profit figures of the periods concerned will be distorted.

EXAMPLE

8.4

During the accounting year that ended on 31 December 2005, Engineers Ltd made a special machine for a customer. At the beginning of 2006, after having a series of tests successfully completed by a subcontractor, the machine was delivered to the customer. The company's normal practice (typical of most businesses and following the realisation convention) is to take account of sales when the product passes to the customer. The sale price of the machine was $50,000.

During 2005, materials costing $7,000 were used on making the machine and 1,200 hours of direct labour, costing $18,600, were worked on the machine. The company uses a direct labour hour basis of charging overheads to jobs, which is believed to be fair because most of its work is labour intensive. The total manufacturing overheads for the company for 2005 were $154,000 and the total direct labour hours worked were 22,000. Testing the machine cost $2,000.

How much profit or loss did the company make on the machine in 2005? How much profit or loss did the company make on the machine in 2006? At what value must the company carry the machine in its accounting system at the end of 2005, so that the correct profit will be recorded for each of the two years?

No profit or loss was made in 2005, following the company's (and the generally accepted) approach to recognising revenues (sales). If the sales were not to be recognised until 2006 it would be illogical to treat the costs of making the machine as expenses until that time.

In 2006 the sale would be recognised and all of the costs, including a reasonable share of overheads, would be set against it in the 2006 income statement, as follows:

	$'000	$'000
Sales price		50,000
Costs		
Direct labour	18,600	
Direct materials	7,000	
Overheads (1,200 × ($154,000 / 22,000))	8,400	
Total incurred in 2003	34,000	
Testing cost	2,000	
Total cost		36,000
2006 profit from the machine		14,000

The machine needs to be shown as an asset of the company at $34,000 at 31 December 2005.

Unless all production costs are charged in the same accounting period as the sale is recognised in the income statement, distortions will occur that will render the income statement much less useful. Thus, it is necessary to deduce the full cost of any production undertaken completely or partially in one accounting period but sold in a subsequent one.

CRITICISMS OF FULL COSTING

Full costing is widely criticised because in practice it tends to use past costs and to restrict its consideration of future costs to outlay costs. It can be argued that past costs are irrelevant, irrespective of the purpose for which the information is to be used. This is basically because it is not possible to make decisions about the past, only about the future. A particular issue that arises relates to the relatively arbitrary nature of overhead allocation. While it can be argued that the use of ABC with careful consideration of the cost drivers can reduce this arbitrariness, it is difficult to see how all of these concerns can be eliminated. A further important point that needs to be recognised is that adding a loading for overheads, which is a reasonable and necessary thing to do, should not be taken to imply that actual costs behave in line with the overhead recovery rate used. This will almost never happen. This means that while full costing is useful in indicating the kind of recovery rates needed for the long-term survival and prosperity of a business, it has the potential to mislead in certain situations. The concept of relevant costs that was discussed in Chapter 7 is paramount in decision making. Full costing, while providing useful guidance for decision making, also has the potential to distort and lead to incorrect decisions. Areas of particular concern relate to the kind of special decisions identified in Chapter 7.

PDH Ltd, a small firm of building contractors, has, on your advice, prepared a budget for the next year and is aiming for increased output in an effort to improve profits.

The actual results for last year have been finalised and both sets of figures are given below.

EXAMPLE 8.5

	Actual $'000	Budget $'000
Sales	1,800	2,250
Direct costs		
Materials	800	1,000
Labour	400	500
	1,200	1,500
Gross profit	600	750
Factory production overheads	200	210
	400	540
Administration and general overheads	280	330
Net profit	120	210

The company has been asked to tender for a contract at a time when work is scarce and staff may have to be laid off. In addition, the output to date is well below the level hoped for, being nearer to last year's actual than this year's budget. Because of this the CEO has prepared his quotation using an overhead recovery rate based on actual proportions achieved last year. The quotation is given below:

	$'000
Direct costs	
Materials	150
Labour	60
	210
Factory overheads—one-sixth of direct costs	35
	245
Administration overheads—one-fifth of factory cost	49
	294
Profit—one-fourteenth of total cost but reduce to	6
Price tendered	300

You ascertain that the materials have been priced at cost and include the following:

1. special window frames which cost $8,000, but are now unlikely to be used and have a disposal value of $3,000. Alternatively they could be converted for use on this contract at a labour cost of $2,000; otherwise, frames that would cost $7,000 would have to be purchased.

2. timber which cost $10,000 but would now cost $18,000 to replace.

Required:

(a) Explain the system of overhead recovery implicit in the quotation.

(b) Discuss the basis on which the quotation was prepared.

(c) Revise the quote where you think is appropriate, giving your reasons.

The problem with the figures shown is that they reflect the assumption that overheads will be based on some kind of average, quite arbitrary, sharing of overheads. Actual overhead costs may be quite different. A revised quotation should be prepared which reflects expected costs.

A further factor is that the contract is at a time of low demand, so there will be no opportunity cost—lost contribution—for labour. The company is short of work and may have to lay off labour. Under these circumstances any job that makes a contribution needs to be considered carefully. The contribution of the job being tendered for can be calculated by comparing the relevant cost (as shown below) with the price quoted.

The revised statement should be something like:

Materials		150,000
less		
the cost of windows which have a lower opportunity cost		(8,000)
plus the opportunity cost of the windows used. Either:		
(a) If used, the scrap value will be lost	3,000	
A further labour cost will be incurred	2,000	
	5,000	
or (b) Replacement frames could be purchased	7,000	
The lower cost option should be used, so		5,000
Timber		
The opportunity cost of using the material, which had cost 10,000		
but which would cost 18,000 to replace, is 18,000, so		
the increased cost (10,000 is already included) is		8,000
Materials cost		155,000
Labour—actual cost		60,000
		215,000

The question as to how the various overheads behave is difficult, but requires consideration. In the figures shown above it is presumed that the overheads will not change just as the result of taking on this job, so there are no relevant cost increases. In practice this may not be the case and a sound understanding of the way in which costs behave is essential.

Any price in excess of this would leave the business better off taking on the contract than not doing so.

The original quotation reflects the kind of price that needs to be charged if PDH Ltd is to be fairly confident of recovering its overheads and making a profit. This confidence is only justified if total revenues and general cost levels are in line with the budget. In a time of low demand the probability of being able to recover the overheads is seriously reduced. Trying to recover overheads in a competitive market might prove impossible. The decision comes down to what the market will bear in price, and how much the job is needed by PDH Ltd. In a case like this the reality is that taking on the contract at any price above $215,000 will minimise loss rather than avoid losses altogether.

ACTIVITY 8.11

Contractors Ltd expects to have spare capacity in the coming year. It has been offered a contract which will take a year to complete at a fixed price of $125,000. The accountant has prepared the following figures and advises rejection of the contract.

Contract price		125,000
Direct costs		
Materials		
Material X 50 tonnes at $500 per tonne	25,000	
Material Y 100 tonnes at $50 per tonne	5,000	
		30,000
Labour		
Direct labour—2 workers at $500 per week for a year	52,000	
Supervisor	34,000	
		86,000
Overheads		
Depreciation	7,500	
Other fixed and variable overheads		
(recovered at a rate of 50% of direct labour)	26,000	33,500
Total cost		149,500
Profit margin (10% of total cost)		14,950
Deficit		39,450

After further investigation you discover the following:

1. Twenty-five tonnes of material X is already in stock. It originally cost $400 per tonne. At present material X can be bought and sold for $450 per tonne. Apart from this contract, it is of no other use to the company.

2. One hundred and fifty tonnes of material Y is in stock. It originally cost $60 per tonne. It is impossible to obtain further supplies of this material. The company originally intended to use the whole of the 150 tonnes on another contract. However, it is possible to use a substitute for the other contract which can be bought for $45 per tonne but which requires processing costing $25 of labour per tonne to put it in a suitable condition for use.

3. Two skilled workers would be required for the contract at a weekly wage of $500 each. One of these could be transferred from another department where at present they are doing work that could be done by a semi-skilled

worker at a rate of $400 per week. The other worker would have to be recruited and would require two weeks' training before work on the contract begins.

4. The supervisor was intending to retire at the end of this year on a company pension of $16,000 a year, but can be persuaded to stay on for another year. This would have no effect on his ultimate annual pension.

5. The contract would require the use of one machine that was bought three years ago for $75,000 and which is being depreciated on a straight-line basis over 10 years. If not used on this contract, the machine could be hired out for the year at a rate of $100 per week.

6. The company has budgeted for the following total overheads, excluding depreciation, during the following year:

Variable overheads	$50,000
Fixed overheads	$175,000
	$225,000

The budgeted direct labour cost for the entire company for the year is $450,000, *excluding this contract*. The company uses a full costing approach and overheads are recovered on the basis of 50% of direct labour cost.

   If the contract were accepted it is estimated that total variable overheads would increase by $5,000 because of increased power costs and administrative costs.

Required:

(a) Explain the rationale of full costing and the system of overhead recovery implicit in the accountant's figures.

(b) Revise the above statement and state whether the contract should be accepted. Explain fully your statement and its assumptions.

(c) Explain the differences between your statement and that of the accountant.

Clearly, when making decisions of a non-routine nature great care needs to be taken. Advocates of full costing would argue that it provides an informative long-run average cost. This is often an important component of any decision, but circumstances arise, as in the case of Example 8.5 and Activity 8.11, where other relevant factors need to be examined.

Despite the criticisms that are made of full costing, it is, according to research evidence, very widely practised.

SUMMARY

In this chapter we have achieved the following objectives in the way shown.

OBJECTIVE	METHOD ACHIEVED
Deduce the full cost of a unit of output in a single-product (single-service) environment	• Illustrated that many, perhaps most, businesses seek to identify the total or full cost of pursuing some objective, typically of a unit of output • Illustration and calculation of full cost • Illustrated that where all units of goods or service produced by a business are identical, this tends to be a fairly straightforward matter—a case of simply finding the total cost for a period and dividing by the number of units of output for the same period
Distinguish between direct and indirect costs	• Explained and illustrated that under the above circumstances the separate identification of costs into direct and indirect costs is important, as normally such businesses identify the direct costs of production—those costs which can be directly measured in respect of a particular unit of output • Explained and differentiated between the two types of cost • Explained and illustrated the nature of overheads • Explained and illustrated how it is necessary to add to the direct costs a share of the overheads according to some formula, which, of necessity, must to some extent be arbitrary • Explained and illustrated the concept of overhead recovery • Calculated and applied overhead recovery rates
Use this distinction to deduce the full cost of a job in a multi-product (multi-service) environment	• Illustrated that where a business's output is of units that are not similar it is necessary to take a less straightforward approach to the problem • Calculated the full cost by adding direct costs and an appropriate overhead recovery rate • Identified direct labour hours as a popular (but not the sole) basis of sharing overheads • Noted that costing individual cost units in this way is known as job costing
Discuss the problem of charging overheads to jobs in a multi-product (multi-service) environment, including the role of activity-based costing	• Explained and illustrated the different outcomes when different rates are applied • Illustrated ways of segmenting the overheads • Illustrated and applied ways of dealing with overheads on a departmental basis
Explain cost drivers	• Noted that there is an element of arbitrariness in the choice between overhead recovery rates • Explained the notion of cost drivers
Explain the nature and role of activity-based costing	• Introduced the idea of activity-based costing, a method which is strongly advocated by many people as providing a more focused approach to applying overheads to jobs, by identifying 'cost drivers' or activities that give rise to overhead costs • Explained activity-based costing • Identified the main criticisms of activity-based costing

OBJECTIVE	METHOD ACHIEVED
Identify and explain the main uses of full cost information	• Identified the main uses of full costing as being for pricing and income measurement • Illustrated the use of full costing
Identify the main criticisms of full costing	• Recognised that full costing is also widely criticised as not providing very helpful and relevant information • Explained the limitations of full costing • Illustrated the ways in which full costing can mislead or be inappropriately used
Apply the concepts of relevant costing and full costing in an appropriate manner in a number of decision-making situations	• Explained, illustrated and applied the concept of relevant costing to a range of situations • Examined a number of decision-making situations where the use of full costing approaches has the potential to mislead, and where the concept of relevant costing needs to come to the fore

DISCUSSION QUESTIONS

EASY

<Obj 1>	8.1	Assuming a simple manufacturing operation in which only one product is produced, what problems arise in determining the unit output cost?
<Obj 1–3>	8.2	How is the term 'full cost' defined?
<Obj 2>	8.3	What is the point of distinguishing direct costs from indirect ones?
<Obj 2>	8.4	Provide a list of direct and indirect costs for a 'hot bread' shop.
<Obj 2>	8.5	Are direct costs and variable costs the same thing?
<Obj 2>	8.6	What other labels are used for 'indirect costs'?
<Obj 5>	8.7	What is a 'cost driver'?

INTERMEDIATE

<Obj 1, 3>	8.8	It is sometimes claimed that the full cost of pursuing some objective represents the long-run break-even selling price. Why is this said and what does it mean?
<Obj 3>	8.9	Under what circumstances does the allocation of overheads on the basis of labour hours lead to product costs distortions?
<Obj 3, 4>	8.10	The textbook discusses segmenting the overheads. What is meant by this term? How does this help in allocating overheads to individual jobs or services?
<Obj 3, 4>	8.11	Distinguish between a 'product cost centre' and a 'service cost centre'.
<Obj 4>	8.12	Under 'full costing' what basis should be used to allocate overhead costs to individual jobs?
<Obj 4>	8.13	What problem does the existence of work-in-progress cause in process costing?
<Obj 4>	8.14	Is it possible to use a different basis to charge overheads to different jobs (i.e. labour hours for one, machine hours for another, material cost for a third)?
<Obj 4>	8.15	What are the potential advantages and limitations of dividing the manufacturing process into separate departments?

<Obj 4>   **8.16** Identify and discuss the changes in manufacturing that have created potential problems for traditional manufacturing overhead allocation.

<Obj 4, 6> **8.17** Identify key differences between 'conventional absorption costing' and 'activity-based costing'.

<Obj 6–8>   **8.18** What are the possible limitations of activity-based costing (ABC)?

<Obj 8, 9> **8.19** How is full cost information used?

APPLICATION EXERCISES

EASY

<Obj 1, 2>   **8.1** Distinguish between:
- job costing
- process costing
- batch costing.

What tend to be the problems specifically associated with each of these?

<Obj 1, 3>   **8.2** Bodgers Ltd operates a job costing system. Towards the end of each financial year, the overhead recovery rate (the rate at which overheads will be charged to jobs) is established for the forthcoming year.

(a) Why does the company bother to predetermine the recovery rate in the way outlined?

(b) What steps will be involved in predetermining the rate?

(c) What problems might arise with using a predetermined rate?

<Obj 2>   **8.3** Gatton Foods Ltd manufactures canned meat foodstuffs. Below is a selection of the costs accumulated by the accounting department for the company. Assuming the cost object is the product, classify each of these costs as direct or indirect. Also classify each cost as variable or fixed in respect of its expected reaction to changes in volume of production.

(a) Raw meat acquired for processing

(b) Purchase of gas for cooking ovens

(c) Cost of tin cans

(d) Repair costs for canning machines

(e) Wages for plant security

(f) Depreciation of cooking ovens

(g) Freight cost of raw materials inwards

(h) Cost of building insurance

(i) Cost of can labels

(j) Cost of cleaning materials for factory

(k) General manager's salary

(l) Advertising costs related to products sold

(m) Factory supervisor's salary

(n) Annual licence fee regarding health regulations

(o) Distribution costs to supply products to customers.

<Obj 4>

8.4 Brumpy Ltd uses a predetermined overhead rate in applying overheads to product costs, using direct labour costs for cost centre A and machine hours for cost centre B. The following details the estimated forecasts for 2004:

	A	B
Direct labour costs	$200,000	$70,000
Production overheads	$140,000	$300,000
Direct labour hours	18,000	7,000
Machine hours	2,000	20,000

Required:
(a) What is the predetermined overhead rate cost for centres A and B?
(b) What would be the overhead rate costs if we used machine hours for A and direct labour hours for B?
(c) What is the main limitation of full costing (also known as absorption costing)?

INTERMEDIATE

<Obj 3>

8.5 Cowling Ltd uses a predetermined overhead rate in applying overheads to product costs, using direct labour costs for cost centre A and machine hours for cost centre B. The following details the estimated forecasts for 2005.

	A	B
Direct labour costs	$90,000	$45,000
Production overheads	$130,000	$160,000
Machine hours	1,200	3,500

Required:
(a) Calculate the predetermined overhead rate for cost centres A and B.

Nuforma is one of the products manufactured by Cowling. The manufacturing process involves the two cost centres A and B. The following data relate to the resources that were used in the manufacture of the product during 2005.

	A	B
Direct materials	$7,600	$8,900
Direct labour	$5,700	$4,300
Machine hours	63	45

(b) Assuming that product Nuforma consists of 4,000 units, what is the unit cost of Nuforma?

<Obj 4>

8.6 Many businesses charge overheads to jobs, in a job costing environment, on a departmental basis. What is the advantage that is claimed for charging overheads to jobs on a departmental basis and why is it claimed?

What circumstances need to exist to make a difference to a particular job according to whether overheads are charged on a 'business-wide' basis or a 'departmental' basis? (Note that the answer to this part of the question is not specifically covered in the chapter. You should, nevertheless, be able to deduce the reason from what you know.)

<Obj 9>   **8.7**   The following statement was made by a junior accountant in the business in which you work.

> In a job costing system it is necessary to divide the business up into departments. Fixed costs (or overheads) will be collected for each department. Where a particular fixed cost relates to the business as a whole it must be divided between the departments. Usually this is done on the basis of floorspace occupied by each department relative to the entire business. When the total fixed costs for each department have been identified, this will be divided by the number of hours that were worked in each department to deduce an overhead recovery rate. Each job that was worked on in a department will have a share of fixed costs allocated to it according to how long it was worked on. The total cost for each job will therefore be the sum of the variable costs of the job and its share of the fixed costs. It is essential that this approach is taken in order to deduce a selling price for the firm's output.

You are required to prepare a table of two columns. In the first column you should show any phrases or sentences from this statement with which you do not agree and in the second column you should show your reason for disagreeing with each one.

<Obj 9>   **8.8**   Pieman Products Ltd makes road trailers to the precise specifications of individual customers.

The following are predicted to occur during the forthcoming year, which is about to start:

Direct materials cost	$100,000
Direct labour costs	$160,000
Direct labour time	16,000 hours
Indirect labour cost	$50,000
Depreciation (wear and tear) of machinery, etc.	$16,000
Rent and rates	$20,000
Heating, lighting and power	$10,000
Indirect materials	$4,000
Other indirect costs	$2,000
Machine time	3,000 hours

All direct labour is paid at the same hourly rate.

A customer has asked the company to build a trailer for transporting a racing motorcycle to races. It is estimated that this will require materials and components that will cost $2,300. It will take 250 direct labour hours to do the job, of which 50 will involve the use of machinery.

Deduce a logical cost for the job and explain the basis of dealing with overheads which you propose.

CHALLENGING

<Obj 3, 4, 9>   **8.9**   The following estimates of total costs are made for a business for the year:

	$
Direct materials	300,000
Direct labour	200,000
Production overheads	100,000

Production cost	600,000
General overheads	120,000
Total cost	720,000
Profit	72,000
Sales	792,000

From these figures it was decided that the overhead recovery rates and profit loadings would be as follows:

Production overheads	50% of direct labour
General overheads	20% of production cost
Profit	10% of total cost

At the end of the first month it became clear that an error had been made in the budget—$50,000 of the labour had been included as direct labour when in fact it was an indirect production cost.

Show the effect of the mistake by setting out tables as shown above for a job for which the direct materials cost was estimated to be $6,000 and direct labour $4,000, using:

(a) the original recovery rates.
(b) the revised recovery rates.

Illustrate the concept of relevant costs, and the dangers implicit in use of full costing, by reference to the following job:

Price	$20,000
Direct materials	$10,000
Direct labour	$6,000

This job will result in the need for overtime (costing $500) on another job and will increase the costs of supervision by $500 and administrative costs by $500.

<Obj 4>

8.10 Davids Ltd makes boat sails. They receive a special order to produce 350 for a retail chain. The order will take 2,100 metres of material that costs $16.10 per metre and will require 1,400 direct labour hours and 525 machine hours. The following are the expected annual costs for Davids Ltd:

Direct labour	$327,600
Direct labour hours	25,795 hours
Direct materials	$193,200
Indirect costs	$98,400
Machine hours	9,840 hours

From the above information calculate the following:

(a) the overhead recovery rate given that the process is labour intensive.
(b) the total costs to Davids Ltd to produce the special order.
(c) the cost of the special order if Davids Ltd chose to use machine time as the basis for allocating overheads.
(d) the minimum price Davids Ltd could accept per sail.

<Obj 5>

8.11 Original Clean Ltd sells vacuum cleaners to three major retail outlet stores. The following reflects sales and service information related to these customers:

Details	Retailer 1	Retailer 2	Retailer 3
Sales ($)	$100,000	$60,000	$200,000
Sales returns			
Number of items	50	13	30
Amount	$20,000	$5,000	$7,000
Sales order numbers			
Standard	40	30	50
Urgent	10	45	30

Original Clean Ltd uses activity-based costing, and the following costs apply:

Activity	Allocation base
Regular order processing	$25 per customer
Rush order processing	$75 per rush order
Returned item processing	$15 per returned item
Customer support	$1,250 per retail outlet

Required:
Assuming a mark-up of 50% on manufacturing cost, what is the contribution of each retailer after considering the above costs?

<Obj 9>

8.12 Premier Computers assembles and sells elite computers. Data relating to February and March 2005 being:

	February	March
Units		
Beginning inventory	0	2,320
Production	5,140	3,760
Sales	2,820	6,080
Variable costs (per unit)		
Manufacturing cost	$410	$430
Non-manufacturing	$105	$108
Fixed costs (total)		
Manufacturing costs	$350,000	$350,000
Non-manufacturing costs	$130,000	$130,000

The selling price of each computer is $1,199

Required:
Present income statements for Premier Computers for February and March 2005 under
(a) variable costing and (b) absorption costing.

<Obj 9>

8.13 Dale Ltd manufacture a component part A356 for its lawnmowers. The current production is 12,000 units annually. The cost per unit for A356 is as follows:

Direct materials	$17.40
Direct labour	$9.60
Variable overhead	$5.70
Fixed overhead	$7.80
Total	$40.50

Of the total fixed overhead assigned to A356, 45% can be eliminated in the short term if the production of this line is dropped.

An outside supplier has offered to sell the part to Dale Ltd for $38.60.

Required:

(a) Should Dale Ltd make or buy part A356?
(b) What is the most Dale Ltd would be willing to pay an outside supplier for the part?
(c) What are other factors (apart from the financial estimates provided) that Dale Ltd should take into account in making the final decision to make or purchase this part?

CASE STUDY

8.1

Moles–Cyer Ltd is a large business which operates on a departmental basis. Each department is responsible for manufacturing one product. The budget for the next year for one such department is shown below.

	Per unit	Total
	$	$'000
Sales revenue 40,000 units	60	2,400
Less costs		
Material A	22	880
Material B	5	200
Labour	28	1,120
Variable overheads	20	800
	75	3,000
Fixed overheads	15	600
Total cost	90	3,600
Loss		1,200

On the basis of this budget the accountant argues that the department should be closed.

The CEO asks you for an independent assessment. You ascertain the following;

1. The company has enough material A in stock to produce 40,000 units of output. This material cannot be sold. If not used in the year it will have to be destroyed at a cost of $75,000.
2. Enough material B is in stock to produce 20,000 units. This originally cost $10 per unit but has been written down to $5 per unit, which is the current replacement cost. If not used on this job it would be used in another department as a substitute for a part costing $3 per unit, or scrapped for $2.50 per unit.
3. Most variable overheads vary with output. However, the variable overhead rate includes supervisory labour and the supervisor is needed only as long as the department exists. The

supervisor is paid $40,000 a year. If the department were to be closed the supervisor would be retired on a pension of $15,000 a year. The rate also includes depreciation of $100,000 a year, based on historic cost. The machinery would be sold as soon as the department closes. It currently has a sale value of $450,000 but after producing the 40,000 units it would realise only about $50,000.

4. The fixed overhead recovery rate is made up of allocated rent, rates and general expenses all of which are unaffected by any decision regarding the department.

5. Management has already decided on the selling price, and that the department will produce 40,000 units next year, or close.

---

1 If you think it necessary, redraft the accountant's statement. Explain your amendments and state your assumptions clearly.

2 Advise the CEO on both the financial and more general factors that should influence the final decision.

Toymakers Ltd, a manufacturer of toys, is considering whether to accept an order for a new toy, called 'MacBain'. It has been agreed that a trial period of two years will be considered, since there is currently spare capacity in the organisation. In each year it is estimated that 6,000 units can be sold at a price of $50 each in the first year and $55 in the second year.

Each MacBain will require the following inputs:

Materials—wooden mouldings	2	
—plastic mouldings	1	
—fixings	1	
Labour direct production	1 hour	

CASE STUDY 8.2

Additional costs will be incurred with regard to supervision and maintenance, variable overheads, administration and distribution.

Further investigation of costs reveals the following:

1. Toymakers has 2,000 wooden mouldings already in stock. These had cost $5 each. If not used on the MacBain the mouldings can be used on an alternative product in place of mouldings which would cost $2.50 each. New mouldings would cost $6 each in the first year and $6.50 each in the second.

2. Five thousand plastic mouldings are in stock. These had cost $7.50 each. They have no alternative use and if not used on the MacBain they would probably be destroyed at a cost of $500. Further mouldings can be purchased for $5 each. No price increases are expected over the next two years.

3. Fixings used are of a type also used on other products. Enough are in stock to produce 3,000 MacBains. They had cost $1.50 each. Further fixings are available at a price of $2.50 each.

4. The labour force currently consists of 20 staff on direct production work and three on supervision and maintenance. Production workers are currently working on short time, for only 30 hours per week. They are currently paid $15 per hour. The three staff involved with supervision and maintenance are fully employed and an additional supervisor will be required if the MacBain is to be produced. These three staff are currently paid $40,000 per annum. One of the existing supervisors is due to retire shortly, on a pension of $20,000 per annum. He has

offered to stay on for an additional year if it will help the situation. If he does he will be paid his normal salary. There will be no effect on his future pension. A pay rise of 10 per cent is expected at the beginning of the second year.

5. Variable overheads are expected to amount to $2.50 per MacBain. If the new toy is to be produced, new machinery costing $110,000 will need to be acquired. This will probably last for five years after which it will have a disposal value of about $10,000. Disposal values at the end of each of the first two years are estimated to be $60,000 and $40,000 respectively. Administration costs are expected to rise by about $2,500 per annum if the MacBain is made, although administration overheads are usually recovered on the basis of 10 per cent on direct costs. Distribution of Toymakers' production currently costs $250,000 in total for each year. This is shared out in proportion to direct costs, using a 10 per cent loading. In actual fact the company considers that it can manage to distribute the MacBains by employing additional part-time drivers at a cost of $15,000 a year, and running the trucks for longer periods of time. Additional vehicle costs will be $10,000 each year. This decision will in turn lead to earlier replacement of one of the trucks, which will need to be replaced a year from now at a cost of $25,000. Replacement was originally planned for two years from now. Toymakers can obtain funds from the bank for capital expenditure of this type at 15 per cent per annum.

1   Set out a statement for each of the next two years of possible production showing the costs and revenues you consider relevant to the decision under consideration. State your assumptions and/or explain the basis of your figures.
2   Make a recommendation as to whether Toymakers Ltd should proceed with the MacBains. Briefly identify any additional information that would be useful.

SOLUTIONS TO ACTIVITIES

Activity 8.1

This is simply found by taking all of the costs and dividing by the number of litres brewed:

$$\$(800 + 250 + 900 + 200) / 4,300 = \$0.50 \text{ per litre}$$

Activity 8.2

Only the electrician's wages earned while working on the particular job and the cost of the actual materials used on the job are direct costs. This is because it is possible to measure how much time (and therefore labour cost) was spent on the particular job and it is possible to measure how many materials were used in the job.

All of the other costs are general costs of running the business and, as such, must form part of the full cost of doing the job, but they cannot be directly measured in respect of the particular job.

Activity 8.3

The answer is all of them will be direct costs, since they can all be related to, and measured in respect of, running the business for a month.

Activity 8.4

The reasons that occurred to us are as follows:

- Large jobs should logically attract large amounts of overheads because they are likely to have been rendered more 'service' by the overheads than small ones. The length of time that they are worked on by direct labour may be seen as a rough and ready way of measuring relative size, although other means of doing this may be found—for example, relative physical size.
- Most overheads are related to time. Rent, heating, lighting, depreciation, supervisors' and managers' salaries, and loan interest, which are all typical overheads, are all more or less time-based. That is to say, the overhead cost for one week tends to be about half that for a similar two-week period. Thus it seems logical to use a basis of apportioning overheads to jobs which takes account of the length of time the units of output benefited from the 'service' rendered by the overheads.
- Direct labour hours are capable of being measured in respect of each job. They will normally be measured to deduce the direct labour element of cost in any case. Thus in the real world it is practical to apply a direct labour hour basis of dealing with overheads.

Activity 8.5

First it is necessary to identify which are the indirect costs and total them as follows:

	$
Indirect labour	27,000
Depreciation	9,000
Rent and rates	15,000
Heating, lighting and power	6,000
Indirect materials	1,500
Other miscellaneous indirect costs	600
Total indirect costs	$59,100

(Note that this list does not include the direct costs. This is because we shall deal with the direct costs separately.)

Since the company uses a direct labour hour basis of charging overheads to jobs, we need to deduce the indirect cost or overhead recovery rate per direct labour hour. This is simply:

$$\$59,100 / 6,000 = \$9.85 \text{ per direct labour hour}$$

Thus the full cost of the sail would be expected to be:

		$
Direct materials	(20 × $6)	120.00
Direct labour	(12 × ($90,000 / 6,000))	180.00
Indirect costs	(12 × $9.85)	118.20
Total cost		$418.20

Activity 8.6

The total overheads will, of course, be the same irrespective of the method of charging them to jobs. Thus the overhead recovery rate, on a machine hour basis, will be:

$$\$59,100 / 2,000 = \$29.55 \text{ per machine hour}$$

Thus the full cost of the sail would be expected to be:

		$
Direct materials	(20 × $6)	120.00
Direct labour	(12 × ($90,000 / 6,000))	180.00
Indirect costs	(5 × $29.55)	147.75
Total cost		$447.75

Activity 8.7

Direct labour hour basis:

Overhead recovery rate = $12,000 / 1,600 = $7.50 per direct labour hour

Machine hour basis:

Overhead recovery rate = $8,000 / 1,000 = $8.00 per machine hour

Overheads charged to jobs:

	Job 1 $	Job 2 $
Direct labour hour basis		
$7.50 × 800	6,000	
$7.50 × 800		6,000
Machine hour basis		
$8.00 × 700	5,600	
$8.00 × 300		2,400
Total	$11,600	$8,400

We can see from this that the total expected overheads figure of $20,000 is charged in total.

Activity 8.8

A service cost centre is one through which jobs do not pass. It renders a service to other cost centres.

Examples include general administration, accounting, stores, maintenance, personnel, catering (canteen, etc.). All of these render services to product cost centres.

Activity 8.9

Identification of the activities that cause costs puts management in a position in which it may well be better able to control them.

Activity 8.10

The answer is no difference at all. ABC is only concerned with the way in which overheads are charged to jobs to derive the full cost.

Activity 8.11

The rationale for full costing is essentially to ensure that overheads are fully recovered by an addition to the other costs charged to customers. In this case, the total overheads of $225,000 (see note 6) are recovered on the basis of direct labour cost. As budgeted direct labour cost is $450,000 and the overheads to be recovered amount to $225,000, the overheads will be fully recovered if an amount equivalent to 50 per cent of the direct labour cost for individual jobs or contracts is added to the other costs, as long as the actual direct labour cost is at least equal to the budgeted figure.

Of course, in this case, the contract is additional to the budget and the justification for adding such a loading is dubious.

Revised statement showing revenues and relevant costs:

Revenues		125,000
Costs		
Materials		
X 25 × $450 (opportunity cost)	11,250	
+ 25 × $450 (cost to buy)	11,250	
Y 100 × (45 + 25) (opportunity cost—will cost this much elsewhere if we use it on this job)	7,000	
Labour		
Direct		
52 × 400 × 1	20,800	
54 × 500 × 1	27,000	
Indirect		
Supervisor (additional cost of keeping versus retiring)	18,000	
Overheads		
Use of machine—lost hire charge 52 × 100	5,200	
Additional variable overheads incurred due to job	5,000	
Total costs		105,500
Contribution of the contract		19,500

The contract is worthwhile.

The main differences relate to:

- identification of opportunity costs rather than historic costs
- identification of relevant costs rather than arbitrary allocations.

OBJECTIVES

When you have completed your study of this chapter you should be able to:

1   define a budget

2   explain how budgets, corporate objectives and long-term plans are related

3   set out the main components of the budget-setting process

4   explain the interlinking of the various budgets within the business

5   identify the main uses of budgeting

6   construct various budgets, including the cash budget, from relevant data

7   use a budget to provide a means of exercising control over the business

8   explain and apply flexible budgeting

9   calculate a series of variances between budget and actual to assist in controlling activity

10 identify the limitations and the behavioural implications of the traditional approach to control through budgets and standards.

BUDGETING

This chapter is concerned with budgets. Budgeting is an activity that most business managers see as one of the most crucial in which they are engaged. We shall consider the purpose of budgets and how they fit into the decision-making and planning process. We shall also consider how budgets are prepared. Lastly, we shall take a look at how budgets are used to help exercise control over the business to try to ensure that plans are achieved.

BUDGETS, LONG-TERM PLANS AND CORPORATE OBJECTIVES

In Chapter 1 we saw that it is important that businesses define what it is they are ultimately seeking to achieve. (You should remember that we identified maximisation of the wealth of the business as the single most valid financial objective in the private sector.)

Clearly just to define a broad objective, such as maximisation of the wealth of the business, is not sufficient to achieve the goal. It is necessary to go into more detail as to how the objective is to be worked towards. Businesses typically do this by producing a long-term plan, perhaps going five years into the future, and a short-term plan, perhaps (usually) looking at the following 12 months.

The relationship between these three planning devices can be shown graphically, as in Figure 9.1. The overall objectives are first defined, then they are translated into long-term plans of action which are achieved through working towards short-term plans or budgets.

FIGURE 9.1 Objectives, plans and budgets

The long-term plan would define the general direction of the business over the next five or so years and would deal, in broad terms, with such matters as:

* the market that the business will seek to serve
* production/service rendering methods
* what the business will offer to its customers
* levels of profit sought
* financial requirements and financing methods
* personnel requirements
* requirements and sources for bought-in goods and services.

The budget would go into far more detail in respect of the forthcoming year and deal with such things as:

* sales and expenses
* cash flows
* short-term credit to be given or taken
* inventory requirements.

There is a clear relationship between objectives, long-term plans and budgets. The objective, once set, is likely to last for quite a long time, perhaps throughout the life of the business (though changes can and do occur). A series of long-term plans identifies how the objective is to be pursued, and budgets identify how the long-term plan is to be fulfilled.

An analogy might be found in terms of someone enrolling in a course of study. His or her objective might be to have a working career that is rewarding in various ways. The person might have identified the course as the most effective way to work towards this objective. In working towards achievement of this, passing a particular stage of the course might be identified as the target for the forthcoming year.

Here the intention to complete the entire course is analogous to a long-term plan and passing each stage is analogous to the budget. Once having achieved the 'budget' for the first year, the 'budget' for the second year becomes passing the second stage.

THE SOURCE OF PLANS AND BUDGETS

It is the function of the management of a business to set long-term plans and budgets. It is not the function of the accountant, although accountants can typically offer technical guidance. The setting of plans and budgets for the next period may be done as a major annual exercise. Alternatively, during the period of the long-term plan/budget it can be extended. For example, each month the budget for the same month next year is set; thus there will always be fairly detailed plans for a full 12 months into the future. Such a budget would be called a **rolling budget**.

It need not necessarily be the case that long-term plans are set for five years and budgets are set for 12 months; it is up to the management of the business concerned, although these are fairly typical of the time periods found in practice. A business involved in certain industries, such as information technology, may feel that five years is too long a planning period since new developments can, and do, occur virtually overnight.

ACTIVITY 9.1

Can you think of any reason why most businesses prepare detailed budgets for the forthcoming year, rather than for a shorter or longer period?

The annual budget sets targets for the year for all levels of the business. It is usually broken down into monthly budgets which define monthly targets. In many cases the annual budget will, in any case, be built up from monthly figures. For example, where the level of sales is the limiting factor the sales staff will be required to achieve sales targets for each month of the budget period. The other budgets will be set, for each month of the budget period, following the kind of links depicted in Figure 9.2 and explained below.

DEFINITION OF A BUDGET

A budget may be defined as a financial plan for a future period of time. *Financial* because the budget is, to a great extent, expressed in financial terms. Note particularly that a budget is a plan, not a forecast. To talk of a plan suggests an intention or determination to achieve the planned targets. Forecasts tend to be predictions of the future state of the environment.

Clearly, forecasts are very helpful to the planner/budget setter. If a reputable forecaster has forecast the particular number of new cars to be purchased in Australia during the next year, it will be valuable for a manager in a car manufacturing business to consider this forecast figure when setting sales budgets. However, the forecast and the budget are distinctly different.

THE INTERRELATIONSHIP OF VARIOUS BUDGETS

For a particular business for a particular period there is not one budget but a number of them, each one relating to a specific aspect of the business. It is generally considered that the ideal situation is that there should be a separate budget for each person who is in a managerial position, no matter how junior. The contents of all of the individual budgets are, in effect, summarised in master budgets which would typically be an income statement (profit and loss account), balance sheet and cash flow statement.

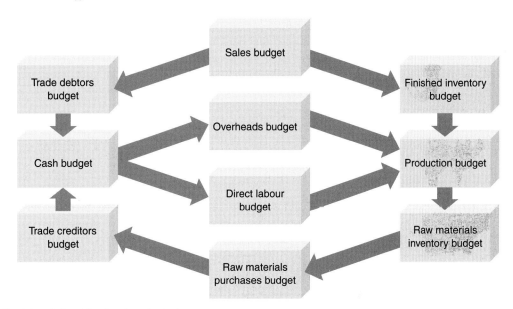

FIGURE 9.2 The interrelationship of various budgets

Figure 9.2 illustrates the interrelationship and interlinking of the individual budgets, using a manufacturing business as an example. Starting at the top of Figure 9.2, the finished inventory requirement would be dictated partly by the level of sales; it would also be dictated by the policy of the business on finished inventory holding. The requirement for finished inventory would define the required production levels, which would in turn dictate the requirements of the individual production departments or sections. The demands of manufacturing will dictate the materials budget and that will, in conjunction with the business's policy on raw material inventory holding, define the stores (raw materials) inventory budget. The purchases budget will be dictated by the stores inventory budget which will, in conjunction with the policy of the business on creditor payment, dictate the creditors budget. One of the inputs into the cash budget will be from the creditors budget; another will be the debtors budget, which itself derives via the debtor policy of the business from the sales budget. Cash will also be affected by selling and distribution costs (themselves indirectly related to sales), by labour and administration costs (themselves linked to production) and by capital expenditure. The factors that affect policies on matters such as inventory holding and debtor and creditor collection periods will be discussed in some detail in Chapter 13.

Assuming that the budgeting process takes the order in which we have just reviewed them, it might be found in practice that there is some constraint to achieving the sales target. For example, the production function of the business may be incapable of providing the necessary levels of output to match the sales budget for one or more months. In this case, it might be reasonable to look at the ways of overcoming the problem. As a last resort, it might be necessary to revise the sales budget to a lower level to enable production to meet the target.

ACTIVITY 9.2

Can you think of any ways in which a short-term shortage of production facilities might be overcome?

There will not only be the horizontal relationships between budgets which we have just looked at, but there will usually be vertical ones as well. For example, the sales budget may be broken down into a number of subsidiary budgets, perhaps one for each regional sales manager. Thus the overall sales budget will be a summary of the subsidiary ones. The same may be true of virtually all of the other budgets, most particularly the production budget. Figure 9.2 gives a very simplified outline of the budgetary framework of the typical manufacturing business.

All of the operating budgets we have just reviewed are set within the framework of the master budgets—that is, the budgeted income statement, balance sheet and cash flow statement.

THE BUDGET-SETTING PROCESS

Budgeting is such an important area for almost all businesses, and other organisations, that they tend to approach it in a fairly methodical and formal way. This is usually seen as involving a number of steps. These are:

1. Establish who will take responsibility for the budget-setting process.
2. Communicate budget guidelines to relevant managers.
3. Identify the key or limiting factor.
4. Prepare the budget for the area of the limiting factor.
5. Prepare draft budgets for all other areas.
6. Review and coordinate the budgets.
7. Prepare the master budgets.
8. Communicate the budgets to all interested parties.
9. Monitor performance relative to the budgets.

It is usually seen as crucial that those responsible for the budget-setting process have real authority in the organisation. Quite commonly a **budget committee** is formed to supervise and take responsibility for the budget-setting process. This committee usually comprises a senior representative of most of the functional areas of the business: marketing, production, personnel, etc. Often a **budget officer** is appointed to carry out, or take immediate responsibility for having carried out, the tasks of the committee. Not surprisingly, given their technical expertise in the activity, accountants are often required to take on the budget officer role.

ACTIVITY 9.3

Why is it crucial that those responsible for the budget-setting process have real authority in the organisation?

Budgets are intended to be the short-term plans that seek to work towards the achievement of long-term plans and the overall objectives of the business. It is therefore important that in drawing up budgets managers are well aware of what the long-term plans are, and how to work towards them in the forthcoming budget period. Managers also need to be made well aware of the commercial and economic environment in which they will be operating. It is the responsibility of the budget committee to see that managers have all of the necessary information.

There will always be some aspect of the business which will stop it from fully achieving its objectives. This is often a limited ability of the business to sell its products. Sometimes it is some production shortage—labour, materials or plant—that is the limiting factor, or, linked to these, a shortage of funds. Often, but not always, production shortages can be overcome by funds—for example, more plant can be bought or leased. It is possible that no amount of money will buy certain labour skills or increase the world supply of some raw material. As has been pointed out earlier in this chapter, it is sometimes possible to ease an initial limiting factor—for example, a plant capacity problem can be eliminated by subcontracting. This means that some other factor, perhaps sales, will replace the production problem, although at a higher level of output. Ultimately, however, the business will hit a ceiling; some limiting factor will prove impossible to ease.

For entirely practical reasons it is important that the limiting factor is identified. Ultimately most, if not all, budgets will be affected by the limiting factor, so if it can be identified at the outset all managers can be informed of the restriction early in the process. The budget for the area of the limiting factor then needs to be prepared. This will quite often be the sales budget, since ability to sell is frequently the limiting factor which simply cannot be avoided. The other budgets are then prepared, complementing the budget for the area of the limiting factor.

There are two broad approaches to setting budgets, namely **top-down** or **bottom-up**. In the top-down approach the senior management of each budget area originates the budget targets, perhaps discussing them with lower levels of management and, as a result, refining them before the final version is produced. With the bottom-up approach the targets are fed upwards from the lowest level. For example, junior sales managers will be asked to set their own sales targets which then become incorporated into the budgets of higher levels of management until the overall sales budget emerges. This approach is probably the one increasingly found in practice. Where the bottom-up approach is adopted it is usually necessary to haggle and negotiate to achieve a consensus, because the plans of some departments may not fit in with those of others.

The budget committee must now review the various budgets and satisfy itself that the budgets complement one another. Part of the process is likely to include preparation of the master budgets, covering the income statement, balance sheet and cash flow statement.

The formally agreed budgets are now passed to the individual managers who will be responsible for their implementation. This is, in effect, the most senior level of management (the board of directors) formally communicating the task of all other managers to them. Communication of the budget effectively *authorises* management to implement its part of the budget.

Finally, the budgetary system requires performance to be monitored relative to the budget. Much of the budget-setting activity will have been pointless unless each manager's actual performance is compared with planned performance, which is embodied in the budget, and remedial action taken where things are going wrong.

THE USES OF BUDGETS

Budgets are generally regarded as having four areas of usefulness:

1. *They tend to promote forward thinking and the possible identification of short-term problems.* In the previous section of this chapter we saw that a shortage of production capacity may be identified during the budgeting process. This discovery, if made in plenty of time, may leave a number of means of overcoming the problem open to exploration. Take, for example, the problem of a shortage of production at a particular time of the year. If the potential problem is picked up early enough, all of the suggestions in the answer to Activity 9.2 and, possibly, other ways of overcoming the problem can be explored and considered rationally. Budgeting should help to achieve this.

2. *They can be used to help coordination between various sections of the business.* It is crucially important that the activities of the various departments and sections of the business are linked so that the activities of one department are complementary to those of another. For example, the activities of the purchasing/procurement department of a manufacturing business should dovetail with the raw materials needs of the production departments. If this is not the case, production could run out of inventory, leading to expensive production stoppages. Alternatively, excessive inventory could be bought, leading to large and unnecessary inventory holding costs.

3. *They can motivate managers to better performance.* Having a stated task can motivate performance. To tell a manager to do his or her best is not very motivating, but to define a required level of achievement is likely to motivate. Managers are particularly well motivated by being able to relate their particular role in the business to overall objectives of the business. Since budgets are directly derived from corporate objectives, budgeting makes this possible.

   It might seem that requiring managers to work towards predetermined targets will stifle managers' skill, flair and enthusiasm. There is this danger if targets are badly set. If, however, the budgets are set in such a way as to offer challenging, yet achievable, targets, the manager is still required to show skill, flair and enthusiasm.

   It is obviously not possible to allow managers to operate in an unconstrained environment. Having to operate in a way that matches the goals of the business is the price of working in an effective business.

4. *They can provide a basis for a system of control.* If senior management wishes to control and to monitor the performance of subordinates it needs some standard or yardstick with which the performance can be compared and against which it can be assessed. There is a temptation, where it is possible to do so, to compare current performance with that of last month or last year, or perhaps with what happens in another business. However, the most logical yardstick is planned performance.

ACTIVITY 9.4

What is wrong with comparing actual performance with past performance or the performance of others in an effort to exercise control?

Experience of the past, and of what happens elsewhere, will be taken into account when budgets are being set.

A definition of control is 'to compel events to conform to a plan'. Even when we talk of controlling a motor vehicle, we mean making the car behave in the manner which the driver planned, even though that plan may have been made less than a second earlier.

If there are data available concerning the actual performance for a period (say, a month) and this can be compared with the planned performance, a basis for control will have been established. Such a basis will facilitate **management by exception**, a technique where senior managers can spend most of their time dealing with those of their subordinates who have failed to achieve the budget, rather than with those who are performing well. It also allows junior managers to exercise self-control—by knowing what is expected of them and what they have actually achieved, they can assess how well they are performing and take steps to correct matters where they are failing to achieve.

AN EXAMPLE OF A BUDGET—THE CASH BUDGET

We shall now look in some detail at one particular budget, the cash budget. There are three reasons for using this as an example:

1. It is at least as good an example as any other budget.
2. Most economic aspects of a business are reflected in cash sooner or later, so that for the typical business the cash budget reflects the whole business more than any other single budget.
3. Very small, unsophisticated businesses (e.g. a corner shop) may feel that full-scale budgeting is not appropriate to their needs, but almost certainly they should prepare a cash budget as a minimum.

We shall also consider other budgets later in the chapter.

Since budgets are documents which are to be used only internally by the business, their style and format is a question of management choice and will therefore vary from one business to the next. However, since managers, irrespective of the business, are likely to be using budgets for similar purposes, there is a tendency for some consistency of approach to exist across most businesses. We can probably say that in most businesses the cash budget would possess the following features:

1. The budget period would be broken down into sub-periods, typically months.
2. The budget would be in columnar form, a column for each month.
3. Receipts of cash would be identified under various headings and a total for each month's receipts shown.
4. Payments of cash would be identified under various headings and a total for each month's payments shown.
5. The surplus of total cash receipts over payments, or of payments over receipts, for each month would be identified.
6. The running cash balance, which would be obtained by taking the balance at the end of the previous month and adjusting it for surplus or deficit of receipts over payments for the current month, would be identified.

Typically all of features 3 to 6 would be useful to management for one reason or another.

Probably the best way to deal with this topic is through an example.

Suppliers Ltd is a wholesale business. The budgeted financial performance (income statement) for the next six months is as follows:

	Jan. $'000	Feb. $'000	Mar. $'000	Apr. $'000	May $'000	June $'000
Sales	52	55	55	60	55	53
Cost of goods sold	30	31	31	35	31	32
Salaries and wages	10	10	10	10	10	10
Electricity	5	5	4	3	3	3

EXAMPLE
9.1

Depreciation	3	3	3	3	3	3
Other overheads	2	2	2	2	2	2
Total expenses	50	51	50	53	49	50
Net profit	2	4	5	7	6	3

The business allows all of its customers one month's credit (i.e. goods bought in January will be paid for in February). Sales during December had been $60,000.

The business plans to maintain inventory at its existing level until March, when it is to be reduced by $5,000. Inventory will remain at this lower level indefinitely. Inventory purchases are made on one month's credit (the December purchases were $30,000). Salaries and wages and 'other overheads' are paid in the month concerned. Electricity is paid quarterly in arrears in March and June. The business plans to buy and pay for a new delivery van in March. This will cost a total of $15,000, but an existing van will be traded in for $4,000 as part of the deal. The business expects to start January with $12,000 in cash.

Show the cash budget for the six months ending in June.

Solution

Cash budget for the six months ended 30 June:

	Jan. $'000	Feb. $'000	Mar. $'000	Apr. $'000	May $'000	June $'000
Receipts						
Debtors (note 1)	60	52	55	55	60	55
Payments						
Creditors (note 2)	30	30	31	26	35	31
Salaries and wages	10	10	10	10	10	10
Electricity			14			9
Other overheads	2	2	2	2	2	2
Van purchase	–	–	11	–	–	–
Total payments	42	42	68	38	47	52
Cash surplus	18	10	(13)	17	13	3
Cash balance (note 3)	30	40	27	44	57	60

Notes

1. The cash receipts lag a month behind sales because customers are given a month in which to pay for their purchases.

2. In most months the purchases of inventory will equal the cost of goods sold. This is because the business maintains a constant level of inventory. For inventory to remain constant at the end of each month the business must exactly replace the amount of inventory that has been used. During March, however, the business plans to reduce its inventory by $5,000. This means that inventory purchases will be lower than the cost of goods sold in that month. The payments for inventory purchases lag a month behind purchases because the business expects to be allowed a month to pay for what it buys.

3. Each month's cash balance is the previous month's figure plus the cash surplus (or minus the cash deficit) for the current month. The balance at the start of January is $12,000, according to the question.

ACTIVITY 9.5

Looking at the cash budget of Suppliers Ltd (above), what conclusions do you draw, and what possible course of action do you recommend regarding the cash balances over the period concerned?

ACTIVITY 9.6

Suppliers Ltd, the wholesale business which was the subject of Example 9.1, now wishes to prepare its cash budget for the second six months of the year. The budgeted financial performance (income statement) for the period is as follows:

	July $'000	Aug. $'000	Sept. $'000	Oct. $'000	Nov. $'000	Dec. $'000
Sales	57	59	62	57	53	51
Cost of goods sold	32	33	35	32	30	29
Salaries and wages	10	10	10	10	10	10
Electricity	3	3	4	5	6	6
Depreciation	3	3	3	3	3	3
Other overheads	2	2	2	2	2	2
Total expenses	50	51	54	52	51	50
Net profit	7	8	8	5	2	1

The business will continue to allow all of its customers one month's credit (i.e. goods bought in July will be paid for in August).

The business plans to increase inventory from the 30 June level by $1,000 each month until, and including, September. During the following three months inventory levels will be decreased by $1,000 each month.

Inventory purchases, which had been made on one month's credit until the June payment, will, starting with the purchases made in June, be made on two months' credit.

Salaries and wages and 'other overheads' will continue to be paid in the month concerned. Electricity is paid quarterly in arrears in September and December.

At the end of December the business intends to pay off part of a loan. This payment is to be such that it will leave the business with a cash balance of $5,000 with which to start next year.

Remember that any information you need which relates to the first six months of the year, including the cash balance which is expected to be brought forward on 1 July, is given in Example 9.1.

Prepare the cash budget for the six months ending in December.

PREPARING OTHER BUDGETS

Although each one will have its own idiosyncrasies, other budgets will tend to follow the same sort of pattern as the cash budget. Take the debtors budget, for example. This would normally show the planned amount owing from credit sales to the business at the beginning and end of each month, the planned total sales for each month

371

and the planned total cash receipts from debtors. The layout of the *debtors budget* would be something like the following:

	Month 1	Month 2	etc.
	$	$	
Opening balance	X	X	
Sales	X	X	
	X	X	
Less cash receipts	X	X	
Closing balance	X	X	

The opening and closing balances represent the amount planned to be owed (in total) to the business by debtors at the beginning and end of the month respectively.

The layout of the *creditors budget* would be something like the following:

	Month 1	Month 2	etc.
	$	$	
Opening balance	X	X	
Purchases	X	X	
	X	X	
Less cash payments	X	X	
Closing balance	X	X	

The opening and closing balances represent the amount planned to be owed (in total) by the business to creditors at the beginning and end of the month respectively.

A *raw materials inventory budget* (for a manufacturing business) would follow a similar pattern, as follows:

	Month 1	Month 2	etc.
	$ (or physical units)	$ (or physical units)	
Opening balance	X	X	
Purchases	X	X	
	X	X	
Less issues to production	X	X	
Closing balance	X	X	

The opening and closing balances represent the amount of inventory, at cost, planned to be held by the business at the beginning and end of the period respectively.

The inventory budget will normally be expressed in financial terms, but may well be expressed in physical terms (e.g. kilograms or metres) as well for individual inventory items.

For a wholesaling or retailing business—that is, one that sells its inventory in much the same condition as it is bought—the fourth line of the inventory budget would be 'Less inventory sold'.

A manufacturing business would normally produce both a raw materials inventory budget and a finished goods inventory budget. A *finished goods inventory budget* (for a manufacturing business) would typically be as follows:

	Month 1	Month 2	etc.
	$ (or physical units)	$ (or physical units)	
Opening balance	X	X	
Finished goods inventory			
transferred from production	X	X	
	X	X	
Less finished goods sold	X	X	
Closing balance	X	X	

ACTIVITY 9.7

Prepare the debtors budget for Suppliers Ltd for the six months from July to December (see Activity 9.6).

Note how the debtors budget links to the cash budget; the cash receipts row of figures is the same. The debtors budget would similarly link to the sales budget. This is how the linking discussed earlier in this chapter is achieved.

ACTIVITY 9.8

Prepare the creditors budget for Suppliers Ltd for the six months from July to December (see Activity 9.6).

Hint: Remember that the creditor payment period alters from the June purchases onwards.

SELF-ASSESSMENT QUESTION 9.1

Antonio Ltd has planned production and sales for the next nine months as follows:

	Production units	Sales units
May	350	350
June	400	400
July	500	400
August	600	500
September	600	600
October	700	650
November	750	700
December	750	800
January	750	750

During the period, the business plans to advertise heavily to generate these increases in sales. Payments for advertising of $1,000 and $1,500 will be made in July and October respectively.

The selling price per unit will be $20 throughout the period. Forty per cent of sales are normally made on two months' credit. The other 60 per cent are settled within the month of the sale.

Raw materials will be held in stock for one month before they are used in production. Purchases of raw materials will be on one month's credit (buy one month, pay the next). The cost of raw materials is $8 per unit of production.

Other direct production expenses, including labour, are planned to be $6 per unit of production. These will be paid in the month concerned.

Various production overheads, which during the period to 30 June had run at $1,800 per month, are expected to rise to $2,000 each month from 1 July to 31 October. These are expected to rise again from 1 November to $2,400 per month and to remain at that level for the foreseeable future. These overheads include a steady $400 each month for depreciation. Overheads are planned to be paid 80 per cent in the month of production and 20 per cent in the following month.

To help meet the planned increased production, a new item of plant will be bought and will be delivered in August. The cost of this item is $6,600; the contract with the supplier will specify that this will be paid in three equal amounts in September, October and November.

Raw materials inventory is planned to be 500 units on 1 July. The balance at the bank the same day is planned to be $7,500.

You are required to draw up:

- a raw materials budget, showing both physical quantities and financial values
- a creditors budget
- a cash budget

for the six months ending 31 December.

The cash budget reveals a potential cash deficiency during October and November. Can you suggest any ways in which a modification of plans could overcome this problem?

USING BUDGETS FOR CONTROL

FLEXIBLE BUDGETS

Earlier in this chapter the point was made that budgets can provide a useful basis for exercising control over the business. This is because control is usually seen as making events conform to a plan. Since the budget represents the plan, making events conform to it is the obvious way to try to control the business. Using budgets in this way is very popular.

As we saw in Chapter 1, for most businesses the routine is as shown in Figure 9.3. These steps in the control process are probably fairly easy to understand. The point is that if plans are sensibly drawn up we have a basis for exercising control over the business. Control also requires us to have the means of measuring actual performance, in the same terms as those in which the budget is stated. If actual and budget figures are not prepared in the same terms comparison will not usually be possible.

Taking steps to exercise control means finding out where and why things did not go according to plan and seeking ways to put things right for the future. One of the reasons why things may not have gone according to plan is that the plans may, in reality, prove to be unachievable. In this case, if budgets are to be a useful basis for exercising

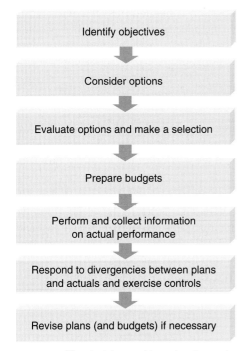

Identify objectives

Consider options

Evaluate options and make a selection

Prepare budgets

Perform and collect information on actual performance

Respond to divergencies between plans and actuals and exercise controls

Revise plans (and budgets) if necessary

FIGURE 9.3 The decision-making, planning and control process

control in the future, it may be necessary to revise the budgets for future periods to bring targets into the realms of achievability.

This last point should not be taken to mean that budget targets can simply be ignored if the going gets tough. However, for a variety of reasons, including unexpected changes in the commercial environment (e.g. unexpected collapse in demand for services of the type in which the business deals), budgets may prove to be totally unrealistic targets. In this case, nothing whatsoever will be achieved by pretending that the targets can be met.

By having a system of budgetary control a position can be established where decision making and responsibility can be delegated to junior management, yet control can still be retained by senior management. This is because senior management can use the budgetary control system to enable it to know which junior managers are meeting targets, and therefore working towards the objectives of the business, and which managers are failing to do so.

COMPARISON OF THE ACTUAL PERFORMANCE WITH THE BUDGET

Since the principal objective of most private sector businesses is to enhance their wealth, and remembering that profit is the net increase in wealth as a result of trading, the most important budget target to meet is the profit target. In view of this we shall begin on that aspect in our consideration of making the comparison between actuals and budgets.

The following are the budgeted and actual performance figures for Baxter Ltd for the month of May:

	Budget		Actual	
Output (production and sales)	1,000	units	900	units
	$		$	
Sales	100,000		92,000	
Raw materials	(40,000)	(40,000 metres)	(36,900)	(37,000 metres)
Labour	(20,000)	(2,000 hours)	(17,500)	(1,750 hours)
Fixed overheads	(20,000)		(20,700)	
Operating profit	$20,000		$16,900	

Clearly, the budgeted profit was not achieved. As far as May is concerned, this is a matter of history. However, the business (at least some aspects of it) is out of control. Senior management must discover where things went wrong during May and try to ensure that they are not repeated in later months. Thus, it is not enough to know that overall things went wrong; we need to know where and why.

ACTIVITY 9.9

Can you see any problems in comparing the various items (sales, raw materials, etc.) for the budget and the actual performance in order to draw conclusions as to which aspects were out of control?

In order to focus on the differences from a control viewpoint, a comparison is needed between actual costs incurred (for the actual volume of production) and those that we would have included in a budget if we had planned to achieve the level of production that we did achieve. In other words, in the above example we need to compare actual costs incurred in producing 900 units (the actual production) with a budget prepared on the assumption that 900 units would be produced.

Flexing the budget

This requires us to 'flex' the budget. In the above example this requires us to calculate the budget that we would have expected had the planned level of output been 900 units rather than 1,000 units. Flexing a budget simply means revising it to that which it would have been had the planned level of output been some different figure.

In the context of control, the budget is usually flexed to reflect the volume which actually occurred. To be able to flex the budget we need to know which items are fixed and which are variable relative to the level of output. Once we have this knowledge, flexing is a simple operation. We shall assume that sales revenue, materials cost and labour cost vary strictly with volume. Fixed overheads, by definition, will not. Whether in real life labour cost does vary in this way is not so certain, but it will serve well enough as an assumption for our purposes.

On the basis of the assumptions regarding the behaviour of costs, the **flexed budget** would be as follows:

	Flexed budget	
Output (production and sales)	900 units	
	$	
Sales	90,000	
Raw materials	(36,000)	(36,000 metres)
Labour	(18,000)	(1,800 hours)
Fixed overheads	(20,000)	
Operating profit	$16,000	

Putting together the original budget, the flexed budget and the actual for May the following is obtained:

	Original budget	*Flexed budget*	*Actual*
Output (production and sales)	1,000 units	900 units	900 units
	$	$	$
Sales	100,000	90,000	92,000
Raw materials	(40,000)	(36,000)	(36,900)
Labour	(20,000)	(18,000)	(17,500)
Fixed overheads	(20,000)	(20,000)	(20,700)
Operating profit	$20,000	$16,000	$16,900

The critical comparison is between the budgeted operating profit and the actual operating profit. What needs to be explained is how the $3,100 reduction in profit occurred. The above table enables us to attribute a reduction in profit of $4,000 to the reduction in volume that has resulted—the difference between the original budget and the flexed budget. Besides this we can see that (comparing the flexed budget with actual costs) an extra $900 was spent on raw materials, $500 less was spent on labour and $700 more was spent on fixed overheads than we would have expected. Also the sales revenue was $2,000 higher than we would have expected, given the level of output, which means that the selling price must have been higher than expected.

Use of the flexed budget figures facilitates a more valid comparison between budget and actual. For example, we can now see that there was a genuine labour cost saving, even after allowing for the output shortfall. Use of the flexed budget also enables us to identify clearly the loss of profit associated with a reduction in volume. The reverse is true: increases in volume would usually be associated with an increase in profit.

ACTIVITY 9.10

What would be the loss of profit arising from the sales shortfall, assuming that everything except sales volume was as planned?

We call this the *sales volume* or *quantity variance*. It is an adverse variance because, taken alone, it has the effect of making the actual profit lower than that which was budgeted. We can therefore say that an 'x' variance is the effect of the change in that factor (x) on the budgeted profit. For example, the sales volume variance measures the effect on profit of a change in sales volume. When looking at some particular aspect such as sales volume we assume that all other factors went according to plan.

ACTIVITY 9.11

What should the senior management of Baxter Ltd do about the May sales volume variance?

Who should be asked about this **variance**? The answer would probably be the sales manager. This person should know why this departure from budget has occurred. This is not the same as saying that it was the sales manager's fault. The reason for the problem could easily have been that the production department was at fault in not having produced the budgeted production, meaning that there were not sufficient items to sell. What is not in doubt is that, in the first instance, it is the sales manager who should know the reason for the problem.

A reconciliation between budgeted profit and actual profit is an essential part of the control process. Where the difference can be broken down by reason, control is increased. Differences are known as variances and the reconciliation can be summarised as follows:

| Budgeted profit | plus | All favourable variances | minus | All adverse variances | equals | Actual profit |

The reconciliation for Baxter Ltd for May is set out below:

	$	$
Budgeted profit		20,000
Less adverse variances		
Sales volume	(4,000)	
Raw materials	(900)	
Fixed overheads	(700)	
		(5,600)

Plus favourable variances
Labour	500	
Sales price	2,000	
		2,500
Actual profit		$16,900

ACTIVITY 9.12

The budget and actual figures for Baxter Ltd for June are as given below. They will be used as the basis for a series of activities that you should work through as we look at variance analysis. The May figures will be used as examples as part of the text and the June ones will provide the information for the activities. Note that the company had budgeted for a higher level of output for June than it did for May.

	Budget for June		Actual for June	
Output (production and sales)	1,100 units		1,150 units	
	$		$	
Sales	110,000		113,500	
Raw materials	(44,000)	(44,000 metres)	(46,300)	(46,300 metres)
Labour	(22,000)	(2,200 hours)	(23,200)	(2,368 hours)
Fixed overheads	(20,000)		(19,300)	
Operating profit	$24,000		$24,700	

The flexible budget is shown below, alongside the original budget and the actual figures. Compare this with the June actuals, and find the sales volume variance.

	Budget		Flexible budget		Actual	
Output (units)	1,100		1,150		1,150	
(production and sales)						
	$		$		$	
Sales	110,000		115,000		113,500	
Raw materials	(44,000)	(44,000 metres)	(46,000)	(46,000 metres)	(46,300)	(46,300 metres)
Labour	(22,000)	(2,200 hours)	(23,000)	(2,300 hours)	(23,200)	(2,368 hours)
Fixed overheads	(20,000)		(20,000)		(19,300)	
Operating profit	$24,000		$26,000		$24,700	

Clearly, what is needed next is a reconciliation of budgeted and actual profits. A comparison of budget and flexed budget enables us to derive the first stage of the reconciliation as follows:

	$
Budgeted profit	24,000
Sales volume variance	2,000
Flexed budget profit	26,000

The next stage is to compare the flexed budget with actual results in detail. There are differences in all lines, which are analysed below.

Backtracking to May with the sales revenue figure, we saw that there was a difference of $2,000 (favourable) between the flexed budget and the actual figures. This could only have arisen from higher prices being charged than were envisaged in the original budget, because any variance arising from the volume difference has already been 'stripped out' in the flexing process. Hence the *sales price variance* of $2,000 which was shown in the reconciliation above for May.

ACTIVITY 9.13

What is the sales price variance for June?

In May there was an overall or *total direct materials variance* of $900 (adverse). Who should be held accountable for this variance? The answer to this question depends on whether the difference arises from excess usage of the raw materials, in which case it is the production manager, or whether it is a higher than budgeted price per metre being paid, in which case it is the responsibility of the buying manager.

Fortunately, we have the means available to go beyond this total variance. We can see from the figures that 37,000 metres of materials were used when the flexed budget suggested that only 36,000 were needed. In other words there was a 1,000 metre excess usage of the raw materials. All other things being equal, this alone would have led to a profit shortfall of $1,000 since the budgeted price per metre is $1. The $1,000 (adverse) variance is known as the *direct materials usage variance*. Normally, this would be the responsibility of the production manager since it is that person's responsibility to supervise the use of the raw material.

ACTIVITY 9.14

What was the direct materials usage variance for June?

The other aspect of direct materials is the *direct materials price variance*. Here we simply take the actual quantity bought and compare what should have been paid for it with what was actually paid for it. In May, for a quantity of 37,000 metres the cost should have been $37,000; it was actually $36,900. Thus we have a favourable price variance of $100.

ACTIVITY 9.15

What was the direct materials price variance for June?

As we have just seen, the total direct materials variance is the sum of the usage variance and the price variance. This is illustrated in Figure 9.4.

Direct labour variances are very similar in style to those for direct materials. The *total direct labour variance* for May was $500 (i.e. $18,000 – 17,500). Again, this information is not particularly helpful since the responsibility for the rate of pay lies primarily with the personnel manager, at least to the extent of being able to explain the

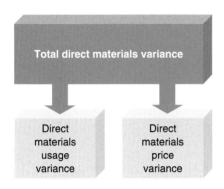

Total direct materials variance

Direct materials usage variance

Direct materials price variance

FIGURE 9.4 The relationship between the total, usage and price variances for direct materials

variance. The number of hours taken to complete a particular quantity of output is, however, the responsibility of the production manager.

The *direct labour efficiency variance* compares the number of hours that would be allowed for the level of production achieved with the actual number of hours, and costs the difference at the allowed hourly rate. Thus, for May, it was (1,800 hours – 1,750 hours) × $10 = $500 (favourable). The variance is favourable because fewer hours were used than would have been expected (allowed) for the actual level of output.

ACTIVITY 9.16

What was the direct labour efficiency variance for June?

The *direct labour rate variance* compares the actual cost of the hours worked with the planned cost. For 1,750 hours worked in May the allowed cost would be $17,500 (i.e. 1,750 × $10). Since this is exactly the amount that was actually paid, there is no rate variance.

ACTIVITY 9.17

What was the direct labour rate variance for June?

The remaining area is that of fixed overheads. Here the *fixed overhead spending (expenditure) variance* is simply the difference between the flexed budget and the actual figures. For May, this was $700 (adverse). In theory, this is the responsibility of whoever controls overheads expenditure. In practice, this tends to be a very slippery area and one that is notoriously difficult to control.

ACTIVITY 9.18

What was the fixed overhead spending variance for June?

We are now in a position to reconcile the original May budget profit with the actual one, in an expanded way, as follows:

	$	$
Budgeted profit		20,000
Favourable variances		
Sales price variance	2,000	
Direct materials price	100	
Direct labour efficiency	500	2,600
		22,600

Adverse variances		
Sales volume	4,000	
Direct materials usage	1,000	
Fixed overhead spending	700	5,700
Actual profit		16,900

ACTIVITY 9.19

Try reconciling the original profit figure for June with the actual June figure.

ACTIVITY 9.20

The following are the budgeted and actual performance figures for Baxter Ltd for the month of July:

	Budget		Actual	
Output (production and sales)	1,000 units		1,050 units	
	$		$	
Sales	100,000		104,300	
Raw materials	(40,000)	(40,000 metres)	(41,200)	(40,500 metres)
Labour	(20,000)	(2,000 hours)	(21,300)	(2,080 hours)
Fixed overheads	(20,000)		(19,400)	
Operating profit	$20,000		$22,400	

Produce a reconciliation of the budgeted and actual operating profit, going into as much detail as possible with the variance analysis.

STANDARD QUANTITIES AND COSTS

The budget is a financial plan for a future period of time. It is built up from standards. **Standards** are planned quantities and costs (or revenues) for individual units of input or output. Thus standards are the building blocks that are used to build the budget. Detailed identification of standards facilitates meaningful variance analysis.

We can say about Baxter Ltd's operations that:

* The standard selling price is $100 per unit of output.
* The standard raw materials cost is $40 per unit of output.
* The standard raw materials usage is 40 metres per unit of output.
* The standard raw materials price is $1 per metre (i.e. per unit of input).
* The standard labour cost is $20 per unit of output.
* The standard labour time is 2 hours per unit of output.
* The standard labour rate is $10 per hour (i.e. per unit of input).

The standards, like the budgets to which they are linked, represent targets and therefore yardsticks by which actual performance is measured. They are derived from experience of what is a reasonable quantity of input (for labour time and materials usage) and from assessments of the market for the product (standard selling price) and for the inputs (labour rate and materials price). These should be subject to frequent review and, where necessary, revision. It is vital if they are to be used as part of the control process that they represent realistic targets.

Calculation of most variances is, in effect, based on standards. For example, the materials usage variance is the difference between the standard materials usage for the level of output and the actual usage, costed at the standard materials price.

Standards can have uses other than in the context of budgetary control. The existence of what should be, and normally are, the various usages and costs associated with the operations of the business provides decision makers with a ready set of information for their decision-making purposes.

REASONS FOR ADVERSE VARIANCES

A constant possible reason why variances occur is that the standards against which performance is being measured are not reasonable targets. This is certainly not to say that the immediate reaction to an adverse variance should be that the standard is unreasonably harsh. On the other hand, standards that are not achievable are useless.

ACTIVITY 9.21

The variances we have considered are:

- sales volume
- sales price
- direct materials usage
- direct materials price
- direct labour efficiency
- direct labour rate
- fixed overhead spending (or expenditure).

Ignoring the possibility that standards may be unreasonable, jot down any ideas that occur to you as possible practical reasons for adverse variances in each case.

There is a very large number of variances that it is possible to calculate, given the range of operations found in practice. We have considered just the most basic of them. They are all, however, based on similar principles.

Though we have tended to use the example of a manufacturing business to explain variance analysis, this should not be taken to imply that variance analysis is not equally applicable and useful in a service sector business.

INVESTIGATING VARIANCES

It is unreasonable to expect that budget targets will be precisely met each month. Whatever the reason for a variance may be, that reason may not be very obvious. This means that to find the reason will take time, and time is costly. Given that small variances are almost inevitable and that investigating variances can be expensive, management needs to establish a policy on which variances to investigate and which to ignore. For example, for Baxter Ltd (the example used earlier in this chapter) the budgeted usage of materials during May was 40,000 metres at a cost of $1 per metre. Suppose that production had been of the budgeted quantity of output, but that

40,005 metres of material had actually been used. Would this adverse variance of $5 be investigated? Probably it would not. What, however, if the variance were $50 or $500 or $5,000?

ACTIVITY 9.22

What broad approach do you feel should be taken on whether to spend money investigating a particular variance?

The only reason that knowing why a variance occurred can have any value is that it might provide management with the means to put things back in control so that future targets can be met. It should be borne in mind here that normally variances will either be zero, or more likely very close to zero. This is to say that achieving targets, give or take small variances, should be normal.

Broadly, we can probably say the following:

✳ Significant adverse variances should be investigated because the fault that they represent could ultimately be very costly. Management must decide what 'significant' means. A certain amount of science can be brought to bear in making this decision, but it must be a matter of managerial judgment as to what is significant. Perhaps a variance of 5 per cent from the budgeted figure would be deemed to be significant.

✳ Significant *favourable* variances should probably also be investigated. Although such variances would not cause such immediate management concern as do adverse ones, they still represent things not going according to plan. If actual performance is significantly better than the target, it may well mean that the target is unrealistically low.

✳ Insignificant variances, although not triggering immediate investigation, should be kept under review. For each aspect of operations the cumulative sum of variances, over a series of control periods, should be zero, with small adverse variances in some periods being compensated for by small, favourable ones in other periods. This should be the case with variances caused by chance factors which will not necessarily repeat themselves.

Where a variance is caused by a more systematic factor that *will* repeat itself, the cumulative sum of the periodic variances will not be zero but an increasing figure. Where the increasing figure represents a set of adverse variances it may well be worth investigating the situation, even though the individual variances may be insignificant. Even where the direction of the cumulative total points to favourable variances, investigation may still be considered to be valuable.

COMPENSATING VARIANCES

There is superficial appeal in the idea that linked favourable and adverse variances will result in compensation and therefore not be considered further. For example, a sales manager believes that she could sell more of the product if prices were lowered and that this would feed through to increased net operating profit.

ACTIVITY 9.23

What possible reason is there why the sales manager should not go ahead with the price reduction?

The solution to this activity illustrates that 'trading off' variances is not automatically acceptable without a more far-reaching consultation and revision of plans.

NECESSARY CONDITIONS FOR EFFECTIVE BUDGETARY CONTROL

It is probably fairly obvious, from what we have seen of control through budgets, that if it is to be successful, a system or a set of routines must be established to enable the potential benefits to be gained.

ACTIVITY 9.24

Jot down a list of any points you can think of which you feel need to be included in any system or routines that will enable control through budgets to be effective.

We have not specifically covered these points, but your common sense, and perhaps your background knowledge, should enable you to think of a few.

LIMITATIONS OF THE TRADITIONAL APPROACH TO CONTROL THROUGH VARIANCES AND STANDARDS

Budgetary control, of the type we have reviewed in this chapter, has obvious appeal and, judging by the wide extent of its use in practice, has value as well. It is somewhat limited at times, however. Some of its limitations are as follows:

* Vast areas of most business and commercial activities simply do not have the same direct relationship between inputs and outputs as is the case with, say, level of output and the amount of raw materials used. Much of the expense of the modern business is in areas such as training and advertising which are discretionary and not linked to the level of output in a direct way.

* Standards can quickly become out of date as a result of both technological change and price changes. This does not pose insuperable problems, but it does require that the potential problem is systematically addressed. Standards which are unrealistic are, at best, useless. At worst they could have adverse effects on performance. A buyer who knows that it is impossible to meet price targets anyway, because of price rises, has a reduced incentive to keep costs as low as possible.

* Sometimes factors that are outside the control of the manager concerned can affect the calculation of the variance for which that manager is held accountable. This is likely to have an adverse effect on the manager's performance. This can often be overcome by a more considered approach to the calculation of the variance which results in separation of that which is controllable by the manager from that which is not.

* In practice, creating clear lines of demarcation between the areas of responsibility of various managers may be difficult. Thus, one of the prerequisites of good budgetary control is lost.

BEHAVIOURAL ASPECTS OF BUDGETARY CONTROL

Budgets, perhaps more than any other accounting statement, are prepared with the objective of affecting the attitudes and behaviour of managers. The point was made earlier in this chapter that budgets are intended to motivate managers. In practice, research evidence generally shows this to be true. More specifically:

* the existence of budgets tends to improve performance
* setting demanding, but achievable, budget targets tends to motivate better than less demanding targets

* unrealistically demanding targets tend to have an adverse effect on managers' performance
* the participation of managers in setting the targets for themselves tends to improve motivation and performance.

It has been suggested that allowing managers to set their own targets will lead to slack being introduced, so making achievement of the target that much easier. On the other hand, in an effort to impress, a manager may select a target that is not really achievable. These points imply that care must be taken in the extent to which managers have unfettered choice of their own targets.

Where a manager fails to meet a budget, care must be taken by that manager's senior in dealing with the failure. A harsh, critical approach may demotivate the manager. Adverse variances may imply that the manager needs help from the senior.

The existence of budgets gives senior managers a ready means to assess the performance of their subordinates. Where promotion or bonuses depend on the absence of variances, senior management must be very cautious.

SELF-ASSESSMENT QUESTION 9.2

Toscanini Ltd makes a standard product, which is budgeted to sell at $12.00 per unit, in a competitive market. It is made by taking a budgeted 0.4 kg of material, budgeted to cost $7.20 per kilogram, which is worked on by hand by an employee, paid a budgeted $12 per hour for a budgeted 12 minutes. Monthly fixed overheads are budgeted at $14,400. The output for May was budgeted at 4,000 units. The actual results for May were as follows:

	$
Sales (3,500 units)	41,460
Materials (1,425 kg)	(10,260)
Labour (690 hours)	(8,070)
Fixed overheads	(14,700)
Actual operating profit	$8,430

No inventory of any description existed at the beginning and end of the month.

Required:

(a) Deduce the budgeted profit for May and reconcile it with the actual profit in as much detail as the information provided will allow.

(b) State which manager should be held accountable, in the first instance, for each variance calculated.

(c) Assuming that the standards were all well set in terms of labour times and rates, and materials usage and price, suggest at least one feasible reason for each of the variances you identified in requirement (a), given what you know about the company's performance for May.

(d) If it were discovered that the actual total world market demand for the company's product was 10 per cent lower than it had been estimated to be when the May budget was set, state how and why the variances you identified in requirement (a) could be revised to provide information that would be potentially more useful.

SUMMARY

In this chapter we have achieved the following objectives in the way shown.

OBJECTIVE	METHOD ACHIEVED
Define a budget	• Defined a budget • Explained the role of budgeting • Illustrated how budgets can be used to try to achieve the business objectives
Explain how budgets, corporate objectives and long-term plans are related	• Considered the relationship between business objectives and short-term plans and how those short-term plans or budgets are derived
Set out the main components of the budget-setting process	• Illustrated how budgets are prepared • Worked through a typical budget-setting process • Identified and explained the role of a budget committee • Introduced the concept of key or limiting factors in relation to the budget • Discussed top-down versus bottom-up approaches to budgeting
Explain the interlinking of the various budgets within the business	• Explained and illustrated how budgets for different facets of the business can be made to coordinate
Identify the main uses of budgeting	• Identified the main uses of budgeting, specifically the tendency to encourage forward thinking, help coordination, motivate better performance and provide a basis for exercising control • Illustrated how budgets can be used to help management exercise control over the business
Construct various budgets, including the cash budget, from relevant data	• Illustrated and prepared budgets from basic information
Use a budget to provide a means of exercising control over the business	• Showed how it is possible, by making a comparison between the actual outcomes and the original budgets, and carrying out further analysis, to identify areas of the business that are not performing according to plan • Identified the limitations of the traditional control model
Explain and apply flexible budgeting	• Explained the rationale for flexible budgeting • Flexed a budget
Calculate a series of variances between budget and actual to assist in controlling activity	• Used flexible budgeting to be able to provide a basis for comparing actual performance with an appropriate standard • Calculated relevant variances • Reconciled the budgeted and actual profits
Identify the limitations and the behavioural implications of the traditional approach to control through budgets and standards	• Indicated that there is an important behavioural dimension to budgeting, in that budgets have the power to motivate or demotivate • Applied your understanding to practical problems

DISCUSSION QUESTIONS

EASY

<Obj 1>	**9.1**	Define a budget. How is a budget different from a forecast?
<Obj 2>	**9.2**	What is the relationship between the budget and the business objectives?
<Obj 4>	**9.3**	What other budgets impact on the 'production budget'?
<Obj 5>	**9.4**	What were the four uses of budgets that were identified in the chapter?
<Obj 8>	**9.5**	What is a 'flexed budget'?
<Obj 9>	**9.6**	What is meant by a variance?
<Obj 9>	**9.7**	What is the alternative title for sales volume variance? How is it calculated? What does it show?
<Obj 9>	**9.8**	Distinguish between a 'materials price variance' and a 'materials usage variance'.
<Obj 9>	**9.9**	What does a sales price variance disclose?
<Obj 9>	**9.10**	How is the labour efficiency variance calculated? What factors may give rise to an unfavourable labour efficiency variance?
<Obj 9>	**9.11**	What does a fixed overhead spending variance disclose?
<Obj 9>	**9.12**	What factors might give rise to a favourable sales volume variance and an unfavourable direct materials usage variance?
<Obj 9>	**9.13**	Which variances should be investigated?
<Obj 9>	**9.14**	What are standards in cost accounting? Why are they used? What are their advantages and limitations?

INTERMEDIATE

<Obj 2>	**9.15**	What would normally be included in the long-term plan of a commercial organisation?
<Obj 2>	**9.16**	Who should be responsible for setting long-term plans and budgets?
<Obj 3>	**9.17**	Two approaches to budget setting are labelled 'top-down' and 'bottom-up'. What is the difference between the two? Discuss the merits and limitations of both.
<Obj 3, 4, 6>	**9.18**	What are the steps involved in the budgeting process?
<Obj 3, 7, 9>	**9.19**	What is meant by the expression 'management by exception'?
<Obj 4>	**9.20**	What are the master budgets?
<Obj 4>	**9.21**	The term 'limiting factor' is important to the budgeting process. What is a limiting factor? How does it impact on the budgeting process?
<Obj 4, 7>	**9.22**	Budgets are said to facilitate coordination between sectors and departments. Do you agree?
<Obj 7, 9>	**9.23**	How do budgets help to identify short-term problems?
<Obj 8>	**9.24**	What is the point in flexing the budget in the context of variance analysis? Does flexing imply that differences between budget and actual in terms of the volume of output are ignored in variance analysis?
<Obj 9, 10>	**9.25**	What are the limitations of the use of standards and control through variance analysis?
<Obj 10>	**9.26**	Under what set of conditions will the budgetary system operate optimally?

CHALLENGING

<Obj 2, 7, 10>	**9.27**	In what way do budgets assist in management control?
<Obj 10>	**9.28**	Assess budgets as a motivational device for staff.

APPLICATION EXERCISES

EASY

<Obj 6>

9.1 The budgeted income statement of Noel Ltd for the year ending 31 December 2005 is as follows:

	$	$
Sales		360,000
Cost of sales		(210,000)
Gross profit		150,000
Depreciation	25,000	
Other expenses	75,000	(100,000)
Net profit		50,000

The budgeted balance sheet amounts related to trading activities are as follows:

		1/1/2005	31/12/2005
Current assets	Cash	10,000	?
	Accounts receivable	38,000	33,000
	Inventory	51,000	57,000
	Prepayments (Expenses)	2,000	3,500
Current liabilities	Accounts payable	27,000	34,000
	Accruals (Expenses)	1,000	2,500

Required:
Prepare an operating cash budget based on the above information.

INTERMEDIATE

<Obj 2, 3, 6, 10>

9.2 You have overheard the following statements:

(a) 'A budget is a forecast of what is expected to happen in a business during the next year.'

(b) 'Monthly budgets must be prepared with a column for each month so that you can see the whole year at a glance, month by month.'

(c) 'Budgets are okay but they stifle all initiative. No manager worth employing would work for a business which seeks to control through budgets.'

(d) 'Activity-based budgeting is an approach that takes account of the volume of activity which is planned to deduce the figures to go into the budget.'

(e) 'Any sensible person would start with the sales budget and build up the other budgets from there.'

(f) 'A budget which attempts to be realistic will not motivate best performance.'

(g) 'Only adverse variances are worth investigating, because favourable variances, by definition, must be good.'

Critically discuss these statements, explaining any technical terms.

<Obj 6>   **9.3**   Finetime Ltd is a new business and started production on 1 April. Planned sales for the next nine months are as follows:

	Sales units
May	500
June	600
July	700
August	800
September	900
October	900
November	900
December	800
January	700

The selling price per unit will be a consistent $100 and all sales will be made on one month's credit. It is planned that sufficient finished goods inventory for each month's sales should be available at the end of the previous month.

Raw materials purchases will be such that there will be sufficient raw materials inventory available at the end of each month precisely to meet the following month's planned production. This planned policy will operate from the end of April. Purchases of raw materials will be on one month's credit. The cost of raw materials is $40 per unit of finished product.

The direct labour cost, which is variable with the level of production, is planned to be $20 per unit of finished production. Production overheads are planned to be $20,000 each month, including $3,000 for depreciation. Non-production overheads are planned to be $11,000 per month of which $1,000 will be depreciation. Various fixed assets costing $250,000 will be bought and paid for during April.

Except where specified otherwise, assume that all payments take place in the same month as the cost is incurred.

The business will raise $300,000 in cash from a share issue in April.

You are required to draw up:

* a finished inventory budget, showing just physical quantities
* a raw materials inventory budget, showing both physical quantities and financial values
* a trade creditors budget
* a trade debtors budget
* a cash budget

for the six months ending 30 September.

<Obj 6>   **9.4**   The summarised balance sheet of Brown & Co. Pty Ltd as at 31 May 2006 is as follows:

BROWN & CO. PTY LTD

Balance sheet as at 31 May 2006		
	$	$
Current assets		
Bank	20,000	
Debtors	200,000	
Inventory	90,000	
		310,000

Non-current assets (net of depreciation)		190,000
		500,000
Current liabilities		
Creditors	80,000	
Accrued wages	2,500	
Accrued general expenses	2,000	
		84,500
Capital and reserves		415,500
		500,000

Creditors represent purchases for May and debtors the sales for April and May at $100,000 per month.

The directors are seeking finance from a bank and have produced the following profit forecast, but the bank, before deciding, has asked for a cash budget for the period showing the maximum anticipated finance needed from month to month.

The profit forecast for 2006 is:

	June	July	August	September	October	November
Sales	100,000	150,000	250,000	250,000	250,000	250,000
Gross profit (20% fixed)	20,000	30,000	50,000	50,000	50,000	50,000
Wages and salaries	20,000	20,000	20,000	30,000	30,000	30,000
Rent	1,670	1,670	1,660	1,670	1,670	1,660
Other expenses	8,000	8,000	8,000	15,000	15,000	15,000
Net profit/(loss)	(9,670)	330	20,340	3,330	3,330	3,340
Stock requirement at month-end	100,000	110,000	180,000	180,000	180,000	180,000

Further information is given below:
1. At each month-end one-eighth of a month's wages and salaries, and a quarter of other expenses, would be outstanding.
2. Rent at the rate of $20,000 per annum is payable quarterly in arrears on 31 August, 30 November, etc.
3. It may be assumed that one month's credit will be taken on purchases as previously, and that debtors will continue to take two months' credit.
4. New fixed assets (additional) will be delivered in June and must be paid for on 31 August; cost $200,000.
5. If the bank grants finance, it will continue an existing $50,000 overdraft facility, and give a five-year loan of a fixed amount as soon as necessary to maintain the overdraft within its limit for the whole period under review.

You are required to produce:
(a) the required cash budget
(b) the income statement for the period
(c) a summary balance sheet as at 30 November 2006.

<Obj 6>   **9.5**   The following table is to be used in completing this question.

	Jan.	Feb.	Mar.	Apr.	May	June
Financial performance:	$	$	$	$	$	$
Sales	100,000	110,000	115,000	110,000	105,000	90,000
Opening stock						
Purchases						
Available						
Closing stock						
Cost of sales						
Gross profit						
Expenses – Cash						
Expenses – Allocation	6,000	6,000	6,000	6,000	6,000	6,000
Net profit						
Cash budget						
Receipts:						
Cash sales						
Debtors current						
Debtors 30 days						
Debtors 60 days						
Payments:						
Cash purchases						
Creditors – Current						
Creditors – 30 days						
Expenses – Cash						

Notes: (1) Sales: 25% cash, 75% credit
    (2) Credit sales collection estimates: 10% current month
                                             40% 30 days
                                             22% 60 days
                                             3% lost
    (3) Purchases 40% cash, 60% credit.
    (4) Credit purchase payment policy: 10% current month
                                          50% 30 days
    (5) Inventory policy: Monthly closing stock equals the estimated next 1.5 months
         'cost of sales'.
    (6) Mark-up: All inventory items are marked up 75%.
    (7) Expenses – Cash equal 11% of that month's sales.
    (8) The business commenced operations on 1 January this year.

Required:
Complete the cash budget for the months January–March. You will find it useful to
complete most of the statement of financial performance budget for January–June to
facilitate computing the cash budget figures.

<Obj 8>   **9.6**   The following forecasts were prepared for a company for a four-week period:

	Forecast A	Forecast B
Sales at $200 each	20,000	50,000
Variable and semi-variable expenses		
Indirect labour	50 workers	80 workers
Power	$80,000	$200,000
Maintenance	$200,000	$380,000
Distribution	$100,000	$160,000

Other relevant information is:
1. Direct materials are 30 per cent of sales.
2. Each person involved on direct labour produces 50 items per month.
3. Depreciation is $320,000.
4. Other fixed costs are $600,000.
5. Selling costs are 5 per cent of sales.
6. Labour wages are $500 per week.

Required:
(a) Prepare comparative forecast profit statements for the period.
(b) If production is 40,000 units and sales are 30,000 units, calculate the appropriate figures you would compare with actual costs for control purposes. (The term 'allowed cost', meaning an appropriate allowance for an expense, given the volume, is frequently used to describe this.)

<Obj 8>   **9.7**   The following summary data are from a performance report for the Graham Ltd for May, during which 10,700 units were produced. The budget reflects the company's normal capacity of 10,000 units.

	Budget (10,000 units)	Actual Costs (10,700 units)	Variances over (under) budget
Raw materials	$35,000	$36,100	$1,100
Direct labour	$70,000	$70,300	$300
Factory overhead: Variable	$24,000	$23,600	($400)
Fixed	$18,000	$18,700	$700
	$147,000	$148,700	$1,700

Required:
What is the general implication of the performance report? Why might the manager question the significance of the report?

Revise the performance report using flexible budgeting and comment on the general implication of the revised report.

<Obj 9>   **9.8**   Antonio Ltd makes product X, the standard cost of which is:

	$
Sales revenue	25
Direct labour (half hour)	(5)
Direct materials (1 kg)	(10)
Fixed overheads	(3)
Standard profit	7

The budgeted output for March was 1,000 units of product X; the actual output was 1,100 units, which were sold for $28,200. There was no inventory of any description at either end of March.

The actual production costs were:

	$
Direct labour (537.5 hours)	5,550
Direct materials (1,170 kg)	11,630
Fixed overheads	3,200

You are required to calculate the variances for March as fully as you are able to from the available information and to use the variances calculated to reconcile the budgeted and actual profit figures.

<Obj 10>   **9.9**   Explain the different reasons why a manager might submit a budget estimate that is biased. How do you guard against this?

<Obj 10>   **9.10** Give some examples of how a manager might achieve his or her budget by methods that are harmful to the organisation. How would you stop this?

CHALLENGING

<Obj 6>   **9.11** Byron Ltd estimated sales for the forthcoming months are:

Nov.	25,000 @ $3.70
Dec.	40,000 @ $3.90
Jan.	20,000 @ $3.80
Feb.	15,000 @ $3.60
Mar.	10,000 @ $3.50
April	5,000 @ $3.50

Past experience has shown that collections from sales average:

25% cash received in the month of the sale
55% in the month following the sale
20% two months following the sale

Opening inventories (units) each month are required to be equal to 75% of the month's expected sales. Production capacity is a maximum of 50,000 units per month. Each finished unit requires 3.6 kg of raw material at a cost of 48 cents per kg. The firm maintains an inventory of 20,000 kg of raw material as replacement stocks are not readily available from suppliers. Purchases are made on 60 days' credit terms.

The costs being: Labour — variable $1.05 per unit
— fixed $4,000 per month
Overheads — variable 5% of sales
— fixed $4,700 ($2,200 non-cash)

The cash balance at 31 December was $12,000 (credit) and the company has an overdraft limit of $50,000.

Prepare the following budgets for January, February and March:
(a) Sales
(b) Purchases
(c) Production
(d) Cash

<Obj 6>   **9.12** Lewisham Ltd manufactures one product line—the Zenith. Sales of Zeniths over the next few months are planned to be as follows:

1. *Demand*

	Units
July	180,000
August	240,000
September	200,000
October	180,000

Each Zenith sells for $3 each.

2. *Debtor receipts*
Debtors are expected to pay as follows:
- 70 per cent during the month of sale
- 28 per cent during the following month.
The remainder of debtors are expected to go bad.
    Debtors who pay in the month of sale are entitled to deduct a 2 per cent discount from the invoice price.

3. *Finished goods inventory*
Finished goods inventories are expected to be 40,000 units at 1 July. The company's policy is that, in future, the inventory at the end of each month should equal 20 per cent of the following month's planned sales requirements.

4. *Raw materials inventory*
Raw materials inventory is expected to be 40,000 kg on 1 July. The company's policy is that, in future, the inventory at the end of each month should equal 50 per cent of the following month's planned production requirements. Each Zenith requires 0.5 kg of the raw material which costs $1.50 per kilogram.
    Raw materials purchases are paid in the month after purchase.

5. *Labour and overheads*
The direct labour cost of each Zenith is $0.50. The variable overhead element of each Zenith is $0.30. Fixed overheads, including depreciation of $25,000, total $47,000 per month.
    All labour and overheads are paid during the month in which they arise.

6. *Cash in hand*

At 1 August the company plans to have a bank balance (in funds) of $20,000.

You are required to prepare the following budgets:

(a) finished goods inventory budget (expressed in units of Zenith) for each of the three months July, August and September

(b) raw materials budget (expressed in kilograms of the raw material) for the two months July and August

(c) cash budget for August and September.

<Obj 8, 9>   **9.13** You are given the following data for a company, for a four-week period, at two forecasted levels of activity.

	Forecast A	Forecast B
Sales at $100 per unit	50,000 units	100,000 units
Indirect labour	80 workers	140 workers
Power	$100,000	$200,000
Maintenance	$300,000	$500,000
Distribution	$208,000	$296,000

In addition the following information applies to both forecasts:

Direct materials	50% of sales value
Direct labour	1 worker produces 50 units a week
Depreciation	$100,000
Other fixed costs	$300,000
Selling costs	2.5% of sales
Labour costs	$500 per week per worker

Required:

(a) Prepare comparative forecast income statements for the two output levels.

(b) Prepare a statement of allowed costs for an actual activity level of 60,000 units of production and 40,000 units of sales.

Actual costs were as follows:

	$
Direct materials	3,180,000
Direct labour	602,000
Indirect labour	180,000
Power	124,000
Maintenance	338,000
Selling and distribution	189,000

In addition you are told that the prices of direct materials rose by 5 per cent at the beginning of the period owing to an increase in tax, while direct and indirect labour rates rose by 3 per cent as a result of a national agreement.

(c) Calculate appropriate variances between budgeted (allowed) and actual, distinguishing those which are controllable from those which are not.

<Obj 9>

9.14 Mowbray Ltd makes and sells one standard product, the standard cost of which is as follows:

	$
Direct materials (3 kg at $5 per kilogram)	15
Direct labour (30 minutes at $9 per hour)	4.50
Fixed overheads	7.20
	26.70
Selling price	40.00
Standard profit margin	13.30

The monthly production and sales are planned to be 1,200 units. The actual results for May were as follows:

	$
Sales	36,000
Direct materials	(14,800) (2,800 kg used)
Direct labour	(4,600) (510 hours)
Fixed overheads	(8,200)
Operating profit	$8,400

There was no inventory of any description either at the start or end of the month.

As a result of poor sales demand during May, the company had reduced the price of all sales by 10 per cent.

You are required to calculate the budgeted profit for May and reconcile it to the actual profit through variances, going into as much detail as is possible from the information available.

CASE STUDY 9.1

Whitbitz Pty Ltd, a company based in Proserpine, produces a single machined part used extensively in boat building and repairs. To date the company has not thought it necessary to use sophisticated costing methods, but much fiercer competition is changing this attitude. A system of flexible budgeting has been developed which effectively provides a standard cost for the product. These costs are shown below.

	$	$	$
Selling price			200
Less costs			
Extrusions 10 kg @ $5 per kilogram		50	
Wages—3 hours @ $20 per hour		60	
Overheads			
Fixed costs (average)	20		
Variable costs	10		
		30	
			140
Standard profit			60

These figures are based on a budget of 1,000 parts in every four weeks (20 days). Products are broadly made to order so you can assume that minimal inventory is held.

During February a summarised income statement shows the following:

	$	$	$
Sales			176,000
Less costs			
Materials—8,100 kg @ $6 per kilogram		48,600	
Labour		63,800	
Overheads			
Fixed costs	22,500		
Variable costs	11,000		
		33,500	
			145,900
Net profit			30,100

The following additional information is available:

1. Selling price was increased by 10 per cent.
2. A strike called by the national union on an Australia-wide basis to support a pay rise for all workers in the industry, resulted in a stoppage for five days. The result of the action was an increase in the hourly rate of pay to $22, backdated to the start of February.
3. Actual hours included some overtime to make up for some of the time lost in the strike, but the rate was only at the new rate of $22 per hour.

_____

1 Prepare a statement reconciling budgeted and actual profits.
2 Discuss briefly:
   (a) the attitudes supervisory management are likely to display in the circumstances to such a report
   (b) what steps might be taken to encourage positive attitudes to this kind of report
   (c) the usefulness of this kind of report.

SOLUTIONS TO ACTIVITIES

Activity 9.1

The reason is that a year represents a long enough time for the budget preparation exercise to be worthwhile, yet is short enough into the future for it to be possible to make detailed plans. The process of formulating budgets can be a time-consuming exercise, but there are economies of scale—for example, preparing the budget for the next 12 months would not normally take twice as much time and effort as preparing the budget for the next six months.

Activity 9.2

We thought of the following:

- Increasing production in previous months and stockpiling to meet the higher demand period(s).
- Increasing the production facility might be possible, perhaps by working overtime and/or acquiring (buying or leasing) additional plant.

- It may be possible to subcontract some production.
- It may be possible to encourage potential customers to change the timing of their buying by offering discounts or other special terms during the months that have been identified as being quiet.

You may well have thought of other approaches.

Activity 9.3

One of the crucial aspects of the process is establishing coordination between budgets so that the plans of one department match and are complementary to those of other departments. This usually requires compromise and adjustment of initial budgets. This usually means that someone at board level (or its equivalent) has to be closely involved. Only people of this rank are likely to have the necessary moral and, in the final analysis, formal managerial authority to force departmental managers to compromise.

Activity 9.4

The answer is that there is no automatic reason to believe that what happened in the past, or is happening elsewhere, represents a sensible target for this year in this business. Considering what happened last year and in other businesses may help in the formulation of plans, but past events and the performance of others should not automatically be seen as the target.

Activity 9.5

There appears, for the size of the business, to be a fairly large and increasing cash balance. Management might consider putting some of the cash into an income-yielding deposit. Alternatively, it could be used to expand the trading activities of the business by, for example, increasing the investment in non-current assets.

Activity 9.6

Cash budget for the six months ended 31 December						
	July $'000	Aug. $'000	Sept. $'000	Oct. $'000	Nov. $'000	Dec. $'000
Receipts						
Debtors	53	57	59	62	57	53
Payments						
Creditors (note 1)	–	32	33	34	36	31
Salaries and wages	10	10	10	10	10	10
Electricity			10			17
Other overheads	2	2	2	2	2	2
Loan repayment (note 2)	–	–	–	–	–	131
Total payments	12	44	55	46	48	191
Cash surplus	41	13	4	16	9	(138)
Cash balance	101	114	118	134	143	5

Notes

1. There will be no payment to creditors in July because the June purchases will be made on two months' credit and therefore paid in August. The July purchases, which will equal the July cost of sales figure plus the increase in inventories made in July, will be paid for in September and so on.
2. The repayment is simply the amount that will cause the balance at 31 December to be $5,000.

Activity 9.7

Debtors budget for the six months ended 31 December						
	July $'000	Aug. $'000	Sept. $'000	Oct. $'000	Nov. $'000	Dec. $'000
Opening balance (note 1)	53	57	59	62	57	53
Sales	57	59	62	57	53	51
	110	116	121	119	110	104
Less cash receipts	53	57	59	62	57	53
Closing balance	57	59	62	57	53	51

This could, of course, be set out in any manner that gives the sort of information management needs in respect of planned levels of debtors and associated transactions.

Note

1. The opening balances will be the sales figures for the previous month, since the business plans to allow its credit customers one month's credit.

Activity 9.8

Creditors budget for the six months ended 31 December						
	July $'000	Aug. $'000	Sept. $'000	Oct. $'000	Nov. $'000	Dec. $'000
Opening balance (note 1)	32	65	67	70	67	60
Purchases	33	34	36	31	29	28
	65	99	103	101	96	88
Less cash payments (note 2)	–	32	33	34	36	31
Closing balance	65	67	70	67	60	57

This could be set out in any manner that gives the sort of information management needs in respect of planned levels of creditors and associated transactions.

Notes

1. The opening balance for July will be the planned purchases figures for the previous month (June), since the business plans, until the June purchases, to take one month's credit from its suppliers. The opening balances for July to December will represent the planned purchases for the previous two months.

2. There will be no payment to creditors planned in July because creditors will be paid two months after the month of purchase, starting with the June purchases which will be paid for in August.

Activity 9.9

The problem is that the actual level of output was not as budgeted. This means that we cannot, for example, say that there was a labour cost saving of $2,500 (i.e. $20,000 – 17,500) and conclude that all is well in that area. This is because the level of output was 10 per cent less than budgeted and we would therefore expect labour costs to be lower than budgeted.

Activity 9.10

The answer is simply the difference between the original and flexed budget profit figures. The only difference between these two profit figures is the assumed volume of sales; everything else was the same. Thus the figure is $4,000.

Activity 9.11

The answer is that inquiries must be made to find out why the volume of sales fell below the budget figure. Only by discovering this information will management be in a position to try to see that it does not occur again in the future.

Activity 9.12

The sales volume variance is $2,000 (favourable) (i.e. $26,000 – 24,000). It is favourable because the original budget profit was lower than the flexed budget profit.

Activity 9.13

The sales price variance for June is $1,500 (adverse) (i.e. $115,000 – 113,500).

Activity 9.14

The direct materials usage variance for June was $300 (adverse) (i.e. (46,300 – 46,000) × $1).

Activity 9.15

The direct materials price variance for June was zero (i.e. ($46,300 – 46,300) × $1).

Activity 9.16

The direct labour efficiency variance for June was $680 (adverse) (i.e. (2,368 – 2,300) × $10).

Activity 9.17

The direct labour rate variance for June was $480 (favourable) (i.e. (2,368 × 10) – 23,200).

Activity 9.18

The fixed overhead spending variance for June was $700 (favourable) (i.e. $20,000 – 19,300).

Activity 9.19

	$	$
Budgeted profit		24,000
Favourable variances		
Sales volume	2,000	
Fixed overhead spending	700	
Direct labour rate	480	
		3,180
		27,180
Adverse variances		
Sales price	1,500	
Direct material usage	300	
Direct labour efficiency	680	
		2,480
Actual profit		$24,700

Activity 9.20

The original budget, the flexed budget and the actual are as follows:

	Original budget	Flexed budget	Actual
Output (production and sales)	1,000 units	1,050 units	1,050 units
	$	$	$
Sales	100,000	105,000	104,300
Raw materials	(40,000)	(42,000)	(41,200)
Labour	(20,000)	(21,000)	(21,300)
Fixed overheads	(20,000)	(20,000)	(19,400)
Operating profit	$20,000	$22,000	$22,400

Reconciliation of the budgeted and actual operating profits for June

	$	$
Budgeted profit		20,000
Favourable variances		
Sales volume (22,000 − 20,000)	2,000	
Direct materials usage {[(1,050 × 40) − 40,500] × $1}	1,500	
Direct labour efficiency {[(1,050 × 2) − 2,080] × $10}	200	
Fixed overhead spending (20,000 − 19,400)	600	4,300
		24,300
Adverse variances		
Sales price variance (105,000 − 104,300)	700	
Direct materials price [(40,500 x $1) − 41,200]	700	
Direct labour rate [(2,080 x $10) − 21,300]	500	1,900
Actual profit		$22,400

Activity 9.21

The reasons we thought of included the following:

Sales volume

- Poor performance by sales personnel.
- Deterioration in market conditions between the setting of the budget and the actual event.
- Lack of availability of inventory to sell as a result of some production problem.

Sales price

- Poor performance by sales personnel.
- Deterioration in market conditions between the setting of the budget and the actual event.

Direct materials usage

- Poor performance by production staff leading to high rates of scrap, etc.
- Substandard materials leading to high rates of scrap, etc.
- Faulty machinery causing high rates of scrap, etc.

Direct materials price

- Poor performance by buying department staff.
- Change in market conditions between setting the standard and the actual event.

Labour efficiency

- Poor supervision.
- A low-skill grade of worker taking longer to do the work than was envisaged for the correct skill grade.
- Low-grade material leading to high levels of scrap and wasted labour time.
- Problems with machinery leading to labour time being wasted.
- Dislocation of material supply leading to workers being unable to proceed with production.

Labour rate

- Poor performance by the personnel function.
- Using a higher grade of worker than was planned.
- Change in labour market conditions between setting the standard and the actual event.

Fixed overheads

- Poor supervision of overheads.
- General increase in costs of overheads not taken account of in the budget.

Activity 9.22

The general approach to this policy must be concerned with cost and benefit. The benefit of knowing why a variance exists needs to be balanced against the cost of obtaining that information.

Activity 9.23

The change in policy will have ramifications for other areas of the business, including:

- More goods would need to be available to sell, which production might not be able to supply. It might not be possible to buy the inventory in from elsewhere.
- Increased sales will involve an increased need for finance to pay for increased production.

Activity 9.24

There is no clear-cut, absolutely correct answer to this activity. However, most businesses that operate successful budgetary control systems (there are many of them) tend to show some common factors. These include the following:

- A serious attitude is taken to the system by all levels of management, right from the very top.
- There is clear demarcation between areas of responsibility of various managers so that accountability can more easily be ascribed for any area that seems to be going out of control.
- Budget targets are reasonable so that they represent a rigorous, yet achievable target. This may be promoted by managers being involved in setting their own targets. This can promote the managers' commitment and motivation.
- There are established data collection, analysis and dissemination routines which take the actual results and the budget figures and calculate and report the variances.
- Reports are targeted at individual managers rather than being general purpose. This avoids managers having to wade through reams of reports to find the part relevant to them.
- There are fairly short reporting periods—typically a month—so that things cannot go too far wrong before they are picked up.
- Variance reports are produced and disseminated shortly after the end of the relevant reporting period.
- Action is taken to get operations back in control if they are shown to be out of control.

OBJECTIVES

When you have completed your study of this chapter you should be able to:

1   explain the role of projected financial statements

2   prepare a simple projected cash flow statement, income statement and balance sheet for a business

3   explain the usefulness of each of the above statements for planning and decision-making purposes

4   evaluate the use of projected financial statements

5   explain sensitivity analysis and illustrate the way in which sensitivity analysis can help in evaluating projected information

6   discuss the role of spreadsheets in the preparation of projected financial statements.

10

PROJECTED FINANCIAL STATEMENTS

In this chapter we consider the preparation and usefulness of projected (pro forma) financial statements. We see that projected financial statements can be useful both for internal planning purposes and for providing information to prospective investors or lenders. This chapter uses the framework of the basic financial statements in a forward-looking way, as distinct from taking an historic perspective. Most successful businesses have fairly well thought-out plans, where all aspects of the plans link together and articulate. A sensible (probably an essential) step in planning is to follow through the plans into the three financial statements that would result if the plans were to succeed. A ratio analysis of the forecasts would enable some objective assessment of likely results to be achieved. If the forecast financial results are unsatisfactory the plans need to be reconsidered. A set of fully linked financial statements provides a useful model to experiment with variations in the plans. For example, the plans may result in good levels of profitability but indicate that cash flows will be problematic. Examination of the forecasts should enable the plans to be modified. For instance, cash flows could be increased by such things as leasing assets rather than buying, chasing debtors for earlier payment and taking longer to pay creditors. Forecast financial statements can provide a really useful model for decision making.

THE ROLE OF PROJECTED FINANCIAL STATEMENTS

Projected financial statements can be particularly valuable when developing long-term strategic plans. When making such plans it is important for managers to consider the financial consequences to the business as a whole of pursuing a particular course of action. Often, managers will be confronted with a number of possible options. Where these are mutually exclusive, it will be necessary to decide which gives the best return in relation to the risks involved. Projected financial statements can be prepared for each option and can be used to assess the likely future returns. On the basis of these statements an informed decision can be made.

You will recall from Chapter 1 (Figure 1.4) that the first three steps in the decision-making, planning and control process were:

1. identify objectives
2. consider options
3. evaluate options and make a selection.

It is this third step where projected financial statements have a valuable role.

Where managers are considering only one course of action, projected financial statements can still be extremely useful. The preparation of projected statements will provide a useful insight on the effect of the plans on future financial performance and position for the business as a whole. They can identify future financing needs and help to assess whether the expected outcomes from the particular course of action are acceptable. Plans may have to be modified to take account of the likely financial outcomes that are revealed.

Where there is considerable uncertainty about the future, managers may wish to examine a range of possible scenarios or states of the world, and prepare more than one set of financial statements. Thus, projected statements may be prepared on the basis of:

* an optimistic view of likely future events
* a pessimistic view of likely future events
* a 'most likely' view of future events.

This type of scenario analysis, as it is sometimes called, can help in assessing the level of risk involved. The degree of probability associated with each 'state of the world' would also require careful assessment.

Projected financial statements are normally prepared for internal purposes only. Managers are usually reluctant to share this information with those outside the business, feeling that its publication could damage the competitive position of the business. They may also feel that those outside the business might not fully understand the nature of projected statements and may not therefore appreciate that the projections may prove to be inaccurate. There may be a significant difference between projected and actual financial outcomes, particularly where the business operates in a turbulent environment. Nevertheless, there are certain occasions when managers are prepared to release projected information to those outside the business.

ACTIVITY 10.1

Can you think of any circumstances under which managers might be prepared to provide projected financial information to those outside the business?

PREPARING PROJECTED FINANCIAL STATEMENTS

For most businesses the most important item in the preparation of projected statements is the projection of sales. The expected level of sales for a period will be influenced by a number of factors, including the degree of competition, the planned expenditure on advertising, the quality of the product, changes in consumer tastes and the general state of the economy. Only some of these factors will be under the control of the business. A reliable sales projection is useful as many other items, including certain expenses, inventory levels, non-current assets and financing requirements, will be determined partially or completely by the level of sales for the period. Other expenses, however, may be unaffected by the level of sales for a period.

ACTIVITY 10.2

Can you name two expenses that are likely to vary directly with the level of sales and two expenses that are likely to stay constant irrespective of the level of sales?

The sales projection of a business may be developed in a number of ways. It may be done by simply aggregating the projections made by the salesforce. These projections may rely heavily on subjective judgment and will usually attempt to take account of various aspects of the market and likely changes in market conditions. However, sales projections may also be based on certain statistical techniques or (in the case of large businesses) economic models. There are no hard and fast rules concerning the most appropriate method of projecting into the future for a business. Each business must assess the available methods, in terms of reliability and accuracy for their particular situation, and estimate the associated costs. The particular techniques of projecting into the future are not the subject of this chapter. Rather we are concerned with the preparation of projected financial statements and their subsequent evaluation.

Projected financial statements are prepared using the same methods and principles we have discussed in relation to historic financial statements. The only real difference lies in the fact that the statements are prepared using *projected* rather than *actual* information. This means that projected statements are less reliable and rely more on the use of judgment.

In order to illustrate the preparation of financial statements let us consider the following example.

EXAMPLE

10.1

Designer Dresses Ltd is a small company to be formed by James and William Clark to sell an exclusive range of dresses from a boutique in a fashionable suburb of Perth. On 1 January 2006 they plan to invest $50,000 cash to purchase 25,000 shares in the company issued at $2 each. Of this, $30,000 is to be invested in new fittings in January. These fittings are to be depreciated over three years on the straight-line basis. (Their scrap value is assumed to be zero at the end of their lives.) A half year's depreciation is to be charged in the first six months. The sales and purchases projections for the company are as follows (all figures are in $'000):

	Jan.	Feb.	Mar.	Apr.	May	June	Total
Sales	10.2	30.6	30.6	40.8	40.8	51.0	204.0
Purchases	20.0	30.0	25.0	25.0	30.0	30.0	160.0
Other costs*	9.0	9.0	9.0	9.0	9.0	9.0	54.0

* These include wages but exclude depreciation.

The sales will all be made by credit card. The credit card company will take one month to pay and will deduct its fee of 2 per cent of gross sales before paying amounts due to Designer Dresses. One month's credit is allowed by suppliers. Other costs shown above do not include rent and rates of $10,000 per quarter, payable on 1 January and 1 April. All other costs will be paid in cash. Closing inventory at the end of June is expected to be $58,000.

Ignoring taxation, and working to the nearest $'000, we now use these figures to prepare the following:

- a cash flow projection for the six months to 30 June 2006
- a projected income statement for the same period
- a projected balance sheet as at 30 June 2006.

PROJECTED CASH FLOW STATEMENT

We have seen in Chapter 5 that the cash flow statement is fairly straightforward to prepare. A typical format is shown below:

Cash flow statement for the year ended 30 June 2006	
Cash flows from operating activities	
Cash receipts from customers	x
Cash paid to suppliers and employees	(x)
Interest paid	(x)
Income taxes paid	(x)
Net cash provided by (used in) operating activities	x/(x)
Cash flows from investing activities	
Purchase of property, plant and equipment	(x)

Acquisition of subsidiary, net of cash acquired	(x)
Proceeds from sale of property, plant and equipment	x
Interest received	x
Dividends received	x
Net cash provided by (used in) investing activities	x/(x)

Cash flows from financing activities

Proceeds from issues of share capital	x
Proceeds from long-term borrowings	x
Repayment of long-term borrowings	(x)
Payment of finance lease liabilities	(x)
Dividends paid	(x)
Net cash provided by (used in) financing activities	x/(x)

Net increase (decrease) in cash and cash equivalents held	x/(x)
Cash and cash equivalents at the beginning of the year	x/(x)
Cash and cash equivalents at the end of the year	x/(x)

This statement simply records the cash inflows and outflows of the business. When preparing this statement for management purposes, the cash flow statement can be broken down into monthly periods. This helps managers to monitor closely any changes in the cash position of the business. In fact, the format used is often slightly different from that of the cash flow statement, being rather more detailed. The format of the typical cash budget was covered in more detail in Chapter 9. Below is an outline cash budget for Designer Dresses for the six months to 30 June 2006. This format is widely used and we recommend that you use it when preparing this type of statement. You should note, however, that there is no set format for the cash budget and managers are free to decide on the form of presentation that best suits their needs.

Projected cash flow statement for the six months to 30 June 2006

	Jan. $'000	Feb. $'000	Mar. $'000	Apr. $'000	May $'000	June $'000	Total $'000
Cash inflows							
Issue of shares							
Receipts from debtors							
Cash outflows							
Payments to creditors							
Rent and rates							
Fittings							
Other costs							
Net cash flow							
Opening balance							
Closing balance							

In this outline each column represents a monthly period. At the top of each column the cash inflows are set out. Below these cash inflows the cash outflows are set out. The difference between the cash inflows and outflows is the net cash flow for the period. If we add this net cash flow to the opening cash balance brought forward from the previous month we derive the cash balance at the end of the month.

When preparing a cash budget or cash flow statement there are two questions you must ask when considering each item of information presented to you:

1. *Does the item of information concern a cash transaction (i.e. does it involve cash inflows or outflows)?* If the answer to this question is 'no' then the information should be ignored for the purposes of preparing this statement. You will find that there are various items of information relating to a particular period, such as the depreciation charge, which do not involve cash movements. If the answer is 'yes' then a second question must be asked:

2. *When did the cash transaction take place?* It is important to identify the particular month in which the cash movement takes place. Often the cash movement will occur after the period in which a particular transaction took place—for example, where sales and purchases are made on credit.

Problems in preparing cash budgets/cash flow statements usually arise because the two questions above have not been properly addressed.

ACTIVITY 10.3

Fill in the outline cash budget for Designer Dresses Ltd for the six months to 30 June 2006 using the information contained in the example.

This form of cash budget should be compared with the more traditional form of the cash flow statement. When set out as a summary cash flow statement the statement for the six months would appear as follows:

Cash flow statement for the six months ended 30 June 2006		
	$'000	$'000
Cash flows from operating activities		
Cash receipts from customers	150	
Cash paid to suppliers and employees (130 + 54 + 20)	(204)	
Interest paid	–	
Income taxes paid	–	
Net cash used in operating activities		(54)
Cash flows from investing activities		
Purchase of property, plant and equipment	(30)	
Acquisition of subsidiary, net of cash acquired	–	
Proceeds from sale of property, plant and equipment	–	
Interest received	–	
Dividends received	–	
Net cash used in investing activities		(30)
Cash flows from financing activities		
Proceeds from issue of share capital	50	
Proceeds from long-term borrowings	–	

Repayment of long-term borrowings	–	
Payment of finance lease liabilities	–	
Dividends paid	–	
Net cash provided by financing activities		50
Net decrease in cash and cash equivalents held		34
Cash and cash equivalents at the beginning of the year		–
Cash and cash equivalents at the end of the year		(34)

In fact this kind of statement is probably more useful than the cash budget for strategic analysis, particularly when modified in the way discussed later in this chapter.

PROJECTED INCOME STATEMENT

When preparing the projected income statement it is important to include all revenues that are realised in the period (whether or not the cash has been received) and all expenses (including non-cash items) that relate to those revenues. Remember that the purpose of this statement is to show the wealth generated during the period and this may bear little relation to the cash generated. The format for the projected income statement will be along the following lines:

Projected income statement for the six months ended 30 June 2006

	$'000	$'000
Sales		X
Less cost of sales		
Opening inventory	X	
Purchases	X	
Less closing inventory	X	X
Gross profit		X
Credit card discounts	X	
Rent and rates	X	
Depreciation of fittings	X	
Other costs	X	X
Net profit		X

ACTIVITY 10.4

Fill in the outline income statement for Designer Dresses Ltd for the six months ended 30 June 2006 using the information contained in the example.

PROJECTED BALANCE SHEET

The projected balance sheet reveals the end-of-period balances and should normally be the last of the three statements to be prepared since the earlier ones provide information to be used when preparing the projected balance sheet: the projected cash flow statement reveals the end-of-period cash balance and the projected income statement reveals the projected retained profit for the period for inclusion in the shareholders' equity section of the balance sheet. The depreciation charge for the period, which appears in the projected income statement, must also be taken into account when preparing the projected balance sheet. The format for the projected balance sheet will be as follows:

Projected balance sheet as at 30 June 2006		
	$'000	$'000
Current assets		
Debtors	X	
Inventory	X	X
Non-current assets		
Fittings at cost	X	
Less Accumulated depreciation	X	X
Total assets		X
Current liabilities		
Trade creditors	X	
Bank overdraft	X	X
Shareholders' equity		
Paid-up share capital	X	
Retained profit	X	X
Total liabilities and shareholders' equity		X

ACTIVITY 10.5

Fill in the outline balance sheet for Designer Dresses Ltd as at 30 June 2006 using the information contained in the example.

ALTERNATIVE FORM OF CASH FLOW STATEMENT FOR FORECASTING

In Chapter 5 we discussed the reconciliation component of the cash flow statement, in which the operating profit was reconciled with the cash flow from operations. In fact the reconciliation of the net profit with the cash flow from operations is generally a more useful approach to forecasting cash flows. The revised format for the first section, which is that derived in Chapter 5, is shown below:

Operating profit (loss) after tax	x/(x)
add non-cash expenses related to non-current assets	
e.g. depreciation/loss on sale of non-current assets	x
Adjust for changes over the period in non-cash current assets/current liabilities	
inventory	x/(x)
accounts receivable (debtors)	x/(x)
prepayments and accruals	x/(x)
accounts payable (creditors)	x/(x)
income tax payable*	x/(x)
equals the cash flow from operating activities	x/(x)

* An alternative way of approaching the tax is to use the profit before tax as the profit figure to be included in the cash flow statement, with the income tax payable being shown as an outflow.

ACTIVITY 10.6

Prepare the cash flow statement for Designer Dresses Ltd using the above approach.

The links between the three statements seem more obvious with this approach, with the profit clearly linking with cash flows and the balance sheet. This approach clearly identifies that profit yielded a positive cash flow, which was further enhanced by the fact that depreciation is not associated with a cash outflow—so together they yield $24,000 cash. The problem lies with the fact that, for this period at least, substantial cash outflows are associated with inventory and debtors build-up, which are only partly offset by increases in creditors. Working capital management is important (see Chapter 13) and the implications of different working capital strategies (good and bad) are more clear-cut using this approach. It is for reasons such as these that this layout is seen as being more useful for strategic decision making.

EVALUATION OF PROJECTED STATEMENTS

Projected financial statements must be evaluated in order to ensure that sensible financial decisions are made. When evaluating such statements you must ask yourself a number of key questions. These include the following:

* How reliable are the projections that have been made?
* What underlying assumptions have been made and are they valid?
* Are the cash flows satisfactory? Can they be improved by changing policies or plans—for example, delaying capital expenditure decisions, requiring debtors to pay more quickly?
* Is there a need for additional financing? Is it feasible to obtain the amount required?
* Can any surplus funds be profitably reinvested?
* Is the level of projected profit satisfactory in relation to the risks involved? If not, what could be done to improve matters?
* Are the levels of sales and individual expense items satisfactory?
* Have all relevant expenses been included?
* Is the financial position at the end of the period acceptable?
* Is the level of gearing acceptable? Is the company too highly geared?

ACTIVITY 10.7

Evaluate the projected financial statements of Designer Dresses Ltd. Pay particular attention to the projected profitability and liquidity of the business.

ACTIVITY 10.8

Dalgleish Ltd is a wholesale supplier of stationery. In recent months the company has experienced liquidity problems. The company has an overdraft at the end of November 2005 and the bank has been pressing for a reduction in this overdraft over the next six months. The company is owned by the Dalgleish family who are unwilling to raise finance through long-term borrowing.

The balance sheet of the business as at 30 November 2005 is as follows:

Balance sheet as at 30 November 2005		
	$'000	'$000
Current assets		
Debtors	120	
Inventory	142	262
Non-current assets		
Fixtures and fittings at cost	174	
Less accumulated depreciation	38	136
Freehold land and premises at cost	250	
Less accumulated depreciation	24	226
		362
Total assets		624
Current liabilities		
Bank overdraft	126	
Trade creditors	145	
Income tax payable	24	
Dividends payable	20	315
Shareholders' equity		
Paid-up share capital (issued at $1)	200	
Retained profits	109	309
Total liabilities and shareholders' equity		624

The following projections for the six months ended 31 May 2006 are available concerning the business:

1. Sales and purchases for the six months ended 31 May 2006 will be as follows:

	Sales $'000	Purchases $'000
December	160	150
January	220	140
February	240	170
March	150	110
April	160	120
May	200	160

2. Seventy per cent of sales are on credit and 30 per cent are cash sales. Cash from credit sales is received in the following month. All purchases are on one month's credit.

3. Wages are $40,000 for each of the first three months. However, this will increase by 10 per cent as from March 2006. All wages are paid in the month they are incurred.

4. The gross profit percentage on goods sold is 30 per cent.

5. Administration expenses are expected to be $12,000 in each of the first four months and $14,000 in subsequent months. These figures include a monthly charge of $4,000 in respect of depreciation of fixed assets ($1,000 for premises and $3,000 for fixtures). Administration expenses are paid in the month they are incurred.

6. Selling expenses are expected to be $8,000 per month except for May 2006 when an advertising campaign costing $12,000 will also be paid for. The advertising campaign will commence at the beginning of June 2006. Selling expenses are paid for in the month they are incurred.

7. The dividend outstanding will be paid in December 2005. The tax is due for payment in August.

8. The company intends to purchase, and pay for, new fixtures and fittings at the end of April 2006 for $28,000. These will be delivered in June 2006.

Required:

(a) Prepare a cash budget for Dalgleish Ltd for each of the six months to 31 May 2006.

(b) Prepare a projected income statement for the six months to 31 May 2006.

(c) Convert this into a cash flow statement using the 'reconcilation' approach discussed above.

(d) Prepare a projected balance sheet as at 31 May 2006.

(e) Briefly discuss ways in which the company might reduce the bank overdraft as required by the bank.

SENSITIVITY ANALYSIS

Sensitivity analysis is useful when evaluating projected financial statements. The technique involves taking a single variable (e.g. volume of sales) and examining the effect of changes in the chosen variable on the likely financial performance and position of the business. An assessment can then be made of the sensitivity of financial performance and position to changes in that variable. Although only one variable is examined at a time, a number of variables considered to be important to the performance of a business may be examined consecutively. There is nothing wrong with changing more than one variable at a time, but that is not strictly sensitivity analysis. It is more akin to scenario analysis when different scenarios are examined and their consequences followed through.

In essence, in sensitivity analysis a series of 'what if' questions is posed. In relation to sales, for example, the following questions might be asked:

✳ What if sales volume is 5 per cent higher than expected?

✳ What if sales volume is 10 per cent lower than expected?

✳ What if sales price is reduced by 4 per cent?

✳ What if sales price is increased by 6 per cent?

In answering these questions it is possible to develop a better 'feel' for the effect of projection inaccuracies on the final outcomes. However, this technique does not assign probabilities to each possible change, nor does it consider the effect of more than one variable on projected outcomes at a time.

PROJECTIONS USING SPREADSHEETS

Preparing projected financial statements is facilitated by the use of spreadsheet packages. In essence, a spreadsheet is simply a matrix of rows and columns that can be loaded into a computer and viewed on the computer screen. The intersection of a row and a column is referred to as a cell, into which it is possible to insert numbers, equations or descriptions. A simple model can be built using this matrix. For example, the projected cash flow statement for Dalgleish Ltd given in the solution to Activity 10.8 may be prepared using the rows and columns of a spreadsheet package as follows:

	A	B	C	D	E	F	G	H
1		Dec.	Jan.	Feb.	Mar.	Apr.	May	Total
2		$'000	$'000	$'000	$'000	$'000	$'000	$'000
3	Cash inflows							
4	Receipts from debtors	120	112	154	168	105	112	771
5	Cash sales	48	66	72	45	48	60	339
6		168	178	226	213	153	172	1,110
7	Cash outflows							
8	Payments to creditors	145	150	140	170	110	120	835
9	Administration costs	8	8	8	8	10	10	52
10	Wages	40	40	40	44	44	44	252
11	Selling expenses	8	8	8	8	8	20	60
12	Fixtures					28		28
13	Dividends	20						20
14		221	206	196	230	200	194	1,247
15								
16	Net cash flow	(53)	(28)	30	(17)	(47)	(22)	(137)
17	Opening balance	(126)	(179)	(207)	(177)	(194)	(241)	(126)
18	Closing balance	(179)	(207)	(177)	(194)	(241)	(263)	(263)

Cell B6 can be made equal to the sum of cells B4 and B5, cell C6 can be made equal to the sum of C4 and C5, etc., so that all calculations are carried out by the software. The total columns would all be calculated using formulae— for example, H4 would be set up using the formula =SUM(B4:G4), H6 would be set up using =H4+H5, etc.

The spreadsheet package is useful if managers wish to carry out sensitivity or scenario analysis on the projected statements. One or more variables may be altered and the spreadsheet will quickly recalculate the totals to show the effect of the change.

As you become more proficient with spreadsheets the relationships and use of formulae become more obvious and useful. The only real advantage of using the simple spreadsheet above is arithmetic. In practice you should be trying to identify as many relationships and formulae as possible. For example, sales volume and price can be input as a variable, with the sales figure being shown using the formula = the grid reference which has the price in it × the grid reference with the sales quantity in it. If we then need to test the sensitivity on cash flows of changes in sales price or quantity, only these two grid contents need to be changed. Of course, cost of sales will be dependent on sales volume, so there is a need to identify the relationship and build it into the spreadsheet model. Taxation will link to profits, so the calculation of the tax figure should be by use of a formula. These and other links will emerge with practice.

It is also important to note that the three main financial statements link and overlap. In the cash flow forecast illustrated above, the cash from sales figures will link (albeit with adjustments) with both the income statement and the balance sheet (through debtors). Depreciation will impact on both the income statement and the balance sheet. There is a multitude of such linkages, as should be clear from the earlier exercises, especially those in Chapter 3 and in Appendix to Chapter 10 where duality or double entry is critical.

Table A10.1 on pp. 433–4 provides a suggested solution to Designer Dresses set out on a spreadsheet. You should check this carefully and ensure that you understand it. You should particularly note that the top section consists of input variables. Any changes in these will be reflected in the subsequent financial forecasts, as these forecasts use formulae which manipulate the input data. Points worth noting include:

EXAMPLE 10.2

In the **income statement**:
- the sales figure is directly linked with H4—the total sales in the input section
- the purchases figure is directly linked with H5—the total purchases in the input section
- the closing inventory is linked with D13—the closing inventory in the input section
- the cost of sales figure uses a formula
- the credit card discounts link sales with the percentage input in D12
- other costs and rent and rates are picked up directly from the input section
- depreciation is calculated by using the input for fittings and the depreciation method/rate.

In the **cash budget** and **cash flow statement**:
- the share proceeds link with the amounts from the input section
- the credit sales figure builds in a lag of one month and a discount
- the other cash outflows link directly with the input
- the net cash flow is calculated by formula
- the initial opening balance is input, the remainder are worked out by formula
- the closing balance is derived by formula
- the increase in debtors links the discount and the time lag with the figures input.

In the **balance sheet**:
- all of these figures link with the input or earlier calculations
- note the link between accumulated depreciation and depreciation in the income statement
- note the profit figure in the income statement, which links with the retained profit figure in the balance sheet.

Table A10.2 on pp. 435–6 shows relevant parts of the spreadsheet set out in a way that shows formulae, thus illustrating the linkages.

It should be apparent to you that the strength of the spreadsheet is in the ease with which changes can be made. What happens if:
- sales in June were $60,000?
- fittings of only $15,000 were purchased?

- purchases were $50,000 in January?

Given the way the spreadsheet has been set up, the answers can be obtained simply by changing the relevant grid in the input section.

In fact, the relationships identified by Designer Dresses are really quite simple. In reality, spreadsheet models are likely to become quite complex as knowledge of relationships expands. Typical complications include:

- For most businesses there will be opening figures to start with, which need to be input, which will have a relationship with the transactions that occur in the year.
- The relationships between sales, debtors and cash need to be understood and modelled in the spreadsheet wherever possible.
- The relationships between purchases, creditors, cash and cost of sales need to be understood and modelled in the spreadsheet wherever possible.
- The cost–volume relationships need to be understood and incorporated.
- Dividends proposed and paid and tax must be dealt with.
- There may be purchase and sale of non-current assets and associated depreciation.

ACTIVITY 10.9

Redo Activity 10.8 on a spreadsheet, then answer the following questions.

What will be the profit and cash flow for the period assuming:

- an increase in sales of 10 per cent
- an increase in the gross profit margin to 33 per cent
- a reduction in administration costs (other than depreciation) to $6,000 a month
- the taking of two months' credit from suppliers
- the reduction in credit to customers to half a month?

SELF-ASSESSMENT QUESTION 10.1

Quardis is an importer of high-quality laser printers which can be used with a range of microcomputers. The balance sheet of Quardis Ltd as at 31 May 2005 is as follows:

	$'000	$'000
Current assets		
Cash	2	
Debtors	34	
Inventory	24	60

Non-current assets		
Fixtures and fittings at cost	35	
Less accumulated depreciation	10	25
Freehold premises at cost	460	
Less accumulated depreciation	30	430
		455
Total assets		515
Current liabilities		
Trade creditors	22	
Income tax payable	14	
Dividends payable	10	46
Non-current liabilities		
Loan—High Country Bank		125
Shareholders' equity		
Paid-up share capital (issued at $1 each)	200	
Retained profits	144	344
Total liabilities and shareholders' equity		515

The following information is available for the year ended 31 May 2006:

1. Sales are expected to be 15,000 units at $20 each, giving $300,000 for the year. Sixty per cent of sales are on credit and it is expected that, at the year end, three months' credit sales will be outstanding. Sales revenues accrue evenly over the year.

2. Purchases of inventory during the year will be $186,000 and will accrue evenly over the year. All purchases are on credit and at the year end it is expected that two months' purchases will remain unpaid. Cost of sales is estimated to be 60 per cent of sales.

3. Fixtures and fittings costing $25,000 will be purchased and paid for during the year. Depreciation is charged at 10 per cent on the cost of fixtures and fittings held at the year end.

4. Depreciation is charged on freehold premises at 2 per cent on cost.

5. On 1 June 2005, $30,000 of the loan from the High Country Bank is to be repaid. Interest is at the rate of 13 per cent per annum and all interest accrued to 31 May 2006 will be paid on that day.

6. Wages for the year will be $54,000. At the year end it is estimated that $4,000 of this total will remain unpaid.

7. Other overhead expenses for the year (excluding those mentioned above) are expected to be $21,000. At the year end it is expected that $3,000 of this total will still be unpaid.

8. A dividend of 5c per share is expected to be announced at the year end. The dividend outstanding at the beginning of the year will be paid during the year.

9. Tax is payable at the rate of 35 per cent. Tax outstanding at the beginning of the year will be paid during the year.

Preferably use a spreadsheet to:

(a) prepare a projected income statement for the year ended 31 May 2006

(b) prepare a projected balance sheet as at 31 May 2006

(c) prepare a projected cash flow statement for the year ended 31 May 2006

(d) comment on the significant features revealed by these statements

(e) identify the impact on the financial results of:

 (i)   an increase in sales volume of 5 per cent—wages and other overheads can be regarded as a fixed cost for any expected sales volume

 (ii)   a reduction in cost of sales to 58 per cent of sales

 (iii)   a tightening of credit to customers to two months.

SUMMARY

In this chapter we have achieved the following objectives in the way shown.

OBJECTIVE	METHOD ACHIEVED
Explain the role of projected financial statements	• Explained the role • Identified their importance in strategic planning • Explained the role of 'what if' questions and scenario analysis • Illustrated that such statements are used mostly for internal planning purposes • Explained why such statements tend to be internal statements
Prepare a simple projected cash flow statement, income statement and balance sheet for a business	• Illustrated that the preparation of projected statements is based on the same principles as those underlying the preparation of historic statements, the only difference being that we employ projected rather than actual data • Illustrated how such statements can be prepared • Prepared projected financial statements
Explain the usefulness of each of the above statements for planning and decision-making purposes	• Illustrated the importance of the three statements • Explained the advantages of the 'alternative' format of the cash flow statement
Evaluate the use of projected financial statements	• Evaluated projected financial statements • Noted that such statements are only useful if the projections made are reliable; hence the starting point in any evaluation of projected statements is the examination of the way in which the projected data are developed and any assumptions made
Explain sensitivity analysis and illustrate the way in which sensitivity analysis can help in evaluating projected information	• Explained sensitivity analysis • Applied sensitivity analysis to projected statements to assist in evaluating and refining plans, and to get a general feel for likely future outcomes
Discuss the role of spreadsheets in the preparation of projected financial statements	• Used a spreadsheet to prepare an integrated financial plan, in a way that shows clearly the interrelationships between the three main financial statements • Developed spreadsheets in a way that facilitates use of sensitivity analysis

DISCUSSION QUESTIONS

EASY

<Obj 2>	**10.1**	What are the two key questions that must be asked/answered when preparing either a cash flow statement or a cash budget?
<Obj 2>	**10.2**	Why is the sales projection often the key to the preparation of projected financial statements?
<Obj 2>	**10.3**	Identify different methods for projecting future sales.
<Obj 2>	**10.4**	It is frequently stated that 'revenues should be realised' before they are recognised in the accounts. In an accounting context, what does this mean?
<Obj 4>	**10.5**	What is the main purpose of the projected income statement?

INTERMEDIATE

<Obj 1>	**10.6**	Consider the relative importance of 'relevance' and 'reliability' in the context of both historic and forecast financial statements.
<Obj 1, 3>	**10.7**	What is the main difference between preparing 'projected' and 'actual' financial reports?
<Obj 2>	**10.8**	Why is the balance sheet prepared last?
<Obj 2, 3>	**10.9**	Discuss the proposition that the modified form of cash flow statement, built around the reconciliation of net profit and cash inflows from operations, is more useful for decision making.
<Obj 3>	**10.10**	Should forecast results be part of the published reports of quoted companies?
<Obj 3>	**10.11**	How do projected financial statements assist decision makers in the decision-making, planning and control process?
<Obj 3, 4>	**10.12**	What questions can be answered from projected financial statements in assessing the financial viability of a project?
<Obj 5>	**10.13**	What is 'scenario analysis'? How does it assist in decision making?
<Obj 5, 6>	**10.14**	Identify the main advantages of using spreadsheets to develop forecast financial statements to assist in strategic decision making.

APPLICATION EXERCISES

INTERMEDIATE

<Obj 2>   **10.1**   The income statement and balance sheet for a business are shown below:

Income statement for the year ended 31 December 2005

	$'000	$'000
Sales		500,000
less cost of sales		400,000
Gross profit		100,000
less expenses	20,000	
Depreciation	50,000	
		70,000
Net profit		30,000

Balance sheet as at 31 December 2005		
	$'000	$'000
Current assets		
Cash	20,000	
Debtors	80,000	
Inventory	50,000	
		150,000
Non-current assets		
Cost	500,000	
Accumulated depreciation	200,000	
		300,000
		450,000
Current liabilities		
Creditors		50,000
Capital		400,000
		450,000

Using the following information, provide a projected set of final accounts for 2006.
1. Sales are expected to increase by 20 per cent.
2. Gross profit will remain at 30 per cent.
3. General expenses (to be paid in cash) are expected to be around $25,000.
4. Depreciation remains at 10 per cent straight line.
5. Average period of credit given to debtors is expected to be two months.
6. Inventory is expected to turn over seven times a year.
7. Creditors turnover is expected to be 11 times a year.
8. All sales and purchases will be on credit.

<Obj 2>   **10.2**   The financial statements of a company contain the following information:

At the end of the year
Current ratio is 1.75
Liquid ratio is 1.25
Working capital is $375,000
Issued capital amounts to $500,000 in ordinary shares
Non-current assets = $300,000
Debtors turnover is 8 times

For the year
Net profit as percentage of issued ordinary capital is 15 per cent
Inventory turnover is 4.8 times
Gross profit is 25 per cent of turnover

At the end of the year there were no prepayments or accruals. Nor were there any liabilities other than creditors, or assets other than those implicit in the above information.

Required:
Construct an income statement and balance sheet in as much detail as possible.

<Obj 2, 3>   **10.3**   Prolog Ltd is a small wholesaler of microcomputers. It has in recent months been selling 50 machines a month at a price of $2,000 each. These machines cost $1,600 each. A new model has just been launched and this is expected to offer greatly enhanced performance. Its selling price and cost will be the same as for the old model. From the beginning of January, sales are expected to increase at a rate of 20 machines each month until the end of June when sales will amount to 170 units per month. They are expected to continue at that level thereafter. Operating costs, including depreciation of $2,000 per month, are forecast as follows (all in $'000):

	Jan.	Feb.	Mar.	Apr.	May	June
Operating costs	6	8	10	12	12	12

Prolog expects to receive no credit for operating costs. Additional shelving for storage will be bought, installed and paid for in April costing $12,000. Tax of $25,000 is due at the end of March. Prolog anticipates that debtors will amount to two months' sales. To give their customers a good level of service Prolog plans to hold enough inventory at the end of each period to fulfil anticipated demand from customers in the following month. The computer manufacturer, however, grants one month's credit to Prolog.

Prolog Ltd's balance sheet appears below.

Balance sheet as at 31 December 2005		
	$'000	$'000
Current assets		
Cash	–	
Debtors	200	
Inventory	112	312
Non-current assets		80
Total assets		392
Current liabilities		
Trade creditors	112	
Income tax	25	
Overdraft	68	205
Shareholders' equity		
Paid-up share capital (issued at 25c per share)	10	
Retained profits	177	187
Total liabilities and shareholders' equity		392

Required:

(a) Prepare a cash forecast for Prolog Ltd showing the cash balance or required overdraft for the six months ending 30 June 2006.

(b) Calculate at 30 June 2006 Prolog's:
  (i)   current ratio
  (ii) acid test ratio.
  You should ignore any possible tax liability or proposed dividend.

(c) State briefly what further information a banker would require from Prolog before granting additional overdraft facilities for the anticipated expansion of sales.

CHALLENGING

<Obj 2–4>

10.4 Davis Travel Ltd specialises in the provision of winter sports holidays but it also organises outdoor activity holidays in the summer. You are given the following information:

Abbreviated balance sheet as at 30 September 2005		
	$'000	$'000
Current assets		
Cash		30
Non-current assets		560
Total assets		590
Current liabilities		
Trade creditors		180
Non-current liabilities		
Loans		110
Shareholders' equity		
Paid-up share capital	100	
Retained profits	200	300
Total liabilities and shareholders' equity		590

Its sales estimates for the next six months are:

	Number of bookings received	Number of holidays taken	Promotion expenditure $'000
October	1,000		100
November	3,000		150
December	3,000	1,000	150
January	3,000	4,000	50
February		3,000	
March		2,000	
Total	10,000	10,000	450

1. Holidays sell for $300 each. Ten per cent is payable when the holiday is booked and the remainder after two months.
2. Travel agents are paid a commission of 10 per cent of the price of the holiday one month after the booking is made.
3. The cost of a flight is $50 per holiday and of a hotel is $100 per holiday. Flights and hotels must be paid for in the month in which the holidays are taken.
4. Other variable costs are $20 per holiday and are paid in the month of the holiday.
5. Administration costs, including depreciation of non-current assets of $42,000, amount to $402,000 for the six months. Administration costs can be spread evenly over the period.
6. Loan interest of $10,000 is payable on 31 March 2006 and a loan repayment of $20,000 is due on that date. For your calculations you should ignore any interest on the overdraft.

7. The creditors of $180,000 at 30 September are to be paid in October.
8. A payment of $50,000 for non-current assets is to be made in March 2006.
9. The airline and the hotel chain base their charges on Davis Travel's forecast requirements and hold capacity to meet those requirements. If Davis is unable to fill this reserved capacity a charge of 50 per cent of those outlined in note 3 above is made.

Required:
(a) Prepare:
   (i) a cash forecast for the six months to 31 March 2006
   (ii) an income statement for the six months ended on that date
   (iii) a balance sheet as at 31 March 2006.
(b) Discuss the main financial problems confronting Davis Travel.

Ignore taxation in your calculations.

<Obj 2–4>   **10.5**   Changes Ltd owns a chain of eight shops selling fashion goods. In the past the company maintained a healthy cash balance. However, this has fallen in recent months and at the end of September 2006 it had an overdraft of $70,000. In view of this, its managing director has asked you to prepare a cash forecast for the next six months. You have collected the following data:

	October $'000	November $'000	December $'000	January $'000	February $'000	March $'000
Sales forecast	140	180	260	60	100	120
Purchases	160	180	140	50	50	50
Wages and salaries	30	30	40	30	30	32
Rent			60			
Rates						40
Other expenses	20	20	20	20	20	20
Refurbishing shops				80		

Inventory at 1 October amounted to $170,000 and creditors were $70,000. The purchases in October, November and December are contractually committed and those shown for January, February and March are the minimum necessary to restock with spring fashions. Cost of sales is 50 per cent of sales and suppliers allow one month's credit on purchases. Taxation of $90,000 is due on 1 January. The rates payment is a charge for a whole year and other expenses include depreciation of $10,000 per month.

Required:
(a) Compute the cash balance at the end of each month for the six months to 31 March 2006.
(b) Compute the inventory levels at the end of each month for the six months to 31 March 2006.
(c) Prepare an income statement for the six months ended 31 March 2006.
(d) What problems might Changes Ltd face in the next six months and how would you attempt to overcome them?

<Obj 2–4>

10.6 Optimists Ltd is developing its plans for the next year. Plans are to be based on the following information.

1. Sales are estimated to be $8 million, spread fairly evenly over the year.
2. Gross profit is expected to be 35 per cent and other expenses are expected to be about 80 per cent of the gross profit.
3. Taxation will be charged at 35 per cent.
4. Working capital will be maintained as follows:
   - inventory will be held for an average of two months
   - debtors turnover will be 8 times a year
   - trade creditors will be based on an assumed three months' payment period
   - other items include taxation and any dividends proposed, together with cash.
5. The company plans to pay a dividend of 10 cents a share.
6. The company has issued 1 million shares at $1 each. At the start of the year the reserves amount to $500,000.
7. Non-current assets at the start of the year consisted of plant and equipment which cost $1.5 million and which had been depreciated by $300,000 (i.e. accumulated depreciation). Depreciation will be charged at 20 per cent on cost. Depreciation is included in the figure for other expenses mentioned in (1) above.

Required:

Prepare a projected income statement for the year and a balance sheet at the year end.

CASE STUDY

10.1

Gadabout Travel Ltd (GT) organises short European holidays which are targeted at Australian visitors to Britain. The London-based company charters planes and books hotels. The charter arrangements are such that the air operators include all UK transport costs, airport charges, etc., in the charter price. The contracts with the hoteliers require them to deal with all local arrangements, including transfers from airports to hotels and local activities where these are a feature of particular holidays. All holidays are advertised throughout Australia as add-ons to European visits and are booked through Australian travel agents. Prices are set in pounds sterling so the client bears any exchange rate risk. By having to deal only with airlines, hotels and travel agents, the company is able to be administratively streamlined and, its management believe, efficient and price competitive.

GT's holidays are of two types: summer 'beach' holidays and winter sports holidays. The company charges a flat rate for all holidays, only distinguishing between the beach holidays and the winter sports ones. An unusual feature of GT's holidays is the fact that full payment must be made with the booking. Although this is unusual, GT is able to sustain this policy by being very price competitive. The management believes that any possible loss of custom through following this policy is outweighed by the knowledge that bookings, once made, are certain from the company's point of view.

Further information about the company and forecasts for next year are as follows:

1. Travel agents deduct a 10 per cent commission from the full price of each holiday before remitting the other 90 per cent to the company at the time of booking.
2. Winter sports holidays have a cost to the customer of £350 each and beach holidays cost £300 each. They are very attractive to young, budget-conscious travellers.
3. Flights and hotel accommodation are booked by GT as soon as the booking is received from a customer. Airline charges for both types of holiday are £100 per passenger. Hotel charges are £125 for beach holidays and £150 for winter sports holidays. Both airline and hotel charges must

be paid in the month in which the holiday was originally due to be taken. If a holiday is cancelled by the time that payment is due to the airline and hotels, they require 60 per cent of these amounts in respect of the cancelled places. Airline and hotel charges for later cancellations have to be made in full. It is not GT's practice to make any refunds to their clients, irrespective of the date of cancellation. The company tends to know from experience what percentage of holidays booked are likely to be cancelled.

4. At 31 December this year the company has received 660 bookings for winter sports holidays. It is estimated that bookings and cancellations will be as follows:

	Holidays booked		Holidays taken		Holidays cancelled	
	Winter	Beach	Winter	Beach	Winter	Beach
Pre-January	660	–	–	–	–	–
January	700	150	540	–	40	–
February	740	980	520	–	50	–
March	120	860	790	–	70	–
April	40	660	230	–	20	–
May	–	450	–	200	–	20
June	–	100	–	370	–	30
July	–	80	–	890	–	80
August	–	80	–	1,070	–	90
September	70	50	–	600	–	60
October	110	–	–	–	–	–
November	360	–	–	–	–	–
December	400	–	–	–	–	–

The holidays cancelled columns of this table show the month for which the cancelled holiday was intended to be taken at the time of booking. Past experience suggests that, of the holidays which are cancelled, 50 per cent will be cancelled before payment is due to the airlines and hotels, and 50 per cent will be cancelled later than this.

GT's outline balance sheet (UK format) as at 31 December this year is expected to look as follows:

	£	£
Fixed assets		
Freehold land and buildings		210,000
Equipment and furniture		57,000
		267,000
Current assets		
Prepaid rate	500	
Cash	21,200	
	21,700	
Current liabilities		
Accrued electricity	1,500	
Trade creditors (660 winter sports × (350 − 10%))	207,900	
	209,400	
		(187,700)
		79,300
Share capital and reserves		79,300

In addition to the above plans for bookings, the company management expects the following during next year:

1. Salaries will be £20,600 for each month. These will be paid during the month in which they are incurred.
2. Electricity is expected to be the same as this year at about £1,500 each quarter, payable on 1 January, 1 April, etc.
3. The business rates are also expected to be the same as this year at £2,000 in total, payable in two equal instalments on 1 April and 1 October.
4. Repairs are expected to cost about £100 each month, payable in the month concerned.
5. Depreciation is to be charged at the rate of 20 per cent on the book value of the equipment and furniture. No depreciation is to be charged on the building.
6. Staff will incur costs for travelling on behalf of the company. These are expected to be at the rate of £3,500 each month during the months when holidays are being taken by clients. During each of the other three months the figure will be £500.

The company has always adopted the policy of realising the profit on a particular holiday in the month in which it is taken.

1   Prepare a month-by-month cash budget and a budgeted income statement, both for next year, and a budgeted balance sheet as at the end of next year. You should also make some comments on the company's plans and on the policy of waiting until holidays have been taken or were due to be taken before realising the profit on them.

SOLUTIONS TO ACTIVITIES

Activity 10.1

Managers will often be prepared to provide financial statements when trying to raise finance for the business. Prospective lenders may require projected financial statements before considering a loan application. When making an offer of new shares to the public, projected statements are published by the company in order to attract investor interest. Projected statements may also be published if the managers feel that the business is under threat. For example, a company that is the subject of a takeover bid to which the managers are opposed may publish projected financial statements in order to give its shareholders confidence in the future of the company as a separate entity and to encourage them to retain their shares in the company.

Activity 10.2

You may have identified cost of sales, materials consumed and salesforce commission as examples of expenses that vary directly with sales. Other expenses, such as depreciation, rent, rates, insurance and salaries, may stay constant during a period irrespective of the level of sales generated. Some expenses have both a variable and fixed element, and so may vary partially with sales output. Energy costs may be an example of such an expense. A certain amount of heating, air conditioning and electricity costs will be incurred irrespective of the level of sales. However, if overtime is being worked due to heavy demand, this expense will increase. The behaviour of different types of expenses in response to changes in the level of output is an important issue which was dealt with in Chapter 7.

Activity 10.3

Your answer to this activity should be as follows:

Projected cash budget for the six months to 30 June 2006

	Jan. $'000	Feb. $'000	Mar. $'000	Apr. $'000	May $'000	June $'000	Total $'000
Cash inflows							
Issue of shares	50	–	–	–	–	–	50
Receipts from debtors	–	10	30	30	40	40	150
	50	10	30	30	40	40	200
Cash outflows							
Payments to creditors	–	20	30	25	25	30	130
Rent and rates	10	–	–	10	–	–	20
Fittings	30	–	–	–	–	–	30
Other costs	9	9	9	9	9	9	54
	49	29	39	44	34	39	234
Net cash flow	1	(19)	(9)	(14)	6	1	(34)
Opening balance	–	1	(18)	(27)	(41)	(35)	–
Closing balance	1	(18)	(27)	(41)	(35)	(34)	(34)

Notes

1. The receipts from credit sales will arise one month after the sale has taken place; hence, cash from January's sales will be received in February, etc. Similarly, trade creditors are paid one month after the goods have been purchased.

2. The closing cash balance for each month is deduced by adding to (or subtracting from) the opening balance the cash flow for the month.

Activity 10.4

Your answer to this activity should be as follows:

Projected income statement for the six months ended 30 June 2006

	$'000	$'000
Credit sales		204
Less cost of sales		
Opening inventory	–	
Purchases	160	
Less closing inventory	58	102
Gross profit		102
Credit card discounts	4	
Rent and rates	20	
Other costs	54	
Depreciation of fittings	5	83
Net profit		19

Note: The credit card discount is shown as a separate expense and not deducted from the sales figure. This approach is more informative than simply netting off the amount of the discount against sales.

Activity 10.5

Your answer to this activity should be as follows:

Projected balance sheet as at 30 June 2006		
	$'000	$'000
Current assets		
Debtors ($51,000 less 2%)	50	
Inventory	58	108
Non-current assets		
Fittings at cost	30	
Less accumulated depreciation	5	25
Total assets		133
Current liabilities		
Trade creditors	30	
Bank overdraft	34	64
Shareholders' equity		
Paid-up share capital	50	
(25,000 shares issued at $2 each)		
Retained profit	19	69
Total liabilities and shareholders' equity		133

Note: The debtors figure represents June credit sales (less the credit card discount). Similarly the creditors figure represents June purchases.

Activity 10.6

Cash flow statement for the six months ended 30 June 2006		
	$'000	$'000
Cash flows from operating activities		
Operating profit (loss) after tax	19	
add non-cash expenses related to		
non-current assets – depreciation	5	
adjust for changes over the period in non-cash		
current assets/current liabilities		
inventory	(58)	
accounts receivable (debtors)	(50)	
prepayments and accruals	–	
accounts payable (creditors)	30	
income tax payable	–	
equals the cash flow from operating activities		(54)
Cash flows from investing activities		
Purchase of property, plant and equipment	(30)	
Proceeds from sale of property, plant and equipment	–	
Interest received	–	
Dividends received	–	
Net cash used in investing activities		(30)

Cash flows from financing activities		
Proceeds from issues of share capital	50	
Proceeds from long-term borrowings	–	
Repayment of long-term borrowings	–	
Dividends paid	–	
Net cash provided by financing activities		50
Net decrease in cash and cash equivalents held		34
Cash and cash equivalents at the beginning of the year		–
Cash and cash equivalents at the end of the year		(34)

Activity 10.7

The projected cash flow statement reveals that the company will have a bank overdraft throughout most of the period under review. The maximum overdraft requirement will be $41,000 in April 2006. Although the company will be heavily dependent on bank finance in the early months, this situation should not last for too long providing the company achieves and then maintains the level of projected profit. The alternative cash flow statement used above highlights that much of the cash flow problem is due to the build-up of inventory and debtors. A build-up of this amount is inevitable when starting from scratch, but is unlikely to continue.

The company is expected to achieve a net profit margin of 9.3 per cent and a return on owners' equity (using end-of-period figures) of 27.5 per cent. This level of return for a new business may be considered acceptable. The return on equity, in particular, seems to be high. However, the business is of a high-risk nature and therefore the owners will be looking to make high returns. As this is a new company involved in a high-risk business it may be very difficult to project into the future with any real accuracy. Thus, the basis on which the projections have been made requires careful investigation.

Some further points regarding profitability can be made. It is not clear from the question whether the wages included in the income statement include any remuneration for James and William Clark. If no remuneration for their efforts has been included, the level of profit shown (as a reward for acting as an entrepreneur) may be overstated. It may not be possible to extrapolate the projected revenues and expenses for the six-month period in order to obtain a projected profit for the year. It may be that the business is seasonal in nature, and therefore the following six-month period may be quite different.

Activity 10.8

Your answer to this activity should be along the following lines:

(a)	Cash budget for the six months ended 31 May 2006						
	Dec.	Jan.	Feb.	Mar.	Apr.	May	Total
	$'000	$'000	$'000	$'000	$'000	$'000	$'000
Cash inflows							
Credit sales	120	112	154	168	105	112	771
Cash sales	48	66	72	45	48	60	339
	168	178	226	213	153	172	1,110
Cash outflows							
Purchases	145	150	140	170	110	120	835
Administration costs	8	8	8	8	10	10	52
Wages	40	40	40	44	44	44	252
Selling expenses	8	8	8	8	8	20	60
Fixtures	–	–	–	–	28	–	28
Dividends	20	–	–	–	–	–	20
	221	206	196	230	200	194	1,247

Net cash flow	(53)	(28)	30	(17)	(47)	(22)	(137)
Opening balance	(126)	(179)	(207)	(177)	(194)	(241)	(126)
Closing balance	(179)	(207)	(177)	(194)	(241)	(263)	(263)

(b) Projected income statement for the six months ended 31 May 2006

	$'000	$'000
Sales		1,130
Less cost of sales (balancing figure)		791
Gross profit (30% of sales)		339
Wages	252	
Selling expenses (excluding advertising campaign)	48	
Administration expenses (including depreciation of 24)	76	
		376
Net loss		37

Notes

1. The advertising campaign relates to the next financial period and will therefore be charged to the income statement (profit and loss account) of that period.

2. Cost of sales = 70 per cent of sales = $791,000.

   Opening inventory + Purchases – Closing inventory = Cost of sales.

   So $142 + 850 - x = 791$

   so x (closing inventory) $= 142 + 850 - 791 = 201$.

(c) Cash flow statement for the six months ended 31 May 2006

	$'000	$'000
Cash flows from operating activities		
Net loss	(37)	
add non-cash expenses related to non-current assets		
e.g. depreciation	24	
adjust for changes over the period in non-cash current		
assets/current liabilities		
increase in inventory	(59)	
increase in accounts receivable (debtors)	(20)	
increase in prepayments (advertising)	(12)	
increase in accounts payable (creditors)	15	
equals the cash flow from operating activities		(89)
Cash flows from investing activities		
Purchase of non-current assets	(28)	
Proceeds from sale of property, plant and equipment	–	
Net cash used in investing activities		(28)

Cash flows from financing activities		
Proceeds from issue of share capital	–	
Proceeds from long-term borrowings	–	
Repayment of long-term borrowings	–	
Dividends paid	(20)	
Net cash used in financing activities		(20)
Net decrease in cash and cash equivalents held		(137)
Cash and cash equivalents at the beginning of the year		(126)
Cash and cash equivalents at the end of the year		(263)

(d) Balance sheet as at 31 May 2006

	$'000	$'000	Notes
Current assets			
Debtors	140		70% of May's sales
Prepaid advertising	12		
Inventory	201	353	see note 2 above
Non-current assets			
Fixtures and fittings at cost	202		increase of $28,000
Less accumulated depreciation	56	146	increase of $18,000
Freehold land and premises at cost	250		
Less accumulated depreciation	30	220	increase of $6,000
		366	
Total assets		719	
Current liabilities			
Bank overdraft	263		from cash flow
Trade creditors	160		May's purchases
Income tax payable	24		due in August
Dividends payable	–	447	paid in December
Shareholders' equity			
Paid-up capital (issued at $1 each)	200		
Retained profits	72	272	109 – 37
Total liabilities and shareholders' equity		719	

(e) You may have thought of a number of possible options. The following (or perhaps some combination of these) might be feasible:

- new equity finance injected by the Dalgleish family or others
- reduce inventory levels
- delay purchase/payment of fixtures
- sell non-current assets
- increase proportion of cash sales

- reduce period of credit to debtors
- delay payment of trade creditors.

Note: The Dalgleish family have ruled out the possibility of raising a loan.

Each of the above options has advantages and disadvantages and these must be carefully assessed before a final decision is made.

Activity 10.9

A possible spreadsheet solution is shown as Table A10.3 on pp. 437–9. The formulae are shown as Table A10.4 on pp. 440–42.

The profit and cash flow for the six months after the modifications are:

	Profit	Cash flow for the year
Base case	– 37	– 137
• an increase in sales of 10 per cent	– 3.1	– 38
• an increase in the gross profit margin to 33 per cent	– 3.1	– 137
• a reduction in administration costs to $6,000 a month	– 45	– 145
• the taking of two months' credit from suppliers	– 37	– 17
• the reduction in credit to customers to half a month	– 37	– 67

APPENDIX TO CHAPTER 10

TABLE A10.1 (1) • Spreadsheet solution to Designer Dresses

	A	B	C	D	E	F	G	H	I	J
1	**Input section**									
2										
3		Jan.	Feb.	Mar.	Apr.	May	June	Total		
4	Sales	10.2	30.6	30.6	40.8	40.8	51	204		
5	Purchases	20	30	25	25	30	30	160		
6	Other costs	9	9	9	9	9	9	54		
7	Rent and rates	10			10			20		
8	Shares	50						50		
9	Fittings	30						30		
10										
11	Depreciation			0.3333						
12	Credit card discount %			2						
13	Closing inventory			58						
14										
15	**Forecast income statement**									
16	Sales				204					
17	Less: cost of sales				102					
18	Purchases			160						
19	Less closing inventory			58						
20	Gross profit				102					
21	Credit card discounts			4						
22	Other costs			54						
23	Rent and rates			20						
24	Depreciation			5						
25					83					
26										
27	Net profit				19					
28										
29										
30	**Cash budget**									
31		Jan.	Feb.	Mar.	Apr.	May	June	Total		Notes
32	*Cash inflows*									
33	Share issue	50						50		
34	Receipts from debtors	0	10	30	30	40	40	150		98% of previous months sales
35										
36		50	10	30	30	40	40	200		
37										
38	*Cash outflows*									
39	Payments to creditors	0	20	30	25	25	30	130		one-month lag
40	Other costs	9	9	9	9	9	9	54		
41	Rent and rates	10	0	0	10	0	0	20		
42	Fittings	30	0	0	0	0	0	30		
43										
44		49	29	39	44	34	39	234		
45	*Net cash flow*	1	−19	−9	−14	6	1	−34		
46	Opening balance	0	1	−18	—27	−41	−35	0		
47										
48	Closing balance	1	−18	−27	−41	−35	−34	−34		
49										

TABLE A10.1 (2) • Spreadsheet solution to Designer Dresses

	A	B	C	D	E	F	G	H	I	J
50										
51	**Cash flow statement**									
52										
53	*Cash flow from operations*									
54	Net profit				19					
55	Adjusted for depreciation				5					
56	Increase in debtors				−50					
57	Increase in inventory				−58					
58	Increase in creditors				30					
59						−54				
60	*Cash flow from investing activities*									
61	Purchase of fittings					−30				
62										
63	*Cash flow from financing activities*									
64	Share issue					50				
65										
66						−34				
67										
68										
69	**Balance sheet**									
70										
71	*Current assets*									
72	Cash				−34					
73	Debtors				50					
74	Inventory				58					
75						74				
76										
77	*Non-current assets*									
78	Fittings – cost				30					
79	Less Depreciation provision				5					
80						25				
81										
82	Total assets					99				
83										
84	*Current liabilities*									
85	Creditors					30				
86										
87	*Shareholders' equity*									
88	Share capital				50					
89	Retained profit				19					
90						69				
91										
92						99				
93										

TABLE A10.2 (1) • Spreadsheet solution to Designer Dresses—relevant formulae

	A	B	C	D	E	F	G	H	I	J
1	**Input section**									
2										
3		Jan.	Feb.	Mar.	Apr.	May	June	Total		
4	Sales	10.2	30.6	30.6	40.8	40.8	51	=SUM(B4:G4)		
5	Purchases	20	30	25	25	30	30	=SUM(B5:G5)		
6	Other costs	9	9	9	9	9	9	=SUM(B6:G6)		
7	Rent and rates	10			10			=SUM(B7:G7)		
8	Shares	50						=SUM(B8:G8)		
9	Fittings	30						=SUM(B9:G9)		
10										
11	Depreciation			0.3333						
12	Credit card discount %			2						
13	Closing inventory			58						
14										
15	**Forecast income statement**									
16	Sales				=H4					
17	Less cost of sales				=D18–D19					
18	Purchases			=H5						
19	Less closing inventory			=D13						
20	Gross profit				=E16–E17					
21	Credit card discounts			=E16*D12/100						
22	Other costs			=H6						
23	Rent and rates			=H7						
24	Depreciation			=H9*D11*6/12						
25					=SUM(D21:D24)					
26										
27	Net profit				=E20–E25					
28										
29										
30	**Cash budget**									
31		Jan.	Feb.	Mar.	Apr.	May	June	Total	Notes	
32	Cash inflows									
33	Share issue	=B8						=SUM(B33:G33)		
34	Receipts from debtors	0	=B4*0.98	=C4*0.98	=D4*0.98	=E4*0.98	F4*0.98	=SUM(B34:G34)	98% of previous months sales	
35										
36		=B33+B34	=C33+C34	=D33+D34	=E33+E34	=F33+F34	=G33+G34	=H33+H34		
37										
38	**Cash outflows**									
39	Payments to creditors	0	=B5	=C5	=D5	=E5	=F5	=SUM(B39:G39)	one-month lag	
40	Other costs	=B6	=C6	=D6	=E6	=F6	=G6	=SUM(B40:G40)		
41	Rent and rates	=B7	=C7	=D7	=E7	=F7	=G7	=SUM(B41:G41)		
42	Fittings	=B9	=C9	=D9	=E9	=F9	=G9	=SUM(B42:G42)		
43										
44		=SUM(B39:B42)	=SUM(C39:C42)	=SUM(D39:D42)	=SUM(E39:E42)	=SUM(F39:F42)	=SUM(G39:G42)	=SUM(H39:H42)		
45	Net cash flow	=B36–B44	=C36–C44	=D36–D44	=E36–E44	=F36–F44	=G36–G44	=H36–H44		
46	Opening balance	0	=B48	=C48	=D48	=E48	=F48	=B46		
47										
48	Closing balance	=B45+B46	=C45+C46	=D45+D46	=E45+E46	=F45+F46	=G45+G46	=H46+H45		
49										

TABLE A10.2 (2) • Spreadsheet solution to Designer Dresses—relevant formulae

	A	B	C	D	E	F	G	H	I	J
50										
51	Cash flow statement									
52										
53	Cash flow from operations									
54	Net profit				=E27					
55	Adjusted for depreciation				=D24					
56	Increase in debtors				=G4*0.98					
57	Increase in inventory				=D13					
58	Increase in creditors				=G5					
59						=SUM(E54:E58)				
60	Cash flow from investing									
61	Purchase of fittings					= −H9				
62										
63	Cash flow from financing									
64	Share issue					=H8				
65										
66						=F59+F61+F64				
67										
68										
69	Balance sheet									
70										
71	Current assets									
72	Cash				=F66					
73	Debtors				−G4*0.98					
74	Inventory				=D13					
75						=E72+E73+E74				
76										
77	Non-current assets									
78	Fittings – cost				=H9					
79	Less accumulated depreciation				=D24					
80						=E78−E79				
81										
82	Total assets					=F75+F80				
83										
84	Current liabilities									
85	Creditors					=G5				
86										
87	Shareholders' equity									
88	Share capital				=H8					
89	Retained profit				=E27					
90						=E88+E89				
91										
92						=F85+F90				
93										

TABLE A10.3 (1) • Spreadsheet solution to Dalgleish Ltd

	A	B	C	D	E	F	G	H	I	J	K
1	**Input section**										
2											
3		Dec.	Jan.	Feb.	Mar.	Apr.	May	Total			
4	Sales	160	220	240	150	160	200	1130			
5	Purchases	150	140	170	110	120	160	850			
6	Wages	40	40	40	44	44	44	252			
7	Administration	8	8	8	8	10	10	52			
8	Depreciation										
9	– Fittings	3	3	3	3	3	3	18			
10	– Land and premises	1	1	1	1	1	1	6			
11	Selling	8	8	8	8	8	8	48			
12	New fixtures					28		28			
13											
14	Adjustments/notes										
15	Advertising prepayment			12							
16	Credit sales as proportion of sales			70%							
17	Gross profit margin			30%							
18	Dividends paid December			20							
19	New fixtures delivery June										
20											
21	**Forecast income statement**										
22											
23	Sales				1130						
24	Less cost of sales				791						
25	Opening inventory			142							
26	Purchases			850							
27											
28				992							
29	Less closing inventory			201							
30	Gross profit				339						
31	Wages			252							
32	Administration			52							
33	Depreciation										
34	– Fittings			18							
35	– Land and premises			6							
36	Selling			48							
37					376						
38											
39	Net profit				−37						
40											
41											

437

TABLE A10.3 (2) • Spreadsheet solution to Dalgleish Ltd

	A	B	C	D	E	F	G	H	I	J	K
42	**Cash budget**										
43											
44		Dec.	Jan.	Feb.	Mar.	Apr.	May	Total		Notes	
45	*Cash inflows*										
46	Cash sales	48	66	72	45	48	60	339			
47	Receipts from debtors	120	112	154	168	105	112	771		closing debtors	140
48											
49		168	178	226	213	153	172	1110			
50											
51	*Cash outflows*										
52	Payments to creditors	145	150	140	170	110	120	835		closing creditors	160
53	Wages	40	40	40	44	44	44	252			
54	Administration	8	8	8	8	10	10	52			
55	Selling	8	8	8	8	8	8	48			
56	Advertising						12	12		Prepayment	
57	Dividends	20						20			
58	Fittings	0	0	0	0	28	0	28		Asset	
59											
60		221	206	196	230	200	194	1247			
61	*Net cash flow*	−53	−28	30	−17	−47	−22	−137			
62	Opening balance	−126	−179	−207	−177	−194	−241	−126			
63											
64	Closing balance	−179	−207	−177	−194	−241	−263	−263			
65											
66											
67	**Cash flow statement**										
68											
69	*Cash flow from operations*										
70	Net profit				−37						
71	Adjusted for depreciation				24						
72	Increase in debtors				−20						
73	Increase in prepayments				−12						
74	Increase in inventory				−59						
75	Increase in creditors				15						
76						−89					
77	*Cash flow from investing activities*										
78	Purchase of fittings					−28					
79											
80	*Cash flow from financing activities*										
81	Dividends					−20					
82											
83						−137					
84											

TABLE A10.3 (3) • Spreadsheet solution to Dalgleish Ltd

	A	B	C	D	E	F	G	H	I	J	K
85											
86	**Balance sheet**		Opening		Closing						
87											
88	*Current assets*										
89	Cash		−126		−263						
90	Debtors		120		140						
91	Prepayments				12						
92	Inventory		142		201						
93				136		90					
94											
95	*Non-current assets*										
96	Fixtures and fittings – cost		174		202						
97	Less accumulated deprec.		−38		−56						
98	Land and premises – cost		250		250						
99	Less accumulated deprec.		−24		−30						
100				362		366					
101											
102	Total assets			498		456					
103											
104	*Current liabilities*										
105	Creditors		145		160						
106	Income tax payable		24		24						
107	Dividends payable		20		0						
108				189		184					
109	*Shareholders' equity*										
110	Paid up share capital		200		200						
111	Retained profits		109		72						
112				309		272					
113											
114				498		456					
115											

TABLE A10.4 (1) • Spreadsheet solution to Dalgleish Ltd—formulae

	A	B	C	D	E	F	G	H	I	J	K
1	**Input section**										
2											
3		Dec.	Jan.	Feb.	Mar.	Apr.	May	Total			
4	Sales	160	220	240	150	160	200	=SUM(B4:G4)			
5	Purchases	150	140	170	110	120	160	=SUM(B5:G5)			
6	Wages	40	40	40	44	44	44	=SUM(B6:G6)			
7	Administration	8	8	8	8	10	10	=SUM(B7:G7)			
8	Depreciation										
9	– Fittings	3	3	3	3	3	3	=SUM(B9:G9)			
10	– Land and premises	1	1	1	1	1	1	=SUM(B10:G10)			
11	Selling	8	8	8	8	8	8	=SUM(B11:G11)			
12	New fixtures					28		=SUM(B12:G12)			
13											
14	Adjustments/notes										
15	Advertising prepayment			12							
16	Credit sales as proportion of sales			0.7							
17	Gross profit margin			0.3							
18	Dividends paid December			20							
19	New fixtures delivery June										
20											
21	**Forecast income statement**										
22											
23	Sales				=H4						
24	Less: cost of sales				=E23–E30						
25	Opening inventory			142							
26	Purchases			=H5							
27											
28				=D25+D26							
29	Less closing inventory			=D28–E24							
30	Gross profit				=E23*D17						
31	Wages			=H6							
32	Administration			=H7							
33	Depreciation										
34	– Fittings			=H9							
35	– Land and premises			=H10							
36	Selling			=H11							
37					=SUM(D31:D36)						
38											
39	Net profit				=E30–E37						
40											
41											

TABLE A10.4 (2) • Spreadsheet solution to Dalgleish Ltd—formulae

	A	B	C	D	E	F	G	H	I	J	K
42	**Cash budget**										
43											
44		Dec.	Jan.	Feb.	Mar.	Apr.	May	Total		Notes	
45	*Cash inflows*										
46	Cash sales	=0.3*B4	=0.3*C4	=0.3*D4	=0.3*E4	=0.3*F4	=0.3*G4	=SUM(B46:G46)			
47	Receipts from debtors	=C90	=0.7*B4	=0.7*C4	=0.7*D4	=0.7*E4	=0.7*F4	=SUM(B47:G47)		closing debtors	=0.7*G4
48											
49		=B46+B47	=C46+C47	=D46+D47	=E46+E47	=F46+F47	=G46+G47	=H46+H47			
50											
51	*Cash outflows*										
52	Payments to creditors	=C105	=B5	=C5	=D5	=E5	=F5	=SUM(B52:G52)		closing creditors	=G5
53	Wages	=B6	=C6	=D6	=E6	=F6	=G6	=SUM(B53:G53)			
54	Administration	=B7	=C7	=D7	=E7	=F7	=G7	=SUM(B54:G54)			
55	Selling	=B11	=C11	=D11	=E11	=F11	=G11	=SUM(B55:G55)			
56	Advertising						12	=SUM(B56:G56)		Prepayment	
57	Dividends	20						=SUM(B57:G57)			
58	Fittings	=B12	=C12	=D12	=E12	=F12	=G12	=SUM(B58:G58)		Asset	
59											
60		=SUM(B52:B58)	=SUM(C52:C58)	=SUM(D52:D58)	=SUM(E52:E58)	=SUM(F52:F58)	=SUM(G52:G58)	=SUM(H52:H58)			
61	*Net cash flow*	=B49–B60	=C49–C60	=D49–D60	=E49–E60	=F49–F60	=G49–G60	=H49–H60			
62	Opening balance	–126	=B64	=C64	=D64	=E64	=F64	=B62			
63											
64	Closing balance	=B61+B62	=C61+C62	=D61+D62	=E61+E62	=F61+F62	=G61+G62	=H62+H61			
65											
66											
67	**Cash flow statement**										
68											
69	*Cash flow from operations*										
70	Net profit				=E39						
71	Adjusted for depreciation				=D34+D35						
72	Increase in debtors				= –(E90–C90)						
73	Increase in prepayments				= –H56						
74	Increase in inventory				= –(E92–C92)						
75	Increase in creditors				=E105–C105						
76						=SUM(E70:E75)					
77	*Cash flow from investing*										
78	Purchase of fittings					= –H12					
79											
80	*Cash flow from financing*										
81	Dividends					= –D18					
82											
83						=F76+F78+F81					
84											

441

TABLE 10.4 (3) • Spreadsheet solution to Dalgleish Ltd—formulae

	A	B	C	D	E	F	G	H	I	J	K
85											
86	**Balance sheet**		Opening		Closing						
87											
88	*Current assets*										
89	Cash		−126		=F83+C89						
90	Debtors		120		=K47						
91	Prepayments				=H56						
92	Inventory		142		=D29						
93				=C89+C90+C92		=SUM(E89:E92)					
94											
95	*Non-current assets*										
96	Fixtures and fittings − cost		174		=C96+H12						
97	Less accumulated deprec.		−38		=C97−D34						
98	Land and premises − cost		250		=C98						
99	Less accumulated deprec.		−24		=C99−D35						
100				=SUM(C96:C99)		=SUM(E96:E99)					
101											
102	Total assets			=D93+D100		=F93+F100					
103											
104	*Current liabilities*										
105	Creditors		145		=K52						
106	Income tax payable		24		=C106						
107	Dividends payable		20		=C107−H57						
108				=SUM(C105:C107)		=SUM(F105:F107)					
109	*Shareholders' equity*										
110	Share capital		200		=C110						
111	Retained profits		109		=C111+E39						
112				=C110+C111		=E110+E111					
113											
114				=D108+D112		=F108+F112					
115											

OBJECTIVES

When you have completed your study of this chapter you should be able to:

1 identify the essential features of investment decisions

2 list examples of investment decisions

3 state the four common capital investment methods

4 demonstrate an understanding of the 'accounting rate of return method' with respect to the formula, decision rule, strengths and weaknesses

5 demonstrate an understanding of the 'payback method' with respect to the formula, decision rule, strengths and weaknesses

6 demonstrate an understanding of the 'net present value method' with respect to the formula, decision rule, strengths and weaknesses

7 demonstrate an understanding of the 'internal rate of return method' with respect to the formula, decision rule, strengths and weaknesses

8 explain the notion of present values

9 identify alternative means of determining present values

10 convert forecast profit flows into cash flows

11 discuss other factors important to capital investment decision making

12 compare the two DCF methods.

11

CAPITAL INVESTMENT DECISIONS

In this chapter we shall look at how businesses can make decisions involving investments in new plant, machinery, buildings and similar long-term assets. Though we shall be considering this topic in the context of businesses making decisions about the type of assets just mentioned, the general principles can be applied equally well to investments in the shares of companies, irrespective of whether the investment is being considered by a business or by a private individual. This is dealt with in more detail in Chapter 12.

THE NATURE OF INVESTMENT DECISIONS

The essential feature of investment decisions, irrespective of who is to make the decision, is the time factor. Investment involves making an outlay of something of economic value, usually cash, at one point in time which is expected to yield economic benefits to the investor at some other point in time. Typically, the outlay precedes the benefits. Also, the outlay is typically one large amount and the benefits arrive in a stream over a fairly protracted period.

Investment decisions tend to be of crucial importance to the investor for the following reasons.

* *Large amounts of resources are often involved.* Many investments made by a business involve outlaying a significant proportion of its total resources. If mistakes are made with the decision, the effects on the business could be significant, if not catastrophic.

* *It is often difficult and expensive to 'bail out' of an investment once it has been undertaken.* It is often the case that investments made by a business are specific to its needs. For example, a manufacturing business may have a factory built which has been specifically designed to accommodate the particular flow of production of that business. This may render the factory unattractive to another potential user with different needs, with the result that its second-hand value is low. If the business found, after having made the investment, that the product being produced in the factory is not selling as well as was planned, the only possible course of action might be to close down production and sell the factory. This would probably mean that much less could be recouped from the investment in the factory than it had originally cost, particularly if the costs of design are included as part of the cost, as they logically should be.

ACTIVITY 11.1

When businesses are making decisions involving capital investments, what should the decision seek to achieve?

METHODS OF INVESTMENT APPRAISAL

Given the importance of investment decisions to the viability of the business, it is essential that proper screening of investment proposals take place. An important part of this screening process is to ensure that appropriate methods of evaluating the profitability of investment projects are employed.

Research shows that there are basically four methods used in practice by businesses to evaluate investment opportunities. It is possible to find businesses which use variants of these four methods. It is also possible to find businesses, particularly smaller ones, which do not use any formal appraisal methods but rely more on the 'gut feeling' of managers. Most businesses, however, seem to use one or more of the four methods, which we shall now review.

To help us to consider each of the four methods it might be useful to look at how each of them would cope with a particular investment opportunity. Let us consider the following example.

EXAMPLE

11.1

Billingsgate Battery Company has carried out some research which shows that it could manufacture and sell a product that the business has recently developed.

Production would require an investment in a machine which would cost $100,000, payable immediately. Production and sales would take place throughout the next five years. At the end of this time, it is estimated that the machine could be sold for $20,000.

Production and sales of the product would be expected to occur as follows:

	Number of units
Next year	5,000
Second year	10,000
Third year	15,000
Fourth year	15,000
Fifth year	5,000

It is estimated that the new product can be sold for $12 a unit and that the relevant material and labour costs will total $8 a unit.

To simplify matters, we shall assume that the cash from sales and for the costs of production are received and paid, respectively, at the end of each year. (This is clearly unlikely to be true in real life; money will have to be paid to employees on a weekly or a monthly basis and customers will pay within a month or two of buying the product. On the other hand, it is probably not a serious distortion. It is a simplifying assumption that is often made in real life and it will make things more straightforward for us now. You should be clear, however, that there is nothing about any of the four approaches which demands that this assumption is made.)

Bearing in mind that each product sold will give rise to a net cash inflow of $4 (i.e. $12 – $8), the cash flows (receipts and payments) over the life of the production will be as follows:

		$'000
Immediately	Cost of machine	(100)
1 year's time	Net profit before depreciation ($4 × 5,000)	20
2 years' time	Net profit before depreciation ($4 × 10,000)	40
3 years' time	Net profit before depreciation ($4 × 15,000)	60
4 years' time	Net profit before depreciation ($4 × 15,000)	60
5 years' time	Net profit before depreciation ($4 × 5,000)	20
	Plus disposal proceeds from the machine	20

Note that, broadly speaking, the net profit before deducting depreciation (i.e. before non-cash items) equals the net amount of cash flowing into the business. We will return to this in more detail later in this chapter.

Having set up the example, we shall go on to look at the techniques used to assess investment opportunities and see how they deal with the decision in the example.

ACCOUNTING RATE OF RETURN (ARR)

The **accounting rate of return** method takes the average accounting profit which the investment will generate and expresses it as a percentage of the average investment in the project as measured in accounting terms. Thus:

$$ARR = \frac{\text{Average annual profit}}{\text{Average investment to earn that profit}} \times 100\%$$

The average profit before depreciation over the five years is $40,000 (i.e. (20 + 40 + 60 + 60 + 20) / 5). Assuming straight-line depreciation (i.e. equal annual amounts), the annual depreciation charge will be $16,000 (i.e. (100 – 20) / 5). Thus the average annual profit after depreciation is $24,000 (i.e. 40 – 16).

The machine will appear in the balance sheet as follows:

		$'000
Beginning of year	1	100
At the end of year	1	84 (i.e. 100 – 16)
	2	68 (i.e. 84 – 16)
	3	52
	4	36
	5	20

The average investment (at closing balance sheet values) will be $60,000 (i.e. (100 + 84 + 68 + 52 + 36 + 20) / 6). This can also be calculated by taking the average of the initial cost and the expected residual value ((100 + 20) / 2). Thus the ARR of the investment is 40 per cent (i.e. (24 / 60) × 100).

ACTIVITY 11.2

Chaotic Industries is considering an investment in a fleet of 10 delivery vehicles to take its products to customers. The vehicles will cost $15,000 each to buy, payable immediately. The annual running costs are expected to total $20,000 for each vehicle (including the driver's salary). The vehicles are expected to operate successfully for six years at the end of which period they will all have to be scrapped with disposal proceeds expected to be about $3,000 per vehicle. At present the business uses a commercial carrier for all of its deliveries. It is expected that this carrier will charge a total of $230,000 each year for the next six years to undertake the deliveries.

What is the ARR of buying the vehicles? Note that cost savings are as relevant a benefit from an investment as are actual net cash inflows.

The accounting rate of return and the return on total assets (ROA) ratio employ the same approach to performance measurement. You may recall from Chapter 6 that ROA is a popular means of assessing the performance of a business *after* the period has passed. However, ARR can be argued to be a useful means of assessing an investment opportunity *before* it takes place. In theory, if all investments made by Chaotic Industries (Activity 11.2) actually proved to have an ARR of 11.1 per cent, then the ROA for that business should be 11.1 per cent. Since private sector businesses are seeking, probably among other things, to increase the wealth of their owners, ARR seems to be a sound method of appraising investment opportunities. Profit can be seen as a net increase in wealth over a period, and relating it to the size of investment made to achieve it seems logical.

A user of ARR would require that any investment undertaken by the business would be able to achieve a minimum ARR. Perhaps the minimum would be the rate which previous investments had achieved (as measured by the ROA), or perhaps it would be the industry average ROA.

Where there are competing projects which all seem capable of exceeding the minimum rate, the one with the higher or highest ARR would normally be selected.

As a method of investment appraisal ARR is said to have a number of advantages. It was mentioned earlier that the ROA is a widely used measure of business performance. Shareholders use this ratio to evaluate management performance and often the financial objective of a business will be expressed in terms of a target ROA. It therefore seems sensible to employ a method of investment appraisal which is consistent with this overall approach to measuring business performance. ARR is also a measure of profitability which many believe is the correct way to evaluate investments, and it produces a percentage figure of return which managers understand and feel comfortable with.

ACTIVITY 11.3

The ARR suffers from a very major defect as a means of assessing investment opportunities. Can you see what this is? Take a look back at the Billingsgate Battery Company example (above).

Hint: The defect is not concerned with the ability of the decision maker to forecast future events, although this too can be a problem.

It can be seen from the solution to Activity 11.3 that the use of ARR can easily cause poor decisions to be made. We shall look in more detail at the reason for timing being so important later in this chapter.

There are other defects associated with the ARR method. For investment appraisal purposes it is cash flows rather than accounting profits that are important. Cash is the ultimate measure of the economic wealth generated. This is because it is cash that is used to acquire resources and for distribution to shareholders. Accounting profit is more appropriate for reporting purposes. It is a measure of productive effort for a particular reporting period such as a year or half-year. ARR also fails to take account of the fact that dollars received at a later date are worth less than dollars received at an earlier date. We will return to this point later in the chapter.

PAYBACK PERIOD (PP)

The **payback period** method seems to go some way to overcoming the timing problem of ARR, or at least at first glance it does.

It might be useful to consider PP in the context of the Billingsgate Battery Company example. You will recall that essentially the project's costs and benefits can be summarised as:

		$'000
Immediately	Cost of machine	(100)
1 year's time	Net profit before depreciation	20
2 years' time	Net profit before depreciation	40
3 years' time	Net profit before depreciation	60
4 years' time	Net profit before depreciation	60
5 years' time	Net profit before depreciation plus disposal proceeds	40 (i.e. 20 + 20)

Note that all of these figures are amounts of cash to be paid or received.

The payback period is the length of time it takes for the initial investment to be repaid out of the net cash inflows from the project. In this case, it will be nearly three years before the $100,000 outlay is covered by the inflows. The payback period can be derived by calculating the cumulative cash flows as follows:

Year		Net cash flows $'000	Cumulative cash flows $'000
Immediately	Cost of machine	(100)	(100)
1 year's time	Net profit before depreciation	20	(80)
2 years' time	Net profit before depreciation	40	(40)
3 years' time	Net profit before depreciation	60	20
4 years' time	Net profit before depreciation	60	80
5 years' time	Net profit before depreciation plus disposal proceeds	40 (20 + 20)	120

We can see that the cumulative cash flows become positive in the third year. If we assume that the cash flows accrue evenly over the year, the precise payback period will be:

2 years + (40 / 60) = 2⅔ years

A decision maker using PP would need to have a maximum payback period in mind. For example, if Billingsgate Battery Company had a required maximum payback period of three years it would accept the project, but it would not go ahead if its required maximum payback period were two years. If there were two competing projects which both met the maximum payback period requirement, the decision maker should select the project with the shorter payback period.

ACTIVITY 11.4

What is the payback period of the Chaotic Industries project from Activity 11.2?

The PP approach has certain advantages. It is quick and easy to calculate and can be easily understood by managers. The logic of using PP is that projects that can recoup their cost quickly are economically more attractive than those with longer payback periods. PP is probably an improvement on ARR in respect of the timing of the cash flows. PP is not, however, the whole answer to the problem. It does not focus on all of the timing issues.

ACTIVITY 11.5

In what respect, in your opinion, is PP not the whole answer as a means of assessing investment opportunities? Use the cash flows arising from the three competing projects given below for purposes of illustration.

		Project 1 $'000	Project 2 $'000	Project 3 $'000
Immediately	Cost of machine	(200)	(200)	(200)
1 year's time	Net profit before depreciation	40	10	80
2 years' time	Net profit before depreciation	80	20	100

3 years' time	Net profit before depreciation	80	170	20
4 years' time	Net profit before depreciation	60	20	200
5 years' time	Net profit before depreciation	40	10	500
	Plus disposal proceeds	40	10	20

Hint: Again the defect is not concerned with the ability of the decision maker to forecast future events. This is a problem, but it is a problem whatever approach we take.

Within the payback period, PP ignores the timing of the cash flows. Beyond the payback period, the method totally ignores the size and the timing of the cash flows. While ignoring cash flows beyond the payback period neatly avoids the practical problems of forecasting cash flows over a long period, it means that relevant information may be ignored.

The PP approach is seen as a means of dealing with the problem of risk by favouring projects with a short payback period. However, this is a fairly crude approach to the problem. There are more systematic approaches to dealing with risk which can be used.

It seems that PP has the advantage of taking some note of the timing of the costs and benefits from the project, but it suffers the disadvantage of ignoring relevant information. ARR ignores timing to a great extent, but it does take account of all of the benefits and costs. What we really need to help us to make sensible decisions is a method of appraisal that takes account of all of the costs and benefits of each investment opportunity, but which also makes a logical allowance for the timing of those costs and benefits.

NET PRESENT VALUE (NPV)

The **net present value** method compares the sum of the present value of all expected cash inflows with the present value of the expected cash outflows related to a given project. Consider the Billingsgate Battery Company example, which can be summarised as follows:

		$'000
Immediately	Cost of machine	(100)
1 year's time	Net profit before depreciation	20
2 years' time	Net profit before depreciation	40
3 years' time	Net profit before depreciation	60
4 years' time	Net profit before depreciation	60
5 years' time	Net profit before depreciation	20
	Plus disposal proceeds	20

Given that the principal financial objective of the business is probably to increase wealth, it would be very easy to assess this investment if all of the cash flows were to occur now (i.e. all at the same time). All that we should need to do is to add up the benefits (total $220,000) and compare them with the cost ($100,000). This would lead us to the conclusion that the project should go ahead, because the business would be better off by $120,000. Of course, it is not as easy as this because time is involved. The cash outflow (payment) will, if the project is undertaken, occur immediately. The inflows (receipts) will arise at a range of later times.

The time factor arises because normal people will not pay out $100 now in order to receive $100 in a year's time—these are not seen as being equivalent in value. If you were to be offered $100 in 12 months, provided that you paid $100 to that person now, you probably would not be prepared to do so unless you wished to do that person (perhaps a friend or relation) a favour.

ACTIVITY 11.6

Why would you see $100 to be received in a year's time as unequal in value to $100 to be paid immediately? (There are basically three reasons.)

We shall now take a closer look at the three factors identified in the solution to Activity 11.6.

Interest lost

If you are to be deprived of the use of your money for a year, you could equally well be deprived of its use by placing it on deposit in a bank or building society. In this case, at the end of the year you could have your money back and have interest as well. Thus, unless the opportunity to invest will offer similar returns you will be incurring an **opportunity cost**. An opportunity cost occurs where one course of action—for example, making an investment in, say, a computer—deprives you of the opportunity to derive some benefit from an alternative action—for example, putting the money in the bank.

From this we can see that any investment opportunity must, if it is to make you more wealthy, do better than the returns that are available from the next best opportunity. Thus, if Billingsgate Battery Company sees putting the money in the bank on deposit as the alternative to investing in the machine, the return from investing in the machine must be better than that from investing in the bank. If the bank offered better returns the business would become more wealthy by putting the money on deposit.

Risk

Buying a machine to manufacture a product to be sold in the market, on the strength of various estimates made in advance of buying the machine, is risky.

ACTIVITY 11.7

Can you suggest some areas where things might not go according to plan?

It is important to remember that the decision whether or not to invest in the machine must be taken before any of the things suggested in the solution to Activity 11.7 are known. After the machine has been purchased things can go wrong—for example, we realise that the level of sales that had been estimated before the event is not going to be achieved. It is not possible to wait until we know for certain whether the market will behave as we expected before we buy the machine. We can study reports and analyses of the market. We can commission sophisticated market surveys and these may give us more confidence in the likely outcome. We can advertise strongly and try to expand sales. Ultimately, however, we have to jump off into the dark and accept the risk.

Normally, people expect to receive greater returns where they perceive risk to be a factor. Examples of this in real life are not difficult to find. One such example is the fact that a bank will tend to charge a higher rate of interest to a borrower whom the bank perceives to be more risky than to one who can offer good security for the loan and can point to a regular source of income from which repayments can be made.

Going back to Billingsgate Battery Company's investment opportunity, it is not enough to say that we would not advise making the investment unless the returns from it are higher than those from investing in a bank deposit.

Clearly, we would want returns above the level of bank deposit interest rates because the logical equivalent investment opportunity to investing in the machine is not putting the money on deposit. It is making an alternative investment which seems to have a risk similar to that of the investment in the machine.

In practice, we tend to expect a higher rate of return from investment projects where the risk is perceived as being higher. How risky a particular project is, and therefore how large this risk premium should be, are matters that are difficult to gauge. In practice, it is necessary to make some judgment on these questions.

Inflation

If you are to be deprived of $100 for a year, when you come to spend that money it will not buy as much in the way of goods and services as it would have done a year earlier. Generally, you will not be able to buy as many tins of baked beans or loaves of bread or bus tickets for a particular journey as you could have done a year earlier. Clearly, the investor needs this loss of purchasing power to be compensated for if the investment is to be made. This is on top of a return that takes account of the returns that could have been gained from an alternative investment of similar risk.

In practice, interest rates observable in the market tend to take inflation into account. Rates which are offered to potential building society and bank depositors include an allowance for the rate of inflation that is expected in the future.

To summarise these factors, we can say that the logical investor, who is seeking to increase his or her wealth, will only be prepared to make investments that will compensate for the loss of interest, the loss of purchasing power of the money invested and the risk (the fact that the returns which are expected may not materialise). This is usually assessed by seeing whether the proposed investment will yield a return that is greater than the basic rate of interest (which would include an allowance for inflation) plus a risk premium.

Naturally, investors need at least the minimum return before they are prepared to invest. However, it is in terms of the effect on their wealth that they should logically assess an investment project. Usually, the investment with the highest percentage return will make the investor most wealthy, but we shall see later in this chapter that this is not always the case. For the time being, therefore, we shall concentrate on wealth.

Let us now return to the Billingsgate Battery Company example. You will recall that the cash flows expected from this investment, were it to be made, are:

		$'000
Immediately	Cost of machine	(100)
1 year's time	Net profit before depreciation	20
2 years' time	Net profit before depreciation	40
3 years' time	Net profit before depreciation	60
4 years' time	Net profit before depreciation	60
5 years' time	Net profit before depreciation	20
	Plus disposal proceeds	20

Let us assume that instead of making this investment the business could make an alternative investment, with similar risk, and obtain a return of 20 per cent a year.

You will recall that we have concluded that it is not possible just to compare the basic figures listed above. It would therefore be useful if we could express each of these cash flows in similar terms so that we could make a direct comparison between the sum of the inflows and the $100,000 investment. In fact we can do this.

We know that Billingsgate Battery Company could alternatively invest its money at a rate of 20 per cent a year. How much do you judge the present (immediate) value of the expected first year receipt of $20,000 to be? In other words, if instead of having to wait a year for the $20,000 and being deprived of the opportunity to invest it at 20 per cent, you could have some money now, what sum to be received now would you regard as exactly equivalent to getting $20,000, but having to wait a year for it?

If we could derive the present value (PV) of each of the cash flows associated with the machine investment, we could easily make the direct comparison between the cost of making the investment ($100,000) and the various benefits that will derive from it in years 1 to 5. Fortunately, we can do precisely this.

We can make a more general statement about the PV of a particular cash flow. It is:

$$PV \text{ of the cash flow of year } n = \text{Actual cash flow of year } n / (1 + r)^n$$

where n is the year of the cash flow (i.e. how many years into the future) and r is the opportunity investing rate expressed as a decimal (instead of as a percentage).

We have already seen how this works for the $20,000 inflow for year 1. For year 2 the calculation would be:

$$PV \text{ of year 2 cash flow} = \$40,000 / (1 + 0.2)^2$$
$$PV = \$40,000 / (1.2)^2 = \$40,000 / 1.44 = \$27,778$$

Thus the PV of the $40,000 to be received in two years' time is $27,778. This can be shown as follows:

	$
Amount available for immediate investment	27,778
Add interest for year 1 (20% x 27,778)	5,556
	33,334
Add interest for year 2 (20% x 33,334)	6,667
	40,001

(The extra $1 is only a rounding error.)

Thus because the investor can turn $27,778 into $40,000 in two years, these amounts are equivalent and we can say that $27,778 is the present value of $40,000 receivable after two years, assuming a 20 per cent investment opportunity.

Now let us deduce the PVs of all of the cash flows associated with the machine project and hence the NPV of the project as a whole. The relevant cash flows and calculations are as follows:

Time	Cash flow $'000	Calculation of PV	PV $'000
Immediately (time 0)	(100)	$(100) / (1 + 0.2)^0$	(100.00)
1 year's time	20	$20 / (1 + 0.2)^1$	16.67
2 years' time	40	$40 / (1 + 0.2)^2$	27.78
3 years' time	60	$60 / (1 + 0.2)^3$	34.72
4 years' time	60	$60 / (1 + 0.2)^4$	28.94
5 years' time	40 (20 + 20)	$40 / (1 + 0.2)^5$	16.08
			24.19

We can now say that, given the investment opportunities available to the business elsewhere, investing in the machine will make the business $24,190 better off. What the above is saying is that the benefits from investing in this machine are worth a total of $124,190 today. Since the business can 'buy' these benefits for just $100,000 the investment should be made. Clearly, at any price up to $124,190 the investment would be worth making as it would be giving a return in excess of the 20 per cent opportunity rate.

Using discount tables

Deducing the PVs of the various cash flows was a little laborious using the approach that we have just taken. To deduce each PV we took the relevant cash flow and multiplied it by $1/(1 + r)^n$. Fortunately, there are quicker ways. Tables exist which show values of this discount factor for a range of values of r and n. Such a table is appended at the end of this chapter. Take a look at it.

Look at the column for 20 per cent and the row for 1 year. We find that the factor is 0.833. Thus the PV of a cash flow of $1 receivable in one year, assuming an opportunity rate of 20 per cent, is $0.833. So the PV of a cash flow of $20,000 receivable in one year's time is $16,667 (i.e. 0.833 × $20,000), the same result as we found doing it longhand. The opportunity rate is usually referred to as the discount rate. It is effectively the reverse of compounding.

Use of financial calculators or spreadsheets to deal with the calculations represents a more practical approach to solving the problems. A familiarity with present value tables is nevertheless encouraged, at least in the early stages, until you have developed a full understanding of the process.

ACTIVITY 11.9

What is the NPV of the Chaotic Industries project from Activity 11.2, assuming a 15 per cent opportunity cost of finance (discount rate)? You should use the discount table at the end of this chapter.

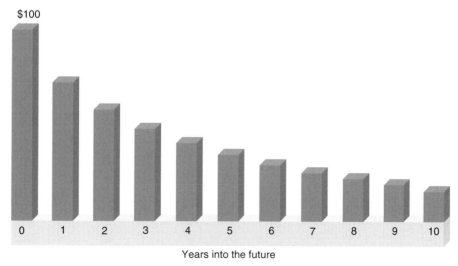

FIGURE 11.1 Present value of $100 receivable at various times in the future, assuming an annual financing cost of 20 per cent

Figure 11.1 shows how the value of $100 diminishes as its receipt goes further into the future, assuming an opportunity cost of finance of 20 per cent per annum. The $100 to be received immediately, obviously, has a PV of $100. As the time before it is to be received grows larger, the present value diminishes significantly.

From what we have seen, NPV seems to be a better method of appraising investment opportunities than either ARR or PP. NPV fully addresses each of the following:

✳ *The timing of the cash flows.* Discounting the various cash flows associated with each project according to when they are expected to arise takes into account the fact that cash flows do not all occur simultaneously. Associated with this is the fact that by discounting, using the opportunity cost of finance (i.e. the return which the next best alternative opportunity would generate), the net benefit after financing costs have been met is identified (as the NPV).

✳ *The whole of the relevant cash flows.* NPV includes all of the relevant cash flows irrespective of when they are expected to occur. It treats them differently according to their date of occurrence, but they are all taken account of in the NPV and they all have, or can have, an influence on the decision.

✳ *The objectives of the business.* NPV is the only method of appraisal where the output of the analysis has a direct bearing on the wealth of the business. (Positive NPVs enhance wealth, negative ones reduce it.) Since most private sector businesses seek to increase their value and wealth, NPV clearly is the best approach to use, at least of all the methods we have considered so far.

There are at least two potential limitations of the use of NPV:

✳ *The actual return percentage is unknown.* Where the NPV is positive (+) you simply know the projected return is higher than the discount rate, or where it is negative (–) it is lower than the discount rate. However, you do not know how much higher or lower. For example, project X has an NPV of +$1,900 after discounting at 12 per cent. We do not know whether the return is 13 per cent or 17 per cent.

✳ *Ranking of alternative projects.* If funds were unlimited, then all projects with positive (+) NPVs would be selected. However, funds are normally restricted and the ranking of alternative projects on the basis of NPV may not lead to the best investment strategy. Problem areas of this type are explained in more detail later in the chapter.

In general, and subject to qualifications dealt with later, users of the NPV approach should adopt the following decision rules:

✳ Take on all projects with positive NPVs, when they are discounted at the opportunity cost of finance.

✳ Where a choice has to be made between two or more projects, select the one with the larger or largest NPV.

DISCOUNTED PAYBACK

We noted earlier that the payback method does not take into account the concept of the time value of money.

One way of changing this is to compare the initial cost with the cash inflows, after discounting.

Suppose a project has an initial cash outflow of $60,000 and cash inflows of $20,000 for each of the next five years. Clearly the payback period is three years. If the cash inflows are discounted at 10% the relevant figures will be:

EXAMPLE 11.2

Cost				$60,000
Inflows	Amount	Discount factors	PV	Cumulative inflows
1	20,000	.909	18,180	18,180
2	20,000	.826	16,520	34,700
3	20,000	.751	15,020	49,720
4	20,000	.683	13,660	63,380
5	20,000	.621	12,420	75,800

The discounted payback is thus approximately 3¾ years.

INTERNAL RATE OF RETURN (IRR)

This is the last of the four main methods of investment appraisal that are found in practice. It is quite closely related to the NPV method in that, like NPV, the **internal rate of return** involves discounting future cash flows.

You will recall that when we discounted the cash flows of the Billingsgate Battery Company machine investment opportunity at 20 per cent, we found that the NPV was a positive figure of $24,190. The fact that the NPV is positive when discounting at 20 per cent implies that the rate of return which the project generates is more than 20 per cent. The fact that the NPV is a pretty large figure implies that the actual rate of return is quite a lot above 20 per cent. We should expect that an increase in the size of the discount rate would reduce NPV because a higher discount rate gives a lower discount factor. Thus, future inflows are more heavily discounted, which will reduce their impact on the NPV. In fact, the IRR is the discount rate that will have the effect of producing an NPV of precisely zero.

It is somewhat laborious to deduce the IRR by hand since it cannot usually be calculated directly. Thus, without access to a financial calculator or computerised spreadsheet, iteration (trial and error) is the only approach.

Let us try a higher rate—say, 30 per cent—and see what happens.

Time	Cash flow $'000	Discount factor	PV $'000
Immediately (time 0)	(100)	1.000	(100.00)
1 year's time	20	0.769	15.38
2 years' time	40	0.592	23.68
3 years' time	60	0.455	27.30
4 years' time	60	0.350	21.00
5 years' time	40 (20 + 20)	0.269	10.76
			(1.88)

In increasing the discount rate from 20 per cent to 30 per cent, we have reduced the NPV from $24,190 (positive) to $1,880 (negative). Since the IRR is the discount rate that will give us an NPV of exactly zero, we can conclude that the IRR of Billingsgate Battery Company's machine project is very slightly under 30 per cent. Further trials could lead us to the exact rate, but there is probably not much point given the likely inaccuracy of the cash flow estimates. Of course, use of a spreadsheet or financial calculator will give a precise figure. You need to recognise that, given the tentative nature of some of the cash flows, such precision could mislead.

The relationship between the NPV method discussed earlier and the IRR is shown graphically in Figure 11.2 using the information relating to the Billingsgate Battery Company. Where the discount rate is zero, the NPV will be the sum of the net cash flows. In other words, no account is taken of the time value of money. However, as the discount rate increases there is a corresponding decrease in the NPV of the project. When the NPV line touches the horizontal axis there will be a zero NPV and that point will also represent the IRR.

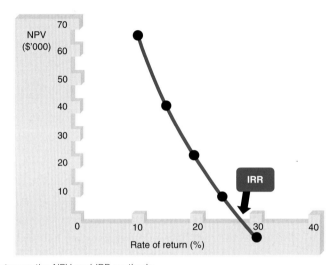

FIGURE 11.2 The relationship between the NPV and IRR methods

 ACTIVITY 11.10

What is the IRR of the Chaotic Industries project from Activity 11.2? You should use the discount table at the end of this chapter. (*Hint*: Remember that you already know the NPV of this project at 15 per cent.)

In answering the above activity, we were fortunate in using a discount rate of 10 per cent for our second iteration as this happened to be very close to the IRR figure. However, what if we had used 6 per cent? This discount factor will provide us with a large positive NPV as we can see below:

Time	Cash flows $'000	Discount factor (from the table)	Present value $'000
Immediately	(150)	1.00	(150.00)
1 year's time	30	0.943	28.29
2 years' time	30	0.890	26.70
3 years' time	30	0.840	25.20
4 years' time	30	0.792	23.76
5 years' time	30	0.747	22.41
6 years' time	60 (30 + 30)	0.705	42.30
	Net present value		18.66

We can see that the IRR will fall somewhere between 15 per cent, which gives a negative NPV, and 6 per cent, which gives a positive NPV. We could undertake further iterations in order to derive the IRR. More realistically, we could use a financial calculator or spreadsheet, either of which will do this very quickly. If, however, you are required to calculate the IRR manually, further iterations can be time consuming. Nevertheless, by linear interpolation we can get close to the answer fairly quickly. Linear interpolation assumes a straight-line relationship between the discount rate and NPV which may be a reasonable approximation over a relatively short range. In order to understand the principles behind this method it is useful to study the diagram in Figure 11.3.

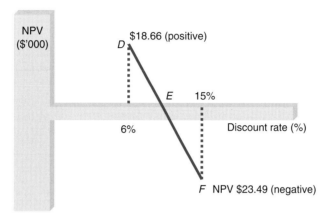

FIGURE 11.3 Finding the IRR of an investment by plotting the NPV against the discount rate

The graph plots the NPV of the investment against the discount rates. Thus point D represents the NPV at a discount rate of 6 per cent and point F represents the NPV at a discount rate of 15 per cent. The point at which the sloping line DF intersects the discount rate line (point E) is the IRR. An alternative way of approaching the calculation is as follows. Set out at least two discount rates and their associated NPVs. Then calculate the rate of change of the NPV for every 1 per cent change as shown below.

	Discount rate (%)	NPV
	15	(23,490)
	6	18,660
Difference	9	42,150

Therefore a 1 per cent change would be associated with a change of $42,150 / 9 = $4,683.

The IRR occurs where the NPV is zero. Hence we could provide an estimate of NPV at different discount rates as follows:

Discount rate (%)	NPV	
15	(23,490)	
14	−23,490 + 4,683	= (18,807)
13	−23,490 + 2(4,683)	= (14,124)
12	−23,490 + 3(4,683)	= (9,440)
11	−23,490 + 4(4,683)	= (4,757)
10	−23,490 + 5(4,683)	= (74)

9	−23,490 + 6(4,683)	=	4,609
8	−23,490 + 7(4,683)	=	9,292
7	−23,490 + 8(4,683)	=	13,975
6	18,660		

Alternatively, we could start at 6 per cent and adjust from the other direction. Clearly, the IRR is just less than 10 per cent. This can be calculated arithmetically by either:

$$15 - 9(23,490 / 42,150) \text{ or } 6 + 9(18,660 / 42,150)$$

both of which give 9.984 per cent.

We can see that the figure derived through this process is slightly different from the figure for the IRR calculated earlier where one of the discount rates used was very close to the actual IRR. It is less accurate because of the linearity assumption employed (which is strictly incorrect) but it is likely to be a reasonable approximation for most purposes. If you refer back to Figure 11.2 you can see that the line curves. Superimposing a curve on Figure 11.3 implies the linear interpolation will be slightly on the high side of the correct figure, but, as pointed out above, this is unlikely to be a problem unless you try to interpolate between substantially different figures. In fact the correct IRR figure is 9 per cent.

Users of the IRR approach normally apply the following decision rules:

✳ For any project to be acceptable, it must meet a minimum IRR requirement. Logically, this minimum should be the opportunity cost of finance.

✳ Where there are competing projects (e.g. the business can choose one of the projects, but not all) the one with the higher or highest IRR would be selected.

The IRR has certain attributes in common with NPV. All cash flows are taken into account and the timing of them is logically handled. The main disadvantage of the IRR is the fact that it does not address the question of wealth generation. It could therefore lead to the wrong decision being made. This is because the IRR focuses on the rate of return and ignores the scale of the project. A project that has an IRR of 25 per cent will be preferred to one that has a return of 20 per cent, as long as the IRR is greater than the opportunity cost of finance. Although this may well lead to the project being taken which could most effectively increase wealth, it nevertheless could have the opposite effect. This is because the IRR completely ignores the scale of investment. For example, if we assume a 15 per cent cost of finance, $1 million invested at 20 per cent would make you richer than $0.5 million invested at 24 per cent. The IRR does not recognise this. It should be acknowledged that it is not usual for projects to be competing where there is such a large difference in scale. Even though the problem may be rare and typically the IRR will give the same signal as NPV, a method that is always reliable must be better to use than the IRR. That method is NPV.

A further problem with the IRR method is that it has difficulty handling projects with unconventional cash flows. In the examples studied so far, each project has a negative cash flow arising at the start of its life and then positive cash flows thereafter. However, in some cases a project may have both positive and negative cash flows at future points in its life. Such a pattern of cash flows can result in the IRR method providing more than one solution.

Also in relation to unconventional cash flows, projects with a higher IRR but with significant cash inflows early in the project may be inferior to projects with a lower IRR but with significant cash inflows later in the project.

ACTIVITY 11.11

Can you see why a project with a higher IRR and bigger cash inflows early in the project may be inferior to a project with a lower IRR and bigger cash inflows later in the project?

Assume that the total project lives are similar, as is the level of risk involved.

SOME PRACTICAL POINTS

THE BASIS OF THE CASH FLOW CALCULATIONS

It is clear that the basis of the figures for discounted cash flow (DCF) techniques should be cash flows. However, it is likely that in many businesses projects will be set out in terms of profit calculations.

Suppose that a business is considering investing in a project costing $120,000. It has prepared the following forecasts:

EXAMPLE

11.3

	Year 1	Year 2	Year 3
Sales 20,000 × $10 each	200,000	200,000	200,000
Variable expenses 20,000 × $5 each	100,000	100,000	100,000
Contribution	100,000	100,000	100,000
Other expenses	40,000	40,000	40,000
Depreciation (straight line)	40,000	40,000	40,000
Profit	20,000	20,000	20,000

The question inevitably arises as to how to convert profit flows into cash flows.

All of the figures for revenues and expenses are associated with cash flows, other than depreciation. The cash flows for each of the years 1–3 can be calculated as:

Sales revenues	200,000
Variable expenses	100,000
	100,000
Less other expenses	40,000
Net cash inflow	60,000

Alternatively, these figures can be derived by adding back depreciation to the profit figures (i.e. $20,000 + $40,000). In fact this is probably the most common way of deriving cash flows from profit forecasts.

The cash flow patterns are thus likely to be:

Year 0	Investment	120,000
Year 1	Net profit plus depreciation	60,000
Year 2	Net profit plus depreciation	60,000
Year 3	Net profit plus depreciation	60,000

This pattern gives an NPV at 12% of $24,120 (using the present value tables) and an IRR at 23%.

In practice the situation is rarely this simple. It is almost certainly the case that inventory will need to be purchased up front. The purchase of a holding of inventory will lead to the need for earlier cash payments than was assumed above. If sales are made on credit the associated cash receipts will be delayed. If credit periods are obtained from suppliers, then cash payments can be delayed.

Suppose that this project involved the holding of an average inventory figure of $25,000, that debtors took 1½ months to pay, and creditors were paid one month after due. In effect this means that the project has an additional amount of working capital tied up, amounting to:

Inventory	$25,000	
Debtors	$25,000	($200,000 × 1½ / 12)
Creditors	($11,667)	(½ of variable expenses + ½ of other expenses, i.e. 140,000 / 12)
Working capital needed	$38,333	

The revised cash flows for the project would now be:

Year 0	
Initial investment	(120,000)
Working capital invested	(38,333)
	(158,333)
Year 1	60,000
Year 2	60,000
Year 3	60,000
Plus the working capital released	38,333

When an adjustment of this type is made the adjusted operating profit (pre-depreciation) will provide a reasonable approximation to cash flows.

Assuming a 12% discount rate this will give an NPV of 13,080 (using the present value tables). The IRR will be 16.3%. There is quite a difference between the figures for the project with and without the working capital adjustments.

This situation is fairly typical. While it is strictly true that the working capital adjustment can be in either direction, the working capital needs are almost invariably positive. Where this is the case, and no adjustment is made, the appraisal gives a more favourable result than is justified.

You should realise that the above procedure is still only an approximation to the likely cash flows. One striking anomaly is that cash flows are frequently assumed to occur at the end of each year. Such an assumption is probably quite realistic for securities and associated returns, where interest and dividends are typically received at the end of the years. It is unlikely to be true of sales of a commodity, where sales and expenses are likely to be spread over each year, sometime fairly evenly, sometimes with a substantial seasonal bias.

For example, consider the previous example, where forecast annual sales were $200,000, annual variable costs were $100,000, depreciation was $40,000, and other expenses were forecast at $40,000 per annum. It is highly unlikely that all of these flows would occur at the year end, and, in order for a more accurate appraisal to be made, a more precise specification of cash flows needs to be drawn up. A monthly analysis of cash flows is probably the best.

The resulting analysis is based upon the following assumptions.

1. Credit sales are spread evenly over the year, namely $16,667 per month.
2. Variable costs are incurred evenly over the year, subject to an initial purchase of stock of $25,000, which is maintained by regular purchases as long as is needed.
3. Other expenses are spread evenly over the year.
4. Debtors from sales will pay on average one and a half months after sales.
5. Creditors for inventory and other expenses will be paid one month after the expenses were incurred.

A forecast cash flow analysis is given on the spreadsheet in Table 11.1.

TABLE 11.1 • Detailed cash flow analysis on a monthly basis

	A	B	C	D	E	F
1	Cash flows					
2						
3	Month	Investment	Inventory	Other expenses	Revenues	Net cash flow
4	0	−120000				−120000
5	1		−25000			−25000
6	2		−8333	−3333		−11666
7	3		−8333	−3333	16667	5001
8	4		−8333	−3333	16667	5001
9	5		−8333	−3333	16667	5001
10	6		−8333	−3333	16667	5001
11	7		−8333	−3333	16667	5001
12	8		−8333	−3333	16667	5001
13	9		−8333	−3333	16667	5001
14	10		−8333	−3333	16667	5001
15	11		−8333	−3333	16667	5001
16	12		−8333	−3333	16667	5001
17	13		−8333	−3333	16667	5001
18	14		−8333	−3333	16667	5001
19	15		−8333	−3333	16667	5001
20	16		−8333	−3333	16667	5001
21	17		−8333	−3333	16667	5001
22	18		−8333	−3333	16667	5001
23	19		−8333	−3333	16667	5001
24	20		−8333	−3333	16667	5001
25	21		−8333	−3333	16667	5001
26	22		−8333	−3333	16667	5001
27	23		−8333	−3333	16667	5001
28	24		−8333	−3333	16667	5001
29	25		−8333	−3333	16667	5001

TABLE 11.1 • Detailed cash flow analysis on a monthly basis

30	26		−8333	−3333	16667	5001
31	27		−8333	−3333	16667	5001
32	28		−8333	−3333	16667	5001
33	29		−8333	−3333	16667	5001
34	30		−8333	−3333	16667	5001
35	31		−8333	−3333	16667	5001
36	32		−8333	−3333	16667	5001
37	33		−8333	−3333	16667	5001
38	34		−8333	−3333	16667	5001
39	35			−3333	16667	13334
40	36			−3333	16667	13334
41	37			−3333	16667	13334
42	38				16667	16667
43						
44		NPV @ 1% per month		16878		
45		IRR per monthly period		1.49%		
46		Hence IRR approximately		0.1788		

The following notes may be needed to explain the figures.

1. The initial inventory purchased is paid for one month later.

2. The annual variable costs of $100,000 will be purchased evenly over the year ($8,333 per month) and will be paid for one month later. Hence month 1 expenses will be paid for in month 2, and so on. However, the regular stock held throughout the project is likely to be run down in the last three months of the project. Hence months 35, 36 and 37 will have no cash outflow for stock purchases. The total payments for inventory will be $25,000 + 33($8,333) = $300,000.

3. The other expenses of $40,000 per annum will be incurred evenly over the year ($3,333 per month) and will be paid for one month later.

4. Depreciation is irrelevant as it is not a cash flow.

5. The annual sales of $200,000 are spread evenly over the year ($16,667 per month) and cash will be received one and a half months later (shown as two months later given the assumption about monthly cash flows)

6. Effectively, the cash flows are set out on a monthly basis, so the discount rate used will be one-twelfth of the annual rate. The IRR will represent a monthly rate so needs to be multiplied by 12 to get an annual rate. You should note that there is nothing magical about monthly cash flows. If cash flows were prepared on a quarterly basis the discount rate would need to be divided by four and the IRR multiplied by 4, and so on.

7. Note that the spreadsheet has two important functions, the IRR function and the NPV function, which facilitate calculation. The IRR function is set out as follows: = IRR (F4:F42), while the NPV function is = NPV(1%,F5:F42) − 120,000. The 1% represents the discount rate per period, while the 120,000 represents the initial investment.

In fact, the calculations using the above approach are reasonably close to the method using accounting flows modified by working capital changes. In general, it is likely that monthly cash flows will show higher NPVs and IRRs, since cash flows are likely to be brought forward.

You should realise that many examination questions do not have such complications, but simply assume that profit flows are cash flows.

MORE PRACTICAL POINTS

When dealing with questions relating to investment appraisal, there are a number of practical points you should bear in mind.

❋ *Relevant costs.* As with all decision making, we should only take account of cash flows that are relevant to the decision in our analysis. Thus, cash flows that will be the same, irrespective of the decision under review, should be ignored. For example, overheads that will be incurred in equal amount whether or not the investment is made should be ignored, even though the investment could not be made without the infrastructure that the overhead costs create. Similarly, past costs should be ignored as they are not affected by, and do not vary with, the decision.

❋ *Opportunity costs.* Opportunity costs arising from benefits forgone must be taken into account. Thus, for example, when considering whether or not to continue to use a machine to produce a new product, the realisable value of the machine may be an important opportunity cost.

❋ *Taxation.* Tax will usually be affected by an investment decision; the profits will be taxed, the capital investment may attract tax relief, etc. Tax is levied on these profits at significant rates. This means that, in real life, unless tax is formally taken account of, the wrong decision could easily be made. In practice, some, if not all, of the taxation relating to the current year's profits will be paid in a later period (usually the following year). The timing of the tax outflow must be taken into account when preparing the cash flows for the project.

❋ *Interest payments.* When using discounted cash flow techniques, interest payments that have been charged to the income statement should not be taken into account in deriving the cash flows for the period (i.e. the relevant figure is net profit before interest and depreciation). The discount factor already takes account of the costs of financing, so to take account of interest charges in deriving cash flows for the period would be double counting.

❋ *Other factors.* Investment decision making must not be viewed as simply a mechanical exercise. The results derived from a particular investment appraisal method will be only one input into the decision-making process. There may be broader issues connected to the decision that have to be taken into account but that may be difficult or impossible to quantify. For example, a regional bus company may be considering an investment in a new bus to serve a particular route which local residents would like to see operated. Although the NPV calculations may reveal that a loss will be made on the investment, it may be that, by not investing in the new bus and not operating the route, the renewal of the company's licence to operate will be put at risk. In such a situation, the size of the expected loss, as revealed by the calculations made, must be weighed against the prospect of losing the right to operate before a final decision is made. The reliability of the forecasts and the validity of the assumptions used in the evaluation will also have a bearing on the final decision.

ACTIVITY 11.12

The directors of Manuff (Steel) Ltd have decided to close one of its factories. There has been a reduction in the demand for the products made at the factory in recent years and the directors of the company are not optimistic about the long-term prospects for these products. The factory is situated in an area to the north of Sydney where unemployment is high.

The factory is leased and four years' worth of the lease is still remaining. The directors are uncertain as to whether the factory should be closed immediately or at the end of the period of the lease. Another company has offered to sub-lease the premises from Manuff (Steel) Ltd at a rental of $40,000 per annum for the remainder of the lease period.

The machinery and equipment at the factory cost $1.5 million and have a written-down value of $400,000. In the event of immediate closure, the machinery and equipment could be sold for $220,000. The working capital at the factory is $420,000 and could be liquidated for that amount immediately if required. Alternatively, the working capital can be liquidated in full at the end of the lease period. Immediate closure would result in redundancy payments to employees of $180,000.

If the factory continues in operation until the end of the lease period, the following operating profits (losses) are expected:

	Year 1 $'000	Year 2 $'000	Year 3 $'000	Year 4 $'000
Operating profit (loss)	160	(40)	30	20

The above figures include a charge of $90,000 per year for depreciation of machinery and equipment. The residual value of the machinery and equipment at the end of the lease period is estimated at $40,000.

Redundancy payments are expected to be $150,000 at the end of the lease period if the factory continues in operation. The company has a required rate of return of 12 per cent. Ignore taxation.

Required:

(a) Calculate the incremental cash flows arising from a decision to continue operations until the end of the lease period rather than to close immediately.

(b) Calculate the net present value of continuing operations until the end of the lease period rather than closing immediately.

(c) What other factors might the directors of the company take into account before making a final decision on the timing of the factory closure?

(d) State, with reasons, whether or not the company should continue to operate the factory until the end of the lease period.

SELF-ASSESSMENT QUESTION 11.1

Beacon Chemicals Ltd is considering the erection of a new plant to produce a chemical named X14. The new plant's capital cost is estimated at $100,000 and if its construction is approved now the plant can be erected and commence production by the end of 2005. $50,000 has already been spent on research and development work. Estimates of revenues and costs arising from the operation of the new plant appear below:

	2006	2007	2008	2009	2010
Sales price ($ per unit)	100	120	120	100	80
Sales volume (units)	800	1,000	1,200	1,000	800
Variable costs ($ per unit)	50	50	40	30	40
Fixed costs ($'000s)	30	30	30	30	30

If the new plant is erected, sales of some existing products will be lost and this will result in a loss of contribution of $15,000 per year over its life.

The accountant has informed you that the fixed costs include depreciation of $20,000 per annum on new plant. They also include an allocation of $10,000 for fixed overheads. A separate study has indicated that if the new plant was built, additional overheads, excluding depreciation, arising from its construction would be $8,000 per year. The plant would require additional working capital of $30,000.

For the purposes of your initial calculations ignore taxation.

Required:

(a) Deduce the relevant annual cash flows associated with building and operating the plant.

(b) Deduce the payback period.

(c) Calculate the net present value using a discount rate of 8 per cent.

Hint: You should deal with the investment in working capital by treating it as a cash outflow at the start of the project and an inflow at the end.

A MORE DETAILED COMPARISON OF THE DCF METHODS

Both the NPV and IRR methods have advantages and disadvantages. In general, the NPV method is regarded as easier to use, since the IRR method requires an iterative process. In practice, this argument is of doubtful validity with the use of spreadsheets. However, the exact meaning of NPV is not readily obvious, whereas the meaning of the IRR is.

For most simple accept or reject decisions relating to a single project the decision should be the same. A project which has a positive NPV must have an internal rate of return which is greater than the discount rate. Sometimes, however, there are differences between the conclusions reached by the two methods. Problem areas arise in:

1. mutually exclusive projects
2. capital rationing situations.

MUTUALLY EXCLUSIVE PROJECTS

In practice, many businesses have more than one way of dealing with a problem. For example, consider a case in which one way of solving a problem is to buy a special purpose machine costing $100,000, which is expected to return $130,000 in one year's time. Another machine, which is more general purpose, could be purchased, which would have a range of alternative uses. The cost would be $200,000, and the project is expected to yield returns of $250,000 in one year's time. The NPV and IRR are as shown below.

	Special purpose	General purpose
Cash flows ($'000)		
Initial	100	200
Inflow after year 1	130	250
Discounted cash flows @ 10% ($'000)		
Initial	100	200
Inflow after year 1	130 × .909 = 118.17	250 × .909 = 227.25
Net present value	18.17	27.25
IRR	30%	25%

The problem in this case is that the NPV and IRR methods give different results. The special purpose equipment has an NPV of $18,170 and an IRR of 30%, while the general purpose equipment has an NPV of $27,250 and an IRR of 25%.

The reason for this is that the two investments are of different sizes. It should be clear that the absolute size of the NPV for the larger project should be larger than that of the smaller project, even though the rate of return is smaller. If there are no limitations on the amount to be spent, the project which gives the largest NPV should be selected.

It may be worth while reviewing this from a different perspective, the *incremental perspective*. The incremental difference between the two projects is as follows:

	Cost $'000	Revenues $'000
Special purpose	100	130
General purpose	200	250
Incremental figures	100	120

The internal rate of return on the incremental cost is 20%.

The net present value (at 10%) on the incremental cost can be obtained by ((120,000 × .909) – $100,080) i.e. $109,080 – $100,000 = $9,080.

Clearly, it is worth while taking on the larger project since the incremental returns are favourable, with a positive NPV of $9,080 and an incremental yield of 20%.

CAPITAL RATIONING

The decision criteria imply that any project with a positive NPV or an IRR in excess of the discount rate, should be accepted. This may not be sensible, nor possible, where there are limits to the amount of capital invested. These limitations may be real, in the sense that further funds are simply not available for new projects, or self-imposed.

 ACTIVITY 11.13

Can you think of any reasons why management might wish to impose limits to the amount invested on new projects with the result that projects yielding a positive NPV might need to be rejected.

Clearly, a number of possible reasons exist for capital rationing. Probably the main reason is that the investment decision is a far more complex one than is implied so far. This point will be returned to later. Whatever the reason, when capital rationing exists, it may well be necessary to rank projects in some way.

Capital rationing causes particular problems for the NPV method. It should be clear that the IRR method relates the return to the amount invested. This is not true of the NPV, since it is not related to the size of the amount invested. However, it is not difficult to overcome this problem with slight adaptations. The two most common methods are:

1. Profitability index or benefit/cost ratio.
2. NPV per $1.

Profitability index or benefit/cost ratio

This method attempts to relate the present value of inflows to the amount invested, as follows:

$$\text{Profitability index} = \frac{\text{PV of inflows}}{\text{Initial investment}}$$

or

$$\text{Benefit/cost ratio} = \frac{\text{PV of inflows}}{\text{PV of outflows}}$$

Using either of these criteria projects should be accepted whenever the result is greater than one. Where a capital rationing situation exists it will be necessary to rank the projects in descending order. The problems relating to mutually exclusive projects remain, so care is needed.

NPV per $1 of investment

This method relates the NPV to the amount invested.

$$\frac{\text{NPV}}{\text{Investment}} = \text{NPV per \$1 of investment}$$

The general rule is to accept projects with a positive NPV. Where capital is limited then a ranking starting with the maximum NPV per $1 of investment will ensure the maximum NPV.

These methods typically cope fairly well with a single period of capital rationing. However, there is one particular problem which we need to guard against. In certain projects the amount of the investment is spread over several periods. In cases such as this care must be taken to relate the ratios to the amount of the constraint.

Where capital restrictions exist for more than one period the above methods become more difficult, and it is likely that mathematical programming techniques will need to be used.

THE ESSENTIAL DIFFERENCE BETWEEN NPV AND YIELD (IRR)

Both the NPV and yield make assumptions, albeit implicit, about the rate of return on cash flows re-invested. Effectively, the yield method assumes that cash re-invested in the course of the life of the project earns at the same rate as the project. The NPV method assumes that the re-investment rate is the discount rate used, namely the cost of capital or the cut-off rate. The justification for either assumption is questionable, and dual rate calculations are made by some organisations.

SUMMARY

In this chapter we have achieved the following objectives in the way shown.

OBJECTIVE	METHOD ACHIEVED
Identify the essential features of investment decisions	Examined and identified the following features: • Significant capital outlays • Returns over an extended period • Difficult or expensive to 'bail out' of the investment
List examples of investment decisions	Examples included: • Purchase of a business • Retain or replace fixed assets • Manufacture or buy components
State the four common capital investment methods	Identified as: • Accounting rate of return (ARR) • Payback period (PP) • Net present value (NPV) • Internal rate of return (IRR)
Demonstrate an understanding of the 'accounting rate of return method' with respect to the formula, decision rule, strengths and weaknesses	Explained ARR: • Method: *ARR* = Average return/Average investment • Decision rules: above a minimum return / accept the highest return • Advantages: easily calculated / readily understood / based on accrual performance • Disadvantages: problems with using the average / based on accrual not cash flows / disregards timing of returns
Demonstrate an understanding of the 'payback method' with respect to the formula, decision rule, strengths and weaknesses	Explained payback: • Method: *PP* = Time taken to recover amount of investment • Decision rules: below a minimum payback period / accept the shortest payback period • Advantages: simple to implement / readily understood / emphasises the short term / based on cash flows • Disadvantages: disregards the timing of cash flows / excludes post payback period cash flows
Demonstrate an understanding of the 'net present value method' with respect to the formula, decision rule, strengths and weaknesses	Explained NPV: • Method: $NPV = PV_{inflows} - PV_{outflows}$ • Decision rules: accept the highest positive NPV / reject all negative NPVs • Advantages: based on all cash flows / incorporates the time value of money / based on wealth increments

OBJECTIVE	METHOD ACHIEVED
	• Disadvantages: more difficult to calculate less readily understood does not determine the actual rate of return does not yield a relative measure of return
Demonstrate an understanding of the 'internal rate of return method' with respect to the formula, decision rule, strengths and weaknesses	Explained IRR: • Method: IRR = The rate at which $PV_{inflows} = PV_{outflows}$ • Decision rule: accept the highest IRR specify a minimum required return • Advantages: based on all cash flows incorporates the time value of money specifies an actual expected return • Disadvantages: more difficult to calculate there may be multiple returns it is not based on wealth increments
Explain the notion of present values	Explained as either: • The amount you need to invest now at a given interest rate to compound to the specified future amount given the time (n) and interest rate (r) or • The future amount discounted to a current amount based on the time period (n) and the discount rate (r). That is, we deduct the interest component
Identify alternative means of determining present values	Identified and illustrated the following: • Formula: $(FV)/(l + r)^n$ • Discount tables
Convert forecast profit flows into cash flows	Illustrated how to convert profit flows into cash flows including: • use of profit plus depreciation as a cash flow surrogate • working capital adjustments • impact of timing
Discuss other factors important to capital investment decision making	Identified and discussed the following factors: • Relevant costs—they cannot be avoided in relation to a particular investment decision • Taxation—tax will normally apply to profits and other gains • Opportunity costs—represents benefits forgone by not taking the next best alternative action • Cash flows—apart from ARR all the other methods focus on cash flows • Interest—should be excluded from the figures as it will be incorporated in the discount rate • Other factors
Compared the two DCF methods	Identified problem areas • mutually exclusive projects • capital rationing Explained the essential difference between the two methods

DISCUSSION QUESTIONS

EASY

<Obj 1>	**11.1** What are the typical characteristics of capital investment decisions?
<Obj 2>	**11.2** Provide examples of typical capital investment decisions.
<Obj 3>	**11.3** What are the four most common investment appraisal methods?
<Obj 6>	**11.4** What is meant by the expression 'the time value of money'?
<Obj 8>	**11.5** Why might you prefer $1,000 now rather than $1,000 in three years' time?
<Obj 8>	**11.6** What would be the formula to calculate the present value of $5,000 to be received in 10 years given an annual interest rate of 8 per cent.

INTERMEDIATE

<Obj 4>   **11.7** Accounting rate of return:
- (a) How is it calculated?
- (b) What is the investment decision rule?
- (c) What are the strengths of this approach?
- (d) What are the limitations of this approach?

<Obj 5>   **11.8** Payback:
- (a) How is it calculated?
- (b) What is the investment decision rule?
- (c) What are the benefits of using the payback method?
- (d) What are the deficiencies of using the payback method?

<Obj 5, 6>   **11.9** The payback method has been criticised for not taking into account the time value of money. Could this limitation be overcome? If so, would this method then be preferable to the NPV method?

<Obj 6>   **11.10** Net present value (NPV):
- (a) How is it calculated?
- (b) What is the investment decision rule?
- (c) What are the advantages of using NPV compared with ARR or PP?
- (d) Are there any limitations of the NPV method?

<Obj 6>   **11.11** An NPV analysis of an investment project yields a +$3,600 magnitude based on a discount rate of 14 per cent.
- (a) What does this mean?
- (b) What does it not tell us about the financial viability of the project?

<Obj 6, 10>   **11.12** How is depreciation accounted for under the cash flow appraisal methods?

<Obj 6, 11>   **11.13** Why is 'interest expense' excluded from the discounted cash flow investment appraisal techniques?

<Obj 7>   **11.14** Internal rate of return (IRR):
- (a) How is it calculated?
- (b) What is the investment decision rule?
- (c) What advantage does it have over NPV?
- (d) What are the deficiencies of this method?

<Obj 7>   **11.15** What is the relationship between NPV and the IRR?

<Obj 7, 11>   **11.16** Research indicates that the IRR method is a more popular method of investment appraisal than the NPV method. Why might this be?

<Obj 9, 12>	**11.17**	Why is the NPV method of investment appraisal considered to be theoretically superior to other methods of investment appraisal found in the literature?
<Obj 10>	**11.18**	Why are cash flows rather than profit flows used in the IRR, NPV and PP methods of investment appraisal?
<Obj 11>	**11.19**	In a decision context:
		(a) What are relevant costs?
		(b) What is the relationship between relevant costs and avoidable costs?
<Obj 11>	**11.20**	Opportunity costs:
		(a) What are opportunity costs?
		(b) How are they important in capital investment decisions?
<Obj 11>	**11.21**	What implications does working capital have for the four investment appraisal approaches?
<Obj 11, 12>	**11.22**	Under what circumstances might it be preferable to accept a project with a lower internal rate of return (e.g. accept B (IRR of 18 per cent) over D (IRR of 21 per cent))?

APPLICATION EXERCISES

EASY

<Obj 3, 5, 6, 7>   **11.1**   The directors of Mylo Ltd are currently considering two mutually exclusive investment projects. Both projects are concerned with the purchase of new plant.

The following data are available for each project.

	Project 1 $	Project 2 $
Cost (immediate outlay)	100,000	60,000
Expected annual net profit (loss)		
Year 1	29,000	18,000
Year 2	(1,000)	(2,000)
Year 3	2,000	4,000
Estimated residual value at the end of year 3	7,000	6,000

The company has a required rate of return of 10 per cent and employs the straight-line method of depreciation for all non-current assets when calculating net profit. Neither project would increase the working capital of the company. The company has sufficient funds to meet all capital expenditure requirements.

(a) Calculate for each project:
   (i) the net present value
   (ii) the approximate internal rate of return
   (iii) the payback period.
(b) State which, if any, of the two investment projects the directors of Mylo Ltd should accept and why.
(c) State, in general terms, which method of investment appraisal you consider to be most appropriate for evaluating investment projects and why.

ACCOUNTING an introduction

<Obj 4, 5, 6>   **11.2**   A special-purpose machine costing $30,000 will save Foster Ltd $9,500 per year in cash operating expenses for the next six years. Straight-line depreciation with a zero salvage value will be used (for accounting and tax purposes), and the minimum desired rate of return is 12 per cent.

Assuming a 30 per cent income tax rate and rounding amounts to the nearest dollar, calculate the following:
(a) average accounting rate of return
(b) cash payback period
(c) net present value.

<Obj 5, 6, 7>   **11.3**   The following summarises an appraisal of four projects using different analysis tools:

Project	Payback (years)	NPV (10%)	IRR (%)
A	4	−$610	8.2
B	3.5	+$2,430	13.8
C	3.8	+$3,610	15.6
D	4.2	+$4,790	10.9

(a) Why was the payback technique inadequate on its own to assess the four projects?
(b) Explain clearly what the −$610 NPV for project A means.
(c) Why does project D have the highest + NPV but the lowest IRR (for projects with + NPV)?
(d) For NPV we use 10 per cent in this example. In reality what should be the required discount rate?
(e) Project C has the highest IRR. Under what circumstances might we prefer project B (with a lower IRR)?

<Obj 5, 6, 10>   **11.4**   Arkwright Mills Ltd is considering expanding its production of a new yarn code name X15. The plant is expected to cost $1 million and have a life of five years and a nil residual value. It will be ready for operation before 31 December 2005 and the initial period will be used to build up inventory; $500,000 has already been spent on development costs of the product and this has been charged to revenue in the year it was incurred.

The following income statements for the new yarn are forecast:

	2006 $m	2007 $m	2008 $m	2009 $m	2010 $m
Sales	1.2	1.4	1.4	1.4	1.4
Costs, including depreciation	1.0	1.1	1.1	1.1	1.1
Profit before tax	0.2	0.3	0.3	0.3	0.3

Tax is charged at 50 per cent on profits and paid one year in arrears. Depreciation has been calculated on a straight-line basis. Additional working capital of $0.6 million will be required at the beginning of the project. You should assume that all cash flows occur at the end of the year in which they arise.
(a) Prepare a statement showing the incremental cash flows of the project relevant to a decision concerning whether or not to proceed with the construction of the new plant.
(b) Calculate the net present value of the project, using a 10 per cent discount rate.
(c) Calculate the payback period to the nearest year. Explain the meaning of this term.

<Obj 5, 6, 10, 11>   **11.5**   The accountant of your company has recently been taken ill through overwork. In his absence his assistant has prepared some calculations of the profitability of a project which are to be discussed soon at the board meeting of your company. His workings, which are set out below, include some errors of principle. You can assume that the statement below includes no arithmetical errors.

	2006 $'000	2007 $'000	2008 $'000	2009 $'000	2010 $'000	2011 $'000
Sales revenue		450	470	470	470	470
Less costs						
Materials		126	132	132	132	132
Labour		90	94	94	94	94
Overheads		45	47	47	47	47
Depreciation		120	120	120	120	120
Working capital	180					
Interest on working capital		27	27	27	27	27
Write-off of development costs		30	30	30		
Total costs	180	438	450	450	420	420
Profit/(loss)	(180)	12	20	20	50	50

Total profit/(loss)   (28,000) = 4.7% return on investment
Cost of equipment 600,000

You ascertain the following additional information:
* The cost of equipment contains $100,000 being the book value of an old machine. If it was not used for this project it would be scrapped with a zero net realisable value. New equipment costing $500,000 will be purchased on 31 December 2006. You should assume that all other cash flows occur at the end of the year to which they relate.
* The development costs of $90,000 have already been spent.
* Overheads have been costed at 50 per cent of direct labour which is the company's normal practice. An independent assessment has suggested that incremental overheads are likely to amount to $30,000 per year.
* The company's required rate of return is 12 per cent.

Ignore taxation in your answer.
(a) Prepare a corrected statement of the incremental cash flows arising from the project. Where you have altered the assistant's figures you should attach a brief note explaining your alterations.
(b) Calculate:
    (i) the project's payback period
    (ii) the project's net present value.
(c) Write a memo to the board advising on the acceptance or rejection of the project.

<Obj 8>   **11.6**   Use the table on page 489 to calculate the following:
(a) the present value factor for $n = 7, r = 15\%$
(b) the present value factor for $n = 10, r = 9.25\%$
(c) the present value factor for $n = 30, r = 12\%$

(d) the present value factor for an annuity ordinary (receipts at the end of the period) of eight annual receipts ($n = 8$) and interest of 7 per cent ($r = 7\%$)

(e) the present value factor for an annuity due (receipts at the beginning of the period) of six annual payments ($n = 6$) and interest of 10 per cent ($r = 10\%$).

INTERMEDIATE

<Obj 6, 10, 11>

11.7 C. George (Controls) Ltd manufactures a thermostat that can be used in a range of kitchen appliances. The manufacturing process is, at present, semi-automated. The equipment used cost $540,000 and has a written-down value of $300,000. Demand for the product has been fairly stable and output has been maintained at 50,000 units per annum in recent years.

The following data, based on the current level of output, have been prepared in respect of the product:

	Per unit	
	$	$
Selling price		12.40
Less		
Labour	3.30	
Materials	3.65	
Overheads—Variable	1.58	
—Fixed	1.60	
		10.13
Profit		2.27

Although the existing equipment is expected to last for a further four years before it is sold for an estimated $40,000, the company has recently been considering purchasing new equipment which would completely automate much of the production process. The new equipment would cost $670,000 and would have an expected life of four years at the end of which it would be sold for an estimated $70,000. If the new equipment is purchased, the old equipment could be sold for $150,000 immediately.

The assistant to the company accountant has prepared a report to help assess the viability of the proposed change which includes the following data:

	Per unit	
	$	$
Selling price		12.40
Less		
Labour	1.20	
Materials	3.20	
Overheads—Variable	1.40	
—Fixed	3.30	
		9.10
Profit		3.30

Depreciation charges will increase by $85,000 per annum as a result of purchasing the new machinery, however other fixed costs are not expected to change.

In the report the assistant wrote:

The figures shown above which relate to the proposed change are based on the current level of output and take account of a depreciation charge of $150,000 per annum in respect of the new equipment. The effect of purchasing the new equipment will be to increase the net profit to sales ratio from 18.3 per cent to 26.6 per cent. In addition, the purchase of the new equipment will enable us to reduce our inventory level immediately by $130,000.

In view of these facts I recommend purchase of the new equipment.
The company has a required rate of return of 12 per cent. Ignore taxation.

(a) Prepare a statement of the incremental cash flows arising from the purchase of the new equipment.
(b) Calculate the net present value of the proposed purchase of new equipment.
(c) State, with reasons, whether the company should purchase the new equipment.
(d) Explain why cash flow forecasts are used rather than profit forecasts to assess the viability of proposed capital expenditure projects.

CHALLENGING

<Obj 4, 5, 6, 10> **11.8** Spark Electrical Company is planning to introduce a toaster-grill to its line of small home appliances. Annual sales of the toaster-grill are estimated at 5,000 units at a price of $69 per unit. Variable manufacturing costs are estimated at $39 per unit, incremental fixed manufacturing costs (other than depreciation) at $30,000 annually, and incremental selling and general expenses relating to the grillers at $35,000 annually.

To build the toaster-grills the company must invest $200,000 in moulds, patterns and special equipment. Since the company expects to change the design of the toaster-grill every five years, this equipment will have a five-year service life with no salvage value. Depreciation will be calculated on a straight-line basis. All revenue and expenses other than depreciation will be received or paid in cash. The company's tax rate is 30 per cent.

(a) Calculate the annual implications of the project for financial performance after tax.
(b) Calculate the cash flow consequences of the project over the life of the first model.
(c) Calculate:
   (i)   accounting rate of return
   (ii) payback
   (iii) net present value assuming a 15 per cent discount rate.

<Obj 6, 10, 11> **11.9** Newton Electronics Ltd has incurred expenditure of $5 million over the past three years researching and developing a miniature hearing aid. The hearing aid is now fully developed and the directors of the company are considering which of three mutually exclusive options should be taken to exploit the potential of the new product. The options are as follows:

Option 1. The company could manufacture the hearing aid itself. This would be a new departure for the company, which has so far concentrated on research and development projects. However, the company has manufacturing space available which it currently rents to another business for $100,000 per annum. The company would have to purchase plant and equipment costing $9 million and invest $3 million in working capital immediately for production to begin.

A market research report, for which the company paid $50,000, indicates that the new product has an expected life of five years. Sales of the product during this period are predicted as follows:

	Predicted sales for the year ended 30 November				
	2006	2007	2008	2009	2010
Number of units (000s)	800	1,400	1,800	1,200	500

The selling price per unit will be $30 in the first year but will fall to $22 in the following three years. In the final year of the product's life, the selling price will fall to $20. Variable production costs are predicted to be $14 per unit and fixed production costs (including depreciation) will be $2.4 million per annum. Marketing costs will be $2 million per annum.

The company intends to depreciate the plant and equipment using the straight-line method and based on an estimated residual value at the end of the five years of $1 million. The company has a cost of capital of 10 per cent.

Option 2. Newton Electronics Ltd could agree to another company manufacturing and marketing the product under licence. A multinational company, Faraday Electricals Ltd, has offered to undertake the manufacture and marketing of the product and, in return, will make a royalty payment to Newton Electronics Ltd of $5 per unit. It has been estimated that the annual number of sales of the hearing aid will be 10 per cent higher if the multinational company rather than Newton Electronics Ltd manufactures and markets the product.

Option 3. Newton Electronics Ltd could sell the patent rights to Faraday Electricals Ltd for $24 million, payable in two equal instalments. The first instalment would be payable immediately and the second instalment would be payable at the end of two years. This option would give Faraday Electricals the exclusive right to manufacture and market the new product.

Ignore taxation.
(a) Calculate the net present value of each of the options available to Newton Electronics Ltd.
(b) Identify and discuss any other factors which Newton Electronics Ltd should consider before arriving at a decision.
(c) State what you consider to be the most suitable option, and why.

<Obj 6, 11>

11.10 You are employed as the accountant of Re New Ltd. The directors of Re New are currently considering two mutually exclusive investment projects. Both projects are concerned with the purchase of new plant. The following data are available for each project.

	Re-tread	Re-line
	$	$
Purchase of plant cost (immediate outlay)	75,000	55,000
Expected annual net profit (loss) *		
Year 1	38,000	12,000
Year 2	27,000	24,000
Year 3	16,000	36,000
Estimated residual value at the end of year 3	24,000	10,000
* Before depreciation		

Re New Ltd has a required rate of return of 10 per cent and employs the straight-line method of depreciation for all non-current assets when calculating net profit. Neither project would increase the working capital of the company. The company has insufficient funds to meet all capital expenditure requirements. The company tax rate is 30 per cent.

(a) Calculate for each project:
  (i) the payback period (assume that the cash flows accrue equally over the year)
  (ii) the net present value.
(b) State which, if either, of the two investment projects the directors of Re New Ltd should select. Justify your answer.

<Obj 10, 11>

11.11 Your company has the following capital investment schemes available for consideration in a particular year.

Project A

This is for a new item of plant costing $210,000. A feasibility study costing $10,000 has already been undertaken. The project will mean the replacement of an old item of plant, and will lead to subsequent annual cost savings of $45,000 on labour, and $10,000 on materials. Installation costs are $15,000 and the old plant could be sold now for $25,000. The new asset will last for five years and will have a residual value of $15,000. No changes in sales are envisaged. The old asset would last another five years and would have a scrap value of $5,000 at the end of this period.

Project B

The purchase of the equipment necessary to produce a new product, at a cost of $300,000. The direct costs of the new product are likely to be $100 per unit, and a 30% loading for overheads is to be made. Fixed costs of running the department are likely to be $14,000 per annum. A selling price of $200 per unit has been agreed on, but it is uncertain how many units will be sold at this price. A market research team has been commissioned at a cost of $5,000, and it has produced the following probability distribution for annual sales:

Quantity	400	600	700	1000
Probability	.1	.5	.3	.1

The equipment will have a life of ten years, and $10,000 will have to be spent to dispose of it at the end of its life.

Project C

Department X has suggested a new product which can be produced by one of two methods:

(a) using 'Acret' equipment, at an original cost of $100,000. Direct costs are likely to be $25 per unit, while the overhead recovery rate is 30% on direct cost. Fixed costs of the department are expected to be $25,000 per annum.
(b) using 'Quik' equipment, at an original cost of $200,000. Direct costs are likely to be $20 per unit, with the same overhead recovery as above. Fixed costs are expected to be $17,000 per annum.

Sales, at $50 per unit, are expected to be 2,000 units for each of the next five years and 1,200 units for each of the five years after that.

Project D

$100,000 could be spent now on a building plot. This would be used in five years time to build a projected new factory. If the land is not purchased it is estimated that an equivalent piece of land in five years time would cost $170,000.

Notes:
Assume all revenue transactions take place at the end of the year.
No projects are divisible.
Cost of capital is 10%.

Required:
(a) Recommendations as to the projects which should be accepted, giving full reasons, assuming capital expenditure budgets for the year in question of:
  (i) $800,000
  (ii) $700,000
  (iii) $600,000
  (iv) $500,000.
(b) What other factors, not mentioned above, need to be considered in capital investment decisions?

<Obj 10, 11>   **11.12**   Creative Products Ltd is at present undertaking a cost reduction program. As part of its program it is considering modernising some of the machine processes. Details of one such proposal, intended to replace three machines with one multipurpose machine, are as follows:

	Existing machines for replacement	Proposed multi-purpose machine
Machine costs		
Purchase costs	$120,000 each	$1,400,000
Installation costs	–	$200,000 including $20,000 own labour
Removal of old machines	$150,000 in total	–
Operating costs		
Labour cost per product	$9.50 per machine	$28
Expenses per product	$17.50 total	$16.50
Maintenance per annum	$100,000*	$90,000
Depreciation of machines per annum	$30,000 total	$150,000
Absorbed factory overheads	$500,000 total	$450,000

*A major overhaul of these machines is due which is estimated to cost an additional $250,000.

The old machines have about another 10 years of life after which each machine is likely to have a residual value of $10,000. However, their present second-hand value is $20,000 each. The new machine would also have a 10-year life and an estimated residual value of $100,000.

Introduction of the new machine would not result in any increased revenue, since the existing machines can provide adequate capacity during the period under consideration. Production (and sales) is estimated to be:

100,000	.1 probability per annum
150,000	.4 probability per annum
200,000	.3 probability per annum
250,000	.2 probability per annum

However, use of the new machine will reduce material scrap so that a saving of 20 cents may be expected in respect of each product.

Management expects each capital investment proposal to earn at least 12 per cent and that it should pay for itself within a period of five years.

(a) Appraise this project and calculate its internal rate of return.

(b) Discuss briefly how you would attempt to take account of risk and uncertainty when appraising capital investment projects.

CASE STUDY

11.1

Your company operates a number of ferry services covering the north-west of the United States and Canada. It currently has a fleet of eight vessels. The company's required rate of return on investment projects is 20 per cent before tax, calculated on a discounted cash flow basis.

A year ago the company was considering the introduction of a new service, estimates of which had been made, as shown below:

1. Cost of the vessel: $5 million
2. Promotional and other initial costs: $1 million in the first year, $0.8 million in the second year.
3. Annual cash flows (estimated only for the next eight years) are expected to be:

Revenues $5 million per annum
Operating costs $3 million per annum (excluding depreciation)
Other overheads $0.4 million per annum

4. At the end of eight years the vessel is expected to be worth approximately $1 million. Depreciation is to be taken on a straight-line basis over the eight years.

The company went ahead with the project, mainly because of the particular interest of one of the directors. In the course of the first year the actual figures turned out to be:

1. Cost of vessel $5.4 million
2. Promotional and other costs $1.3 million (extra needed to boost revenue as demand not as high as expected).
3. Revenues $4.8 million
   Operating costs $2.9 million
   Other overheads $0.4 million

Estimates of revenues for the remainder of the life of the project have now been revised downwards to $4.8 million per annum. Estimates for expenses remain unchanged. The vessel could currently be sold for $4 million net, if it decided to close down the service now.

Being a little unhappy about these figures you consult the market research team that prepared both the initial and revised forecasts. In discussions with them it becomes clear that while expenses were always seen as being fairly easy to predict, and relatively fixed, the forecast for the revenues was a *most likely* forecast. *Optimistic* and *pessimistic* forecasts had also been prepared, showing revenues at $6 million for the optimistic forecast and at $4 million for the pessimistic. Under the revised forecasts these two figures were scaled down to $5.8 million and $3.8 million respectively.

The market research team considered that their estimates of total revenue range ($4 million–$6 million and $3.8 million–$5.8 million) were fairly accurate, but that the spread of probabilities of occurrence within that range was far less certain. They had thus assumed a 30 per cent probability of occurrence in the range $4 million–$4.6 million, a 40 per cent probability of occurrence of returns in the $4.6 million–$5.4 million range, and a 30 per cent probability of returns in the $5.4 million–$6 million range. The new ranges to which these probabilities related were $3.8 million–$4.4 million, $4.4 million–$5.2 million and $5.2 million–$5.8 million. In the original calculations revenues had been based simply on the most likely figures.

1 Should the original project have been accepted (workings required)?
2 Evaluate the revised project in the light of the above comments. Make recommendations and indicate what further information you would like to have to improve your decision making.

For simplicity assume cash flows occur at the end of each year, other than those relating to the cost of the vessel.

CASE STUDY 11.2

The chapter has focused on practical, financially oriented approaches to investment decisions. In practice there are many other aspects that need to be considered, particularly where decisions are made largely on strategic lines. Behavioural factors are also important in successful choice and implementation of investment decisions. Below is an article from the October 2002 *Australian CPA*, which addresses some of these issues. Read the article and consider the questions that follow.

Evaluating investment decisions

David Emsley says making good investment decisions requires the science of technical analysis and the art of managing behavioural threats

Investment and capital expenditure decisions are important because of their long term implications for profitability and surveys indicate that most companies routinely evaluate potential investments using discounted cashflow analysis (DCFs). But while the logic of DCFs is simple and compelling, just how effective are they at screening out unprofitable investments?

This question was prompted during a series of roundtable discussions with accountants from commerce and industry who all used DCFs to evaluate investments and held them to be highly effective in screening out unprofitable investments. But hardly anyone could actually recall any investment proposal being rejected using DCF analysis (even though they had no difficulty in identifying investments that should have been rejected). This finding raises questions about the effectiveness of DCFs to screen out unprofitable investment decisions.

There are two basic threats to making good investment decisions: technical and behavioural. Technical threats concern the ability to quantify the risk and profitability of investments and this threat can be minimised by using techniques such as DCFs. Managers' enthusiasm for technical solutions to problems have resulted in considerable resources being directed to understanding DCFs and producing the information needed to drive them, such as calculating the weighted average cost of capital. By contrast, behavioural threats concern the opportunism of managers sponsoring investments to manipulate or circumvent DCF analysis (because they see the investment as a stepping stone to promotion or as a pet project they are emotionally committed to). Compared to the technical threats, these behavioural threats are not so obvious and consequently attract far less management attention, even though the results of behavioural threats are readily apparent when investments fail—look no further than One.Tel.

A CLOSER LOOK AT DCFs

While DCFs are widely perceived as important for screening out unprofitable investments, a little critical (and honest) reflection reveals that this perception is often unfounded. For example, top management can bypass DCF analysis for investments initiated by themselves on the basis that there are "strategic benefits" that cannot be quantified in a DCF analysis. While there may be an element of truth in this, it can nevertheless serve as a convenient smokescreen for top management's own pet projects or hunches, and underlines the fact that such controls can be circumvented.

In contrast, for investment proposals that are initiated elsewhere in the organisation, top management often insist that before the proposals reach them, they are independently evaluated by the accounting department using DCF analysis. This evaluation process might appear rigorous but for opportunistic managers it is relatively easy to engineer a favourable evaluation by providing biased data, such as overly optimistic demand forecasts. Such biased information is difficult to distinguish from information that is simply uncertain and inevitably leads to a greater chance the investment will fail.

MAKING IMPROVEMENTS

Any resulting unease about the quality of investment decisions tends to focus on the quality of the DCF analysis because it is the most specific and visible control.

Consequently, improvements to investment decisions tend also to look no further than improving DCF analysis which might, for example, lead to incorporating a real-options approach (that enables the strategic value of investments to be evaluated). While there is undoubtedly value in understanding the principle behind the real-options approach, incorporating real-option techniques into the investment evaluation is likely to be impracticable and consume a disproportionate amount of management time and resources (for example, *The Economist* reported recently that finance directors would need a PhD in applied mathematics to understand real-options properly). However, the relevant point to make is that no matter how good these analytical techniques are, they cannot overcome the behavioural threats of opportunistic managers.

A BETTER BALANCE

A more balanced approach to controlling investment decisions requires greater recognition of the need to control behaviour threats, which in turn requires thinking more laterally about the controls that can affect individuals' behaviour across all stages of the investment decision (not just the evaluation stage). This is often unfamiliar territory for accountants who tend to think about, and have jurisdiction over, accounting controls, such as DCF analysis and responsibility reporting, and tend to leave the non-accounting (behavioural) controls to general managers. Without integrating these different controls, overall control will become fragmented, which provides scope for opportunists.

While the accountants in the roundtable discussions initially considered investment controls almost exclusively in terms of DCF analysis, once they reflected on the behavioural threats, they had little trouble in identifying ways they could be controlled, as indicated by the following three examples.

The first is that arguably it is the generation of investment ideas that is more important to control than evaluating them using DCF analysis because if only sound investment ideas are generated then it matters less how they are evaluated—this is analogous to quality management techniques which aim to ensure that a quality product is produced in the first place rather than inspecting quality after it has been made. Generating sound investment proposals depends on recruiting capable employees but the recruitment process can also be extended to gauge the level of opportunism in potential employees by using psychological tests and role playing exercises during the recruitment process. Consequently, putting resources into recruitment processes can reduce the likelihood of opportunism in investment decisions.

The second is that the strategic planning process can control behavioural threats by acting as a conduit through which investments need to pass. Obliging managers sponsoring the investment to describe how an investment helps to achieve the strategic plan serves to effectively pre-evaluate part of the investment proposal. For example, if the strategic planning process has separately established through rigorous argument and debate that growth via acquisitions is appropriate, an investment proposal to make an acquisition does not need to argue why acquisitions in general are appropriate (because that has already been done in the strategic planning process) but only why the particular acquisition under consideration is appropriate. Requiring investments to be linked to a well-thought-out strategic plan, minimises the likelihood that they are strategically mismatched and means that greater attention can then be focused on the remaining factors that are relevant to the particular acquisition. Consequently, the scope for opportunism can be reduced by enhancing the strategic planning process and then obliging managers to show how investments fit into the strategy.

Finally, behavioural controls can also supplement DCF analysis through a genuine peer review in an open and constructive (but adversarial) interactive forum where the assumptions and the logic of the analysis are openly challenged by a diverse range of suitably motivated staff. Such a forum is more likely to expose inappropriate assumptions and biases disingenuously introduced by opportunists sponsoring the investment.

These examples show how behavioural threats can be controlled and, while there are many other ways to achieve this, the important point to recognise is that behavioural threats are unlikely to be controlled using analytical techniques. Indeed the existence of analytical techniques provides opportunistic managers with the potential to manipulate the analysis and provide credibility where it is unwarranted. Making good investment decisions requires both the science of technical analysis and the art of managing the behavioural threats but while the technical analysis continues to monopolise management's mindset, the behavioural threats will continue to cause more failed investments than they should.

David Emsley is a senior lecturer in accounting at Macquarie University.
Reprinted by kind permission of the author.

1 In screening investment proposals what kind of things might prevent an investment being seriously considered?
2 Do you consider that strategic decisions can be made using DCF? What role do you think DCF plays in strategic decision making?
3 What kind of risks might lead to an investment being rejected even though it showed a positive present value?
4 How might bias or manipulation by sponsoring managers be prevented?
5 It can be argued that decisions are made on strategic lines with a present value calculation being only used to confirm the decision. Do you agree? Why/why not?
6 It is the generation of good ideas, rather than the generation of figures, which is the most important part of investment decision making? Discuss.

SOLUTIONS TO ACTIVITIES

Activity 11.1

The answer to this question must be that any decision must be made in the context of the objectives of the business concerned. For a private sector business, this is likely to include increasing the wealth of the shareholders of the business through long-term profitability.

Activity 11.2

The vehicles will save the business $30,000 a year (i.e. 230 – (20 × 10)), before depreciation, in total. Thus the inflows and outflows will be:

		$'000
Immediately	Cost of vans	(150)
1 year's time	Net saving before depreciation	30
2 years' time	Net saving before depreciation	30
3 years' time	Net saving before depreciation	30
4 years' time	Net saving before depreciation	30
5 years' time	Net saving before depreciation	30
6 years' time	Net saving before depreciation	30
	Plus disposal proceeds from the vans	30

The total annual depreciation expense (assuming a straight-line approach) will be $20,000 (i.e. (150 – 30) / 6). Thus the average annual saving, after depreciation, is $10,000 (i.e. 30 – 20).

The vehicles will appear in the balance sheet as follows:

		$'000
At beginning of year	1	150
At the end of year	1	130 (i.e. 150 – 20)
	2	110 (i.e. 130 – 20)
	3	90
	4	70
	5	50
	6	30

The average investment (at reporting date values) will be $90,000 (i.e. (150 + 130 + 110 + 90 + 70 + 50 + 30) / 7) or (150 + 30) / 2. Thus the ARR of the investment is 11.1 per cent (i.e. (10 / 90) × 100).

Activity 11.3

ARR suffers from a major defect in that it almost completely ignores the time factor. In the Billingsgate Battery Company example, exactly the same ARR would have been calculated under any of the following three scenarios:

		Original $'000	Option 1 $'000	Option 2 $'000
Immediately	Cost of machine	(100)	(100)	(100)
1 year's time	Net profit before depreciation	20	10	160
2 years' time	Net profit before depreciation	40	10	10

3 years' time	Net profit before depreciation	60	10	10
4 years' time	Net profit before depreciation	60	10	10
5 years' time	Net profit before depreciation	20	160	10
	Plus disposal proceeds	20	20	20

Since the same total profit over the five years arises in all three of these cases, the average net profit after depreciation must be the same in each case. In turn, this means that each case will give rise to the same ARR of 40 per cent.

Given a financial objective of increasing the wealth of the business, any rational decision maker faced with these three scenarios as a choice between three separate investments would strongly favour option 2. This is because most of the benefits from the investment come in within 12 months of spending the $100,000 to establish the project. The original scenario would rank second and option 1 would come a poor third in the rankings. Any appraisal technique that is not capable of distinguishing between these three situations is seriously flawed.

Activity 11.4

The inflows and outflows are expected to be:

		Net cash flows $'000	Cumulative net cash flows $'000
Immediately	Cost of vehicles	(150)	(150)
1 year's time	Net saving before depreciation	30	(120)
2 years' time	Net saving before depreciation	30	(90)
3 years' time	Net saving before depreciation	30	(60)
4 years' time	Net saving before depreciation	30	(30)
5 years' time	Net saving before depreciation	30	0
6 years' time	Net saving before depreciation plus disposal proceeds	60 (i.e. 30 + 30)	60

The payback period here is five years—that is, it is not until the end of the fifth year that the vans will pay for themselves out of the savings they are expected to generate.

Activity 11.5

Any rational decision maker would prefer project 3 to either of the other two scenarios, yet PP sees them as being the same—that is, there is a three-year payback period. The method cannot distinguish between those projects that pay back a significant amount before the three-year payback period and those that do not. Project 3 is by far the best bet because the cash flows come in earlier and they are greater in total, yet PP would not identify it as the best.

The cumulative cash flows of each project are set out in Figure 11.4.

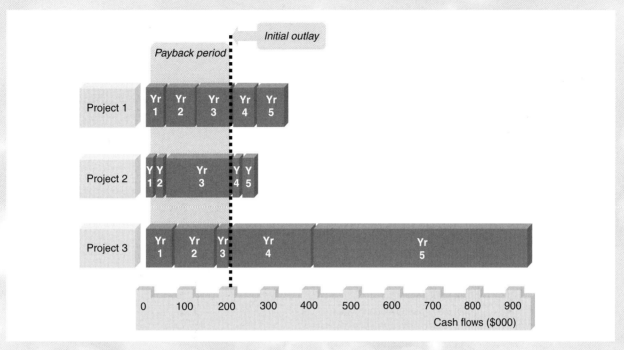

FIGURE 11.4 The cumulative cash flows of each project

Activity 11.6

The reasons are:

- interest lost
- effects of inflation
- risk.

Activity 11.7

You may have came up with the following:

- The machine might not work as well as expected; it might breakdown, leading to loss of production and to loss of sales.
- Sales of the product may not be as buoyant as expected.
- Labour costs may prove to be higher than were expected.
- The sales proceeds of the machine could prove to be less than were estimated.

Activity 11.8

We should obviously be happier to accept a lower amount if we could get it immediately than if we had to wait a year. This is because we could invest it at 20 per cent (in the alternative project). Logically, we should be prepared to accept the amount which, with a year's income, will grow to $20,000. If we call this amount PV (for present value) we can say:

$$PV + (PV \times 20\%) = \$20,000$$

That is, the amount plus income from investing the amount for the year equals the $20,000.

If we rearrange this equation we find:

$$PV \times (1 + 0.2) = \$20,000$$

Note that 0.2 is the same as 20 per cent, but expressed as a decimal.

Further rearranging gives:

$$PV = \$20,000 / (1 + 0.2)$$
$$PV = \$16,667$$

Thus, rational investors who have the opportunity to invest at 20 per cent a year would not mind whether they have $16,667 now or $20,000 in a year's time. In this sense we can say that, given a 20 per cent investment opportunity, the present value of $20,000 to be received in one year's time is $16,667.

Activity 11.9

Remember that the inflows and outflows are expected to be:

		$'000
Immediately	Cost of vans	(150)
1 year's time	Net saving before depreciation	30
2 years' time	Net saving before depreciation	30
3 years' time	Net saving before depreciation	30
4 years' time	Net saving before depreciation	30
5 years' time	Net saving before depreciation	30
6 years' time	Net saving before depreciation plus disposal proceeds	60 (30 + 30)

The calculation of the NPV of the project is as follows:

Time	Cash flows $'000	Discount factor (from the table)	Present value $'000
Immediately	(150)	1.000	(150.00)
1 year's time	30	0.870	26.10
2 years' time	30	0.756	22.68
3 years' time	30	0.658	19.74
4 years' time	30	0.572	17.16
5 years' time	30	0.497	14.91
6 years' time	60 (30 + 30)	0.432	25.92
		Net present value	(23.49)

The fact that the project has a negative NPV means that the benefits from the investment are worth less than the cost of entering into it. Any cost up to $126,510 (the present value of the benefits) would be worth paying, but not $150,000.

Activity 11.10

Since we know (from a previous activity) that at a 15 per cent discount rate the NPV is a relatively large negative figure ($23,490), our next trial is using a lower discount rate, say 10 per cent.

Time	Cash flows $'000	Discount factor (from the table)	Present value $'000
Immediately	(150)	1.000	(150.00)
1 year's time	30	0.909	27.27
2 years' time	30	0.826	24.78
3 years' time	30	0.751	22.53
4 years' time	30	0.683	20.49
5 years' time	30	0.621	18.63
6 years' time	60 (30 + 30)	0.564	33.84
		Net present value	(2.46)

We can see that NPV rose about $21,000 (from negative $23,490 to negative $2,460) for a 5 per cent drop in the discount rate—that is, about $4,200 per 1 per cent. We need to know the discount rate for a zero NPV—that is, a fall of a further $2,400. This logically would be roughly 0.6 per cent. Thus the IRR is close to 9.4 per cent. However, to say that the IRR is about 9 per cent is near enough for most purposes.

Activity 11.11

The answer relates to reinvestment. The project with the higher IRR (say, 22 per cent) will generate returns early that may only be able to be reinvested at a much lower rate (say, 14 per cent). The project with the lower IRR (say, 19 per cent) will yield the 19 per cent return over a longer period with a lesser amount having to be reinvested at the lower rates.

It is possible to modify the IRR method to incorporate reinvestment and calculate an overall average rate of return on the total project.

Activity 11.12

Your answer to this activity should be as follows.

(a) Incremental cash flows:

	Years				
	0 $'000	1 $'000	2 $'000	3 $'000	4 $'000
Operating cash flows (profit plus depreciation)		250	50	120	110
Sale of machinery	(220)				40
Redundancy costs	180				(150)
Sub-lease rentals		(40)	(40)	(40)	(40)
Working capital invested	(420)				420
	(460)	210	10	80	380

The sale value of the machinery represents an opportunity cost of keeping the factory operational, as does the sub-lease rentals lost if the factory keeps going.

(b)

Discount rate 12%	1.00	0.893	0.797	0.712	0.636
Present value	(460)	187.5	8.0	57.0	241.7
Net present value	34.2				

(c) Other factors that may influence the decision include:

- *The overall strategy of the company.* The company may need to set the decision within a broader context. It may be necessary to manufacture the products made at the factory because they are an integral part of the company's product range. The company may wish to avoid redundancies in an area of high unemployment for as long as possible.

- *Flexibility.* A decision to close the factory is probably irreversible. If the factory continues, however, there may be a chance that the prospects for the factory will brighten in the future.

- *Creditworthiness of sub-lessee.* The company should investigate the creditworthiness of the sub-lessee. Failure to receive the expected sub-lease payments would make the closure option far less attractive.

- *Accuracy of forecasts.* The forecasts made by the company should be examined carefully. Inaccuracies in the forecasts or any underlying assumptions may change the expected outcomes.

(d) The NPV of the decision to continue operations rather than close immediately is positive. Hence, shareholders would be better off if the directors took this course of action. The factory should therefore continue in operation rather than close down. This decision is likely to be welcomed by employees, as unemployment is high in the area.

Activity 11.13

Several reasons may exist:

1. Management may be fairly cautious.

2. Returns of future projects may well be more profitable than those currently on offer.

3. The ability of the organisation to raise more funds by new equity or borrowings may be limited in the short term.

4. The expected profitability, and the likely commitment to dividends, may have an unfavourable affect on cash flows.

5. In the final analysis it must be recognised that projects are usually fairly risky. In the event that cash flows were unfavourable it is likely that a fully committed portfolio of projects would put some strain on the business.

6. Many businesses adopt a policy of strategic positioning which requires considerable flexibility of resources.

7. If certain projects can be postponed without major problems, they may be delayed for reasons of prudence, without any significant loss.

8. If the business has a well developed corporate plan it is likely that any decisions about capital rationing are likely to be an explicit or implicit part of that process.

APPENDIX TO CHAPTER 11

PRESENT VALUE TABLE

Present value of $1, i.e. $(1 + r)^{-n}$

Where r = discount rate

n = number of periods until payment

					Discount rates (r)						
Periods											
(n)	1%	2%	3%	4%	5%	6%	7%	8%	9%	10%	
1	0.990	0.980	0.971	0.962	0.952	0.943	0.935	0.926	0.917	0.909	1
2	0.980	0.961	0.943	0.925	0.907	0.890	0.873	0.857	0.842	0.826	2
3	0.971	0.942	0.915	0.889	0.864	0.840	0.816	0.794	0.772	0.751	3
4	0.961	0.924	0.888	0.855	0.823	0.792	0.763	0.735	0.708	0.683	4
5	0.951	0.906	0.863	0.822	0.784	0.747	0.713	0.681	0.650	0.621	5
6	0.942	0.888	0.837	0.790	0.746	0.705	0.666	0.630	0.596	0.564	6
7	0.933	0.871	0.813	0.760	0.711	0.665	0.623	0.583	0.547	0.513	7
8	0.923	0.853	0.789	0.731	0.677	0.627	0.582	0.540	0.502	0.467	8
9	0.914	0.837	0.766	0.703	0.645	0.592	0.544	0.500	0.460	0.424	9
10	0.905	0.820	0.744	0.676	0.614	0.558	0.508	0.463	0.422	0.386	10
11	0.896	0.804	0.722	0.650	0.585	0.527	0.475	0.429	0.388	0.350	11
12	0.887	0.788	0.701	0.625	0.557	0.497	0.444	0.397	0.356	0.319	12
13	0.879	0.773	0.681	0.601	0.530	0.469	0.415	0.368	0.326	0.290	13
14	0.870	0.758	0.661	0.577	0.505	0.442	0.388	0.340	0.299	0.263	14
15	0.861	0.743	0.642·	0.555	0.481	0.417	0.362	0.315	0.275	0.239	15

	11%	12%	13%	14%	15%	16%	17%	18%	19%	20%	
1	0.901	0.893	0.885	0.877	0.870	0.862	0.855	0.847	0.840	0.833	1
2	0.812	0.797	0.783	0.769	0.756	0.743	0.731	0.718	0.706	0.694	2
3	0.731	0.712	0.693	0.675	0.658	0.641	0.624	0.609	0.593	0.579	3
4	0.659	0.636	0.613	0.592	0.572	0.552	0.534	0.516	0.499	0.482	4
5	0.593	0.567	0.543	0.519	0.497	0.476	0.456	0.437	0.419	0.402	5
6	0.535	0.507	0.480	0.456	0.432	0.410	0.390	0.370	0.352	0.335	6
7	0.482	0.452	0.425	0.400	0.376	0.354	0.333	0.314	0.296	0.279	7
8	0.434	0.404	0.376	0.351	0.327	0.305	0.285	0.266	0.249	0.233	8
9	0.391	0.361	0.333	0.308	0.284	0.263	0.243	0.225	0.209	0.194	9
10	0.352	0.322	0.295	0.270	0.247	0.227	0.208	0.191	0.176	0.162	10
11	0.317	0.287	0.261	0.237	0.215	0.195	0.178	0.162	0.148	0.135	11
12	0.286	0.257	0.231	0.208	0.187	0.168	0.152	0.137	0.124	0.112	12
13	0.258	0.229	0.204	0.182	0.163	0.145	0.130	0.116	0.104	0.093	13
14	0.232	0.205	0.181	0.160	0.141	0.125	0.111	0.099	0.088	0.078	14
15	0.209	0.183	0.160	0.140	0.123	0.108	0.095	0.084	0.074	0.065	15

OBJECTIVES

When you have completed your study of this chapter you should be able to:

1 identify reasons for investing in financial assets

2 explain the normal approach to security valuation

3 value fixed-term bonds and perpetual bonds, under specified assumptions

4 identify and explain the factors that influence the value of shares

5 identify and explain the factors that influence the value of businesses

6 explain the relationship between risk and security valuation

7 explain what is meant by efficient capital markets.

12

SECURITY AND BUSINESS VALUATIONS

This chapter is seen as an extension of investment appraisal, with the emphasis being on the appraisal of financial assets rather than physical assets. The chapter aims to provide a broad introduction to security and business valuation. In practice this is an area which requires considerable experience. In valuing businesses it is likely that several years knowledge and experience in the particular industry or industries concerned is needed to be able to do the job properly.

INVESTMENT IN FINANCIAL ASSETS

Business organisations tend to invest mainly in real assets—plant, machinery, stocks, etc.—although sometimes they invest in **financial assets**, namely securities issued by other organisations—both business and public sector organisations. Possible reasons for investing in financial assets include the following:

* The objectives of certain organisations (e.g. investment companies) may include investing partially or wholly in financial assets.
* Investment in financial assets may be a practical means of risk reduction through diversification.
* Financial assets provide a useful revenue earning repository for short-term cash surpluses. It should be noted that this is only likely to be true of securities which are quoted on the stock exchange, where the purchase and sale of such assets is quick and easy.
* Financial assets may be acquired in order to obtain control over the assets of another organisation. Control can be achieved by obtaining sufficient ordinary shares to achieve voting control. The number of shares needed to obtain effective control is dependent on how widespread the ownership is.

In addition to business organisations, a great many individuals and non-business organisations invest in financial assets, and the remaining sections of this chapter apply equally to them.

In broad terms, the same type of evaluation and appraisal techniques used for investment in real assets can be applied to financial assets. However, in practice, discounted cash flow techniques (DCF) are the most widely used, and the majority of the valuation models proposed follow this logic. The use of DCF requires some assessment of future cash flows, and the identification of an appropriate discount rate. Thus, the estimation of such things as future earnings, dividends, market values, taxation rates and changes therein must be seen as an essential part of the valuation process.

The prediction of future events and results relies largely on information about:

* the national economy
* the industry
* the particular organisation concerned.

Estimates of the likely future state of the economy can be aided by information obtained from a variety of statistical sources, particularly government publications. The main economic trends need to be identified, along with additional factors such as productivity, employment, credit, balance of payments and price indices. Many of the statistics used in this first part of the analysis will also provide extremely useful industrial information, and are likely to provide a basis for estimating market size, capital expenditure needs, likely cost escalation and profitability, etc.

Any assessment of the individual organisation involves a detailed examination of past performance, the current situation and future prospects. The main thrust of this examination is likely to centre on the analysis of past accounting information, in order to help in the prediction of future events; this topic has been dealt with in

Chapters 6 and 10. However, past information is not always a reliable indicator of likely future performance, and other factors and sources of information need to be considered.

SECURITY VALUATION—THE APPROACH TO THE PROBLEM

Once the returns available from a security have been estimated, the valuation problem can be viewed as a discounted cash flow problem, with expected cash flows being discounted by the rate of return required by security holders.

The required rate of return is the minimum rate of return necessary to induce investors to buy or hold a security. It must be recognised that not all securities carry an equal risk. Thus, higher risk securities will need to yield higher returns than lower risk securities if investors are to invest in them. For example, it is unlikely that investors will be prepared to buy shares in a gold prospecting company which yields the same rate of return as a government bond. The higher risk associated with prospecting, including complete loss, will require a higher expected return. Expected return generally is taken as the sum of the various probable outcomes multiplied by their respective probabilities.

EXAMPLE

12.1

The range of possible outcomes for three investments are shown below:

A—government bond		B—prospecting business		C—retailing business	
Outcome	*Probability*	*Outcome*	*Probability*	*Outcome*	*Probability*
6%	1	0%	.6	0%	.1
		20%	.2	10%	.4
		40%	.15	20%	.4
		500%	.05	30%	.1

The expected (i.e. weighted average) returns are therefore:

A   6%

B $(0 \times .6) + (20 \times .2) + (40 \times .15) + (500 \times .05) = 35\%$

C $(0 \times .1) + (10 \times .4) + (20 \times .4) + (30 \times .1) = 15\%$

These three potential investments are quite different with substantially different levels of risk. Most investors are risk averse, and will choose between investments using certain criteria:

• for investments which have the same expected return, they will choose the one with the least risk (i.e. volatility)
• for investments which have the same risk, they will choose the one with the highest return.

This means that neither B nor C will be chosen unless they give a higher yield than A. However, the above criteria do not help us in choosing between these three investments. Clearly A is the least risky, B is extremely risky, with high probability of loss but a small probability of substantial gain, while C is in between, and offers higher returns than A with moderate volatility. How are we to choose between them?

Essentially, the final choice is a personal one, reflecting the attitude to risk of the person at the time. However, in practice, other investors will be making similar decisions, and as information is built up a set of required rates of return for different categories of investment will emerge from the market for these investments.

For any given risky security, the required rate of return is equal to the risk-free rate plus a risk premium. The current yield on government securities is normally taken to be the risk-free rate. The relationship between risk and required return can be illustrated graphically as shown in Figure 12.1 and is known as the **securities market line (SML)**.

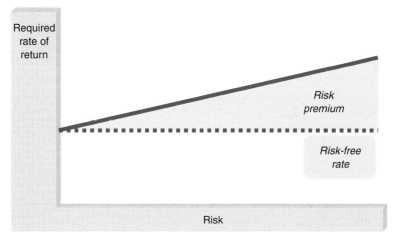

FIGURE 12.1 The relationship between risk and return

The figure illustrates the point that the required rate of return for a security with high risk will be higher than that for one with a lower risk. Higher required rates of return will be associated with lower prices and vice versa. The risk index can be measured in a number of ways, usually dealing with volatility of outcomes, including the standard deviation of expected returns, but the most common measure is the beta coefficient, a measure of the correlation of individual security returns with those of the market.

Changes in the level of interest rates will change the risk-free rate, so the line will move up and down by the amount of that change. Higher levels of inflation will generally be associated with higher risk-free rates. Changes in investors' attitudes towards risk may result in changes in the slope of the line. If investors become more averse to risk, the line will become steeper, implying a higher required return for the same degree of risk. If they become less averse to risk, the line will become flatter. In times of economic depression, investors tend to become more **risk averse** (i.e. try to avoid risk) so the SML will be steeper, while optimistic times are associated with a flatter SML.

BOND VALUATION

Fixed-term bonds

These are securities which pay interest, and repay the capital sum at some agreed future time.

A bond of this type can be valued as follows:

$$PV = \Sigma \frac{I}{(1 + k)^n} + \frac{M}{(1+k)^n} \qquad \text{where } \Sigma \text{ means sum of}$$

or

$$\frac{I}{(1 + k)} + \frac{I}{(1 + k)^2} + \frac{I}{(1 + k)^3} \text{ and so on until } \frac{(1 + M)}{(1 + k)^n}$$

where:

  PV is the current value
  I is the annual interest payable
  M is the **maturity value** (the amount repaid at a future date, excluding interest)
  k is the required rate of return
  n is the remaining life of the security

EXAMPLE

12.2

What is the likely price for a government security (nominal value $100), paying 4 per cent interest and redeemable by the government in four years' time, if the current required rate of return is 6 per cent.

  The value, assuming a required rate of return of 6 per cent, can be derived as follows.

$$PV = \frac{4}{(1 + 0.06)} + \frac{4}{(1 + 0.06)^2} + \frac{4}{(1 + 0.06)^3} + \frac{(4 + 100)}{(1 + 0.06)^4}$$

Using discount tables this reduces to:

$$(4 \times .943) + (4 \times .890) + (4 \times .840) + (104 \times .792) = \$93.06$$

ACTIVITY 12.1

What would the value of the bond be assuming the current required rate of return is:

(a) 10 per cent

(b) 16 per cent

(c) 2 per cent?

It should be noted that so far knowledge of the discount rate (i.e. the required rate of return) has been presumed, along with knowledge of future cash flows. This has enabled calculations to be made of the appropriate value of the security. If the value of the security were known, along with its associated cash flows, the yield or IRR of that particular investment could be calculated. The problem is merely approached from a different direction.

EXAMPLE

12.3

Find the yield to maturity of a bond—currently priced on the market at $80—with a par value of $100, a 6 per cent coupon rate (the percentage based on the par or nominal value) and which is redeemable in four years' time at a premium of 10 per cent.

  If the cash flows are discounted at 10 per cent and 20 per cent the following present values are obtained.

Year	Cash flow	at 10% discount factor	PV	at 20% discount factor	PV
0 (initial flow)	(80)	1.0	(80)	1.0	(80)
1	6	.909	5.45	.833	5.00

2	6	.826	4.96	.694	4.16
3	6	.751	4.51	.579	3.47
4	116	.683	79.23	.482	55.91
Net present value			14.15		(11.46)

Clearly the yield is greater than 10 per cent and less than 20 per cent. By a process of interpolation (see chapter 11) the yield can be approximated as follows:

$$10\% + (14.15 / 25.61)\ 10\% = 15.5\%$$

Alternatively use of a financial calculator or spreadsheet will give a more accurate figure.

It is worth noting that the use of annuity tables can considerably reduce the amount of arithmetical calculation needed.

It should also be recognised that the techniques illustrated above can also be applied to preference shares, which have similar cash flow characteristics to fixed-term bonds.

ACTIVITY 12.2

A bond is purchased on 1 April 2005 for $800. It was originally issued on 1 April 2003 with the following characteristics:

- par value of $1,000
- coupon rate 6 per cent
- interest paid at six-monthly intervals
- term—7 years
- repayment at a premium of 10 per cent.

(a) If the required rate of return is 10 per cent per annum at what price should the bond have been purchased? *Hint*: cash flows occur semi-annually. You should use periods of six months at half the discount rate for the year.

(b) What is the yield on the bond?

Perpetual bonds

Perpetual bonds are securities which pay a fixed amount of interest indefinitely, with no repayment of the capital sum outstanding. They are not part of the Australian environment and are largely confined to countries such as Britain, where political circumstances (e.g. world war) created an environment in which they could be sold.

A bond of this type can be valued as follows.

$$PV = \frac{I}{(1 + k)} + \frac{I}{(1 + k)^2} + \ldots\ldots\ldots + \frac{I}{(1 + k)^n}$$

where:

PV is the current value

I is the annual interest payable,

k is the required rate of return

n is the remaining life of the security

For a perpetuity (i.e. n = infinity) this reduces to:

$$PV = I/k$$

EXAMPLE

12.4

$100 of government bonds (nominal value) pay $4 annual interest. The current rate of interest on government bonds is 5 per cent. The price for the bonds is thus likely to be:

$$PV = 4/0.05 = \$80$$

Put another way, the acquisition of $100 of 4 per cent government bonds at a price of $80 will give a 5 per cent return.

ACTIVITY 12.3

If the current market interest rate (and required rate of return) were 10 per cent what would you expect the price to be?

If the current rate of interest were 16 per cent or 2 per cent the figures would be $25 and $200 respectively.

From the above example it is apparent that *interest rate changes* are likely to have a significant effect on the price of perpetual bonds. However, it is unlikely that price changes would occur with the precision implied above, since these figures are based on permanent changes in the interest rate. Short-term changes in interest rate are unlikely to have very much effect. Rather, it is the expectations of the long-term interest rate which are likely to be paramount.

ACTIVITY 12.4

Assume that $100 of perpetual bonds pay annual interest of $4, and the current value is $80.

There is a run on the dollar which leads to an increase in the short-term interest rate from 5 per cent to 10 per cent.

Would you expect the value of the bonds to halve?

At this point the reason for discussing perpetuities becomes clearer. A perpetual bond is the ultimate in terms of period of the bond. It represents one extreme point in the bond valuation exercise. Comparison of the prices calculated for different required rates of return for the perpetuity and the four-year bond (example 12.2) indicates clearly that the longer the period to maturity of a security, the greater its price change in response to a given change in interest rates. This greater interest rate risk which is associated with perpetuities explains why short-term bonds usually have lower yields than long-term bonds, in spite of similar levels of confidence in the returns. It also explains the reluctance of most managers to hold their near-cash reserves in the form of long-term debt securities.

VALUATION OF ORDINARY SHARES

In theory, the same ideas apply as in the last section. The value of a share ought to be the sum of future dividends, discounted at an appropriate rate, that is:

$$P = \frac{D_1}{(1+k)} + \frac{D_2}{(1+k)^2} + \frac{D_3}{(1+k)^3} \ldots\ldots\ldots + \frac{D_n}{(1+k)^n}$$

where   P = current value
        D_n = dividends in period n
        k = required rate of return

However, in practice several difficulties occur with share valuations, which pose problems for the above model.

❋ The degree of certainty with regard to earnings, dividends and share prices is considerably reduced.

❋ Unlike loan interest and preference dividends, ordinary dividends and share prices are usually expected to grow, thus making the application of standard formulae more difficult.

❋ Rather different values will be given to shares, depending upon whether they are private or public companies, and quoted or unquoted.

❋ In certain cases, the question arises as to whether a purchase of shares gives a majority (i.e. controlling) holding or a minority holding, resulting in possible differences in share values.

A number of models or approaches to the valuation of ordinary shares are given below. However, it must be recognised that share valuation is an imprecise art, and no perfect models have yet been put forward. A considerable amount of research has taken place over the years in a attempt to identify the factors which influence or explain share pricing. The most common explanatory variables include the following:

1. the level of earnings
2. expected growth in earnings
3. the level of dividends and/or the dividend payout ratio
4. expected growth in dividends
5. historic share price variability
6. historic earnings variability.

These are reflected in the models given below. However, several research findings include rather less obvious explanatory variables including the following:

7. some measure of correlation between earnings of the particular organisation and those of the market
8. a measure of gearing
9. an index of operating asset liquidity
10. a measure of firm size.

Growth models

A model to incorporate growth can be developed as follows:

$$P_0 = \frac{D_1 + P_1}{(1 + k)}$$

where D_1 is the dividend at the end of year 1
         P_0 is the market price at the end of year 0
         P_1 is the market price at the end of year 1
         k is the required rate of return

Therefore

$$P_0 = \frac{D_1 + P_0(1 + g)}{(1 + k)} = \frac{D_1 + P_0 + P_0 g}{(1 + k)}$$

where g is the expected growth rate in market price.

This reduces to:

$$P_0 + P_0 k = D_1 + P_0 + P_0 g$$

Therefore

$$P_0 k - P_0 g = D_1$$

So

$$P_0 = \frac{D_1}{(k - g)}$$

In applying this model to growth situations, it must be recognised that to be valid for more than one period a constant growth rate must be assumed in earnings, dividends and market price.

EXAMPLE

12.5

Mr X is thinking of buying a share in A Ltd which he intends to hold for one year. An annual dividend of 50c per share has just been paid. Dividends have been growing at about 6 per cent per annum for several years, and this rate is expected to continue. The current rate of return on risk-free stocks is 10 per cent and Mr X considers that a risk premium of 4 per cent is appropriate for an organisation such as A Ltd.

How much should Mr X be prepared to pay for a share in A Ltd?

The answer is given below. The required rate of return for a company in this particular risk category is 14 per cent (10 per cent risk free plus 4 per cent risk premium).

$$P_0 = \frac{D_1}{(k - g)}$$

where D_1 = 53c
       k = 0.14 (14%)
       g = 0.06 (6%)

Therefore

$$P_0 = \frac{0.53}{(0.14 - 0.06)} = \frac{0.53}{0.08} = \$6.625$$

In practice, organisations typically go through phases where growth occurs at rather different rates. In such a case the above approach can be modified to arrive at a present price.

EXAMPLE

12.6

B Ltd is expected to grow at a rate of about 20 per cent for the next four years, then at 10 per cent for the next three years and finally settle down to a growth rate of 5 per cent for the indefinite future. The company's ordinary shares currently pay a dividend of 50c per share, but dividends are expected to increase in proportion to the growth of the firm.

What value should be placed on the ordinary shares if a 10 per cent return is required?

Estimates of dividends can be made for the first two periods of growth, and these can be discounted at the required rate (assumed to be 10 per cent) as shown below, to give the present value of the dividend stream for the next seven years.

Year	Dividends	discount factor	PV
1	60	.909	54.5
2	72	.826	59.5
3	86.4	.751	64.9
4	103.7	.683	70.8
5	114	.621	70.8
6	125.5	.564	70.8
7	138	.513	70.8
			462.1c = $4.62

At the beginning of year 8 (end of year 7) a period of constant annual growth (5 per cent) is entered. The shares could thus be expected to be valued at:

$$P_7 = \frac{D_8}{(k-g)}$$

$$= \frac{144.9^* \text{ cents}}{(0.10 - 0.05)} = \$28.98$$

$$^* (138 + 5\%)$$

This value is calculated as at the beginning of Year 8 (which is taken to be the end of Year 7 for discounting purposes). This needs to be further discounted to bring the value back to the present. Its present value is thus $28.98 \times 0.513 = \$14.87$

Then we need to add the PV of dividends from years 1–7, which was $4.62. An ordinary share in B Ltd should thus be valued at $19.49 (i.e. $14.87 + $4.62).

Shares with zero growth effectively reduce to a perpetuity, i.e.

$$P_0 = \frac{D_1}{k} \quad \text{which converts to} \quad k = \frac{D_1}{P_0}$$

which implies that the required rate of return on a share with no growth prospects is simply the dividend yield.

Market yields and multipliers

Over the years a number of factors have been used by the market to identify important relationships. The two most common factors are:

✴ the dividend yield
✴ the price-earnings ratio.

The method of calculation for each is given below:

$$\text{Dividend yield} = \frac{\text{Dividends per share}}{\text{Market price per share}} \times 100$$

$$\text{Price-earnings ratio} = \frac{\text{Share price}}{\text{Earnings per share}}$$

Securities in similar risk categories are likely to have similar ratios, and estimates of share price can be made by applying these market figures to dividends or earnings. Actual PE ratios are published. The major difficulty is assessing whether the PE ratio is stable, or whether other things are working to change it. The PE ratio is effectively the inverse of the earnings yield i.e. a PE ratio of 10 would give an earnings yield of 10 per cent and a PE ratio of 20 would give an earnings yield of 5 per cent. So if there is a perception that the future is more risky than the past, in other words the future risk associated with a particular company is greater relative to competitors, the required earnings yield will increase, with a consequent reduction in the PE ratio. What constitutes an appropriate future PE ratio is problematic. It will reflect the views of many analysts and investors and their evaluation of various fundamental factors. The major determinants of PE ratios are growth rates in earnings and risk. There is also an inverse relationship between PE ratios and financial leverage, above a certain level. High PE ratios tend to be associated with organisations with perceived growth prospects.

EXAMPLE

12.7

An organisation has annual profits after tax of $1m, and 2 million shares. If an investor regards a price–earnings (PE) ratio of 10 as appropriate to such a share—taking risk and other factors into account—what value would be placed on each share?

$$\text{Earnings per share (EPS)} = \frac{\$1m}{2m} = 50c$$

If the

$$\text{PE ratio} = \frac{\text{Share price}}{\text{Earnings per share}}$$

then

$$\text{Share price} = \text{PE ratio} \times \text{EPS} = 10 \times 50c = \$5 \text{ per share}$$

ACTIVITY 12.5

Using the information provided immediately above this activity:

(a) If there was a perception that the company described had serious problems with its management, what might you expect to happen to the PE ratio?

(b) If the PE ratio moved to 7, what would happen to the share price?

Private/public—quoted/unquoted

In valuing shares, differences are likely to arise because of the ease (or otherwise) of transferability of shares. Private companies usually impose restrictions on the rights of shareholders to transfer their shares and so are generally regarded as more risky than public companies as finding a buyer for unwanted shares may be difficult. Similarly, if an organisation's securities are quoted on the stock exchange, these securities can be disposed of much more quickly and easily than those of an unquoted organisation, and this will have an effect on share prices.

Majority/minority holdings

The value which an investor places on a share is also likely to be influenced by whether he or she acquires:

* a minority shareholding
* a majority holding.

The price set for the acquisition of a minority holding is likely to be largely determined by the dividend yield since, in practical terms, such a holding does not give the shareholder any opportunity to influence future decisions. The investment decision will thus probably have to be based upon expectations about future dividends. Acquisition of a majority holding facilitates the consideration of other factors because of the greater freedom of action obtained by the investor (in terms of control of the organisation thus acquired).

The use of charts

Certain analysts argue that the use of charts, showing trends in share prices for past periods, can be extremely beneficial. Such analysts, known as Chartists, argue that share prices follow certain well-defined patterns, and that critical decision points can be isolated by graphing the patterns for particular securities. Many other analysts are critical of this viewpoint, but it must be recognised that some use is undoubtedly made of charts. This is important in that if sufficient investors believe that a particular event will occur it may well actually happen. For example, if a large number of people believe that the shares of Smith Ltd will rise to a price of $4 each, they will buy them at prices below $4, thus causing that price to be achieved. A similar logic applies to the use of charts.

RISK AND SECURITY VALUATION

In the context of security valuation, risk may be considered to be the extent to which the actual returns from a security could vary from those expected. This can be subdivided into two aspects.

1. **Specific risk** is that part of the total risk which arises from features of the organisation itself, and from features of the industry within which it operates. Examples include things like marketing, industrial relations and specific contracts.
2. **Systematic risk** is that part of the total risk which arises from features of the economy generally—system wide. Examples include recessions, inflation, high interest rates, and events of significant political importance which impact on current trading conditions.

The difference between these two is extremely important, since specific risk can be eliminated by any particular shareholder merely by holding a **portfolio** of securities of different organisations from different industries. By contrast, systematic risk cannot be eliminated or even reduced by holding portfolios of shares. The relationship between total risk and the number of securities in a portfolio is shown in Figure 12.2.

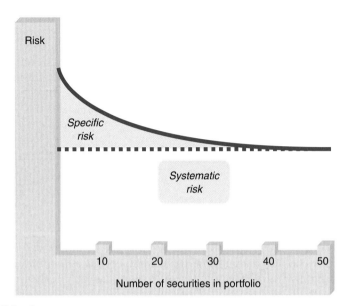

FIGURE 12.2 Total risk and portfolio size

Figure 12.2 clearly shows that much of the total risk attaching to any individual organisation can be eliminated by holding a *portfolio of securities*. This explains why investors typically hold securities in portfolios. Figure 12.2 also shows that most of the specific risk can be eliminated by holding a portfolio of as little as 10 securities. It further indicates that, irrespective of how many securities are held, there remains part of the total risk—the systematic risk—which the investor is forced to bear.

Most rational investors will tend to develop portfolios of securities which minimise the volatility of the portfolio returns. Securities which have returns which are counter-cyclical are likely to be attractive to investors from a portfolio viewpoint, and will be priced accordingly.

Since specific risk can be eliminated easily and cheaply, investors cannot expect to obtain large returns to compensate them for bearing the risk. However, they can and do require compensation in the form of larger returns for bearing systematic risk. Systematic risk will not affect individual companies equally. Interest rate changes may have dramatically different implications for different types of companies, e.g. building companies are likely to find that increases in interest rates will depress demand substantially, whereas they are unlikely to greatly affect a business retailing foodstuffs.

Systematic risk is measured by a factor known as a **beta coefficient**. It measures the degree of correlation between the returns for an individual security and those of the market generally. Theoretically, the higher the coefficient, the higher the risk premium associated with the security. A security with a beta coefficient of zero should have no risk premium. Securities with negative or low coefficients should have negative risk premiums, i.e. their price is likely to be 'bid up' because of their attractiveness as part of a portfolio, thus reducing the returns obtainable. In practice, securities with negative or zero beta coefficients are very difficult to find.

The capital asset pricing model (CAPM) is a model which sees the required rate of return as being equal to the risk-free rate of return plus its risk premium, *where its risk reflects the effects of diversification*. More formally, this transforms the relationship graphed earlier in Figure 12.1, to:

$$k = k_{RF} + (k_M - k_{RF})\, b$$

where   k = the required rate of return on the shares in question
    k_{RF} = the risk-free rate, usually that of long-term government bonds
    b = the beta coefficient of the shares in question
    k_M = the required rate of return on average risk shares (or of a market portfolio of all shares)

You should note that the part of the equation which follows i.e. $(k_M - k_{RF})$ represents the risk premium. The difference between the SML and CAPM is the formal inclusion of beta, which focuses clearly on the diversification issue. The SML suggests that returns can be higher the higher the risk. CAPM suggests that specific risk has the potential to be diversified away (partly at least). This means that if specific risk can be diversified away relatively easily, very little in the way of a risk premium will be available. An analysis of risk therefore needs to take place at a portfolio level rather than at an individual security level.

The market risk premium represents the difference between the average return on shares and the long-term government bond rate—the risk-free rate. So, if a market portfolio of shares yields 12 per cent while the risk-free rate is 7 per cent, the market risk premium is 5 per cent.

The beta recognises that the systematic risk will impact on individual securities in different ways and is a measure of this variability in comparison with a market portfolio. The beta for the market portfolio is assumed to be 1, so the required rate of return for a market portfolio (using the figure from the previous paragraph) would be:

$$k = k_{RF} + (k_M - k_{RF})\, b$$

$$k = 7\% + (12\% - 7\%)\, 1 = 12\%$$

If a security has a beta of 0.5, implying considerably less volatility than a market portfolio, the required rate of return for that security should theoretically be:

$$k = 7\% + (12\% - 7\%)\, 0.5 = 9.5\%$$

For a security with a beta of 2, implying considerably more volatility than a market portfolio, the required rate of return for that security should theoretically be:

$$k = 7\% + (12\% - 7\%)\, 2 = 17\%$$

CAPM has a number of assumptions which tend to weaken it, e.g. all investors may lend and borrow at the same rate, the absence of transactions costs. Nevertheless, the empirical tests that have been run have broadly supported CAPM as an explainer of past events. The evidence on betas as predictors of the future is a lot less clear.

What is clear is that rational investors should diversify to the extent necessary to eliminate most of the specific risk from their portfolios. There are no rewards for bearing specific risk.

SHARE VALUES AND EFFICIENT CAPITAL MARKETS

While certain doubts exist with regard to the applicability of some of the particular techniques or models discussed above, there appears to be a general acceptance that the market (i.e. the stock exchange) is, overall, fairly efficient. In other words, the prices obtaining at any moment in time reflect a balance of all the views in the market. If such a view is accepted, the question must be asked as to whether it is worthwhile spending time and effort in trying to value quoted securities. It would appear that share valuation is only worth undertaking where unquoted securities are involved or if efficiency is doubted. It is something of a paradox that efficiency only exists as long as people continue to try to 'beat' the market.

BUSINESS VALUATIONS

The valuation of a business is, in concept, no different from the valuation of a share or shares. However, a number of other factors are worthy of consideration.

1. Estimated cash inflows will generally relate to earnings rather than dividends. Where appropriate, opportunity costs should be included (e.g. salaries drawn by an owner for work done in the business), so as to ensure that a correct figure is obtained for returns from the amount invested.

2. Knowledge of asset values can be useful. Replacement costs (RC) enable a potential investor to ascertain how much it would cost to acquire the physical assets necessary to start such a business from scratch. Net realisable values (NRV) provide an indication as to the bailout facility should the project go wrong. There is no logical financial reason for a business to be sold at a figure which is lower than the total of the NRVs of assets, less any external debts.

3. In acquiring a business as a going concern, some consideration needs to be given to the fact that acquisition brings with it certain advantages which would not be available to a new business, e.g. reputation, clientele, experienced work force. These advantages are generally referred to as goodwill, and must be paid for. In certain industries conventions exist with regard to the amount paid for goodwill, but in the final analysis the amount is the result of negotiation by the parties to the agreement.

SELF-ASSESSMENT QUESTION 12.1

(a) Marko Ltd issued 10 year 10 per cent coupon debentures on 1 June 2001 with a par value of $100. Redemption is at a premium of 10 per cent. Coupons are paid every 31 May.

Current yields of similar bonds on 1 June 2006 are 8 per cent.

What is the likely current price of the security?

(b) If the current price were $80, what would be the yield?

(c) If interest were to be paid twice a year, how would you modify your approach to get a more accurate result?

(d) Davo Ltd has enjoyed many years of uneven growth. It is now seen as entering a period of steady growth. What would the price per share be if the required return is 15 per cent, the current dividend per share is 50 cents, and the projected growth rate is 5 per cent?

(e) Paulo Ltd expects to enter a period of growth as follows:

—next three years—10 per cent

—thereafter—5 per cent

The current dividend is 50 cents per share.

The required rate of return is 15 per cent.

What is the likely share price?

SUMMARY

In this chapter we have achieved the following objectives in the way shown.

OBJECTIVE	METHOD ACHIEVED
Identify reasons for investing in financial assets	• Listed and explained reasons for investing in financial assets
Explain the normal approach to security valuation	• Identified the main evaluation and appraisal techniques used • Discussed basis of predictions
Value fixed-term bonds and perpetual bonds, under specified assumptions	• Illustrated basis of valuation of fixed-term bonds and perpetual bonds • Illustrated link between length of bond period and interest rates
Identify and explain the factors that influence the value of shares	• Explained main variables influencing share values • Illustrated use of growth model • Explained market yields and multipliers • Explained importance of public and private distinction
Explain the relationship between risk and security valuation	• Explained the difference between specific and systematic risk • Explained the significance of diversification • Explained the capital asset pricing model and its implications for diversification and risk reduction
Explain what is meant by efficient capital markets	• Explained the nature of efficient capital markets
Identify and explain the factors that influence the value of businesses	• Identified main factors

DISCUSSION QUESTIONS

EASY

<Obj 1>	12.1	What are the main reasons why a business might invest in financial assets?
<Obj 2>	12.2	How might you gather information about the state of the economy?
<Obj 4>	12.3	Discuss the main factors determining PE ratios.
<Obj 6>	12.4	Explain the securities market line. What are the difficulties associated with measuring risk? How might it be measured?

INTERMEDIATE

<Obj 2>	12.5	Explain the nature of the valuation problem.
<Obj 3>	12.6	Discuss the link between interest rate changes, period to maturity and price of a bond.
<Obj 4>	12.7	What characteristic of ordinary shares make them far more difficult to value than bonds?
<Obj 4>	12.8	What is the link between growth and share price, in broad terms?
<Obj 5>	12.9	What additional factors need to be considered when purchasing a business, as distinct from shares.
<Obj 6, 7>	12.10	Distinguish between specific and systematic risk
<Obj 6, 7>	12.11	Explain why investors typically diversify. What is the link between diversification and risk reduction?

APPLICATION EXERCISES

EASY

<Obj 2>

12.1 Return is generally identified as being the increase in wealth for a period expressed as a percentage of the amount invested. What is the return expressed as a percentage in the following cases?

a) A company invests $1m in a project and by the end of the year net profits are $150,000.

b) An investor purchases $100 worth of preference shares at par which had a fixed rate of dividend of 8 per cent.

c) Suppose that the $100 of preference shares referred to in b) above had been purchased for $90, what would have been the return?

d) Why might the preference share price have reduced?

<Obj 2>

12.2 With regard to share purchase the general actual return can be expressed as:

$$\frac{\text{Increase in wealth} \times 100}{\text{Beginning wealth}}$$

a) An ordinary share which was valued at the start of the year at $2 had a value at the year end of $2.20. During the year no dividends were paid. What is the return on the investment?

b) An ordinary share which was valued at the start of the year at $2 had a value at the end of the year of $2.20. During the year dividends of 20 cents a share were paid. What is the return on the investment?

<Obj 2>

12.3 Return figures are usually calculated on the basis of expectations. An ordinary share currently valued at $2 is expected to have a value of $2.15 at the year end and is expected to pay a dividend of 30 cents a share.

What return might be expected on the investment?

<Obj 2>

12.4 Formally, expected return (the rate of return expected to be realised from an investment) is the mean value of a probability distribution of possible outcomes.

(a) Suppose that a business estimates that a particular investment has a range of possible outcomes. It has estimated the following:

There is a .5 (i.e. 50 per cent) probability that it will yield returns of 15 per cent

There is a .25 (i.e. 25 per cent) probability that it will yield returns of 20 per cent

There is a .25 (i.e. 25 per cent) probability that it will yield returns of 10 per cent

What is the expected return?

(b) Suppose that the distribution was:

.2 probability of a return of –20 per cent (in other words a small chance of a really poor outcome)

.3 probability of a return of 10 per cent

.3 probability of a return of 20 per cent

.2 probability of a return of 50 per cent

What is the expected return?

(c) Suppose that the distribution was:

.1 probability of a return of –20 per cent (in other words a small chance of a really poor outcome)

.3 probability of a return of 10 per cent

.4 probability of a return of 20 per cent

.2 probability of a return of 30 per cent

What is the expected return?

(d) Comment on the relative risks associated with each set of figures.

(e) How might you choose between them?

<Obj 2>   **12.5**   Suppose that the shares of two companies are available for investment.

The first is a supermarket with little risk and an expected return of 15 per cent.

The second is in a high-risk sector of the IT industry and also has an expected return of 15 per cent.

Both shares initially sell at $1 each.

What do you think would happen to share prices over the next period. Why?

<Obj 2>   **12.6**   What return would you require in order to be prepared to invest $1,000 in the following:

a)   government bonds

b)   Telstra shares

c)   shares in a wool farm

d)   shares in Dreamworld.

Explain your underlying rationale for each of these figures.

INTERMEDIATE

<Obj 3, 4>   **12.7**   Summarised accounts for Jons Enterprises Ltd for last year are shown below.

Income statement

Operating profit	1,000,000
Less debenture interest	100,000
	900,000
Less taxation	300,000
Net profit after taxation	600,000
Less dividends	500,000
Added to reserves	100,000
Retained profits b/f	1,500,000
Retained profits c/f	1,600,000

Balance sheet

Current assets

Inventory		2,000,000
Debtors		900,000
Cash		300,000
		3,200,000
Non-current assets		
Cost	5,000,000	
Less accumulated depreciation	1,400,000	
		3,600,000
Total assets		6,800,000

Current liabilities	
Creditors	1,200,000
Long-term debt (5% debentures)	2,000,000
Equity	
Ordinary share capital issues at $1 per share	2,000,000
Reserves	1,600,000
Total liabilities and shareholders' equity	6,800,000

Required:

Calculate the following from the given data:

(a) Balance sheet value of a $1 Ordinary share of Jons Enterprises Ltd.

(b) Market value of a $1 ordinary share on the basis that the current dividend yield on similar shares is 8 per cent.

(c) Ratio of net profit after tax to ordinary shareholders interest.

(d) Market value of $100 debenture stock, ex div, if the appropriate yield is 7 per cent and the stock is redeemable at par in exactly 10 years.

<Obj 3, 4, 6> **12.8** (a) Find the yield to maturity of a bond currently on the market at $110, with a par value of $100, an 8 per cent coupon rate, which is redeemable in five years time at a premium of 10 per cent.

(b) You are thinking of buying a share in H Ltd, which you intend to hold for one year. An annual dividend of $1 per share has just been paid. Dividends have been growing at an average rate of 5 per cent per annum and this is expected to continue for the foreseeable future. The current rate of return on risk-free securities is 8 per cent and you consider that a risk premium of 4 per cent is appropriate for a share with the degree of risk associated with companies like H Ltd.

How much should you be prepared to pay for the share?

(c) Distinguish between specific and systematic risk.

<Obj 4, 5> **12.9** The summarised accounts of a property company for last year were as follows.

Income statement		
Net rental income		6,000,000
Less		
Interest on debentures	3,000,000	
Depreciation	150,000	
		3,150,000
		2,850,000
Interest received		100,000
		2,950,000
Less taxation		1,000,000
Net profit after tax		1,950,000
Less dividends		1,000,000
Added to reserves		950,000

Balance sheet

Current assets		3,000,000
Non-current assets		
Properties at cost	90,000,000	
Investments at cost		
5% debentures redeemable in 10 years,		
shown at cost at time of issue to the company	1,200,000	
		91,200,000
Total assets		94,200,000
Current liabilities		10,000,000
Non-current liabilities		
Debentures 6%		50,000,000
Total liabilities		60,000,000
Shareholders' equity		
Ordinary share capital (10 million shares)	25,000,000	
Reserves	9,200,000	
Total shareholders' equity		34,200,000
Total liabilities and shareholders' equity		94,200,000

Required:

From the above figures show:

(a) The market value of an ordinary share, on the basis of the price: earnings ratio of similar shares being 11.

(b) Earnings as a percentage of equity.

(c) The times covered for dividends

(d) An estimate of the value of the investment owned. The market yield on similar debentures is around 6 per cent and the debentures are redeemable in 10 years at a premium of 5 per cent.

<Obj 4, 5>   **12.10** The following are the summarised accounts for the last financial year of a small company making and selling soft drinks and dairy products for the local market.

Income statement

Revenue	1,500,000
Expenses	1,200,000
Net profit before tax	300,000
Taxation	100,000
Net profit after tax	200,000
Dividends	100,000
Added to retained profits	100,000

Balance sheet

Current assets	500,000
Non-current assets	1,000,000
Total assets	1,500,000

Current liabilities	300,000
Equity	
Share capital (issued at $1 per share)	1,000,000
Retained profits	200,000
Total liabilities and shareholders' equity	1,500,000

The shares are owned by two local businesspeople. The company was formed six years ago.

You have been approached by the two owners to see whether you are interested in buying shares in the company. They are prepared to issue a further 200,000 shares in the business. The owners have expressed the view that with this amount of additional capital they believe that the current rate of return can be maintained and that they would not envisage the dividend per share reducing below the current level.

Returns from companies in the same kind of business, quoted on the stock exchange, are on average as follows:

Dividend yield	5 per cent
Dividend cover	3 times
Price earnings ratio	10 times

The current going concern value of the non-current assets of the business is around $1.4m.

Return on capital has been fairly steady over the life of the business to date.

Required:

Suggest a reasonable price that you might be prepared to offer for each of the shares on offer. Explain the logic and identify other questions you would like answered before making a final decision.

<Obj 5>   **12.11**   Paul owns a light engineering business which is run by a manager who receives a salary of $60,000 a year. Paul does not work in the business but draws out $30,000 a year. He is now thinking of selling the business and his accountant has provided the following information.

Profits after tax and after drawings (all retained)

2003	$90,000
2004	$96,000
2005	$93,000

Balance sheet as at 31 December 2005

Current assets		
Inventory		35,000
Debtors		15,000
Short-term investments		80,000
Cash		1,000
		131,000
Non-current assets		
Goodwill	50,000	
Land & buildings	180,000	
Equipment (net of depreciation)	150,000	
		380,000
Total assets		511,000

Current liabilities	
Creditors	33,000
Capital	
Original contribution	200,000
Reserves	278,000
Total liabilities and owner's equity	511,000

Paul estimates that the land and buildings could be sold for $350,000 and that the market value of the securities is $60,000. He thinks that equipment in a similar condition to that used in the business could be bought for $200,000.

His accountant tells him that the market normally uses a 7:1 ratio of market value to profits after tax in arriving at a price for this type of business.

Required:

On the basis of the information provided calculate what the minimum and maximum prices Paul might reasonably expect.

What other factors might impact on the final price?

CHALLENGING

<Obj 4, 5, 6>

12.12 In order to achieve vertical integration Colleen Ltd offered at 1 January 2006 to acquire all the share capital of David Ltd. The purchase consideration for each share in David Ltd was:

Ordinary shares issued at $1 per share—one share in Colleen issued at $1 per share.

7% preference shares (issued at $1)—$1.20 in cash.

All shares are quoted on the stock exchange.

Relevant accounting data is set out below:

Balance sheets	Colleen Ltd $'000s	David Ltd $'000s
Net current assets	9,000	13,000
Non-current assets (Net)	55,000	70,000
Goodwill	10,000	4,000
	74,000	87,000
Loans and debentures	14,000	20,000
Ordinary share capital ($1)	20,000	30,000
7% Preference shares ($1)	–	5,000
Reserves	40,000	32,000
	74,000	87,000

Profits		
2003	7,000	10,000
2004	8,000	5,000
2005	12,000	11,000

Dividends		
2003	20 cents per share	10 cents per share
2004	20 cents per share	8 cents per share
2005 forecast	20 cents per share	15 cents per share

Ordinary share price

2003	$2–$2.50	$1.80–$2.80
2004	$2.80–$5	$2.20–$4
2005	$4–$4.60	$3.20–$4

Required:

Provide a brief report to your client who owns 10,000 ordinary shares and 2,000 preference shares in David Ltd, advising on the offer.

<Obj 4, 5, 6, 7>

12.13 Matt Ltd and James Ltd are both manufacturers of similar products. Their summarised income statements and balance sheets are as shown below:

	Matt Ltd $'000s	James Ltd $'000s
Income statement for the year ending 31 December 2005		
Sales	90,000	20,000
Operating expenses	84,000	17,000
Net profit before tax	6,000	3,000
Tax	2,000	1,000
Net profit after tax	4,000	2,000
Dividends	2,000	2,000
Added to reserves	2,000	–
Balance sheet as at 31 December 2005		
Net current assets	10,000	1,500
Non-current assets	32,000	6,000
	42,000	7,500
Ordinary share capital issued at $1	10,000	5,000
Reserves	32,000	2,500
	42,000	7,500

Dividends were paid on the last day of the year.

The current market value (December 31 2005) of Matt Ltd shares is $2.10 a share. For some time the company has adopted a dividend payout ratio of 50%. The company intends to retain this policy as it has resulted in an annual growth rate of 6% in profits and dividends. This growth rate is expected to continue indefinitely.

James Ltd shares are currently valued at $1.05 each. Profit has been stable for many years and this is unlikely to change in the foreseeable future. Associated with this is a decision to pay out all of its profits as a dividend.

The Directors of Matt Ltd are now considering whether to buy out the shares of James Ltd in full. They believe that they could increase the returns by a further $1,000,000 in the next year. They could also rationalise the non-current assets needed and would sell off some of James Ltd's assets for $800,000. They consider that the takeover would reduce the risk of the combined businesses with a consequent reduction in the required rate of return of 1 per cent. The 50 per cent dividend payout ratio would remain, with an expectation that the growth rate of 5 per cent would then apply to the enlarged business.

Required:

(a) Calculate the maximum price that Matt Ltd should be prepared to pay for shares of James Ltd.

(b) Determine the minimum price that the ordinary shareholders of James Ltd should be prepared to accept for their shares.

(c) Discuss briefly any other factors that the directors and shareholders of both companies might consider in assessing the desirability of the proposed takeover.

<Obj 5>

12.14 One of your clients is considering purchasing the consultancy practice of a local business whose latest balance sheet is as follows:

Balance sheet as at 31 December 2005		
Current assets		
Debtors		75,000
Non-current assets		
Freehold premises at cost		500,000
Equipment at cost	70,000	
Less accumulated depreciation	20,000	
		50,000
Vehicles at cost	75,000	
Less accumulated depreciation	40,000	
		35,000
Total assets		660,000
Current liabilities		
Creditors and accruals	30,000	
Bank overdraft	50,000	
		80,000
Capital		
Opening balance	600,000	
Net profit for the year	180,000	
	780,000	
less Drawings	200,000	
		580,000
Total liabilities and owner's equity		660,000

Your client estimates the current value of the non-current assets as:

	Replacement cost	Realisable value
Premises	800,000	750,000
Equipment	75,000	30,000
Vehicles	50,000	35,000

In addition to the non-current assets your client expects to take over the current assets and liabilities of the business. However, he believes that around $8,000 of the debtors are likely to prove bad.

The profits for the business over the last five years are as shown below:

2001	200,000
2002	160,000
2003	190,000
2004	175,000
2005	180,000

Your client has recently inherited $2 million, which is currently invested in a very low-risk area and is currently earning an annual rate of interest of 6 per cent. If he buys the business he will purchase it out of the inheritance. He is currently employed and is earning $80,000 pa. He would probably give this job up if he were to take over and work in the business.

Required:

Advise your client as to how much he might offer for the business.

Explain any calculations that support your recommendations and indicate what other information would be useful before a final decision is made.

CASE STUDY

12.1

The chapter discusses risk and risk premiums. It does not address the attitude of individuals to risk. The two short articles below provide some interesting implications.

The articles were from *The Age* of 6 November 2004, the Business section page 5, both by Simon Hoyle. The first provided 'A guide for the upwardly mobile with a fear of heights'. The second was entitled 'Risk tolerance: how do you rate?'

Read them and then consider the questions that follow.

A guide for the upwardly mobile with a fear of heights

Adventure companies are adept at nudging clients into the zone between comfort and panic — a crucial skill for a financial planner. Simon Hoyle reports

WHETHER you're hanging from a rope at the top of a sheer cliff, or about to commit your life savings to the sharemarket, the last thing you want to do is lose sight of why you're there, how you got there and what you must do next.

Brett Sheridan, director of marketing and strategic development for the adventure experiences company Corporate Adrenalin, says measuring, controlling and understanding the risks you're facing is the best way to minimise the chances of panicking and making an incorrect — and possibly catastrophic — decision.

'We call it RAM: risk assessment management. It means identifying risks and measuring on a scale where there are critical risks, or something we can avoid by doing something differently,' he says.

An individual's personality and tolerance for taking risks will dictate how far Sheridan allows an experience to go — but regardless of personality type, the principles are the same.

'If you draw a circle, draw a ring around it, and draw another ring around that, we go out of the circle into the first ring, and that's out of your comfort zone. The second ring, that's an area you do not want to operate in. If you go into the "fear zone", it becomes detrimental.

'The more educated you are, the less risk-averse you become. What I mean by that is, if you're standing at the top of a cliff, if your instruction is right, if you've been taught to trust in your equipment and you're told to just concentrate on having a good time or enjoying the task — people's acceptance of the risks, through knowledge, goes up.'

Risk means different things to different people. Geoff Davey, managing director of financial risk assessment group FinaMetrica, says there are four broad categories of risk: physical, financial, social and ethical. Physical risk is self-explanatory: it's the risk of being injured or killed. Financial risk is the risk of losing money. Social risk is the fear of embarrassment, and ethical risk is the fear of being shamed by your actions.

'People behave consistently within a category, but not across categories,' Davey says. In other words, you might be quite willing to dangle from a rope at the top of a cliff but are scared stiff of investing in the sharemarket.

Sheridan has seen senior financial services figures reduced to gibbering wrecks at a cliff edge—the same people who don't blink when it comes to making significant and far-reaching financial decisions.

That's why it can be tricky to assess accurately how much risk an investor might be prepared to take with their investments. Outwardly, they might seem to be a risk taker—they enjoy extreme sports, for example—but this attitude does not translate to money matters. It might, but it ain't necessarily so.

Nevertheless, getting a good handle on your attitude towards risk, and your capacity to cope with it, is an absolutely crucial first step in putting together an effective financial plan.

Davey says there are two elements to a risk assessment: the first is risk capacity, the second, risk tolerance. 'Risk capacity is a hard financial number, which you get from doing an analysis of an individual's financial affairs. The other you get from an analysis of the investor's psyche.'

Both are important. The first is an assessment of your actual resources, and your ability to physically withstand a loss of money. The odd thing is that risk capacity and risk tolerance aren't always linked. A high risk capacity does not necessarily mean you have a high risk tolerance.

Why are both important?

Most investors have fairly optimistic goals. We wouldn't be human if we didn't. In many cases, the goals aren't achievable with the level of financial resources we have. In other words, we might want to retire with $1 million in our pockets, but if we're earning $50,000 a year, and we have other commitments such as school fees and mortgages, that target is unreasonable.

That is where a financial planner brings together an understanding of both risk tolerance and risk capacity. By assessing your financial resources today and knowing where you want to be, and understanding your risk tolerance assessment, they can try to bridge the inevitable gap.

It might mean educating us on what risk is and why we might need to take a bit more of it if we want to get to where we're aiming, or it might mean lowering our expectations a bit. Or both.

Risk tolerance: how do you rate?

UNDERSTANDING your tolerance for risk is as important when investing as it is when you're about to undertake a dangerous physical activity.

FinaMetrica's managing director, Geoff Davey, feels so strongly about its importance that he's put his risk assessment tool on the internet.

Anyone can log on to www.myrisktolerance.com and, for a fee, fill out a questionnaire and receive a rigorous assessment of his or her risk tolerance.

It's the same questionnaire a financial planner who uses the FinaMetrica assessment would use, but now that it's online you can learn about your attitude towards and tolerance for financial risk even before you discuss strategies and investment options with a planner.

There are 25 questions in the FinaMetrica assessment. They range from whether you would fix the interest rate on all or part of your home loan, or stay with your lender's variable rate, to how much you believe your investments could decline in value before you would start to feel uneasy.

Davey says the questions are structured so that the same sort of information is sought in a couple of different ways, to ensure consistency.

Some questions are quite explicit while others are subtle. For example, there's a question about a house you inherit that could increase significantly in value if you spent money on it, but there's a chance of a freeway being built nearby that could harm its value—would you spend the money?

1. What is your attitude to risk when it comes to investing?

 Specifically, if you were retiring, what kind of risks would you take?

 By way of illustration, Unisuper, the superannuation fund responsible for university staff, has a range of investment options which include cash, capital stable, conservative balanced, balanced, growth, socially responsible shares and shares. Returns and risks are quite different across these categories. How would you choose between them?

2. If you were aged 60 and retiring what category would you select? What other factors might influence your decision?

3. Would your attitude towards risk change if you were talking about a one-off investment that represented quite a small portion of your savings?

4. Do you agree with the assertion that 'the more educated you are the less risk averse you become'? Why/why not?

5. Do you agree with the statement that 'people behave consistently within a category, but not across categories'? Why/why not?

6. How might fundamentally different attitudes to extreme sport and financial investments occur?

7. Which of risk capacity or risk tolerance represents the limiting factor for you in decision making? Explain.

8. What circumstances might lead to the situation in which someone who has a high risk capacity might have a low risk tolerance, and vice-versa?

9. In the second article there is reference to a question about a house that you inherit which could increase significantly in value if you spend money on it, but there is a chance of a freeway being built nearby that could harm its value. How would you deal with this situation?

10. There is also a question about when you might choose to fix the interest rate on your mortgage. How would you make a decision of this sort?

CASE STUDY
12.2

The article in this case study provides an interesting perspective on the bond market that is rather different from usual. The article, from *Australian CPA*, August 2003, pages 52–3, looks at the implications of past government policy and the benefits provided by the current bond market. Read the article and then consider the questions that follow.

Shaken, not stirred, the Aussie bond market

Plans by Howard and co to scrap government bonds have been rethought. Susan Campbell looks at the implications of their debt-free dream and the benefits provided by the current market

Bitter debate on the appropriate level of government debt has raged for years. Is it really too high? Do governments need to carry it round their necks like a millstone? Generally, the anti-debt factions have appeared to have the upper hand for a while now. But in an interesting turn of events some financial market experts are now saying that public sector debt is too small and that our elected representatives must take an active role to keep the government bonds market alive.

 Last year prime minister John Howard and his fellow parliamentarians seriously considered winding down the government debt market. Treasurer Peter Costello had indicated he was inclined to allow the market to continue to contract by using assets sales to repay debt. With that backdrop, in late October 2002, treasury's debt management review team released *Review of the*

Commonwealth Government Securities Market, a 160-page paper (go to http://debtreview. treasury.gov.au). The market responded with 40 written submissions and 120 consultative meetings with most interested parties arguing that eliminating government bonds would impede efficient risk management measures for fund managers and traders.

The bond market was genuinely concerned that its market was being threatened by Costello's ambition to be the world's first treasurer overseeing a debt-free government. These fears were allayed, however, when he committed to retaining the Commonwealth government bond market.

In May 2003, the then head of the debt review team, Blair Comley, in a presentation to the finance and treasury association's Adding Value to Government Financing conference, indicated that the commonwealth had accepted the view that the CGS market assists efficient interest rate risk management, and that diversity within the financial system helped reduce vulnerability to shocks. Comley, now acting head of the Australian office of financial management, added: 'That the decision is not specifically targeted at meeting investor demand for risk-free financial assets.'

The government has now accepted the argument that the market should be kept alive and indicated it would structure issuance of bonds to underpin liquidity for the key three-year and 10-year bond futures contracts used by many financial market players to manage risk exposures. The government will aim to have about $5 billion in stock for each of the eight or so maturity lines of debt needed for effective liquidity which means just over $40bn of outstanding debt.

Paul Bide, head of debt markets division, Macquarie Bank, considers that last year's review was a useful exercise. 'The proposition that financial markets, the banking system and proper risk management and identification were inextricably linked was allowed to be tested by the process treasury undertook and the government bond market is better off for that having taken place as its role is better understood by a broader group of people.'

To put this into perspective it is worth considering the total size of the Australian bond market currently. According to ANZ Investment Bank head of credit research, Kate Birchall, there was a total pool of $154bn of bonds on issue as at May this year. The largest sector is actually the semi-government bond market at 35 per cent, followed by the Commonwealth government bond market at 31 per cent. The corporate bond market, which has seen rapid growth in the 1990s, comes in at 27 per cent.

Birchall does not believe that the changes indicated in the 2003–2004 budget will have any material impact on the financial markets and ANZ believe that the CGB market will retain its traditional role of proving a risk-free alternative for investors.

Estimates suggest that CGS outstandings will increase marginally from $60.4bn to $63.4bn.

Macquarie Bank's Bide sees the treasurer's statement in the recent budget (Budget Paper No. 7) as endorsing the CGS market as having a central, unique and important role to play as facilitating risk management in the economy.

He says: 'That bodes well for the future of the market.

'The right size of the market is a hard issue to be explicit about. Where this issue has rested is that the government has committed to maintain the CGS market to the point where the Sydney futures exchange can offer and administer its two bond futures contracts.

'It is generally understood that to run these two contracts, the CGS market needs to be at least large enough to have $15bn of stock in at least three lines for each contract plus $15bn of stock in lines "outside" the stock that would be included in each contract.'

Toby Johnston, investment strategist, Alliance Capital Management Australia Ltd, says that the projected Budget surpluses are actually quite small due to tax cuts, extra spending on defence and the delayed sale of the remainder of Telstra. 'These surpluses are highly dependent on the government's economic growth forecasts,' he points out. 'If growth is weaker than forecast, the surpluses will be smaller and in fact the Budget may go into deficit. This uncertainty underscores the importance of maintaining a viable bond market.'

In addition, some aspects of government spending benefit both the current and future generations. An example is increased defence spending. Why should today's taxpayers share the whole burden of paying for a service that is critical to the security of current and future generations? In other words, issuing long-dated debt to pay for projects that benefit future generations is an equitable and efficient way to fund such projects. 'Maintaining an active and viable bond market makes both economic and social sense,' adds Johnston.

James Wright, head of fixed interest at ING Investment Management, believes that the volume of government debt on issue has huge implications for Australian fixed interest investors. 'Over the past few years,' he says, 'the fall in government bonds on issue has been offset by the increase in corporate borrowers raising funds in the public capital markets [shifting from traditional bank funding].

'However, the growing demands from Australian superannuation funds for investment grade fixed interest assets is overwhelming the potential supply.'

A shortage of conventional fixed income assets will force Australians to invest in foreign bonds and by doing so they will have to take on foreign currency, sovereign and credit risks.

With the equity market continuing to look risky, bonds are becoming increasingly popular for superannuation and other fund managers.

Under most circumstances envisaged, and despite the government's commitment to maintain the current level of liquid benchmark bonds (around $45bn), it is likely that there will be greater flows offshore to international sovereign and credit portfolios. 'Domestic credit markets will continue to be well supported, although they are likely to fall in percentage terms as the international component of fixed interest assets held by superannuation funds increases,' adds Wright.

And what about the semi-government debt securities? Though this is still an active market it is unlikely we are going to see any state government increase the size of its debt in the near term. This restriction on supply will ensure that yields remain low for investors. Super funds and private investors have been pushing up the demand for secure good credit investments such as Commonwealth and semi-government bonds which will keep the price continually bid.

But another big question arises now that the government is committed to keeping the bond market alive, what will it do with the proceeds? This is also a question that should concern all taxpayers in Australia. What will the government do with the surplus? Any government must be accountable for the surplus funds. The most talked about usage of a surplus is to apply the cash balances as a sinking fund to the unfunded superannuation liabilities. The unfunded superannuation liability is already beginning to bite at state and local government levels. Some local councils already have to put up rates to meet the shortfall in their funding.

Overall, Bide from Macquarie Bank feels that the final impact on the financial markets of the governments decision is very positive. 'It allows those who are currently managing financial risks in the CGS framework to feel comfortable that key infrastructure will remain. Systemic stability is not threatened and the ability to raise debt capital and ability to identify and trade financial risks is assured, or is at least as good as we can do as a financial market.'

Susan Campbell is a treasury consultant and freelance business writer.

---

1   What do you think are the main advantages of retaining the bond market?
2   What is the size and nature of the Australian bond market?
3   What is the traditional role of the Commonwealth government bond market?
4   What is the importance of the bond market in facilitating risk management in the economy?
5   Explain the advantages of the bond market for inter-generational equity issues such as the amount of funding spent on long-term defence needs.
6   Explain the importance of the bond market for superannuation funds.

SOLUTIONS TO ACTIVITIES

Activity 12.1

Similar calculations for the other three required rates of return give prices of $80.98 (10 per cent return), $66.39 (16 per cent return) and $107.65 (2 per cent return).

Activity 12.2

(a) The price will be arrived at by working out the present value of the cash inflows, discounted at the required rate of return. Given that interest is paid semi-annually, the cash flows can be calculated over 10 periods using a discount rate of 5 per cent per period. The calculation is shown below:

Period	cash flow	discount factor	PV
1	30	.952	28.56
2	30	.907	27.21
3	30	.864	25.92
4	30	.823	24.69
5	30	.784	23.52
6	30	.746	22.38
7	30	.711	21.33
8	30	.677	20.31
9	30	.645	19.35
10	1,130	.614	693.82
			907.09

The price should have been $907.

   A quicker method would be to use annuity tables or formulae as follows:

   PV of an annuity of $30 over 10 periods, discounted at 5 per cent = 30 × 7.722 = 231.66,

   plus PV of the maturity value = 1,100 × .614 = 675.4

   which totals $907.

(b) When comparing the cost with the present value of the inflows the NPV at 10 per cent is $107 ($907 − 800). This implies that the yield (or internal rate of return) is greater than 10 per cent. How much more? If we try 14 per cent the PV of the inflows will be:

   PV of an annuity of $30 over 10 periods, discounted at 7 per cent = 30 × 7.024 = 210.72, plus

   PV of the maturity value = 1,100 × .508 = 558.8

   which totals $770.

The NPV at 14 per cent is therefore −30 (−800 + 770), so the yield is less than 14 per cent.

By interpolation the yield is 10% + (107 / 137)4 = 13.1%

Activity 12.3

$$PV = 4 / 0.10 = \$40$$

Activity 12.4

No, because there is probably no expectation that the long-term interest rate will rise. Rather this increase is likely to be relatively short term. It is expectations of the long-term rate which are the more important.

Activity 12.5

(a) The result is likely to be that investors see higher risks and greater uncertainty resulting and will require higher returns. Hence the PE ratio will fall.

(b) If the earnings remained the same, the share price would fall to 7 × 50c = $3.50.

Of course, it isn't that simple. The process of moving from 10 to 7 is unclear. If earnings did not fall, confidence might be re-established with a move back up towards 10.

OBJECTIVES

When you have completed your study of this chapter you should be able to:

1 list the items making up working capital

2 discuss the nature and importance of working capital

3 illustrate the working capital cycle

4 demonstrate an understanding of the importance of inventory and the techniques available to facilitate efficient and effective management of this asset

5 discuss the provision of credit to customers and utilise various management tools in monitoring and controlling this asset

6 explain the reasons for holding cash and the basis of management and control

7 summarise the key aspects of creditor management.

THE MANAGEMENT OF WORKING CAPITAL

13

In this chapter we consider the factors that must be taken into account when managing the working capital of a business. Each element of working capital will be identified and the major issues surrounding them will be discussed.

THE NATURE AND PURPOSE OF WORKING CAPITAL

Working capital is usually defined as current assets less current liabilities.

The main elements of current assets are:

* inventory
* accounts receivable (trade debtors)
* cash (in hand and at bank).

The main element of current liabilities is:

* accounts payable (trade creditors).

The size and composition of working capital can vary between industries. For some types of business, the investment in working capital can be substantial. For example, a manufacturing company will invest heavily in raw materials, work-in-progress and finished goods and will often sell its goods on credit thereby incurring trade debtors. A retailer, on the other hand, will hold only one form of inventory (finished goods) and will usually sell goods for cash.

Working capital represents a net investment in short-term assets. These assets are continually flowing into and out of the business and are essential for day-to-day operations. The various elements of working capital are interrelated and can be seen as part of a short-term cycle. For a manufacturing business, the working capital cycle can be depicted as shown in Figure 13.1.

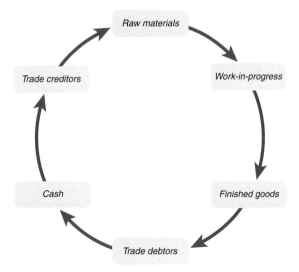

FIGURE 13.1 The working capital cycle

The management of working capital is an essential part of the short-term planning process. It is necessary for management to decide how much of each element should be held. As we shall see later, there are costs associated with holding both too much and too little of each element. Management must be aware of these in order to manage effectively. Management must also be aware that there may be other, more profitable, uses for the funds of the business. Hence, the potential benefits must be weighed against the likely costs in order to achieve the optimum investment.

Working capital needs are likely to change over time as a result of changes in the business environment. This means that working capital decisions are rarely 'one-off' decisions. Managers must try to identify changes occurring so as to ensure that the level of investment in working capital is appropriate.

ACTIVITY 13.1

What kind of changes in the business environment might lead to a decision to change the level of investment in working capital? Try to identify four possible changes that could affect the working capital needs of a business.

In addition to changes in the external environment, changes arising within the business, such as changes in production methods (resulting, perhaps, in a need to hold less inventory) and changes in the level of risk managers are prepared to take, could alter the required level of investment in working capital.

The management of working capital is a significant issue because this item often represents a substantial investment for a business. The significance depends on the nature of the business. The Coles Myer group, for example, had current assets in the early 2000s amounting to 80 per cent of the figure for non-current assets. Approximately half of the current assets could be said to be funded by current liabilities, but the investment in working capital remains considerable. By comparison, BHP typically had current assets at a level that amounted to less than 25 per cent of the non-current assets, with a substantial portion of these current assets being funded by current liabilities. The difference reflects the fundamentally different nature of their businesses.

In the sections that follow we will consider each element of working capital separately. We will examine the factors that must be considered to ensure their proper management.

THE MANAGEMENT OF INVENTORIES

A business may hold inventories for various reasons. The most common reason is, of course, to meet the immediate day-to-day requirements of customers and production. However, a business may hold more than is necessary for this purpose if it is believed that future supplies may be interrupted or scarce. Similarly, if the business believes that the cost of inventory will rise in the future it may decide to stockpile.

For some types of business the inventory held may represent a substantial proportion of the total assets held. For example, a car dealership that rents its premises may have nearly all of its total assets in the form of inventory. In the case of manufacturing businesses, inventory levels tend to be higher than in many other forms of business as it is necessary to hold three kinds of inventory—raw materials, work-in-progress and finished goods. Each form of inventory represents a particular stage in the production cycle. For some types of business the level of inventory held may vary substantially over the year due to the seasonal nature of the industry—for example, greetings card manufacturers—whereas for other businesses inventory levels may remain fairly stable throughout the year.

Where a business holds inventory simply to meet the day-to-day requirements of its customers and production, it will normally seek to minimise the amount held. This is because there are significant costs associated with holding inventories. These include storage and handling costs, financing costs, the risks of pilferage and obsolescence, and the opportunities forgone in tying up funds in this form of asset. However, a business must also recognise that if the level of inventory held is too low there will be associated costs.

 ACTIVITY 13.2

What costs might a business incur as a result of holding too low a level of inventory? Try to jot down at least three types of cost.

To try to ensure that inventories are properly managed, a number of procedures and techniques may be employed. These are reviewed below.

Forecasts of future demand

In order for there to be inventory available to meet future sales a business must produce appropriate forecasts. These forecasts should deal with each product line. It is important that every attempt is made to ensure the accuracy of these forecasts as they will determine future ordering and production levels. These forecasts may be derived in various ways. They may be developed using statistical techniques such as time series analysis, or may be based on the judgment of the sales and marketing staff.

Financial ratios

One ratio that can be used to help monitor inventory levels is the inventory turnover period which we examined in Chapter 6. You may recall that this ratio is calculated as follows:

$$\text{Inventory turnover period} = \frac{\text{Average inventory held}}{\text{Cost of sales}} \times 365$$

This will provide a picture of the average period for which inventory is held and can be useful as a basis for comparison. It is possible to calculate the turnover period for individual product lines as well as for inventory as a whole.

Recording and re-ordering systems

The management of inventory in a business of any size requires a sound system of recording inventory movements. There must be proper procedures for recording purchases and sales. Periodic checks may be required to ensure the amount of physical inventory held is consistent with the inventory records.

There should also be clear procedures for the re-ordering of inventory. Authorisation for both the purchase and issue of inventory should be confined to a few senior staff if problems of duplication and lack of coordination are to be avoided. To determine the point at which inventory should be re-ordered, information concerning the lead time (i.e. the time between the placing of an order and the receipt of the goods) and the likely level of demand will be required.

ACTIVITY 13.3

An electrical retailer keeps a particular type of light switch as part of its inventory. The annual demand for the light switch is 10,400 units and the lead time for orders is four weeks. Demand for the inventory is steady throughout the year. At what level of inventory should the company re-order, assuming that the company is confident of the figures mentioned above?

In most businesses there will be some uncertainty surrounding the above factors and so a buffer or safety stock level may be maintained in case problems occur. The amount of safety stock to be held is really a matter of judgment and will depend on the degree of uncertainty concerning the above factors. However, the likely costs of running out of inventory must also be taken into account.

Levels of control

Management must make a commitment to the management of inventory. However, the cost of controlling inventory must be weighed against the potential benefits. It may be possible to have different levels of control according to the nature of the inventory held. The **ABC system of inventory control** is based on the idea of selective levels of control.

A business may find that it is possible to divide its inventory into three broad categories—A, B and C. Each category will be based on the value of inventory held. Category A will represent the high-value items. It may be the case, however, that although the items are high in value and represent a high proportion of the total value of inventory held, they are a relatively small proportion of the total volume of inventory held. For example, 10 per cent of the physical inventory held may account for 65 per cent of the total value. For these items, management may decide to implement sophisticated recording procedures, exert tight control over inventory movements and have a high level of security at the inventory location.

Category B will represent less valuable items held. Perhaps 30 per cent of the total volume of inventory may account for 25 per cent of the total value held. For this category a lower level of recording and management control would be appropriate. Category C will represent the least valuable items. Say 60 per cent of the volume of inventory may account for 10 per cent of the total value held. For these items the level of recording and management control would be lower still. Categorising inventory in this way (see Figure 13.2) can help to ensure that management effort is directed to the most important areas and that the costs of controlling stocks are commensurate with their value.

Stock/inventory management models

It is possible to use decision models to help manage inventory. The **economic order quantity (EOQ)** model is concerned with answering the question, 'How much inventory should be ordered?' In its simplest form the EOQ model assumes that demand is constant, so that inventories will be depleted evenly over time and will be replenished just at the point the inventory runs out. These assumptions would lead to a 'sawtooth' pattern to represent inventory movements within a business, as shown in Figure 13.3.

The EOQ model recognises that the total cost of inventory is made up of the cost of holding inventory and the costs of ordering inventory. It calculates the optimum size of a purchase order by taking account of both of these cost elements. The cost of holding inventory can be substantial and so management may try to reduce the average amount of inventory held to as low a level as possible. However, by reducing the level of inventory held, and therefore the holding costs, there will be a need to increase the number of orders during the period and so ordering costs will rise.

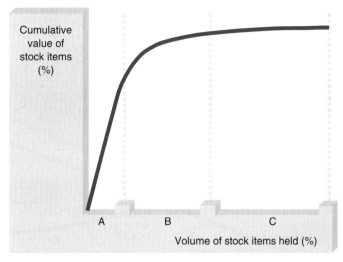

FIGURE 13.2 ABC method of analysing and controlling stock

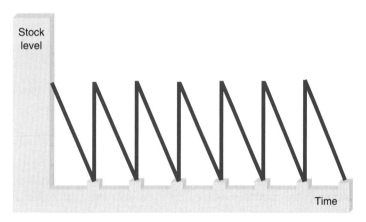

FIGURE 13.3 Pattern of inventory movements over time

Figure 13.4 shows that as the level of inventory and the size of orders increase, the annual costs of placing orders will probably decrease because fewer orders will be placed. However, the cost of holding inventory will increase as there will be higher inventory levels. The total costs curve, which is a function of the holding costs and ordering costs, will fall to a minimum level. Thereafter, total costs begin to rise. The point of minimum costs corresponds with an inventory level E as shown in the figure.

The EOQ model seeks to identify the size of the order that minimises the total costs. If this can be achieved the EOQ will represent the optimum amount which should be ordered on each occasion.

The EOQ can be calculated by using the following equation:

$$EOQ = \sqrt{\frac{2DC}{H}}$$

where D = the annual demand for the item of stock
         C = the cost of placing an order
         H = the cost of holding one unit of stock for one year.

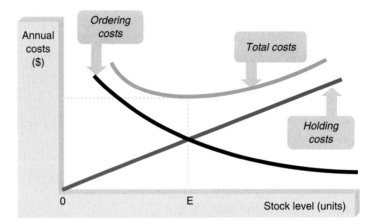

FIGURE 13.4 Stockholding and stock order costs

ACTIVITY 13.4

HLA Ltd sells 2,000 units of product X each year. It has been estimated that the cost of holding one unit of the product for a year is $4. The cost of placing an order for stock is estimated at $25.

Calculate the EOQ for the product.

The EOQ model has a number of limiting assumptions. In particular, it assumes that demand for the product can be predicted with accuracy and that this demand is even over the period and does not fluctuate through seasonality or other reasons. It also assumes that no 'buffer' stock is required. However, these limiting assumptions do not mean we should dismiss the model as being of little value. The model can be developed to accommodate the problems of uncertainty and uneven demand. Many businesses use this model (or a development of it) to help in the management of inventory.

Materials requirements planning (MRP) systems

Materials requirements planning takes as its starting point forecasts of sales demand. It then uses computer technology to help schedule the timing of deliveries of bought-in parts and materials to coincide with production requirements to meet the demand. It is a coordinated approach which links materials and parts deliveries to their scheduled input to the production process. By ordering only those items that are necessary to ensure the flow of production, inventory levels may therefore be reduced. MRP is really a 'top-down' approach to inventory management which recognises that inventory ordering decisions cannot be viewed as being independent from production decisions. In more recent years this approach has been extended so as to provide a fully integrated approach to production planning which also takes account of other manufacturing resources such as labour and machine capacity.

Just-in-time (JIT) stock/inventory management

In recent years some manufacturing businesses have tried to eliminate the need to hold inventory by adopting a '**just-in-time**' approach. This method was first used in the US defence industry during the Second World War but in more recent times has been widely used by Japanese businesses. The essence of this approach is, as the name suggests, to have supplies delivered to a business just in time for them to be used in the production process. By adopting this approach the stockholding problem rests with the suppliers rather than the business.

In order for this approach to be successful it is important for the business to inform suppliers of their production plans and requirements in advance and for suppliers to deliver materials of the right quality at the agreed times. Failure to do so could lead to a dislocation of production and could be very costly. Thus, a close relationship between the business and its suppliers is required.

Although a business will not have to hold inventory, there may be certain costs associated with this approach. As the suppliers will be required to hold inventory for the business they may try to recoup this additional cost through increased prices. The close relationship necessary between the business and its suppliers may also prevent the business from taking advantage of cheaper sources of supply when they become available.

Many people view JIT as more than simply an inventory control system. The philosophy underpinning this method is concerned with eliminating waste and striving for excellence. There is an expectation that suppliers will always deliver parts on time and that there will be no defects in the parts supplied. There is also an expectation that the production process will operate at maximum efficiency. This means there will be no production breakdowns and the queuing and storage times of products manufactured will be eliminated as only that time spent directly on processing the products is seen as adding value. While these expectations may be impossible to achieve, they do help to create a culture that is dedicated to the pursuit of excellence.

THE MANAGEMENT OF DEBTORS

Selling goods or services on credit results in costs being incurred by a business. These costs include credit administration costs, bad debts and opportunities forgone in using the funds for more profitable purposes. However, these costs must be weighed against the benefits of increased sales resulting from the opportunity for customers to delay payment.

Selling on credit is very widespread and appears to be the norm outside the retail trade. When a business offers to sell its goods or services on credit it must have clear policies concerning:

* which customers it is prepared to offer credit to
* what length of credit it is prepared to offer
* whether discounts will be offered for prompt payment
* what collection policies should be adopted.

In this section we will consider each of these issues.

Which customers should receive credit?

A business offering credit runs the risk of not receiving payment for goods or services supplied. Thus, care must be taken over the type of customer to whom credit facilities are offered. When considering a proposal from a customer for the supply of goods or services on credit the business must take a number of factors into account. The following 'five Cs of credit' provide a business with a useful checklist:

* *Capital.* The customer must appear to be financially sound before any credit is extended. Where the customer is a business, its accounts should be examined. Particular regard should be given to the profitability and liquidity of the customer, and any onerous financial commitments must be taken into account.

* *Capacity.* The customer must appear to have the capacity to pay amounts owing. Where possible, the payment record of the customer to date should be examined. If the customer is a business, the type of business operated and the physical resources of the business will be relevant. The value of goods that the customer wishes to buy on credit must be related to the total financial resources of the customer.

* *Collateral.* On occasions it may be necessary to ask for some kind of security for goods supplied on credit. When this occurs, the business must be convinced that the customer is able to offer a satisfactory form of security.

* *Conditions.* The state of the industry in which the customer operates and the general economic conditions of the particular region or country may have an important influence on the ability of a customer to pay the amounts outstanding on the due date.

* *Character.* It is important for a business to make some assessment of the character of the customer. The willingness to pay will depend on the honesty and integrity of the individual with whom the business is dealing. Where the customer is a limited company this will mean assessing the characters of its directors. The business must feel satisfied that the customer will make every effort to pay any amounts owing.

Once a customer has been found creditworthy, credit limits for the customer should be established and procedures should be laid down to ensure that these credit limits are adhered to.

ACTIVITY 13.5

Assume you are the credit manager of a business and that a limited company approached you with a view to buying goods on credit. What sources of information might you decide to use to help assess the financial health of the potential customer?

Length of credit period

A business must determine what credit terms it is prepared to offer its customers. The length of credit offered to customers can vary significantly between businesses and may be influenced by various factors. These factors may include:

* the typical credit terms operating within the industry
* the degree of competition within the industry
* the bargaining power of particular customers
* the risk of non-payment
* the capacity of the business to offer credit
* the marketing strategy of the business.

The last point identified may require some explanation. The marketing strategy of a business may have an important influence on the length of credit allowed. For example, if a business wishes to increase its market share it may decide to liberalise its credit policy in order to stimulate sales. Potential customers may be attracted by the offer of a longer period in which to pay. However, any such change in policy must take account of the likely costs and benefits arising.

To illustrate this point consider the following example.

EXAMPLE

13.1

Senior Ltd was formed in 2005 in order to produce a new type of golf putter. The company sells the putter to wholesalers and retailers and has an annual sales turnover of $1.2 million. The following data relate to each putter produced.

	$	$
Selling price		72
Variable costs	36	
Fixed cost apportionment	12	48
Net profit		24

The cost of capital (before tax) of Senior Ltd is estimated at 15 per cent.

Senior Ltd wishes to expand sales of this new putter and believes this can be done by offering a longer period in which to pay. The average collection period of the company is currently 30 days. The company is considering three options in order to increase sales. These are as follows:

	Option		
	1	2	3
Increase in average collection period (days)	10	20	30
Increase in sales ($)	60,000	90,000	100,000

Prepare calculations to show which credit policy the company should offer its customers.

In order to decide on the best option to adopt, the company must weigh the benefits of each option against their respective costs. The benefits arising will be represented by the increase in profit from the sale of additional putters. From the cost data supplied we can see that the contribution (i.e. sales less variable costs) is $36 per putter. This represents 50 per cent of the selling price. The fixed costs can be ignored in our calculations as they will remain the same whichever option is chosen.

The increase in contribution under each option will therefore be:

	Option		
	1	2	3
50 per cent of increase in sales	30,000	45,000	50,000

The increase in debtors under each option will be as follows:

	Option		
	1	2	3
Planned level of debtors			
1,260,000 × 40 / 365	138,082		
1,290,000 × 50 / 365		176,712	
1,300,000 × 60 / 365			213,699

Less current level of debtors
1,200,000 × 30 / 365

98,630	98,630	98,630
39,452	78,082	115,069

The increase in debtors which results from each option will mean an additional cost to the company, since the company has an estimated cost of capital of 15 per cent. Thus the increase in the additional investment in debtors will be:

	Option	
1	2	3

Cost of additional investment (15 per cent of increase in debtors)	(5,918)	(11,712)	(17,260)

The net increase in profits will be:

	Option	
1	2	3

Cost of additional investment (15 per cent of increase in debtors)	(5,918)	(11,712)	(17,260)
Increase in contribution (see above)	30,000	45,000	50,000
Net increase in profits	24,082	33,288	32,740

The calculations show that option 2 will be the most profitable one for the company. However, there is little to choose between options 2 and 3.

The above example illustrates the way in which a business should assess changes in credit terms. However, if there is a risk that, by extending the length of credit, there will be an increase in bad debts this should also be taken into account in the calculations. Similarly, if additional collection costs are incurred this should also be taken into account.

Cash discounts (early settlement)

A business may decide to offer a cash discount in order to encourage prompt payment from its credit customers. The size of any discount will be an important influence on whether a customer decides to pay promptly.

From the point of view of the business, the cost of offering discounts must be weighed against the likely benefits in the form of a reduction in the cost of financing debtors and any reduction in the amount of bad debts.

In practice, there is always the danger that a customer may be slow to pay and yet may still take the discount offered. Where the customer is important to the business it may be difficult for the business to insist on full payment. Some businesses may charge interest on overdue accounts in order to encourage prompt payment. However, this is only possible if the business is in a strong bargaining position with its customers. For example, the business may be the only supplier of a particular product in the area.

SELF-ASSESSMENT QUESTION 13.1

Williams Wholesalers Ltd at present requires payment from its customers by the end of the month after the month of delivery. On average it takes customers 70 days to pay. Sales amount to $4 million per year and bad debts to $20,000 per year.

It is planned to offer customers a cash discount of 2 per cent for payment within 30 days. Williams estimates that 50 per cent of customers will accept this facility but that the remaining customers, who tend to be slow payers, will not pay until 80 days after the sale. At present the company has a partly used loan facility costing 13 per cent per annum. If the plan goes ahead, bad debts will be reduced to $10,000 per annum and there will be savings in credit administration expenses of $6,000 per annum.

Should Williams Wholesalers Ltd offer the new credit terms to customers? You should support your answer with any calculations and explanations you consider necessary.

Collection policies

A business offering credit must ensure that amounts owing are collected as quickly as possible. An efficient collection policy requires an efficient accounting system. Invoices must be sent out promptly along with regular monthly statements. Reminders must also be despatched promptly where necessary.

When a business is faced with customers who do not pay there should be agreed procedures for dealing with them. However, the cost of any action to be taken against delinquent debtors must be weighed against the likely returns. For example, there is little point in pursuing a customer through the courts and incurring large legal expenses if there is evidence that the customer does not have the necessary resources to pay. Where possible, the cost of bad debts should be taken into account when pricing products or services.

Management can monitor the effectiveness of collection policies in a number of ways. One method is to calculate the ratio we dealt with in Chapter 6 for the average settlement period for debtors. This ratio, you may recall, is calculated as follows:

$$\text{Average settlement period for debtors} = \frac{\text{Average trade debtors}}{\text{Credit sales}} \times 365$$

Although this ratio can be useful it is important to remember that it produces an average figure for the number of days debts are outstanding. This average may be badly distorted by a few large customers who are also very slow payers.

A more detailed and informative approach to monitoring debtors is to produce an **ageing schedule of debtors**. Debts are divided into categories according to the length of time the debt has been outstanding. An ageing schedule can be produced for managers on a regular basis in order to help them see the pattern of outstanding debts. An example of an ageing schedule is set out below:

Ageing schedule of debtors

	Days outstanding			
Customer	1–30 days	31–60 days	61–90 days	>91 days
	$	$	$	$
A Ltd	20,000	10,000	–	–
B Ltd	–	24,000	–	–
C Ltd	12,000	13,000	14,000	18,000
Total	32,000	47,000	14,000	18,000

Thus, we can see from the schedule that A Ltd has $20,000 outstanding for 30 days or less and $10,000 outstanding for between 31 and 60 days. This information can be very useful for credit control purposes.

The use of computers can make the task of producing such a schedule simple and straightforward. Many accounting software packages now include this ageing schedule as one of the routine reports available to managers.

A slightly different approach to exercising control over debtors is to identify the pattern of receipts from credit sales that occur on a monthly basis. This involves monitoring the percentage of trade debtors that pay (and the percentage of debts that remain unpaid) in the month of sale and the percentage who pay in subsequent months. In order to do this, credit sales for each month must be examined separately. To illustrate how a pattern of credit sales receipts is produced, consider a business that achieved credit sales of $250,000 in June and received 30 per cent of the amount owing in the same month, 40 per cent in July, 20 per cent in August and 10 per cent in September. The pattern of credit sales receipts and amounts owing will be:

Pattern of credit sales receipts

Month	Receipts from June credit sales	% received	Amount outstanding from June sales at month end	% outstanding
	$		$	
June	75,000	30	175,000	70
July	100,000	40	75,000	30
August	50,000	20	25,000	10
September	25,000	10	–	–

The table above shows how sales received for June were received over time. This information can be used as a basis for control. The actual pattern of receipts can be compared to the expected (budgeted) pattern of receipts in order to see if there was any significant deviation (see Figure 13.5). If this comparison shows that debtors are paying more slowly than expected, management may decide to take corrective action.

 **ACTIVITY 13.6**

What kind of corrective action might the managers of a business decide to take if they found that debtors were paying more slowly than anticipated?

THE MANAGEMENT OF WORKING CAPITAL   chapter 13

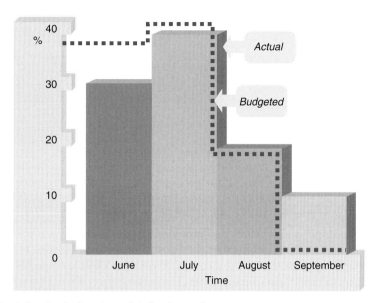

FIGURE 13.5 Pattern of budgeted and actual cash receipts for June sales

THE MANAGEMENT OF CASH

Why hold cash?

Most businesses will hold a certain amount of cash as part of the total assets held. The amount of cash held, however, may vary considerably between businesses.

ACTIVITY 13.7

Why do you think a business may decide to hold at least some of its assets in the form of cash?

We have identified that there are three reasons for holding cash: transactionary, precautionary and speculative (see solution to Activity 13.7).

How much cash should be held?

Although cash can be held for each of the reasons identified in the solution to Activity 13.7, it may not always be necessary to hold cash for these purposes. If a business is able to borrow quickly, the amount of cash it needs to hold can be reduced. Similarly, if the business holds assets that can easily be converted to cash (e.g. marketable securities such as shares in stock exchange-listed companies, government bonds) the amount of cash held can be reduced.

The decision as to how much cash a particular business should hold is a difficult one. Different businesses will have different views on the amount of cash it is appropriate for them to hold.

Controlling the cash balance

A number of models have been proposed to help control the cash balance of a business. One model proposes the use of upper and lower control limits for cash balances and of a target cash balance. The model assumes the business will invest in marketable investments that can easily be liquidated. These investments will be purchased or sold, as necessary, in order to keep the cash balance within the control limits.

The model proposes two upper and two lower control limits (see Figure 13.6). If the business finds that it has exceeded an outer limit, the managers must decide whether or not the cash balance is likely to return to a point within the inner control limits set over the next few days. If this seems likely then no action is required. If, on the other hand, this does not seem likely management must change the cash position of the business by either buying or selling marketable securities.

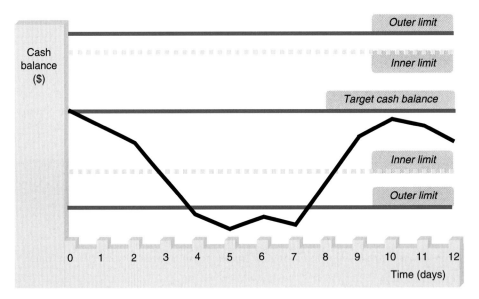

FIGURE 13.6 Controlling the cash balance

In Figure 13.6 we can see that the lower outer control limit has been breached for four days. If a four-day period is unacceptable, managers must sell marketable securities in order to replenish the cash balance.

The model relies heavily on management judgment to determine where the control limits are set and the time period within which breaches of the control limits are acceptable. Past experience may be useful in helping managers to decide on these issues. There are other models, however, that do not rely on management judgment; instead, they use quantitative techniques to determine an optimal cash policy.

Cash flow statements and the management of cash

In order to manage cash effectively it is useful for a business to prepare a cash flow statement and/or cash budget. This is a very important tool for both planning and control purposes. Cash budgets were considered in Chapters 9 and 10 and it is therefore not necessary to consider them again in detail. However, it is worth repeating the point that these statements enable the managers of a business to see the expected outcome of planned events on the cash balance. The cash budgets will identify periods when cash surpluses or cash deficits are expected.

When a cash surplus is expected to arise managers must decide on the best use of the surplus funds. When a cash deficit is expected to arise managers must make adequate provision by borrowing, liquidating assets or rescheduling cash payments and receipts to deal with this. Cash budgets are also useful in helping to control the cash held. The actual cash flows can be compared to the budgeted cash flows for the period. If there is a significant divergence between the budgeted cash flows and the actual cash flows, explanations must be sought and corrective action taken where necessary.

To refresh your memory, an example of a cash budget is given below. Remember that there is no set format for this statement. Managers can determine how best to present the information. However, the format set out below appears to be in widespread use. Cash budgets covering the short term are usually broken down into monthly periods in order to allow a close monitoring of cash movements. In addition, cash inflows are usually shown above cash outflows and the difference between these (i.e. the net cash flow) for a month is separately identified along with the closing cash balance.

EXAMPLE 13.2

Cash flow statement for the six months to 30 November 2006

	June $	July $	Aug. $	Sept. $	Oct. $	Nov. $
Cash inflows						
Credit sales	–	–	4,000	5,500	7,000	8,500
Cash sales	4,000	5,500	7,000	8,500	11,000	11,000
	4,000	5,500	11,000	14,000	18,000	19,500
Cash outflows						
Motor vehicles	6,000					
Equipment	10,000					7,000
Freehold premises	40,000					
Purchases	–	29,000	9,250	11,500	13,750	17,500
Wages/salaries	900	900	900	900	900	900
Commission	–	320	440	560	680	680
Overheads	500	500	500	500	650	650
	57,400	30,720	11,090	13,460	15,980	26,730
Net cash flow	(53,400)	(25,220)	(90)	540	2,020	(7,230)
Opening balance	60,000	6,600	(18,620)	(18,710)	(18,170)	(16,150)
Closing balance	6,600	(18,620)	(18,710)	(18,170)	(16,150)	(23,380)

Although cash flow statements are prepared primarily for internal management purposes they are sometimes required by prospective lenders when a loan to a business is being considered.

Operating cash cycle

When managing cash it is important to be aware of the **operating cash cycle** of the business. This may be defined as the time period between the outlay of cash necessary for the purchase of inventory and the ultimate receipt of cash from the sale of the goods. In the case of a business that purchases goods on credit for subsequent resale on credit, the operating cash cycle can be shown in diagrammatic form in Figure 13.7. Figure 13.7 shows that payment for goods acquired on credit occurs some time after the goods have been purchased and therefore no immediate cash outflow arises from the purchase. Similarly, cash receipts from debtors will occur some time after the sale is made and so there will be no immediate cash inflow as a result of the sale. The operating cash cycle is the time period between the payment made to the creditor for goods supplied and the cash received from the debtor.

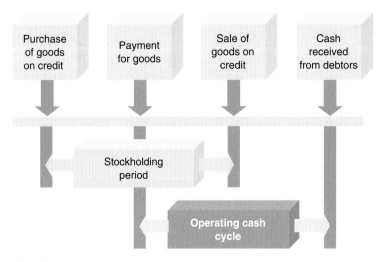

FIGURE 13.7 Operating cash cycle

The operating cash cycle is important because it has a significant influence on the financing requirements of the business. The longer the cash cycle the greater the financing requirements of the business and the greater the financial risks. For this reason, a business is likely to want to reduce the operating cash cycle to a minimum if possible.

For the type of business mentioned above, the operating cash cycle can be calculated from the financial statements by the use of certain ratios. The cash cycle is calculated as follows:

Average inventory holding period
+ Average settlement period for debtors
− Average payment period for creditors

ACTIVITY 13.9

The accounts of Freezeqwik Ltd, a distributor of frozen foods, are set out below for the year ended 31 December 2005.

Income statement for the year ended 31 December 2005		
	$'000	$'000
Sales		820
Less cost of sales		
Opening inventory	142	
Purchases	568	
	710	
Less closing inventory	166	544
Gross profit		276
Administration expenses	120	
Other expenses	127	247
Net profit		29
Income tax		7
Net profit after tax		22

Balance sheet as at 31 December 2005		
	$'000	$'000
Current assets		
Cash	24	
Trade debtors	264	
Inventory	166	
		454
Non-current assets		
Motor vans at written down value	102	
Fixture and fittings at written-down value	82	
Freehold premises at valuation	180	
		364
Total assets		818
Current liabilities		
Trade creditors	159	
Income tax payable	7	
		166
Shareholders' equity		
Ordinary share capital	300	
Preference share capital	200	
Retained profit	152	
		652
Total liabilities and shareholders' equity		818

All purchases and sales are on credit.

(a) Calculate the operating cash cycle for the company.

(b) Suggest how the company may seek to reduce the cash cycle.

Cash transmission

A business will normally wish to receive the benefits from providing goods or services at the earliest opportunity. The benefit received is immediate where payment is made in cash. However, when payment is made by cheque there is normally a delay of three to four working days before the cheque can be cleared through the banking system. The business must therefore wait for this period before it can benefit from the amount paid in. In the case of a business that receives large amounts in the form of cheques, the opportunity cost of this delay can be very significant.

In order to avoid this delay a business could require payments to be made in cash, but this is not usually very practical for a number of reasons. Another option is to ask for payment to be made by standing order or by direct debit from the customer's bank account. This will ensure that the amount owing is transferred from the bank account of the customer to the bank account of the business on the day that has been agreed.

It is also possible now for funds to be directly transferred to a business's bank account. As a result of developments in computer technology, a customer can pay for items by using a card (rather like a cheque card) which results in his or her account being instantly debited and the business's bank account being instantly credited with the required amount. This method of payment is being increasingly used by large retail businesses and may well extend to other forms of business.

THE MANAGEMENT OF TRADE CREDITORS

Trade credit is regarded as an important source of finance by many businesses. It has been described as a 'spontaneous' source of finance as it tends to increase in line with the increase in the level of sales achieved by a business. Trade credit is widely regarded as a 'free' source of finance and therefore as a good thing for a business to have. However, there may be real costs associated with taking trade credit.

Customers who pay on credit may not be as well favoured as those who pay immediately. For example, when goods are in short supply credit customers may receive lower priority when allocating the inventory available. In addition, credit customers may be given lower priority in terms of delivery dates or the provision of technical support services. Sometimes the goods or services provided may be more costly if credit is required. In most industries, however, trade credit is the norm and as a result the above costs will not apply unless, perhaps, the credit facilities are abused by the customer. A business purchasing supplies on credit may also have to incur additional administration and accounting costs in order to deal with the scrutiny and payment of invoices, the maintaining and updating of creditors' accounts, etc.

Where a supplier offers discount for prompt payment a business should give careful consideration to the possibility of paying within the discount period. An example may be useful to illustrate the cost of forgoing possible discounts.

EXAMPLE
13.3

Simat Ltd takes 70 days to pay for goods supplied by its supplier. In order to encourage prompt payment the supplier has offered the company a 2 per cent discount if payment for goods is made within 30 days.

Simat Ltd is not sure whether it is worth taking the discount offered. What is the annual percentage cost to Simat Ltd of forgoing the discount?

If the discount is taken, payment could be made on the last day of the discount period (i.e. the thirtieth day). However, if the discount is not taken, payment will be made after 70 days. This means that by not taking the discount Simat Ltd will receive an extra 40 days' (i.e. 70 – 30) credit. The cost of this extra credit to the company will be the 2 per cent discount forgone. If we annualise the cost of this discount forgone we have:

$$2\% \times 365 / 40 = 18.3\%$$

You should note that this is an approximate annual rate. For the more mathematically minded the precise rate is:

$$(1 + 2 / 98)^{365/40} - 1 = 20.24\%$$

We can see that the annual cost of forgoing the discount is quite high and it may be profitable for the company to pay the supplier within the discount period even if it means that it will have to borrow in order to do so.

The above points are not meant to imply that taking credit is a burden to a business. There are, of course, real benefits that can accrue. Provided that trade credit is not abused by a business it can represent a form of interest-free loan. It can be a much more convenient method of paying for goods and services than paying by cash and, during a period of inflation, there will be an economic gain by paying later rather than sooner for goods and services purchased. For many businesses these benefits will exceed the costs involved.

Controlling trade creditors

In order to monitor the level of trade credit taken, management can calculate the average settlement period for creditors. You may recall from Chapter 6 that this ratio was as follows:

$$\text{Average settlement period} = \frac{\text{Average trade creditors}}{\text{Credit purchases}} \times 365$$

Once again this provides an average figure, which can be distorted. A more informative approach would be to produce an ageing schedule for creditors. This would look much the same as the ageing schedule for debtors described earlier. Alternatively, a pattern of credit payments could be prepared similar to the pattern of credit receipts discussed earlier.

SUMMARY

In this chapter we have achieved the following objectives in the way shown.

OBJECTIVE	METHOD ACHIEVED
List the items making up working capital	Identified as current assets (cash + debtors + inventories) less current liabilities (creditors)
Discuss the nature and importance of working capital	Identified working capital as the pool of short-term assets necessary for the day-to-day operations of the entity
Illustrate the working capital cycle	Showed the net period that funding has to be provided for trading activities (inventory turnover period plus debtors turnover period less creditors turnover period)
Demonstrate an understanding of the importance of inventory and the techniques available to facilitate efficient and effective management of this asset	Discussed issues and techniques relating to inventory as follows: • The costs/benefits of too little and too much inventory • Forecasting inventory needs • Calculating the inventory turnover period • Calculating the economic order quantity (EOQ) • Applying the ABC system of inventory control • Implementing materials requirements planning (MRP) • Assessing just-in-time (JIT) inventory management
Discuss the provision of credit to customers and utilise various management tools in monitoring and controlling this asset	Discussed credit and the following related issues: • The costs/benefits of selling on credit • Evaluating credit applications • Determining the credit period • Understanding early settlement discounts • Tools for assessing collection policies: —average collection period —aged listing of debtors —pattern of credit sales receipts
Explain the reasons for holding cash and the basis of management and control	Explained the costs/benefits of holding cash Discussed the following aspects of cash management and control: • Determining the level of cash to hold: —cash flow statements —operating cash cycle • Efficient cash transmission to the business
Summarise the key aspects of creditor management	Explained the costs/benefits of using creditors' finance Identified and discussed the following tools for assessing creditor management: • Average payment period • Aged listing of creditors • Pattern of credit purchase payments

DISCUSSION QUESTIONS

EASY

<Obj 1, 2>   **13.1**   Distinguish between the working capital structure of:

(a) a cabinet maker

(b) a cash and carry store

(c) a public accountant.

<Obj 2>   **13.2**   What is working capital?

<Obj 3>   **13.3**   The working capital cycle:

(a) What is it?

(b) How does it vary between different entity types?

(c) Why is it important for management to review this cycle?

<Obj 4>   **13.4**   What are the reasons for holding inventory? Are these reasons different from the reasons for holding cash?

<Obj 4>   **13.5**   Contrast the benefits and costs of holding excess inventory.

<Obj 5>   **13.6**   The textbook discusses the 'five Cs of credit'. Distinguish between 'capital' and 'character'.

<Obj 5>   **13.7**   What are the possible costs involved in extending the credit period for customers?

<Obj 6>   **13.8**   Why do businesses hold cash?

<Obj 6>   **13.9**   What are the potential benefits to management of preparing a cash budget?

<Obj 6>   **13.10**   Identify the costs of holding:

(a) too little cash

(b) too much cash.

<Obj 6>   **13.11**   Identify alternative means a business can utilise to minimise the cash transmission period (from customer to the bank).

<Obj 6>   **13.12**   Why do some suppliers of resources (e.g. councils) offer such high early settlement discounts (e.g. 10 per cent)?

INTERMEDIATE

<Obj 4>   **13.13**   How might each of the following affect the level of inventory held by a business?

- An increase in the number of production bottlenecks experienced by the business.
- A rise in the level of interest rates.
- A decision to offer customers a narrower range of products in the future.
- A switch of suppliers from an overseas business to a local business.
- A deterioration in the quality and reliability of bought-in components.

<Obj 4>   **13.14**   What are the possible deficiencies in using the average inventory turnover period as a management tool in controlling working capital?

<Obj 4>   **13.15**   How would you establish re-order points for inventory items?

<Obj 4>   **13.16**   What is the rationale behind the ABC system of inventory control?

<Obj 4>   **13.17**   JIT inventory management has many advantages, but what are some of the potential deficiencies?

<Obj 5>   **13.18**   In controlling debtors we can calculate:

- average settlement period
- aged schedule of debtors
- pattern of credit sales receipts.

(a) In summary, what is the purpose of each calculation?

(b) Is there any benefit in calculating all three, or does each one largely duplicate the information provided by the others?

<Obj 5>   **13.19**   Tariq is the credit manager of Heltex Ltd. He is concerned that the pattern of monthly sales receipts shows that credit collection is poor compared to budget. The sales director believes that Tariq is to blame for this situation, but Tariq insists he is not. Why might Tariq not be to blame for the deterioration in the credit collection period?

<Obj 6>   **13.20**   Is it possible to have a negative cash cycle (e.g. –10 days)?

APPLICATION EXERCISES

EASY

<Obj 4>   **13.1**   Calculate the economic order quantity for inventory given:
- annual sales of 3,000 units
- order costs of $36 per order.

<Obj 5>   **13.2**   An analysis of collection receipts is given below.

Sales month	Credit sales $	Jan. $	Feb. $	Mar. $	Apr. $	Collection May $	June $	July $	Aug. $	Sept. $	Oct. $
Jan.	110,000	33,000	55,000	16,500	5,500	–	–	–	–	–	–
Feb.	90,000	–	25,200	43,200	15,300	6,300	–	–	–	–	–
Mar.	100,000	–	–	26,000	47,000	19,000	6,000	2,000	–	–	–
Apr.	120,000	–	–	–	28,800	55,200	21,600	8,400	6,000	–	–
May	130,000	–	–	–	–	28,600	57,200	22,100	7,800	7,800	6,500
June	150,000	–	–	–	–	–	30,000	63,000	24,000	12,000	10,500

Analyse the above by compiling the pattern of credit sales receipts.

<Obj 5>   **13.3**   It is policy of a company to allow 30 days' credit. Management wishes to encourage debtors to pay invoices earlier and offers clients a 2 per cent discount if invoices are paid within five days.
(a) What is the effective annual equivalent percentage from such an offer? Assuming management believes that the resultant annual equivalent percentage is too high, make a recommendation to management to reduce the annual equivalent percentage to approximately 18 per cent.
(b) What will such a percentage mean in terms of the discount percentage to be offered if invoices are to be paid within 10 days to obtain the discount?

<Obj 6>   **13.4**   The accountant for Nu Way Ltd has calculated the following ratios for his company for the last four years.

	2003	2004	2005	2006
Receivables turnover	8.1	7.7	7.2	6.9
Inventory turnover	4.2	3.9	3.7	3.5
Payables turnover	6.3	6.7	7.2	8.1

(a) Calculate the cash cycle period for each year.
(b) Comment on the management of working capital as revealed by this analysis.

<Obj 7>   **13.5**   During the last year Global Homeware purchased $180,000 stock on credit from House of Fashion. At the beginning of the year Global Homeware owed House of Fashion $40,000 and at the end of the year $36,000. In an effort to improve the payment rate from Global Homeware, House of Fashion is offering them a 2 per cent discount for payments made within 30 days.

(a) Calculate Global Homeware's average settlement period for its creditor.

(b) What is the annual percentage cost to Global Homeware if it does not take advantage of the discount offered?

INTERMEDIATE

<Obj 2, 3>   **13.6**   The following information is available for Jones Ltd:

Ratios	Year 1	Year 2	Year 3
Current ratio (times)	2.61:1	1.94:1	1.32:1
Receivables turnover period (days)	37	43	47
Inventory turnover period (days)	48	54	65
Payables turnover period (days)	8	9	31
(Credit terms: 2.10, n/30—meaning there is 2% discount for payment within 10 days, normal credit 30 days)			
Non-current assets (indexed, year 1 as base)	100	118	141
Long-term finance (indexed, year 1 as base)	100	109	115

Evaluate the management of working capital for Jones Ltd in relation to changes in the operating cycle and the financing scheme.

<Obj 4, 5>   **13.7**   The managing director of Sparkrite Ltd, a trading company, has just received summary sets of accounts for 2005 and 2006.

SPARKRITE LTD

Income statements for years ended 30 September 2005 and 2006

	2005		2006	
	$'000	$'000	$'000	$'000
Sales		1,800		1,920
Less cost of sales				
Opening inventory	160		200	
Purchases	1,120		1,175	
	1,280		1,375	
Less closing inventory	200		250	
		1,080		1,125
Gross profit		720		795
Less expenses		680		750
Net profit		40		45

Balance sheets as at 30 September 2005 and 2006				
	2005		2006	
	$'000	$'000	$'000	$'000
Current assets				
Bank	4		2	
Debtors	375		480	
Inventory	200		250	
		579		732
Non-current assets		950		930
Total assets		1,529		1,662
Current liabilities		195		225
Shareholders' equity				
Paid-up ordinary share capital	825		883	
Retained profits	509		554	
		1,334		1,437
Total liabilities and shareholders' equity		1,529		1,662

The financial director has expressed concern at the deterioration in inventory and debtors levels.

(a) Show by using the data given how you would calculate ratios that could be used to measure inventory and debtor levels in 2005 and 2006.

(b) Discuss the ways in which the management of Sparkrite Ltd could exercise control over:

  (i) inventory levels

  (ii) debtor levels.

<Obj 5> **13.8** Your superior, the general manager of Plastics Manufacturers Ltd, has recently been talking to the chief buyer of Plastic Toys Ltd, which manufactures a wide range of toys for young children. At present it is considering changing its supplier of plastic granules and has offered to buy its entire requirement of 2,000 kg per month from you at the going market rate, providing you will grant it three months' credit on its purchases. The following information is available:

1. Plastic granules sell for $10 per kilogram, variable costs are $7 per kilogram and fixed costs are $2 per kilogram.

2. Your own company is financially strong and has sales of $15 million per year. For the foreseeable future it will have surplus capacity and it is actively looking for new outlets.

3. Extracts from Plastic Toys' accounts:

	2003	2004	2005
	$'000	$'000	$'000
Sales	800	980	640
Profit before interest and tax	100	110	(150)
Capital employed	600	650	575
Current assets	—	—	—
Debtors	140	160	160
Inventory	200	220	320
	340	380	480

Current liabilities			
Creditors	180	190	220
Overdraft	100	150	310
	280	340	530
Net current assets	60	40	(50)

(a) Write some short notes suggesting sources of information you would use in order to assess the creditworthiness of potential customers who are unknown to you. You should critically evaluate each source of information.

(b) Describe the accounting controls you would use to monitor the level of your company's trade debtors.

(c) Advise your general manager on the acceptability of the proposal. You should give your reasons and do any calculations you consider necessary.

CHALLENGING

<Obj 2, 3, 7> **13.9** Presented below are the financial details relating to the assessment of working capital by two businesses, Quick-Service and Priced-Right.

	Quick-Service		Priced-Right	
	For period*	Year end	For period*	Year end
	$	$	$	$
Net credit sales	360,000		480,000	
Cost of sales	234,000		264,000	
Cash		27,400		18,700
Accounts receivable	45,000	41,700	68,600	72,300
Inventory	46,800	42,400	66,000	70,400
Accounts payable	38,600	36,700	47,500	50,300

*Represents average for asset and liability accounts

(a) For each company calculate:
   (i) Working capital
   (ii) Current ratio
   (iii) Quick ratio
   (iv) Inventory turnover period in days
   (v) Debtors turnover period in days
   (vi) Creditors turnover period in days
   (vii) Operating cycle in days.

(b) Contrast the two businesses from the perspective of the:
   (i) creditor/lender
   (ii) investor/owner.

<Obj 5> **13.10** Mayo Computers Ltd has an annual turnover of $20 million before taking into account bad debts of $0.1 million. All sales made by the company are on credit and at present credit terms are negotiable by the customer. On average, the settlement period for trade debtors is 60 days. The company is currently reviewing its credit policies to see whether more efficient and profitable methods could be employed. Only one proposal has so far been put forward concerning the management of trade credit.

The credit control department has proposed that customers should be given a 2½ per cent discount if they pay within 30 days. For those who do not pay within this period, a maximum of 50 days' credit should be given. The credit department believes that 60 per cent of customers will take advantage of the discount by paying at the end of the discount period and the remainder will pay at the end of 50 days. The credit department believes that bad debts can be effectively eliminated by adopting the above policies and by employing stricter credit investigation procedures that will cost an additional $20,000 per annum. The credit department is confident that these new policies will not result in any reduction in sales. At present Mayo has an overdraft facility with its bank at 14 per cent per annum.

Calculate the net annual cost (savings) to the company of abandoning its existing credit policies and adopting the proposals of the credit control department. (*Hint*: In order to answer this question you must weigh the costs of administration and cash discounts against the savings in bad debts and interest charges.)

<Obj 5>   **13.11** International Electric Ltd at present offers its customers 30 days' credit. Half the customers, by value, pay on time. The other half take an average of 70 days to pay.

The company is considering offering a cash discount of 2 per cent to its customers for payment within 30 days. It anticipates that half of the customers who now take an average of 70 days to pay will pay in 30 days. The other half will still take an average of 70 days to pay. The scheme will also reduce bad debts by $300,000 per year.

Annual sales of $365 million are made evenly throughout the year. At present the company has a large overdraft ($60 million) with its bank at 12 per cent per annum.

(a) Calculate the approximate equivalent annual percentage cost of a discount of 2 per cent that reduces the time taken by debtors to pay from 70 days to 30 days. (This part can be answered without reference to the narrative above.)

(b) Calculate debtors outstanding under both the old and new schemes.

(c) How much will the scheme cost the company in discounts?

(d) Should the company go ahead with the scheme? State what other factors, if any, should be taken into account.

(e) Outline the controls and procedures a company should adopt to manage the level of its debtors.

<Obj 5>   **13.12** Prepare an analysis of credit sales receipts based on the following information:

| Month | Credit sales | Collection on credit sales in following months | | | | |
| | | Current | Second | Third | Fourth | Fifth |
	$	$	$	$	$	$
January	127,000	17,780	72,390	36,830	0	0
February	136,000	17,680	74,800	36,720	6,800	0
March	154,000	18,480	80,080	36,960	13,860	4,620
April	146,000	16,060	71,540	32,120	16,060	10,220
May	141,000	14,100	64,860	29,610	21,150	11,280
June	165,000	14,850	72,600	33,000	23,100	21,450

<Obj 6>   **13.13** Hercules Wholesalers Ltd has been particularly concerned with its liquidity position in recent months. The most recent income statement and balance sheet of the company are as follows:

Income statement for the year ended 31 May 2006

	$	$
Sales		452,000
Less cost of sales		
Opening inventory	125,000	
Add purchases	341,000	
	466,000	
Less closing inventory	143,000	323,000
Gross profit		129,000
Expenses		132,000
Net loss for the period		(3,000)

Balance sheet as at 31 May 2006

	$	$
Current assets		
Debtors	163,000	
Inventory	143,000	
		306,000
Non-current assets		
Motor vehicles at cost less depreciation	52,000	
Fixtures and fittings at cost less depreciation	25,000	
Freehold premises at valuation	280,000	
		357,000
Total assets		663,000
Current liabilities		
Trade creditors	145,000	
Bank overdraft	140,000	
		285,000
Non-current liabilities		
Loans		120,000
Shareholders' equity		
Ordinary share capital	100,000	
Retained profits	158,000	
		258,000
Total liabilities and shareholders' equity		663,000

The debtors and creditors were maintained at a constant level throughout the year.

(a) Explain why Hercules Wholesalers Ltd is concerned about its liquidity position.

(b) Explain the term 'operating cash cycle' and state why this concept is important in the financial management of a business.

(c) Calculate the operating cash cycle for Hercules Wholesalers Ltd based on the information above.

(d) State what steps may be taken to improve the operating cash cycle of the company.

<Obj 7>

13.14 The accountant for Dulex Ltd has calculated the following ratios for his company for the last four years.

	2002	2003	2004	2005
Receivables turnover	6.8	7.2	7.9	8.4
Inventory turnover	9.2	9.4	9.7	10.2
Payables turnover	8.7	8.4	8.1	7.6

Required

(a) Compute the working capital period (cash cycle) for each year.

(b) Comment on the management of working capital as revealed by this analysis.

CASE STUDY 13.1

Creditors (Accounts payable) are often treated as an afterthought. The article below suggests that this is a mistake, and that use of modern technology has the potential to make significant savings. Read the article and answer the questions that follow.

What's that you say? Paying bills quickly really pays off

Richard Gamble

Treasury and Risk Management, July/August 2004

For some companies, the ROI on EIPP comes faster and bigger than expected

When Topeka-based Payless ShoeSource Inc. decided to automate its supply chain by using a payer-centric electronic invoice presentment and payment (EIPP) solution from Xign Corp., it predicted that the budget for accounts payable would drop significantly. And it did: The company has been able to cut its A/P staff, from 21 to 17 full-time equivalents.

What Vic Nation, manager of accounts payable and receivable at Payless, didn't quite factor in was how substantial the savings would be for the discount shoe seller given the simple reality that it now was able to pay its bills on time and therefore take advantage of prompt-pay discounts it used to miss. In fact, by using a Xign feature called 'Discount Manager' and extending its standard terms from 30 to 45 days, Payless could even expand those savings by encouraging suppliers that didn't normally offer discounts to give one in return for immediate payment—or by paying slower when they did not. 'Those discounts bring a much higher effective return on our cash than we could get from paying later and investing the money at today's low rates,' Nation observes.

Uphill struggle for billing model

The bottom line for Payless: Nation and his staff were able to realise most of the goals of the projected three-year return on investment in just one year. 'We were so successful so quickly that my boss accused us of sandbagging our business plan,' Nation laughs. 'He was just kidding, I hope.'

And Chris Rauen, Xign's manager of marketing communications, would happily tell any CFO that the Payless results are fairly typical for payer-centric EIPP. Companies usually spend anywhere from $8 to $20 to process and pay a paper invoice, and EIPP can cut that to about $2, he observes. But the biggest gain comes from discounts for paying quickly, which often add up to an annual return on cash in the range of 24% to 30%, Rauen claims.

So why is it the case, after years of process improvements in EIPP systems, that many—if not, most—treasury professionals still regard automated payment and billing with such hopelessness? Simply put, not every company has the clout with either its customers or suppliers that a high-volume retailer like Payless does. 'If a payer has quite a bit of control over its suppliers, it can impose a payer-centric solution. And when the biller has quite a bit of control over its customers, it can impose a biller-centric solution,' explains Steve Hooper, vice president and product line manager for electronic payments at Mellon Bank and co-chair of the Council for Electronic Billing and Presentment at NACHA, the Electronic Payments Association. 'But when neither is the case, progress has come slowly, one company at a time.' The route around this impasse for frustrated EIPP vendors? Find industries where an established network of payers and billers exists and convert them to EIPP, says Kevin Tissot, vice president for receivables business management at Citigroup, an early and aggressive EIPP advocate. 'We're having our serious discussions with vertical exchanges that represent a community of buyers and sellers,' Tissot explains.

According to Tissot, vertical exchanges, a favorite in the dot-com heyday, are making a comeback. While he won't identify his hot prospects, he says that they are in the global shipping and logistics space. This makes sense since one of Citi's biggest EIPP success stories is Cargo Network Services (CNS). A long-established middleman, based in Garden City, NY, CNS represents the commercial crossroads, so to speak, for a relatively compact and closed group of airlines and airfreight forwarders. CNS didn't have to coax billers or payers to participate; it simply converted an existing network from paper to EIPP.

Despite Tissot's enthusiasm, the market niche of vertical exchanges is somewhat thin. Hence, up until now, the key to the limited success EIPP has enjoyed is the lack of flexibility in systems to accept output in a variety of popular formats. In general, this has given the edge to payer-centric models á la Payless offered by vendors such as Xign and US Bank's PowerTrack, notes Beth Robertson, senior analyst at Needham, Mass.-based TowerGroup, rather than biller-centric offerings that generally just deliver invoices in the billers' formats. That may be okay since automating the payment process seems to be a higher priority for most companies right now than automating billing. Web invoicing ranked just behind imaging and workflow in automation priorities, according to a survey that Charlotte-based Paystream Advisors took at a recent meeting of the International Association of Purchasing Professionals (IAPP), notes Henry Ijams, managing director. 'They want to bring invoices into their automated workflow processes. There is a lot of talk now about whether to build a supplier portal for receiving invoices or join a network like Xign,' he explains.

That may be changing, thanks to providers such as San Francisco-based Avolent Inc., which now sells software to billers that generates electronic invoices that can be viewed online and printed or imported by payers in their favored A/P format, ranging from EDI to Quickbooks. E-invoices can be routed to whomever needs to approve them in the payer's shop, reports Avolent CEO Doug Roberts. Payers can even see a two-year archive of past bills online, he adds.

An early adopter of the Avolent system was Delray Beach, Fla.-based Office Depot Inc. with $13 billion in annual sales. After carefully testing the system for customer acceptance and satisfaction, Office Depot rolled out the Avolent EIPP in February 2003. Some 20% of Office Depot's customers now use the high-tech system, which basically images all documents and posts them online. 'They can look at images of invoices, proof of delivery, even see who signed for it,' says Nancy Mackey, manager of the strategic project for billing and payment. Statements now are available any day of the month. 'We don't mail out paper statements any more,' she notes. Also extinct: collection calls that stall when the customer needs to see a copy of the invoice.

Since the project was rolled out in early 2003, DSO (days sales outstanding) has been cut by seven days, in part because of this project, Mackey says. What can be tied exclusively to this initiative is $1.7 million of net savings. 'After July, we expect to save more than $2 million a year,' Mackey says. 'Besides DSO, we've reduced staff, postage, even paper envelopes. There is tremendous savings potential for both us and our customers,' she declares. It's not the perfect solution—yet. Because it is based on Web site visits, not a computer-to-computer interface, Office Depot's largest customers rarely use it, Mackey concedes. But it is a big step toward supply chain automation. That 20% adoption means that by June, the company had already reached its goal for year-end 2004. 'I think we'll be closer to 30%,' Mackey predicts. 'Acceptance has been tremendous. We understand that EIPP adoption in the first couple years usually runs between 1% and 7%.'

Getting systems to cooperate

But while Office Depot's clients may be lapping it up, other companies seem stuck in the mud on EIPP. Still, many vendors—particularly the banks—remain bullish. Traditionally, two events were visible to the biller: when the invoice was sent and when the check arrived, notes Saw Hooi Him, head of EIPP for Deutsche Bank's global cash management unit. Every step happening in between, he says, was invisible. EIPP opens a huge window on that process and lets both parties plan, investigate, communicate, resolve and execute online, Saw explains. How can that not be a benefit that every businessperson wouldn't eventually want and need?

Down the road, biller-centric and payer-centric systems will build links, so that their systems can exchange documents without requiring individual mapping, predicts TowerGroup's Robertson. 'The need for individual mapping has led some vendors to take a broader view and start a move toward facilitating integration and document exchange between trading partners using different solutions,' she observes. 'This lets both parties leverage the value of their internal solutions. The end game is an open exchange for parties using different solution types.'

1 What are the main reasons why Payless was able to make substantial savings in the area of accounts payable (creditors)?
2 Under what conditions are EIPP systems likely to be acceptable and thrive?
3 What are the advantages of systems such as those designed by Avolent?
4 Identify the areas in which savings occurred in the Office Depot project?
5 What are included as likely future directions in the development of EIPP systems?

CASE STUDY

13.2

Savings from improvements in working capital management can be considerable. However, working capital vary depending on both the nature of the business, and the nature of both the economic and technological environment. The following article provides some interesting insights into this area. Read the article and answer the questions that follow.

Go with the flow

Niles Lo

CFO Asia, March 2005

Being the CFO of a company that stock analysts regard as a proxy for the growth of a nation's economy has its pleasures. 'It's been a rather glamorous 18 months, with sales just huge,' says John Slack, CFO of PT Astra International, the US$4 billion in sales Indonesian automaker. Indonesia is on the growth path again, and a new breed of consumer is hungry for a first vehicle—motorcycles—as well as Astra's more premium brands of Hondas and Toyotas. And one of the most beautiful parts of the proposition is that working capital management seems to be taking care of itself.

'Depending on the business, and counting trade receivables only, we have between eight and 19 days working capital,' which Slack reckons is manageable given the company's stellar growth. One of the reasons that working capital has not expanded at the rate of the business is inventory, or rather the dearth of it. 'We're in a market that responds very strongly to new products,' says Slack, 'and the presales of products are very high. We have advanced orders from four to six months, with deposits paid, and this helps our cash position.' Best of all, as soon as a vehicle is off the assembly line, it's out to the dealer. 'We have low inventory costs and the product lines are very easy to move.'

He adds: 'That's the fundamental thing. It's consumer driven, and demand has forced us to produce more, which is good and bad.' The good is that working capital doesn't grow as fast as the company grows. The bad is that if Astra doesn't produce its motorcycles and cars fast enough, it loses market share. This is where Slack's analytical skills—and perhaps a little of market clairvoyance—pay off. Building too much capacity would be a mistake, because economists expect the Indonesian market to cool eventually, and competition will eventually ease the now-monumental thirst for Astra vehicles. That would lead to waste, including high inventory costs and working capital woes. But to build too little would also be a mistake. Right now Slack is happy enough with Astra's balance on this fine line, but he's ever vigilant.

More an embarrassment of riches than a nagging problem, Slack's situation is shared with the companies that occupy the top tier of CFO Asia's and REL Consultancy's fifth annual ranking of working capital in the region. In choice sectors within a handful of economies—most notably Indonesia, India, South Korea, and Taiwan—the top performers are all improving their working capital management, despite periods of intense growth. To show this phenomenon, we've offered a different slice of the numbers than in previous years, showing percentage changes in key figures, including days working capital (DWC), over the previous two years. We've then ranked the bunch by performance on days working capital, showing the top and bottom players in a given sector. Beneath that, for benchmarking purposes, we've given an average for the sector.

The historical information is instructive. Astra, for example, decreased its DWC by 14 percent between 2001 and 2002 and then 23 per cent in the following year. (Astra's figure on the ranking is a DWC of 20 days. The figures that Slack gives above are a more recent reckoning.) The top player in that sector, Sanyang Industry Company, a US$627 million auto manufacturer from Taiwan, held its reduction of DWC by 17 percent steady over two years, resulting in three days DWC. Siemens India, a US$376 million maker of electronic components, can boast of a negative 15 DWC and an improvement of 35 per cent over the previous year. Likewise, Hindustan Lever, the US$2.4 billion household products maker, enjoys a negative 19 DWC driven by an improvement of 26 per cent over the previous year. The US$924 million diversified industrial company Sterlite Industries (India) has an enviable negative three DWC based on an improvement of 135 per cent from the prior year.

Given the improvements in so many sectors, it would be natural to assume that Asia's overall averages for working capital performance would be improving. Sadly, this is not so. In 2003, net working capital of Asian companies deteriorated slightly on 2002, with a 1.6 per cent increase in DWC. This still brings the total fall to 8.6 per cent over the past two years, because of an improvement in 2001, but, of course, indicates a slowing of what looked to be a positive trend. The reason behind this, according Peter Rabjohns, an analyst with REL in Singapore, is that Asia-wide, companies have managed to bring in receivables at a better rate, but this improvement has been offset by a 2.6 per cent increase in days inventory outstanding and a 5.3 per cent decline in days payables outstanding.

Even if the overall performance deteriorated slightly in 2003 on 2002, it is interesting to notice that out of a total of 47 sectors, two-thirds of them have shown improved DWC, while a third deteriorated. Among the biggest improvers were manufacturers of computer-related hardware, consumer and household services, and containers and packaging. Heavy industries, such as mining, oil, and telecom companies did better. Among the sectors that took a dive were airlines, electric utilities, media, and home construction. Even some of the sectors that comprise the outstanding companies mentioned above have declined on an overall basis, including household products and electronic components.

Reading trends in this business is never easy, as the demands and conditions for working capital differ from sector to sector. But Rabjohns sees a kind of bifurcation in working capital skills around the region that would explain the decline. 'This year, the gap is wider between the top tier and the bottom tier in most of the sectors,' says Rabjohns. 'There's a bigger difference between who's better and who's worse.' For most of the sectors, excess working capital, or 'opportunity', has grown in the bottom tier. REL calculates its excess figure by comparing working capital performance of a company against an average for the top quartile of a given sector. Essentially, this excess liquidity is tied up in invoices not being paid by companies' customers, suppliers being paid too early, and inventories lying unsold on warehouse shelves. Looked at this way, at the top 1,000 Asian companies US$140 billion of cash is tied up in excess working capital, representing 38 per cent of all the receivables, inventories, and payables on their books. In both Europe and the US, the amount of total receivables, inventories, and payables that can be classified as excess working cap amounts to 27 percent in each region. 'This suggests that there is a larger distribution of performance within each working capital component among Asian companies,' says Rabjohns.

This means that Asia, a traditional laggard in working capital management, retains this lowly mantle due to the performance of companies like Del Monte Pacific, the US$206 million Singapore-based food producer with a 162 DWC, compared with a sector average of 54; Metropolitan Construction, the US$257 million Taiwan heavy construction company in a class by itself with 795 DWC, compared with a sector average of 79; and Cipla, the US$303 million Indian pharmaceutical manufacturer with 188 DWC, stacked against a sector average of 98. The reasons given for the wider gap between the 'champs' and the 'chumps' are the traditional candidates that dog working capital management in the region. These include a greater geographical dispersal of supply chains, ungainly or inoperable infrastructure, perhaps exemplified by India's battered roads, and businesses built on 'relationships' in the Asian milieu, that allow suppliers to go easy on collecting receivables for long-standing customers.

While these drawbacks remain impediments, the greatest lesson in this year's ranking is that, to quote Ira Gershwin, 'It ain't necessarily so'. Companies like Astra and Hindustan Lever, in markets once thought impossible, are showing significant improvements. CFOs like Slack attribute this to close attention to the fundamentals. In the case of Astra, this includes careful management of dealer and banking relationships. Slack says that as soon as the vehicles are sold to dealers, the dealers obtain a line of credit from the banks to pay. Therefore, Astra gets its money on a pre-paid basis and transfers the problem of collecting receivables over to the dealers. If the dealers fail to meet a certain threshold, Astra stops shipping more cars. In return for taking on this risk, the dealers are able to get concessions from the banks, in the form of low interest rates on loans, lower rates on mortgages, and better conditions on collateral. In this type of arrangement, an advantage emerges in the transparency a single bank can provide. It's easier to spot problems as they emerge and act quickly.

The salutary role of banks in working capital management is one reason that J Gopalkrishnan, the CFO of Indian cement manufacturer Grasim, says that cashflow has improved in his business. As the ranking shows, the improvements have been steady. Birla Corporation, Grasim's owner, tops the building materials category with 11 DWC, having reduced its days working capital by 38 per cent between 2003 and 2002, and 38 per cent a year earlier.

He flatly states that better management is a result of banking competition that has allowed the company to move from traditional bankers, the state-owned Indian institutions, to more competitive private institutions and the foreign banks that partner with them. These banks have invested in technology, allowing a visibility over cashflow unheard of five years ago.

In India, and in the cement business, that visibility can breed distinct advantages. Gopalkrishnan says that, on a typical day Grasim has 10 billion rupees (US$229 million) in receivables outstanding, and because many of those sales are on India's rural byways, it takes six to eight days to collect. Five years ago, he says, 'we'd have 20 million rupees in a state bank on one side of India, and on the other side of the country, we'd be drawing on an overdraft of 10 crores (about the same amount) the same day.' Now, Grasim's banks have the ability to make cash across the country visible and available when they need it. What's more, says Gopalkrishnan, 'today, I know for sure that cement and metals businesses of Birla have tied up with these banks, even in remote centers. There's an early clear every morning, and it's all on-line.'

The advantage, he says, is that 'we can use the float early in the morning,' he says. 'It helps reduce funding costs, because we don't have to borrow while all this cash is parked somewhere that we can't tap. We can put it in a mutual fund, where the return it earns also helps us reduce costs.'

Nick Franck, head of CFO Solutions consultancy in Singapore, is less willing to hand laurels to technology and banks. He says that improvements in top Indian companies are more likely due to better internal processes. 'Banks may have been importing "Western"-style systems,' he says, 'but the real improvements surely come from better processes within the companies.'

This suggests that companies that want to find their way into the top tier of working capital performers can't buy their way into a solution. Like their counterparts at Astra and Birla, they will have to roll up their sleeves.

1   Why is PT Astra able to keep its inventory low?
2   What are the risks Astra faces by keeping inventory low?
3   Why has net working capital of Asian companies deteriorated slightly over the last year?
4   In which sectors did DWC improve or deteriorate?
    Can you think of any explanations?
5   What reasons were given to explain the wide variance in performance in this area?
6   How did Astra manage to obtain the improvements?
7   How have the banks enabled working capital management to improve in India?

SOLUTIONS TO ACTIVITIES

Activity 13.1

In answering this activity, you may have thought of the following:

- changes in interest rates
- changes in market demand
- changes in the seasons
- changes in the state of the economy.

You may have also thought of others.

Activity 13.2

In answering this activity, you may have thought of the following costs:

- loss of sales, from being unable to provide the goods required immediately
- loss of goodwill from customers, for being unable to satisfy customer demand
- high transportation costs incurred to ensure inventories are replenished quickly
- lost production due to shortage of raw materials
- inefficient production scheduling due to shortages
- purchasing inventories at a higher price than may otherwise have been possible in order to replenish inventories quickly.

Activity 13.3

The average weekly demand for the inventory item is 10,400 / 52 = 200 units. During the time between ordering the inventory and receiving the goods the inventory sold will be 4 × 200 units = 800 units. So the company should re-order no later than when the inventory level goes down to 800 units in order to avoid a stockout (i.e. running out of stock).

Activity 13.4

Your answer to this activity should be as follows:

$$EOQ = \sqrt{\frac{2 \times 2,000 \times 25}{4}}$$

$$= 158 \text{ units (to the nearest whole unit)}$$

This will mean that the business will have to order product X about 13 times each year in order to meet sales demand.

Activity 13.5

There are various sources of information available to a business to help assess the financial health of a customer. You may have thought of some of the following:

- *Trade references*. Some businesses ask a potential customer to furnish them with references from other suppliers who have had dealings with them. This may be extremely useful, providing the references supplied are truly representative of the opinions of a customer's suppliers. There is a danger that a potential customer will attempt to be highly selective when furnishing details of other suppliers in order to gain a more favourable impression than is deserved.
- *Bank references*. It is possible to ask the potential customer for a bank reference. Although banks are usually prepared to oblige, the contents of a reference are not always very informative. If customers are in financial difficulties the bank will usually be unwilling to add to their problems by supplying poor references.
- *Annual accounts*. All public limited companies and all large proprietary companies are required to prepare an annual report. Under the circumstances the company that is being asked to grant credit could reasonably expect to receive a copy of the financial report, whether it is legally required or not. A company that is not prepared to provide a copy of its report is potentially a greater risk to the business considering credit.
- *The customer*. You may wish to interview the directors of the company and visit its premises in order to gain some impression about the way the company conducts its business. Where a significant amount of credit is required, the business may ask the company for access to internal budgets and other unpublished financial information to help assess the level of risk to be taken.
- *Credit agencies*. Specialist agencies exist to provide information that can be used to assess the creditworthiness of a potential customer. The information that a credit agency supplies may be gleaned from various sources, including the accounts of the customer, court judgments and news items relating to the customer from both published and unpublished sources.

Activity 13.6

Managers might decide to do one or more of the following:

- offer cash discounts to encourage prompt payment
- change the collection period
- improve the accounting system to ensure customers are billed more promptly, reminders sent out promptly, etc.
- change the eligibility criteria for customers who receive credit.

Activity 13.7

According to economic theory there are three motives for holding cash. These may be identified as follows:

- *Transactionary motive*. In order to meet day-to-day commitments a business requires a certain amount of cash. Payments in respect of wages, overhead expenses, goods purchased, etc., must be made at the due dates. Cash has been described as the 'life blood' of a business. Unless it 'circulates' through the business and is available for the payment of maturing obligations, the survival of the business will be put at risk. We saw in an earlier chapter that profitability alone is not enough. A business must have sufficient cash to pay its debts when they fall due.
- *Precautionary motive*. If future cash flows are uncertain for any reason it would be prudent to hold a balance of cash. For example, a major customer which owes a large sum to the business may be in financial difficulties. Given this situation, the business can retain its capacity to meet its obligations by holding a cash balance. Similarly, if there is some uncertainty concerning future outlays a cash balance will be required.
- *Speculative motive*. A business may decide to hold cash in order to be in a position to exploit profitable opportunities as and when they arise. For example, by holding cash a business may be able to acquire a competitor business that suddenly becomes available at an attractive price. Holding cash has an opportunity cost for the business which must be taken into account. Thus, when evaluating the potential returns from holding cash for speculative purposes, the cost of forgone investment opportunities must also be considered.

Activity 13.8

Factors that influence the decision as to how much cash will be held are varied and may include:

- *The nature of the business*. Some businesses, such as utilities (water companies, electricity companies, gas companies, etc.), may have cash flows that are both predictable and reasonably certain. This will enable them to hold lower cash balances. For some businesses cash balances may vary greatly according to the time of year. A seasonal business may accumulate cash during the high season to enable it to meet commitments during the low season.
- *The opportunity cost of holding cash*. Where there are profitable opportunities it may not be wise to hold a large cash balance.
- *The level of inflation*. The holding of cash during a period of rising prices will lead to a loss of purchasing power. The higher the level of inflation the greater will be this loss.
- *The availability of near-liquid assets*. If a business has marketable securities or inventories that may easily be liquidated the amount of cash held may be reduced.
- *The availability of borrowing*. If a business can borrow easily (and quickly) there is less need to hold cash.
- *The cost of borrowing*. When interest rates are high the option of borrowing becomes less attractive.
- *Economic conditions*. When the economy is in recession businesses may prefer to hold on to cash in order to be well placed to invest when the economy improves. In addition, during a recession, businesses may experience difficulties in collecting debts. They may therefore hold higher cash balances than usual in order to meet commitments.
- *Relationships with suppliers*. Too little cash may hinder the ability of the business to pay suppliers promptly. This can lead to a loss of goodwill. It may also lead to discounts forgone.

Activity 13.9

The operating cash cycle may be calculated as follows:

Number of days

Average inventory holding period:

$$\frac{\text{(Opening inventory + closing inventory) / 2}}{\text{Cost of sales}} \times 365 = \frac{(142 + 166) / 2}{544} \times 365 = \quad 103$$

Add
Average settlement period for debtors (based on closing debtors' balance, as average debtors figure not available):

$$\frac{\text{Trade debtors}}{\text{Credit sales}} \times 365 = \frac{264}{820} \times 365 = \qquad\qquad \underline{118}$$

$$\underline{221}$$

Less
Average settlement period for creditors (based on closing creditors' balance, as average creditors' figure not available):

$$\frac{\text{Trade creditors}}{\text{Credit purchases}} \times 365 = \frac{159}{568} \times 365 = \qquad \underline{102}$$

Operating cash cycle $\qquad\qquad\qquad\qquad\qquad\qquad\qquad \underline{119}$

The company can reduce the operating cash cycle in a number of ways. The average inventory holding period seems quite long. At present, average inventory held supports more than three months' sales. This may be reduced by reducing the level of inventory held. Similarly, the average settlement period for debtors seems long. Debtors represent nearly four months' sales. This may be reduced by imposing tighter credit control, offering discounts, charging interest on overdue accounts, etc. However, any policy decisions concerning inventory and debtors must take account of current trading conditions.

The operating cash cycle could also be reduced by extending the period of credit taken to pay suppliers. However, for reasons mentioned below, this option must be given careful consideration.

OBJECTIVES

When you have completed your study of this chapter you should be able to:

1 identify the main sources of finance available to a business

2 explain the advantages and disadvantages of each form

3 describe the concept of gearing and its influence on the long-term financing decision

4 explain the reasons that influence whether or not long-term or short-term finance is used

5 identify the so-called internal sources of finance and explain them

6 explain the role and nature of the stock exchange

7 explain the role of venture capital organisations in financing businesses

8 discuss the ways in which share capital may be issued and identify the underlying reasons why a particular method might be chosen.

14

FINANCING THE BUSINESS

In this chapter we examine various aspects of financing the business. We begin by considering the various sources of finance available to a business and the factors to be considered in choosing an appropriate source of finance. We then go on to consider various aspects of the capital markets, including the role of the stock exchange, the role of venture capital organisations and the ways in which share capital may be issued.

SOURCES OF FINANCE

In order to examine the various sources of finance for a business it is useful to distinguish between *external* and *internal* sources of finance and, when considering the various external sources of finance, it is probably helpful to distinguish between *long-term* and *short-term* sources. Figure 14.1 summarises the main sources of long-term and short-term external finance.

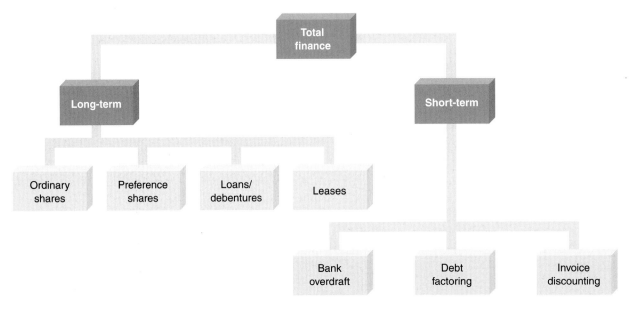

FIGURE 14.1 The main external sources of finance

In the sections that follow we consider the various sources of external finance under each of the headings in Figure 14.1. We then go on to consider the various sources of internal finance available.

LONG-TERM SOURCES OF FINANCE

For the purpose of this chapter long-term sources of finance are defined as sources of finance that are not due for repayment within one year. Figure 14.1 reveals that the main forms of long-term external finance are:

✳ ordinary shares
✳ preference shares
✳ loans
✳ finance leases and sale and lease-back arrangements.

In order to decide on the most appropriate form of external finance, we must be clear about the advantages and disadvantages of each.

Ordinary shares

Ordinary shares form the backbone of the financial structure of a company. Ordinary share capital represents the risk capital of a company. There is no fixed rate of dividend, and ordinary shareholders will only receive a dividend if profits available for distribution still remain after other investors (preference shareholders and lenders) have received their dividend or interest payments. If the company is wound up, the ordinary shareholders will receive any proceeds from asset disposals only after lenders and creditors and, often, preference shareholders have received their entitlements. Because of the high risks associated with this form of investment, ordinary share-holders will normally require a higher rate of return from the company.

Although ordinary shareholders have limited loss liability, based on the amount they have agreed to invest, the potential returns from their investment are unlimited. Ordinary shareholders have control over the company. They have voting rights and thus they have the power to elect the directors and also to remove them from office.

From the company perspective, ordinary shares can be a valuable form of financing as, at times, it is useful to be able to avoid paying a dividend. In the case of a new expanding company, or a company in difficulties, the requirement to make a cash payment to investors can be a real burden. Where the company is financed by ordinary shares, this problem need not occur. However, the costs of financing ordinary shares may be high over the longer term for the reasons mentioned earlier. Moreover, the company does not obtain any tax relief on dividends paid to shareholders, whereas interest on borrowings is tax deductible.

Preference shares

Preference shares offer investors a lower level of risk than equity shares. Providing there are sufficient profits available, preference shares will normally be given a fixed rate of dividend each year and preference dividends will be paid before ordinary dividends are paid. Where the company is wound up, preference shareholders may be given priority over the claims of ordinary shareholders. Because of the lower level of risk associated with this form of investment, investors will be offered a lower level of return than that offered for ordinary shares.

There are various types of preference shares which may be issued by a company. Cumulative preference shares give investors the right to receive arrears of dividends that have arisen as a result of the company having insufficient profits in previous periods. The unpaid dividends will accumulate and will be paid when the company has generated sufficient profits. Non-cumulative preference shares do not give investors the right to receive arrears of dividends. Thus, if a company is not in a position to pay the preference dividend due for a particular period, the preference shareholder loses the right to receive the dividend. Participating preference shares give investors the right to a further share in the profits available for dividends after they have been paid the fixed rate due on the preference shares and after ordinary shareholders have been awarded a dividend. Redeemable preference shares allow the company to buy back the shares from shareholders at some agreed future date. Redeemable preference shares are seen as a lower-risk investment than non-redeemable shares and so often carry a lower dividend.

ACTIVITY 14.1

Would you expect the market price of ordinary shares or preference shares to be the more volatile? Why?

Preference shares are no longer a major source of new finance for companies. An important reason why this particular form of fixed-return capital has declined in popularity is that dividends paid to preference shareholders are not allowable against taxable profits, whereas interest on loan capital is an allowable expense. A further reason relates to changes in accounting rules, which mean that preference shares are no longer seen as equity, but debt, in terms of assessing debt capacity.

Loans and debentures

Many companies rely on loan capital in order to finance operations. Lenders will enter into a contract with the company in which the rate of interest, dates of interest payments and capital repayments, and security for the loan are clearly stated. In the event that the interest payments or capital repayments in respect of the loan are not made on the due dates, the lender will usually have the right, under the terms of the contract, to seize the assets on which the loan is secured and sell them in order to repay the amount outstanding. Security for a loan may take the form of a fixed charge on particular assets of the company (freehold land and premises are often favoured by lenders) or a floating charge on the whole of the company's assets. A floating charge will 'crystallise' and fix on particular assets in the event that the company defaults on its obligations.

ACTIVITY 14.2

What do you think is the advantage for the company of having a floating charge rather than a fixed charge on its assets?

Investors will normally view loans as being less risky than preference shares or equity shares. Lenders have priority over any claims from shareholders and will usually have security for their loans. As a result of the lower level of risk associated with this form of investment, investors are usually prepared to accept a lower rate of return.

One form of long-term loan associated with limited companies is the **debenture**. This is simply a loan that is evidenced by a trust deed. The debenture loan is frequently divided into units (rather like share capital) and investors are invited to purchase the number of units they require. The debenture loan may be redeemable or irredeemable. Debentures of public limited companies are often traded on the stock exchange and their listed value will fluctuate according to the fortunes of the company, movements in interest rates, etc.

Another form of long-term loan finance is the **eurobond**. Eurobonds are issued by listed companies (and other organisations) in various countries and the finance is raised in countries other than the country of the denominated currency. They are bearer **bonds** which are often issued in US dollars but may also be issued in other major currencies such as Australian or New Zealand dollars. Interest is normally paid on an annual basis. Eurobonds are part of an emerging international capital market and are not subject to regulations imposed by authorities in particular countries. There is a secondary market for eurobonds which has been created by a number of financial institutions throughout the world. The issue of eurobonds is usually made by placing them with large banks and other financial institutions which may either retain them as an investment or sell them to their clients.

ACTIVITY 14.3

Why might a company prefer to issue eurobonds in preference to more conventional forms of loan capital?

Interest rates on loan finance may be either floating or fixed. A floating rate means that the required rate of return from lenders will rise and fall with market rates of interest. However, the market value of the lenders' investment in the business is likely to remain fairly stable over time. The converse will normally be true for fixed-interest loans and debentures. The interest payments will remain unchanged with rises and falls in market rates of interest, but the resale value of the investment (the loan) will fall when interest rates rise and will rise when interest rates fall.

A company may issue redeemable loan capital which offers a rate of interest below the market rate. In some cases, the loan capital may have a zero rate of interest. Such loans are issued at a discount to their redeemable value and are referred to as **deep discount bonds**. Thus, a company may issue loan capital at (say) $80 for every $100 of nominal value. Although lenders will receive little or no interest during the period of the loan, they will receive a gain when the loan is finally redeemed. The redemption yield, as it is referred to, is often quite high and, when calculated on an annual basis, may compare favourably with returns from other forms of loan capital with the same level of risk. Deep discount bonds may have particular appeal to companies with short-term cash flow problems. They receive an immediate injection of cash and there are no significant cash outflows associated with the loan until the maturity date. Deep discount bonds are likely to appeal to investors who do not have short-term cash flow problems as they must wait for the loan to mature before receiving a significant return.

Convertible loans and debentures

Convertible loans or debentures give the investor the right to convert the loan into equity shares at a given future date and at a specified price. The investor remains a lender to the company and will receive interest on the amount of the loan until such time as the conversion takes place. The investor is not obliged to convert the loan or debenture to equity shares. This will normally only be done if the market price of the shares at the conversion date exceeds the agreed conversion price.

An investor may find this form of investment a useful hedge against risk. This may be particularly useful when investment in a new company is being considered. Initially, the investment is in the form of a loan and regular interest payments will be made. If the company is successful the investor can then decide to convert the investment into equity shares.

The company may also find this form of financing useful. If the company is successful the loan becomes self-liquidating as investors will exercise their option to convert. The company may also be able to offer a lower rate of interest to investors because investors expect future benefits arising from conversion. However, there will be some dilution of both control and earnings for existing shareholders if holders of convertible loans exercise their option to convert.

Warrants

Holders of **warrants** have the right, but not the obligation, to acquire ordinary shares in a company at a given price. In the case of both convertible loan capital and warrants, the price at which shares may be acquired is usually higher than the market price prevailing at the time of issue. The warrant will usually state the number of shares the holder may purchase and the time limit within which the option to buy shares can be exercised. Occasionally, perpetual warrants are issued which have no set time limits. Warrants do not confer voting rights or entitle the holders to make any claims on the assets of the company.

Share warrants are often provided as a 'sweetener' to accompany the issue of loan capital or debentures. The issue of warrants in this way may enable the company to offer lower rates of interest on the loan or to negotiate less restrictive loan conditions. The issue of warrants enables the lenders to benefit from future company success providing the option to purchase is exercised. However, an investor will normally only exercise this option if the market price exceeds the option price within the time limit specified. Share warrants may be detachable, which means that they can be sold separately from the loan capital.

Mortgages

A **mortgage** is a form of loan that is secured by freehold property. Financial institutions such as banks, insurance companies and superannuation funds are often prepared to lend to businesses on this basis. The mortgage loan may be extended over a long period, often over 25–30 years. In addition to the possible capital gain from holding the freehold property, businesses also benefit from a decline in the real value of the capital sum owing because of inflation. However, lenders usually compensate for this fall in value, as mentioned earlier, by increasing the rate of interest payable.

Loan covenants

When drawing up a loan agreement the lender may impose certain obligations and restrictions in order to protect the investment in the business. **Loan covenants** (as they are referred to) often form part of a loan agreement and may deal with such matters as:

* *Accounts.* The lender may require access to the financial accounts of the business on a regular basis.
* *Other loans.* The lender may require the business to ask permission before taking on further loans.
* *Dividend payments.* The lender may require dividends to be limited during the period of the loan.
* *Liquidity.* The lender may require the business to maintain a certain level of liquidity during the period of the loan.

Any breach of these restrictive covenants can have serious consequences for the business. The lender may require immediate repayment of the loan in the event of a serious breach.

> **ACTIVITY 14.4**
>
> Both preference shares and loan capital are forms of finance which require the company to provide a particular rate of return to investors. What factors may be taken into account by a company when deciding between these two sources of finance?

A further point that has not been dealt with so far is that preference shares issued form part of the permanent capital base of the company; that is, the funds contributed (and placed at risk, however small) by shareholders. If they are redeemed at some future date, the law requires that they are replaced, either by a new issue of shares or by a transfer from reserves, in order to ensure that the capital base of the company stays intact. However, loans are not viewed, in law, as part of the permanent capital base of the company and therefore there is no requirement to replace any loan capital that has been redeemed by the company.

Finance leases and sale and lease-back arrangements

Instead of buying an asset directly from a supplier, a business may decide to arrange for a financial institution, such as a bank, to buy the asset and then agree to lease the asset from the institution. A finance lease is, in essence, a form of lending. Although legal ownership of the asset rests with the financial institution (the lessor), a finance lease agreement transfers virtually all the rewards and risks that are associated with the item being leased to the business (the lessee). The lease agreement covers a significant part of the life of the item being leased and often cannot be cancelled.

In recent years some important benefits associated with finance leasing have disappeared. Changes in the tax laws no longer make it such a tax-efficient form of financing, and changes in accounting disclosure requirements make it no longer possible to conceal this form of 'borrowing' from investors. Nevertheless, the popularity of finance leases has continued to increase. Other reasons must therefore exist for businesses to adopt this form of financing. These reasons are said to include the following:

* *Ease of borrowing.* Leasing may be obtained more easily than other forms of long-term finance. Lenders normally require some form of security and a profitable track record before making advances to a business. However, a lessor may be prepared to lease assets to a new business without a track record and to use the leased assets as security for the amounts owing.

* *Cost.* Leasing agreements may be offered at reasonable cost. As the asset leased is used as security, standard lease arrangements can be applied and detailed credit checking of lessees may be unnecessary. This can reduce administration costs for the lessor and thereby help in providing competitive lease rentals.

* *Flexibility.* Leasing can help to provide flexibility where there are rapid changes in technology. If an option to cancel can be incorporated into the lease, the business may be able to exercise this option and invest in new technology as it becomes available. This will help the business avoid the risk of obsolescence.

* *Cash flows.* Leasing, rather than purchasing an asset outright, means that large cash outflows can be avoided. The leasing option allows cash outflows to be smoothed out over the asset's life. In some cases it is possible to arrange for low lease payments to be made in the early years of the asset's life, when cash inflows may be low, and for these to increase over time.

A **sale and lease-back** arrangement involves a business selling freehold property to a financial institution in order to raise finance. However, the sale is accompanied by an agreement to lease the freehold property back to the business to allow it to continue to operate from the premises. The rent payable under the lease arrangement is allowable against profits for taxation purposes. There are usually rent reviews at regular intervals throughout the period of the lease and the amounts payable in future years may be difficult to predict. At the end of the lease agreement, the business must either try to renew the lease or find alternative premises, as there is no guarantee that the customer may recover ownership at the end of the lease. Although the sale of the premises will result in an immediate injection of cash for the business, it will lose benefits from any future capital appreciation on the property. Where a capital gain arises on the sale of the premises to the financial institution, a liability for taxation may also arise.

GEARING AND THE LONG-TERM FINANCING DECISION

In Chapter 6 we saw that gearing occurs when a business is financed, at least in part, by contributions from fixed-charge capital such as loans, debentures and preference shares. We also saw that the level of gearing associated with a business is often an important factor in assessing the risk and returns to ordinary shareholders. In the example that follows we consider the implications of making a choice between a geared and an ungeared form of raising long-term finance.

EXAMPLE

14.1

The following is a shortened version of the accounts of Woodhall Engineers Ltd, a company that is not listed on a stock exchange.

WOODHALL ENGINEERS LTD

Income statement for the year ended 31 December

	2005 $m	2004 $m
Sales turnover	50	47
Operating costs	47	41
Operating profit	3	6
Interest expense	2	2
Profit on ordinary activities before tax	1	4
Taxation on profit on ordinary activities	=	=
Profit on ordinary activities after tax	1	4
Dividends	1	1
Profit retained for the financial year	–	3

Balance sheet as at 31 December

	2005 $m	2004 $m
Current assets		
Cash at bank	1	3
Debtors	17	16
Inventory	18	10
	36	29
Non-current assets (less depreciation)	20	21
Total assets	56	50
Current liabilities		
Short-term debt	11	5
Trade creditors	10	10
	21	15
Non-current liabilities		
Long-term loans (secured)	15	15
Shareholders' equity		
Paid-up share capital ordinary shares issued at 25c	16	16
Retained profits	4	4
	20	20
Total liabilities and shareholders' equity	56	50

The company is making plans to expand its factory. New plant will cost $8 million and an expansion in output will increase working capital needs by $4 million. Over the 15 years' life of the project, incremental profits arising from the expansion will be $2 million per year before interest and tax. In addition, 2006 profits before tax from its existing activities are expected to return to 2004 levels.

Two alternative methods of financing the expansion have been discussed by Woodhall's directors. The first is the issue of debt totalling $12 million, at an annual rate of interest of 15 per cent, repayable in 2010. The second is a rights issue of 40 million ordinary shares issued at 30 cents per share.

The company has substantial tax losses, so you can ignore taxation in your calculations. The 2006 dividend per share is expected to be the same as that for 2005.

Prepare a forecast of Woodhall's income statement (excluding sales turnover and operating costs) for the year ended 31 December 2006, and of its shareholders' equity, long-term loans and number of shares outstanding at that date assuming:

(a) the company issues debt

(b) the company issues ordinary shares.

The first part of the question requires the preparation of a forecast income statement under each financing option. These statements will be as follows:

Forecast income statement for the year ended 31 December 2006

	Debt issue $m	Equity issue $m
Profit before interest and taxation	8.0	8.0
Loan interest	3.8	2.0
Profit before tax	4.2	6.0
Taxation	–	–
Profit after tax	4.2	6.0
Dividends	1.0	1.625*
Retained profit for the year	3.2	4.375

* For forecasting purposes it is presumed that the dividends per share will remain the same. Given that there were originally 64 million shares and there are now 104 million the dividends will increase by the ratio 104/64 = $1.625 million.

The capital structure of the company under each option will be as follows:

Shareholders' equity

Share capital ordinary shares—64 million issued at 25c	16.0	16.0
Share capital ordinary shares—40 million issued at 30c		12.0
Retained profit	7.2	8.375
	23.2	36.375
No. of shares in issue (25c shares)	64 million	104 million

ACTIVITY 14.5

Calculate Woodhall's interest cover and earnings per share for the year ended 31 December 2006 and its gearing on that date, assuming:

(a) the company issues debt

(b) the company issues ordinary shares.

ACTIVITY 14.6

What would your views of the proposed schemes in Activity 14.5 be in each of the following circumstances?

1. You are a banker and you are approached for a loan.

2. You are a shareholder in Woodhall and you are asked to subscribe to a rights issue.

SELF-ASSESSMENT QUESTION 14.1

Ashcroft Ltd, a family-controlled company, is considering raising additional funds to modernise its factory. The scheme is expected to cost $2.34 million and will increase annual profits before interest and tax from 1 January 2006 by $0.6 million. A summarised balance sheet and income statement are shown below. Currently the share price is $2.

Two schemes have been suggested. First, 1.3 million shares could be issued at $1.80 (net of issue costs). Second, a consortium of six Melbourne-based institutions has offered to buy debentures from the company totalling $2.34 million. Interest would be at the rate of 13 per cent per annum and capital repayments of equal instalments of $234,000 starting on 1 January 2007 would be required.

ASHCROFT LTD

Balance sheet as at 31 December 2005

	$m
Current assets	
Debtors	2.2
Inventory	2.4
	4.6
Non-current assets	1.4
Total assets	6.0
Current liabilities	
Creditors	2.7
Income tax payable	0.6
Dividends payable	0.2
	3.5

Shareholders' equity	
Paid-up share capital issued at 25c a share	1.0
Retained profits	1.5
	2.5
Total liabilities and shareholders' equity	6.0

Income statement for the year ended 31 December 2005	
	$m
Sales	11.2
Profit on ordinary activities before tax	1.2
Income tax	0.6
Profit after tax	0.6
Dividends	0.3
Retained profit for the year	0.3

For illustration purposes assume tax at the rate of 50 per cent.

Required:

(a) Calculate the earnings per share for 2006 under the equity (share issue) alternative and the debt (debenture) alternative.

(b) Discuss the considerations the directors should take into account before deciding upon debt or equity finance.

SHORT-TERM SOURCES OF FINANCE

A short-term source of borrowing is one that is available for a short time period. Although there is no agreed definition of what 'short term' means, we will define it as being up to one year. The main sources of short-term borrowing are as follows.

Bank overdraft

This represents a very flexible form of borrowing. The size of the overdraft can (subject to bank approval) be increased or decreased according to the financing requirements of the business. It is relatively inexpensive to arrange and interest rates are often very competitive. The rate of interest charged on an overdraft will vary, however, according to how creditworthy the bank perceives the customer to be. It is also fairly easy to arrange— sometimes an overdraft can be agreed by a telephone call to the bank. In view of these advantages it is not surprising that this is an extremely popular form of short-term finance.

Banks prefer to grant overdrafts that are self-liquidating—that is, the funds applied will result in cash inflows that will extinguish the overdraft balance. The banks may ask for forecast cash flow statements from the business to see when the overdraft will be repaid and how much finance is required. The bank may also require some form of security on amounts advanced. One potential drawback with this form of finance is that it is repayable on demand. This may pose problems for a business that is illiquid. In practice, many businesses operate using an overdraft and this form of borrowing, although in theory regarded as short-term, can often become effectively a long-term source of finance. Banks, however, are likely to put pressure on businesses to re-finance to other long-term forms of debt, if the overdraft balance does not fluctuate sufficiently, or if the firm is unable to generate cash flows to reduce overdraft debt periodically.

Debt factoring

Debt factoring is a form of service that is offered by a financial institution (a factor). Many of the large factors are subsidiaries of commercial banks. Debt factoring involves the factor taking over the sales ledger (i.e. the debtors' accounts) of a company. In addition to operating normal credit control procedures, a factor may offer to undertake credit investigations and to provide protection for approved credit sales. The factor is usually prepared to make an advance to the company of up to 85 per cent of approved trade debtors. The charge made for the **factoring** service is based on total turnover and is often around 2–3 per cent of turnover. Any advances made to the company by the factor will attract a rate of interest similar to the rate charged on bank overdrafts.

A company may find a factoring arrangement very convenient. It can result in savings in credit management and can create more certain cash flows. It can also release the time of key personnel for more profitable ends. This may be extremely important for smaller companies which rely on the talent and skills of a few key individuals. However, there is a possibility that some will see a factoring arrangement as an indication that the company is experiencing financial difficulties. This may have an adverse effect on confidence in the company. For this reason, some businesses try to conceal the factoring arrangement by collecting debts on behalf of the factor. When considering a factoring agreement, the costs and likely benefits arising must be identified and carefully weighed.

Invoice discounting

Invoice discounting involves a business approaching a factor or other financial institution for a loan based on a proportion of the face value of credit sales outstanding. If the institution agrees, the amount advanced is usually 75–80 per cent of the value of the approved sales invoices outstanding. The business must agree to repay the advance within a relatively short period—perhaps 60 or 90 days. The responsibility for collection of the trade debts outstanding remains with the business and repayment of the advance is not dependent on the trade debt being collected. Invoice discounting will not result in such a close relationship developing between the client and the financial institution as that in factoring. Invoice discounting may be a one-off arrangement whereas debt factoring usually involves a longer-term arrangement between the customer and the financial institution.

Nowadays, invoice discounting is a much more important source of funds to companies than factoring. Invoice discounting is believed to have amounted to more than $20 billion in Australia in 2004, more than double the turnover in 2001. Factoring, on the other hand, probably turned over less than $4 billion. There are various reasons for this. First, it is a confidential form of financing which the client's customers will know nothing about. Second, the service charge for invoice discounting is only about 0.2–0.3 per cent of turnover, compared to 2–3 per cent of turnover for factoring. Finally, many companies are unwilling to relinquish control over their sales ledger. Customers are an important resource of the business and many companies wish to retain control over all aspects of their relationship with their customers.

LONG-TERM VERSUS SHORT-TERM BORROWING

Having decided that some form of borrowing is required to finance the business, the managers must then decide whether long-term borrowing or short-term borrowing is more appropriate. There are a number of issues that should be taken into account when deciding between long-term and short-term borrowing. These include the following:

✱ *Matching.* The business may attempt to match the type of borrowing with the nature of the assets held. Thus, assets that form part of the permanent operating base of the business, including non-current assets and a certain level of current assets, will be financed by long-term borrowing. Assets held for a short period, such as current assets held to meet seasonal increases in demand, will be financed by short-term borrowing (see Figure 14.2).

A business may wish to match the asset life exactly with the period of the related loan; however, this may not be possible because of the difficulty of predicting the life of many assets.

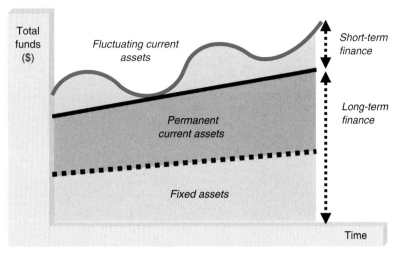

FIGURE 14.2 Short- and long-term financing requirements

ACTIVITY 14.7

Some companies may take up a less—or more—conservative financing position than shown in Figure 14.2. How would the diagram differ under each of these options?

✳ *Flexibility.* Short-term borrowing may be useful in order to postpone a commitment to taking on a long-term loan. This may be seen as desirable if interest rates are high and it is forecast that they will fall in the future. Short-term borrowing does not usually incur penalties if there is early repayment of the amount outstanding, whereas some form of financial penalty may have to be paid if long-term debt is repaid early.

✳ *Re-funding risk.* Short-term borrowing has to be renewed more frequently than long-term borrowing. This may create problems for the business if it is already in financial difficulties or if there is a shortage of funds available for lending.

✳ *Interest rates.* Interest payable on long-term debt is often higher than for short-term debt. (This is because lenders require a higher return where their funds are locked up for a long period.) This fact may make short-term borrowing a more attractive source of finance for a business. However, there may be other costs associated with borrowing (e.g. arrangement fees) to be taken into account. The more frequently borrowings must be renewed, the higher these costs will be.

INTERNAL SOURCES OF FINANCE

In addition to external sources of finance there are certain internal sources that a business may use to generate funds for particular activities. These sources usually have the advantage that they are flexible. They may also be obtained quickly—particularly working capital sources—and may not require the permission of other parties. The main sources of internal funds are described below and summarised in Figure 14.3.

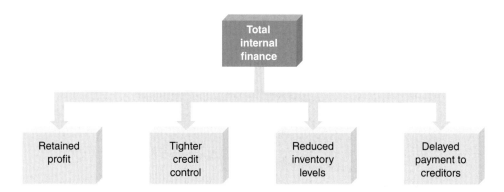

FIGURE 14.3 Main internal sources of finance

Retained profit

Retained profit is the main source of finance for most companies. By retaining profits within the company rather than distributing them to shareholders in the form of dividends, the funds of the company are increased.

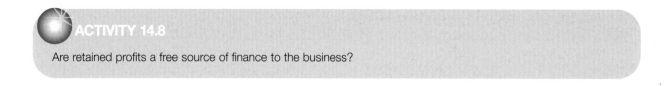

ACTIVITY 14.8

Are retained profits a free source of finance to the business?

The reinvestment of profit rather than the issue of new ordinary shares can be a useful way of increasing equity capital. There are no issue costs associated with retaining profits and the amount raised is certain. When issuing new shares the issue costs may be substantial and there may be uncertainty over the success of the issue. Retaining profits will have no effect on the control of the company by existing shareholders. However, where new shares are issued to outside investors there will be some dilution of control by existing shareholders.

The retention of profits is something that is determined by the directors of the company. They may find it easier simply to retain profits rather than ask investors to subscribe to a new share issue. Retained profits are already held by the company and so the company does not have to wait to receive the funds. Moreover, there is often less scrutiny when profits are being retained for reinvestment purposes than when new shares are being issued. Investors and their advisers will examine closely the reasons for any new share issue.

Some shareholders may prefer profits to be retained by the company rather than distributed in the form of dividends. By ploughing back profits, it may be expected that the company will expand and share values will increase as a result. Income tax paid by shareholders only arises on realised profits, so an unrealised capital gain in the form of a share price rise is normally not taxable. The shareholder has a choice as to when the gain is realised. Research indicates that investors are often attracted to particular companies according to the dividend/retention policies they adopt.

Tighter credit control

By exerting tighter control over trade debtors it may be possible for a business to reduce the proportion of assets held in this form and to release funds for other purposes. It is important, however, to weigh the benefits of tighter credit control against the likely costs in the form of lost customer goodwill and lost sales. To remain competitive a business must take account of the needs of its customers and of the credit policies adopted by rival companies within the industry.

ACTIVITY 14.9

H. Rush Ltd produces a single product that is used in a variety of electronic products. Details of the product are as follows:

	$	Per unit $
Selling price		20
Less variable costs	14	
Fixed costs	4	18
Net profit		2

Sales are $10 million per annum and are all on credit. The average credit period taken by customers is 45 days, although the terms of credit require payment within 30 days. Bad debts are currently $100,000 per annum. Debtors are financed by a bank overdraft costing 15 per cent per annum.

The credit control department believes it can eliminate bad debts and reduce the average credit period to 30 days if new credit control procedures are implemented. These will cost $50,000 per annum and are likely to result in a reduction in sales of 5 per cent per annum.

Should the company implement the new credit control procedures? (*Hint*: In order to answer this activity it is useful to compare the current cost of trade credit with the costs under the proposed approach.)

Reduced inventory levels

This is an internal source of funds which may prove attractive to a business. If a business has a proportion of its assets in the form of inventory there is an opportunity cost as the funds tied up cannot be used for more profitable opportunities. (This is also true, of course, for investment in trade debtors.) By liquidating inventory, funds become available for other purposes. However, a business must ensure there is sufficient inventory available to meet likely future sales demand. Failure to do so will result in lost customer goodwill and lost sales.

The nature and condition of the inventory held will determine whether it is possible to exploit this form of finance. A business may be overstocked as a result of poor buying decisions in the past. This may mean that a significant proportion of inventory held is slow moving or obsolete and cannot therefore be liquidated easily.

Delayed payment to creditors

By delaying payment to creditors, funds are retained within the business for other purposes. This may be a cheap form of finance for a business. However, as we saw in Chapter 13, there may be significant costs associated with this form of financing.

Spontaneous sources of funds

Accrued wages are significant sources of spontaneous finance for firms. Most employees are not paid daily, but either weekly or fortnightly. As such the employees are effectively providing funds for the firm until the end of the pay cycle. The withholding of pay-as-you-go tax instalments has the same effect, as does the deduction of superannuation contributions and delayed payment into the superannuation fund.

SELF-ASSESSMENT QUESTION 14.2

Helsim Ltd is a wholesaler and distributor of electrical components. The most recent financial statements of the company revealed the following:

HELSIM LTD

Income statement for the year ended 31 May 2005

	$m	$m
Sales		14.2
Opening stock	3.2	
Purchases	8.4	
	11.6	
Closing stock	3.8	7.8
Gross profit		6.4
Other expenses		5.9
Net profit before taxation		0.5
Tax		0.2
Net profit after taxation		0.3

Balance sheet as at 31 May 2005

	$m	$m
Current assets		
Cash	0.1	
Trade debtors	3.6	
Inventory	3.8	
		7.5
Non-current assets		
Motor vehicles	0.5	
Equipment	0.9	
Land and buildings	3.8	
		5.2
Total assets		12.7
Current liabilities		
Bank overdraft	3.6	
Trade creditors	1.8	
		5.4

Non-current liabilities		
Debentures (secured on freehold land)		3.5
Shareholders' equity		
Share capital		
Ordinary capital issued at $1	2.0	
Reserves		
Retained profits	1.8	
		3.8
Total liabilities and shareholders' equity		12.7

Notes

1. Land and buildings are shown at their current market value. Equipment and motor vehicles are shown at their written-down values.

2. No dividends have been paid to ordinary shareholders for the past three years.

In recent months trade creditors have been pressing for payment. The managing director has therefore decided to reduce the level of trade creditors to an average of 40 days outstanding. In order to achieve this he has decided to approach the bank with a view to increasing the overdraft to finance the necessary payments. The company is currently paying 12 per cent interest on the overdraft.

Required:

(a) Comment on the liquidity position of the company.

(b) Calculate the amount of finance required in order to reduce trade creditors, as shown on the balance sheet, to an average of 40 days outstanding.

(c) State, with reasons, how you consider the bank would react to the proposal to grant an additional overdraft facility.

(d) Evaluate four sources of finance (internal or external, but excluding a bank overdraft) which may be used to finance the reduction in trade creditors and state, with reasons, which of these you consider the most appropriate.

THE ROLE OF THE STOCK EXCHANGE

Earlier we considered the various forms of long-term capital that are available to a company. In this section we examine the role that the stock exchange plays in the provision of finance for companies. The stock exchange acts as an important primary and secondary market in capital for companies. As a primary market, the function of the stock exchange is to enable companies to raise new capital. As a secondary market, its function is to enable investors to transfer their securities (i.e. shares and loan capital) with ease. Thus, it provides a 'second-hand' market where shares and loan capital already in issue may be bought and sold.

In order to issue shares or loan capital through the stock exchange, a company must be listed. This means that it must meet fairly stringent stock exchange requirements concerning size, profit history, disclosure, etc. Some share issues on the stock exchange arise from the initial listing of the company. Other share issues are undertaken by companies that are already listed on the stock exchange and which are seeking additional finance from investors.

The secondary market role of the stock exchange means that shares and other financial claims are easily transferable. This can bring real benefits to a company as investors may be more prepared to invest if they know their investment can be easily liquidated whenever required. It is important to recognise, however, that investors are not obliged to use the stock exchange as the means of transferring shares in a listed company. Nevertheless, it is usually the most convenient way of buying or selling shares. Prices of shares and other financial claims are usually determined by the market in an efficient manner and this should also give investors greater confidence to purchase shares. The company may benefit from this greater investor confidence by finding it easier to raise long-term finance and by obtaining this finance at a lower cost as investors will view their investment as being less risky.

A stock exchange listing can, however, have certain disadvantages for a company. The stock exchange imposes strict rules on listed companies and requires additional levels of financial disclosure to that already imposed by law and by the accounting profession (e.g. half-yearly financial reports must be published). The activities of listed companies are closely monitored by financial analysts, financial journalists and other companies, and such scrutiny may not be welcome, particularly if the company is dealing with sensitive issues or experiencing operational problems. It is often suggested that listed companies are under pressure to perform well over the short term. This pressure may detract from undertaking projects that will only yield benefits in the longer term. If the market becomes disenchanted with the company and the price of its shares falls, this may make it vulnerable to a takeover bid from another company.

VENTURE CAPITAL AND LONG-TERM FINANCING

Venture capital is long-term capital provided by certain institutions to help businesses exploit profitable opportunities. The businesses of interest to the venture capitalist will have higher levels of risk (and hence higher potential earnings) than would normally be acceptable to traditional providers of finance such as the major clearing banks. Venture capital providers may be interested in a variety of businesses, including:

* business start-ups
* acquisitions of existing businesses by a group of managers
* providing additional capital to young, expanding businesses
* the buyout of one of the owners from an existing business.

The risks associated with the business can vary, in practice, but are often due to the nature of the products or to the fact that it is a new business which either lacks a trading record or has new management. Although the risks are higher, the businesses also have potentially higher levels of return—hence their attraction to the venture capitalist. The types of businesses helped by venture capitalists are normally small or medium size rather than large companies listed on the stock exchange.

The venture capitalist will often make a substantial investment in the business and this will normally take the form of ordinary shares. In order to keep an eye on the sum invested, the venture capitalist will usually require a representative on the board of directors as a condition of the investment. The venture capitalist may not be looking for a quick return and may well be prepared to invest in a business for five years or more. The return may take the form of a capital gain on the realisation of the investment.

ACTIVITY 14.10

When examining prospective investment opportunities, what kind of non-financial matters do you think a venture capitalist will be concerned with?

SHARE ISSUES

A company may issue shares in a number of different ways. These may involve direct appeals by the company to investors or the use of financial intermediaries. The most common methods of share issue are as follows:

* rights issues
* bonus issues
* **offer for sale**
* public issue
* **private placing**.

RIGHTS ISSUES

The company may offer existing shareholders the right to acquire new shares in the company, in exchange for cash. The new shares will be allocated to shareholders in proportion to their existing shareholdings. In order to make the issue appear attractive to shareholders, the new shares are often offered at a price significantly below the current market value of the shares. Rights issues are now the most common form of share issue. For companies, it is a relatively cheap and straightforward way of issuing shares. Issue expenses are quite low and issue procedures are simpler than for other forms of share issue. The fact that those offered new shares already have an investment in the company that presumably suits their risk–return requirements is likely to increase the chances of a successful issue.

    Control of the company by existing shareholders will not be diluted providing they take up the rights offer. A rights offer allows existing shareholders to acquire shares in the company at a price below the current market price. This means that entitlement to participate in a rights offer is a source of value to existing shareholders. Those who do not wish to take up the rights offer can sell their rights to other investors, so long as the offer is made on a renouncable basis (the right to receive shares is able to be sold in the market). In contrast, non-renouncable offers must either be taken up or allowed to lapse. Calculating the value of the rights offer received by shareholders is quite straightforward. An example can be used to illustrate how this is done.

EXAMPLE 14.2

Shaw Holdings Ltd has 20 million ordinary shares which were issued at 50 cents each. These shares are currently valued on the stock exchange at $1.60 per share. The directors of Shaw Holdings believe the company requires additional long-term capital and have decided to make a one-for-four issue (i.e. one new share for every four shares held) at $1.30 per share.

    The first step in the valuation process is to calculate the price of a share following the rights issue. This is known as the ex-rights price and is simply a weighted average of the price of shares before the issue of rights and the price of the rights shares. In the above example we have a one-for-four rights issue. The theoretical ex-rights price is therefore calculated as follows:

	$
Price of four shares before the rights issue (4 x $1.60)	6.40
Price of taking up one rights share	1.30
	7.70
Theoretical ex-rights price	= 7.70 / 5
	= $1.54

As the price of each share, in theory, should be $1.54 following the rights issue and the price of a rights share is $1.30, the value of the rights offer will be the difference between the two:

$$\$1.54 - \$1.30 = \$0.24 \text{ per share}$$

Market forces will usually ensure that the actual price of rights and their theoretical price will be fairly close.

ACTIVITY 14.11

An investor with 2,000 shares in Shaw Holdings Ltd has contacted you for investment advice. She is undecided whether to take up the rights issue, sell the rights or allow the rights offer to lapse.

Calculate the effect on the net wealth of the investor of each of the options being considered.

When considering a rights issue the directors of a company must first consider the amount of funds it needs to raise. This will depend on the future plans and commitments of the company. The directors must then decide on the issue price of the rights shares. Generally speaking, this decision is not of critical importance. In the example above, the company made a one-for-four issue with the price of the rights shares set at $1.30. However, it could have raised the same amount by making a one-for-two issue and setting the rights price at $0.65, or a one-for-one issue and setting the price at $0.325, etc. The issue price that is finally decided upon will not affect the value of the underlying assets of the company or the proportion of the underlying assets and earnings of the company to which the shareholder is entitled. The directors of the company must, however, ensure that the issue price is not above the current market price of the shares in order for the issue to be successful.

BONUS ISSUES

A bonus issue should not be confused with a rights issue of shares. A bonus, or scrip, issue also involves the issue of new shares to existing shareholders in proportion to their existing shareholdings. However, shareholders do not have to pay for the new shares issued. The bonus issue is effected by transferring a sum from the reserves to the paid-up share capital of the business and then issuing shares, equivalent in value to the amount transferred, to existing shareholders. As the reserves are already owned by the shareholders they do not have to pay for the shares issued. In effect, a bonus issue will simply convert reserves into paid-up capital. In order to understand this conversion process, and its effect on the financial position of the company, let us consider the following example.

EXAMPLE

14.3

Wickham Ltd has the following abbreviated balance sheet as at 31 March 2006.

	$m
Net assets	20
Share capital issued at $1 per share	10
Reserves	10
	20

The directors decide to convert $5 million of the reserves to paid-up capital. As a result, it was decided that a one-for-two bonus issue should be made. Following the bonus issue, the balance sheet of Wickham Ltd will be as follows:

	$m
Net assets	20
Share capital issued at $1 ordinary per share	15
Reserves	5
	20

A relevant question to ask is: are the shareholders in Wickham Ltd better off as a result of receiving bonus shares?

We can see that the share capital of the company has increased and there has been a corresponding decrease in the reserves of the company. The net assets of the company remain unchanged by the bonus issue.

Although each shareholder will own more shares following the bonus issue, the proportion held of the total number of shares in issue will remain unchanged and so the stake in the business and the net assets of the business will remain unchanged. Thus, bonus issues do not, of themselves, result in an increase in shareholder wealth. They will simply switch part of the owners' claim from reserves to share capital.

ACTIVITY 14.12

Assume that the market price per share in Wickham Ltd before the bonus issue was $2.10. What will be the market price per share following the share issue?

You may wonder from the calculations above why bonus issues are made by companies, particularly as the effect of a bonus issue may be to reduce the reserves available for dividend payments. A number of reasons have been put forward to explain this type of share issue.

* *Share price.* The share price of a company may be very high and, as a result, may become more difficult to trade on the stock exchange. It seems that shares which trade within a certain price range generate more interest and activity in the market. By increasing the number of shares issued, the market value of each share will be reduced, which may have the effect of making the shares more marketable.

* *Lender confidence.* The effect of making a transfer from distributable reserves to paid-up share capital will be to increase the permanent capital base of the business. This move may increase confidence among lenders. In effect, a bonus issue will reduce the risk of the company reducing its equity capital through dividend distributions and, thereby, leaving lenders in an exposed position.

* *Market signals.* The directors may use a bonus issue as an opportunity to signal to investors their confidence in the future prospects of the business. The issue may be accompanied by the announcement of good news concerning the company (e.g. securing a large contract or achieving an increase in profits). Under these

circumstances, the share price of the company may rise in the expectation that earnings/dividends per share will be maintained. Shareholders would therefore be better off following the issue. However, it is the information content of the bonus issue, rather than the issue itself, that will create this increase in wealth.

✷ *Dividends.* A bonus issue of shares can be provided to shareholders as an alternative to a cash dividend. Those shareholders who decide to receive bonus shares rather than cash will increase their stake in the total value of the business and will therefore increase their wealth.

OFFER FOR SALE

This type of issue can involve a public limited company selling a new issue of shares to a financial institution known as an issuing house. However, shares that are already in issue may also be sold to an issuing house. In this case, existing shareholders agree to sell their shares to the issuing house. The issuing house will, in turn, sell the shares purchased from either the company or its shareholders to the public. The issuing house will publish a prospectus that sets out details of the company and the type of shares to be sold and investors will be invited to apply for shares. The advantage of this type of issue from the company's viewpoint is that the sale proceeds of the shares are certain. The issuing house will take on the risk of selling the shares to investors. This type of issue is often used when a company seeks a listing on the stock exchange and wishes to raise a large amount of funds.

PUBLIC ISSUE

This form of issue involves the company making a direct invitation to the public to purchase shares in the company. Typically, this is done through a newspaper advertisement. The shares may once again be a new issue or shares already in issue. An issuing house may be asked by the company to help administer the issue of the shares to the public and to offer advice concerning an appropriate selling price. However, the company, rather than the issuing house, will take on the risk of selling the shares. An offer for sale and a public issue will both result in a widening of share ownership in the company.

When making an issue of shares, the company or the issuing house will usually set a price for the shares. However, establishing a share price may not be an easy task, particularly where the market is volatile or where the company has unique characteristics. If the share price is set too high, the issue will be undersubscribed and the company (or issuing house) will not receive the amount expected. If the share price is set too low, the issue will be oversubscribed and the company (or issuing house) will receive less than could have been achieved.

One way of dealing with the problem is to make a **tender issue** of shares. This involves the investors determining the price at which the shares are issued. Although the company (or issuing house) may publish a reserve price to help guide investors, it will be up to the individual investor to determine the number of shares to be purchased and the price the investor wishes to pay. Once the offers from investors have been received, a price at which all the shares can be sold will be established (known as the *strike price*). Investors who have made offers at, or above, the strike price will be issued shares at the strike price and offers received below the striking price will be rejected. Although this form of issue is adopted occasionally, it is not popular with investors and is therefore not in widespread use.

PRIVATE PLACING

This method does not involve an invitation to the public to subscribe to shares. Instead the shares are 'placed' with selected investors, such as large financial institutions. This can be a quick and relatively cheap form of raising funds as savings can be made in advertising and legal costs. However, it can result in the ownership of the company being concentrated in a few hands. Usually, unlisted companies seeking relatively small amounts of cash will employ this form of issue. Moreover, both listed and unlisted firms often follow a private placement with a rights issue to their shareholders to allow current shareholders the opportunity to increase their holdings on favourable terms.

SUMMARY

In this chapter we have achieved the following objectives in the way shown.

OBJECTIVE	METHOD ACHIEVED
Identify the main sources of finance available to a business	• Identified and discussed the main sources of long-term finance available to businesses, including ordinary shares, preference shares, loans, debentures and leases • Identified and discussed the main sources of short-term finance available to businesses, including overdraft, debt factoring and invoice discounting
Explain the advantages and disadvantages of each form	• Explained the advantages and disadvantages
Describe the concept of gearing and its influence on the long-term financing decision	• Described the concept of gearing • Analysed the implications of making a choice between a geared and an ungeared form of raising long-term finance
Explain the reasons that influence whether or not long-term or short-term finance is used	• Identified the main factors that influence the choice between short-term or long-term finance and between the various forms of finance available
Identify the so-called internal sources of finance and explain them	• Identified the main internal sources of finance and their significance, including retained profit, tighter credit control, reduced inventory levels and delayed payment to creditors
Explain the role and nature of the stock exchange	• Examined the role of the stock exchange and saw that the stock exchange performs two main roles: a primary role in raising finance for companies and a secondary role in ensuring that investors can buy and sell securities with ease
Explain the role of venture capital organisations in financing businesses	• Explained venture capital • Identified the main purposes to which venture capital is usually put
Discuss the ways in which share capital may be issued and identify the underlying reasons why a particular method might be chosen	• Identified the main forms of share issue • Explained the advantages and disadvantages of each

DISCUSSION QUESTIONS

EASY

<Obj 1> **14.1** List the main sources of long-term finance.

<Obj 1, 2> **14.2** What category of investor would purchase preference shares rather than ordinary shares? Preference shares have different labels. Briefly explain the following terminology linked to certain categories of preference shares:
(a) cumulative versus non-cumulative
(b) redeemable versus non-redeemable
(c) participating versus non-participating.

<Obj 1, 2>	**14.3**	From the company's viewpoint what is the disadvantage of preference shares?
<Obj 1, 2>	**14.4**	If you were a significant lender to a business, what conditions (covenants) might you attach to the loan? Give the reason for having each restriction.
<Obj 1, 2>	**14.5**	Leases can be classified as either 'operating' or 'finance' leases.

(a) What is the difference between the two?

(b) Why do firms prefer to have their leases classified as 'operating' rather than 'finance'?

<Obj 2>	**14.6**	From the viewpoint of the business, what are the potential disadvantages of using overdraft finance?
<Obj 4>	**14.7**	What factors should be taken into account in determining the balance between short-term and long-term debt finance?
<Obj 6>	**14.8**	Distinguish between an offer for sale and a public issue of shares.
<Obj 6>	**14.9**	How does the stock exchange benefit:

(a) investors?

(b) corporate regulators?

(c) business entrepreneurs?

<Obj 8>	**14.10**	From the company perspective a rights issue makes a lot of sense when additional equity capital is required. Why?
<Obj 8>	**14.11**	Who benefits from a bonus issue of shares?

INTERMEDIATE

<Obj 1, 2>	**14.12**	Distinguish between invoice discounting and debt factoring.
<Obj 1, 2>	**14.13**	Prepare a case to support invoice discounting or debt factoring as a source of short-term finance.
<Obj 1, 2>	**14.14**	In recent years many banks have sold their freehold property and entered into long-term lease-back arrangements.

(a) Why would they do this?

(b) How will the transaction be recorded in their financial statements?

<Obj 3>	**14.15**	How would you go about determining the appropriate level of gearing for a specific business?
<Obj 4>	**14.16**	Distinguish between warrants and options.
<Obj 4>	**14.17**	What are the benefits of issuing share warrants for a company?
<Obj 6>	**14.18**	Why might a public company which has a stock exchange listing revert to being an unlisted company?
<Obj 7>	**14.19**	Venture capital:

(a) What is it?

(b) Which organisations seek venture capital?

(c) What criterion is important to venture capitalists in making investment decisions?

<Obj 8>	**14.20**	Under what circumstances would a business choose the following share issue approaches?

(a) offer for sale

(b) public issue

(c) private placement.

APPLICATION EXERCISES

EASY

<Obj 1, 2>

14.1 H Brown Ltd produces a range of air conditioning systems for sale to builders' merchants. As a result of increasing demand for its products, the directors have decided to expand production. The cost of acquiring new plant and machinery and the increase in working capital requirements is planned to be financed by a mixture of long-term and short-term debt.

(a) Discuss the main factors that should be taken into account when deciding on the appropriate mix of long-term debt and short-term debt necessary to finance the expansion program.

(b) Discuss the main factors that a lender should take into account when deciding whether to grant a long-term loan to the company.

(c) Identify three conditions that might be included in a long-term loan agreement and state the purpose of each.

<Obj 1, 2, 3>

14.2 Answer all three questions below.

(a) Discuss the main factors that should be taken into account when choosing between long-term debt and equity finance.

(b) Explain the term 'convertible loan stock'. Discuss the advantages and disadvantages of this form of finance from the viewpoint of both the company and investors.

(c) Explain the term 'debt factoring'. Discuss the advantages and disadvantages of this form of finance.

INTERMEDIATE

<Obj 3, 8>

14.3 Business is going well for Lazer Technology Ltd. The board of directors of this family-owned company believes that Lazer Technology Ltd could earn an additional $800,000 in profit before interest and taxes each year by expanding its range of products. However, the $4 million that the business needs for growth cannot be raised within the family. The directors, who strongly wish to retain family control of the firm, must consider issuing securities to outsiders. They are considering three financing plans.

Plan A is to borrow at 11 per cent over five years.

Plan B is to issue 100,000 ordinary shares at $40 each.

Plan C is to issue 40,000 non-voting preference shares at $100, with each share entitled to an annual preference dividend of $8.80.

Lazer Technology Ltd presently has 500,000 ordinary shares issued. All three plans will raise the required $4 million. The income tax rate is 30 per cent.

Required:
Prepare an analysis of the alternatives for the board members to consider.

<Obj 7>

14.4 Venture capital may represent an important source of finance for a business.

(a) What is meant by the term 'venture capital'? What are the distinguishing features of this form of finance?

(b) What types of business venture may be of interest to a venture capitalist seeking to make an investment?

(c) When considering a possible investment in a business, discuss the main factors a venture capitalist would take into account.

ACCOUNTING an introduction

<Obj 8>

14.5 Carpets Direct Ltd wishes to increase its number of retail outlets in southern Queensland. The board of directors has decided to finance this expansion program by raising the funds from existing shareholders through a one-for-four rights issue. The most recent income statement of the company is as follows:

Income statement for the year ended 30 April 2006	
	$m
Sales turnover	164.5
Profit before interest and taxation	12.6
Interest	6.2
Profit before taxation	6.4
Income tax	1.9
Profit after taxation	4.5
Ordinary dividends	2.0
Retained profit for the year	2.5

The share capital of the company consists of 120 million ordinary shares issued at $0.50 per share. The shares of the company are currently being traded on the stock exchange at a price/earnings ratio of 22 times and the board of directors have decided to issue the new shares at a discount of 20 per cent on the current market value.

Required:
(a) Calculate the theoretical ex-rights price of an ordinary share in Carpets Direct Ltd.
(b) Calculate the price at which the rights in Carpets Direct Ltd are likely to be traded.
(c) Identify and evaluate, at the time of the rights issue, each of the options arising from the rights issue for an investor who holds 4,000 ordinary shares before the rights announcement.

CHALLENGING

<Obj 1, 2>

14.6 Gainsborough Fashions Ltd operates a small chain of fashion shops in Auckland. In recent months the company has been under pressure from its trade creditors to reduce the average credit period taken from three months to one month. To be able to comply with the creditors' demands the directors of the company have approached the bank to ask for an increase in the existing overdraft for one year. The most recent accounts of the company are as follows:

GAINSBOROUGH FASHIONS LTD

Balance sheet as at 31 May 2006		
	$	$
Current assets		
Trade debtors	3,000	
Inventory	198,000	
		201,000
Non-current assets		
Fixtures and fittings at cost	90,000	
Less accumulated depreciation	23,000	
	67,000	

582

	$	$
Motor vehicles at cost	34,000	
Less accumulated depreciation	27,000	
	7,000	
		74,000
Total assets		275,000
Current liabilities		
Trade creditors	162,000	
Accrued expenses	5,000	
Bank overdraft	7,000	
Income taxation payable	10,000	
Dividends payable	10,000	
		194,000
Non-current liabilities		
12% Debentures 2009/10		40,000
Shareholders' equity		
Ordinary shares issued at $1	20,000	
General reserve	4,000	
Retained profits	17,000	
		41,000
Total liabilities and shareholders' equity		275,000

Abbreviated income statement for the year ended 31 May 2006

	$
Sales	740,000
Net profit before interest and taxation	38,000
Interest charges	5,000
Net profit before taxation	33,000
Taxation	10,000
Net profit after taxation	23,000
Dividend proposed	10,000
Retained profit for the year	13,000

Notes

1. The debentures are secured by personal guarantees from the directors.
2. The current overdraft bears an interest rate of 12 per cent.

Required:

(a) Identify and discuss the main factors that a bank would take into account before deciding whether or not to grant an increase in the overdraft of a company.

(b) State whether, in your opinion, the bank should grant the required increase in the overdraft for Gainsborough Fashions Ltd. You should provide reasoned arguments and supporting calculations where necessary.

<Obj 3, 4, 8>

14.7 Telford Engineers Ltd, a medium-sized manufacturer of automobile components, has decided to modernise its factory by introducing a number of robots. These will cost $20 million and will reduce operating costs by $6 million per year for their estimated useful life of 10 years. To finance this scheme the company can either:

- raise $20 million by the issue of 20 million ordinary shares at $1, or
- raise $20 million debt at 14 per cent interest per year with capital repayments of $3 million per year commencing at the end of 2008.

Extracts from Telford Engineers' accounts appear below:

TELFORD ENGINEERS LTD

Summary of balance sheet as at 31 December

	2002	2003	2004	2005 (estimated)
	$m	$m	$m	$m
Current assets	55	67	57	55
Non-current assets	48	51	65	64
Total assets	103	118	122	119
Current liabilities				
Creditors	20	27	25	18
Overdraft	5	–	6	8
	25	27	31	26
Non-current liabilities	30	30	30	30
Share capital and reserves	48	61	61	63
Total liabilities and shareholders' equity	103	118	122	119
Number of shares issued at 25c per share (millions)	80	80	80	80
Share price	$1.50	$2	$1	$1.45

Summary of income statement for the year ended 31 December

	2002	2003	2004	2005 (estimated)
	$m	$m	$m	$m
Sales	152	170	110	145
Profit before interest and taxes	28	40	7	15
Interest payable	4	3	4	5
Profit before tax	24	37	3	10
Income tax	12	16	0	4
Profit after tax	12	21	3	6
Dividends	6	8	3	4
Retained	6	13	0	2

For your answer you should assume that the company tax for 2004 is 40 per cent, that sales and operating profit will be unchanged except for the $6 million cost saving arising from the introduction of the robots and that Telford Engineers will pay the same dividend per share in 2006 as in 2005.

Required:

(a) Prepare, for each scheme, Telford Engineers' income statement for the year ended 31 December 2006 and a statement of its share capital, reserves and loans on that date.

(b) Calculate Telford's earnings per share for 2006 for both schemes.

(c) Calculate the level of earnings (profit) before interest and tax at which the earnings per share for each scheme is equal.

(d) Which scheme would you advise the company to adopt? You should give your reasons and state what additional information you would require.

Small and medium enterprises (SMEs) often have particular problems not shared by larger businesses. Reproduced below is an article relating to this issue, from *Australian CPA*, August 2004, pages 35–7.

Read this article and consider the questions that follow.

CASE STUDY

14.1

Anyone got a fiver?

Rising interest rates and falling property prices could cut loans to SMEs that are attempting to grow. Ed Charles looks at the borrowing options and how the money lenders measure up

One of the eternal problems for start-up businesses or growing SMEs is getting access to credit.

Susan Campbell, finance policy adviser at CPA Australia and principal consultant at Argyll Financial Consulting, says that often small businesses use family homes or investment properties as asset backing, creating an easy cheap source of credit.

The Commonwealth Bank's Steve Morgan – regional executive manager, business banking – says that the backbone of the Australian economy are sole traders or small partnerships, who typically secure lending on the home. Some have regular mortgages, others are lines of credits, overdrafts or loans. A typical debt structure would be some sort of term loan for the core of the debt, working overdraft and a business credit card.

Campbell says the changing property market is having an impact on SMEs: 'When you need more money at a time when house prices are going up you can say "I'll keep increasing my loan". But when your house price starts going down, you can't go and increase your loan.'

She says the problems are exacerbated for fast growing businesses or companies that don't understand the profit and cash flow of their business.

'Some businesses have had the luxury during the last few years of easy access to money. But that could well be drying up and could dry up quite rapidly during 2004.'

Usually banks will lend between 70 and 80 per cent of value of the house. Campbell says that the banks are usually interested in where the money is going and how the all-important business plan is shaping up. Many mortgage brokers, however, aren't so interested in where the money is going. She warns that people involved with such brokers risk being forced to sell their house should the business implode.

Keith Rodwell, managing director of GE Commercial Finance, says that a lot of asset-backed bank facilities are a five-year term but with annual review points. Under bank regulations facilities less than 12 months require less equity.

He says that in the eyes of the banks the 12-month loan is lower risk and as a result it can be priced cheaper. Rodwell says: 'The risk though is then passed to the customer because now they don't have a five-year commitment. It is probably a less known issue at the moment because we have gone through such a long period of economic strength.

'If you go back to the early 1990s you will see that this happened significantly. This is an issue for companies today. They need to think about what they would do if they had to pay back more of their facilities.

'How would they handle that?'

CPA Australia's Campbell says that although the prospect of a severe fall in house prices may be some way off, companies should be thinking now about reviewing their property-backed borrowing facilities.

'It's now the time to do it – not when the crunch has come and you are panicking.

'If you want to go sourcing for funds you want to do it from a position of power,' she explains.

She adds that it is not easy to find alternative sources of finance. 'People don't always want to have partners involved in their business or other potential investors who may take the idea or kick them out.'

Alternatives are venture capitalists and business angels, where the options are few and far between. Many people as a last resort look to family and friends. But Campbell warns to shy away from handshake deals and to ensure that investors understand the details and that the terms are put into writing.

'I've seen examples when people have borrowed from family or friends who thought they were actually investing in the firm and sharing in the capital growth. But the people who owned the firm just thought it was a loan,' she says.

GE's Rodwell says that SMEs inevitably reach the point where directors want to separate personal assets and business assets.

'If you've been running your business for 10 or 20 years at some point you feel like you deserve to release your home,' he says.

'A lot of the business lending is effectively home-loan lending. Again, short-term in nature and secured by your home. And at some point the business needs to stand on its own two feet.'

One of the problems for SMEs is having the clout and expertise to negotiate with banks in addition to identifying the best deal structures and deals on finance.

Andrew Nicholls, director, NCS Nicholls Corporate Services, had over 20 years experience as a senior strategist and adviser at the National. He says that as small businesses grow into larger, more profitable ones, their finance requirements and structures need to change. He says that borrowing at the smaller end of the market is very difficult.

'The general banking market is not tolerant of new business unless they've got the bricks and mortar to support them.'

He says that as the banks have segmented their market many clients have found they are being ostracised and pushed onto telephone platforms.

'They were, and still are, screaming out to have that bank manager as the confidante to the business. But unless a company makes a lot of money for the bank, nowadays relationship banking is a thing of the past down at the smaller end.

'Even at the larger SME level, while there are relationship managers in place, obviously they are pushing their own bank's products.'

What Nicholls does is not only help find new funding for companies but also restructures their existing arrangements. The advice goes beyond debt funding to including transactional cash management advice as well as risk management on interest rates and foreign exchange.

The main concern for established businesses or mature businesses is that the directors often want to split their personal assets away from the business assets.

Nicholls says: 'Nowadays there are ways where businesses can finance their operations purely on the balance sheet.'

One method is debt finance, a form of factoring but invisible to the customer. 'It doesn't have the traditional ramifications,' Nicholls explains.

Traditional factoring is known as 'lender of last resort' when a company is running into trouble. Nowadays the twist on factoring is that invoices can be mortgaged to the bank, which provides 80 per cent of finance.

The company, rather than the bank, invoices the client direct. This finance, however, is for companies with a financial track record of two to three years, a turnover of at least $1m to $2m, and a debt requirement from a few hundred thousand dollars upwards.

Nicholls says another source of finance is leasing. But he cautions businesses to be careful of the cost of this option. For example, the high depreciation of IT equipment means that the lease costs are higher than, for instance, a car. 'But it suits people and certainly protects company's and individual's cash flows,' he points out.

Many businesses survive on overdrafts and credit cards but these are costly ways to finance a business.

Nicholls says: 'Most businesses are unaware how expensive it actually is to run an overdraft. The premiums are enormous. They are a fantastic facility for come-and-go requirements for companies that are cash-strapped over a few months.

'The whole reason for having an overdraft is to cover those peaks and troughs in cash requirements.

'What a lot of companies tend to do is have it become their easy form of long-term finance. And what they need to understand is that they are paying enormous margins on it.'

Some banks specialise under $2m. Both the Commonwealth and St George are targeting small business.

The Commonwealth's Morgan says that the bank focuses on cash flow and the track record of the people running the business more than asset backing in its relationships.

He says that the prospects of changing economic conditions and falling house prices aren't causing concern in the bank's risk management.

'It's probably from our point of view business as normal,' he says. 'There's always going to be cycles in most markets.

'When we are making a lending decision it's not so much on the ups and downs of the market but the underlying cash flow of the business.

'The vast majority of what we do is based on the fundamentals—the track record of the business, the cash flow of the business and perhaps the collateral that's gone in there.

'The security is only a fall-back position.

'Obviously banks aren't in the business of trying to sell assets and wind up loans. That's not good for either party.'

Bob Greves, executive manager, small business at the Commonwealth, says that SMEs looking for finance should put a great deal of effort into their business plans.

'No one is going to come near you unless you spend a lot of time on the viability of the business going forward,' he stresses.

'You've got to show some sort of track record. Even venture capitalists—they'll look at the business plan but they will also look at the individuals that are running it and how they have gone in the past.'

Morgan says that typically a bank will want to review three years of financial records. Many decisions are made after visiting a company's offices.

'Typically,' he says, 'you get a good sense of how a business is travelling when you walk through the premises.'

Reproduced by kind permission of the author.

1   What is the significance to SMEs of a potential fall in the property market?
2   Do you believe that the majority of SME finance is related to housing?
3   What are the potential impacts on SMEs of a fall in the housing market, either in the form of a soft landing or a dramatic crash?
4   Do you consider that lenders have been irresponsible in recent years, with more lending being carried out on the strength of the current value of property as distinct from being based on a proper business plan?
5   What are the alternative sources of finance available to SMEs and what is the likelihood of these being available
6   What are the dangers in borrowing from family and friends?
7   What are the inherent difficulties facing SMEs in raising finance that are identified by the article?
8   What comments are made regarding the cost of running an overdraft?
9   The article comments that from the banks' perspective it is 'business as normal'. What does the article imply is meant by 'business as normal'? What kind of information is required by banks in the normal course of events?

CASE STUDY

14.2

Set out below is an article from *Australian CPA*, August 2003, pages 58–9. This article looks at the contribution that accountants can make to the venture capital process. Read the article and consider the questions that follow.

Crunching venture capital

Accountants are an essential part of the hungry venture capitalist's retinue. Philip Latham looks at why their input is so valued

The short-listing of compatible venture capitalists has given accountants an increasingly important role to play in any fund-raising process. The changes, while occurring a fair while back down the track, mean that accountants working on venture capital projects must now prepare and assist in the presentation of: cashflow forecasts; historical financial statements; aged debtor, creditor and stock turnover issues; and historical tax summaries. Accountants should also be familiar with standard confidentiality agreements and deal with legal advisers on this matter.

Once you have confirmed a mutual interest in progressing discussions through the sharing of high level information, it is prudent to request a list of references with whom you can speak and seek external guidance on the potential venture capital partners. Ideally this will be a mix of management, or joint shareholders of businesses that the proposed partner has worked with in the past, along with a selection of exited investments.

Venture capitalists are a significant consumer of accounting resources, and therefore represent a fertile market for accounting and tax services. There are a number of key occasions throughout the investment lifecycle in which number crunchers have the opportunity to act as a service provider to venture capitalists.

Accounting services are required to establish due diligence when considering investment entry. As highlighted above, accountants have a central role to play (on both sides of the table) in the due diligence activities that occur before investment. Venture capitalists will almost always seek accountants to assist in confirming their assumptions regarding the investment.

These activities can extend from undertaking aged debtor analysis, to reviewing past audit notes, through to assisting the venture capitalist identify the commercial risks associated with the investment (for example seasonality of cashflows or exposure to key suppliers). The typical focus of due diligence is to provide an insight into the sustainable earnings and cashflows of a business, and all material liabilities and assets.

As with any transactional service, it is very important for accountants to agree on the scope of activities to be undertaken and document these in the form of an engagement letter.

All organisations have a core need for financial reporting and tax advice. As financial investors, venture capitalists in most cases will typically impose a higher reporting threshold than the norm. This arises due to the venture capitalists being relatively remote from the business (in that, they are not usually actively involved in management) and therefore seeking to place a greater reliance on the reported financial information. Moreover, as cashflow is paramount, the tax efficiency of the organisation will also be a key concern and likely to receive greater focus than it would from a strategic shareholder.

A financial investor will also place greater emphasis on the external audit, and seek to realise extended value from its outcomes. For example, performance improvement recommendations are likely to be actively sought and followed up.

Accounting firms able to offer management and investment consultancy services are also likely to benefit from the involvement of a venture capitalist. Such service offerings are consistent with the proposition that venture capitalists will actively seek to work with the management team to increase shareholder value. Such activities are often best achieved with external resources to assist in the identification and implementation of performance improvement opportunities.

The final step in the investment lifecycle is the disposal of the venture capitalists' shareholding. The role for the accountant here is the opposite to the tasks noted above when assisting due diligence from an investment perspective. That is, the accountant's role is to assist in preparing the organisation for due diligence, and then facilitating the due diligence review on behalf of the vendor. The key activity is ensuring that the financial statements and management information systems are robust and reliable. This preparation activity can often commence up to six months in advance of a formal due diligence process.

For further information the Australian Venture Capital Industry Association has a good website (www.avcal.com.au) which not only lists members and their investment parameters, but also carries a range of articles about venture capital and its growing role in Australia.

Philip Latham is the founder and managing director of RMB Ventures, which manages a portfolio of 10 private equity investments.

---

1   Identify the range of issues that might involve the accountant in raising venture capital.
2   What kind of issues do you think would be considered in a due diligence exercise?
3   Given the fact that many venture capitalists do not become actively involved in day to day management there is much more reliance on the reported financial information. What are the key elements of reported financial performance to a venture capitalist?
4   What role can the accountant play in the disposal of a venture capitalist's interests?

CASE STUDY
14.3

Raising capital requires answers to a number of questions. The article below from *Australian CPA*, April 2003, pages 40–1, deals with some of these, albeit focused on private equity. Read the article and consider the following questions.

Finding the perfect match

Philip Latham has the lowdown on raising capital for your client from private equity sources

Businesses raise capital for all sorts of reasons: to expand the production line, to acquire a new business, to reduce the burden of bank debt, to buy out current shareholders ... and even sometimes to bridge a difficult period of high or unexpected cash burn. The sources of such capital are many and varied and each form of capital comes with different conditions attached. In these uncertain economic times, it is not a simple matter to approach the public equity or debt markets, and often it can take considerable time and distract management from what they do best. For many businesses, a private equity fund is an ideal source of new capital, while providing new relationships and a willing partner to assist the growth of your client's business.

What is private equity?

Literally, 'private' means not publicly traded, and 'equity' means non-debt. It's a very flexible form of finance and can be structured via a variety of instruments including convertible notes, ordinary shares and preferred shares. Private equity financiers typically have a long-term investment horizon of between three and five years, and because their return is linked to the performance of the organisation, they are more willing and able to support the growth of the company through mechanisms such as board representation and strategic corporate introductions. In 2001 there was over $1 billion of private equity funding invested in Australian organisations.

Who do I approach?

There is a large range of private equity sources, which is typified by the various terminology such as angel funding and venture capital, which represent sub-segments of the private equity market. The breadth of private equity funding solutions means it is necessary to refine the search for the most suitable partner for your client's business. This search is best guided by answering the following preparatory questions:

- What is the quantum of funding?
- What industry does the organisation operate in?
- What has been, and what is expected to be, the financial performance of the business?
- What is the purpose to which the funds will be put?
- Will more capital raisings be required in the medium term?

Funding requirement

Financiers are segmented according to their preferred investment size. To illustrate, RMB Ventures prefers to make an investment of between $10 million and $20m per business. Other funders may have a mandate to invest between $1m and $3m. The preferred investment size is typically quoted in marketing material, and can be used to select which providers to approach based on your organisation's needs.

Industry exposure

Various industries encompass unique risks, such as aquaculture, agriculture, infrastructure and property development. Private equity funders often seek to limit investments to those industries that they understand. In most cases the industry preferences for a private equity fund will be expressed as exclusions, and be readily apparent in marketing material. When reviewing financiers it is worthwhile exploring their existing investments and industry experience, since this could prove to be a valuable source of assistance and knowledge following the investment.

Company performance

The size, growth stage and current and expected performance of the business will dictate how you should approach private equity funders. Private equity providers are segmented into a number of groups, including early stage (funding start-up or embryonic businesses), expansion stage and later stage financiers. In addition, they can be segmented by industry sector (some have a preference for a particular industry) or by the amount of funding that they have available per transaction.

If your client's business is not cashflow positive, is seriously under-performing, or has sales revenues of below $20m, then it is likely that the appropriate source of private equity capital will be from one of the smaller start-up, expansion capital or specialist turnaround funds, rather than a later stage financier. In the very small businesses (below $10m sales revenue) it may be more appropriate to seek capital from early stage or 'angel' funds.

Use of funds

One of the early questions that a provider will ask you is 'What is the purpose of the funding?' The answer to this question will narrow the range of funds that will be appropriate for your purposes. Some funds are only interested in funding the majority, or total buy-out of the current shareholders. Others are more interested in funding expansions (such as venture capital funds), in which case they may seek a minority shareholding. Where an organisation is seeking funds to effect a turnaround from poor performance, or to reduce the current burden of debt on the balance sheet, the field of private equity providers willing to take on such risks narrows dramatically.

Under such circumstances, it will be necessary to put together a strong argument for the incoming shareholder to believe in the potential turnaround.

Some providers are better than others at taking on such risks and are also able to provide valuable assistance at board and/or management level for such tasks.

Again, by way of example, RMB Ventures' most common reasons for funding businesses are (a) to provide a management team with the capital to buy the business from owners who wish to sell, and/or (b) to provide the current shareholders of a business with the capital to acquire a competitor or complementary business.

Future funding requirements

Ongoing funding requirements will mean that a client is best served by sourcing funding from a partner that is able to maintain the relationship over the long term and continue to provide new capital. A need for ongoing funding should dictate that you search for providers that have access to suitable funds and are not bound by prudential obligations that may limit their ability to provide follow-on funding.

Where do I get private equity?

The *Australian Venture Capital Guide* lists over 100 members and most of these can be broadly described as venture capital businesses. Various other publications list the range and types of providers available and the website of the Australian Venture Capital Association (www.avcal. com.au) is a useful starting point. Choosing the appropriate firm to approach will depend on the answers to the earlier questions.

CPAs have an important role to play in supporting organisational growth by facilitating the fundraising process. The CPA is the lynchpin to preparing the financial statements and working with the board and executives to prepare the necessary business plan and financial forecasts.

This preparation is essential for allowing the financier to understand the business, its growth potential and the way in which the capital can be structured and applied to support that growth.

Philip Latham is the founder and managing director of RMB Ventures, which manages a portfolio of 10 private equity investments.

1   What are the main reasons identified in the article for raising capital?
2   What is 'private equity'?
3   What is the usual term of any investment provided by private equity?
4   What kind of preparatory questions are likely to need to be asked and answered?
5   Summarise the likely view of providers of private equity in the areas of amounts of funding, industry exposure and company performance.
6   A number of uses for private equity funds were identified including turnabout from poor performance. What kind of information do you think would be needed to convince a potential investor that the business is capable of being turned around?

SOLUTIONS TO ACTIVITIES

Activity 14.1

The dividends of preference shares tend to be fairly stable over time and there is usually an upper limit on the returns that can be received. As a result, the share price, which reflects the expected future returns from the share, will normally be less volatile than for ordinary shares.

Activity 14.2

A floating charge on assets will allow the managers of the company greater flexibility in their day-to-day operations than a fixed charge. Assets can be traded without reference to the lenders.

Activity 14.3

Companies are often attracted to eurobonds because of the size of the international capital market. Access to a large number of international investors is likely to increase the chances of a successful issue. In addition, the lack of regulation in the eurobond market means that national restrictions regarding loan issues may be overcome.

Activity 14.4

The main factors are as follows:

- Preference shares have a higher rate of return than loan capital. From the investor's point of view, preference shares are more risky. The amount invested cannot be secured and the return is paid after the returns paid to lenders.
- A company has a legal obligation to pay interest and make capital repayments on loans at the agreed dates. A company will usually make every effort to meet its obligations as failure to do so can have serious consequences. (These consequences have already been mentioned earlier.) Failure to pay a preference dividend, on the other hand, is less important. There is no legal obligation to pay a preference dividend if profits are not available for distribution.

Although failure to pay a preference dividend may prove an embarrassment for the company, the preference shareholders will have no redress against the company if there are insufficient profits to pay the dividend due.

- It was mentioned above that the taxation system in Australia and New Zealand permits interest on loans to be allowable against profits for taxation, whereas preference dividends are not. Because of the tax relief which loan interest attracts, the cost of servicing loan capital is usually much less for a company than the cost of servicing preference shares.
- The issue of loan capital may result in the management of a company having to accept some restrictions on their freedom of action. We have seen earlier that loan agreements often contain covenants which can be onerous. However, no such restrictions can be imposed by preference shareholders.

Activity 14.5

Your answer should be as follows:

	Debt issue	Equity issue
Interest cover ratio		
$= \dfrac{\text{Profit before interest and tax}}{\text{Interest expense}}$	$= \dfrac{(4.2 + 3.8)}{3.8}$	$\dfrac{(6.0 + 2.0)}{2.0}$
	$=$ 2.1 times	4.0 times
Earnings per share		
$= \dfrac{\text{Earnings available to ordinary shareholders}}{\text{No. of ordinary shares}}$	$= \dfrac{4.2}{64,000,000}$	$\dfrac{6.0}{104,000,000}$
	$=$ 6.6c	5.8c
Gearing ratio		
$= \dfrac{\text{Long-term liabilities}}{\text{Share capital + Reserves + Long-term liabilities}}$	$= \dfrac{27,000,000}{(23,200,000 + 27,000,000)}$	$\dfrac{15,000,000}{(36,375,000 + 15,000,000)}$
	$=$ 53.8%	29.2%

Activity 14.6

A banker may be unenthusiastic about lending the company funds. The gearing ratio of 53.8 per cent is rather high and would leave the bank in an exposed position. The existing loan is already secured on assets held by the company and it is not clear whether the company is in a position to offer an attractive form of security for the new loan. The interest cover ratio of 2.1 is also rather low. If the company is unable to achieve the expected returns from the new project, or if it is unable to restore profits from the remainder of its operations to 2004 levels, this ratio would be even lower.

Equity investors may need some convincing that it would be worthwhile to make further investments in the company. The return to equity for shareholders in 2004 was 20 per cent. The incremental profit from the new project is $2 million and the investment required is $12 million, which represents a return of 16.7 per cent. Thus, the returns from the project are expected to be lower than for existing operations. In making their decision, investors should discover whether the new investment is of a similar level of risk to their existing investment and whether the returns from the investment compare with those available from other opportunities with similar levels of risk.

Activity 14.7

A less conservative position would mean relying on short-term finance to help fund part of the permanent capital base. A more conservative position would mean relying on long-term finance to help finance the fluctuating assets of the business.

Activity 14.8

It is tempting to think that retained profits are a 'cost-free' source of funds for a company. However, this is not the case. If profits are reinvested rather than distributed to shareholders this means that the shareholders cannot reinvest the profits made in other forms of investment. They will therefore expect a rate of return from the profits reinvested which is equivalent to what they would receive if the funds had been invested in another opportunity with the same level of risk.

Activity 14.9

The current cost of trade credit is:

	$
Bad debts	100,000
Overdraft [($10m × 45 / 365) × 15%]	184,931
	284,931

The cost of trade credit under the new policy will be:

	$
Overdraft [($9.5m × 30 / 365) × 15%]	117,123
Cost of control procedures	50,000
Net cost of lost sales [($10m / $20 × 5%)(20 − 14*)]	150,000
	317,123

*Selling price less variable costs

The above figures reveal that the business will be worse off if the new policies were adopted.

Activity 14.10

The venture capitalist will be concerned with such matters as the quality of management, the personal stake or commitment made by the owners to the business, the quality and nature of the product and the plans made to exploit the business opportunities, as well as financial matters.

Activity 14.11

If the investor takes up the rights issue she will be in the following position:

	$
Value of holding after rights issue [(2,000 + 500) × $1.54]	3,850
Less cost of buying the rights shares (500 × $1.30)	650
	3,200

If the investor sells the rights she will be in the following position:

	$
Value of holding after rights issue (2,000 × $1.54)	3,080
Sale of rights (500 × $0.24)	120
	3,200

If the investor lets the rights offer lapse, she will be in the following position:

	$
Value of holding after rights issue (2,000 × $1.54)	3,080

As we can see, the first two options should leave her in the same position concerning net wealth. However, she will be worse off if she allows the rights offer to lapse than under the other two options. In practice, however, the company may sell the rights offer on behalf of the investor and pass on the proceeds in order to ensure that she is not worse off as a result of the issue.

Activity 14.12

The company has made a one-for-two issue. A holder of two shares would therefore be in the following position before the bonus issue:

Two shares held at $2.10 market price $4.20

As the wealth of the shareholder has not increased as a result of the issue, the total value of the shareholding will remain the same. This means that, as the shareholder holds one more share following the issue, the market value per share will now be:

$$\frac{\$4.20}{3} = \$1.40$$

OBJECTIVES

When you have completed your study of this chapter you should be able to:

1 define corporate governance

2 outline the principles of corporate governance set out by the ASX

3 outline and discuss a range of social and environmental issues in accounting

4 explain the stakeholder concept

5 explain what is meant by corporate social responsibility

6 explain the Ceres principles

7 list and explain the main methods of accounting for corporate social responsibility

8 explain triple bottom line reporting

9 outline the global reporting initiative and discuss in broad terms the main framework

10 outline the major components of strategic decision making

11 discuss the role of the management accountant in strategy development

12 explain the balanced scorecard approach and its advantages.

15

TRENDS AND ISSUES IN ACCOUNTING

This chapter aims to provide a brief introduction to some of the more important trends and issues in accounting, with an emphasis on reporting. The first area covered relates to corporate governance issues. The second area covered relates to continued improvements in the provision of accounting information concerning areas such as social and environmental aspects of accounting. This is extended by specific reference to triple bottom line reporting. The remainder of the chapter deals with strategic management accounting, which provides better linkage between corporate strategy and accounting. It also covers the balanced scorecard approach. These areas require a rather different view of accounting information, expanding the traditional model.

CORPORATE GOVERNANCE

In Chapter 1 the role of accounting information was introduced, and the main user groups were identified. Chapter 2 introduced a number of different accounting entities, and quite an amount of time was spent discussing companies. The size and nature of companies requires rather more complex rules of governance than do sole proprietors or partnerships. For this reason Chapter 2 dealt with issues such as:

✸ types of companies
✸ roles and responsibilities of directors
✸ different types of shares and the rights associated with them
✸ the role of the regulatory bodies relating to company operations and financial reporting.

    Issues covered in the last of these included:

✸ the role of the stock exchange
  —in transferring ownership
  —in extending the accounting rules for listed companies e.g. in takeovers, interim reporting
  —in relation to auditing
✸ rights of shareholders to withdraw capital
✸ the directors' duty to account
  —in company law, including preparation of financial statements, provision of a directors' report, and a directors' statement
  —by complying with accounting standards
  —by providing an audit report.

    Generally, all these issues raised relate to the idea of developing sound systems of corporate governance. **Corporate governance** is the system by which corporations are directed and controlled. As such it typically details rights and responsibilities of different participants of the corporation. This explains the emphasis found to date on such things as rules relating to the directors, the board as a whole, different types of shareholders and other stakeholders. Governance also typically requires some detailed rules and procedures for decision making, including objective setting and performance evaluation.

    In spite of this, corporate governance remains an ongoing issue. This has emerged as a serious concern since the late 1980s, when the global share market collapsed. A number of high profile corporate failures—e.g. Bond Corporation and Quintex Corporation (Christopher Skase)—added fuel to the debate and resulted in some changes being made. More recently, the collapses of Enron, Ansett, One.Tel and HIH have led to something of a crisis of confidence. The collapse of Arthur Andersen, a major auditor with a worldwide reputation, added fuel to the fire.

The reactions in different parts of the world are not the same. In the USA the resulting legislation has aimed to curtail the misbehaviour and excesses of senior managers, with the emphasis being on ensuring the correctness of the financial statements. In Australia the following occurred:

* A Royal Commission was held relating to the HIH collapse.
* The Australian Stock Exchange (ASX) set up a council on corporate governance.
* The Corporate Law Economic Reform Program (CLERP) gave the Australian Securities and Investments Commission (ASIC) power to fine companies for breaches of the disclosure rules.

The HIH Royal Commission basically found that HIH was mismanaged, that decisions were ill-conceived and that the management culture was unsound.

ACTIVITY 15.1

Do you think that mismanagement could be avoided by imposition of governance systems and structures that are highly prescriptive? Why/why not?

In general the report found that imposing highly prescriptive governance systems and structures is fraught with danger. A 'one size fits all' approach will not work. The report focused rather more on the role of boards and directors, and the associated cultures. The culture of the organisation that was HIH and its board was seen as having major shortcomings. There were no significant recommendations for change.

ACTIVITY 15.2

What does this imply about the difficulties in ensuring that reports are sound, in terms of setting in place detailed rules of corporate governance?

The ASX set up a Corporate Governance Council in 2002, with the overriding mission being:

to develop and deliver an industry-wide, supportable and supported framework for corporate governance which could provide a practical guide for listed companies, their investors, the wider market and the Australian community. (Foreword)

The ASX Corporate Governance Council states that '*the enhancement of corporate accountability and the adoption of this framework is a major evolution in corporate governance practice in Australia*' (Foreword).

The Council requires that the guidelines are applied, arguing that '*maintaining an informed and efficient market and preserving investor confidence remain the constant imperatives*' (Foreword). Disclosure requirements under ASX Listing Rule 4.10 are that companies must provide a statement in their annual report disclosing the extent to which they have followed the best practice recommendations provided, in the reporting period. Where recommendations have not been followed these must be identified and reasons given for not following them. Disclosure is only required where either a recommendation is not met, or disclosure is specifically required under the ASX listing rules mentioned. Disclosure requirements apply for listed companies for financial periods commencing after 1 January 2003.

The Council defines and supports corporate governance as follows.

Corporate governance is the system by which companies are directed and managed. It influences how the objectives of the company are set and achieved, how risk is monitored and assessed, and how performance is optimised.

Good corporate governance structures encourage companies to create value (through entrepreneurism, innovation, development and exploration) and provide accountability and control systems commensurate with the risks involved. (p. 3)

The Council points out that there is no single model of good corporate governance, and that the recommendations, in themselves, cannot prevent failure or mistakes, but they can provide a reference point to minimise problems, and to optimise performance and accountability.

The essential corporate governance principles identified by the ASX Corporate Governance Council (p. 11) are set out below.

A company should:

1. **Lay solid foundations for management and oversight**

   Recognise and publish the respective roles and responsibilities of board and management

2. **Structure the board to add value**

   Have a board of an effective composition, size and commitment to adequately discharge its responsibilities and duties

3. **Promote ethical and responsible decision-making**

   Actively promote ethical and responsible decision-making

4. **Safeguard integrity in financial reporting**

   Have a structure to independently verify and safeguard the integrity of the company's financial reporting

5. **Make timely and balanced disclosure**

   Promote timely and balanced disclosure of all material matters concerning the company

6. **Respect the rights of shareholders**

   Respect the rights of shareholders and facilitate the effective exercise of those rights

7. **Recognise and manage risk**

   Establish a sound system of risk oversight and management and internal control

8. **Encourage enhanced performance**

   Fairly review and actively encourage enhanced board and management effectiveness

9. **Remunerate fairly and responsibly**

   Ensure that the level and composition of remuneration is sufficient and reasonable and that its relationship to corporate and individual performance is defined

10. **Recognise the legitimate interests of stakeholders**

    Recognise legal and other obligations to all legitimate stakeholders

SOCIAL ISSUES IN ACCOUNTING

GENERAL BACKGROUND

In Chapter 1 we identified a range of groups that use accounting information. These included owners and managers, plus a variety of other users including employees, community groups, governments and other interest groups. Over a considerable number of years the focus of accounting has changed from an emphasis on stewardship to decision usefulness. In more recent years the idea of decision usefulness has broadened considerably, with considerable emphasis being directed towards the provision of information that is useful to a larger range of interested parties.

Of particular significance is the far greater interest and involvement in issues that go beyond the confines of a particular business, which impact on society at large.

Throughout the period since the Industrial Revolution there have been inherent conflicts between entrepreneurs and society at large. A reading of books such as *How Green was my Valley*, a story by Richard Llewellyn, set in South Wales in the late nineteenth and early twentieth century, brings out issues such as unashamed greed and excessive use of economic power and wealth, appalling working and living conditions of employees, including health and safety, and environmental issues. In the book the valley became a huge slag heap, which impacted (and still impacts) on life in the valleys.

As wealth and power becomes more widely spread so perspectives change. The accounting information provided has slowly adapted to these changes. The stakeholder concept provides a useful framework to use to explain the broadening of needs.

STAKEHOLDER CONCEPT

The notion of stewardship accounting, and even of decision usefulness for owners and managers, has been the driving force of accounting until the last 20 or so years. This has meant that the main focus of accounting has been on the provision of information that enables owners to make money. The stakeholder concept recognises that there are other interested parties who have a legitimate interest or stake in the business. In Chapter 1 the following user groups were identified:

✳ owners/shareholders

✳ managers

✳ employees and their representatives

* customers
* government
* lenders
* suppliers
* investment analysts
* competitors
* community representatives.

ACTIVITY 15.5

Do you regard these as all having a legitimate stake in a business? Why/why not?

ACTIVITY 15.6

Can you think of a town, city or region where prosperity is, or has been, dependent on one employer?

The importance of the particular business to the various groups of stakeholders might differ considerably, and might change over time for a particular stakeholder group, but generally the stakeholder concept is useful. Other potential additions to the list might include potential customers, socially oriented action groups, including environmentalists, and other pressure groups.

Businesses ignore the views and needs of these groups at their peril. Even if we were to assume that the underlying objective of the business remains as wealth maximisation, the business needs to be very conscious of the views of the various stakeholders and the possible impact on its future should it ignore these views. Recent examples include the boycott on tuna products instigated by the Dolphin Coalition. This was directed against an industry-wide fishing practice which netted and killed large numbers of dolphins. This led to changes both in the fishing practice and in the labelling of cans of tuna as 'dolphin safe'. Health issues raised over the last few years have invariably resulted in pressure from interested groups, which has led to considerable changes in products and packaging.

Probably the main impacts these stakeholder groups have had are:

* greater emphasis on social responsibility
* greater understanding that the direct costs of actions of a particular business can represent only a small part of the total costs, with the rest being borne by the community at large, which has led to environmental or 'green' issues becoming significant
* the recognition that the workforce and its quality are major contributors to the success (or failure) of a business.

This has led to the development of corporate social reporting, environmental accounting (really a sub-set of corporate social reporting) and triple bottom line reporting.

WHAT IS SOCIAL RESPONSIBILITY?

As pointed out earlier many businesses and businesspeople have been criticised for their lack of social responsibility. For example, James Hardie has been subject to severe criticism in recent years for its apparent unsupportive attitude over the long-term illnesses developed by their employees who have been associated with asbestos production.

 ACTIVITY 15.7

Can you think of any businesses that have been seen as having behaved in a way which you do not regard as being socially responsible? What are the underlying reasons for this belief?

By and large, social responsibility is defined in a fairly broad manner. Increasingly, there is an expectation that due consideration will be given by a business to the impact on society at large of its actions. Factors such as pollution, health and safety issues, and impact on employment and job creation or destruction, are often seen as coming within this ambit. Of course, there are cases where one objective might be in conflict with another. For example, it can be argued that coal-fired power stations provide more pollution than nuclear-powered stations, but nuclear power brings its own dilemmas.

Being socially responsible can be said to be putting in place policies, procedures and practices that will ensure that an entity (business or other organisation) acts as a good citizen. A key part of this requires a particular entity to give due consideration to the social costs and benefits that result from an action.

This view is not however shared by all. The emphasis on an objective of shareholder wealth maximisation can be interpreted in a way which totally ignores social costs, other than those that clearly impact directly on the returns of the particular business. This might imply that this objective is consistent with a view that 'it's OK as long as you can get away with it'. How does a business justify in financial terms to its shareholders the choice of a more expensive production process that will yield lower pollution levels but also lower profits than an alternative process? If a competitor goes down the lower cost, higher pollution route it will probably be able to sell at a more competitive price and threaten the competitive position of the first business. There are clearly some inherent conflicts in this area.

 ACTIVITY 15.8

Can you think of reasons why a business might still engage in less profitable activities that would be socially beneficial?

So how might business as a whole be encouraged to engage in more socially responsible behaviour? Several possibilities exist:

* make shirking of responsibilities more costly, by regulation and law and public awareness
* market the good citizen concept, e.g. the growth of 'green' consumerism, where consumers' decisions are strongly influenced by the nature of the business, the product or the method of production

❋ business groupings can combine to deal with aspects of their business in a socially responsible way

❋ government action, which might include legislation, imposition of penalties for non-compliance, or provision of subsidies.

CORPORATE SOCIAL RESPONSIBILITY (CSR)—WHAT DOES IT MEAN?

While definitions can vary slightly the following definition provides a useful starting point.

> 'CSR is about how companies manage the business processes to produce an overall positive impact on society.'

This definition is from Mallen Baker (see www.mallenbaker.net/csr/CSRfiles/definition.html)—the Mallen Baker website provides interesting insights into the whole area of **corporate social responsibility**. The site is frequently updated, issues based, international in focus and has the potential to be an agent for change. It is recommended.

Mallen Baker goes on to say that companies need to consider two aspects of their operations:

1. The quality of their management—both in terms of people and practices
2. The nature of, and quantity of, their impact on society in the various areas.

He argues that outside stakeholders are taking a far greater interest in the activities of the company, typically what the company has actually done, good or bad, in terms of its products and services, in terms of its impact on the environment and on local communities, or in its treatment and development of its workforce.

The World Business Council for Sustainable Development (2000) defined CSR as follows:

> Corporate Social Responsibility is the continuing commitment by business to behave ethically and contribute to economic development while improving the quality of life of the workforce and their families as well as of the local community and society at large. (Holme and Watts, 2000, p. 8)

This approach tends to be associated with capacity building for sustainable livelihoods, respect for different cultures, and skill development.

Mallen Baker has argued that definitions of this sort are much more inclusive than the typical approach found in the USA, where CSR is defined more in terms of a philanthropic model. In Europe the emphasis seems to be more on operating in a socially responsible way, while at the same time still investing in communities for solid business reasons. This latter approach is probably more sustainable, in that it:

❋ links inextricably the social responsibility with wealth creation

❋ is likely to continue when times are hard, whereas philanthropy is likely to be the first to go.

There is little doubt that pressure will grow on businesses to play a role in social issues. This is particularly true for the transnational companies, which are often economic giants that have more economic power than many nation states.

By way of illustration, consider the example of Ceres. Ceres is a US-based coalition of environmental, investor and advocacy groups working together for a sustainable future, with a mission to move businesses, capital and markets to advance lasting prosperity by valuing the health of the planet and its people (see www.ceres.org). The aim is to find solutions to today's environmental challenges. Ceres has developed a set of principles, which is effectively a 10-point code of environmental conduct. The **Ceres principles** are set out below.

Protection of the Biosphere

We will reduce and make continual progress towards eliminating the release of any substance that may cause environmental damage to the air, water, or the earth or its inhabitants. We will safeguard all habitats affected by our operations and will protect open spaces and wilderness, while preserving biodiversity.

Sustainable Use of Natural Resources

We will make sustainable use of renewable natural resources, such as water, soils and forest. We will conserve non-renewable natural resources through efficient use and careful planning.

Reduction and Disposal of Wastes

We will reduce and where possible eliminate waste through source reduction and recycling. All waste will be handled and disposed of through safe and responsible methods.

Energy Conservation

We will conserve energy and improve the energy efficiency of our internal operations and of the goods and services we sell. We will make every effort to use environmentally safe and sustainable energy sources.

Risk Reduction

We will strive to minimise the environmental, health and safety risks to our employees and the communities in which we operate through safe technologies, facilities and operating procedures, and by being prepared for emergencies.

Safe Products and Services

We will reduce and where possible eliminate the use, manufacture or sale of products and services that cause environmental damage or health or safety hazards. We will inform our customers of the environmental impacts of our products or services and try to correct unsafe use.

Environmental Restoration

We will promptly and responsibly correct conditions we have caused that endanger health, safety or the environment. To the extent feasible, we will redress injuries we have caused to persons or damage we have caused to the environment and will restore the environment.

Informing the Public

We will inform in a timely manner everyone who may be affected by conditions caused by our company that might endanger health, safety or the environment. We will regularly seek advice and counsel through dialogue with persons in communities near our facilities. We will not take any action against employees for reporting dangerous incidents or conditions to management or to appropriate authorities.

Management Commitment

We will implement these principles and sustain a process that ensures that the Board of Directors and Chief Executive Officer are fully informed about pertinent environmental issues and are fully responsible for environmental policy. In selecting our Board of Directors, we will consider demonstrated environmental commitment as a factor.

Audits and Reports

We will conduct an annual self-evaluation of our progress in implementing these Principles. We will support the timely creation of generally accepted environmental audit procedures. We will annually complete the Ceres Report, which will be made available to the public. (Reproduced with permission.)

The main work carried out by Ceres in recent years relates to:

* climate change, and
* corporate environmental reporting.

As part of the latter work Ceres launched the **Global Reporting Initiative (GRI)**. The Sustainability Reporting Guidelines prepared by the GRI are among the most widely accepted standards for corporate **sustainability reporting** worldwide. We will return to them later.

ACTIVITY 15.9

The Ceres principles might be seen as representing one end of a fairly large spectrum. Can you identify what possible arguments might be used against corporate social responsibility?

Of course some of the arguments that are put forward against CSR are not strong, and many are based on an incomplete understanding of CSR. For example, it can be argued that an emphasis on philanthropy as an appropriate reaction to CSR illustrates a complete misunderstanding of CSR, and indeed, of the nature of business. If business is about relationship building with a range of stakeholders, the case for a broader approach to CSR is easily put. Arguments about 'not having time' also fail. If you don't have time to look at the wider issues you may be missing opportunities and, possibly more importantly, given the particular context we are in, of missing threats. With regard to the role being largely political or government based, the problems arise when businesses presume that the issues are being addressed when they are not, and when the particular business realises that it has not kept its eye on the ball. In some cases, given the size and nature of the industry and associated companies, better progress will be achieved by full involvement with the main corporate players than with national governments. Many companies spend a lot of time and money on activities which shape public policy, for good or evil. It is significant that quite a number of the most respected companies are respected because of their role in CSR.

ACTIVITY 15.10

Identify several companies that are currently in the news and identify the issues that make them newsworthy. What kind of CSR issues are found?

The whole area of corporate social responsibility is particularly challenging. There is little doubt that a company cannot ignore what are seen as legitimate responsibilities. However, there is no clear checklist to go with this. The public view is changing continuously. The Ceres principles might appear to be, at best, optimistic, but the changes in attitude that seem to pervade much of the thinking of the developed world seem to all be pointing in one direction, to greater acceptance of social responsibility, in a fairly broadly based way. Whether the same is true of the developing nations is a matter for continued debate.

ACCOUNTING FOR CORPORATE SOCIAL RESPONSIBILITIES

In Australia there are no accounting standards relating to social responsibility accounting. However, there has been a move towards voluntary disclosure, especially for large listed companies. Reasons for voluntary disclosure include the following.

✳ In making decisions that impact on perceived social responsibilities a business needs to be aware of the costs and benefits, at least in broad terms, in order to be able to make informed decisions. If the information is available there could be advantages in sharing it.

* As mentioned earlier, companies may achieve a competitive advantage by being seen as acting in a socially responsible manner, thus being seen as a good corporate citizen that ought to be supported. Voluntary disclosure provides a framework for a good marketing and public relations team to be able to put pressure on non-disclosing competitors, by highlighting what it is doing in a pro-active way, compared to what might or might not be being done by the non-disclosing competitor.

* Cultivation of the 'green' and 'ethical' consumer markets.

Voluntary reporting has grown considerably over time. In 1979, Trotman surveyed the annual results of the 100 largest companies listed in Australia. At this time 69 provided some disclosures relating to social responsibility. The majority of the disclosures related to human resources (including health and safety, working conditions and training) and the environment (including pollution control, protecting and improving the environment, and recycling of products), with a smaller number of disclosures relating to community (including philanthropy and opening facilities to the public), energy (including reduction of energy consumption and use of waste resources) and products (including making products safer and reducing pollution). Under the heading of 'others' were included work experience programs and use of local suppliers.

To summarise some later studies:

* Trotman and Bradley (1981) examined the characteristics of companies that provided information of this type. They found that such companies were larger, had higher systematic risk and placed greater emphasis on the long term.

* Guthrie and Parker (1990) found that disclosure was greater in the UK and the USA than in Australia. They also found that no company provided 'bad news', suggesting a desire to counter any potential criticism.

* This was reinforced by Gray, Owen and Adams (1996) who summarised research in the UK and showed that the percentage of companies making voluntary and mandatory disclosures relating to the environment and to energy had grown significantly between 1986 and 1991. In excess of 70% of UK companies provided information relating to the environment by 1991 (pp. 173–4).

* Deegan and Gordon (1996) reviewed the 1991 accounts of 197 Australian companies. They discovered that there was a significant increase in disclosures during the period 1988–91, that there were more positive than negative reports, and that disclosures were mainly qualitative in nature. Disclosures seemed to reflect the general increase in public interest in a number of issues, which were no longer seen as being solely the domain of fringe groups. The research tended to reinforce the idea that disclosures of this type were seen as a component of the public relations effort of the business. It also provided a quite extensive list of examples of environmental disclosures, both positive and negative. Some of these are listed below:

Positive
* Use of environmentally sensitive management techniques.
* Compliance with government environmental reports and standards.
* Pollution or waste control in the manufacturing process.
* Maintenance or implementation of a strategy to protect the environment.
* Rehabilitation of mining sites.
* Implementation of tree replanting schemes.
* Positive outcomes from government inquiries.
* Introduction of environmental audits.
* Recycling of materials.

- Use of environmentally safe products in manufacturing.
- Undertaking of environmental impact or assessment studies.
- Sponsoring or receiving environmental achievement awards.
- Evidence of public support/approval of the company's environmental activities.

Negative

- Company in conflict with government view on its environmental activities.
- Admission of causing environmental, including health-related, problems for residents through the company's environmental activities.
- Explicit admission of excessive pollution emissions.
- Government investigation into, and court action concerning, the company's environmental activities.
- Non-compliance with regulations.

In recent years attention has focused more strongly on triple bottom line (TBL) reporting and the global reporting initiative (GRI), both of which are dealt with in more detail later. Before moving on to them it is worth reflecting on methods of accounting for social responsibility in broad terms. Many of the underlying problems remain under the TBL and GRI approaches.

METHODS OF ACCOUNTING FOR CORPORATE SOCIAL RESPONSIBILITY

It is clear that corporate social responsibility is about accountability where the social and environmental impacts of the organisation are reported to stakeholders, including the community at large. Just what form this accountability takes is less clear. A number of approaches are possible, and the following have been identified:

* the inventory approach
* an approach based on cost
* a program management approach, and
* a cost–benefit approach.

Most companies have not moved past the first of these, for reasons which may be justifiable.

The inventory approach

This is essentially an approach which simply prepares and discloses a list of activities it regards as having a bearing on its social responsibilities. As such it should also make reference to areas where it has not been socially responsible, but this tends not to happen.

Typically the list covers some or all of the following:

* physical resources and environmental contributions, usually including pollution reduction, natural resource conservation, recycling activities, restoration of the environment, and similar activities
* energy, which usually includes reduction in energy consumption and use of waste
* human resources, usually with an emphasis on the well-being of employees, including training programs, improvement in working conditions, health and safety, provision of other benefits such as child care, and affirmative action programs
* product or service contribution, which might include quality and safety

* community involvement, which typically emphasises those activities of benefit to the general public, including corporate philanthropy
* 'other', which might include work experience and use of local suppliers.

This is undoubtedly the most common approach used by Australian companies. Unfortunately, it has the drawback of being somewhat ad hoc, with limited ability to compare performance between businesses, or even to measure the social responsibility of a business.

Cost approach

With this approach the costs incurred on each activity will be disclosed. This poses some interesting dilemmas for the accountant in determining what proportion of any expenditure should be treated as the expense for the year.

ACTIVITY 15.11

How might an amount that is spent on improving production systems with the aim of reducing both energy costs and the level of pollution be dealt with?

Program management approach

With this approach a longer term program is identified, and the report will show the extent to which the objectives have been met. For example, a program might have an objective of increasing the number of women, people with disabilities, or ethnic minorities in the workforce to a certain level by a specified date. The report can provide details of progress to date.

With this approach there is a clear need to explain the underlying rationale, including objectives, for the program or programs. This is followed by an indication as to how much progress has been made towards these objectives. Unfortunately, achievement of these objectives does not necessarily mean that social benefits have actually been achieved.

Cost–benefit approach

This approach requires a detailed cost–benefit analysis of those activities which have a social (or environmental) impact. This is rather more difficult than any of the three methods discussed so far. While direct costs to the business are fairly clear, the indirect (social) costs are less clear, and the benefits can prove difficult to measure.

ACTIVITY 15.12

What kind of benefits might accrue from a pollution reduction strategy initiated by a business?

What difficulties might you experience in trying to measure these benefits?

All of the methods described are either inadequate, incomplete, or require extremely difficult calculations. Attempts have been made to pull together these ideas into a framework which could be used fairly consistently, which would broaden the reporting context to reflect the needs of today. The two main frameworks are dealt with below.

TRIPLE BOTTOM LINE REPORTING

Given the problems identified above there emerged a need to develop a reporting framework which was more comprehensive than the traditional reporting framework. What was needed was a new form of disclosure which integrated financial, environmental and social reporting. **Triple bottom line reporting** emerged in the late 1990s. The phrase 'triple bottom line' was coined by John Elkington in his book *Cannibals with Forks: the Triple Bottom Line of 21st Century Business* (1997). The essence of triple bottom line reporting is sustainable development. Sustainable development requires much greater collaboration between industry, government and society at large. In reporting on a particular entity (which might include business corporations, governments and local governments) we need to devise a system which reports in a manner which will facilitate sustainable development, or at least identify actions which move us towards, or away from, this ideal. This requires a report that focuses on three areas:

✳ economic prosperity

✳ environmental quality

✳ social justice.

So far in this book we have tended to deal with things which can be measured. Not everything in the triple bottom line agenda falls easily into this category. What is needed is a set of performance indicators relating to these three elements.

Companies generally aim to create wealth, primarily for their shareholders. Typically, they want to do this for the long term, so they should be interested in what has been described as 'sustainable value creation'. This is likely to mean that companies need to meet society's need for goods and services without destroying natural or social capital. It has been argued that this approach increases the time over which performance should be measured.

Basically, the triple bottom line focuses on three components:

✳ economic value added

✳ environmental value added

✳ social value added

which together give total value added.

Of course in many cases the impact of some activity on the environment or society might be negative. In many cases the impact is not easily measured as was discussed above. A major challenge with triple bottom line reporting is not the production of each of the three parts, but rather the integration of the three components.

In spite of this, triple bottom line reporting has gained in support and sophistication. Many companies see clear benefits arising from its use and development. Benefits that might accrue include:

✳ embedding good corporate governance and ethics systems, which has had the effect of producing a values-driven, integrated culture

✳ better management of risk and resource allocation

✳ formalising and enhancing communication with key stakeholders

✳ attracting better staff

✳ better benchmarking, leading to an enhanced ability to develop competitive advantage

✳ better access to financial markets.

A recent KPMG (2002) survey found that 45% of the world's top 250 companies now produce a separate corporate report with details of social and environmental performance, an increase from 35% in 1999. There were substantial differences by country, with Japan having the largest proportion at 72%. Australia was ranked 12th at 14%. PricewaterhouseCoopers has recently collected historical data to examine the nature, extent and quality of triple bottom line performance-reporting by 40 of Australia's largest listed companies. The report suggested the following:

✳ the triple bottom line is very important to some companies

✳ there is greater emphasis on the social bottom line than the environmental bottom line

✳ companies report high levels of favourable news.

The report raises questions about the extent to which companies are using the Concise Annual Report to explain the triple bottom line, seeing current use as a missed opportunity. A concise annual report is a condensed version of the annual report which companies may substitute, by agreement with individual shareholders, which avoids fully detailed accounting disclosures. Clearly the PricewaterhouseCoopers report considers that a report of this nature could be used very constructively to reflect the three aspects covered by the triple bottom line, but that this is not happening. The report also questions whether the motivation for reporting is to influence market perceptions regarding quality of management, and its ability to create innovative solutions and resolve conflicts between economic, environmental and social considerations.

In passing it is worth noting that triple bottom line reporting is not limited to companies. By way of illustration Maroochy Shire Council in Queensland produces *monthly* triple bottom line report cards which include the following items (reproduced with permission from Maroochy Shire Council):

Financial report card

Focuses on variations to budget and the cash position and reviews:

✳ annual operating performance

✳ cash management

✳ debt management

✳ short-term viability of the organisation

✳ long-term viability of the organisation.

Environmental report card

Considers:

✳ waste water quality

✳ recycled solid waste

✳ roadside weed control

✳ greenhouse gas reduction

✳ volunteers working on conservation projects

Social report card

Considers:

❋ employee safety
❋ workplace stability
❋ community support
❋ listening to the community
❋ community works.

This suggests that the triple bottom line concept can be a critical component is setting the ethos of an organisation, and translating this into effective day-to-day management practices.

Given that triple bottom line reporting is a relatively new phenomenon there are no clear formats (though see the next section on the GRI) or rules to follow. Broad guidelines might include that the report should:

❋ be balanced, including negatives as well as positives
❋ have some external verification or back up
❋ be timely
❋ encourage interactive exchange and links with stakeholder groups
❋ be distributed widely in a number of modes
❋ link with existing financial reports.

The next section on the global reporting initiative takes the concept of triple bottom line reporting into a new phase.

THE GLOBAL REPORTING INITIATIVE (GRI)

The Global Reporting Initiative (GRI) is a multi-stakeholder process and independent institution whose mission is to develop and disseminate globally applicable Sustainability Reporting Guidelines. These Guidelines are for voluntary use by organisations for reporting on the economic, environmental, and social dimensions of their activities, products, and services. The GRI incorporates the active participation of representatives from business, accountancy, investment, environmental, human rights, research and labour organisations from around the world. Started in 1997, GRI became independent in 2002, and is an official collaborating centre of the United Nations Environment Programme (UNEP) and works in cooperation with UN Secretary-General Kofi Annan's Global Compact. (See GRI website www.globalreporting.org/about/brief.asp.)

GRI released its *Sustainability Reporting Guidelines* in 2002. In doing so:

GRI recognises that developing a globally accepted reporting framework is a long-term endeavour. In comparison, financial reporting is well over half a century old and still evolving amidst increasing public attention and scrutiny. The 2002 Guidelines represent the GRI Board's view of a consensus on a reporting framework at this point in time that is a blend of a diverse range of perspectives. (p. i)

The Guidelines document is very comprehensive. It identifies a number of trends, which are listed below (pp. 1–3):

✳ expanding globalisation—with corporate activity remaining the driving force, but all parties seeking new forms of accountability that credibly describe the consequences of business activities wherever, whenever and however they occur

✳ search for new forms of global governance—with a key theme being increased transparency

✳ reform of corporate governance—with higher standards being expected in terms of ethics, transparency, sensitivity and responsiveness

✳ global role of emerging economies, particularly countries such as Brazil, India and South Africa

✳ rising visibility of, and expectations for, organisations

✳ measurement of progress toward sustainable development—with a need to align future goals with a complex range of external factors and partners, and an increased urgency in defining broadly accepted sustainability performance indicators

✳ governments' interest in sustainability reporting

✳ financial markets' interest in sustainability reporting

✳ emergence of next-generation accounting.

The last section is particularly interesting as it points to the future directions of accounting and sets them firmly in context.

The late 20th century saw worldwide progress in harmonizing financial reporting. Indeed, the rich tradition of financial reporting, continually evolving to capture and communicate the financial condition of the organization, has inspired GRI's evolution. Yet today, many observers, including accountants themselves, recognise that characterising the 'bricks and mortar' economy of the past will not suffice as a basis for characterizing today's information economy. Valuing intangible assets—human capital, environmental capital, alliances and partnerships, brand and reputation—must complement the valuation of conventional tangible assets—factories, equipment, and inventory. Under the rubric of 'business reporting', 'intangible assets analysis', and 'value reporting', a number of accounting groups have launched programmes to explore how accounting standards should be updated to enhance such value drivers. New concepts of risk, opportunity, and uncertainty are likely to emerge.

The future directions of accounting are clear, at least in broad terms. There remains an enormous amount of work to be done in order to achieve the aspirations of the GRI.

Perceived benefits are (Guidelines, pp. 3–4):

✳ effective management in a global economy—where information travels at Internet speed

✳ need to engage in continual dialogue with stakeholders—with reporting being seen as assisting in the communication process

✳ increased emphasis on company relationships with external parties

✳ sustainability reporting provides linkages between functions

✳ process of developing a sustainability report provides early warning of trouble spots in terms of supply chains, communities, regulators, reputation and brand management

✳ sustainability reporting helps sharpen management's ability to assess the organisation's contribution to natural, human and social capital

✳ sustainability reporting might reduce share price volatility.

The Guidelines organise 'sustainability reporting' in terms of economic, environmental and social performance. This brings it in line with triple bottom line reporting, which was discussed earlier in the chapter. GRI recognises that the triple bottom line approach has obtained a fair degree of consensus and it is sensible to use this approach as a *reasonable entry into a complex issue*' (p. 9).

In the main the new form of report will be designed in a way that reflects the unique nature of an organisation, and the context within which it operates. Key issues will be:

* defining boundaries
* providing additional content
* designing an appropriate format.

The boundary issue is interesting, given the arguably limited perspective found in financial reporting. Just how far out should the boundaries be set? The Guidelines suggest that engagement with stakeholders would facilitate the second issue regarding additional content.

The Guidelines suggest (p. 17) that the frequency and medium of reporting might be rather more varied than is found with traditional financial reporting, with an expectation of annual, quarterly and even real-time data.

The Guidelines indicate an awareness of the need for credibility of the report and suggest that reports include (p. 18) a statement of:

* the reporting organisation's policies and internal practices to enhance the credibility and quality of its sustainability report
* the reporting organisation's policy and current practice with regard to providing independent assurance about the full report.

Again, the GRI recognises that this is an area in the early stages of development. The Guidelines provide a detailed set of principles to underpin the reports. These are summarised and organised as shown in Figure 15.1. Many of these have their genesis in financial reporting.

ACTIVITY 15.13

Which of these principles represent a shift away from those developed for financial reporting, in principle or in application?

The form of the report

The guidelines suggest that the report should contain the following (p. 35):

* Vision and strategy statement—a description of the reporting organisation's strategy with regard to sustainability, including a statement from the CEO.
* Profile—an overview of the reporting organisation's structure and operations and of the scope of the report.
* Governance structure and management systems—description of reporting organisation's organisational structure, policies and management systems, including stakeholder engagement efforts.

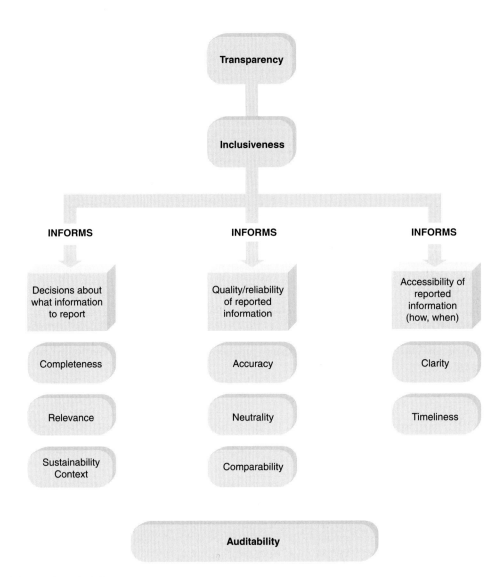

FIGURE 15.1 GRI reporting principles

Source: GRI, *Sustainability Reporting Guidelines*, p. 23.

* GRI content index—a table supplied by the reporting organisation identifying where the information listed in part C of the Guidelines (which covers reporting content requirements) is located within the organisation's report.
* Performance indicators—measures of the impact or effect of the reporting organisation divided into integrated, economic, environmental, and social performance indicators.

The hierarchy of indicators is shown in Figure 15.2 (see Guidelines, p. 36). This highlights the differences between traditional reporting and sustainability reporting, with increased emphasis on environmental and social performance indicators, and the increase in qualitative performance indicators.

CATEGORY	ASPECT
ECONOMIC Direct Economic Impacts	Customers Suppliers Employees Providers of capital Public sector
ENVIRONMENTAL Environmental	Materials Energy Water Biodiversity Emissions, effluents and waste Suppliers Products and services Compliance Transport Overall
SOCIAL Labour Practices and Decent Work	Employment Labour/management relations Health and safety Training and education Diversity and opportunity
Human Rights	Strategy and management Non-discrimination Freedom of association and collective bargaining Child labour Forced and compulsory labour Disciplinary practices Security practices Indigenous rights
Society	Community Bribery and corruption Political contributions Competition and pricing
Product Responsibility	Customer health and safety Products and services Advertising Respect for privacy

FIGURE 15.2 GRI hierarchy of performance indicators

Source: GRI, *Sustainability Reporting Guidelines*, p. 36.

The GRI content is spelled out in detail on pp. 38–59. Given the limited aims of this chapter it is not possible to go through these in detail. However, the following pages identify the main themes.

Under vision and strategy

✳ It is important that the main issues for the organisation relating to the theme of sustainable development are identified, and an explanation given as to just how these issues are reflected in the organisation's values and integrated into its strategies.

✳ The CEO is required to commit to targets and report on performance against industry benchmarks.

Under profile

❋ Consideration must be given to provision of information relating to indirect employees.

❋ There is a requirement to identify stakeholders, their key attributes, and their relationship with the organisation.

❋ The report scope should identify its boundaries.

❋ Any decisions not to apply GRI principles should be identified.

Under structure and governance

❋ The process for determining the expertise board members need to guide the strategic direction of the organisation, including issues related to environmental and social risks and opportunities, should be outlined.

❋ Outline approaches to stakeholder consultation.

❋ Note any applicable externally developed, voluntary economic, environmental and social charters.

❋ Identify policies and systems for managing upstream and downstream impacts.

❋ Outline the reporting organisation's approach to managing indirect economic, environmental and social impacts resulting from its activities.

❋ Outline programs and procedures pertaining to economic, environmental and social performance including priority and target setting, internal communication, performance monitoring and auditing.

ACTIVITY 15.14

What do you think is meant by the terms 'upstream' and 'downstream'?

Quite detailed guidelines are provided for the performance indicators, covering core indicators and additional indicators. Performance indicators relating to *economic performance* direct impacts required are shown in Table 15.1.

TABLE 15.1 GRI economic performance indicators

Element of concern	Core indicators	Additional indicators
Customers	• Net sales • Geographic breakdown of markets	
Suppliers	• Cost of goods, materials, services • Percentage of contracts paid in accordance with agreed terms	• Supplier breakdown by organisation and country
Employees	• Total payroll and benefits	
Providers of capital	• Distributions to providers broken down by interest and dividends of all classes of shares • Increase/decrease in retained earnings	
Public sector	• Total sum of all taxes • Subsidies by country or region • Donations to community, civil society and other groups, broken down into cash and in kind	• Total spent on non-core business infrastructure

Indirect economic impacts need to be identified.

For *environmental performance*, requirements are set out as summarised in Table 15.2.

TABLE 15.2 GRI environmental performance indicators

Element of concern	Core indicators	Additional indicators
Materials	• Total materials used • Percentage of materials used that are waste	
Energy	• Direct energy used, segmented by primary source • Indirect energy	• Initiatives to use renewable energy sources and increase energy efficiency • Annualised lifetime energy requirements of major products • Other indirect energy use and implications
Water	• Total water use	• Water sources and related ecosystems/habitats significantly affected by use of water • Annual withdrawals of ground and surface water as a percentage of annual renewable quantity of water available from the sources • Total recycling and reuse of water
Biodiversity	• Location and size of land owned, leased or managed in biodiversity rich habitats • Description of major impacts on biodiversity associated with activities and/or products and services in terrestrial, freshwater and marine environments	• Total amount of land owned, leased or managed for production activities or extractive use • Amount of impermeable surface as a percentage of land purchased or leased • Impact of activities and operations in protected and sensitive areas • Changes to natural habitats resulting from activities and operations and percentage of habitat protected or restored • Objectives, programs and targets for protecting and restoring native ecosystems and species in degraded areas • Number of IUCN Red List species with habitats in areas affected by operations • Business units currently operating or planning operations in or around sensitive areas
Emissions, effluent and waste	• Reporting separate totals for each gas, for both direct and indirect emissions • Use and emissions of ozone depleting substances • Various specific emissions, by type • Total amounts of waste, by type and destination • Significant discharges to water, by type • Significant spills of chemicals, oils and fuels, by number and volume	• All relevant indirect greenhouse gas emissions • All production, transport import or export of any waste deemed hazardous under the terms of the Basel convention • Water sources and related ecosystems/habitats significantly affected by discharges of water and runoff

Element of concern	Core indicators	Additional indicators
Suppliers		• Performance of suppliers relative to environmental components of programs and procedures
Products and services	• Significant environmental impacts of principal products and services • Percentage of the weight of the products sold that is reclaimable at the end of the product's useful life and percentage that is actually reclaimed	
Compliance	• Incidents and fines for non-compliance with all applicable international declarations, conventions and treaties, and national, sub-national, regional and local regulations associated with environmental issues	
Transport		• Significant environmental impacts of transportation used for logistical purposes
Overall		• Total environmental expenditures by type

In the area of social performance, indicators are suggested in the areas of labour practices and decent work, human rights, society, and product responsibility, as shown below. Indicators for *labour practices and decent work* are shown in Table 15.3.

TABLE 15.3 GRI performance indicators for labour practices and decent work

Element of concern	Core indicators	Additional indicators
Employment	• Breakdown of workforce by region, status, employment type and contract • Identify workforce retained in conjunction with other employers • Net employment creation and average turnover by region/country	• Employee benefits beyond those mandated
Labour/Management relations	• Percentage of employees with trade union representation etc., broken down geographically • Policy and procedures involving information, consultation and negotiation with employees over changes in operations e.g. restructuring	• Provision for formal worker representation in decision making or management
Health and safety	• Practices on recording and notification of occupational accidents and diseases etc. • Description of formal joint health and safety committees • Standard injury, lost day and absentee rates and number of work-related fatalities	• Evidence of substantial compliance with the International Labour Organization (ILO) guidelines for Occupational Health Management Systems

	• Description of policies on programs on HIV/AIDS	
Training and education	• Average hours of training per year per employee by category of employee	• Description of programs to support the continued employability of staff and to manage career endings • Specific policies and programs for skills management or for lifelong learning
Diversity and opportunity	• Description of equal opportunity policies or governance, and compliance • Might include harassment • Composition of senior management and governance bodies, including male/female ratios and other indicators of cultural diversity	

The suggested indicators for *human rights* are as shown in Table 15.4.

TABLE 15.4 GRI performance indicators for human rights

Element of concern	Core indicators	Additional indicators
Strategy and management	• Description of policies, guidelines, corporate structure and procedures relating to human rights • Evidence of consideration of human rights impacts as part of investment and procurement decisions, including suppliers • Description of policies and procedures to evaluate and address human rights performance within the supply chain and contractors etc.	• Employee training on policies and practices concerning all aspects of human rights relating to operations
Non-discrimination	• Description of global policy and procedures/programs preventing all forms of discrimination in operations, and associated monitoring systems	
Freedom of association and collective bargaining	• Description of policy and extent to which universally applied, and description of associated procedures and programmes	
Child labour	• Description of policy excluding child labour as defined by the ILO convention, and extent to which policy visibly stated and applied, plus description of associated procedures and programs, together with monitoring systems and results of monitoring	
Forced and compulsory labour	• Description if policy to prevent forced and compulsory labour and extent to which policy visibly stated and applied, plus	

	description of associated procedures and programs, together with monitoring systems and results of monitoring	
Disciplinary practices	• Description of appeal practices • Description of non-retaliation policy and effective confidential employee grievance systems	
Security practices	• Human rights training for security personnel	
Indigenous rights	• Description of policies, guidelines and procedures to address the needs of indigenous people • Description of jointly managed community grievance mechanisms • Share of operating revenues redistributed to local communities	

Indicators relating to *society* are identified in Table 15.5.

TABLE 15.5 GRI performance indicators for society

Element of concern	Core indicators	Additional indicators
Community	• Description of policies to manage impacts on communities affected by activities, plus description of associated procedures and programs, together with monitoring systems and results of monitoring	• Awards received relevant to social, ethical and environmental performance
Bribery and corruption	• Description of the policy, procedures, management systems and compliance mechanisms addressing bribery and corruption	
Political contributions	• Description of the policy, procedures, management systems and compliance mechanisms for managing political lobbying and contributions	• Amount of money paid to political parties and institutions whose prime function is to fund political parties or their candidates
Competition and pricing		• Court decision cases regarding anti-trust and monopoly legislation • Description of the policy, procedures, management systems and compliance mechanisms for preventing anti-competitive behaviour

Many of these reflect key issues in the USA, particularly the anti-trust legislation, and will inevitably need to be modified in practice to reflect slightly different views of the world.

Suggested indicators for *product responsibility* are given in Table 15.6.

TABLE 15.6 GRI performance indicators for product responsibility

Element of concern	Core indicators	Additional indicators
Customer health and safety	• Description of policy for preserving customer health and safety during use of products and services, extent to which policy is visibly stated, plus description of associated procedures and programs, together with monitoring systems and results of monitoring	• Number and type of non-compliances, including fines • Number of complaints upheld by regulatory or similar official bodies • Voluntary code compliance, product labels or awards with respect to social and/or environmental responsibility
Products and services	• Description of policies, procedures, management systems and compliance mechanisms related to product information and labelling	• Number and type of non-compliance with regulations, and fines • Description of policies, procedures, management systems and compliance mechanisms related to customer satisfaction, by geographic area
Advertising		• Description of policies, procedures, management systems and compliance mechanisms for adherence to standards and voluntary codes in advertising • Number and types of breaches of advertising and marketing regulations
Respect for privacy	• Description of policies, procedures, management systems and compliance mechanisms for consumer privacy	• Number of substantiated complaints regarding breaches of consumer privacy

Just how far most companies are prepared to go in this whole area remains unclear. It is probably unrealistic to expect all countries to move forward at the same rate, given that the pressures economically, politically and possibly culturally are quite different. However, there is little doubt that pressures for greater disclosure will continue to grow in the developed world, as will the rewards for being a good corporate citizen. Continuing development in this area is almost certain to happen.

MANAGEMENT ACCOUNTING AND STRATEGY

Not surprisingly, many of the issues dealt with to date in this chapter also form part of management accounting. One of the perceived benefits of the GRI work is that it broadens perspectives, not least of management. Management now is forced to think far more carefully about such things as:

❋ long-term effects on the environment

❋ the need for and value of a good team of staff (and hence about how to maintain and further develop the team)

❋ the value of a brand or brands

❋ how it is perceived by various communities, how this perception might be improved or how it might be damaged.

In other words, the need to develop and successfully implement a sound strategy is more important than ever and the role of the accountant needs to be extended to cover **strategic management accounting**. There is little doubt that the management accountant has a major role to play in this development. In Chapter 1 an outline decision making, planning and control process was set out. While this process is sound, it probably is simplistic when it comes to strategy development, at least in terms of the first three items (identify objectives, consider and evaluate options, and make a decision). Strategic decisions are rather more complex than indicated.

Essentially when dealing with strategy development the decision-making process can be summarised as below (based on Smith, 1997, p. 114).

TABLE 15.7 Framework for strategic management accounting

Objectives	Corporate goals congruent with targets
Situation analysis	Financial/competition/market analyses
	Environmental/social impact analyses
Benchmarking	Similar analyses of competitor performance to determine areas of relative strength and weakness
Strategy alternatives	Formulate and implement optimum offensive/defensive strategies
Evaluation of achievement	Monitoring with financial/non-financial measures
Accounting system implications	Changed information sources/measures/reporting practices to create relevant internal management

The starting point is to identify objectives. These need to be broadly based in the first instance. There is a need to develop a mission statement for the organisation, together with a plan of action which sets out targets and performance indicators. More frequently now than in the past, statements of values are found, again reflecting the broad trends discussed in this chapter to date.

Then comes a consideration of options. Many of the options examined in the book to this point were options at an operational level, where choices could be made relatively easily on the basis of numbers. In many of these cases a given strategy could be assumed. However, in developing strategy we are clearly talking about strategic options, which require a much more broadly based approach. Development of strategic options requires a detailed situational analysis, to identify just where the business is at the moment, and what potential directions it might take in the future. A variety of possible approaches exist. Common methods used are portfolio matrices, with the most common being a SWOT analysis, in which strengths, weaknesses, opportunities and threats are set out on a matrix as illustrated below.

FIGURE 15.3 SWOT analysis

Not surprisingly, the main areas that need to be addressed are financial performance, competitiveness, market situation, environmental factors and, increasingly, social factors. Typically this last item has not been seen as a major role of the management accountant, but inevitably the role will be expanded to include it.

Financial performance in detail is clearly the domain of the accountants. Clearly, historic, broadly based accounts are the domain of the financial accountant. More detailed analysis and forecasting is more likely to be the domain of the management accountant. A great deal of benchmarking and comparison is likely to be needed, some of which might be quite difficult for companies (conglomerates) with a large number of unrelated business subsidiaries. All of the ratios used in Chapter 6 are likely to need to be used carefully.

Competitive and market analyses requires identification of such things as just what businesses the company wants to be in, who the main competitors are, what their strengths and weaknesses are, whether the business has any competitive advantage, and if so, what it is and how it can be maintained and enhanced. Questions need to be asked about such things as:

* industry leadership
* market shares
* economies of scale and cost leadership
* innovation and product differentiation
* niche market opportunities
* brand equity
* impact of green policies both within and outside of the business
* government intervention and subsidies and likely changes therein
* macroeconomic factors such as exchange and interest rates, whether the government is running a large deficit, inflation levels etc.
* technological advantage/disadvantage and potential, and timelines for change
* labour costs
* management policies e.g. inventory holdings, staff development.

 ACTIVITY 15.15

For which of the items listed do you think the management accountant could play a part?

 ACTIVITY 15.16

Can you identify any key factors that might facilitate innovation and competitive advantage?

Environmental and social factors include the kind of things discussed earlier in the chapter.

Alongside the situational analysis we need to develop benchmarking. In the earlier chapters of the book we covered budgeting and variance analysis, which was effectively a comparison of actual figures with planned figures. Serious attempts need to be made to benchmark externally as well as internally if good strategy is to be developed. In practice this is quite difficult, given questions of confidentiality, different accounting systems etc.

When analysing alternative options it is necessary to look at them at a strategic level. Hence decisions are likely to be made at this level before (or at the same time as) a detailed financial appraisal (typically using discounted cash flow techniques). A key component of this strategic analysis relates to diversification. Diversification can be within a particular industry, within broadly similar industries, or completely unrelated industries. Different practices occur in different parts of the world. Generally in the USA the diversification tends to be related i.e. the areas of business can be linked in some way. For example, one major US company has defined as its broad market anything that can be found in a supermarket shopping trolley. It therefore diversified from its base as a tobacco company into retailing, liquor and canning, and sold off a shipping subsidiary. Another with a strong background in hotels and gambling sold its shipping subsidiary, largely because the CEO had no experience within that particular industry. The target market was seen broadly as the leisure industry and cargo shipping did not fit well. However, in the UK there are many companies with subsidiaries in five to eight major areas of business, often completely unrelated. These kind of companies are known as conglomerates. Ideally, where different parts of the corporation are unrelated it makes sense to try to find areas which are counter-cyclical, but this is quite difficult to do. Diversification into related businesses may be horizontal, e.g. new products into existing markets, or vertical, e.g. suppliers' or customers' products or markets.

A further factor that needs to be understood is the concept of a product life cycle. Basically, this recognises that there are four or five components of a product life cycle. These are the introduction and growth phases, which are then followed by a period of maturity, then decline and demise. Just how long the growth and, more particularly, the maturity, phases last is dependent on a multiplicity of factors which need to be considered. The last phases are the decline phase, which may or may not be followed by a rejuvenation phase before final decline, and demise. A clear understanding of the various life cycles is important in developing strategy. In practice this is more difficult than it might appear.

The Boston Consulting Group (BCG) portfolio matrix has proved useful over the last 20-plus years in enabling businesses to understand how each section of the business contributes to the whole, and assists in deciding on strategic directions. Basically, the various arms of the business—which might be subsidiary companies—are plotted on the matrix. The placing of the various components can then be analysed strategically.

The market growth rate provides an indicator of industry attractiveness, while the competitive position is measured by relative market share. Stars are subsidiaries that are market leaders, being profitable and having high growth potential. They often require further investment. When the growth slows, they become cash cows. Cash cows are subsidiaries in mature markets with good growth, and often low investment needs. Dogs are uncompetitive in low growth, static or declining markets. No further investment funds should be spent and consideration needs to be given to eliminating them. The question mark group needs careful consideration. This group has good market potential but to move to star status the companies probably need investment. If this does not happen they tend to turn into dogs. The strategies that emerge from this matrix are fourfold:

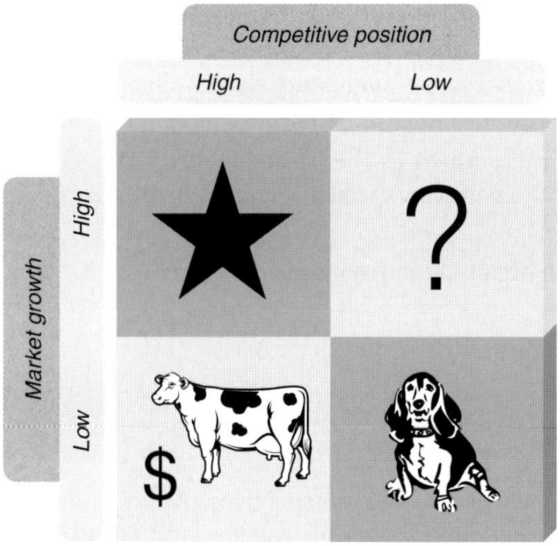

FIGURE 15.4 BCG portfolio matrix

* build—i.e. invest to build market share
* hold—i.e. preserve market share
* harvest—use cash cows to fund other businesses
* divest—get rid of inefficient businesses.

In reviewing strategy it is important to monitor achievements to date. This requires a comparison with the corporate goals to see whether achievements are in line with the original goals, what needs to be done if the goals have not been achieved, and whether the goals themselves need to be changed.

When decision making at a strategic level is to occur the information needed is far more broadly based than that needed for decisions dealt with in this book to date. In fact, the information needed for this internal decision making is very similar to, and has considerable overlap with, the kind of information required by the GRI. The role of the accountant seems destined to broaden over time.

THE BALANCED SCORECARD APPROACH

The final topic in the book, the **balanced scorecard**, provides an indication of the potential overlapping of the role of management and financial accountants. It also reinforces the view that the measurement role of the accountancy profession is likely to be expanded into new areas.

Essentially, the balanced scorecard is both a management system and a system for measuring and reporting performance, which integrates financial and operating performance measures in a way that highlights and communicates the strategic goals of the organisation. It was developed in the 1990s by Kaplan and Norton in a series of articles in the *Harvard Business Review*. They argued that in today's information age companies must aim to create future value through investment in customers, suppliers, employees, processes, technology and innovation. The emphasis has changed from production to customers, from tangible assets to intangible, from top-down management to bottom up, and incremental change has become transformational change. The changes are significant in driving value. Intangible assets such as brands, intellectual property, and people now drive value in many companies.

The traditional accounting statements are not particularly useful as indicators of future value, if in fact value is driven differently. What is needed is information to assist in both strategy development, and in communicating to users information that will assist them in making judgments about value, both now and in the future. The aim of the balanced scorecard approach is therefore to build management systems based on strategy.

The balanced scorecard has been described as the 'strategic chart of accounts'. It aims to capture both the financial and non-financial elements of a company's strategy, and to explain the relationships that drive the business results.

The balanced scorecard views the organisation from four perspectives:

* financial
* business process
* customer
* learning and growth.

It aims to provide and analyse data on all four perspectives. A key component of the balanced scorecard approach is measurement. Ways must be found to identify the key strategic drivers and then find some criteria by which these can be measured. A major part of the process is examination of outcomes as defined by agreed measures, followed by tracking of these results and their feedback to further develop and refine strategy. Key components are:

* strategic analysis of the present status of the company
* determination of appropriate measures of performance
* feedback on the performance measures
* analysis of trends in performance over time
* development of decision support tools and systems.

The financial perspective

Financial information remains a core component of decision making and strategy development. As the balanced scorecard system is implemented it would be expected that a comprehensive corporate database would be developed and that more of the financial data would be centralised and automated. There is almost certainly going to be a need to include some additional financial information, especially in the risk management area, and in the social and environmental areas, where cost–benefit information is likely to be needed. However, the essence of the balanced scorecard message is that reliance solely on financial data will provide an incomplete or unbalanced approach.

The business process perspective

This perspective is all about how the business is running internally. Questions that need to be asked might include the following.

* Are the products and services appropriate to customer and market needs? If not what needs to be done to rectify the situation?
* Are the support services providing the desired support in a timely and efficient manner? How can they be improved?
* How efficient are the production processes?
* How is the interaction with stakeholders organised?

The aim should be to identify the key elements of the business process that impact on strategy, and then decide on measures that enable performance in these areas to be tracked. Measures might include things such as:

* percentage of systems automated
* percentage of production completed within standard
* production days lost for a variety of different reasons.

The customer perspective

A focus on customers and customer satisfaction is central to success. Dissatisfied customers will fairly quickly lead to the demise of a business. Poor performance in this area is a good lead indicator of future decline. Detailed questions need to be asked in this area and measures devised for tracking and analysis. Measures might include such things as:

* some kind of customer satisfaction index
* market share
* number of new products
* number of new customers
* number of new markets, by type.

The learning and growth perspective

In the modern information age people are a key strategic asset. In some companies people are the only asset of significance. Financial accounting has never really handled assets of this type well, yet this perspective is central to the strategy of many organisations. Focus needs to be put on things such as:

* quality, experience and skills of staff
* systems for continuous training and development, professional updating and development of a philosophy of life-long learning
* availability of technical and other specialist staff
* time and support available for research and development.

This key perspective then requires some measurable performance indicators to be devised.

The balanced scorecard aims to link all four perspectives around vision and strategy. The management accountant is likely to become a central part of this process, primarily because of the emphasis on measurement, which is what accountants are good at. A number of advantages are claimed:

* decisions are based on fact
* development of strategy occurs through a much broader staff base
* translates strategy into operational reality
* because drivers are grounded in strategy, far more staff will have a better understanding of big picture strategy issues, with the (expected) result that strategy will be improved, so the organisation should be better aligned to the strategy, and strategy becomes part of everyone's job
* continual feedback and review occurs in a strategic context, so strategy development is better informed and becomes a continual process.

ACTIVITY 15.18

Identify the similarities in thinking between the GRI approach and the balanced scorecard approach.

OVERALL CONCLUSION

Demand from a variety of users is growing for the provision of much more broadly based information than has historically been provided. It is no longer sufficient for a business to be focused solely on maximisation of wealth as it relates to the shareholder group. Social and environmental concerns are now serious and there is a great deal of emphasis on sustainability. Sustainability demands come from every sector—society, environmentalists, customers, employees and the shareholders. There is increasing evidence that in fact management itself needs to address a much broader set of questions and issues than it has in the past in order to develop sound strategy. Whether all of this translates into broad acceptance of the GRI, with further development of measurement systems that will certainly expand the role of accountants, remains to be seen. As we have seen in discussing triple bottom line reporting, and more particularly the balanced scorecard, management will need to expand its information base considerably if it is to compete in the information economy. It would seem reasonable to suppose that both management and society at large are moving in the same direction. Just what pace both are going at is debatable. Whatever conclusion you reach, it seems inevitable that the issues raised in this chapter will not go away. Accountants will need to develop a set of expanded skills in these areas.

SUMMARY

In this chapter we have achieved the following objectives in the way shown.

OBJECTIVE	METHOD ACHIEVED
Define corporate governance	Defined and set in context
Outline the principles of corporate governance set out by the ASX	Set out and explained
Outline and discuss a range of social and environmental issues in accounting	Provided a general background
Explain the stakeholder concept	• Described and illustrated the stakeholder concept • Set in the context of social and environmental issues
Explain what is meant by corporate social responsibility	• Explained social responsibility • Defined corporate social responsibility • Illustrated by examples
Explain the Ceres principles	• Set out principles • Described context

OBJECTIVE	METHOD ACHIEVED
List and explain the main methods of accounting for corporate social responsibility	Provided detail of methods used including • Inventory approach • Cost approach • Program approach • Cost–benefit approach
Explain triple bottom line reporting	Described and explained triple bottom line reporting
Outline the global reporting initiative and discuss in broad terms the main framework	• Set the GRI in context • Explained the benefits • Described and detailed the reporting principles • Described the form of the report • Provided a hierarchy of performance indicators • Listed the main performance indicators
Outline the major components of strategic decision making	• Described the implications for management accounting of links with strategy • Provided a framework for strategic management accounting • Illustrated role of SWOT analysis • Described and explained the BCG portfolio matrix
Discuss the role of the management accountant in strategy development	Discussed and illustrated the role
Explain the balanced scorecard approach and its advantages	• Described the underlying rationale behind the balanced scorecard • Explained its benefits • Indicated ways in which its use will expand the role of the management accountant

BIBLIOGRAPHY

ASX Corporate Governance Council, *Principles of Good Corporate Governance and Best Practice Recommendations*, March 2003.

Deegan, C. & Gordon, B., 'A study of the environmental disclosure practices of Australian corporations', *Accounting & Business Research*, Summer 1996, pp. 187–99.

Elkington, J., *Cannibals with Forks: the Triple Bottom Line of 21st Century Business*, Capstone, 1997.

Global Reporting Initiative, *Sustainability Reporting Guidelines*, GRI, Amsterdam, The Netherlands, 2002 <www.globalreporting.org>.

Gray, R., Owen, D. & Adams, C., *Accounting and Accountability—Changes and Challenges in Corporate Social and Environmental Reporting*, Prentice Hall, London, 1996.

Guthrie, J. & Parker, L.D., 'Corporate social disclosure practice: A comparative international analysis', *Advances in Public Interest Accounting*, Vol. 3, 1990, pp. 159–76.

Holme, R. & Watts, P., *Corporate Social Responsibility: Making Good Business Sense*, World Business Council for Sustainable Development, UK, January 2000.

KPMG Global Sustainability Services, *KPMG International Corporate Sustainability Reporting*, 2002.

Smith, M., *Strategic Management Accounting*, Butterworths, Sydney, 1997.

Trotman, K.T., 'Social responsibility disclosures by Australian companies', *The Chartered Accountant in Australia*, March 1979, pp. 24–8.

Trotman, K.T. & Bradley, G.W., 'Associations between social responsibility disclosures and characteristics of companies', *Accounting, Organisations and Society*, 1981, pp. 355–62.

DISCUSSION QUESTIONS

EASY

<Obj 5> **15.1** What do you understand by corporate social responsibility?

<Obj 6> **15.2** Examine the Ceres principles. To what extent do you think that these principles can ever be a practical guide to business?

INTERMEDIATE

<Obj 1, 2> **15.3** What do you think are the consequences of the various scandals that have occurred in recent years for confidence? What direction do you expect corporate governance to take over the next five years?

<Obj 2> **15.4** Do you think that the current trends in governance are going over the top?

<Obj 3> **15.5** Just how much responsibility should an organisation take for social and environmental issues?

<Obj 3, 4> **15.6** Assume that you are the CEO of a company which is the major employer in a small town in rural New South Wales. What responsibility would you see yourself having for your employees? Would your company size make any difference to your thinking?

<Obj 3, 6, 7> **15.7** Is there any evidence that companies that are socially responsible in terms of pollution and waste avoidance benefit in terms of profits?

<Obj 4, 7> **15.8** To what extent are social and environmental concerns consistent with a shareholder wealth maximisation objective?

<Obj 7> **15.9** While many of the underlying ideas of corporate social reporting are sound, the fact remains that many are unmeasurable. To what extent does this detract from this style of reporting?

<Obj 9> **15.10** How realistic do you see the GRI being for anything other than the largest transnational companies? To what extent do you think the basic principles might be used by smaller, domestic companies?

<Obj 11> **15.11** To what extent do you think that the training of a typical accountant equips him or her to take on the expanded roles implicit in the GRI?

CHALLENGING

<Obj 7> **15.12** Why might we expect a voluntary CSR policy to work?

<Obj 8, 9> **15.13** Is the form of the GRI report too complex? Will it lead to information overload?

<Obj 9> **15.14** To what extent do you see the perceived benefits from the GRI actually becoming real tangible benefits?

<Obj 9> **15.15** Can you think of any other major environmental or social issues not covered in the performance indicators?

<Obj 10, 11> **15.16** To what extent does the strategic decision-making process result in a downplaying of financial measures such as net present value?

<Obj 12> **15.17** In working through the balanced scorecard approach what difficulties do you see in actually balancing the four perspectives?

APPLICATION EXERCISES

<Obj 3–9>   **15.1**   Try to find out as much as you can about two major transnational corporations and comment on their social and environmental practices over time. (BP and Nike might be good starting points.)

<Obj 3–9>   **15.2**   Use the web to find examples of corporate social responsibility reporting, summarise them, and comment on them. (Westpac recently produced a comprehensive social impact report.)

<Obj 7>   **15.3**   Try to obtain examples of companies that have undertaken major cost–benefit analyses before undertaking a particular action which has been good (or bad) for the environment.

<Obj 10–11>   **15.4**   Many capital investment decisions are seen as strategic. But many of these are made to fit within a strategic context. Does this mean that capital investment decisions using discounted cash flow techniques are in fact only a small, and relatively automatic, part of the strategic investment process? If so, what are the implications for decision making of this type? If not, where does finance fit into the strategic decision-making process?

The following article provides commentary on corporate governance guidelines. Read the article and answer the questions that follow.

CASE STUDY
15.1

Views from the top

Peter Matruglio, Partner, Business Risk Services, Ernst & Young

Australian CPA
April 2004, pp. 42–3

In the aftermath of a host of corporate collapses Ernst & Young has held a series of interviews among leading directors of ASX 100 companies to learn their views on the 'comply or explain' philosophy of the ASX Corporate Governance Council (CGC) principles. Directors were also asked what impact the CGC principles and best practice recommendations had on them personally and if the practices advocated by the CGC would change corporate and board behaviour.

All directors who spoke with Ernst & Young said new corporate governance regulation had to happen. All generally embrace the spirit of the principles, feeling that they are sound and make good business sense. However, concerns were raised about some of the suggested best practices. Many directors also have concerns about rigid adherence to the guidelines fearing a focus on merely ticking boxes as opposed to fostering real, long-lasting change.

It is said that at the core of good corporate governance is a sound culture that allows the principles of good governance to thrive. The directors who spoke with Ernst & Young were unanimous in this view, feeling that values and culture are not something that can be regulated but yet are the ultimate drivers of how a company operates.

With culture so important it was agreed that ultimately no amount of governance regulation can prevent all corporate collapses. After all, companies fail for a number of reasons. One of the directors interviewed suggested that corporate collapses could be categorised as occurring as a result of either (or a combination of): technological development; changes in consumer preferences; fraud; and incompetent management.

Companies that fail to respond accordingly to technological change or movement in consumer preferences run the heightened risk of failure. Good governance practices will not save these companies.

The directors agreed companies need to have effective and efficient processes in place to detect fraud. While good governance practices cannot ensure that fraud will not occur, sound practices can go a long way to ensuring fraud will be detected at a sufficiently early stage.

One director said you cannot 'legislate against incompetence'. Rather, board members should 'weed out' incompetent management. Good governance practices should highlight those managers who are not performing at a level required to ensure the success of the company and directors should have processes in place to act on this information in a timely manner.

Over-regulation was a cause of concern raised by some directors. It was feared that it could cause companies to become risk averse and stifle growth. There was concern that boards may not respond quickly to new opportunities. Boards may become too risk averse as a result of the focus on compliance and companies could miss out on opportunities or improved returns. It was felt that the core of any company's success is the need to be entrepreneurial. Companies need to take risks, albeit measured and informed risks, in order to succeed and grow.

Many directors feel that in the current environment, the lines of responsibility within companies have become blurred. The message from directors, though, was, 'Let directors direct and managers manage'. At present directors are feeling the pressure to have a greater involvement in the management of the company and are spending more time managing than directing. Likewise shareholders, rather than requiring disclosure of what the company is doing, want to be involved in directing the business. This is not an effective way to run a company and hinders commercial transactions.

One size does not fit all

Directors point out that each company is different. What may be appropriate in one company in terms of 'directing' may not be appropriate at another. For example, the manner in which directors obtain comfort about governance and compliance matters will vary from company to company and indeed from case to case, changing from an approach of 'tell me' to 'show me' depending upon the circumstances. Directors were also concerned that rating agencies would only evaluate if a company had or had not 'ticked the box' rather than rating a company on the level of disclosure or the appropriateness of the reason for non-compliance.

Directors that spoke to Ernst & Young fully support the concept of continuous disclosure believing that transparency is necessary to build trust and inspire confidence. But where do you draw the line? Directors feel that commercial transactions, such as proposed mergers or potential acquisitions, could be put at risk if directors are forced to make disclosure of these events. A director asked, 'what is the benefit to shareholders of being 'aware', if that awareness jeopardises the transaction itself?' It was pointed out that the real issue should be to ensure that selective disclosure does not occur.

Directors recognise the role they play in ensuring corporate governance compliance. They feel it is definitely their responsibility to ensure compliance but feel they also need to ensure requirements are added in a manner that adds value to the company.

And what about the role of the regulator? Of concern to directors was the specifics of how governance and the wider financial reporting function should be regulated. It was suggested that regulators are focused on creating a process to achieve good governance rather than focusing on improving the output.

Directors said regulators should be focused on ensuring that the market is appropriately informed. Rather than regulating what should be done, (potentially adding to the 'tick box' mentality) they should be concerned with ensuring that the market is well informed about what the company is actually doing and how this achieves the aim of good governance.

As Charles Macek, chair of the Financial Reporting Council, has said: 'The best regulator is an educated, informed investor acting in a market where there is adequate disclosure.'

1   What are the main concerns raised by the directors spoken to?
2   What are seen as the ultimate drivers of how a company operates?
3   What reasons were given for corporate failures?
4   Which of these reasons could have been eliminated with good governance?
5   Explain the comments made around the quotation that you cannot 'legislate against incompetence'?
6   Why were some directors concerned about over regulation?
7   Explain the concerns raised about blurring of responsibilities between management and board.
8   Explain the concerns about the idea that 'one size fits all'.
9   How can transparency be reconciled with 'commercial in confidence'?
10 Explain the role of the regulators as perceived by the directors interviewed.

The second article deals with corporate social responsibility. Read the article and answer the questions that follow.

The social bottom line

Gary O'Donovan

Australian CPA
December 2002, pp. 66–9

CASE STUDY

15.2

→

Judy Wicks is the proprietor of the White Dog Café, which since its opening in 1983 has become an institution in the US city of Philadelphia. The story of the White Dog Café is the story of Wicks' evolving understanding that you can use the market as a vehicle for serving humanity. Since its opening, the White Dog Café has become internationally known and valued for Wicks' just relationships with employees, her social and environmental activism, and, of course, her focus on good cooking. Two examples of Wicks' social responsiveness include paying her entry-level employees above the minimum wage and exclusively using humanely raised animal produce.

The White Dog Café is an example of a small business embracing corporate social responsibility and making it work for the business, the planet and society. In the 21st century, big business is seeing the benefits of becoming more socially responsible. An international survey in 2000 conducted by the Prince of Wales' Business Leaders Forum found that: 'Corporate social responsibility has shifted decisively from the "nice to do" to the "need to do"'.

What is corporate social responsibility (CSR)?
CSR can be broadly described as the ethical behaviour of a corporation towards society. Reporting on CSR is about the interaction of the corporation with the legal and social obligations of the societies in which it operates, and how it accounts for those obligations.

The dimensions of CSR vary among different definitions but typically include the following issues:
• Workplace issues such as recruitment policies, treatment of employees, health and safety issues
• Environmental issues
• Human rights
• Community involvement and development
• Market place issues such as product safety and marketing practices
• Financial issues

- Accountability
- Corporate governance and ethics.

CSR and the triple bottom line (TBL)

The concept of the TBL (see below) expands the traditional performance measures of an entity, in particular corporate entities, from a financial measure to that of an all-embracing measure which incorporates the social and environmental effects entities operations have on society.

During the past decade, corporations have focused on reporting environmental performance, and research indicates that environmental reporting is more prevalent and more advanced at this stage than social reporting. Environmental performance appears to be regarded as a concept more easily defined than social performance and while measurement and reporting issues are complex for both, it is more straightforward for entities to report on environmental impacts and initiatives than it is on social issues. Reporting on social performance has developed more slowly. The diverse range of social issues and impacts corporations face makes it difficult to develop a consistent and reliable measurement and reporting framework on which to develop meaningful, comparable social reports.

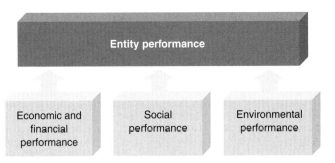

Entity performance model

Why do companies report on CSR?

Notwithstanding the difficulties in measuring social performance, the number of stand-alone social reports, as well as the disclosure of social information in the annual report, is increasing. Corporations increasingly see a need to legitimise their social performance, engage stakeholders and establish reputations as good corporate citizens. In a recent study by Ernst & Young (2002), 147 senior executives from the Global 1000 group of companies were interviewed. Nearly all (94 per cent) of the respondents believed that practising and reporting CSR could deliver real business benefits. Interestingly, 76 per cent of the companies published some CSR information and 46 per cent produced a separate CSR report but only 11 per cent claimed to have made significant progress in implementing a CSR strategy in their organisation. This indicates that, at this stage, the usefulness and relevance of the reports and strategies might be questionable.

Actions by customers and the community based on perceptions of good or bad social performance can affect corporate profits and, in worst case scenarios, an entity's existence. For example, in an Environics International survey—*The Millennium Poll on Corporate Social Responsibility*, 51 percent of Australians claim they punished companies they viewed as socially irresponsible. Likewise, a study by Resnik/KPMG found that approximately 80 per cent of the survey group said they had purchased products and services on the basis of social or environmental issues.

Examples of social reporting

There are many examples of social reporting available. These may be as detailed as a comprehensive stand-alone report or may be as simple as a general statement of CSR policy included in an annual report. For example, in Australia the Westpac Banking Corporation produced a comprehensive Social Impact Report this year. Some of the issues covered in the 44-page report include:

- CSR management
- Employee CSR including employee turnover and job creation, employee satisfaction, top management remuneration, female-male salary ratio and non-work aspects of career management
- Retail banking including transparency of fees and charges; responsible lending accessibility and availability of banking services; improving accessibility for the disabled
- Institutional banking including third world debt; global country profile
- Suppliers including social and environmental performance screening of key suppliers.

In contrast, a vastly different example of CSR and CSR reporting is practiced by Canadian company BC Hydro, one of the largest electric utilities in Canada. BC Hydro is a Crown corporation owned by the province of British Columbia, which is home to 197 First Nations bands (Aboriginal groups). BC Hydro has facilities on at least 168 of these band's reserve lands. Consequently, they believe that building sustainable, mutually beneficial relationships with Aboriginal peoples is critical for BC Hydro.

To implement this strategy, BC Hydro developed an approach to build relations with the Aboriginals by addressing the past, building for the future, and effectively managing its Aboriginal relations initiatives. Key components of the relationship building strategy are facilitating participation in resource management and development decisions, fostering economic development, supporting education for Aboriginal peoples, and contributing to community projects and events. Some of the specific CSR practices BC Hydro has initiated include:

- Negotiating contracts for work on start-up and expansion grants to Aboriginal-owned businesses are provided and in some cases joint ventures are explored;
- Developing an Aboriginal Business Directory that is used throughout the corporation and is available to government and private sector companies as a source for products and services;
- Providing cross-cultural training programs that address historical facts, court decisions, and cultural issues. More than 4,700 BC Hydro employees have taken at least one half day, cross-cultural, training course.

The future

There is little doubt that CSR is here to stay and that the social, environmental and ethical performance of companies is under increased scrutiny. One needs to look no further for evidence of this than the annual publishing of the *Age* and *Sydney Morning Herald Good Reputation Indices*, which ranks the top 100 Australian companies by social, environmental and financial performance. Moreover the growth of socially responsible investment funds and other ethical investment services in Australia and internationally indicate that society is becoming more discerning in relation to where they will invest their money and from whom they will buy consumer products. This spells out an urgent need for companies to manage their social responsibilities as diligently as they do their financial responsibilities.

Associate Professor O'Donovan is Head of School and Deputy Dean in the Faculty of Commerce at the University of Tasmania.

---

1   Why do you think that environmental reporting is more prevalent and more advanced than social accounting?

2 According to the article, why do companies engage in CSR?

3 According to the article, what employee information was provided in the Westpac Social Impact Report? Why do you think Westpac provided this information?

4 What do you think is socially significant about the information provided by Westpac on retail banking?

5 Discuss the possible reasons for the BC Hydro approach to indigenous issues described in the article.

CASE STUDY 15.3

The third article is about the use (and non-use) of the balanced scorecard in Hong Kong. Read the article and answer the questions that follow.

Hong Kong strikes a perfect balance

Hong Kong China CPA Division Strategic Management Centre of Excellence Cell

Australian CPA
November 2002, pp. 62–4

Traditionally, companies have emphasised financial indicators such as profit and turnover as measures of performance. The Balanced Scorecard (BSC) is an approach to performance measurement that combines traditional financial measures with contemporary, non-financial ones. It enables companies to clarify their business strategy and vision into operational objectives, and measure targets using these different but complementary methods.

The BSC translates a company's strategy into objectives and performance measures. It links the past outcome measures with the future driver measures and considers the organisation's vision and strategy as central to determining objectives. It includes both financial and non-financial measures and indicators and represents a balance between external and internal measures, aligning individual goals with the corporate strategy.

BSC emphasises the importance of lead indicators that drive the future performance of the organisation. The lead (and lag) indicators can be classified into four groups—customers, internal business processes, organisational learning and entity growth. This is in contrast to the traditional lag indicators of financial outcomes that only report past performance.

The framework of the BSC (on page 637) shows the interaction between financial, customer-based, internal business process and learning/growth indicators.

Kaplan and Norton introduced the BSC in a seminal article published in the *Harvard Business Review* in 1992. Since then, the BSC has been widely adopted by many organisations worldwide as a management tool. Early adopters in the US included Mobil North American Marketing and Refining Division, CIGNA Property and Casualty Insurance Company, and Chemical Bank.

Implementing the BSC is not always easy. Instances where it has failed are not unknown. The critical success factors include top management's commitment, leadership and the company's ability to manage any internal resistance to change.

Successful implementation of the BSC involves four key steps:

1. Define the BSC architecture by developing an in-depth understanding of the business—this enables formulation of the long-term strategy of the organisation by top management.

2. Define a set of strategic objectives that are built around the strategy and based on input from executives through regular meetings and group sessions.

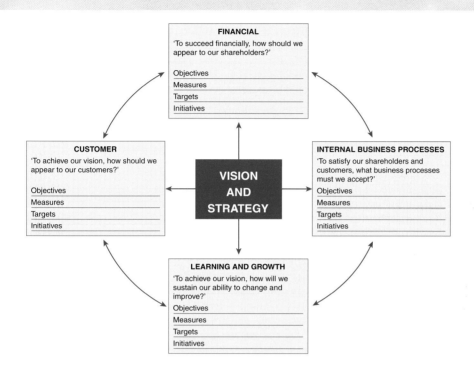

3. Define and select the best scorecard measures—called key performance indicators (KPIs)—that are aligned with each other and that will track the progress of the strategy.
4. Develop an implementation plan to facilitate communication at different levels, develop information and reporting systems and conduct appropriate staff training on the BSC project.

Benefits of the Balanced Scorecard

As a performance measurement system, the benefits of the BSC are realised when it is transformed from a measurement system to a management one. The management processes built around the BSC enable organisations to become aligned and focused on implementing a long-term strategy. In an information and knowledge economy, the BSC becomes the foundation for managing today's organisations, which place more reliance on intangible assets.

With the adoption of the BSC, executives can measure how business units create value for current and future customers. In addition, they can measure how they must build and enhance internal capabilities and an investment in people, systems and procedures that is necessary to improve future performance. Since the BSC enables financial and non-financial measures to be part of business information systems for employees at all levels of the organisations, employees can understand the financial consequences of their decisions and actions, while senior executives can understand the drivers of long-term financial success.

Objectives

Adoptions of the BSC by organisations from a wide range of industries in Western countries has increased awareness of it in Asia. In response to this, CPA Australia's strategic business management centre of excellence cell—Hong Kong China division, conducted a study to gauge public awareness of the BSC as a formal system of performance measurement. The specific objectives of the study were to explore the general awareness and knowledge of the BSC approach among professional accountants in Hong Kong; whether Hong Kong organisations have a formal system in place to measure their performance and, in particular, the BSC approach; the reasons for implementing the BSC and its real benefits; the difficulties, if any, encountered in the implementation of the BSC; the general perceptions on the BSC approach in terms of its applicability in the Hong Kong business environment.

A questionnaire survey was prepared to explore:

1. Whether the respondents' organisations were adopting the BSC.
2. Their awareness and perception of the BSC.
3. The benefits and problems in implementing the BSC.
4. Demographic information of respondents and their organisations.

Data was collected through a survey of 200 members of the CPA Australia—Hong Kong China division, who attended a seminar. The members were selected not only as a convenient sample, but also as they were expected to be involved in strategic planning and designing performance measurement systems within their organisations to increase their opportunity of exposure to the BSC.

There were 199 usable responses—56 per cent had been with their current organisation for longer than two years, 40 per cent were employed as managers, senior managers, CFO or CEO and 53 per cent were from companies with 100 or more employees.

Industries represented in the results include wholesale/trading (21 per cent), professional services (16 per cent), manufacturing (13 per cent), finance/banking (7 per cent), real estate/construction (7 per cent), IT (6 per cent), education (5 per cent) and public/government services (4 per cent)—the remaining represented other industries.

Respondents were asked to classify the management style of their organisation—44 per cent classified their organisations as using a Western style, 42 per cent Hong Kong Chinese, 5 per cent Japanese, 3 per cent mainland Chinese and 6 per cent as other Asian styles.

Awareness of the BSC

Of the 199 respondents, 51 per cent indicated that their organisations had a formal system to measure performance, but only 25 per cent (49) were familiar with the BSC approach to performance measurement. Specifically among these 49 respondents, 84 per cent had some knowledge, 10 per cent had an in-depth understanding, 4 per cent were actively involved while 2 per cent had just heard about it. Given that the BSC has been around for about a decade, the findings are surprising. It may suggest that a majority of the respondents have been qualified accountants for over 10 years and may not, therefore, have been exposed to BSC through their education.

General perceptions of BSC

The BSC was generally perceived as more than an evaluation system. It was also seen as a management system primarily used for determining strategic direction and required organisations to be strategy driven. The BSC was also seen as good for corporate governance. Quite a significant number of respondents agreed that the advantages of the BSC outweigh the disadvantages. They also viewed it primarily as fitting a Western management approach.

These results suggest that a majority of the 46 respondents have correct ideas about the BSC. However, their perceptions that the BSC was a radical change from their existing performance measurement system and was expensive to implement might deter adoption of the BSC. A majority of respondents were neutral to the opinions that the BSC required too much disclosure of confidential information, could be implemented quickly and was not suited to Hong Kong.

Adoption in Hong Kong

Disappointingly, only nine respondents' firms indicated adoption of the BSC at various levels. Of these firms, six were of medium to large size (100 or more employees), seven considered themselves to use a Western management style, while only two classified their management style as Hong King Chinese.

The adopters were from various industries. They implemented the BSC mainly due to strategic reasons and to integrate management and measurement systems. Also, with the BSC, these firms aimed to make senior and middle managers more accountable for results.

By implementing the BSC, the realised benefits included better staff motivation (30 per cent), improved competitive position (20 per cent), increased customer satisfaction (15 per cent), increased profitability (10 per cent) and rapid growth (5 per cent).

In implementing the BSC, a majority of these firms experienced difficulties in defining key performance indicators. Further, it was found that sudden organisational changes made some performance measurements obsolete.

Some respondents found implementing the BSC was more expensive and took longer than expected. Difficult too was the fact that middle management and staff resistance was encountered.

Also, implementing the BSC caused problems with existing systems—many changes in operations and IT systems were required as a result of implementation.

The way forward

With this small sample size, we cannot conclude the extent of the BSC adoption in Hong Kong. The results could imply that Hong Kong is lagging far behind reported rates of BSC adoption in other parts of the economically developed world.

Although the BSC should not be regarded as a Western approach, copying the BSC implementation in the US may not be feasible in Hong Kong. Implementing changes in any management accounting practice involved people. To avoid resistance to change and to ensure success in implementing the BSC it is paramount to understand the organisational and national culture that represents people's beliefs and behaviour.

The BSC is not just about combining financial and non-financial measures. It encompasses an integrated system that motivates employees at all levels to achieve different performance measures—more than measures specific only to their job role but part of the bigger organisational picture—and link these multiple measures to a single organisational strategy.

The study also shows that a low number of firms use formal performance measurement systems. This could result in a further barrier to acceptance of BSC within these organisations as it would require a huge leap from not having any formal performance appraisal to a strategy-focused, and performance-focused, measure. To encourage a wide adoption of the BSC to enhance the competitive advantage of Hong Kong organisations, we should endeavour to increase awareness of this management approach among accounting professionals. Unless they have a better idea of why, and how, to implement the BSC, it would be difficult for them to introduce it into their organisations and achieve the anticipated benefits.

Reproduced with the permission of CPA Australia.

1 Explain in your own words the four steps for successful implementation of the balanced scorecard.
2 What are the objectives and benefits of the balanced scorecard, as explained in the article?
3 Summarise the results of the questionnaire.
4 Why might the balanced scorecard not be suited to Hong Kong?
5 Do you believe that the balanced scorecard represents a radical change from existing performance management systems?
6 The article says that it is paramount to understand the organisational and national culture that represents people's beliefs and behaviour. In the context of this particular study, what kind of things might be important in this location?

SOLUTIONS TO ACTIVITIES

Activity 15.1

No. Because rules and regulations do not eliminate mismanagement. More time would be spent on trying to get around these rules and regulations.

Activity 15.2

This is very difficult to do. There is a need to provide more broadly based information relating to culture, management practices, as well as developing a set of reasonable governance guidelines.

Activity 15.3

The following areas have not been covered to date:

- skills assessment and balance/quality of staff/staff potential
- management of risk/risk measurement
- rewards.

    There are a number of fundamental questions which need to be considered:

- Just what are the information needs of a modern investment community?
- How to deal with the broadening of stakeholders and changing priorities?
- Just what information is material for an extended stakeholder group?

    Debates are likely to continue, with concerns about over regulation and the broadening of stakeholder interests.

Activity 15.4

- Working conditions/pay/prospects for employees
- Pollution/impact on the environment
- Use of energy.

Activity 15.5

Some of these have clear and undeniable stakes. For example, employees often have a very considerable stake in the ongoing business, its profitability, its attitude to things such as health and safety, and its long-term success. This is particularly true where a business provides a large portion of the workforce needs of a town or city.

Others have legitimate interests in relatively small parts. There are still some problems in the idea that competitors have legitimate interests.

Activity 15.6

In Australia, places such as Adelaide and Wollongong tend to rely heavily on the car or steel industries. Newcastle until recently relied on steel and port facilities. In the UK in the 1980s large areas of the north of England suffered wholesale decline due to reliance on coal and vehicles. Cities such as Newcastle upon Tyne and Glasgow have suffered in the past for their reliance on shipbuilding.

Activity 15.7

There are examples where pollution, loss of jobs, health and safety issues have been identified as being problematic. For example Nike has been severely criticised in the past for use of child labour (though see comments under Activity 15.10).

Activity 15.8

- Expected future legislation
- Enlightened self-interest
- Publish results and compare, thus putting pressure on competitors
- Market as a good citizen (public relations).

Activity 15.9

- Businesses are owned by the shareholders—any money they choose to spend on so-called social responsibility reduces the amount available for them. Shareholders can choose for themselves whether to be philanthropic.
- Many companies don't have time for this—they are too busy running their main business activity.
- It's not the responsibility of individual businesses, rather it is up to politicians and governments.
- Corporations do not really care about CSR.

Activity 15.10

At the time of writing the website of Mallen Baker had sections on companies in the news. These included Nike and BP.

Nike has been the target of a number of pressure groups relating to human rights, with particular emphasis on employment of children, and working conditions in developing nations. Nike has put in place a code of conduct for all of its suppliers, and is working to review many of these factories. Audits have taken place to which Nike has responded together with a plan to put things right.

BP is clearly associated with the energy industry, and is one of the largest companies in the world. It is high profile in terms of its commitment to changing to suit the needs of a more sustainable future. It is clearly identified with fossil fuels. It is currently trying to become a sustainable energy company. The issues are the sheer scale of the potential environmental impact of its activities, including climate change and emissions, human rights in developing countries, ethical business practices, sustainability of employment, and its democratic legitimacy when dealing with nation states with a smaller economic power base than BP itself.

Other current issues at the time of writing included:

- Should senior managers be responsible for actions taken by the company which lead to accidental loss of human life?
- How should drug companies play their part in combating the AIDS catastrophe in Africa?
- When should companies pull out of a particular country because of the nature of the regime?

Activity 15.11

Capitalise costs and depreciate capital cost, so effectively the depreciation charge represents the cost for the year. This is not very effective as a measure of expense in terms of sustainability.

Activity 15.12

- Reduction in greenhouse gases
- Improvement in health and quality of life
- Improvement in international relations.

  The chief difficulty is how to quantify these.

Activity 15.13

- Transparency probably requires a significant shift in application, rather than in principle.
- Inclusiveness means that all stakeholders will now need to be seriously considered.
- Auditability may well prove more difficult given the need to provide more qualitative information. GRI recognises the need for more work on assurance of sustainability reports.
- Completeness requires careful attention to the boundaries of the report, which are now likely to be much more widely drawn.
- Sustainability context represents the biggest shift.
- Clarity—under financial reporting the primary user is generally seen to be the owners. This is not the case under sustainability reporting.

Activity 15.14

Suppliers and related impacts, and customers and related impacts.

Activity 15.15

Information relating to economies of scale, brand equity, subsidies and quantification of government intervention, macroeconomic factors, labour costs, tax effects and inventory holdings.

Activity 15.16

- Availability (or non-availability) of resources
- Sophistication of markets
- Market saturation might encourage
- Network of support industries
- Rivalry.

Activity 15.17

- Technical advances rendering current products/technology obsolete
- Climate change
- Shortage of natural resources
- Demographics
- Legal changes e.g. employment law, health and safety, advertising, patents, anti-trust legislation, ACCC rulings, ASIC regulations, planning laws and taxation
- Economic changes at a macro level
- Changes in the government of the day
- Political risk—coups.

Activity 15.18

Very similar coverage e.g. environmental, people-oriented, value systems-oriented, recognition of social elements.

SOLUTIONS TO SELF-ASSESSMENT QUESTIONS

SELF-ASSESSMENT QUESTION 1.1

Income statement for day 1

	$
Sales (70 × $0.80)	56
Cost of sales (70 × $0.50)	35
Profit	21

Cash flow statement for day 1

	$
Opening balance	40
Add Cash from sales	56
	96
Less Cash for purchases (80 × $0.50)	40
Closing balance	56

Balance sheet as at end of day 1

	$
Cash balance	56
Stock of unsold goods (10 × $0.50)	5
Helen's business wealth	61

Income statement for day 2

	$
Sales (65 × $0.80)	52.0
Cost of sales (65 × $0.50)	32.5
Profit	19.5

Cash flow statement for day 2

	$
Opening balance	56.0
Add Cash from sales	52.0
	108.0
Less Cash for purchases (60 × $0.50)	30.0
Closing balance	78.0

Balance sheet as at end of day 2

	$
Cash balance	78.0
Stock of unsold goods (5 × $0.50)	2.5
Helen's business wealth	80.5

Cash flow statement for day 3

	$
Sales (20 × $0.80 + 45 × $0.40)	34.0
Cost of sales (65 × $0.50)	32.5
Profit	1.5

Cash flow statement for day 3

	$
Opening balance	78.0
Add Cash from sales	34.0
	112.0
Less Cash for purchases (60 × $0.50)	30.0
Closing balance	82.0

Balance sheet as at end of day 3

	$
Cash balance	82.0
Stock of unsold goods	–
Helen's business wealth	82.0

SELF-ASSESSMENT QUESTION 2.1

1. The summarised balance sheet of Bonanza Ltd immediately following the rights and bonus issue is as follows:

Balance sheet as at 31 December 2005	
Net assets (235 + 40 (cash from the rights issue))	$275,000
Shareholders' equity	
Share capital	
100,000 shares at an issue price of $1.30 each	130,000
50,000 shares at an issue price of $2	
(20,000 rights plus 30,000 bonus)	100,000
Retained profits	45,000
	$275,000

Note that the bonus issue is taken from revaluation reserve first, as this is not distributable as a cash dividend, leaving $23,000 to be taken from the retained profits. This leaves $45,000 still available in retained profits—which is distributable as a cash dividend. If the bonus issue had all come from retained profits, only $8,000 would have remained in a distributable reserve.

2. There may be pressure from a potential creditor for the company to limit its ability to pay dividends. This would place creditors in a more secure position because the maximum 'buffer' or safety margin, between the value of the assets and the amount owed by the company, is maintained. It is not unusual for potential creditors to insist on some measure to lock up shareholders' funds in this way, as a condition of granting the loan.

3. The summarised balance sheet of Bonanza Ltd immediately following the rights and bonus issues (assuming a minimum dividend potential objective) is as follows:

Balance sheet as at 31 December 2005	
Net assets (235 + 40 (cash from the rights issue))	$275,000
Shareholders' equity	
Share capital	
100,000 shares at an issue price of $1.30 each	130,000
50,000 shares at an issue price of $2	
(20,000 rights plus 30,000 bonus)	100,000
Revaluation reserve	37,000
Retained profits	8,000
	$275,000

4. Before the bonus issue the maximum dividend was $68,000. Now it is $8,000. Thus the bonus issue has the effect of locking up an additional $60,000 of the assets of the company in terms of the company's ability to pay dividends.

5. *Lee's position*

   Before the issues Lee had 100 shares, each worth $2.35 (i.e. $235,000/100,000), or $235 in total.

   Lee would be offered 20 shares in the rights issue at $2 each, or $40 in total. After the rights issue Lee would have a total of 120 shares, each worth $2.2917 (i.e. $275,000/120,000), or $275 in total. The bonus issue would give 30 additional shares to Lee. After the bonus issue Lee would have 150 shares, each worth $1.833 (i.e. $275,000/150,000), or $275 in total.

   None of this affects Lee's wealth. Before the issues Lee had $235 worth of shares and $40 more in cash. After the issues Lee has the same total, but all $275 is in the value of the shares.

SELF-ASSESSMENT QUESTION 3.1

The balance sheet you prepare should be set out as follows:

SIMONSON ENGINEERING COMPANY

Balance sheet as at 30 September 2005		
	$	$
Current assets		
Cash in hand	1,500	
Trade debtors	48,000	
Inventory	45,000	
		94,500
Non-current assets		
Fixtures and fittings	9,000	
Motor vehicles	15,000	
Plant and machinery	25,000	
Freehold premises	72,000	
		121,000
Total assets		215,500

Current liabilities		
Bank overdraft	26,000	
Trade creditors	18,000	
		44,000
Non-current liabilities		
Loan		51,000
Total liabilities		95,000
Capital		
Opening balance	117,500	
Add Profit	18,000	
	135,500	
Less Drawings	15,000	
		120,500
Total liabilities and owner's equity		215,500

SELF-ASSESSMENT QUESTION 3.2

The balance sheet provides an insight into the 'mix' of assets held. Thus, it can be seen that, in percentage terms, approximately 60 per cent of assets held are in the form of non-current assets and that freehold premises comprise more than half of the non-current assets held. Current assets held are largely in the form of inventory (approximately 46 per cent of current assets) and debtors (approximately 42 per cent of current assets).

The balance sheet also provides an insight into the liquidity of the business. The current assets are $104,000 and can be viewed as representing cash or near-cash assets held, compared to $42,000 in current liabilities. In this case it appears that the business is fairly liquid as the current assets exceed the current liabilities by a large amount. Liquidity is very important in order to maintain the capacity of the business to pay debts.

The balance sheet gives an indication of the financial structure of the business. In the statement provided, it can be seen that the owner is providing $63,000, and long-term lenders are providing $160,000. This means that outsiders contribute, in percentage terms, more than 71 per cent of the total long-term finance required and the business is therefore heavily reliant on outside sources of finance. The business is under pressure to make profits which are at least sufficient to pay interest and make capital repayments when they fall due.

SELF-ASSESSMENT QUESTION 4.1

TT LTD

Balance sheet as at 31 December 2005

	+	−	Net		+	−	Net
Current assets				Current liabilities			
Cash	50,000	25,000	750	Creditors	143,000	121,000	22,000
	35,000	500					
	132,000	1,200					

	12,000					
	33,500					
	1,650					
	12,000					
	121,000					
	9,400					
Debtors	152,000	132,000	19,600	Accruals	630	1,250
		400			620	
Prepayments	5,000		5,300			
	300			Capital	50,000	76,900
					26,900	
Inventory	143,000	74,000	65,000			
	12,000	16,000				
Non-current assets						
Delivery vehicle	12,000	2,500	9,500	Total liabilities and		
Total assets			100,150	owner's equity		100,150

Income statement for the year ended 31 December 2005

Cost of sales	74,000	90,000	Sales	152,000	187,000
	16,000			35,000	
Rent	20,000*	20,000			
Rates	500	1,400			
	900**				
Wages	33,500	34,130			
	630				
Electricity	1,650	2,270			
	620				
Bad debts	400	400			
Vehicle depreciation	2,500	2,500			
Vehicle expenses	9,400	9,400			
		160,100			
Net profit		26,900			
		187,000			187,000

* An alternative approach would have been to show the $25,000 initially as an expense and at the year-end transfer $5,000 of this to the prepayment.

** An alternative approach would have been to show the $1,200 and subsequently transfer $300 to the prepayment.

SELF-ASSESSMENT QUESTION 4.2

Sales increased by more than 30 per cent over the previous year but the 'bottom line' fell from a net profit of $37,000 to a loss of $58,000. The rapid expansion of the business has clearly brought problems in its wake. In the previous period, the business was making a gross profit of more than 31c for every $1 of sales made. This reduced in the year to 31 May 2006 to around 26c for every $1 of sales made. This seems to suggest that the rapid expansion was fuelled by a reduction in prices. The gross profit increased in absolute terms by $20,000; however, there was a drastic decline in net profits during the period. In the previous period, the business was making a net profit of nearly 6c for every $1 of sales, whereas for the year to 31 May 2006 this reduced to a loss of nearly 7c for every $1 of sales made. This means that overhead expenses have increased considerably. Some increase in overhead expenses may be expected in order to service the increased level of activity. However, the increase appears to be exceptional. If we look at the list of overhead expenses we can see that the bad debts written off figure seems very high (more than 10 per cent of total sales). This may be a further effect of the rapid expansion that has taken place. In order to generate sales, insufficient regard may have been paid to the creditworthiness of customers. A comparison of overhead expenses with those of the previous period would be useful.

SELF-ASSESSMENT QUESTION 4.3

PEAR LTD

Income statement for the year ended 30 September 2006

	$000	$000
Sales (1,456 + 18)		1,474
Cost of sales		768
Gross profit		706
Less Expenses		
Salaries	220	
Depreciation (249 + 12)	261	
Other operating expenses (131 + (2% × 200=4) + 2)	137	
		618
Net profit before interest and tax		88
Interest expense (15 + 15)		30
Net profit before tax		58
Taxation (58 × 30%)		17
Net profit after tax		41
Dividends proposed		25
Profit retained for the year		16

PEAR LTD

Balance sheet as at 30 September 2006

	$000	$000
Current assets		
Cash at bank	21	
Trade debtors (182 + 18 − 4)	196	
Inventory	207	
		424
Non-current assets		
Cost (1,570 + 30)	1,600	
Accumulated depreciation (690 + 12)	(702)	
		898
Total assets		1,322
Current liabilities		
Bank overdraft	105	
Tax payable	17	
Trade creditors	88	
Other creditors (20 + 30 + 15 + 2)	67	
Dividends payable	25	
		302
Non-current liabilities		
10% debentures—repayable 2009		300
Total liabilities		602
Shareholders' equity		
Paid-up capital	600	
Retained profit (104 + 16)	120	
		720
Total liabilities and shareholders' equity		1,322

SELF-ASSESSMENT QUESTION 5.1

TOUCHSTONES LTD

Workings

Cash received from customers

Opening balance of debtors	16
plus sales for the period	207
gives the amount we might expect to receive for the year	223
less closing balance of debtors	(26)
equals the cash received from customers	197

Cash paid to suppliers, etc.

Opening balance of creditors	26
plus purchases of inventory for the period (see below)	100
gives the amount we might expect to pay for the year	126
less closing balance of creditors	(23)
equals the cash paid to creditors	103

Calculation of purchases figure

Opening inventory	25
plus purchases	$x = 100$
equals the amount available for sale	$x + 25$
less closing inventory—the amount unsold	(24)
equals the cost of sales—the cost of the amount sold	101

Non-current assets

Land and buildings — *Net*

Balance at the start of the year	94
less any disposals	–
	94
plus new acquisitions	$x = 22$
plus any revaluations	–
less depreciation for the year	(6)
equals closing balance	110

Plant and machinery — *Net*

Balance at the start of the year	53
less any disposals	–
	53
plus new acquisitions	$x = 19$
plus any revaluations	–
less depreciation for the year	(10)
equals closing balance	62

Dividends paid

Of the dividends proposed in the income statements, only part appears in each of the balance sheets as a liability. The difference must therefore be interim dividends. Hence payments in 2006 were 2005 final proposed dividends plus the interim dividends which must have been $4 (18 – 14).

Cash flow statement for the year ended 31 December 2006

	$m	$m
Cash flows from operating activities		
Cash receipts from customers (197 + 4)	201	
Cash paid to suppliers and employees (103 + 48 – 16)	(135)	
Interest paid	(4)	
Income taxes paid (2005 liability)	(8)	
Net cash provided by operating activities		54

Cash flows from investing activities

Interest received	2
Purchase of property, plant and equipment (22 + 19)	(41)
Proceeds from sale of property, plant and equipment	–
Net cash used in investing activities	(39)

Cash flows from financing activities

Proceeds from long-term borrowings	20
Dividends paid (12 + interim dividend of (18 – 14))	(16)
Net cash provided by financing activities	4
Net increase in cash and cash equivalents held	19
Cash and cash equivalents at the beginning of the financial year	8
Cash and cash equivalents at the end of the financial year	27

The **reconciliation between operating profit and operating cash flows** is as follows:

Operating profit	44
Adjusted for:	
Depreciation	16
Increase in debtors	(10)
Decrease in inventory	1
Reduction in creditors	(3)
Increase in tax liability	8
Interest revenue (not operating)	(2)
	54

SELF-ASSESSMENT QUESTION 6.1

In order to answer this question you may have used the following ratios:

	A Ltd	B Ltd
Current ratio	$= \dfrac{869}{438.4}$ = 2.0 times	$= \dfrac{833.9}{310.5}$ = 2.7 times
Acid test ratio	$= \dfrac{(869 - 592)}{438.4}$ = 0.6 times	$= \dfrac{(833.9 - 403)}{310.5}$ = 1.4 times
Gearing ratio	$= \dfrac{190}{(687.6 + 190)} \times 100$ = 21.6%	$= \dfrac{250}{(874.6 + 250)} \times 100$ = 22.2%
Interest cover ratio	$= \dfrac{(131.9 + 19.4)}{19.4}$ = 7.8 times	$= \dfrac{(139.4 + 27.5)}{27.5}$ = 6.1 times

Dividend payout ratio	$= \dfrac{135.0}{99.9} \times 100$	$= \dfrac{95.0}{104.6} \times 100$
	$= 135\%$	$= 91\%$
Earnings per share	$= \dfrac{99.9}{320}$	$= \dfrac{104.6}{250}$
	$= 31.2¢$	$= 41.8¢$
Price earnings ratio	$= \dfrac{\$6.50}{31.2¢}$	$= \dfrac{\$8.20}{41.8¢}$
	$= 20.8$ times	$= 19.6$ times

A Ltd has a much lower current ratio and acid test ratio than that of B Ltd. The reasons for this may be partly due to the fact that A Ltd has a lower average settlement period for debtors. The acid test ratio of A Ltd is substantially below 1.0. This may suggest a liquidity problem.

The gearing ratio of each company is quite similar. Neither company has excessive borrowing. The interest cover ratio for each company is also similar. The respective ratios indicate that both companies have good profit coverage for their interest charges.

The dividend payout ratio for each company seems very high indeed. In the case of A Ltd the dividends announced for the year are considerably higher than the earnings generated during the year which are available for dividends. As a result part of the dividend was paid out of retained profits from previous years. This is an unusual occurrence. Although it is quite legitimate to do this, such action may nevertheless suggest a lack of prudence on the part of the directors.

The PE ratio for both companies is high which indicates market confidence in their future prospects.

SELF-ASSESSMENT QUESTION 7.1

(a) The break-even point if only product A were made would be:

Fixed costs / (sales revenue per unit – variable cost per unit)
= $40,000 / ($30 – (15 + 6)) = 4,445 units (per annum).

(b) Product	A (per unit)	B (per unit)	C (per unit)
	$	$	$
Selling price	30	39	20
Variable materials	(15)	(18)	(10)
Variable production costs	(6)	(10)	(5)
Contribution	9	11	5
Time on machines (hours)	2	3	1
Contribution per hour on machines	$4.50	$3.67	$5.00
Order of priority	2nd	3rd	1st

(c)   *Contributions ($)*

Produce:

5,000 product C using	5,000 hours generating	25,000
2,500 product A using	5,000 hours generating	22,500
	10,000 hours	47,500
Less Fixed costs		40,000
Profit		$7,500

Leaving a demand for 500 units of product A and 2,000 units of product B unsatisfied.

SELF-ASSESSMENT QUESTION 8.1

(a) The budget may be summarised as follows:

Sales revenue	$196,000	
Direct materials	(38,000)	
Direct labour	(32,000)	
Total overheads	(77,000)	(i.e. 2,400 + 3,000 + 27,600 + 36,000 + 8,000)
Profit	$49,000	

The job may be priced on the basis that both overheads and profit should be apportioned on the basis of direct labour cost, as follows:

	$	
Direct materials	4,000	
Direct labour	3,600	
Overheads	8,663	(i.e. $77,000 × 3,600/32,000)
Profit	5,513	(i.e. $49,000 × 3,600/32,000)
Price	$21,776	

This answer assumes that variable overheads vary in proportion to direct labour cost.

Various other bases of charging overheads and profit could have been adopted. For example, materials cost could have been included (with direct labour) as the basis for profit loading, or even apportioning overheads.

(b) This part of the question, in effect, asks for comments on the validity of 'full cost plus' pricing. This approach can be useful as an indicator of the effective long-run cost of doing the job. On the other hand, it fails to take account of such factors as the state of the market and other external factors.

SELF-ASSESSMENT QUESTION 9.1

Raw materials inventory budget for the six months ending 31 December (in units):

	July	August	September	October	November	December
Opening balance	500	600	600	700	750	750
Purchases	600	600	700	750	750	750
	1,100	1,200	1,300	1,450	1,500	1,500
Less Issued to production	500	600	600	700	750	750
Closing balance	600	600	700	750	750	750

Raw materials inventory budget for the six months ending 31 December (in financial terms):

	July	August	September	October	November	December
Opening balance	4,000	4,800	4,800	5,600	6,000	6,000
Purchases	4,800	4,800	5,600	6,000	6,000	6,000
	8,800	9,600	10,400	11,600	12,000	12,000
Less Issued to production	4,000	4,800	4,800	5,600	6,000	6,000
Closing balance	4,800	4,800	5,600	6,000	6,000	6,000

Creditors budget for the six months ending 31 December:

	July	August	September	October	November	December
Opening balance	4,000	4,800	4,800	5,600	6,000	6,000
Purchases	4,800	4,800	5,600	6,000	6,000	6,000
	8,800	9,600	10,400	11,600	12,000	12,000
Less Payments	4,000	4,800	4,800	5,600	6,000	6,000
Closing balance	4,800	4,800	5,600	6,000	6,000	6,000

Cash budget for the six months ending 31 December:

	July	August	September	October	November	December
Inflows						
Receipts from debtors	2,800	3,200	3,200	4,000	4,800	5,200
Cash sales	4,800	6,000	7,200	7,800	8,400	9,600
Total inflows	7,600	9,200	10,400	11,800	13,200	14,800
Outflows						
Payment to creditors	4,000	4,800	4,800	5,600	6,000	6,000
Direct costs	3,000	3,600	3,600	4,200	4,500	4,500
Advertising	1,000	–	–	1,500	–	–
Overheads						
80%	1,280	1,280	1,280	1,280	1,600	1,600
20%	280	320	320	320	320	400
New plant	–	–	2,200	2,200	2,200	–
Total outflows	9,560	10,000	12,200	15,100	14,620	12,500
Net inflows	(1,960)	(800)	(1,800)	(3,300)	(1,420)	2,300
Balance b/f	7,500	5,540	4,740	2,940	(360)	(1,780)
Balance carried forward	5,540	4,740	2,940	(360)	(1,780)	520

Note how budgets are linked: in this case the materials budget to the creditors budget and the creditors budget to the cash budget.

The following are possible means of relieving the cash shortages revealed by the budget:
- make a higher proportion of sales on a cash basis;
- collect the money from debtors more promptly—for example, during the month following sale;
- hold lower inventories, both of raw materials and finished goods;
- increase the creditor payment period;

- delay the payment for advertising;
- obtain more credit for the overhead cost—at present only 20 per cent is on credit;
- delay the payment for the new plant.

SELF-ASSESSMENT QUESTION 9.2

(a) and (b)

Toscanini Ltd Budget					
	Original	*Flexed*		*Actual*	
Output (units) production and sales	4,000	3,500		3,500	
	$	$		$	
Sales	48,000	42,000		41,460	
Raw materials	(11,520)	(10,080)	(1,400 kg)	(10,260)	(1,425 kg)
Labour	(9,600)	(8,400)	(700 hours)	(8,070)	(690 hours)
Fixed overheads	(14,400)	(14,400)		(14,700)	
Operating profit	12,480	9,120		8,430	

Reconciliation			
	$	$	*Manager accountable*
Budgeted profit		12,480	
Sales volume variance*			
(12,480 − 9,120)	3,360 A		Sales
Sales price variance			
(42,000 − 41,460)	540 A		Sales
Materials price variance			
(1,425 × $7.20) − 10,260	−		
Materials usage variance			
[(3,500 × 0.40) − 1,425] × $7.20	180 A		Production
Labour rate variance			
(690 × $12) − 8,070	210 F		Personnel
Labour efficiency			
[(3,500 × 0.20) − 690] × $12	120 F		Production
Fixed overhead spending			
14,400 − 14,700	300 A		Various, depending on the nature of the overheads
Total net variances		$4,050 A	
Actual profit		$8,430	

*The sales volume variance can also be calculated as follows:

The contribution to fixed costs and profit for every unit of production can be calculated as:

Selling price per unit	12
Materials per unit	2.88
Labour per unit	2.40
Contribution per unit	6.72

This means that if the volume is 500 less than budgeted, the loss of contribution would be 500 x 6.72 = $3,360.

(c) Feasible explanations include the following:

Sales volume	The unanticipated fall in world demand would account for 400 of the reduced sales (demand would fall 10% from 4,000 to 3,600), with the remaining 100 being attributable to other causes. The remainder is probably caused by ineffective marketing, although a lack of availability of inventory to sell may be a reason.
Sales price	Ineffective selling seems the only logical reason.
Materials usage	Inefficient use of materials, perhaps because of poor performance by labour or substandard materials.
Labour rate	Less overtime worked or lower production bonuses paid as a result of lower volume of activity.
Labour efficiency	More effective working, perhaps because fewer hours were worked than planned.
Overheads	Ineffective control of overheads.

(d) Clearly not all of the sales variance can be attributed to poor marketing, given a 10 per cent reduction in demand.

It will probably be useful to distinguish between that part of the variance that arose from the general shortfall in general demand (a planning variance) and a volume variance which is more fairly attributable to the manager concerned. Thus accountability will be more fairly imposed.

Planning variance (10% × 4,000)—based on a flexed budget of 3,600 (or 400 × $6.72)	2,688
'New' sales volume variance reflecting the difference between the budgeted profit on a flexed budget at 3,600 and 3,500 (100 × 6.72)	672
Original sales volume variance	$3,360

SELF-ASSESSMENT QUESTION 10.1

Quardis

	A	B	C	D	E	F	G
1	**Input section**						
2							
3	**Opening balance sheet**						
4	*Assets*				*Liabilities and shareholders' equity*		
5	Cash	2			Creditors		22
6	Debtors	34			Tax		14
7	Inventory	24			Dividends		10
8	Premises – cost	460			Loan		125
9	– Agg Depcn	–30			Share capital		200
10	Fixtures – cost	35			Reserves		144
11	– Agg Depcn	–10					
12							
13		515					515
14							
15							
16				proportion			
17	Sales volume ('000s)	15		on			
18	Sales price	20		credit	debtors t/o*		* equal to 3 months' credit
19	Sales ($000s)	300		0.6	4		
20					creditors t/o		
21	Purchases	186		1	6		
22	Cost of sales as % of sales	0.6					
23	Wages	54		4	accrual		
24	Other overheads	21		3	accrual		
25	Dividends	0.05					
26	Tax	0.35					
27	New fixtures	25		0.1	depreciation (straight line)		
28	Premises			0.02	depreciation (straight line)		
29	Loan (repaid)/raised	–30		0.13	interest		
30							
31	**Projected income statement**						
32							
33	Sales				300		
34	Less Cost of sales				180		
35	Opening inventory			24			
36	Purchases			186			
37							
38				210			
39	Less Closing inventory			30			
40	Gross profit				120		
41	Wages			54			
42	Other overheads			21			
43	Loan interest			12.35			
44	Depreciation						
45	– Fixtures and fittings			6			
46	– Land and premises			9.2			
47					102.55		
48							
49	Net profit				17.45		

ACCOUNTING an introduction

Quardis

	A	B	C	D	E	F	G
50	Tax				6.11		
51							
52	Net profit after tax				11.34		
53	Dividends				10		
54							
55	Retained profit for the year				1.34		
56							
57							
58	**Projected cash flow statement**						
59							
60	*Cash flow from operations*						
61	Net profit				11.34		
62	Adjusted for depreciation				15.2		
63	Reduction in tax due				− 7.89		
64	Increase in debtors				− 11		
65	Increase in prepayments				0		
66	Increase in inventory				− 6		
67	Increase in creditors				9		
68	Increase in accruals				7		
69						17.65	
70	*Cash flow from investing activities*						
71	Purchase of non-current assets					− 25	
72							
73	*Cash flow from financing activities*						
74	Dividends				− 10		
75	Loan repaid				− 30	− 40	
76							
77						− 47.35	
78							
79							
80	**Projected closing balance sheet**						
81	*Assets*				*Liabilities and shareholders' equity*		
82	Cash	− 45.35			Creditors		31
83	Debtors	45			Accruals		7
84	Inventory	30			Tax		6.11
85	Premises − cost	460			Dividends		10
86	− Agg Depcn	− 39.2			Loan		95
87	Fixtures − cost	60			Share capital		200
88	− Agg Depcn	− 16			Reverses		145.34
89							
90		494.45					494.45
91							
92							
93	Changes		Profit	Cash			
94	(i) sales volume plus 5%		23.45	− 34.6			
95	(ii) reduction in COS to 58%		23.45	− 47.35			
96	(iii) credit down to two months		17.45	− 32.35			
97							
98							

SELF-ASSESSMENT QUESTION 11.1

BEACON CHEMICALS LTD

(a) *Relevant cash flows*

	2005 $000	2006 $000	2007 $000	2008 $000	2009 $000	2010 $000
Sales revenue	–	80	120	144	100	64
Loss of contribution		(15)	(15)	(15)	(15)	(15)
Variable costs		(40)	(50)	(48)	(30)	(32)
Fixed costs		(8)	(8)	(8)	(8)	(8)
Operating cash flows		17	47	73	47	9
Working capital	(30)					30
Capital cost	(100)					
Net relevant cash flows	(130)	17	47	73	47	39

(b) *Payback period*

Cumulative cash flows	(130)	(113)	(66)	7

Thus the plant will have repaid the initial investment by the end of the third year of operations. More specifically, the payback period is close to two years, eleven months.

(c) *Net present value*

Discount factor	1.000	.926	0.857	0.794	0.735	0.681
Present value	(130)	15.74	40.28	57.96	34.55	26.56
Net present value	45.09					

SELF-ASSESSMENT QUESTION 12.1

(a) Base point 1 June 2006

Price = present value of future cash flows

		Annual inflows—interest	
May 31		Discount factor (8%)	PV
2007	10	.926	9.26
2008	10	.857	8.57
2009	10	.794	7.94
2010	10	.735	7.35
2011	10	.681	6.81
			39.93
Maturity value	110	.681	74.91
Current price (1 June 2006)		114.84	

(b) Yield to maturity if the price were to be $80:

NPV at 8% = 114.84 − 80 = 34.84 i.e. greater than 8%

Try at 14%:

	(80)	1	(80)
Price	(80)	1	(80)
2007	10	.877	8.77
2008	10	.769	7.68
2009	10	.675	6.75
2010	10	.592	5.92
2011	10	.519	5.19
Maturity value	110	.519	57.09
NPV			11.40

By extrapolation the yield is $14\% + \dfrac{(11.40) \times 6\%}{(34.84 - 11.40)} = 16.9\%$

(c) If interest were to be paid semi-annually all we need to do is to re-work the above using six-monthly periods for income at half the discount rates.

(d) $P_0 = \dfrac{D_1}{(k - g)}$

so P_0 = (50 cents × 105%) / (.15 − .05)

= 52.5 / .10 = 525 cents or $5.25

(e) Dividend stream is:

year	
1	55 (i.e. 50 + 10%)
2	60.5
3	66.55
4	69.88

The value of the future dividend stream at the end of year 3 is

$P_0 = \dfrac{D_1}{(k - g)}$

so the value of the share at the end of year 3 is likely to be 69.88 / (.15 − .05) = $6.99

Current value of the share can be derived by discounting the following cash flows at 15%:

Year	Dividends	DF	PV
1	55c	.870	48c
2	60.5c	.756	46c
3	66.55c + $6.99	.658	5.03
			5.97

SELF-ASSESSMENT QUESTION 13.1

	$	$
Existing level of debtors ($4,000,000 × 70/365)		767,123
New level of debtors		
$2,000,000 × 80/365	438,356	
$2,000,000 × 30/365	164,384	602,740
Reduction in debtors		164,383
Cost and benefits of policy		
Cost of discount ($2,000,000 × 2%)		40,000
Less Savings		
Interest payable ($164,383 × 13%)	21,370	
Administration costs	6,000	
Bad debts	10,000	37,370
Net cost of policy		2,630

The above calculations reveal that the company will be worse off by offering the discounts.

SELF-ASSESSMENT QUESTION 14.1

(a)

	Equity $m	Debt $m
Profit before interest and tax	1.80	1.80
Interest expense	–	0.30
Profit before tax	1.80	1.50
Less taxation	0.90	0.75
Profit available to equity	0.90	0.75
Shares issued	5,300,000	4,000,000
EPS	17.0¢	18.8¢

(b) The following factors should be taken into account:
- stability of sales and profits;
- stability of cash flows;
- interest cover and gearing levels;
- equity investors' attitude towards risk;
- dilution of control by new share issue;
- security available to offer lenders;
- effect on earnings per share and future cash flows.

SELF-ASSESSMENT QUESTION 14.2

(a) The liquidity position may be assessed by using the liquidity ratios discussed in Chapter 6.

$$\text{Current ratio} \quad = \quad \frac{\text{Current assets}}{\text{Current liabilities (Creditors due within one year)}}$$

$$= \quad \frac{\$7.5m}{\$5.4m} = 1.4 \text{ times}$$

$$\text{Acid test ratio} \quad = \quad \frac{\text{Current assets (less inventory)}}{\text{Current liabilities}}$$

$$= \quad \frac{\$3.7m}{\$5.4m} = 0.7 \text{ times}$$

The ratios calculated above reveal a fairly weak liquidity position. The current ratio seems quite low and the acid test ratio seems very low. This latter ratio suggests that the company does not have sufficient liquid assets to meet its maturing obligations. It would, however, be useful to have details of the liquidity ratios of similar companies in the same industry in order to make a more informed judgement. The bank overdraft represents 67 per cent of the short-term liabilities and 40 per cent of the total liabilities of the company. The continuing support of the bank is therefore important to the ability of the company to meet its commitments.

(b) The finance required to reduce trade creditors to an average of 40 days outstanding is calculated as follows:

	$m
Trade creditors at reporting date	1.80
Trade creditors outstanding based on 40 days' credit	
40/365 × $8.4 (i.e. credit purchases)	0.92
Finance required	0.88

(c) The bank may not wish to provide further finance to the company. The increase in overdraft will reduce the level of trade creditors but will increase the exposure of the bank. The additional finance invested by the bank will not generate further funds and will not therefore be self-liquidating. The question does not make it clear whether the company has sufficient security to offer the bank for the increase in overdraft facility. The profits of the company will be reduced and the interest cover ratio, based on the profits generated to the year ended 31 May 2005 would reduce to 1.7 times if the additional overdraft was granted (based on interest charged at 12 per cent per annum). This is very low and means that a relatively small decline in profits would result in interest charges not being covered.

(d) A number of possible sources of finance might be considered. Four possible sources are as follows:

Issue of equity shares. This option may be unattractive to investors. The return on equity is fairly low at 7.9 per cent and there is no evidence that the profitability of the business will improve. If profits remain at their current level the effect of issuing more equity will be to reduce further the returns to equity.

Issue of loans. This option may also prove unattractive to investors. The effect of issuing further loans will have a similar effect to that of increasing the overdraft. The profits of the business will be reduced and the interest cover ratio will decrease to a low level. The gearing ratio of the company is already quite high at 48 per cent and it is not clear what security would be available for the loan.

Chase debtors. It may be possible to improve cash flows by reducing the level of credit outstanding from debtors. At present the average settlement period is 93 days, which seems quite high. A reduction in the average settlement period by approximately one-third would generate the funds required. However, it is not clear what effect this would have on sales.

Reduce inventory. This appears to be the most attractive of the four options discussed. At present the average stockholding period is 178 days, which seems to be very high. A reduction in this stockholding period by less than one-third would generate the funds required. However, if the company holds a large amount of slow-moving and obsolete inventory it may be difficult to reduce inventory levels easily.

SOLUTIONS TO SELECTED APPLICATION EXERCISES

CHAPTER 3

3.5 Balance sheet as at a particular point in time:

Balance sheet		
	$000	*$000*
Current assets		
Trade debtors	34	
Inventory	46	
		80
Non-current assets		
Delivery vans	54	
Plant and machinery	127	
Freehold premises	245	
		426
Total assets		506
Current liabilities		
Trade creditors	23	
Bank overdraft	22	
		45
Non-current liabilities		
Loan from NAB		100
Total liabilities		145
Capital		361
Total liabilities and owner's equity		506

3.6 (a)

CRAFTY ENGINEERING

Balance sheet as at 30 June 2006		
	$000	*$000*
Current assets		
Debtors	185	
Inventory	153	
		338
Non-current assets		
Motor vehicles	38	
Machinery and tools	207	
Freehold premises	320	
		565
Total assets		903

Current liabilities	
Bank overdraft	116
Creditors	86
	202
Non-current liabilities	
Loan from St George Bank	260
Total liabilities	462
Capital	441
Total liabilities and owner's equity	903

(b) The balance sheet reveals a high level of investment in non-current assets. In percentage terms, we can say that more than 60 per cent of the total investment in assets has been in non-current assets. The nature of the business may require a heavy investment in non-current assets. The investment in current assets exceeds the current liabilities by a large amount (approximately 1.7 times). As a result, there are no obvious signs of a liquidity problem. However, the balance sheet reveals that the company has no cash balance and is therefore dependent on the continuing support of the bank (in the form of a bank overdraft) in order to meet obligations when they fall due. When considering the long-term financing of the business, we can see that about 37 per cent of the total long-term finance for the business has been supplied by loan capital and about 63 per cent by the owners. This level of borrowing seems quite high but not excessive. However, we would need to know more about the ability of the company to service the loan capital (i.e. to make interest payments and loan repayments) before a full assessment could be made.

CHAPTER 1

4.4

FIFO
SPRATLEY LTD

	No. of tonnes	Purchases Cost per tonne $	Total $	No. of tonnes	Cost of sales Cost per tonne $	Total $
September						
1	20	18	360			
2	48	20	960			
4	15	24	360			
6	10	25	250			
7				20	18	360
				40	20	800
	93		1,930	60		1,160

Opening inventory + purchases	1,930
Cost of sales	1,160
Closing inventory	770 (i.e. 8 @ $20 + 15 @ $24 + 10 @ $25)

LIFO

| | Purchases | | | | Cost of sales | | |
	No. of tonnes	Cost per tonne $	Total $		No. of tonnes	Cost per tonne $	Total $
September							
1	20	18	360				
2	48	20	960				
4	15	24	360				
6	10	25	250				
7					10	25	250
					15	24	360
					35	20	700
	93		1,930		60		1,310

Opening inventory + purchases	1,930	
Cost of sales	1,310	
Closing inventory	620	(i.e. 20 @ $18 + 13 @ $20)

AVCO

| | Purchases | | | | Cost of sales | | |
	No. of tonnes	Cost per tonne $	Total $		No. of tonnes	Cost per tonne $	Total $
September							
1	20	18	360				
2	48	20	960				
4	15	24	360				
6	10	25	250				
	93	20.8	1,930				
7					60	20.8	1,248

Opening inventory + purchases	1,930
Cost of sales	1,248
Closing inventory	682

4.13

TT LTD

Balance sheet as at 31 December 2006

Cash at bank	49,730	Accrued expenses	1,550
(+ 750 – 20,000 – 15,000 – 1,300 – 13,000		(860 + 690)	
– 36,700 – 1,820 – 8,000 + 54,000 + 178,000			
– 71,000 – 16,200)			

Prepaid expenses (+325)	325		
Trade debtors (+ 19,600 + 179,000 − 178,000)	20,600	Trade creditors (+ 22,000 + 67,000 − 71,000)	18,000
Inventory (+ 65,000 + 67,000 + 8,000 − 89,000 − 25,000)	26,000		
Delivery van (+ 9,500 + 13,000 − 5,000)	17,500	Capital (+ 76,900 − 20,000 + 37,705)	94,605
	114,155		114,155

Income statement for the year ended 31 December 2006

	$	$
Sales (+ 179,000 + 54,000)		233,000
less: Cost of sales (+ 89,000 + 25,000)		114,000
Gross profit		119,000
less:		
Rent (5,000 + 15,000)	20,000	
Rates (300 + 975)	1,275	
Wages (− 630 + 36,700 + 860)	36,930	
Electricity (− 620 + 1,820 + 690)	1,890	
Van depreciation (2,500 + 2,500)	5,000	
Van expenses (16,200)	16,200	
		81,295
Net profit for the year		37,705

The balance sheet can now be rewritten in a better style:

TT LTD

Balance sheet as at 31 December 2006

	$	$
Current assets		
Cash	49,730	
Trade debtors	20,600	
Prepaid expenses	325	
Inventory	26,000	
		96,655
Non-current assets		
Motor vehicles–cost	25,000	
Accumulated depreciation	7,500	17,500
Total assets		114,155
Current liabilities		
Trade creditors	18,000	
Accrued expenses	1,550	
		19,550

Capital		
Original	50,000	
Retained profit	44,605	
		94,605
Total liabilities and owner's equity		114,155

CHAPTER 5

5.10 *Juno Ltd—cash flows from operations:*

Cash receipts from customers (24 + 572 − 23)	573	
Cash paid to suppliers and employees	(327)	
(300 + (80 − 55) − 27 + 31 + 15 − 17)		
Interest paid	(5)	
Net cash flow from operations	241	
Reconciliation:		
Net profit	187	
Adjust for		
Depreciation	55	
Decrease in debtors	1	
Increase in inventory	(4)	
Increase in creditors	2	
	241	

5.16 (a)

Workings

Cash received from customers	*$000*
Opening balance of debtors	60
plus sales for the period	379
gives the amount we might expect to receive for the year	439
less closing balance of debtors	80
equals the cash received from customers	359

Cash paid to suppliers, etc.	
Opening balance of creditors	100
plus purchases of inventory for the period	250
gives the amount we might expect to pay for the year	350
less closing balance of creditors	80
equals the cash paid to creditors	270

Non current assets			
Plant	*Cost*	*DP*	*Net*
Balance at the start of the year	50	30	20

plus new acquisitions	x = 20		20
less depreciation for the year	–	5	(5)
equals closing balance	70	35	35

Vehicles	Cost	DP	Net
Balance at the start of the year	25	12	13
less any disposals	–10	–6	–4
	15	6	9
plus new acquisitions	x = 15		15
less depreciation for the year	–	4	(4)
equals closing balance	30	10	20

Premises
The increase of $10,000 represents acquisitions

Cash flow statement for the year ended 31 December 2006

	$m	$m
Cash flows from operating activities		
Cash receipts from customers	359	
Cash paid to suppliers and employees (270 + 44)	(314)	
Interest paid	(7)	
Income taxes (last year's liability)	(20)	
Net cash provided by operating activities		18
Cash flows from investing activities		
Purchase of property, plant and equipment (20 + 15 + 10)	(45)	
Proceeds from sale of property, plant and equipment	7	
Net cash used in investing activities		(38)
Cash flows from financing activities		
Repayments of long-term borrowing	(30)	
Proceeds from issuance of share capital	20	
Dividends paid (last year's proposed)	(10)	
Net cash used in financing activities		(20)
Net decrease in cash and cash equivalents for the year		(40)
Cash and cash equivalents at the beginning of the financial year		50
Cash and cash equivalents at the end of the financial year		10

The reconciliation between operating profit and operating cash flows is as follows:

Operating profit after tax (102 – 25)	77
Adjusted for:	
Depreciation (5 + 4)	9
Gain on sale (7 – 4)	(3)
Increase in debtors	(20)
Increase in inventory	(30)

Reduction in creditors	(20)	
Increase in tax liability	5	
		18

(b) There is a positive cash flow from operating activities, but the reconciliation shows that it could be higher. Specifically, we would expect inventory, debtors and creditors all to be moving in the same direction. This raises questions as to why creditors were reduced. If the creditors had been maintained at the same level, cash flows would have been higher by $20,000. Also, given that sales increased from $350,000 to $379,000, an increase of less than 10 per cent, why did debtors increase by a third and inventory by close on 50 per cent? Serious questions about working capital management need to be asked.

In the investing area a net $38,000 has been spent on new non-current assets. In addition, the financing section reveals that new shares were issued, partially replacing the loan repaid.

The company has put itself under unnecessary pressure but certainly looks able to turn the cash flows around in the next year, depending on the plans for further acquisitions of non-current assets.

CHAPTER 6

6.4 C. George (Western) Ltd The effect of each of these changes on ROA is not always easy to predict.

(a) Usually we would expect an increase in the gross profit margin to lead to an increase in ROA. However, an increase in the gross profit margin may lead to a decrease in ROA in particular circumstances. If the increase in the margin resulted from an increase in price which, in turn, led to a decrease in sales, a fall in ROA can occur. A fall in sales can reduce the net profit (the numerator in ROA) if the overheads of the business did not decrease correspondingly.

(b) A reduction in sales can reduce ROA for reasons mentioned above.

(c) An increase in overhead expenses will reduce the net profit and this, in turn, will result in a reduction in ROA.

(d) An increase in inventory held will increase the amount of assets employed by the business (the denominator in ROA). This will, in turn, reduce ROA.

(e) Repayment of the loan at the year end will reduce the assets employed and this will increase the ROA.

(f) An increase in the time taken for debtors to pay will result in an increase in assets. This will reduce ROA.

6.5 (a) This part of the question has been dealt with in the chapter.

(b) The ratios reveal that the debtors turnover ratio for business A is 63 days, whereas for business B the ratio is only 21 days. Business B is therefore much quicker in collecting amounts outstanding from customers. Nevertheless, there is not much difference between the two businesses in the time taken to pay trade creditors. Business A takes 50 days to pay its creditors, whereas business B takes 45 days. It is interesting to compare the difference in the debtor and creditor collection periods for each business. As business A allows an average of 63 days credit to its customers, yet pays creditors within 50 days, it will require greater investment in working capital than business B which only allows an average of 21 days to its debtors but takes 45 days to pay its creditors.

Business A has a much higher gross profit percentage than business B. However, the net profit percentage for the two businesses is identical. This suggests that Business A has much higher overheads than business B. The inventory turnover period for business A is more than twice that of business B. This may be due to the fact that business A maintains a wider range of inventory in order to meet customer requirements. The evidence suggests that business A is the business that prides itself on personal service. The higher average settlement period is consistent with a more relaxed attitude to credit collection (thereby maintaining customer goodwill) and the high overheads are consistent with the incurring of additional costs in order to satisfy customer requirements. The high inventory levels of business A are consistent with maintaining a wide range of stock in order to satisfy a range of customer needs.

Business B has the characteristics of a more price competitive business. The gross profit percentage is much lower than that for business A, indicating a much lower gross profit per $1 of sales. However, overheads are kept low in order to ensure that the net profit percentage is the same as for business A. The low inventory turnover period and average collection period for debtors are consistent with a business which wishes to reduce investment in current assets to a minimum, thereby reducing costs.

CHAPTER 7

7.4 The contribution per unit is $5. Since fixed costs are $20,000 it is necessary to sell $20,000/5 = 4,000 units to break even.

If a profit of $25,000 is to be made it is necessary to recover a total contribution of $20,000 + $25,000. The level of sales necessary for this can be derived by dividing this amount by $5 (the contribution per unit) = 9,000 units.

If sales revenues are $90,000 (6,000 units @ $15) the variable costs must be $60,000 (6,000 units @ $10—or two-thirds of the sales revenue), giving a contribution of $30,000. Since fixed costs are $20,000 the profit on this sales revenue will be $10,000.

7.8

	Period 6	Period 7	Difference	VC	FC
Materials	300,000	360,000	60,000	30	–
Labour	212,000	247,000	35,000	17.50	37,000
Overheads	418,000	453,000	35,000	17.50	243,000
				65	280,000

Sales price $100 per unit

Contribution $35 per unit

Break-even point is 280,000/35 = 8,000 units per period.

With new machine, fixed costs increase to $396,000.
Variable costs decrease to $55.

Therefore, the new break-even point is 396,000/45 = 8,800 units per period.

To maintain profits at $140,000, need to recover $536,000.
Therefore, need to produce 536,000/45 = 11,911 units per period.

7.13 **(a)** Total time required on **cutting machines** = (2,500 × 1.0) + (3,400 × 1.0) + (5,100 × 0.5)
= 8,450 hours.

Total time available on **cutting machines** = 5,000 hours (i.e. a limiting factor).

Total time required on **assembling machines** = (2,500 × 0.5) + (3,400 × 1.0) + (5,100 × 0.5) = 7,200 hours.

Total time available on **assembling machines** = 8,000 hours (i.e. not a limiting factor).

Product	A (per unit)	B (per unit)	C (per unit)
	$	$	$
Selling price	25	30	18
Direct materials	(12)	(13)	(10)
Variable production costs	(7)	(4)	(3)
Contribution	6	13	5
Time on cutting machines (hours)	1.0	1.0	0.5
Contribution per hour on cutting machines	$6	$13	$10
Order of priority	3	1	2

Therefore, produce: 3,400 units of product B using   3,400 hours
             3,200 units of product C using   1,600 hours
                                        5,000 hours

(b) Assuming that the company would make no savings in variable production costs by subcontracting, it would be worth paying up to the contribution per unit ($5) for the units of product C—that is, $5 × (5,100 – 3,200) = $9,500 in total.

Similarly it would be worth paying up to $6 per unit for the units of product A or $6 × 2,500 = $15,000 in total.

7.16 **(a) and (b)**

Deduce the total contribution per product and the contribution per dollar of labour and, hence, the relative profitability of the three products, given a shortage of labour.

Product	Alpha $	Beta $	Gamma $
Variable costs			
Materials	6,000	4,000	5,000
Labour	9,000	6,000	12,000
Expenses	3,000	2,000	2,000
Total variable cost	18,000	12,000	19,000

Sales	39,000	29,000	33,000
Contribution	21,000	17,000	14,000
Contribution per $ of labour	2.333	2.833	1.167
Order of profitability	2	1	3

Since 50 per cent of each budget (and therefore $13,500 of labour) is committed, only $6,500 of labour is left uncommitted (i.e. $20,000 – 13,500).

The $6,500 should be deployed as:

Beta	$3,000
Alpha	3,500
	$6,500

Total labour committed to each product and resultant profit are as follows:

Product	Alpha $	Beta $	Gamma $	Total $
Labour				
50% of budget	4,500	3,000	6,000	
Allocated above	3,500	3,000	–	
Total	8,000	6,000	6,000	20,000
Contribution per $ of labour	2.333	2.833	1.167	
Contribution per product	18,664	16,998	7,002	42,664
Less Fixed costs				33,000
Maximum profit (subject to minor rounding errors)				$9,664

This answer assumes that all costs are variable, except where it is indicated to the contrary, and also that the budgeted sales figures are the maximum sales that can be achieved.

(c)   Other factors that might be considered include the following.
- Could all of the surplus labour be used to produce Betas (the most efficient user of labour)—that is, could the business sell more than $29,000 of this product? It might be worth reducing the price of this product, though still keeping the contribution per labour dollar above $2.33, in order to expand sales.
- Could the commitment to 50 per cent of budget on each product be dropped in favour of producing the maximum of the higher yielding products?
- Could another source of labour be found?
- Could the labour-intensive part of the work be subcontracted?

CHAPTER 8

8.1   All three of these costing techniques are means of deducing the full cost of some activity. The distinction between them lies essentially with the difference in the style of the production of the goods or services involved.

- *Job costing* is used where each unit of output or 'job' differs from others produced by the same business. Because the jobs are not identical, it is not normally acceptable to those who are likely to use the cost information to treat the jobs as if they are identical. This means that costs need to be identified, job by job. For this purpose, costs fall into two categories: direct costs and indirect costs (or overheads).

  Direct costs are those that can be measured directly in respect of the specific job, such as the amount of labour that was directly applied to the job, or the amount of the material that has been incorporated into it. To this must be added a share of the indirect costs. This is usually done by taking the total overheads for the period concerned and charging part of them to the job. This, in turn, is usually done according to some measure of the job's size and importance relative to the other jobs done during the period. The number of direct labour hours worked on the job is a commonly used measure of size and/or importance.

  The main problem with job costing tends to be the method of charging indirect costs to jobs. Indirect costs, by definition, cannot be related directly to jobs and must, if full costs are to be deduced, be charged on a basis which is more or less arbitrary. If indirect costs accounted for a small proportion of the total, the arbitrariness of charging them would probably not matter. Indirect costs, in many cases, however, form the majority of total costs, so arbitrariness is a problem.

- *Process costing* is the approach taken where all output is of identical units. These can be treated, therefore, as having identical cost. Sometimes a process costing approach is taken even where the units of output are not strictly identical. This is because process costing is much simpler and cheaper to apply than the other option, job costing. Provided that users of the cost information are satisfied that treating units as identical when they are not strictly so is acceptable, the additional cost and effort of job costing is not justified.

  In process costing, the cost per unit is found by dividing total costs for the period by the total number of units produced in the period.

  The main problem with process costing tends to be that at the end of any period/beginning of the next period there will probably be partly completed units of output. An adjustment needs to be made for this work-in-progress if the resulting cost per unit figures are not to be distorted.

- *Batch costing* is really an extension of job costing. Batch costing tends to be used where production is in batches. A batch consists of more than one, perhaps many, identical units of output. The units of output differ from one batch to the next. For example, a clothing manufacturing business may produce 500 identical jackets in one batch. This is followed by a batch of 300 identical skirts.

  Each batch is costed as one job, using a job costing approach. The full cost of each garment is then found by dividing the cost of the batch by the number of garments in the batch.

  The main problem of batch costing is exactly that of job costing, of which it is an extension. This is the problem of dealing with overheads.

8.2 (a) The company predetermines the rate at which overheads are to be charged to jobs because, for most of the reasons that full costing information could be useful, costs usually need to be known either before the job is done or, more or less, immediately afterwards. The two main reasons why businesses identify full costs are for pricing decisions and income measurement purposes.

  For pricing, usually the customer will want to know the price in advance of placing the order. Thus it is not possible to wait until all the costs have actually been incurred, and are known, before the price can be deduced. Even where production is not for an identified customer, the business still needs to have some idea of whether it can produce the good or service at a price which the market will bear.

In the context of income measurement, valuing inventory and work-in-progress is the purpose for which full costs are required. If managers and other users are to benefit as much as possible from accounting information, that information must speedily follow the end of the period to which it relates. This usually means that waiting to discover actual cost is not practical.

(b) Predetermining the rate at which overheads are charged to jobs requires three judgements to be made:

(i) predicting the overheads for the period concerned;

(ii) deciding on the basis of charging overheads to job (e.g. rate per direct labour hour); and

(iii) predicting the number of units of the basis factor (e.g. number of direct labour hours) which are expected to occur during the period concerned.

Judgements (i) and (iii) are difficult to do, but there will normally be some past experience — for example, the current period, which might provide guidance; (ii) is obviously a matter of judgement and opinion.

(c) The problems of using predetermined rates are really linked to the ability to predict (i) and (iii) above. The desired result is that the total of the overheads, but no more than the total of the overheads, becomes part of the cost of the various jobs worked on in the period. Only if (i) and (iii) are both accurately predicted will this happen, except on lucky coincidence. There is clearly the danger that jobs will either be undercharged or overcharged with overheads relative to the total amount of overheads incurred during that period. In fact, it is almost certain that one of these two will happen, to some extent, simply because perfect prediction is impossible. Minor errors will not matter, but major ones could well lead to bad decisions.

8.7	*Offending phrase*	*Explanation*
	'Necessary to divide the business up into departments'	This can be done, but it will not always be to much benefit to do so. Only in quite restricted circumstances will it give significantly different job costs.
	'Fixed costs (or overheads)'	This implies that fixed costs and overheads are the same thing. They are not really connected with one another. 'Fixed' is to do with how costs behave as the level of output changes; 'overheads' is to do with the extent to which costs can be directly measured in respect of a particular unit of output. Though it is true that many overheads are fixed, not all are. Also, direct labour is usually a fixed cost. All of the other references to fixed and variable costs are wrong. The person should have referred to indirect and direct costs.
	'Usually this is done on the basis of floor space'	Where overheads are apportioned to departments, they will be apportioned on some logical basis. For

certain costs (e.g. rent) floor areas may be the most logical. For others (e.g. machine maintenance costs) floor area would be totally inappropriate.

'When the total fixed costs for each department have been identified, this will be divided by the number of hours that were worked'

Where overheads are dealt with on a departmental basis, they may be divided by the number of direct labour hours to deduce a recovery rate. However, this is only one basis of applying overheads to jobs. For example, machine hours or some other basis may be more appropriate to the particular circumstances involved.

'It is essential that this approach is taken in order to deduce a selling price'

In practice, it is relatively unusual for the 'job cost' to be able to dictate the price at which the manufacturer can price its output. Job costing may have its uses, but setting prices is usually not one of them.

CHAPTER 9

9.6 The *forecast income statement* is given below:

	A	B
	$	$
Sales	4,000,000	10,000,000
Direct materials	1,200,000	3,000,000
Direct labour (400 and 1,000)	800,000	2,000,000
Indirect labour (50 and 80)	100,000	160,000
Power	80,000	200,000
Maintenance	200,000	380,000
Distribution	100,000	160,000
Selling costs (5% of sales)	200,000	500,000
Depreciation	320,000	320,000
Other fixed costs	600,000	600,000
Total expenses	3,600,000	7,320,000
Net profit	400,000	2,680,000

The *statement of allowed costs* would need to be calculated by revising the production expenses in line with a flexed budget of 40,000 units and selling expenses in line with sales of 30,000 units. This would result in the following:

	$
Sales	6,000,000
Direct materials	2,400,000
Direct labour (800 men)	1,600,000
Indirect labour (70 men)	140,000

Power	160,000
Maintenance	320,000
Distribution	120,000*
Selling costs (5% of sales)	300,000*
Depreciation	320,000**
Other fixed costs	600,000**

* based on sales
** fixed
remainder based on production

The figures shown above in the statement of allowed costs provide an appropriate basis for comparison with the actual figures.

Should a profit calculation be required it will be necessary to value the stock of the 10,000 units produced but not sold.

9.8

ANTONIO LTD

Budget

	Original	Flexed		Actual	
Output (units) (production and sales)	1,000	1,100		1,100	
	$	$		$	
Sales	25,000	27,500		28,200	
Labour	(5,000)	(5,500)	550 hours	(5,550)	(537.5 hrs)
Raw materials	(10,000)	(11,000)	(1,100 kg)	(11,630)	(1,170 kg)
Fixed overheads	(3,000)	(3,000)		(3,200)	
Operating profit	$7,000	$8,000		$7,820	

Sales variances
Volume ($7,000 – $8,000)   = $1,000 F
Price ($27,500 – $28,200)   = $700 F

Direct labour variances
Efficiency (550 hours – 537.5 hours) × $10   = $125 F
Rate (537.5 × $10) – $5,550   = $175 A

Direct materials variances
Usage (1,100 kg – 1,170 kg × $10)   = $700 A
Price ((1,170 × $10) – $11,630   = $70 F

Fixed overhead expenditure
($3,200 – $3,000)   = $200 A

Total variances $820 F
Budgeted profit $7,000
Actual profit $7,820

CHAPTER 10

10.2 Steps are:

Working capital = $375,000

$$CA - CL = 375,000$$
$$CA/CL = 1.75$$
$$CA = 1.75CL$$

Substituting:

$$1.75CL - CL = 375,000$$
$$0.75CL = 375,000$$
$$\therefore CL = 500,000 \text{ and } CA = \$875,000$$

Liquid assets (LA) = 625,000 $(1.25 \times CL)$

inventory = $CA - LA$ = 250,000
Inventory turnover = 4.8 times
$\therefore$ **Cost of sales** = 4.8 $\times$ $250,000 = $1,200,000

Gross profit = 25% of turnover
$\therefore$ cost of sales = 75% of turnover
$\therefore$ **turnover** = $1,600,000

Debtors turnover = 8
$\therefore$ **debtors** = 1,600,000/8 = $200,000

So **cash** = $875,000 − (250,000 + 200,000) = $425,000

Net profit = 15% of issued capital = 15% $\times$ $500,000 = $75,000

Balance sheet

	$		$
Current assets		*Current liabilities*	500,000
Cash	425,000		
Debtors	200,000		
Inventory	250,000	*Issued capital*	500,000
	875,000	*Reserves*	175,000
Non-current assets	300,000		
	1,175,000		1,175,000

Income statement

	$
Sales	1,600,000
Cost of sales	1,200,000
Gross profit	400,000
Expenses	325,000
Net profit	75,000

10.3 (a)

Cash forecast (budget) for the six months to 30 June 2006

	Jan. $000	Feb. $000	Mar. $000	Apr. $000	May $000	June $000
Receipts						
Cash from debtors	100	100	140	180	220	260
Payments						
To creditors	112	144	176	208	240	272
Operating expenses	4	6	8	10	10	10
Shelving				12		
Taxation			25			
	116	150	209	230	250	282
Net cash flow	(16)	(50)	(69)	(50)	(30)	(22)
Opening balance	(68)	(84)	(134)	(203)	(253)	(283)
Closing balance	(84)	(134)	(203)	(253)	(283)	(305)

(b) (i) Current ratio $= \dfrac{(272 \text{ inventory} + (300 + 340) \text{ debtors})}{(305 \text{ overdraft} + 272 \text{ creditors})} = \dfrac{912}{577} = 1.6$ times

(ii) Acid test ratio $= \dfrac{(300 + 340)}{(305 + 272)} = \dfrac{640}{577} = 1.1$ times

(c)   A banker may require various pieces of information before granting additional overdraft facilities. These may include:
- security available for the loan;
- details of past profit performance;
- profit projections for the next 12 months;
- cash projections beyond the next six months to help assess the prospects of repayment;
- details of the assumptions underlying the projected figures supplied;
- details of the contractual commitment between Prolog Ltd and its supplier;
- details of management expertise (i.e. can they manage the expansion program?);
- details of the new machine and its performance relative to competing models;
- details of funds available from owners to finance the expansion.

CHAPTER 11

11.1   MYLO LTD

(a) Analysis of the projects:

In the analysis that follows the figures of net profit plus depreciation should be seen as a way of arriving at the cash flows from operating activities.

Annual depreciation can be calculated as:

$$\text{Depreciation} = (\text{Cost less residual value})/\text{Life}$$

Thus: Project 1   ($100,000 − 7,000)/3 = $31,000

       Project 2   ($60,000 − 6,000)/3 = $18,000

Project 1	*Year 0* *$000*	*Year 1* *$000*	*Year 2* *$000*	*Year 3* *$000*
Net profit (loss)		29	(1)	2
Depreciation		31	31	31
Capital cost	(100)			
Residual value				7
Net cash flows	(100)	60	30	40
Discount factor @ 10%	1.000	0.909	0.826	0.751
Present value	(100.00)	54.54	24.78	30.04
Net present value	9.36			

Clearly the IRR lies above 10 per cent; try 15 per cent:

Discount factor @ 15%	1.000	0.870	0.756	0.658
Present value	(100.00)	52.20	22.68	26.32
Net present value	1.20			

Thus the IRR lies a little above 15 per cent, around 16 per cent. More formally the IRR can be calculated as:

$$15\% + \frac{(1.20)}{(9.36 - 1.2)} \times 5 = 15.7\%$$

Cumulative cash flows	(100)	(40)	(10)	30

Thus the payback will occur after about two years, three months (assuming that the cash flows accrue equally over the year).

Project 2	*Year 0* *$000*	*Year 1* *$000*	*Year 2* *$000*	*Year 3* *$000*
Net profit (loss)		18	(2)	4
Depreciation		18	18	18
Capital cost	(60)			
Residual value				6
Net cash flows	(60)	36	16	28
Discount factor @ 10%	1.000	0.909	0.826	0.751
Present value	(60.00)	32.72	13.22	21.03
Net present value	6.97			

Clearly the IRR lies above 10 per cent; try 15 per cent:

Discount factor @ 15%	1.000	0.870	0.756	0.658
Present value	(60.00)	31.32	12.10	18.42
Net present value	1.84			

Thus the IRR lies a little above 15 per cent, around 17 per cent.

$$(15 + 5 (1.84/(6.97 - 1.84)) = 16.7 \text{ per cent.}$$

Cumulative cash flows	(60)	(24)	(8)	20

Thus the payback will occur after about two years, four months (assuming that the cash flows accrue equally over the year).

(b) Presuming that Mylo Ltd is pursuing a wealth maximisation objective, project 1 is preferable since it has the higher NPV. The difference between the two NPVs is not significant, however. The decision may therefore be susceptible to forecast error.

(c) NPV is the preferred method of assessing investment opportunities because it fully addresses each of the following:
- *The timing of the cash flows.* By discounting the various cash flows associated with each project according to when it is expected to arise, the fact that cash flows do not all occur simultaneously is accommodated. Associated with this is the fact that by discounting, using the opportunity cost of finance (i.e. the return that the next best alternative opportunity would generate), the net benefit after financing costs have been met is identified (as the NPV).
- *The whole of the relevant cash flows.* NPV includes all of the relevant cash flows irrespective of when they are expected to occur. It treats them differently according to their date of occurrence, but they are all taken account of in the NPV and they all have, or can have, an influence on the decision.
- *The objectives of the business.* NPV is the only method of appraisal where the output of the analysis has a direct bearing on the wealth of the business. (Positive NPVs enhance wealth, negative ones reduce it.) Since most private sector businesses seek to increase their value and wealth, NPV clearly is the best approach to use, at least out of the methods we have considered so far.

11.9   NEWTON ELECTRONICS LTD

(a) Option 1

	Immediately $m	2006 $m	2007 $m	2008 $m	2009 $m	2010 $m
Plant and equipment	(9.0)					1.0
Sales		24.0	30.8	39.6	26.4	10.0
Variable costs		(11.2)	(19.6)	(25.2)	(16.8)	(7.0)
Fixed costs (excl. depr'n)		(0.8)	(0.8)	(0.8)	(0.8)	(0.8)
Working capital	(3.0)					3.0
Marketing costs		(2.0)	(2.0)	(2.0)	(2.0)	(2.0)
Opportunity costs		(0.1)	(0.1)	(0.1)	(0.1)	(0.1)
	(12.0)	9.9	8.3	11.5	6.7	4.1
Discount factor	1.000	0.909	0.826	0.751	0.683	0.621
Present value	(12.0)	9.0	6.9	8.6	4.6	2.5
NPV	19.6					

Option 2

	Immediately $m	2006 $m	2007 $m	2008 $m	2009 $m	2010 $m
Royalties	–	4.4	7.7	9.9	6.6	2.8
Discount factor	1.000	0.909	0.826	0.751	0.683	0.621
Present value	–	4.0	6.4	7.4	4.5	1.7
NPV	24.0					

Option 3

	Immediately $m	2007 $m
Instalments	12.0	12.0
Discount factor	1.000	0.826
Present value	12.0	9.9
NPV	21.9	

(b) Before making a final decision the following factors should be considered:
- The long-term competitiveness of the business may be affected by the sale of the patents.
- At present, the company is not involved in manufacturing and marketing products. Is this change in direction desirable?
- The company will probably have to buy in the skills necessary to produce the product itself. This will involve costs, and problems will be incurred. Has this been taken into account?
- How accurate are the forecasts made and how valid are the assumptions on which they are based?

(c) Option 2 has the highest NPV and is therefore the most attractive to shareholders. However, the accuracy of the forecasts should be checked before a final decision is made.

CHAPTER 12

12.7

(a) Equity is $3,600,000 spread over 2 million shares so the book value per share is $1.80.

(b) Dividends are 25 cents per share (ie 500,000/2,000,000).
Dividend yield for similar shares 8 per cent.
Value per share = 25 cents × 100/8 = $3.125.

(c) Net profit after tax to ordinary shareholders' interest =
600,000 × 100/(2,000,000 + 1,500,000*) = 17 per cent.
* reserves at the start of the year

(d) Cash inflows per $100 debenture

Years 1–10	$5	PV at 7% = 7.023 × 5 = 35.1
Years 10 terminal value (par)	$100	PV is .508 × 100 = 50.8
Value		$85.9 say $86

12.11 On an assets basis the following might represent a minimum price based on realisable values.

Land & buildings	350,000
Securities	60,000
Equipment	200,000
	610,000
Current assets	
Inventory	35,000
Debtors	15,000
Cash	1,000
	51,000
Less Creditors	33,000
	18,000
	628,000

On a market yield basis multiplying profits by a factor of 7 provides a useful starting point. Average profits before tax and drawings are (90,000 + 96,000 + 93,000 + 30,000 + 30,000 + 30,000)/3 = $369,000/3 = $123,000. Hence value would be $123,000 × 7 = $861,000.

The question that needs to be considered is whether or not the real goodwill is worth $861,000 – $628,000 or $233,000. Paul clearly felt that there was goodwill when he purchased the business amounting to $50,000. Prospective purchasers will need to satisfy themselves of this value. Given the intangible nature of goodwill it is suggested that the value set out above probably represents a maximum price likely to be obtained.

What other factors need to be considered?

- How certain are the disposal figures listed above? Can be a tendency to have unrealistic expectations.
- Paul is not actively involved in the business. Would someone new be prepared to work at it and boost profits?
- Given the relatively significant sums retained over the last three years has the reinvestment (even after taking into account purchase of securities) led to much of an increase in profits?
- The returns on Paul's book equity have been quite good.
  Return for 2005 was $123,000.
  Equity at the start of 2005 was $385,000 (478,000 – 93,000).
  So return to equity was 123 × 100/385 = 32%.

From a purchaser's point of view a price of $628,000 represents a virtually riskless opportunity to buy into a business that yields around 30 per cent. Even at a purchase price of $861,000 the returns would be 123 × 100/861 = 14.3%.

The price likely to be achieved is probably closer to the top end of the range suggested.

CHAPTER 13

13.10   MAYO COMPUTERS LTD

New proposals from credit department

	$000	*$000*
Current level of investment in debtors		
[$20m × (60/365)]		3,288
Proposed level of investment in debtors		
[($20m × 60%)(30/365)]	986	
[($20m × 40%)(50/365)]	1,096	2,082
Reduction in level of investment		1,206

The reduction in overdraft interest as a result of the reduction in the level of investment will be:

$$\$1,206,000 \times 14\% = \$169,000$$

	$000	*$000*
Cost of cash discounts offered ($12m × 2½%)		300
Additional cost of credit administration		20
		320
Bad debt savings	100	
Interest charge savings (see above)	169	269
Net annual cost of policy		51

These calculations show that the company would incur additional annual costs in order to implement this proposal. It would therefore be cheaper to stay with the existing credit policy.

13.13 **(a)** The liquidity ratios of the company seem low. The current ratio is only 1.1 and its acid test ratio is 0.6. The latter ratio suggests that the company has insufficient liquid assets to pay its short-term obligations. A cash flow projection for the next period would provide a better insight into the liquidity position of the business. The bank overdraft seems high and it would be useful to know if the bank is pressing for a reduction and what overdraft limit has been established for the company.

(b) This term is described in the chapter.

(c) The operating cash cycle may be calculated as follows:

No. of days

Average stockholding period

$$\frac{[(\text{Opening inventory} + \text{closing inventory})/2]}{\text{Cost of sales}} \times 365 = \frac{[(125 + 143)/2]}{323} \times 365 \qquad 151$$

Average settlement period for debtors

$$\frac{\text{Trade debtors*} \times 365}{\text{Credit sales}} = \frac{163}{452} \times 365 \qquad\qquad 132$$

* Average debtors figure not available   283

Less

Average settlement period for creditors

$$\frac{\text{Trade creditors}^{**} \times 365}{\text{Credit purchases}} = \frac{145}{341} \times 365$$

155

** Average creditors figure not available

Operating cash cycle

128

(d) The company can reduce the operating cash cycle in a number of ways. The average stockholding period seems quite long. At present, average inventories held are sufficient to support almost five months' sales. This may be reduced by reducing the level of inventory held. Similarly, the average settlement period for debtors seems long. Debtors represent more than four months' sales. This may be reduced by imposing tighter credit control, offering discounts, charging interest on overdue accounts, etc. However, any policy decisions concerning inventory and debtors must take account of current trading conditions.

The operating cash cycle could also be reduced by extending the period of credit taken to pay suppliers. However, for reasons mentioned in the chapter, this option must be given careful consideration.

CHAPTER 14

14.1 (a) The main factors to take into account are:
- *Risk*. If a business borrows, there is a risk that, at the maturity date of the loan, the business will not have the funds to repay the amount owing and will be unable to find a suitable form of replacement borrowing. With short-term loans, the maturity dates will arrive more quickly and the type of risk outlined will occur at more frequent intervals.
- *Matching*. A company may wish to match the life of an asset with the maturity date of the borrowing. In other words, long-term assets will be purchased with long-term loan funds. A certain level of current assets which form part of the long-term asset base of the business may also be funded by long-term borrowing. Those current assets that fluctuate owing to seasonality, etc. will be funded by short-term borrowing. This approach to funding assets will help to reduce risks for the company.
- *Cost*. Interest rates for long-term loans may be higher than for short-term loans as investors may seek extra compensation for having their funds locked up for a long period. However, issue costs may be higher for short-term loans as there will be a need to refund at more frequent intervals.
- *Flexibility*. Short-term loans may be more flexible. It may be difficult to repay long-term loans before the maturity period.

(b) When deciding to grant a loan the following factors should be considered:
- security;
- purpose of the loan;
- the ability of the borrower to repay;
- the loan period;

- the availability of funds;
- the character and integrity of the senior managers.

(c) Loan conditions may include:
  - the need to obtain permission before issuing further loans;
  - the need to maintain a certain level of liquidity during the loan period;
  - a restriction on the level of dividends and directors' pay.

14.2 (a) When deciding between long-term debt and equity finance, the following factors should be considered:
  - *Cost*. The cost of equity is higher over the longer term than the cost of loans. This is because equity is a riskier form of investment. Moreover, loan interest is tax deductible, whereas dividend payments are not. However, when profits are poor, there is no obligation to pay equity shareholders, whereas the obligation to pay lenders will continue.
  - *Gearing*. The company may wish to take on additional gearing in order to increase the returns to equity. This can be achieved providing the returns from the loans invested exceed the cost of servicing the loans.
  - *Risk*. Loan capital increases the level of risk to equity shareholders who will in turn require higher rates of return. If the level of gearing is high in relation to industry norms the credit standing of the business may be affected. Managers, although strictly concerned with the interests of shareholders, may feel their own positions are at risk if a high level of gearing is obtained. However, they may be more inclined to take on additional risk if their remuneration is linked to the potential benefits that may flow from higher gearing.

(b) Convertible loan stock provides the investor with the right, but not the obligation, to convert the loan stock into ordinary shares at a specified future date and a specified price. The investor will only exercise this option if the market value of the shares is above the 'exercise price' at the specified date. The investor will change status from that of lender to that of owner when the option to convert is exercised.

If the company is successful, the convertible loan stock will be self-liquidating, which can be convenient for the company. The company may also be able to negotiate lower rates of interest or fewer loan restrictions because of the potential gains on conversion.

Convertible loan stock is often used in takeover deals. The target company shareholders may find this form of finance attractive if they are uncertain as to the future prospects of the combined business. The investors will be guaranteed a fixed rate of return and, if the combined business is successful, they will be able to participate in this success through the conversion process. However, convertible loan stock can be viewed as part loan and part equity finance and some investors may find it difficult to assess the value to be placed on such securities.

(c) Debt factoring is a service provided by a financial institution whereby the sales ledger of a client company is managed, and credit evaluation and credit protection services may also be offered. The factor will also be prepared to advance funds to the client company of up to 85 per cent of approved sales outstanding. The advantage of factoring is that it can provide an efficient debt collection service and can release the managers to do other things. This may be of particular value to small and medium-sized businesses. The company also receives an immediate injection of finance and there is greater certainty concerning cash receipts. The level of finance provided through factoring will increase in line with the increase in the level of activity of the business.

In the past, factoring has been viewed as a form of last resort lending and so customers may interpret factoring as a sign of financial weakness. However, this image is now fast disappearing. Factoring is quite expensive—a service charge of up to 3 per cent of turnover is levied. Setting up the factoring agreement can be time consuming and so factoring agreements are not suitable for short-term borrowing requirements.

GLOSSARY

ABC system of inventory control A method of applying different levels of inventory control, based on the value of each category of inventory.

Accelerated depreciation An approach to the calculation of depreciation expense which results in depreciation expenses being higher in the early years of an asset's life than in later years.

Accounting The process of identifying, measuring and communicating information to permit informed judgements and decisions by users of the information.

Accounting rate of return (ARR) The average profit from an investment, expressed as a percentage of the average investment made.

Accounting standards Rules established by the professional accounting bodies, which should be followed by preparers of the annual accounts of companies.

Accrued expenses Expenses which are outstanding at the end of the accounting period.

Activity-based costing (ABC) A technique for more accurately relating overheads to specific production or provision of a service. It is based on acceptance of the fact that overheads do not just occur: they are caused by activities, such as holding products in stores, which 'drive' the costs.

Ageing schedule of debtors A report dividing debtors into categories, depending on the length of time outstanding.

Asset A resource held by a business which has certain characteristics.

Auditors Professionals whose main duty is to make a report as to whether, in their opinion, the accounting statements of a company do that which they are supposed to do, namely, to show a true and fair view and comply with statutory, and accounting standard, requirements.

Average settlement period The average time taken for debtors to pay the amounts owing or for a business to pay its creditors.

Balance sheet A statement of financial position which shows the assets of a business and the claim on those assets.

Balanced scorecard Both a management system and a system for measuring and reporting performance, which includes information relating to financial, business processes, customer, and learning and growth, thus giving a more comprehensive (and strategic) view of a business.

Batch costing A technique for identifying full cost, where the production of many types of goods and services, particularly goods, involves producing a batch of identical or nearly identical units of output, but where each batch is distinctly different from other batches.

BCG portfolio matrix A matrix which maps market growth rate and industry attractiveness as an aid to determining business strategy.

Beta coefficient A measure of the correlation between the returns of an individual security and those of the market.

Bond A long-term loan.

Bonus shares Reserves which are converted into shares and given 'free' to shareholders.

Bottom up A term applied to decisions in which great weight is given to the views of relatively junior staff, who often have good experience and knowledge in detail of what is going on in the business and its markets. The term is often used in budgeting, where budgets are driven by the views of staff such as sales representatives.

Break-even point A level of activity where revenue will exactly equal total cost, so there is neither profit nor loss.

Budget A financial plan for the short term, typically one year.

Budget committee A group of managers formed to supervise and take responsibility for the budget-setting process.

Budget officer An individual, often an accountant, appointed to carry out, or take immediate responsibility for having carried out, the tasks of the budget committee.

Business entity convention The convention which holds that, for accounting purposes, the business and its owner(s) are treated as quite separate and distinct.

Cash flow statement A statement which shows the sources and uses of cash for a period.

Ceres principles A set of principles which is effectively a 10-point code of environmental conduct.

Claim An obligation on the part of the business to provide cash or some other benefit to an outside party.

Conservatism/prudence convention The convention which holds that financial reports should err on the side of caution, effectively anticipating losses but only recognising profits when they are realised.

Consistency convention The accounting convention which holds that when a particular method of accounting is selected to deal with a transaction, this method should be applied consistently over time.

Contra asset An account that goes together with another account but represents a reduction in that account. For example, 'Accumulated depreciation—equipment' is a contra account that goes with the 'Equipment' account.

Contribution per unit Sales revenue per unit less variable costs per unit.

Control Compel events to conform to plan.

Conventions Rules that have been devised over time in order to deal with practical problems experienced by preparers and users.

Convertible loans Loan capital which can be converted into equity share capital at the option of the holders.

Corporate governance The system by which corporations are directed and controlled.

Corporate social responsibility How companies manage the business processes to produce an overall positive impact on society.

Cost The amount of resources, usually measured in monetary terms, sacrificed to achieve a particular objective.

Cost centre Some area, object, person or activity for which costs are separately collected.

Cost drivers Activities which cause costs.

Cost plus pricing An approach to pricing output which is based on full cost, plus a percentage profit loading.

Current assets Assets which are not held on a continuing basis. They include cash itself and other assets which are expected to be converted to cash at some future point in time, usually within 12 months.

Current liabilities Amounts due for repayment to outside parties within 12 months of the statement of financial position date.

Debenture A long-term loan, usually made to a company, evidenced by a trust deed.

Debt factoring A form of service that is offered by a financial institution in which the institution (the factor) takes over the list of debtors and effectively controls debt collection.

Deep discount bonds Redeemable bonds which are issued at a low or zero rate of interest and which are issued at a large discount to their redeemable value.

Depreciation A measure of that portion of the cost (less residual value) of a fixed asset which has been consumed during an accounting period.

Direct costs Costs which can be identified with specific cost units, to the extent that the effect of the cost can be measured in respect of each particular unit of output.

Directors Individuals who are elected to act as the most senior level of management of a company.

Dividend yield The return attributable to shares, calculated as dividends per share/market price per share, expressed as a percentage.

Dividends Transfers of assets made by a company to its shareholders.

Dual aspect convention The accounting convention which holds that each transaction has two aspects and that each aspect must be recorded in the financial statements.

Economic order quantity (EOQ) The quantity of stocks that should be purchased in order to minimise total stock costs.

Eurobonds Bearer bonds which are issued by listed companies and other organisations in various countries, with the finance being raised on an international basis.

Expense A measure of the outflow of assets (or increase in liabilities) which is incurred as a result of generating revenues.

Factoring A method of raising short-term finance. A financial institution ('factor') will manage the sales ledger of the business and will be prepared to advance sums to the business based on the amount of trade debtors outstanding.

Financial assets Securities issued by other organisations, e.g. bonds.

Fixed cost A cost which stays fixed (the same) when changes occur to the volume of activity.

Flexed budget A budget which is modified to reflect costs that would have been expected for the actual activity.

Full cost The total amount of resources, usually measured in monetary terms, sacrificed to achieve a particular objective.

Fully paid shares Shares on which the shareholders have paid the full issue price.

Gearing The existence of fixed-payment-bearing securities (e.g. loans) in the capital structure of a business.

Global Reporting Initiative (GRI) A multi-stakeholder institution whose mission is to develop and disseminate globally applicable *Sustainability Reporting Guidelines*.

Going concern (or continuity) convention The accounting convention which holds that the business will continue operations for the foreseeable future. In other words, there is no intention or need to liquidate the business.

Gross profit The difference between sales and cost of sales.

Historic cost convention The accounting convention which holds that assets should be recorded at their historic (acquisition) cost.

Impairment Relates to the valuation of assets and the amount by which the assets' recoverable amount (in use and/or sale) exceeds its carrying amount.

Income Increases in economic benefits for the accounting period in the form of inflows of assets or decreases in liabilities that result in increases in equity, other than those relating to ownership contributions.

Income statement The statement which measures and reports how much wealth (profit) has been generated in a period.

Indirect costs (or overheads) All costs except direct costs—that is, those which cannot be directly measured in respect of each particular unit of output.

Intangible assets Assets which, while providing expected future benefits, have no physical substance—for example, copyrights, patents.

Internal rate of return (IRR) The discount rate for a project which will have the effect of producing a zero NPV.

Invoice discounting A loan provided by a financial institution based on a proportion of the face value of credit sales outstanding.

Job costing A technique for identifying the full cost per unit of output, where that output is not similar.

Just-in-time (JIT) A system of stock management which aims to have supplies delivered to production just in time for their required use.

Limited company An artificial legal person which has an identity separate from that of those who own and manage it.

Limiting factor Some aspect of the business (for example, lack of sales demand) which will stop it from achieving its objectives to the maximum extent.

Loan covenants Conditions contained within a loan agreement which are designed to protect the lenders.

Management by exception Term used to describe a system of control in which attention is given to areas which are out of line with plans—that is, are exceptional.

Margin of safety The extent to which the planned level of output or sales lies above the break-even point.

Marginal cost The addition to total cost which will be incurred by making/providing one more unit of output.

Matching convention The accounting convention which holds that, in measuring income, expenses should be matched to the revenues they helped generate, in the same accounting period as those revenues were realised.

Materiality convention The convention which says that items need to be separately disclosed if they would be seen as important (material) by users. Items not deemed to be important enough to justify separate disclosure can be grouped together.

Maturity value The amount of principal that will be returned at the end of the agreed life of a security.

Money measurement The accounting convention which holds that accounting should only deal with those items which are capable of being expressed in monetary terms.

Mortgage A loan secured on property.

Net present value (NPV) The sum of the cash flows associated with a project, after discounting at an appropriate rate, reflecting the time value of money and risk.

Net realisable value (NRV) The estimated selling price less any further costs that may be necessary to complete the goods and any costs involved in selling and distributing those goods.

Non-current assets Assets held with the intention of being used to generate wealth rather than being held for resale. They can be seen as the tools of the business and are normally held by the business on a continuing basis.

Non-current liabilities Those amounts due to other parties which are not liable for repayment within the next 12 months after the statement of financial position date.

Objectivity convention The convention which holds that, insofar as is possible, the financial statements prepared should be based on objective verifiable evidence rather than matters of opinion.

Offer for sale An issue of shares which involves a public limited company (or its shareholders) selling the shares to a financial institution which will, in turn, sell the shares to the public.

Operating cash cycle The time period between the outlay of cash to purchase supplies and the ultimate receipt of cash from the sale of goods.

Operating cycle Normally represents the time between the acquisition of the assets and their ultimate realisation in cash or cash equivalents.

Opportunity cost The cost of the best alternative strategy.

Ordinary shares Shares of a company owned by those who are due the benefits of the company's activities after all other stakeholders have been satisfied.

Overheads (or indirect costs) All costs except direct costs—that is, those that cannot be directly measured in respect of each particular unit of output.

Owner's equity The claim of the owner(s) on the assets of the business.

Partnership The relationship that exists between two or more persons carrying on a business with a view to profit.

Payback period (PP) The time taken for the initial investment in a project to be repaid from the net cash inflows of the project.

Perpetual bonds Bonds that have an indefinite life on which interest is paid in perpetuity.

Portfolio A holding of a reasonable number of shares in different companies.

Preference shares Shares which have a fixed rate of dividend that must be paid before any ordinary dividend can be paid. Often preference shares have higher priority than ordinary shares in the event of the company going into liquidation.

Price earnings (P/E) ratio The ratio of share price to earnings per share.

Private placing An issue of shares which involves the company 'placing' the shares with selected investors such as large financial institutions.

Process costing A technique for deriving the full cost per unit of output, where the units of output are exactly similar, or it is reasonable to treat them as being so.

Product cost centre Some area, object, person or activity for which costs are separately collected, in which cost units have costs added.

Realisation convention The convention which states that revenue will only be recognised when it is realised—usually when the transaction is substantially complete, can be objectively measured, and it is reasonably certain that the money will be received.

Reducing-balance method A method of depreciation in which a fixed percentage is applied to the written-down value of the asset.

Reserves Amounts reflecting increases in owners' claims.

Retained profit The amount of profit made over the life of the business which has not been taken out by owners in the form of drawings or dividends.

Return on total assets (ROA) Net profit expressed as a percentage of the assets employed.

Revenues Increases in the owners' claim as a result of operations.

Rights issue An issue of shares for cash to existing shareholders on the basis of the number of shares already held.

Risk aversion The situation in which an investor choosing between investments with the same return, will choose the one with the least risk, or for investments with the same risk, will choose the one with the highest return.

Rolling budget A budget (typically covering a year) which is modified regularly (typically monthly) by changing the dates covered by the budget. For example an annual budget might be prepared to cover the period January–December. At the end of January the budget is reviewed and revised to cover the period February–January of the next year. A rolling budget of this type is likely to be more accurate than a budget prepared once a year.

Sale and lease-back An agreement to sell an asset (usually property) to another party and simultaneously to lease the asset back in order to continue using the asset.

Schedule approach An approach to constructing the cash flow statement that makes adjustments to the income statement by a series of relatively standard pluses and minuses.

Securities market line A graph which illustrates the relationship between risk and return.

Semi-fixed (semi-variable) cost A cost which has both an element of fixed and variable cost.

Sensitivity analysis An analysis in which variables in a decision are changed one at a time, with the view to identifying which variables are most important to the success of the decision, plan or project.

Service cost centre Some area, object, person or activity for which costs are separately collected, in which cost units do not have cost added, because service cost centres only render services to product cost services and to other service cost centres.

Sole proprietorship An individual in business on his or her own account.

Specific risk The risk that can be diversified away with an appropriate holding of shares.

Stable monetary unit convention The accounting convention which holds that money, which is the unit of measurement in accounting, will not change in value over time.

Standards Planned quantities and cost (or revenues) for individual units of input or output. Standards are the building blocks used to produce the budget.

Stock exchange A market where 'second hand' shares may be bought and sold and new capital raised.

Straight-line method A method of accounting for depreciation which allocates the amount to be depreciated evenly over the useful life of the asset.

Strategic management accounting A framework which recognises that management accounting needs to take a far more strategic perspective.

Sustainability reporting A system of reporting which attempts to report on key issues that impact on environmental and social sustainability.

Systematic risk Risk that is system-wide that cannot be reduced by diversification.

Tangible assets Those assets that have a physical substance (e.g. plant and machinery, motor vehicles).

Tender issue Shares for sale to investors for which the investors must state the amount they are prepared to pay for the shares.

Top-down An approach to budgeting, where the senior management of each budget area originates the budget targets, perhaps discussing them with lower levels of management.

Total cost The sum of the variable and fixed costs of pursuing some activity.

Triple bottom line reporting A system of reporting which focuses on economic performance, environmental performance and social performance.

Unimpaired The carrying amount of the asset exceeds the amount of expected future net cash inflows arising from the use and/or sale of that asset.

Variable cost A cost which varies according to the volume of activity.

Variance The financial effect, on the budgeted profit, of the particular factor under consideration, being more or less than budgeted.

Venture capital Long-term capital provided by certain institutions to small and medium-sized businesses to exploit relatively high-risk opportunities.

Warrant A document giving the holder the right, but not the obligation, to acquire ordinary shares in a company at an agreed price.

INDEX